W9-CEG-111

CURRICULUM AND EVALUATION

READINGS IN EDUCATIONAL RESEARCH

American Educational Research Association
READINGS IN EDUCATIONAL RESEARCH
Merlin C. Wittrock, EDITOR OF THE SERIES

PHILOSOPHY OF EDUCATIONAL RESEARCH
Harry S. Broudy | Robert H. Ennis | Leonard I. Krimerman

INTELLECTUAL DEVELOPMENT
Pauline S. Sears

SOCIAL DEVELOPMENT AND PERSONALITY
George G. Thompson | Francis J. DiVesta | John E. Horrocks

LEARNING AND INSTRUCTION
Merlin C. Wittrock

EDUCATIONAL ORGANIZATION AND ADMINISTRATION
Donald A. Erickson

EXPERIMENTAL DESIGN AND INTERPRETATION
Raymond O. Collier, Jr. | Thomas J. Hummel

CURRICULUM AND EVALUATION
Arno A. Bellack | Herbert M. Kliebard

CURRICULUM AND EVALUATION

Arno A. Bellack
Herbert M. Kliebard, EDITORS

McCutchan Publishing Corporation
2526 Grove Street
Berkeley, California 94704

Series Preface

This book is one of a series entitled "Readings in Educational Research," sponsored and prepared by the American Educational Research Association (AERA). The titles of the seven volumes are:

1. Philosophy of Educational Research
2. Intellectual Development
3. Social Development and Personality
4. Learning and Instruction
5. Educational Organization and Administration
6. Experimental Design and Interpretation
7. Curriculum and Evaluation

The object of this preface is to state the purposes of the series, to describe briefly the history of its development, and to acknowledge the people who created the series. For several years they donated their time and considerable abilities to its preparation.

The two purposes for publishing the series have in common the liberal theme of building understanding across the different areas and specialties of educational research and of preventing insularity among educators and educational researchers. The major purpose is to promote a systematic development of the quickly growing field of educational research. A multivolume series encompassing different fields of educational research, such as educational administration and research design and analysis, is one appropriate way for AERA to further the cohesiveness of educational research. The second purpose of the series is to make available to students, teachers, researchers, and administrators a comprehensive, useful, and organized set of outstanding published papers representing major fields of educational research.

These two objectives have guided the editors in their selection of the papers and articles that comprise the series. Each paper is included in the series because it contributes to the two purposes mentioned above. Each paper makes important points about significant issues or problems of education and each complements the logical organization of the series and the volume editors' conceptions of the significant divisions of their fields of research.

Lee Cronbach conceived the idea for the series. He is absolved of any inadequacies it may have. When he was president of AERA, he appointed a committee to investigate the advisability and value of having AERA sponsor the series. The members of this committee were John DeCecco, Arthur P. Coladarci, Leland K. Medsker, David G. Ryans, and M. C. Wittrock, chairman.

The committee recommended that the preparation of a multivolume series of readings was an appropriate endeavor for AERA, provided that the series encompassed several major areas of educational research. The series would not then compete with individual researchers' single-volume treatments of their fields of educational research. More important, the series would help to accomplish the objectives mentioned above.

A second committee was then appointed to provide a tentative design for the series and to select a Board of Editors to prepare the series. The second committee consisted of Luvern Cunningham, Ellis Page, Ole Sand, George Thompson, Robert Travers, and M. C. Wittrock, chairman. This committee nominated people to serve as the Board of Editors.

The Board of Editors was given the responsibility of designing and preparing the seven volumes. This board consisted of the following people who prepared the volumes: Arno Bellack, Harry Broudy, Raymond Collier, Francis Di Vesta, Robert Ennis, Donald Erickson, John Horrocks, Thomas Hummel, Herbert Kliebard, Leonard Krimmerman, Pauline Sears, George Thompson, and Merlin Wittrock, W. W. Charters, Jr., and Robert Travers worked at large with the preparation of all of the volumes. Richard Atkinson, William Cooley, and Robert Glaser helped with one or more of the volumes.

Lack of space allows me to mention only a few of the other people involved in the preparation of the series. The Central AERA staff were of invaluable help. The successive presidents of AERA and their respective Association Councils were, without exception, highly supportive of the series and most helpful in its development. I wish to thank the staff of the McCutchan Publishing Corporation, especially John McCutchan, Elizabeth Sklut, and Jo Ann Gutin, for their important contributions to the series, and Elizabeth Delgass for the preparation of the indices of all the volumes in the series.

It is my hope that "Readings in Educational Research" helps to accomplish the goals set for it by the Board of Editors. We have prepared it to further the development and organization of educational research and to provide its readers with intellectual stimulation that will warrant its continued use in coming years.

M. C. Wittrock
Editor of the Series
Readings in Educational Research

Preface

The term "curriculum" as used in educational discourse is notoriously ambiguous. Even a cursory review of recent and contemporary literature dealing with curriculum problems reveals lack of agreement regarding the meaning of the term.* Indeed, there are almost as many conceptions of curriculum and curriculum-making as there are established practitioners and scholars. In spite of the manifest pluralism of curricular positions and movements, curriculum-making and the systematic study of curriculum-making are recognized specialties in education. Curriculum as a professional field encompassing these specialties is currently characterized by a variety of viewpoints and doctrines regarding certain perennial questions that serve as continuing foci of debate and controversy. Rather than attempting to legislate still another definition of curriculum, this volume is organized around and presents principal viewpoints on five persistent and perplexing questions that have historically characterized the curriculum field:

1. How should curriculum problems be studied?
2. What purposes should the curriculum serve?
3. How should knowledge be selected and organized for the curriculum?
4. How should the curriculum be evaluated?
5. How should the curriculum be changed?

---

*See, for example, the eleven issues of the *Review of Educational Research* dealing with the curriculum published from 1931 to 1969 by the American Educational Research Association.

These questions and the controversies surrounding them are seen as giving definition to the curriculum field as well as giving direction and meaning to curriculum research. Although the questions chosen are global in nature and probably will never be answered in any absolute sense, they invite responses that imply decision and action. This distinctive feature directs attention to the eminently practical nature of curriculum-making, which calls upon those involved at various levels of school governance to make decisions regarding what to teach, how to teach, how to evaluate teaching, and the like. How to make intelligent instructional decisions is the basic concern of curriculum practitioners; how to go about studying these practical decisions to gain understanding of them and thus contribute to their improvement is the primary concern of curriculum scholars.

Because virtually all facets of the educational enterprise relate in some way to the instructional programs of the schools, all those involved in the practice and study of education touch on problems of curriculum, directly or indirectly. Curriculum practitioners and scholars obviously play key roles in curriculum-making and in the study of curriculum-making, yet educational philosophers, psychologists, sociologists, and evaluation experts are also involved in the study of curriculum problems. In this volume, therefore, we present the viewpoints not only of self-styled curriculum specialists, but also of other educators and philosophers who address themselves to fundamental curriculum questions.

Within the context of each section an effort was made to include articles representative of the most prominent and the most responsible positions in the field. Practical restrictions of size, of necessity, have eliminated many articles of worth and many scholars of renown. But, in our attempt to accomplish a kind of "mapping out" of the field, the editors also sought to achieve some balance between the established, perhaps predominant, positions and approaches in the curriculum field and those emerging and promising positions that have not reached wide acceptance or even a wide audience. Our notion is that the curriculum field does not consist of particular techniques for accomplishing certain widely accepted ends. Our bias lies in seeing the curriculum field in terms of the widest possible diversity and complexity and in viewing the established ways of thinking and acting within the field as problematic. This volume is not to be seen, therefore, as a mere repository for the accumulated wisdom in the field of curriculum. It is anything but a technical manual. Rather, it is intended to reflect something of the wide range of ways the central questions in the field may be approached, studied, and acted upon.

The enormous task of choosing articles for inclusion in the volume was made easier by the invaluable assistance of Linda M. McNeil. Her additional contribution of the bibliographical essay that appears at the end of this volume is most warmly appreciated by the editors.

Arno A. Bellack
Herbert M. Kliebard

Contents

CURRICULUM AND EVALUATION

CHAPTER 1

How Should Curriculum Problems Be Studied?

We are becoming aware that in adjusting a curriculum, it is not sufficient to agree that some specific subject should be taught. We have to ask many questions and to make many experiments before we can determine its best relation to the whole body of educational influences which are to mould the pupil.

Alfred North Whitehead
"Science in General Education"

A wide range of approaches and ideologies guides curriculum workers in developing instructional programs for the schools. Decisions and actions in curriculum building obviously include normative commitments as well as empirical procedures, and there is no consensus about what values should give direction and meaning to these decisions and actions. Nor is there conclusive evidence gained through research regarding the observable consequences of contrasting approaches to curriculum development. Curriculum theorists and researchers to date have had little success in developing concepts and methods uniquely relevant to the practical problems of the field. It is for this reason that the very question of how the curriculum should be studied remains a central one. But this chapter is, in one sense, a reflection of the continuing dialogue that must exist in any field as to its domain, its heritage, and its ways of attacking problems.

The articles included in this chapter reflect only some of the diversity that characterizes the various approaches to the field's central problems. The diversity, in and of itself, is not an unhealthy sign. What is needed in the field generally, however, is further research into and analysis of some of the presuppositions and probable consequences of the positions taken. Indeed, a critical tradition in the curriculum field is virtually lacking, and many of its most hallowed doctrines remain to be analyzed or even challenged.

That part of curriculum thought and practice which concentrates on the curriculum in general as opposed to the curriculum in specific subject fields is commonly identified as *curriculum theory*. In the first reading in this chapter, Mauritz Johnson attempts to map out the dimensions of this field and includes a review of contrasting approaches to curriculum. He ends with a kind of curriculum taxonomy. In the following reading, George Beauchamp addresses himself to the question of what constitutes curriculum theory. This involves not only a brief consideration of theory building generally, but particular problems of definition and terminology that are characteristic of the field. Joseph Schwab's "The Practical: A Language for Curriculum" (reading #3) begins with a pessimistic assessment of the field of curriculum, but Schwab then analyzes the sources of this state of affairs and recommends a concentration of curriculum efforts on what he calls the eclectic, the practical, and the quasi-practical.

A classic position in the field is the one enunciated in reading #4 by Ralph W. Tyler in "The Organization of Learning Experiences." Drawn from a widely cited collection of theoretical papers entitled, *Toward Improved Curriculum Theory* (edited by Tyler and Virgil E. Herrick in 1950), Tyler's article reflects the widely accepted "Tyler rationale" (stated in *Basic Principles of Curriculum and Instruction*), a position central to much research and practice in the field. In reading #5, Kliebard raises questions about some of the presuppositions that are reflected in Tyler's position.

The final pair of readings in this section deals with the relationship of the curriculum field to two cognate fields. The field that has probably had the most profound influence on curriculum is psychology as reflected in such areas as learning theory, motivation, and human development. In his article (reading #6), Dwayne Huebner attempts to disentangle some of the psychological language that has become imbedded in curricular language. Kenneth Charlton's article (reading #7), by contrast, deals with another field, history, which is all too frequently ignored in curriculum discourse. Charlton attempts to establish the ways in which historical thinking can provide a model for curriculum.

1. DEFINITIONS AND MODELS IN CURRICULUM THEORY

Mauritz Johnson, Jr.

Educational researchers have traditionally been more concerned with improving education than with understanding it. This observation by Lazarsfeld and Sieber[1] seems valid for educationists in general, whether engaged in research or some other endeavor, such as "curriculum development." And, indeed, the noneducationist scholars who have of late interested themselves in curriculum reform projects also are more concerned with *improving* school programs than with gaining increased insight into the nature of curriculum. As scholars, all of them are, of course, interested in some kind of theory, but not in *curriculum* theory. Their views regarding curriculum may be sound, but they are no more firmly grounded in theory than those of education professors.

At the same time, educational practitioners—teachers, administrators, and even those with titles indicating specific responsibility for curriculum development—while interested in curriculum, are not particularly concerned with curriculum *theory*. After all, they feel, their concern is the practical one of improving the curriculum, not studying it. A perusal of the curriculum literature of the past twenty years will reveal, moreover, that the professors of education who have achieved reputations as "curriculum specialists" have chiefly been experts on *how* to organize and direct professional and lay groups effectively for curriculum improvement by applying principles of group-dynamics and human-relations. These specialists have seemed more concerned with improving the

SOURCE. *Educational Theory* 17 (No. 1, April 1967), pp. 127–40.

process of curriculum development than with any specific improvement in the curriculum itself, and whatever interest they may have had in *organizational* theory and the psychology of groups, they have evidenced little concern for curriculum theory.

Thus the majority of educationists, educational practitioners, and scholars active in curriculum reform are oriented toward improvement rather than understanding, action and results rather than inquiry. Nevertheless, a small but increasing number of students of education are directing their attention to questions of curriculum theory for no other immediate purpose than to increase understanding of curricular phenomena. The theoretical clarification they bring about may ultimately benefit both scholars and practitioners in their efforts to improve curriculum, but this possibility is not the immediate motive for attempting to construct a curriculum theory. The theorist cannot allow himself to be forced into justifying his inquiry solely on the basis of its immediate utility.

THEORIES AND PLATFORMS

Current theoretical work on curriculum is of two types—programmatic (doctrinal) and analytic. Phenix[2], who subtitled his book, A Philosophy of the Curriculum for General Education,'' engaged in both analysis and prescription. He analyzed various disciplines and built a taxonomy of meanings. He also proposed certain criteria for curriculum selection and organization. But at the same time he advocated a specific program of general education.

Similarly, Broudy, Smith, and Burnett[3] subtitled their work ''A Study in Curriculum Theory,'' and while they, too, examined criteria and classified the uses of knowledge, they also delineated a program of general education for the secondary schools. Beauchamp, likewise, explored in some detail the problems of formulating a theory, but his own illustrative model of a curriculum theory was programmatic with respect to process (planning), rather than substance or structure. He acknowledged that his own ''curriculum position was imposed upon the field of curriculum theory as organized in the classification scheme. . . .''[4]

All of these current scholars are well aware of the difference between a curriculum position and curriculum theory. In the past, however, even the ''giants'' of the profession seemed not to note this distinction. One of the most remarkable collaborations of eminent educational thinkers occurred in 1924-26 when Bagley, Bobbitt, Bonser, Charters, Counts, Courtis, Horn, Judd, F.J. Kelly, Kilpatrick, H. Rugg, and Works joined in preparing a composite statement on ''The Foundations of Curriculum-Making.'' Despite the fact that every member felt obliged to append his own reservations about the report, the Committee's 58 ''principles'' represented a consensual *position*, rather than a curriculum theory. That the Committee considered it to be a theory is evident, however, from an announcement in the introductory section that ''each member . . . has not insisted upon the acceptance of his own curriculum theory . . . ."[5] On the other hand, it had been stated previously that the group was explicitly concerned with " . . . writing a platform of *practical forward steps* in curriculum-making . . . ." In this same paragraph the confusion is increased by Rugg's reference to " . . . this platform of curriculum theory . . . ."[6]

Clearly, platforms and theories are two different things. Platforms propose policies, theories provide explanations. Included among the "principles" proposed by the 1926 Committee were many normative statements. Not until the 28th item was any definition of curriculum provided, and that was clearly "programmatic," as Scheffler uses the term.[7] "The curriculum," stated the Committee, "should be conceived . . . in terms of a succession of experiences and enterprises having a maximum of lifelikeness for the learner."[8] By considering "experiences and enterprises" to be the essential elements of curriculum, the Committee obscured the distinction between curriculum and instruction; by qualifying these elements with "lifelikeness," it engaged in exhortation instead of explanation.

But the Committee was aware of the problem of terminology. "From the beginning of our discussion," Rugg reported, "it was apparent that we did not understand each other. The chief task which we confronted was the erection of a common vocabulary."[9] Vocabulary is still one of the chief problems in curriculum theory. Note, for example, the confusion evidenced as late as 1962 in the ASCD pamphlet, "What are the Sources of the Curriculum?"[10], in which "curriculum" is confused with "curriculum development" and "source" is confused with "determinant."

CURRICULUM AND INSTRUCTION AS SYSTEMS

Some current theorists (Macdonald; Faix[11]) favor a "systems" or process model for curriculum, in which the elements are inputs, processes, outputs, and feedbacks. They recognize the necessity of explicating the relation between curriculum and instruction, but in viewing curriculum cybernetically, they, too, confuse curriculum *per se* with the curriculum development process. Macdonald has included both content and process in his "curriculum system," but since the system " . . . is made up of people as its basic units . . ."[12] and its output is "transmitted . . . to the instructional setting (also a separate social system),"[13] one finds it difficult to identify the curriculum itself, either *as* or *in* the system. Surely curriculum does not consist of people.

In Macdonald's model some of the variables conventionally labelled as "sources" are considered to be "inputs."[14] This only makes sense if the system in question is construed as the "curriculum development system." To consider these variables "inputs" into the curriculum itself makes no more sense than to consider them "sources" of the curriculum.

Maccia[15] and Macdonald disagree on the relationship of curriculum to instruction. To Macdonald these are separate concepts (systems?) that overlap to some extent. Maccia, on the other hand, holds that curriculum is a component of instruction by virtue of being a variable in "teacher behavior."[16] Thus, she sees curriculum not as a system but as "instructional content." This content consists of "rules." Rules are conceived as "structures," which, in sets, constitute "disciplines."[17]

The role of curriculum in instruction is implicit in Maccia's definition of instruction as "influence toward rule-governed behavior." Since curriculum equals rules,[18] its function must be to *govern,* i.e., regulate, behavior. But there are two levels of discourse here. Whose behavior does curriculum govern? Is curriculum the set of rules that *learners* are influenced through instruction to govern their behavior by, or does curriculum, as rules, govern the *teacher's* behavior in instruction? By Maccia's formula, $B_t = I_cRM_c$ (the only one in which curriculum, I_c, appears), it seems to be the teacher's behavior that curriculum governs. But the teacher's behavior in instruction influences students' behavior toward governance by rules. Are these the same rules that constitute curriculum? What *is* a curriculum?

THE CONCEPT OF CURRICULUM

Accepted usage identifies curriculum with "planned learning experiences." This definition is unsatisfactory, however, if "curriculum" is to be distinguished from "instruction." Whether experiences are viewed subjectively in terms of the sensibility of the experiencing individual or objectively in terms of his actions in a particular setting, there is in either case no experience until an interaction between the individual and his environment actually occurs. Clearly, such interaction characterizes *instruction*, not curriculum.

A concept of curriculum that limits it to a *post hoc* account of instruction is of little value. Surely curriculum must play some role in *guiding* instruction. If so, it must be viewed as anticipatory, not reportorial. Curriculum implies intent.

Surely, too, a useful concept of curriculum must leave some room for creativity and individual style in instruction. In other words, decisions regarding the learning experiences to be provided are the result of instructional planning, not of curriculum development. The curriculum, though it may limit the range of possible experiences, cannot specify them. Curriculum must be defined in other terms.

In view of the shortcomings of the currently popular definition, it is here stipulated that curriculum is a *structured series of intended learning outcomes*. Curriculum prescribes (or at least anticipates) the *results* of instruction. It does not prescribe the *means*, i.e., the activities, materials, or even the instructional content, to be used in achieving the results. In specifying outcomes to be sought, curriculum is concerned with *ends,* but at the level of attainable learning products, not at the more remote level at which these ends are justified. In other words, curriculum indicates *what* is to be learned, not *why* it should be learned.

This view of curriculum seems to be in substantial accord with that of Gagné who defines curriculum as " . . . a series of content units . . . ," a content unit being " . . . a capability to be acquired under a single set of learning conditions. . . . "[19] Eisner, too, appears to endorse this view when he states that a teacher is engaged in curriculum building when he decides " . . . what to teach and how to order what he teaches,"[20] but then appears to depart from it when he stipulates later that " . . . the basic unit of the curriculum is an activity."[21] The central thesis of the present paper is that curriculum has reference to what it is intended that students *learn*, not what it is intended that they *do*.

There seems to be rather general agreement as to what *can* be learned, i.e., what the categories of learning outcomes are. Three "domains" are commonly recognized: the cognitive,[22] the affective,[23] and the psychomotor. Other classification schemes may be preferred, but the component types of outcomes are well recognized and accepted. They include factual knowledge, symbolic equivalents, concepts, generalizations, intellectual skills, manipulative skills, attitudes, interests, values, and appreciations.

The nature of a particular intended learning outcome limits the range of possible appropriate learning experiences and thus guides instructional planning. A learning experience has an activity component and a content component, i.e., it involves some kind of activity with some kind of content. A curriculum item that deals with a skill-type outcome restricts the range of appropriate activities, but may or may not impose any limitations on the content. On the other hand, an item which concerns facts, concepts or generalizations specifies content, but leaves considerable option with respect to activity. When an affective outcome is specified, neither content nor activity may be greatly restricted, although most affects have fairly definite referents (implying content) and schools are concerned that most affective outcomes be intellectually grounded (implying activity).

No curriculum item fully defines instructional *content*. Instructional content includes not only that which is implied or specified in the curriculum, but also a large body of *instrumental* content selected by the teacher, not to be learned, but to facilitate the desired learning. Concepts and generalizations are not learned directly but rather through numerous encounters with specific manifestations, the selection of which is an instructional, rather than curricular, function.

Every curriculum item defines instructional *activity* to some degree. Although there are many ways of developing a concept of a skill, the accepted approaches to each kind of outcome are finite. When the intended outcome is specified, therefore, certain possible activities are ruled out and others favored.

The *order* of learning experiences also is influenced by curriculum. A curriculum is not a random series of items, but a *structured* one, even if only to the extent of indicating that the order in which certain outcomes are achieved is immaterial. Insofar as the sequence of development is not considered to be a matter of indifference, the curriculum must be specific about the proper order. But structure is not merely a matter of temporal sequence. It also refers to hierarchical relations among items.

CURRICULUM STRUCTURE

That curriculum implies such ordering is obviously the assumption underlying the widespread current attention to the structure of knowledge, especially of that knowledge derived from inquiry which constitutes the disciplines. It is implicit in the analysis by Phenix[24] and explicit in that of Schwab[25] that disciplines are structured both conceptually and syntactically (methodologically). Presumably, therefore, curriculum items assume their significance and meaning from their relationship to one another and to the mode of inquiry on the basis of which this relationship was derived or verified.

Thus, if a and b are appropriate curricular items, than aRb is likely to be appropriate also. If a and b are concepts, aRb is a generalization. It may be classificatory (e.g., Addition and multiplication are binary operations), correlational (e.g., Men tend to be taller than women), a function (e.g., $F = ma$), a definition of another concept (e.g., Density is mass per unit of volume), or in some other way relate two concepts within some structure.

Curriculum must indicate such relationships. Concepts and generalizations do not occur singly. They form clusters, and a decision to include one of them is often tantamount to a decision to include a whole cluster. A teacher or curriculum developer is not free to include a concept such as "capillarity" and to exclude, for example, "surface tension." These clusters are not equivalent, however, to "instructional units." The curriculum does not specify what organizational units are to be used in instruction, but it does indicate organizational relationships among the intended outcomes. In this sense, curriculum is a *structured* series of intended learning outcomes.

SOURCE OF CURRICULUM

It is necessary to account for the source of these intended outcomes. In most discussions of this question the sources of the curriculum are regarded to be (1) the needs and interests of the learners, (2) the values and problems of the society and (3) the disciplines or organized subject matter. All three of these may indeed impose criteria for the selection of curriculum items, but only the third can be considered a *source* of them. At that, it is only a partial source, since it ignores the body of unorganized knowledge and related skills and attitudes that lie outside of the recognized disciplines. The source of curriculum—the only possible source—is the total available culture. This was recognized by Bellack in

1956 when he identified " . . . the expanding content of the culture as the source of curriculum content,'' which he defined, in turn, as " . . . those elements of the content of the culture which are considered appropriate or relevant to the instructional aims of the school.''[26] This is not to say what the curriculum *should* be, but what it *is*. When Rugg and Withers[27] say that the curriculum *should be* "culture-centered," they mean something quite different from the present assertion that the curriculum is *necessarily* "culture-derived."

Not all cultural content is of a sort that could be incorporated into the curriculum. Only that which is teachable and available is eligible for inclusion. Artifacts and social institutions are components of a culture, but they are not teachable. Even some knowledge and skills, though teachable and very much a part of the culture, are not available for curriculum, since they are kept secrets by families, craft groups, corporations, or governments.

SELECTION OF CURRICULUM ITEMS

It is obvious that all that is available and teachable in the culture cannot be included in a given curriculum. Selection is essential. Although who does the selecting is an important educational policy question, it is not a concern of curriculum theory. What is of concern, however, is that whatever criteria are used be made explicit.

There are many possible criteria, some sensible, others silly, depending on one's ideology. Some factions insist that curriculum items bear upon persistent problems of living or current social problems; others emphasize the significance of items to the understanding of an organized field of study; still others favor selection on the basis of the experiences and interests of the potential learners. Some of these preferences are more applicable to instructional organization than to curriculum selection. Those who insist on applying them to selection are, of course, free to do so, but the notion of curriculum clusters restricts their freedom to select items at will without regard for structural considerations.

Moreover, a distinction can be made between curriculum selection for training and for education. Training implies learning for use in a predictable situation; education implies learning for use in unpredictable situations. The development of a training curriculum begins with a job analysis in which the tasks to be performed and the knowledge, skills, and attitudes needed to perform them are identified. The uses of training are, in the terminology of Broudy, Smith, and Burnett,[28] replicative and applicative. The uses of education are associative and interpretative.[29]

Man's systematic efforts to interpret his experiences are represented by those organized bodies of knowledge, skills, and attitudes known as disciplines. An educational curriculum is developed by selecting among and within these disciplines those elements which analysis identifies as having the greatest potential interpretive value. Once the disciplines considered most relevant in the interpretation of experience have been identified, internal selection criteria become dominant. Which specific curriculum items are selected depends on how fundamental and crucial they are to the discipline, how well they explicate its structure, how powerful they are in furthering its characteristic thought processes and modes of inquiry. Phenix has called attention to the simplifying, coordinating, and generative features of disciplines. Appropriate selection criteria would maximize the probability of retaining these features in the curriculum and, hence, in instruction. Phenix holds that "a discipline is knowledge organized for instruction."[30]

CURRICULUM AND INSTRUCTION

Although curriculum is not a system, it may be viewed as the output of a "curriculum-development system" and as an input into an "instructional system." (See Figure 1.)

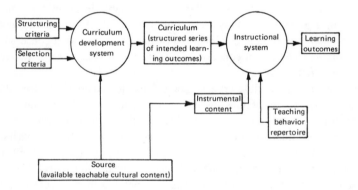

FIGURE 1

A Model Showing Curriculum as an Output of One System and an Input of Another

The instructional system has three components: planning, execution (instruction), and evaluation. Instructional planning occurs at various levels, varying in their temporal proximity to the actual instruction. Most remote is that strategic planning which results in the design of "courses" and "instructional units" within courses. Here an appropriate number of curriculum items (intended learning outcomes) are selected and organized for instructional purposes. Course and unit planners have considerable freedom in their selection and organization, so long as they do not violate curriculum stipulations with respect to hierarchy (clusters) and order. In a graded school organization, several versions of each course and unit may have to be planned to take into account differences in students' ability and readiness. Actually, each version is a different course and should be so designated, though this is seldom the case. In a nongraded instructional program, the curriculum can be arranged into a single series of courses through which students pass at varying rates.

Individual teachers continue the process of instructional planning up to and throughout the execution stage. It is they who make the final choice of learning activities and instrumental content in terms of the characteristics of the students, the availability of resources, and the exigencies of the ongoing instructional process. Even at this point, decisions must be governed by the intended outcomes stipulated by the curriculum and incorporated into the course and unit plans.

The evaluation aspect of instruction obviously involves a comparison of actual learning outcomes with the intended learning outcomes. For purposes of such comparison it is necessary to create a situation in which the student can exhibit behavior indicative that he has learned, i.e., has achieved the intended learning outcome. It is in this evaluation context that Mager's injunction[31] to specify objectives operationally as terminal behaviors at defined levels of performance under defined conditions applies. This is not to say, however, that learning consists of a change in behavior or that learning has not occurred if a behavioral change cannot be demonstrated. Nor is it the case that there has been no teaching where learning cannot be shown to have occurred. Teaching occurs whenever appropriate actions intended to produce learning are taken. Because the intentions are not fulfilled or no evidence of their being fulfilled is available does not in any way disqualify the actions as teaching.

Instruction consists of two sets of interaction. One is Dewey's "transaction" between the student and the environment manipulated by the teacher. As indicated earlier, both the content of the environment and the activities of the student are governed by the curriculum. The second interaction is the interpersonal one between the teacher and students. Flanders and Amidon[32] have developed a procedure for analyzing this interaction, and Bellack,[33] Smith,[34] Ryans,[35] and others have examined the linguistic, logical, and information-processing characteristics of the classroom discourse that facilitates the interaction. Maccia[36] has pointed out that the interaction has both motivational and content bases. The content base is clearly either derived from or inspired by curriculum, and unless the motivational base is entirely nonrational (sentimental, hedonistic, or magisterial), it, too, is curriculum-relevant.

It seems evident that many, if not most, of the so-called "curriculum reform" projects of the past decade have been concerned with instruction far more than with curriculum. Indeed, some of them have never made their curriculum explicit, whereas they have trespassed heavily in the instructional planning domain, going as far as to specify not only the learning activities to be provided but the instructional materials to be used, as well. These suggestions may well be excellent ones, so long as it is not assumed that alternative activities and materials could not possibly be devised to carry out the same curriculum as well or better. It seems probable that some of these projects have encroached upon instructional planning in a deliberate, if cynical, effort to make the curriculum "teacher-proof." On the other hand, syllabuses, courses of study, and curriculum guides have for years been freighted with lengthy compilations of suggested activities, materials, evaluation procedures, and other instructional advice, whereas, aside from an extensive list of vague objectives and an expository outline of so-called "content," they have seldom presented any curriculum at all, in the sense the term has been used in this paper.

CURRICULUM EVALUATION AND RESEARCH

Macdonald[37] has correctly pointed out that curriculum evaluation is all too often conducted at the output point of instruction rather than at the input position. Thus curriculum evaluation is confounded with instructional evaluation. Curriculum serves as the criterion for instructional evaluation; variations in instruction cannot be permitted to enter into the evaluation of curriculum. If curriculum is to be evaluated empirically on the basis of instructional outputs, then differences in instructional effectiveness must be controlled, randomized, or partialed out. Gagné has suggested a scaling method whereby instructional output data may be used " . . . to provide information about the sequence of a curriculum," but notes that it " . . . does not provide an *evaluation* of a curriculum." "It does *not* tell us how good the curriculum is." To determine the effectiveness of an entire curriculum-instruction system, Gagné suggests that "one must actually put the curriculum into use, and then measure the results in terms of student achievement, or some other specified criterion."[38]

It is probable that feedback from instruction can furnish evidence regarding the *structural* validity of a curriculum. On the basis of instructional experience, curriculum items might be found to be incorrectly ordered or hierarchical clusters might be found to be incomplete or contain superfluities. But the validity of curriculum *selection*, i.e., the omission of significant items and the inclusion of insignificant ones, must rest on some criterion other than instructional results. Cronbach[39] and Stake[40] have explored this problem at some length, and it may be expected that further progress will be made on it at the Center for Instructional Research and Curriculum Evaluation at the University of Illinois. Essential, however, to such progress is a clear delineation of curriculum and instruction.

Similarly, research on curriculum can only be conducted on the basis of some theoretical framework. As Ryans has observed, " . . . the chief function of theory is *not* to describe once and for all how certain kinds of phenomena . . . operate, but rather to provide a framework for observation and analysis."[41]

Whether the formulation of curriculum presented here will serve this purpose remains to be seen.

A schema in which curriculum is viewed as something other than "learning experiences" preserves the autonomy of creative instructional planning, free of remote prescription under the guise of curriculum development. It also clarifies the curricular research domain. Immediately susceptible to competent investigation are such questions are:

> What are the rules relating intended outcomes and more general educational and training objectives?
>
> What are the rules for selection of curriculum items within the contexts of education and training?
>
> What are the rules for ordering curriculum items and for determining when order is unimportant?
>
> What are the rules by which hierarchical clusters of curriculum items are identified?
>
> What are the architectonics of nondisciplined cultural content?
>
> What standard system of symbols would be most useful in communicating a curriculum?

SUMMARY

Some problems in current efforts at theorizing about curriculum have been discussed. Little interest in curriculum theory has been manifest by educational practitioners, academic scholars, or curriculum specialists. Curriculum theory has been confused with valuative positions regarding curriculum. The conventional definition of curriculum in terms of "planned learning experiences" has prevented a clear distinction between curriculum and instruction. Consequently, many alleged curriculum documents are primarily prescriptions or suggestions for instruction.

Recent considerations of curriculum theory have focused attention on disciplinary structures, but curriculum has been confused with the curriculum-development system of which it is an output, or it has been considered a part of the instructional system of which it is an input. An attempt was made, therefore, to develop a schema in which curriculum was defined as a structured series of intended learning outcomes. For purposes of clarity and convenience, this schema is summarized below.

A SCHEMA FOR CURRICULUM

1. A curriculum is a structured series of intended learning outcomes.
   Corollary. Curriculum does not consist of planned learning experiences.

Corollary. Curriculum is not a system but the output of one system and an input into another.

1.1 Learning outcomes consist of three classes:

    1.11 Knowledge

        1.111 Facts: items of verifiable information

        1.112 Concepts: mental constructs epitomizing facts about particular referents

        1.113 Generalizations: (including laws, principles, rules) statements of relationship among two or more concepts

    1.12 Techniques (processes, skills, abilities)

        1.121 Cognitive: methods of operating on knowledge intellectually

        1.122 Psycho-motor: methods of manipulating the body and material things effectively with respect to purposes

    1.13 Values (affects)

        1.131 Norms: societal prescriptions and preferences regarding belief and conduct

        1.132 Predilections: individual preferential dispositions (attitudes, interests, appreciations, aversions)

1.2 Whenever a curriculum is used in instruction, the intention (to achieve the outcomes) is implicit regardless of the curriculum's origin or sanction.

2. *Selection* is an essential aspect of curriculum formulation.

    2.1 The *source* from which curriculum is selected is the available culture.

    Corollary. Societal problems and the needs and interests of children are not sources of curriculum.

    2.11 Modern communication makes available cultural content that is not indigenous to the society in which the curriculum is formulated.

    2.12 Some indigenous cultural content may be unavailable due to the secrecy of those in possession of it.

    2.2 Cultural content available for curriculum is of two types: disciplinary and nondisciplinary.

    2.21 The *content* embodied in organized *disciplines* is derived from systematic inquiry conducted within a framework of assumptions and procedures accepted by scholars competent to conduct such inquiry.

    2.22 *Nondisciplinary content* is derived empirically from experience other than deliberate inquiry.

    2.3 Various *criteria* may govern the selection of curriculum from available cultural content.

    2.31 The only *necessary,* albeit insufficient, criterion for curriculum selection is that the content be *teachable*.

        2.311 Teachability implies learnability, but the converse does not necessarily hold.

        2.312 Cultural content is *teachable* if the learning of it by one person can be facilitated by direct or remote interaction with another person.

        2.313 *Teaching* is the process by which one person interacts with another with the *intention* of influencing his learning.

2.3131 There can be teaching where there is no learning.

2.3132 There can be learning without teaching.

2.314 Learning is the process by which an individual invests cultural content with *meaning,* thereby becoming capable of acting differently toward that item, or another item, of cultural content.

Corollary. Learning does not necessarily change behavior, but it changes the potential for behavior.

2.3141 Learning can be detected only by contriving a situation in which a change in behavior can be manifested.

2.3142 Learning is independent of any demonstration of its occurrence.

2.315 Cultural content is *learnable* if meaning can be perceived in it.

2.3151 Cultural content has *meaning* for an individual to the extent that he recognizes appropriate rules by which his actions toward it may be governed.

2.3152 Meanings may be symbolic, empiric, esthetic, ethic, synoetic, or synoptic (Phenix, 1964).

2.32 *Ideology* determines what additional criteria are imposed in curriculum selection.

2.321 A given society may demand that curriculum be selected in conformity with a specified set of political, social, economic, or moral *values*

2.322 Curriculum content may be selected with regard to its *utility* in the social order or in the present or anticipated life situations of learners.

2.323 Curriculum content may be selected with regard to its *significance* in the structure of intellectual disciplines.

2.33 The basis of curriculum selection differs for *training* and for *education.*

2.331 *Training* is the process of preparing an individual to perform defined functions in a predictable situation.

2.332 *Education* is the process of equipping an individual to perform undefined functions in unpredictable situations.

2.333 The selection of curriculum content for training is based on an *analysis* of the specific functions to be performed and the specific situation in which they are to be performed.

2.334 The selection of curriculum content for education is based on its having the widest possible *significance* and greatest possible *explanatory* power.

2.34 The selection of some curriculum items necessitates the selection of related items.

2.341 A set of closely related items is a curriculum *cluster*.

2.342 A curriculum cluster may consist of one type or mixed types of curriculum items.

3. *Structure* is an essential characteristic of curriculum.

3.1 Curriculum structure reveals orderings that are mandatory for instruction.

3.11 The ordering of some curriculum items is indifferent.

3.12 The ordering of some curriculum clusters determines the gross ordering of constituent items, but not their internal order.

3.13 Some curriculum clusters are ordered internally.

3.14 Curriculum ordering disregards instructional temporal spacing (grade or age placement).

3.2 Curriculum structure reveals taxonomic (hierarchical) relationships, whether or not order of items is significant.

4. Curriculum guides instruction.

4.1 Instruction is the interaction between a teaching agent and one or more individuals intending to learn.

4.2 Instruction engages intended learners in activities with cultural content.

4.21 The teaching agent influences the activities of those intending to learn.

4.22 The range of appropriate instructional activities is limited by the *type* of curriculum item.

4.23 Instructional content includes both curricular and instrumental content.

4.231 Curricular content is that cultural content explicitly intended to be learned.

4.232 Instrumental content is optional cultural content introduced into the instructional situation, not to be learned but to facilitate the intended learning.

4.24 Instructional planning consists of the selection and ordering of instructional activities and instrumental content on the basis of curriculum.

4.25 A *learning experience* is the subjective concomitant of activities with instructional content on the part of an individual engaging in them.

4.3 Instruction is episodic.

4.31 An instructional episode consists of a series of teaching cycles relevant to one or more curriculum items.

4.311 A teaching cycle involves perception, diagnosis, and action or reaction by a teaching agent and intended learners (Smith, 1961).

4.312 Teaching cycles are initiated by structuring or soliciting moves (Bellack and Davitz, 1963).

4.313 Teaching cycles include reflexive response or reaction moves (Bellack and Davitz, 1963).

4.314 Actions and reactions in teaching cycles are linguistic, performative, or expressive (Smith, 1961).

4.32 Several instructional episodes may relate to the same curriculum item, just as a given instructional episode may relate to a number of curriculum items.

5. Curriculum evaluation involves validation of both selection and structure.

5.1 Empirical evidence based on instruction can identify structural errors and omissions in selection (Gagné, 1966).

5.2 Judgmental and consensual methods are required to validate priorities and identify superfluities in selection.

6. Curriculum is the criterion for instructional evaluation.

    6.1 The effectiveness of instruction is represented by the extent to which actual outcomes correspond with intended outcomes.

    6.2 Comparisons among instructional plans and among instructors using the same instructional plan can be made only in terms of a given curriculum.

NOTES

1. Paul Lazarsfeld and Sam Sieber, *Organizing Educational Research* (Englewood Cliffs, N.J.: Prentice-Hall, 164), p. 33.

2. Philip Phenix, *Realms of Meaning* (New York: McGraw-Hill, 1964).

3. Harry S. Broudy, B. Othanel Smith, and Joe R. Burnett, *Democracy and Excellence in American Secondary Education* (Chicago: Rand McNally, 1964).

4. George A. Beauchamp, *Curriculum Theory* (Wilmette, Ill.: Kagg Press, 1961), p. 116.

5. Harold Rugg *et al., Foundations of Curriculum-Making*. Twenty-sixth Yearbook of the National Society for the Study of Education. Part II (Chicago: Public School Publishing Co., 1927), p. 11.

6. *Ibid.,* p. 6.

7. Israel Scheffler, *The Language of Education* (Springfield, Ill.: Charles C. Thomas, 1970), p. 19.

8. Harold Rugg *et al., Foundations of Curriculum-Making, op. cit.,* p. 18.

9. *Ibid.,* p. 4.

10. Association for Supervision and Curriculum Development, "What are the Sources of the Curriculum? A Symposium." Mimeo, 1962.

11. Thomas L. Faix, "Structural-Functional Analysis as a Conceptual System for Curriculum Theory and Research." Paper presented at American Educational Research Association meeting, February 1966. Mimeo.

12. James B. Macdonald, "Curriculum Theory: Problems and a Prospectus." Paper presented at Professors of Curriculum meeting, Miami Beach, April 3, 1964. Mimeo, p. p. 6.

13. *Ibid.,* p. 12.

14. His inputs include "Cultural Heritage," "Social Pressures," "Behavioral Knowledge," and "Professional Knowledge." Macdonald, *op. cit.,* p. 5. See similar terminology with respect to sources in Association for Supervision and Curriculum Development, "What are the Sources of the Curriculum?" *op. cit.*

15. Elizabeth S. Maccia, "Curriculum Theory and Policy." Educational Theory Center and Social Studies Curriculum Center, Occasional Paper 65–176, Ohio State University, 1965. Mimeo; "Instruction as Influence Toward Rule-Governed Behavior." Educational Theory Center, Occasional Paper 64–155, Ohio State University, 1964. Mimeo; "The Scientific Perspective: Only One Curricular Model." Center for the Construction of Theory in Education, Occasional Paper 63–143, Ohio State University, 1963. Mimeo.

16. $I=f (B_tRB_s)$ $B_t=I_cRM_c$ where I denotes instruction; B_t, teacher behavior; B_s, student behavior; I_c, instructional content or curriculum; and M_c, motivational content. Maccia, "Curriculum Theory and Policy," *op. cit.*, p. 8.

17. Maccia, "Curriculum Theory and Policy," *op. cit.*, p. 8; "The Scientific Perspective," *op. cit.*, p. 6.

18. "A rule is a reason or criterion which leads to one behavior rather than another. It is a way of behaving. . . ," ". . . a way of solving problems. . . ." "In an individual a rule is a cognitive structure." Maccia, "Instruction as Influence," *op. cit.*, p. 14.

19. Robert M. Gagné, "Curriculum Research and the Promotion of Learning." Invited address to AERA meeting, February 1966. Mimeo, p. 6.

20. Elliot Eisner, "Levels of Curriculum and Curriculum Research," *Elementary School Journal* 66 (December 1965), p. 156.

21. *Ibid.*, p. 158.

22. Benjamin Bloom (ed.), *Taxonomy of Educational Objectives.* Handbook I: *Cognitive Domain* (New York: Longmans, Green, 1956).

23. David R. Krathwohl, Benjamin S. Bloom, and Bertram B. Masia, *Taxonomy of Educational Objectives.* Handbook II: *Affective Domain* (New York: David McKay Co., 1964).

24. Philip Phenix, *Realms of Meaning, op. cit.*; "The Disciplines as Curriculum Content," in A.H. Passow (ed.), *Curriculum Crossroads* (New York: Teachers College Press, Columbia University, 1962), pp. 57–65.

25. Joseph J. Schwab, "Problems, Topics and Issues," in Stanley Elam (ed.), *Education and the Structure of Knowledge* (Chicago: Rand McNally, 1964), pp. 4–42; "Structure of the Disciplines: Meanings and Significances," in G.W. Ford and Lawrence Pugno (eds.), *The Structure of Knowledge and The Curriculum* (Chicago: Rand McNally, 1964), pp. 6–30.

26. Arno Bellack, "Selection and Organization of Curriculum Content: An Analysis," in *What Shall the High School Teach?* Association for Supervision and Curriculum Development Yearbook, 1956, p. 99.

27. Harold Rugg and William Withers, *Social Foundations of Education* (Englewood Cliffs, N.J.: Prentice-Hall, 1955), p. 669.

28. Broudy, Smith, and Burnett, *Democracy and Excellence, op. cit.*, pp. 48–54.

29. *Ibid.*, pp. 46–48, 54–55.

30. Phenix, "Disciplines as Curriculum Content," *op. cit.*, p. 58.

31. Robert F. Mager, *Preparing Objectives for Programmed Instruction* (Belmont, Cal.: Fearon Publishers, 1961), p. 12.

32. Edmund J. Amidon and Ned A. Flanders, *The Role of the Teacher in the Classroom* (Amidon and Associates, 1963).

33. Arno Bellack and Joel R. Davitz, *The Language of the Classroom* (New York: Institute of Psychological Research, Teachers College, Columbia University, 1963).

34. B. Othanel Smith, "A Concept of Teaching," in B.O. Smith and Robert H. Ennis (eds.), *Language and Concepts in Education* (Chicago: Rand McNally, 1961).

35. David G. Ryans, "A Model of Instruction Based on Information System Concepts," in James B. Macdonald and Robert L. Leeper (eds.), *Theories of Instruction.* Association for Supervision and Curriculum Development, 1965, pp. 36–61.

36. Maccia, "Instruction as Influence," *op. cit.*

37. James B. Macdonald, "Researching Curriculum Output: The Use of a General Systems Theory to Identify Appropriate Curriculum Outputs and Research Hypotheses." Paper presented at AERA meeting, February 1965.

38. Robert M. Gagné, "Curriculum Research and the Promotion of Learning," *op. cit.,* p. 14.

39. Lee J. Cronbach, "Evaluation for Course Improvement," in Robert W. Heath (ed), *New Curricula* (New York: Harper and Row, 1964), pp. 231–48; "The Psychological Background for Curriculum Experimentation," in Paul C. Rosenbloom (ed.), *Modern Viewpoints in the Curriculum* (New York: McGraw-Hill, 1964) pp. 19–35.

40. Robert E. Stake, "The Countenance of Educational Evaluation," Center for Instructional Research and Curriculum Evaluation, University of Illinois, 1966. Mimeo.

41. Ryans, "A Model of Instruction," *op. cit.,* p. 38.

2. BASIC COMPONENTS OF A CURRICULUM THEORY

George A. Beauchamp

In this article, I present a point of view on the basis components of a curriculum theory. I have broken the discussion into three topics: (1) a brief statement of theory-building processes, (2) a discussion of sources of potential curriculum postures, and (3) a statement outlining my own curriculum theory position. My major purpose in writing this article is to help stimulate more dialogue on curriculum theory.

BASIC THEORY-BUILDING PROCESSES

There is general agreement that a theory is a set of related statements explaining some series of events. From theory to theory, there may be variations in definition and in the character of the statements made. And the sets of events are, admittedly, always peculiar to the field within which the theorizing takes place. Nonetheless, any theorist is obliged to generate statements that provide satisfactory explanations for the particular sets of events he has under consideration.

The fundamental behaviors of a theorist, particularly in the social sciences, seem to be quite common. They are sufficiently common that we can identify certain rules for behavior in theorizing. A first and necessary task for a theorist is to fence in his field of inquiry. An important mechanism for doing so is to identify the technical language including unique or specialized terms, subjects, and

SOURCE. *Curriculum Theory Network* 10 (Fall 1972), pp. 16–22.

processes that appear to be essential to the set of events the theorist is to delineate and explain. Once the technical language has been identified, a theorist must carefully define and consistently use it throughout his theoretical work. By performing this set of tasks, the theorist satisfies the first rule in theorizing: namely, to discipline his use of technical terms. The identification and definition of technical terms assist the theorist in defining his field, and, to a great extent, in establishing the rough boundaries of the field.

In order to further the definition of the field and to begin the process of explaining the characteristics of the sets of events and the relationships among them, two more basic tasks of theorizing must be enjoined. One is to classify the accumulated information within the sets of events presumed to be in the field of inquiry. A second is to describe the circumstances and conditions under which the identified sets of events occur. When these two tasks are completed, a theorist has satisfied a second rule in theorizing: that is, to identify the principal ingredients essential to the field of concern.

Then the theorist can move to the more sophisticated processes of theory-building, which result in the establishment of relationships among the identified phenomena in the field. The performance of the complicated tasks involved here satisfies the third role of theorizing, which is to identify relationships among the various parts, or the theoretical statements, and to explain the character of those relationships. Most theories are complex wholes. The various parts may have individual meaning or significance, but meaning and significance are enhanced as the parts are related to the whole. We hear a lot about prediction as a sophisticated process in theory-building, but it takes a great deal of study of theoretical events before predictive relationships among them can be established.

The above are relatively simple rules for theory-building. Defining, describing, classifying, relating are fundamental to the more general process of explanation, which is the primary purpose of theory-building. I believe they are of cardinal importance in the guidance of efforts in the development of any curriculum theory.

SOURCES OF CURRICULUM POSTURES

In my judgment, most of the discourse on curriculum theory avoids the principal issues that must be faced if theory development in the field of curriculum is to mature. So far, I have sketched briefly what I consider to be the principal rules of theory-building that tend to be ignored. In particular the rule with respect to the careful definition of technical terms has been violated.

The field of curriculum has grown up with a proliferation of meanings associated with key technical terms, and the associated meanings often are in conflict; that is, distinctly different meanings may be associated with the same term. The most critical term for theory-building in the field of curriculum is *curriculum*. The term *curriculum* is most critical because the associated meanings accepted by the theorist identify the dimensions of the total set of events to be explained by the theory. Different meanings would involve different sets of events, and explanations for different sets of events would produce different theories.

Persons who use different meanings of *curriculum* fall into three groups. One group thinks of a curriculum as a plan for subsequent action. In this case, a curriculum is principally organized so as to reveal the decisions of the planners in response to the question of what ought to be taught in the school, or schools, for which the curriculum is intended. Normally, the intended subsequent action is instruction. In most cases, the plan is assumed to be in written form. The intended characteristics of the written form may vary considerably, but these variations provide food for discourse on the nature of curriculum design.

A significant number of curriculum authorities—the majority, in fact—operate as if *curriculum* and *instruction* were synonymous or a unified concept. There are differences in emphasis within this majority group, however. Critical to these differences is the degree to which curriculum planning and instructional planning are to be explained under the heading "curriculum," as well as distinctions among various arenas for curriculum planning and planning for instruction. For example, one person may advocate a series of steps including curriculum planning by scholars in the disciplines, curriculum planning for an individual school, and the development of specific instructional strategies by individual teachers—all under the caption of curriculum. Another might add to these the action of the classroom. A third person might propose that curriculum planning and instructional planning be accomplished simultaneously. No doubt there are others. There have been attempts within professional organizations to discriminate between curriculum theory and instructional theory, but to no avail; and in my judgment, the failure to develop theoretical postures in the two areas is due primarily to the unwillingness of people to discriminate between curriculum and instruction as two different but related dimensions of schooling.

Others, a smaller group of curriculum authorities, take an even broader view of *curriculum* than do those referred to in the paragraph above. For them, *curriculum* is a very broad term that includes the psychological processes of the learner as he acquires educational experiences. In a sense, proponents of this interpretation of *curriculum* subsume instruction, learning, and often evaluation within the concept of *curriculum*. What happens to the school pupil is so important to these authorities that they would state that each pupil has his own curriculum. I believe that advocates of this position use the term *curriculum* as synonymous with experience in the sense in which John Dewey used the term.

These different conceptual interpretations of *curriculum* should lead to the development of alternative curriculum theories because of variation induced in the sets of events. But all who engage in curriculum theory formulation are obligated to follow the basic rules of theory-building.

A POSITION ON CURRICULUM THEORY

Now I will use my own posture in curriculum theory to illustrate some of the consequences of selection from basic conceptual notions about curriculum as well as the application of theory-building rules. Since an initial decision that must be reached by a theorist is his interpretation of the word *curriculum,* I shall begin there. I choose to use the word in three ways: (1) to refer to a *curriculum,* (2) to refer to a *curriculum system,* or (3) to refer to *curriculum as a field of study.* A *curriculum* is a document designed to be used as a point of departure for instructional planning. A *curriculum system* refers to what has conventionally been called curriculum planning, curriculum implementation, and curriculum appraisal. These events I choose to call curriculum engineering. *Curriculum as a field of study,* or *a field of inquiry,* encompasses: (1) curriculum design, (2) curriculum engineering, and (3) the research and theory-building necessary to explain curriculum design and curriculum engineering.

As I previously stated, the word *curriculum* is the most important technical term within the field. All of its associations must be clearly defined by the theorist in order to prescribe the boundaries of the events he is explaining, to communicate his position to others, and to consistently do the kinds of theoretical work necessary to establish relationships among the phenomena within his field. In this connection, operational definitions are of very great value to theorists. Certainly, any single curriculum theory cannot be based upon all of the diverse ways that the word *curriculum* is used in the present literature. To try to do so would be a violation of the rule of consistency in definition and use of technical terms and a failure to fence in the theoretical field. It has helped me to formulate a few positive assertions with respect to each of the three ways I use the word.

The first is that *what* ought to be taught in schools is the primary curriculum question. Responses to this primary curriculum question would define the subject matter of a school, and the subject matter for a school constitutes the bulk of the content of a curriculum. *Why* that material ought to be taught is in partial justification for the "ought to" decision. Frequently, responses to why content should be taught in a school are spelled out in the form of objectives. *How* the subject matter of a school ought to be taught is a question for the domain of instruction, and therefore is not a primary problem for the curriculum theorist. *What happens* as a result of instruction is the primary question for evaluation with inferences for both curriculum and instruction. From this rationale, I conclude that a curriculum is a written plan for subsequent action. Basically, a curriculum plan should include a statement of goals for the school and the content (subject matter, if you please) that has been selected for the achievement of the goals. There may be other ingredients added to a curriculum, but goals and content in accordance with the administrative organization of the school constitute the basic dimensions of curriculum *design*.

In order for curricula to be created, implemented in schools, and appraised, it is necessary for curriculum workers to establish some means of engineering those decisions within the schools. This I choose to call *a curriculum system*. The fundamental processes of a curriculum system are the choice of the arena in which curriculum decisions are to be made; the selection of personnel to work within the system; the selection, ordering, and execution of working procedures; the establishment of implementation procedures; and the establishment of procedures for appraising and revising the curriculum. The primary output of a curriculum system is, of course, a curriculum.

The location of a curriculum system has a great deal to do with the choices a theorist makes with respect to the fundamental processes of the system. In countries like France, Italy, Spain, and Sweden, the arenas of decisionmaking are split. Curriculum planning takes place in the national arena, but implementation processes are invoked at local school levels. In the United States, most decisions about what shall be taught in schools are made at the level of the local school district. Politically, the local board of education is responsible for the decisions. Ideas about curriculum content generated through national projects, textbooks, state laws, or the work of scholarly groups may be treated as influences upon, or inputs to, curriculum systems located in local school districts.

To me, *curriculum as a field of inquiry* and as an arena for theory-building is defined by all of the concepts and processes associated with curriculum *design* and curriculum *engineering*. The task of the curriculum theorist is to identify, classify, and otherwise explain these various sets of events associated with design and engineering. In my opinion, some of my colleagues who write in the area of curriculum theory tend to restrict themselves to one or the other of these dimensions of the total field. I believe that this is a fundamental error, except in those cases where the individuals tacitly assume that theoretical work in design or in engineering are recognized subordinate components to the total field of curriculum theory. Certainly, we need both, but it is unrealistic to claim that one of these constitutes the entire field.

Every serious curriculum thinker realizes that research is the fundamental tool to be used by the theorist as he attempts to reach acceptable generalizations that explain or predict relationships within the field of curriculum. Most of the research that to date has been done in the field of curriculum has been in the area of curriculum engineering, and, needless to say, there is a lot more that needs to be done. We drastically need research in curriculum design. Curriculum designers today have too few choices available to them. The vast majority of the curricula that have been planned for schools are subject or discipline centered. Any variations are within this basic construct. We have some proposals for variation in the contents of curriculum, but even those variations are subject centered.

CONCLUDING COMMENTS

In the preceding paragraphs, I have identified some basic theory-building processes that ought to be utilized by anyone who is concerned with the development of curriculum theory. Sources for potentially different curriculum postures were identified. Finally, I outlined the principal ingredients of my own theoretical position.

A curriculum theorist who starts with a conceptual posture different from mine necessarily works with different sets of events, and he will arrive at different conclusions. However, it is my conviction that those who adopt different positions should proceed in a systematic way. For instance, those who take the position that curriculum and instruction are all one ball of wax should explain the complex set of events inherent in the position by carefully defining their technical terms, by describing the character of the events, and by identifying relationships among them. Obviously, the resulting propositions about curriculum design and curriculum engineering would be vastly different from those I have set forth. No doubt different research demands would be indicated. Such theoretical postures are not clearly presented in the literature at the present time, and we need them to stimulate organized dialogue on curriculum theory.

3. THE PRACTICAL: A LANGUAGE FOR CURRICULUM[1]

Joseph J. Schwab

I shall have three points. The first is this: that the field of curriculum is mori-bund, unable by its present methods and principles to continue its work and des-perately in search of new and more effective principles and methods.

The second point: the curriculum field has reached this unhappy state by inveterate and unexamined reliance on theory in an area where theory is partly inappropriate in the first place and where the theories extant, even where appro-priate, are inadequate to the tasks which the curriculum field sets them. There are honorable exceptions to this rule but too few (and too little honored) to alter the state of affairs.

The third point, which constitutes my thesis: there will be a renaissance of the field of curriculum, a renewed capacity to contribute to the quality of American education, only if the bulk of curriculum energies are diverted from the theoretic to the practical, to the quasi-practical and to the eclectic. By "eclectic" I mean the arts by which unsystematic, uneasy, but usable focus on a body of problems is effected among diverse theories, each relevant to the problems in a different way. By the "practical" I do *not* mean the curbstone practicality of the mediocre administrator and the man on the street, for whom the practical means the easily achieved, familiar goals which can be reached by familiar means. I refer, rather, to a complex discipline, relatively unfamiliar to the academic and differing radically from the disciplines of the theoretic. It is the discipline concerned with

SOURCE. *School Review* 78 (November 1969), pp. 1–23. Copyright © 1969 by Joseph J. Schwab. Published by the University of Chicago Press.

choice and action, in contrast with the theoretic, which is concerned with knowledge. Its methods lead to defensible decisions, where the methods of the theoretic lead to warranted conclusions, and differ radically from the methods and competences entailed in the theoretic. I shall sketch some of the defining aspects of practical discipline at the appropriate time.

A CRISIS OF PRINCIPLE

The frustrated state of the field of curriculum is not an idiopathology and not a condition which warrants guilt or shame on the part of its practitioners. All fields of systematic intellectual activity are liable to such crises. They are so because any intellectual discipline must begin its endeavors with untested principles. In its beginnings, its subject matter is relatively unknown, its problems unsolved, indeed, unidentified. It does not know what questions to ask, what other knowledge to rest upon, what data to seek or what to make of them once they are elicited. It requires a preliminary and necessarily untested guide to its enquiries. It finds this guide by borrowing, by invention, or by analogy, in the shape of a hazardous commitment to the character of its problems or its subject matter and a commitment to untried canons of evidence and rules of enquiry. What follows these commitments is years of their application, pursuit of the mode of enquiry demanded by the principles to which the field has committed itself. To the majority of practitioners of any field, these years of enquiry appear only as pursuit of knowledge of its subject matter or solution of its problems. They take the guiding principles of the enquiry as givens. These years of enquiry, however, are something more than pursuit of knowledge or solution of problems. They are also tests, reflexive and pragmatic, of the principles which guide the enquiries. They determine whether, in fact, the data demanded by the principles can be elicited and whether, if elicited, they can be made to constitute knowledge adequate to the complexity of the subject matter, or solutions which, in fact, do solve the problems with which the enquiry began.

In the nature of the case, these reflexive tests of the principles of enquiry are, more often than not, partially or wholly negative, for, after all, the commitment to these principles was made before there was well-tested fruit of enquiry by which to guide the commitment. The inadequacies of principles begin to show, in the case of theoretical enquiries, by failures of the subject matter to respond to the questions put to it, by incoherencies and contradictions in data and in conclusions which cannot be resolved, or by clear disparities between the knowledge yielded by the enquiries and the behaviors of the subject matter which the knowledge purports to represent. In the case of practical enquiries, inadequacies begin to show by incapacity to arrive at solutions to the problems, by inability to realize the solutions proposed, by mutual frustrations and cancellings out as solutions are put into effect.

Although these exhaustions and failures of principles may go unnoted by practitioners in the field, at least at the conscious level, what may not be represented in consciousness is nevertheless evidenced by behavior and appears in the literature and the activities of the field as signs of the onset of a crisis of principle. These signs consist of a large increase in the frequency of published papers and colloquia marked by *a flight from the subject of the field*. There are usually six signs of this flight or directions in which the flight occurs.

SIGNS OF CRISIS

The first and most important, though often least conspicuous, sign is a flight of the field itself, a translocation of its problems and the solving of them from the nominal practitioners of the field to other men. Thus one crucial frustration of the science of genetics was resolved by a single contribution from an insurance actuary. The recent desuetude of academic physiology has been marked by a conspicuous increase in the frequency of published solutions to physiological problems by medical researchers. In similar fashion, the increasing depletion of psychoanalytic principles and methods in recent years was marked by the onset of contributions to its lore by internists, biochemists, and anthropologists.

A second flight is a flight upward, from discourse about the subject of the field to discourse about the discourse of the field, from *use* of principles and methods to *talk* about them, from grounded conclusions to the construction of models, from theory to metatheory and from metatheory to metametatheory.

A third flight is downward, an attempt by practitioners to return to the subject matter in a state of innocence, shorn not only of current principles but of all principles, in an effort to take a new, a pristine and unmediated look at the subject matter. For example, one conspicuous reaction to the warfare of numerous inadequate principles in experimental psychology has been the resurgence of ethology, which begins as an attempt to return to a pure natural history of behavior, to intensive observation and recording of the behavior of animals undisturbed in their natural habitat, by observers, equally undisturbed by mediating conceptions, attempting to record anything and everything they see before them.

A fourth flight is to the sidelines, to the role of observer, commentator, historian, and critic of the contributions of others to the field.

A fifth sign consists of marked perseveration, a repetition of old and familiar knowledge in new languages which add little or nothing to the old meanings as embodied in the older and familiar language, or repetition of old and familiar formulations by way of criticisms or minor additions and modifications.

The sixth is a marked increase in eristic, contentious, and *ad hominem* debate.

I hasten to remark that these signs of crisis are not all or equally reprehensible. There is little excuse for the increase in contentiousness nor much value in the flight to the sidelines or in perseveration, but the others, in one way or another, can contribute to resolution of the crisis. The flight of the field itself is one of the more fruitful ways by which analogical principles are disclosed, modified, and adapted to the field in crisis. The flight upward, to models and metatheory, if done responsibly, which means with a steady eye on the actual problems and conditions of the field for which the models are ostensibly constructed, becomes, in fact, the proposal and test of possible new principles for the field. The flight backward, to a state of innocence, is at least an effort to break the grip of old habits of thought and thus leave space for needed new ones, though it is clear that in the matter of enquiry, as elsewhere, virginity, once lost, cannot be regained.

In the present context, however, the virtue or vice of these various flights is beside the point. We are concerned with them as signs of collapse of principles in a field, and it is my contention, based on a study not yet complete, that most of these signs may now be seen in the field of curriculum. I shall only suggest, not cite, my evidence.

THE CASE OF CURRICULUM

With respect to flight of the field itself, there can be little doubt. Of the five substantial high school science curricula, four of them—PSSC, BSCS, Chems and CBA—were instituted and managed by subject-matter specialists; the contribution of educators was small and that of curriculum specialists near vanishing point. Only Harvard Project Physics, at this writing not yet available, appears to be an exception. To one of two elementary science projects, a psychologist appears to have made a substantial contribution but curriculum specialists very little. The other—the Elementary Science Study—appears to have been substantially affected (to its advantage) by educators with one or both feet in curriculum. The efforts of the Commission on Undergraduate Education in the Biological Sciences have been carried on almost entirely by subject-matter specialists. The English Curriculum Study Centers appear to be in much the same state as the high school science curricula: overwhelmingly centered on subject specialists. Educators contribute expertise only in the area of test construction and evaluation, with here and there a contribution by a psychologist. Educators, including curriculum specialists, were massively unprepared to cope with the problem of integrated education and only by little, and late, and by trial and error, put together the halting solutions currently known as Head Start. The problems posed by the current drives toward ethnicity in education find curriculum specialists even more massively oblivious and unprepared. And I so far find myself very much alone with respect to the curriculum problems immanent in the phenomena of student protest and student revolt. (Of the social studies curriculum efforts, I shall say nothing at this time.)

On the second flight—upward—I need hardly comment. The models, the metatheory, and the metametatheory are all over the place. Many of them, moreover, are irresponsible—concerned less with the barriers to continued productivity in the field of curriculum than with exploitation of the exotic and the fashionable among forms and models of theory and metatheory: systems theory, symbolic logic, language analysis. Many others, including responsible ones, are irreversible flights upward or sideways. That is, they are models or metatheories concerned not with the judgment, the reasoned construction, or reconstruction of curriculums but with other matters—for example, how curriculum changes occur or how changes can be managed.

The flight downward, the attempt at return to a pristine, unmediated look at the subject matter, is, for some reason, a missing symptom in the case of curriculum. There are returns—to the classroom, if not to other levels or aspects of curriculum—with a measure of effort to avoid preconceptions (e.g., Smith, Bellack, and studies of communication nets and lines), but the frequency of such studies has not markedly increased. The absence of this symptom may have significance. In general, however, it is characteristic of diseases that the whole syndrome does not appear in all cases. Hence, pending further study and thought, I do not count this negative instance as weakening the diagnosis of a crisis of principle.

The fourth flight—to the sidelines—is again a marked symptom of the field of curriculum. Histories, anthologies, commentaries, criticisms, and proposals of curriculums multiply.

Perseveration is also marked. I recoil from counting the persons and books whose lives are made possible by continuing restatement of the Tyler rationale, of the character and case for behavioral objectives, of the virtues and vices of John Dewey.

The rise in frequency and intensity of the eristic and *ad hominem* is also marked. Thus one author climaxes a series of petulances by the remark that what he takes to be his own forte "has always been rare—and shows up in proper perspective the happy breed of educational reformer who can concoct a brand new, rabble-rousing theory of educational reform while waiting for the water to fill the bathtub."

There is little doubt, in short, that the field of curriculum is in a crisis of principle.

A crisis of principle arises, as I have suggested, when principles are exhausted—when the questions they permit have all been asked and answered—or when the efforts at enquiry instigated by the principles have at last exhibited their inadequacy to the subject matter and the problems which they were designed to attack. My second point is that the latter holds in the case of curriculum: the curriculum movement has been inveterately theoretic, and its theoretic bent has let it down. A brief conspectus of instances will suggest the extent of this theoretic bent and what is meant by "theoretic."

CHARACTERISTICS OF THEORY

Consider first the early, allegedly Herbartian efforts (recently revived by Bruner). These efforts took the view that ideas were formed by children out of received notions and experiences of things, and that these ideas functioned thereafter as discriminators and organizers of what was later learned. Given this view, the aim of curriculum was to discriminate the right ideas (by way of analysis of extant bodies of knowledge), determine the order in which they could be learned by children as they developed, and thereafter present these ideas at the right times with clarity, associations, organization, and application. A theory of mind and knowledge thus solves by one mighty coup the problem of what to teach, when, and how; and what is fatally theoretic here is not the presence of a theory of mind and a theory of knowledge, though their presence is part of the story, but the dispatch, the sweeping appearance of success, the vast simplicity which grounds this purported solution to the problem of curriculum. And lest we think that this faith in the possibility of successful neatness, dispatch, and sweeping generality is a mark of the past, consider the concern of the National Science Teachers Association only four years ago "with identifying the broad principles that can apply to any and all curriculum development efforts in science," a concern crystallized in just seven "conceptual schemes" held to underlie all science. With less ambitious sweepingness but with the same steadfast concern for a single factor—in this case, a supposed fixed structure of knowledge—one finds similar efforts arising from the Association of College Teachers of Education, from historians, even from teachers of literature.

Consider, now, some of the numerous efforts to ground curriculum in derived objectives. One effort seeks the ground of its objectives in social need and finds its social needs in just those facts about its culture which are sought and found under the aegis of a single conception of culture. Another grounds its objectives in the social needs identified by a single theory of history and of political evolution.

A third group of searches for objectives are grounded in theories of personality. The persuasive coherence and plausibility of Freudianism persuaded its followers to aim to supply children with adequate channels of sublimation of surplus libido, appropriate objects and occasions for aggressions, a properly undemanding ego ideal, and an intelligent minimum of taboos. Interpersonal theories direct their adherents to aim for development of abilities to relate to peers, "infeers," and "supeers," in relations nurturant and receiving, adaptive, vying, approving and disapproving. Theories of actualization instruct their adherents to determine the salient potentialities of each child and to see individually to the development of each.

Still other searches for objectives seek their aims in the knowledge needed to "live in the modern world," in the attitudes and habits which minimize dissonance with the prevailing mores of one's community or social class, in the skills required for success in a trade or vocation, in the ability to participate effectively as member of a group. Still others are grounded in some quasi-ethics, some view of the array of goods which are good for man.

Three features of these typical efforts at curriculum making are significant here, each of which has its own lesson to teach us. First, each is grounded in a theory as such. We shall return to this point in a moment. Second, each is grounded in a theory from the social or behavioral sciences: psychology, psychiatry, politics, sociology, history. Even the ethical bases and theories of "mind" are behavioral. To this point, too, we shall return in a moment. Third, they are theories concerning *different* subject matters. One curriculum effort is grounded in concern for the individual, another in concern for groups, others in concern for cultures, communities, societies, minds, or the extant bodies of knowledge.[2]

NEED FOR AN ECLECTIC

The significance of this third feature is patent to the point of embarassment: no curriculum grounded in but one of these subjects can possibly be adequate, defensible. A curriculum based on theory about individual personality, which thrusts society, its demands and its structure, far into the background or ignores them entirely, can be nothing but incomplete and doctrinaire, for the individuals in question are in fact members of a society and must meet its demands to some minimum degree since their existence and prosperity as individuals depend on the functioning of their society. In the same way, a curriculum grounded only in a view of social need or social change must be equally doctrinaire and incomplete, for societies do not exist only for their own sakes but for the prosperity of their members as individuals as well. In the same way, learners are not only minds or knowers but bundles of affects, individuals, personalities, earners of livings. They are not only group interactors but possessors of private lives.

It is clear, I submit, that a defensible curriculum or plan of curriculum must be one which somehow takes account of all these sub-subjects which pertain to man. It cannot take only one and ignore the others; it cannot even take account of many of them and ignore one. Not only is each of them a constituent and a condition for decent human existence but each interpenetrates the others. That is, the character of human personalities is a determiner of human society and the behavior of human groups. Conversely, the conditions of group behavior and the character of societies determine in some large part the personalities which their members develop, the way their minds work, and what they can learn and use by way of knowledge and competence. These various "things" (individuals, societies, cultures, patterns of enquiry, "structures" of knowledge or of enquiries, apperceptive masses, problem solving), though discriminable as separate subjects of differing modes of enquiry, are nevertheless parts or affectors of one another, or coactors. (Their very separation for purposes of enquiry is what marks the outcomes of such enquiries as "theoretic" and consequently incomplete.) In practice, they constitute one complex, organic agency. Hence, a focus on only one not only ignores the others but vitiates the quality and completeness with which the selected one is viewed.

It is equally clear, however, that there is not, and will not be in the foreseeable future, one theory of this complex whole which is other than a collection of unusable generalities. Nor is it true that the lack of a theory of the whole is due to the narrowness, stubbornness, or merely habitual specialism of social and behavioral scientists. Rather, their specialism and the restricted purview of their theories are functions of their subject, its enormous complexity, its vast capacity for difference and change. Man's competence at the construction of theoretical knowledge is so far most inadequate when applied to the subject of man. There have been efforts to conceive principles of enquiry which would encompass the whole variety and complexity of humanity, but they have fallen far short of adequacy to the subject matter or have demanded the acquisition of data and modes of interpretation of data beyond our capabilities. There *are* continuing efforts to find bridging terms which would relate the principles of enquiry of one subfield of the social sciences to another and thus begin to effect connections among our knowledges of each, but successful bridges are so far few and narrow and permit but a trickle of connection. As far, then, as theoretical knowledge is concerned, we must wrestle as best we can with numerous, largely unconnected, separate theories of these many, artificially discriminated subsubjects of man.

I remarked in the beginning that renewal of the field of curriculum would require diversion of the bulk of its energies from theory to the practical, the quasi-practical, and the eclectic. The state of affairs just described, the existence and the necessarily continuing existence of separate theories of separate subsubjects distributed among the social sciences, constitutes the case for one of these modes, the necessity of an eclectic, of arts by which a usable focus on a common body of problems is effected among theories which lack theoretical connection. The argument can be simply summarized. A curriculum grounded in but one or a few subsubjects of the social sciences is indefensible; contributions from all are required. There is no foreseeable hope of a unified theory in the immediate or middle future, nor of a metatheory which will tell us how to put those subsubjects together or order them in a fixed hierarchy of importance to the problems of curriculum. What remains as a viable alternative is the unsystematic, uneasy, pragmatic, and uncertain unions and connections which can be effected in an eclectic. And I must add, anticipating our discussion of the practical, that *changing* connections and *differing* orderings at different times of these separate theories, will characterize a sound eclectic.

The character of eclectic arts and procedures must be left for discussion on another occasion. Let it suffice for the moment that witness of the high effectiveness of eclectic methods and of their accessibility is borne by at least one field familiar to us all—Western medicine. It has been enormously effective, and the growth of its competence dates from its disavowal of a single doctrine and its turn to eclecticism.

THE PLACE OF THE PRACTICAL

I turn now, from the fact that the theories which ground curriculum plans pertain to different subsubjects of a common field, to the second of the three features which characterize our typical instances of curriculum planning—the fact that the ground of each plan is a theory, a theory as such.

The significance of the existence of theory as such at the base of curricular planning consists of what it is that theory does not and cannot encompass. All theories, even the best of them in the simplest sciences, necessarily neglect some aspects and facets of the facts of the case. A theory covers and formulates the *regularities* among the things and events it subsumes. It abstracts a general or ideal case. It leaves behind the nonuniformities, the particularities, which characterize each concrete instance of the facts subsumed. Moreover, in the process of idealization, theoretical enquiry may often leave out of consideration conspicuous facets of *all* cases because its substantive principles of enquiry or its methods cannot handle them. Thus the constantly accelerating body of classical mechanics was the acceleration of a body in "free" fall, fall in a perfect vacuum, and the general or theoretical rule formulated in classical mechanics is far from describing the fall of actual bodies in actual mediums—the only kinds of fall then known. The force equation of classical dynamics applied to bodies of visible magnitudes ignores friction. The rule that light varies inversely as the square of the distance holds exactly only for an imaginary point source of light. For real light sources of increasing expanse, the so-called law holds more and more approximately, and for very large sources it affords little or no usable information. And what is true of the best of theories in the simplest sciences is true a fortiori in the social sciences. Their subject matters are apparently so much more variable, and clearly so much more complex, that their theories encompass much less of their subjects than do the theories of the physical and biological sciences.

Yet curriculum is brought to bear not on ideal or abstract representatives but on the real thing, on the concrete case in all its completeness and with all its differences from all other concrete cases on which the theoretic abstraction is silent. The materials of a concrete curriculum will not consist merely of portions of "science," of "literature," of "process." On the contrary, their constituents will be particular assertions about selected matters couched in a particular vocabulary, syntax, and rhetoric. They will be particular novels, short stories, or lyric poems, each, for better or for worse, with its own flavor. They will be particular acts upon particular matters in a given sequence. The curriculum will be brought to bear not in some archetypical classroom but in a particular locus in time and space with smells, shadows, seats, and conditions outside its walls which may have much to do with what is achieved inside. Above all, the supposed beneficiary is not the generic child, not even a class or kind of child out of the psychological or sociological literature pertaining to the child. The beneficiaries will consist of very local kinds of children and, within the local kinds, individual children. The same diversity holds with respect to teachers and what they do. The generalities about science, about literature, about children in general, about children or teachers of some specified class or kind, may be true. But they attain this status in virtue of what they leave out, and the omissions affect what remains. A Guernsey cow is not only something more than cow, having specific features omitted from description of the genus; it is also cowy in ways differing from the cowiness of a Texas longhorn. The specific not only adds to the generic; it also modulates it.

These ineluctable characteristics of theory and the consequent ineluctable disparities between real things and their representation in theory constitute one argument for my thesis, that a large bulk of curriculum energies must be diverted from the theoretic, not only to the eclectic but to the practical and the quasi-practical. The argument, again, can be briefly summarized. The stuff of theory is abstract or idealized representations of real things. But curriculum in action treats real things: real acts, real teachers, real children, things richer and different from their theoretical representations. Curriculum will deal badly with its real things if it treats them merely as replicas of their theoretic representations. If, then, theory is to be used well in the determination of curricular practice, it requires a supplement. It requires arts which bring a theory to its application: first, arts which identify the disparities between real thing and theoretic representation; second, arts which modify the theory in the course of its application, in the light of the discrepancies; and, third, arts which devise ways of taking account of the many aspects of the real thing which the theory does not take into account. These are some of the arts of the practical.

THEORIES FROM SOCIAL SCIENCES

The significance of the third feature of our typical instances of curriculum work—that their theories are mainly theories from the social and behavioral sciences—will carry us to the remainder of the argument for the practical. Nearly all theories in all the behavioral sciences are marked by the coexistence of competing theories. There is not one theory of personality but twenty, representing at least six radically different choices of what is relevant and important in human behavior. There is not one theory of groups but several. There is not one theory of learning but half a dozen. All the social and behavioral sciences are marked by "schools," each distinguished by a different choice of principle of enquiry, each of which selects from the intimidating complexities of the subject matter the small fraction of the whole with which it can deal.

The theories which arise from enquiries so directed are, then, radically incomplete, each of them incomplete to the extent that competing theories take hold of different aspects of the subject of enquiry and treat it in a different way. Further, there is perennial invention of new principles which bring to light new facets of the subject matter, new relations among the facets and new ways of treating them. In short, there is every reason to suppose that any one of the extant theories of behavior is a pale and incomplete representation of actual behavior. There is similar reason to suppose that if all the diversities of fact, the different aspects of behavior treated in each theory, were somehow to be brought within the bounds of a single theory, that theory would still fall short of comprehending the whole of human behavior—in two respects. In the first place, it would not comprehend what there may be of human behavior which we do not see by virtue of the restricted light by which we examine behavior. In the second place, such a single theory will necessarily interpret its data in the light of its one set of principles, assigning to these data only one set of significances and establishing among them only one set of relations. It will remain the case, then, that a diversity of theories may tell us more than a single one, even though the "factual" scope of the many and the one are the same.

It follows, then, that such theories are not, and will not be, adequate by themselves to tell us what to do with human beings or how to do it. What they variously suggest and the contrary guidances they afford to choice and action must be mediated and combined by eclectic arts and must be massively supplemented, as well as mediated, by knowledge of some other kind derived from another source.

Some areas of choice and action with respect to human behavior have long since learned this lesson. Government is made possible by a lore of politics derived from immediate experience of the vicissitudes and tangles of legislating and administering. Institution of economic guidances and controls owes as much to unmediated experience of the marketplace as it does to formulas and theories. Even psychotherapy has long since deserted its theories of personality as sole guides to therapy and relies as much or more on the accumulated, explicitly nontheoretic lore accumulated by practitioners, as it does on theory or eclectic combinations of theory. The law has systematized the accumulation of direct experience of actual cases in its machinery for the recording of cases and opinions as precedents which continuously monitor, supplement, and modify the meaning and application of its formal "knowledge," its statutes. It is this recourse to accumulated lore, to experience of actions and their consequences, to action and reaction at the level of the concrete case, which constitutes the heart of the practical. It is high time that curriculum do likewise.

THE PRACTICAL ARTS

The arts of the practical are onerous and complex; hence only a sampling must suffice to indicate the character of this discipline and the changes in educational investigation which would ensue on adoption of the discipline. I shall deal briefly with four aspects of it.

The practical arts begin with the requirement that existing institutions and existing practices be preserved and altered piecemeal, not dismantled and replaced. It is further necessary that changes be so planned and so articulated with what remains unchanged that the functioning of the whole remain coherent and unimpaired. These necessities stem from the very nature of the practical—that it is concerned with the maintenance and improvement of patterns of purposed action, and especially concerned that the effects of the pattern through time shall retain coherence and relevance to one another.

This is well seen in the case of the law. Statutes are repealed or largely rewritten only as a last resort, since to do so creates confusion and diremption between old judgments under the law and judgments to come, confusion which must lead either to weakening of law through disrepute or a painful and costly process of repairing the effects of past judgments so as to bring them into conformity with the new. It is vastly more desirable that changes be instituted in small degrees and in immediate adjustment to the peculiarities of particular new cases which call forth the change.

The consequence, in the case of the law, of these demands of the practical is that the servants of the law must know the law through and through. They must know the statutes themselves, the progression of precedents and interpretations which have effected changes in them, and especially the present state of affairs— the most recent decisions under the law and the calendar of cases which will be most immediately affected by contemplated additions to precedent and interpretation.

The same requirements would hold for a practical program of improvement of education. It, too, would effect its changes in small progressions, in coherence with what remains unchanged, and this would require that we know *what is and has been going on in American schools.*

At present, we do not know. My own incomplete investigations convince me that we have not the faintest reliable knowledge of how literature is taught in the high schools, or what actually goes on in science classrooms. There are a dozen different ways in which the novel can be read. Which ones are used by whom, with whom, and to what effect? What selections from the large accumulation of biological knowledge are made and taught in this school system and that, to what classes and kinds of children, to what effect? To what extent is science taught as verbal formulas, as congeries of unrelated facts, as so-called principles and conceptual structures, as outcomes of enquiry? In what degree and kind of simplification and falsification is scientific enquiry conveyed, if it is conveyed at all?

A count of textbook adoptions will not tell us, for teachers select from textbooks and alter their treatment (often quite properly) and can frustrate and negate the textbook's effort to alter the pattern of instruction. We cannot tell from lists of objectives, since they are usually so vastly ambiguous that almost anything can go on under their aegis or, if they are not ambiguous, reflect pious hopes as much as actual practice. We cannot tell from lists of "principles" and "conceptual structures," since these, in their telegraphic brevity are also ambiguous and say nothing of the shape in which they are taught or the extent.

What is wanted is a totally new and extensive pattern of *empirical* study of classroom action and reaction; a study, not as basis for theoretical concerns about the nature of the teaching or learning process, but as a basis for beginning to know what we are doing, what we are not doing, and to what effect—what changes are needed, which needed changes can be instituted with what costs or economies, and how they can be effected with minimum tearing of the remaining fabric of educational effort.

This is an effort which will require new mechanisms of empirical investigation, new methods of reportage, a new class of educational researchers, and much money. It is an effort without which we will continue largely incapable of making defensible decisions about curricular changes, largely unable to put them into effect and ignorant of what real consequences, if any, our efforts have had.

A very large part of such a study would, I repeat, be direct and empirical study of action and reaction in the classroom itself, not merely the testing of student change. But one of the most interesting and visible alterations of present practice which might be involved is a radical change in our pattern of testing students. The common pattern tries to determine the extent to which *intended* changes have been brought about. This would be altered to an effort to find out what changes have occurred, to determine side effects as well as mainline consequences, since the distinction between these two is always in the eye of the intender and side effects may be as great in magnitude and as fatal or healthful for students as the intended effects.

A second facet of the practical: its actions are undertaken with respect to identified frictions and failures in the machine and inadequacies evidenced in felt shortcomings of its products. This origin of its actions leads to two marked differences in operation from that of theory. Under the control of theory, curricular changes have their origin in new notions of person, group or society, mind or knowledge, which give rise to suggestions of new things curriculum might be or do. This is an origin which, by its nature, takes little or no account of the existing effectiveness of the machine or the consequences to this effectiveness of the institution of novelty. If there is concern for what may be displaced by innovation or for the incoherences which may ensue on the insertion of novelty, the concern is gratuitous. It does not arise from the theoretical considerations which commend the novelty. The practical, on the other hand, because it institutes changes to repair frictions and deficiencies, is commanded to determine the whole array of possible effects of proposed change, to determine what new frictions and deficiencies the proposed change may unintentionally produce.

The other effective difference between theoretical and practical origins of deliberate change is patent. Theory, by being concerned with new things to do, is unconcerned with the successes and failures of present doings. Hence present failures, unless they coincide with what is repaired by the proposed innovations, go unnoticed—as do present successes. The practical, on the other hand, is directly and deliberately concerned with the diagnosis of ills of the curriculum.

These concerns of the practical for frictions and failures of the curricular machine would, again, call for a new and extensive pattern of enquiry. The practical requires curriculum study to seek its problems where its problems lie— in the behaviors, misbehaviors, and nonbehaviors of its students as they begin to evince the effects of the training they did and did not get. This means continuing assessment of students as they leave primary grades for the secondary school, leave secondary school for jobs and colleges. It means sensitive and sophisticated assessment by way of impressions, insights, and reactions of the community which sends its children to the school; employers of students, new echelons of teachers of students; the wives, husbands, and cronies of exstudents; the people with whom exstudents work; the people who work under them. Curriculum study will look into the questions of what games exstudents play; what, if anything, they do about politics and crime in the streets; what they read, if they do; what they watch on television and what they make of what they watch, again, if anything. Such studies would be undertaken, furthermore, not as mass study of products of the American school, taken in toto, but as studies of significantly separable schools and school systems—suburban and inner city, Chicago and Los Angeles, South Bend and Michigan City.

I emphasize sensitive and sophisticated assessment because we are concerned here, as in the laying of background knowledge of what goes in schools, not merely with the degree to which avowed objectives are achieved but also with detecting the failures and frictions of the machine: what it has not done or thought of doing, and what side effects its doings have had. Nor are we concerned with successes and failures only as measured in test situations but also as evidenced in life and work. It is this sort of diagnosis which I have tried to exemplify in a recent treatment of curriculum and student protest.[3]

A third facet of the practical I shall call the anticipatory generation of alternatives. Intimate knowledge of the existing state of affairs, early identification of problem situations, and effective formulation of problems are necessary to effective practical decision but not sufficient. It requires also that there be available to practical deliberation the greatest possible number and fresh diversity of alternative solutions to the problem. The reason for this requirement, in one aspect, is obvious enough: the best choice among poor and shopworn alternatives will still be a poor solution to the problem. Another aspect is less obvious. The problems which arise in an institutional structure which has enjoyed good practical management will be novel problems, arising from changes in the times and circumstances and from the consequences of previous solutions to previous problems. Such problems, with their strong tincture of novelty, cannot be solved by familiar solutions. They cannot be well solved by apparently new solutions arising from old habits of mind and old ways of doing things.

A third aspect of the requirement for anticipatory generation of alternatives is still less obvious. It consists of the fact that practical problems do not present themselves wearing their labels around their necks. Problem situations, to use Dewey's old term, present themselves to consciousness, but the character of the problem, its formulation, does not. This depends on the eye of the beholder. And this eye, unilluminated by possible fresh solutions to problems, new modes of attack, new recognitions of degrees of freedom for change among matters formerly taken to be unalterable, is very likely to miss the novel features of new problems or dismiss them as "impractical." Hence the requirement that the generation of problems be anticipatory and not await the emergence of the problem itself.

To some extent, the *theoretical* bases of curricular change—such items as emphasis on enquiry, on discovery learning, and on structure of the disciplines—contribute to this need but not sufficiently or with the breadth which permits effective deliberation. That is, these theoretic proposals tend to arise in single file, out of connection with other proposals which constitute alternatives, or, more important, constitute desiderata or circumstances which affect the choice or rejection of proposals. Consider, in regard to the problem of the "single file," only one relation between the two recent proposals subsumed under "creativity" and "structure of knowledge." If creativity implies some measure of invention, and "structure of knowledge" implies (as it does in one version) the systematic induction of conceptions as soon as children are ready to grasp them, an issue is joined. To the extent that the latter is timely and well done, scope for the former is curtailed. To the extent that children can be identified as more or less creative, "structure of knowledge" would be brought to bear on different children at different times and in different ways.

A single case, taken from possible academic resources of education, will suggest the new kind of enquiry entailed in the need for anticipatory generation of alternatives. Over the years, critical scholarship has generated, as remarked earlier, a dozen different conceptions of the novel, a dozen or more ways in which the novel can be read, each involving its own emphases and its own arts of recovery of meaning in the act of reading. Novels can be read, for example, as bearers of wisdom, insights into vicissitudes of human life and ways of enduring them. Novels can also be read as moral instructors, as sources of vicarious experience, as occasions for aesthetic experience. They can be read as models of human creativity, as displays of social problems, as political propaganda, as revelations of diversities of manners and morals among different cultures and classes of people, or as symptoms of their age.

Now what, in fact, is the full parade of such possible uses of the novel? What is required by each in the way of competences of reading, discussion, and thought? What are the rewards, the desirable outcomes, which are likely to ensue for students from each kind of reading or combinations of them? For what kinds or classes of students is each desirable? There are further problems demanding anticipatory consideration. If novels are chosen and read as displays of social problems and depictions of social classes, what effect will such instruction in literature have on instruction in the social studies? What will teachers need to know and be able to do in order to enable students to discriminate and appropriately connect the *aperçus* of artists, the accounts of historians, and the conclusions of social scientists on such matters? How will the mode of instruction in science (e.g., as verified truths) and in literature (as "deep insights" or artistic constructions or matters of opinion) affect the effects of each?

The same kinds of questions could be addressed to history and to the social studies generally. Yet, nowhere, in the case of literature, have we been able to find cogent and energetic work addressed to them. The journals in the field of English teaching are nearly devoid of treatment of them. College and university courses, in English or education, which address such problems with a modicum of intellectual content are as scarce as hen's teeth. We cannot even find an unbiased conspectus of critical theory more complete than *The Pooh Perplex,* and treatments of problems of the second kind (pertaining to interaction of literature instruction with instruction in other fields) are also invisible.

Under a soundly practical dispensation in curriculum the address of such questions would be a high priority and require recruitment to education of philosophers and subject-matter specialists of a quality and critical sophistication which it has rarely, if ever, sought.

As the last sampling of the practical, consider its method. It falls under neither of the popular platitudes: it is neither deductive nor inductive. It is deliberative. It cannot be inductive because the target of the method is not a generalization or explanation but a decision about action in a concrete situation. It cannot be deductive because it deals with the concrete case, not abstractions from cases, and the concrete case cannot be settled by mere application of a principle. Almost every concrete case falls under two or more principles, **and**

every concrete case will possess some cogent characteristics which are encompassed in no principle. The problem of selecting an appropriate man for an
important post is a case in point. It is not a problem of selecting a representative
of the appropriate personality type who exhibits the competences officially
required for the job. The man we hire is more than a type and a bundle of
competences. He is a multitude of probable behaviors which escape the net of
personality theories and cognitive scales. He is endowed with prejudices, man-
nerisms, habits, tics, and relatives. And all of these manifold particulars will
affect his work and the work of those who work for him. It is deliberation which
operates in such cases to select the appropriate man.

COMMITMENT TO DELIBERATION

Deliberation is complex and arduous. It treats both ends and means and must
treat them as mutually determining one another. It must try to identify, with
respect to both, what facts may be relevant. It must try to ascertain the relevant
facts in the concrete case. It must try to identify the desiderata in the case. It must
generate alternative solutions. It must make every effort to trace the branching
pathways of consequences which may flow from each alternative and affect
desiderata. It must then weigh alternatives and their costs and consequences
against one another and choose, not the right alternative, for there *is* no such
thing, but the best one.

I shall mention only one of the new kinds of activity which would ensue on
commitment to deliberation. It will require the formation of a new public and
new means of communication among its constituent members. Deliberation
requires consideration of the widest possible variety of alternatives if it is to be
most effective. Each alternative must be viewed in the widest variety of lights.
Ramifying consequences must be traced to all parts of the curriculum. The
desirability of each alternative must be felt out, "rehearsed," by a representative variety of all those who must live with the consequences of the chosen
action. And a similar variety must deal with the identification of problems as well
as with their solution.

This will require penetration of the curtains which now separate educational
psychologist from philosopher, sociologist from test constructor, historian from
administrator; it will require new channels connecting the series from teacher,
supervisor, and school administrator at one end to research specialists at the
other. Above all, it will require renunciation of the specious privileges and
hegemonies by which we maintain the fiction that problems of science curriculum, for example, have no bearing on problems of English literature or the
social studies. The aim here is *not* a dissolving of specialization and special
responsibilities. Quite the contrary: if the variety of lights we need are to be

obtained, the variety of specialized interests, competences, and habits of mind which characterize education must be cherished and nurtured. The aim, rather, is to bring the members of this variety to bear on curriculum problems by communication with one another.

Concretely, this means the establishment of new journals, and education of educators so that they can write for them and read them. The journals will be forums where possible problems of curriculum will be broached from many sources and their possible importance debated from many points of view. They will be the stage for display of anticipatory solutions to problems, from a similar variety of sources. They will constitute deliberative assemblies in which problems and alternative solutions will be argued by representatives of all for the consideration of all and for the shaping of intelligent consensus.

Needless to say, such journals are not alone sufficient. They stand as only one concrete model of the kind of forum which is required. Similar forums, operating viva voce and in the midst of curriculum operation and curriculum change, are required: of the teachers, supervisors, and administrators of a school; of the supervisors and administrators of a school system; of representatives of teachers, supervisors, and curriculum makers in subject areas and across subject areas; of the same representatives and specialists in curriculum, psychology, sociology, administration, and the subject-matter fields.[4]

The education of educators to participate in this deliberative process will be neither easy nor quickly achieved. The education of the present generation of specialist researchers to speak to the schools and to one another will doubtless be hardest of all, and on this hardest problem I have no suggestion to make. But we could begin within two years to initiate the preparation of teachers, supervisors, curriculum makers, and graduate students of education in the uses and arts of deliberation—and we should.

For graduate students, this should mean that their future enquiries in educational psychology, philosophy of education, educational sociology, and so on, will find more effective focus on enduring problems of education, as against the attractions of the current foci of the parent disciplines. It will begin to exhibit to graduate students what their duties are to the future schoolmen whom they will teach. For teachers, curriculum makers, and others close to the classroom, such training is of special importance. It will not only bring immediate experience of the classroom effectively to bear on problems of curriculum but enhance the quality of that experience, for almost every classroom episode is a stream of situations requiring discrimination of deliberative problems and decision thereon.

By means of such journals and such an education, the educational research establishment might at last find a means for channeling its discoveries into sustained improvement of the schools instead of into a procession of ephemeral bandwagons.

NOTES

1. A version of this paper was delivered to Section B of the American Educational Research Association, Los Angeles, February 1969. This paper has been prepared as part of a project supported by a grant from the Ford Foundation.

2. It should be clear by now that "theory" as used in this paper does *not* refer only to grand schemes such as the general theory of relativity, kinetic-molecular theory, the Bohr atom, the Freudian construction of a tripartite psyche. The attempt to give an account of human maturation by the discrimination of definite states (e.g., oral, anal, genital), an effort to aggregate human competences into a small number of primary mental abilities— these too are theoretic. So also are efforts to discriminate a few large classes of persons and to attribute to them defining behaviors: e.g., the socially mobile, the culturally deprived, the creative.

3. *College Curriculum and Student Protest* (Chicago: University of Chicago Press, 1969).

4. It will be clear from these remarks that the conception of curricular method proposed here is immanent in the Tyler rationale. This rationale calls for a diversity of talents and insists on the practical and eclectic treatment of a variety of factors. Its effectiveness in practice is vitiated by two circumstances. Its focus on "objectives," with their massive ambiguity and equivocation, provides far too little of the concrete matter required for deliberation and leads only to delusive consensus. Second, those who use it are not trained for the deliberative procedures it requires.

4. THE ORGANIZATION OF LEARNING EXPERIENCES

Ralph W. Tyler

In developing basic concepts with which to think about curriculum problems, less progress has been made with regard to the organization of learning experiences than with the other aspects of the curriculum. To eliminate the confusion over the widely varying classifications of curriculum learning and learning in extracurriculum activities, students of the curriculum have developed a definition of "school curriculum" upon which there is a surprising amount of agreement. The "school curriculum" is commonly defined as all of the learning which is planned and guided by the school, whether or not it is carried on in classes, on the playground, or in other segments of the pupils' lives.

There is also considerable agreement among curriculum workers regarding the nature of objectives. Current curriculum theory views the ends sought as desired changes in the behavior of pupils, "behavior" being used in the broad sense to include thinking, feeling, and acting. The aim of the school curriculum is to develop in pupils those reaction patterns that are of greatest significance. There are, of course, varying conceptions of what reaction patterns are of greatest significance, but the nature of educational objectives as changes in pupil behavior is a common concept of curriculum theories.

Furthermore, there are several well-defined techniques for attacking the

SOURCE. In Virgil E. Herrick and Ralph W. Tyler (eds.), *Toward Improved Curriculum Theory*. Supplementary Educational Monograph No. 71 (Chicago: University of Chicago Press, 1950), pp. 59-67. Copyright © 1950 by the University of Chicago.

problem of objectives, each of which has some theoretical explanation and support. For example, one attack upon objectives is to analyze the activities, interests, problems, and deficiencies of the pupils to identify pupil needs that might serve as the bases for the educational objectives. Another is to analyze contemporary society—its problems and the activities and difficulties of adults in society—to identify social demands and needs that imply educational goals. The various techniques that have been developed for attacking the problem of objectives are not mutually consistent, nor are they altogether adequate; but theory is evolving to provide a more coherent guide for action in dealing with problems of this type. The attack upon curriculum objectives has been given most attention in curriculum theory.

The problem of selecting and designing learning experiences to attain the desired objectives has been given much less attention in its theoretical aspects, but theories of learning have contributed greatly to our concepts in this field. For example, the associationist theory of learning, with its emphasis upon exercise and effect, has played a large part in the planning of many curriculums. This theory places emphasis upon learning experiences in which the pupils practice the behavior desired as the objective and in which the pupils derive satisfaction from these experiences. On the other hand, dynamic theories of learning are also guiding many current curriculum developments. These theories stress learning experiences which involve goals already recognized by the pupils and which provide opportunity for the pupils to attain the goals or to move toward their attainment. With the aid of developing theories of learning, more adequate theory for the selection of the learning experiences of the curriculum appears to be emerging.

THE IMPORTANCE OF ORGANIZATION

In attacking the problem of the organization of learning experiences, very little theoretical structure has been developed and widely tested. Yet this is a very significant problem in curriculum construction. One of the most important respects in which a curriculum differs from the informal and incidental learnings that take place on the street, on the playground, or at other places outside the school is in the conscious effort to organize the learning experiences of the curriculum. Without organization, learning experiences are isolated, chaotic, and haphazard. No matter how effective an individual learning experience may be, if it is not followed up in subsequent phases, it is not likely that significant changes will take place in the learner. Some of the major changes in learners that the school seeks—changes in basic habits, in ways of thinking, in skills, in attitudes, in interests—are changes which require a considerable period of time to develop and which involve continuous attention; that is, they require a large number of learning experiences focused upon the same outcomes. Hence, the organization of learning experiences is an important phase of curriculum construction.

COMPLEXITY OF THE PROBLEM OF ORGANIZATION

The organization of learning experiences not only is an important aspect of curriculum construction but is also a difficult and complex phase. It poses such questions as these:

How can the learning experiences of next week and next month best reinforce those of this week and this month so as to produce a maximum cumulative effect?

How can the learning experiences of this semester not only reinforce those of last semester but go more deeply and more broadly into the field so as to get increasingly deeper and broader understandings on the part of students?

How can the learning experiences in English be related to those in social studies so that appropriate and efficient reinforcement may be provided?

These are questions that can be answered only in the light of a comprehensive theory of curriculum organization based upon the psychology of learning and upon experience and experimentation in schools. Without a comprehensive theory for guidance, the organization of the curriculum is likely to be partial, spasmodic, and relatively ineffective. Hence, an important task for students of the curriculum is to develop a comprehensive theory regarding the organization of learning experiences.

It is not the purpose of this paper to present a comprehensive theory of organization, for no such theory has thus far been formulated by curriculum workers. It is my purpose not only to indicate the importance of formulating an adequate theory of organization but also to outline some of the basic topics that must be treated in it.

DEFINING THE LIMITS OF ORGANIZATION

Before suggesting the subjects with which a theory of organization must deal, it is desirable to indicate the limits of organization in relation to the total task of curriculum building. For purposes of analysis, it is possible to distinguish four major tasks in curriculum construction.

The first of these is the formulation of the educational objectives, or goals, of the curriculum. The formulation and definition of valid educational objectives is necessary to provide a guide for the further development of the curriculum and also to assure that the school is focusing its major attention upon important and significant ends rather than frittering away its time upon less imperative objectives.

After the objectives of the curriculum have been formulated, a second step is to select learning experiences that are likely to attain the objectives. The learning experiences which pupils have are the means by which the objectives of the curriculum are to be achieved. Obviously, it is important that the learning experiences provided should be calculated to attain the ends of the school program. The formulation of the objectives will have provided a guide which, together with our knowledge of the psychology of learning, will make it possible to select learning experiences that are likely to contribute to the attainment of the objectives.

This, then, brings us to the third major task: that of organizing learning experiences effectively and efficiently. It is with this step of organization that we are now concerned. It is assumed that appropriate theory has already been developed to deal with the formulation of objectives and with the selection of learning experiences. In this paper the problem of theory has to do with the organization of these experiences and not with their selection.

It is not my purpose to discuss the fourth step involved in curriculum construction: that of evaluation. Evaluation is necessary in curriculum building to determine how far the objectives are actually being realized and at what points the curriculum needs revision and replanning. A theory of evaluation has, however, been formulated more adequately than has a theory of organization.

THE FUNCTION OF ORGANIZATION

The first topic to be considered in developing a theory of organization of learning experiences is the educational function of organization. Much of the discussion in curriculum journals treats organization as though its primary functions were to arouse the learner's interest or to safeguard the logic of particular subjects. My own theoretical view is that neither of these is the primary function of organization. The primary educational function of organization is to relate the various learning experiences which together comprise the curriculum so as to produce the maximum cumulative effect in attaining the objectives of the school. The significant question to ask about any scheme of organization is: How adequately does it provide reinforcement of the several learning experiences so that they produce a maximum cumulative effect?

No doubt it is true that some curriculum organizations provide a more interesting educational program for the students than do others. This may imply that a secondary criterion for curriculum organization is the effect of the organization upon pupil motivation. But the first consideration is whether the organization serves to maximize the total effect of the various learning experiences.

The assertion that curriculum organization should parallel the logic of the school subject assumes 'that the logic used to build or expound the subject indicates the desirable order of learning experiences for those studying the subject. For some subjects and for some students, the logic used in building the subject coincides with an organization of learning experiences that maximizes the desired learning. In such cases the learning and teaching should follow the logic of the subject itself. It should be clear, however, that the logic of the subject, in itself, has nothing to do with an effective organization for learning. An effective organization for learning provides an order of experiences based on the student's development, not on the relations of content within the subject.

The foregoing statement of my own view of the function of curriculum organization is made, not to deny other formulations, but rather to illustrate the need, in any theory of organization, for stating explicitly the primary function of curriculum organization.

EXTENT OF THE LEARNER'S EXPERIENCES TO BE ORGANIZED

When learning experiences are to be organized, the question that arises early in the planning is this: For a given learner or group of learners, which of all the learning experiences are to be included in the plan of organization? If one considers a pupil's total learning experiences over a period of time, there will be experiences within the school's course of study and in extracurriculum activities. There will also be learning outside the school—at home, at play, and at work. There will be not only the experiences the pupil has today but those of tomorrow, next week, next month, next year, and so on. In practice, no plan of organization could expect to relate effectively all the experiences of the learner during the years he is attending school. Too many of these experiences are completely outside the control of the school and even beyond the control of parents, churches, and youth agencies or other social organizations. An effective theory of organization should indicate the extent of these experiences that need to be organized for practical, efficient, and effective learning.

Probably all theorists would agree that, within each major subject or field of study, the learning experiences from one week to the next, from one semester to the next, from one year to the next, should be organized so that the subsequent experiences build on the earlier ones. This may be referred to as "vertical organization." An example would be the way in which the experiences in reading during the second grade are related to those in the first grade, and those in the third grade are related to those in the first and second grades, and so on. But how far should this vertical organization extend? Is it necessary for the intermediate grades to build upon the primary grades, for the junior high school to build upon the intermediate grades, for the senior high school to build upon the junior high school, the college to build upon the senior high school, and the university and graduate school to build upon the college? Obviously, each school does build upon the work of the preceding school, but should conscious effort be made to organize experiences across these levels so as to produce a maximum cumulative effect? A comprehensive theory of organization would need to treat this question in terms both of possible values to be attained and of feasibility.

The question of the extent of learning experiences to be organized also involves the extent of horizontal organizations, that is, the relationships among the learning experiences in the several subjects and areas of the pupil's life. For example, to what extent should the work in arithmetic be reinforced by work in science, or the writing taught in English be reinforced by the writing activities in the various content fields?

Probably most curriculum specialists would maintain that there should be some planning of relationships among the learning experiences of the several subjects which the pupil is taking concurrently. But there seems to be little agreement regarding the plans that should be made to relate the activities of the curriculum with those of the extracurriculum, or the activities of the school with those outside the school. It is certainly true that, when the pupil's activities outside the school are in conflict with his learning experiences within the school, maximum learning does not result, but no adequate formulation of theory on the desirable and practicable degree of horizontal organization has thus far been made. Clearly, the extent to which the learning experiences within the school and outside the school, from one year to another, and from one school to a higher school, need to be planned so as to provide effective organization is a subject of importance for any theory which is to guide practice.

THE ORGANIZING ELEMENTS

A third matter for treatment in a comprehensive theory of organization is the specification of the elements of learning experiences that are actually to be related in an effective organization. These elements are the threads, the warp and woof, of the fabric of curriculum organization. Obviously, effective organization does not mean simply that the student has the same experience week after week and year after year. This would be boring and not likely to produce the maximum cumulative effect. On the other hand, there does need to be some connection between the experiences of this week and those of last week, and the elements which provide this connection need to be recognized and consciously planned for.

In examining many curriculum guides and course of study, I have identified some of the more common kinds of elements that are now used as the basis for the organization of learning experiences. Concepts comprise one of these common types of elements. For example, the concept of the interdependence of human beings occurs again and again in many courses of study, beginning with the kindergarten and running through the senior high school. This concept of interdependence is one which can be understood in a limited way by kindergarten children as they learn to depend upon each other for setting the table and for sharing blocks, and as they see something of the role of the grocer and the baker in providing some of their needs and their families, in turn, help the grocer and baker by paying for food. This concept of interdependence can be broadened and deepened as the children move from the primary school up through the senior high school, until eventually it is expected that the student will have a conception of the interdependence of peoples upon each other all over the world, including the interdependence of nations. A curriculum which plans for this is using the concept of interdependence as a thread that helps tie together the organization of the social studies from the primary grades through the senior high school. The concept serves as the vertical warp of the curriculum fabric. This particular concept also serves, in some courses of study, as an organizing element for horizontal organization. Interdependence is brought out not only in the social studies but in the language arts, on the playground, and in some of the other parts of the school curriculum as well. In this sense, the use of the same element in the several fields helps tie together the organization at a horizontal level; that is, the concept serves as the horizontal woof of the curriculum fabric. In going over current courses of study and curriculum guides, I have noted several hundred concepts which are being used as organizing elements to tie together the curriculum structure.

A second type of organizing element to be found in current courses of study is that of skills. A skill like reading serves as an element that is acquired at a very simple level in the early grades and is broadened and deepened as the pupil moves on through the elementary school and the high school. The conscious effort to provide for continued emphasis on this skill at an ever broadening and deepening level truly makes this skill an element of organization helping to tie together the curriculum. This skill, too, usually serves both as an element of vertical organization and as an element of horizontal organization, since reading skill is commonly emphasized in the content subjects as well as in the language arts. Many other skills are to be found as organizing elements in current courses of study, including study skills, arithmetic skills, and social skills.

A third type of element which sometimes appears in curriculum guides and courses of study is that of values. When values serve as the organizing element, the educational program is planned to develop loyalty to certain ideals or interest in certain objects and activities. One value which is commonly stressed in social-studies courses is respect for the dignity and worth of every individual regardless of his race, religion, occupation, nationality, or social class. This value is emphasized in the kindergarten, through the elementary school, and on through the senior high school. It thus serves as an element of vertical organization. It is also commonly found as an element for horizontal organization, since it is a value which is emphasized not only in the social studies but in the language arts, in the various content fields, and on the playground and in extracurriculum activities. Values appear to represent the organizing elements related to objectives such as the development of attitudes, interests, and appreciation.

There may be other organizing elements which are being used in curriculum building, but I have not been able to identify them. In any event, it is important as part of a comprehensive theory of organization to indicate just what kinds of elements will serve satisfactorily as organizing elements. And in a given curriculum it is important to identify the particular elements that shall be used.

THE ORGANIZING PRINCIPLES

The fourth subject with which a comprehensive theory of organization must deal is the specification of the organizing principles—the generalizations regarding the way in which experiences of one level can be effectively related to those of another level and the experiences of one area can be effectively related to those in another area. As was suggested earlier, an effective curriculum will not have the same experiences at each level. This would be boring and ineffectual. Instead, it is necessary that subsequent experiences build upon the earlier ones but that they go more broadly and deeply into the matters with which they deal. What kind of connection between experiences can provide for this broadening and deepening in the vertical organization? What kind of connection between experiences can provide for appropriate reinforcement on the horizontal level? No comprehensive statement of theory on these questions has been formulated. However, examination of current curriculum guides and courses of study reveals certain organization principles which seem to be in use.

One commonly found in the primary grades is to begin with experiences close to the personal life of the child and then move out into the home, then into the school, then into the community, and ultimately into the state and nation. This might be referred to as an extension geographically from the learner's immediate personal life. This principle, no doubt, has validity for certain purposes, but we see at once that it is not a universally applicable principle. Some kinds of learning require experience and perspective before the pupil can understand even though the learning concerns matters very close at home. Thus, adolescents are much more sensitive with reference to their own immediate behavior and relations to their parents than they are to the behavior of people they do not know. Hence, it is probably less effective to begin with these sensitive spots than to examine human relations in other cultures or other groups before moving to those which are so vital in the adolescents' own lives.

Another inadequacy of this principle lies in the fact that in some cases the child's ability to comprehend certain aspects of an experience is not dependent upon geographic closeness. Children may more easily understand the primitive culture of the Indian or the Eskimo than the complex organization of their own local urban community. It seems quite clear, then, that the principle of geographic expansion is not adequate as a sole organizing principle for the curriculum.

A second organizing principle commonly found in current courses of study is the chronological one. This is to be found particularly in history, where the learning experiences of this month relate to periods of time that are later than those of last month, while the experiences of next month will deal with periods more recent than those of this month. It is probably true that, when the purpose is to give students an understanding of a consecutive narrative, a chronological organization is useful; but it is hard to see that chronological organization is the best means of developing understanding of basic concepts or of supplying training in skills.

A third organizing principle sometimes followed, particularly in the early stages of learning, is to provide a great many concrete experiences before abstractions are bought in, and then to have pupils abstract the desired concepts from these concrete experiences. Mary Boole's early work with English children in teaching arithmetic showed clearly that, in the case of both computation and mathematical concepts, it is valuable to provide a great deal of concrete experiences with objects, varied in number and size, from which the pupil is led to abstract various notions of number and quantity. However, at what point simple abstractions can serve as the basis for more difficult abstractions without the use of further concrete experiences has not been worked out, either theoretically or empirically. Hence, the way in which this principle can best be used as a basis for organization up through the grades needs to be indicated.

A fourth principle to be found in current courses of study is to begin with experiences that involve simple reactions and then move on to more complex ones. The principle of moving from the simple to the more complex appears to be acceptable to many theorists, but the problem of determining what is simple and what is more complex from the standpoint of the learner is by no means easy. An operational definition of this principle is necessary in order to make use of it, and such definitions are lacking.

In summarizing, it can be said that, although organizing principles are often used to guide the planning of courses of study, there has been no precise definition of these principles, nor any adequate appraisal of them either in terms of the learning theory they imply or in terms of their effect, as shown by actual trial in school experimentation, in providing efficient cumulative learning. Hence, the nature of sound organizing principles is an important subject to be dealt with in any comprehensive theory of the organization of learning experience.

THE ORGANIZING STRUCTURES

A fifth subject with which a comprehensive theory must deal is that of the appropriate organizing structures which can be used effectively at various levels of school and college work. By "structure" I mean the way in which the time of the school is divided up so as to provide a series of periods in which learning experiences are set up and organized. In most schools there is a clearly defined structure in which the pupil's day is divided into approximately equal periods for each of the several school subjects. This differentiation of the school day may provide for many specific subjects, sometimes eight to ten—such specific subjects as reading, spelling, language, penmanship, arithmetic, nature study, geography, history, and the like. Other schools may set up four or five larger structural divisions, so-called "broad fields" like the language arts, mathematics, science, social studies, and the fine arts. Some schools do not divide up the day in any formal plan. They have an undifferentiated structure. This is found most often in the kindergarten.

In setting up the organizing structure of the curriculum, consideration must be given not only to the way of dividing up the school day into specific subjects, broad fields, or an undifferentiated period, but also to vertical differentiation. In some schools each daily lesson, in itself, is the basis for the vertical differentiation of the curriculum structure. This was quite common in the training programs of the armed services. A certain subject might be treated in thirty lessons, each lesson being a unit to itself. On the other hand, in American elementary and secondary schools there has been an increasing tendency to employ larger structural units. A learning unit organized around one or more problems and continuing for several weeks is a fairly common type of curriculum structure. Some schools divide courses into topics which may run for several days or several weeks.

Although the obvious trend seems toward the unit structural organization, there has been no adequate comparison of the relative values of the various structures. Some criteria for evaluation have, however, been suggested, such as: (1) flexibility, to permit modification of plans in the light of pupil needs and significant situations that may arise, (2) ease of planning vertical and horizontal relations, and (3) contribution to pupil motivation. (It is recognized, of course, that motivation is affected by other factors as well as the organizing structure of the curriculum.)

The problem of appropriate structures for the organization of learning experiences in the curriculum requires a clear and comprehensive theoretical formulation. Such a theory should indicate what the basic considerations are and the criteria to be used in judging the relative values of the several possible structures. Until this is done, the selection of curriculum structures will be made in terms of personal preference rather than on the basis of considered theory supported by principles of learning and by evidence obtained from experience and experimentation.

CRITERIA FOR A THEORY OF ORGANIZATION

The foregoing discussion has dealt with the need for a theory of curriculum organization and has suggested topics to be treated in such a theoretical formulation. It may also be helpful to suggest some of the criteria which an adequate theory of organization should meet.

In the first place, a satisfactory theory of organization should outline the nature of an organizing scheme that can achieve an efficient cumulative effect in curriculum learning and explain why such a scheme is effective. This means that the theory should explain what is required for effective sequence (vertical organization) and effective integration (horizontal organization), and why.

In the second place, the theoretical constructs outlined and the explanations must be consistent with defensible theories of behavior and of learning and be appropriate to the curriculum objectives sought.

Much debate on curriculum organization is now guided largely by rules of thumb and by opinions arrived at without sufficient basis in research. It is not possible for the curriculum to be maximally effective without careful planning and appropriate organization. The practice of curriculum construction needs to be guided by a theory which has been carefully developed, utilizing an acceptable philosophy of education, based upon known principles of learning, and taking into account the results of school experience and experimentation. Our educational institutions have more serious responsibilities than they have ever had before. The sheer existence of our society depends upon an educated citizenship that must have knowledge, ideals, habits, and intelligence far greater than has been required in any other age. The only possibility of meeting these imperative demands for an educated citizenship, with all that this implies, is an efficient curriculum that produces the maximum cumulative effect in the time which schools can devote to education. Sound theory is needed to guide the making of this effective organization.

5. THE TYLER RATIONALE

Herbert M. Kliebard

One of the disturbing characteristics of the curriculum field is its lack of historical perspective. New breakthroughs are solemnly proclaimed when in fact they represent minor modifications of early proposals, and, conversely, anachronistic dogmas and doctrines maintain a currency and uncritical acceptance far beyond their present merit. The most persistent theoretical formulation in the field of curriculum has been Ralph Tyler's syllabus for Education 360 at the University of Chicago, *Basic Principles of Curriculum and Instruction,* or, as it is widely known, the Tyler rationale.[1] Tyler's claims for his rationale are modest, but, over time, his proposal for rationally developing a curriculum has been raised almost to the status of revealed doctrine. In the recent issue of the *Review of Educational Research* devoted to curriculum, Goodlad, commenting on the state of the field, reports that "as far as the major questions to be answered in developing a curriculum are concerned, most of the authors in [the] 1960 and 1969 [curriculum issues of the *Review*] assume those set forth in 1950 by Ralph Tyler." Later, he concludes with obvious disappointment, "General theory and conceptualization in curriculum appear to have advanced very little during the last decade."[2] Perhaps the twentieth anniversary of the publication of the Tyler rationale is an appropriate time to reexamine and reevaluate some of its central features.

SOURCE. *School Review* 78 (No. 2, February 1970), pp. 259–72. Published by The University of Chicago Press. Copyright © 1970 by the University of Chicago.

Tyler's rationale revolves around four central questions which Tyler feels need answers if the process of curriculum development is to proceed:

1. What educational purposes should the school seek to attain?
2. What educational experiences can be provided that are likely to attain these purposes?
3. How can these educational experiences be effectively organized?
4. How can we determine whether these purposes are being attained?[3]

These questions may be reformulated into the familiar four-step process by which a curriculum is developed: stating objectives, selecting "experiences," organizing "experiences," and evaluating.[4] The Tyler rationale is essentially an elaboration and explication of these steps. The most crucial step in this doctrine is obviously the first since all the others proceed from and wait upon the statement of objectives. As Tyler puts it, "If we are to study an educational program systematically and intelligently we must first be sure as to the educational objectives aimed at."[5]

THE SELECTION OF EDUCATIONAL OBJECTIVES

Tyler's section on educational objectives is a description of the three sources of objectives: studies of learners, studies of contemporary life, and suggestions from subject-matter specialists, as well as an account of how data derived from these "sources" are to be "filtered" through philosophical and psychological "screens." The three sources of educational objectives encapsulate several traditional doctrines in the curriculum field over which much ideological blood had been spilled in the previous several decades. The doctrines proceeded from different theoretical assumptions, and each of them had its own spokesmen, its own adherents, and its own rhetoric. Tyler's proposal accepts them all, which probably accounts in part for its wide popularity.

While we are aware that compromise is the recourse frequently taken in the fields of diplomatic or labor negotiation, simple eclecticism may not be the most efficacious way to proceed in theorizing. When Dewey, for example, identified the fundamental factors in the educative process as the child and the "values incarnate in the matured experience of the adult," the psychological and the logical, his solution was not to accept them both but "to discover a reality to which each belongs."[6] In other words, when faced with essentially the same problem of warring educational doctrines, Dewey's approach is to creatively reformulate the problem; Tyler's is to lay them all out side by side.

Subject Matter as a Source of Objectives

Of the three "sources"—studies of the learners themselves, studies of contemporary life, and suggestions about objectives from subject-matter specialists—the last one seems curiously distorted and out of place. Perhaps this is because Tyler begins the section by profoundly misconceiving the role and function of the Committee of Ten. He attributes to the Committee of Ten a set of objectives which, he claims, has subsequently been followed by thousands of secondary schools. In point of fact, the notion of objectives in the sense that Tyler defines the term was not used and probably had not even occurred to the members of the Committee of Ten. What they proposed were not objectives, but "four programmes": Classical, Latin-Scientific, Modern Languages, and English. Under each of these rubrics is a listing of the subjects that constitute each of the four courses of study. This recommendation is followed by the reports of the various individual committees on what content should be included and what methods should be used in the various subject fields. Unless Tyler is using the term "objective" as being synonymous with "content" (in which case it would lose all its importance as a concept), then the use of the term "objectives" in the context of the report of the Committee of Ten is erroneous. Probably the only sense in which the term "objective" is applicable to the Committee of Ten report is in connection with the broad objective of mental training to which it subscribes.

An even more serious error follows: "It seems clear that the Committee of Ten thought it was answering the question: What should be the elementary instruction for students who are later to carry on much more advanced work in the field. Hence, the report in History, for example, seems to present objectives [sic] for the beginning courses for persons who are training to be historians. Similarly the report in Mathematics outlines objectives [sic] for the beginning courses in the training of a mathematician."[7]

As a matter of fact, one of the central questions that the Committee of Ten considered was, "Should the subject be treated differently for pupils who are going to college, for those who are going to a scientific school, and for those, who, presumably, are going to neither?"[8] The Committee decided unanimously in the negative. The subcommittee on history, civil government, and political economy, for example, reported that it was "unanimously against making such a distinction"[9] and passed a resolution that "instruction in history and related subjects ought to be precisely the same for pupils on their way to college or the scientific school, as for those who expect to stop at the end of grammar school, or at the end of the high school."[10] Evidently, the Committee of Ten was acutely aware of the question of a differentiated curriculum based on probable destination. It simply rejected the doctrine that makes a prediction about one's future status or occupation a valid basis for the curriculum in general education. The objective of mental training, apparently, was conceived to be of such importance as to apply to all, regardless of destination.

Tyler's interpretation of the Committee of Ten report is more than a trivial historical misconception. It illustrates one of his fundamental presuppositions about the subjects in the curriculum. Tyler conceives of subjects as performing certain "functions." These functions may take the form of a kind of definition of the field of study itself such as when he sees a function of science to be enabling the student to obtain a "clearer understanding of the world as it is viewed by the scientist and man's relation to it, and the place of the world in the larger universe"; or the subject may perform external functions such as the contribution of science to the improvement of individual or public health or to the conservation of natural resources. The first sense of function is essentially a way of characterizing a field of study; in the second sense of function, the subject field serves as an instrument for achieving objectives drawn from Tyler's other two sources. Tyler's apparent predisposition to the latter sense of function seems to be at the heart of his misreading of the Committee of Ten report. To Tyler, studying history or algebra (as was universally recommended by the Committee of Ten), if they are not meeting an obvious individual or social need, is a way of fulfilling the vocational needs of a budding historian or mathematician. Otherwise, how can one justify the existence of mathematics qua mathematics in the curriculum? As such, "suggestions from subject-matter specialists" is really not a source in the sense that the other two are. Subject matter is mainly one of several means by which one fulfills individual needs such as vocational aspirations or meets social expectations.

Needs of the Learner as a Source of Objectives

The section on the "learners themselves as a source of educational objectives," although it is less strained and more analytical than the one on subject matter, is nevertheless elliptical. Tyler proceeds from the assumption that "education is a process of changing behavior patterns of people."[11] This notion, of course, is now widely popular in this country, but, even if one were to accept such a view, it would be important to know the ways in which education would be different from other means of changing behavior, such as, hypnosis, shock treatment, brainwashing, sensitivity training, indoctrination, drug therapy, and torture. Given such a definition, the differences between education and these other ways of changing behavior are not obvious or simple.

Tyler proceeds from his basic definition of education to a consideration of the reason for wanting to study the learner: "A study of the learners themselves would seek to identify needed changes in behavior patterns of the students which the educational institution should seek to produce."[12] There follows an extended discussion of "needs," how they are determined, and how they contribute to the determination of educational objectives. The notion of needs as a basis for curriculum development was not a new one when Tyler used it in 1950. It had been a stable element in the curriculum literature for about three decades.[13] When tied to the biological concept of homeostasis, the term "needs" seems to have a clear-cut meaning. Hunger, for example, may be conveniently translated into a need for food when one has in mind a physiological state of equilibrium. Need becomes a much trickier concept when one speaks of the "need of a haircut" or the "need for a good spanking." These needs involve rather complex social norms on which good men and true may differ sharply. Tyler astutely recognized that the concept of need has no meaning without a set of norms, and he described the kind of study he envisioned essentially as a two-step process: "first, finding the present status of the students, and second, comparing this status to acceptable norms in order to identify the gaps or needs."[14] This formulation is virtually identical to what Bobbitt referred to as "shortcomings" in the first book written exclusively on the curriculum, published in 1918.[15] The key term, in Tyler's version, of course, is "acceptable norms." They are neither self-evident nor easy to formulate.

One of Tyler's illustrations of the process he advocates is a case in point: A "discovery" is made that 60 percent of ninth-grade boys read only comic strips. The "unimaginative" teacher, Tyler says, might interpret this as suggesting the need for more attention to comic strips in the classroom; the imaginative teacher uses the data as a justification "for setting up objectives gradually to broaden and deepen these reading interests."[16] What is the acceptable norm implicit in Tyler's illustration? Apparently, it is not a statistical norm since this could imply that the 40 percent minority of boys should be encouraged to emulate the 60 percent majority. The norm seems to be the simple conviction that having broader and deeper reading interests is better than limiting oneself to the reading of comic strips. The question is what does the 60 percent figure contribute to the process of stating educational objectives. What difference would it have made if the figure were 80 percent or 40 percent? The key factor seems to be the nature and strength of the teacher's conviction as the acceptable norm, toward which the status study contributes very little.

The whole notion of need has no meaning without an established norm, and, therefore, it is impossible even to identify "needs" without it. As Archambault put it, "An objective need can be discovered, but only within a completely defined context in which the normal level of attainment can be clarified."[17] Furthermore, even when a genuine need is identified, the role of the school as an institution for the remediation of that or other needs would have to be considered. Even the course that remediation should take once the need and the responsibility have been established is an open question. These serious value questions associated with the identification and remediation of needs make the concept a deceptively complex one whose advantages are more apparent than real. Komisar, for example, has described this double use of need, "one to report deficiencies and another to prescribe for their alleviation," as so vague and elusive as to constitute a "linguistic luxury."[18]

As already mentioned, Tyler is acutely aware of the difficulties of "deriving" educational objectives from studies of the child. His last word on the subject in this section is to suggest to his students that they compile some data and then try using those data as the basis for formulating objectives. He suggests this exercise in part to illustrate the difficulty of the process. Given the almost impossible complexity of the procedure and the crucial but perhaps arbitrary role of the interpreter's value structure or "philosophy of life and of education," one wonders whether the concept of need deserves any place in the process of formulating objectives. Certainly, the concept of need turns out to be of no help in so far as avoiding central value decisions as the basis for the selection of educational objectives, and without that feature much of its appeal seems to disappear. As Dearden concluded in his analysis of the term: "the concept of 'need' is an attractive one in education because it seems to offer an escape from arguments about value by means of a straightforward appeal to the facts empirically determined by the expert. But . . . it is false to suppose that judgments of value can thus be escaped. Such judgments may be assumed without any awareness that assumptions are being made, but they are not escaped."[19]

Studies of Contemporary Life as a Source of Objectives

Tyler's section on studies of contemporary life as a source of curricular objectives follows the pattern set by the section on the learner. His conception of the role that such studies play in determining objectives is also similar in many respects to that of his spiritual ancestor, Franklin Bobbitt, who stimulated the practice of activity analysis in the curriculum field. Like Bobbitt, Tyler urges that one "divide life" into a set of manageable categories and then proceed to collect data of various kinds which may be fitted into these categories. One of Tyler's illustrations is especially reminiscent of Bobbitt: "Students in the school obtain[ed] from their parents for several days the problems they were having to solve that involved arithmetic. The collection and analysis of this set of problems suggested the arithmetic operations and the kinds of mathematical problems which are commonly encountered by adults, and became the basis of the arithmetic curriculum."[20]

Tyler tends to be more explicitly aware than Bobbitt of the traditional criticisms that have been directed against this approach. Bode, for example, once pointed out that "no scientific analysis known to man can determine the desirability or the need of anything." The question of whether a community with a given burglary rate needs a larger police force or more burglars is entirely a question of what the community wants.[21] Tyler's implicit response to this and other traditional criticism of this approach is to argue that in his rationale studies of contemporary life do not constitute the sole basis for deriving objectives, and, of course, that such studies have to be checked against "an acceptable educational philosophy."[22] In this sense, the contemporary life source is just as dependent on the philosophical screen as is the learner source.

THE PHILOSOPHICAL SCREEN

Tyler's treatment of the section on the learner and on contemporary life as sources of educational objectives are roughly parallel. In each case, Tyler is aware of the serious shortcomings of the source but assumes that they can be overcome, first, by not relying exclusively on any one of them—in a sense counting on his eclecticism to blunt the criticism. And second (and probably more important), he appeals to philosophy as the means for covering any deficiencies. This suggests that it is philosophy after all that is the source of Tyler's objectives and that the stipulated three sources are mere window dressing. It is Tyler's use of the concept of a philosophical screen, then, that is most crucial in understanding his rationale, at least in so far as stating the objectives is concerned.

Even if we were to grant that people go through life with some kind of primitive value structure spinning around in their heads, to say that educational objectives somehow flow out of such a value structure is to say practically nothing at all. Tyler's proposal that educational objectives be filtered through a philosophical screen is not so much demonstrably false as it is trivial, almost vacuous. It simply does not address itself in any significant sense to the question of which objectives we leave in and which we throw out once we have committed ourselves to the task of stating them. Filtering educational objectives through a philosophical screen is simply another way of saying that one is forced to make choices from among the thousands or perhaps millions of objectives that one can draw from the sources that Tyler cites. (The number of objectives is a function of the level of specificity.) Bobbitt was faced with the same predicament when he was engaged in his massive curriculum project in Los Angeles in 1921–23. Bobbitt's solution was to seek "the common judgment of thoughtful men and women,"[23] an appeal to consensus. Tyler's appeal is to divine philosophy, but the effect is equally arbitrary as long as we are still in the dark as to how one arrives at a philosophy and how one engages in the screening process.

Take, for example, one of Tyler's own illustrations of how a philosophy operates: "If the school believes that its primary function is to teach people to adjust to society it will strongly emphasize obedience to present authorities, loyalty to the present forms and traditions, skills in carrying on the present techniques of life; whereas if it emphasizes the revolutionary function of the school it will be more concerned with critical analysis, ability to meet new problems, independence and self-direction, freedom, and self-discipline. Again, it is clear that the nature of the philosophy of the school can affect the selection of educational objectives."[24] Although Tyler appears elsewhere to have a personal predilection for the latter philosophy, we really have no criterion to appeal to in making a choice. We are urged only to make our educational objectives consistent with our educational philosophy, and this makes the choice of objectives precisely as arbitrary as the choice of philosophy. One may, therefore, express a philosophy that conceives of human beings as instruments of the state and the function of the schools as programming the youth of the nation to react in a fixed manner when appropriate stimuli are presented. As long as we derive a set of objectives consistent with this philosophy (and perhaps make a brief pass at the three sources), we have developed our objectives in line with the Tyler rationale. The point is that, given the notion of educational objectives and the necessity of stating them explicitly and consistently with a philosophy, it makes all the difference in the world *what* one's guiding philosophy is since that consistency can be as much a sin as a virtue. The rationale offers little by way of a guide for curriculum making because it excludes so little. Popper's dictum holds not only for science, but all intellectual endeavor: *"Science does not aim, primarily, at high probabilities. It aims at high informative content, well backed by experience. But a hypothesis may be very probable simply because it tells us nothing or very little. A high degree of probability is therefore not an indication of 'goodness'—it may be merely a symptom of low informative content."*[25] Tyler's central hypothesis that a statement of objectives derives in some manner from a philosophy, while highly probable, tells us very little indeed.

SELECTION AND ORGANIZATION OF LEARNING EXPERIENCES

Once the crucial first step of stating objectives is accomplished, the rationale proceeds relentlessly through the steps of the selection and organization of learning experiences as the means for achieving the ends and, finally, evaluating in terms of those ends. Typically, Tyler recognizes a crucial problem in connection with the concept of a learning experience but passes quickly over it: The problem is how can learning experiences be *selected* by a teacher or a curriculum maker when they are defined as the *interaction* between a student and his environment. By definition, then, the learning experience is in some part a function of the perceptions, interests, and previous experience of the student. At least this part of the learning experience is not within the power of the teacher to select. While Tyler is explicitly aware of this, he nevertheless maintains that the teacher can control the learning experience through the "manipulation of the environment in such a way as to set up stimulating situations—situations that will evoke the kind of behavior desired."[26] The Pavlovian overtones of such a solution are not discussed.

EVALUATION

"The process of evaluation," according to Tyler, "is essentially the process of determining to what extent the educational objectives are actually being realized by the program of curriculum and instruction."[27] In other words, the statement of objectives not only serves as the basis for the selection and organization of learning experiences, but the standard against which the program is assessed. To Tyler, then, evaluation is a process by which one matches initial expectations in the form of behavioral objectives with outcomes. Such a conception has a certain commonsensical appeal, and, especially when fortified with models from industry and systems analysis, it seems like a supremely wise and practical way to appraise the success of a venture. Actually, curriculum evaluation as a kind of product control was set forth by Bobbitt as early as 1922,[28] but product control when applied to curriculum presents certain difficulties.

One of the difficulties lies in the nature of an aim or objective and whether it serves as the terminus for activity in the sense that the Tyler rationale implies. In other words, is an objective an end point or a turning point? Dewey argued for the latter: "Ends arise and function within action. They are not, as current theories too often imply, things lying outside activity at which the latter is directed. They are not ends or termini of action at all. They are terminals of deliberation, and so turning points *in* activity."[29] If ends arise only *within* activity it is not clear how one can state objectives before the activity (learning experience) begins. Dewey's position, then, has important consequences not just for Tyler's process of evaluation but for the rationale as a whole. It would mean, for example, that the starting point for a model of curriculum and instruction is not the statement of objectives but the activity (learning experience), and whatever objectives do appear will arise within that activity as a way of adding a new dimension to it. Under these circumstances, the process of evaluation would not be seen as one of matching anticipated consequences with actual outcomes, but as one of describing and of applying criteria of excellence to the activity itself. This view would recognize Dewey's claim that "even the most important among all the consequences of an act is not necessarily its aim,"[30] and it would be consistent with Merton's important distinction between manifest and latent functions.[31]

The importance of description as a key element in the process of evaluation has also been emphasized by Cronbach: *"When evaluation is carried out in the service of course improvement, the chief aim is to ascertain what effects the course has. . . .* This is not to inquire merely whether the course is effective or ineffective. Outcomes of instruction are multidimensional, and a satisfactory investigation will map out the effects of the course along these dimensions separately."[32] The most significant dimensions of an educational activity or any activity may be those that are completely unplanned and wholly unanticipated. An evaluation procedure that ignores this fact is plainly unsatisfactory.

SUMMARY AND CONCLUSION

The crucial first step in the Tyler rationale on which all else hinges is the statement of objectives. The objectives are to be drawn from three sources:

studies of the learner, studies of society, and suggestions from subject-matter specialists. Data drawn from these sources are to be filtered through philosophical and psychological screens. Upon examination, the last of the three sources turns out to be no source at all but a means of achieving objectives drawn from the other two. Studies of the learner and of society depend so heavily for their standing as sources on the philosophical screen that it is actually the philosophical screen that determines the nature and scope of the objectives. To say that educational objectives are drawn from one's philosophy, in turn, is only to say that one must make choices about educational objectives in some way related to one's value structure. This is to say so little about the process of selecting objectives as to be virtually meaningless. One wonders whether the long-standing insistence by curriculum theorists that the first step in making a curriculum be the specification of objectives has any merit whatsoever. It is even questionable whether stating objectives at all, when they represent external goals allegedly reached through the manipulation of learning experiences, is a fruitful way to conceive of the process of curriculum planning. Certainly, the whole concept of a learning experience requires much more analysis than it has been given. Finally, the simplistic notion that evaluation is a process of matching objectives with outcomes leaves much to be desired. It ignores what may be the more significant latent outcomes in favor of the manifest and anticipated ones, and it minimizes the vital relationship between ends and means.

One reason for the success of the Tyler rationale is its very rationality. It is an eminently reasonable framework for developing a curriculum; it duly compromises between warring extremes and skirts the pitfalls to which the doctrinaire are subject. In one sense, the Tyler rationale is imperishable. In some form, it will always stand as the model of curriculum development for those who conceive of the curriculum as a complex machinery for transforming the crude raw material that children bring with them to school into a finished and useful product. By definition, the production model of curriculum and instruction begins with a blueprint for how the student will turn out once we get through with him. Tyler's version of the model avoids the patent absurdity of, let us say, Mager's by drawing that blueprint in broad outline rather than in minute detail.[33]

For his moderation and his wisdom as well as his impact, Ralph Tyler deserves to be enshrined in whatever hall of fame the field of curriculum may wish to establish. But the field of curriculum, in its turn, must recognize the Tyler rationale for what it is: Ralph Tyler's version of how a curriculum should be developed—not *the* universal model of curriculum development. Goodlad once claimed that "Tyler put the capstone on one epoch of curriculum inquiry."[34] The new epoch is long overdue.

NOTES

1. Ralph W. Tyler, *Basic Principles of Curriculum and Instruction* (Chicago: University of Chicago Press, 1950). Note differences in pagination in 1969 printing.

2. John I. Goodlad, "Curriculum: State of the Field," *Review of Educational Research* 39 (1969):374.

3. Tyler, pp. 1–2.

4. I have argued elsewhere that the characteristic mode of thought associated with the field of curriculum frequently manifests itself in enumeration and particularization as a response to highly complex questions. Herbert M. Kliebard, "The Curriculum Field in Retrospect," in Paul W. F. Witt (ed.), *Technology and the Curriculum* (New York: Teachers College Press, 1968), pp. 69–84.

5. Tyler, p. 3.

6. John Dewey, "The Child and the Curriculum," in Reginald D. Archambault (ed.), *John Dewey on Education* (New York: Random House, 1964), pp. 339–40. (Originally published by University of Chicago Press in 1902.)

7. Tyler, p. 17.

8. National Education Association, *Report of the Committee on Secondary School Studies* (Washington, D.C.: Government Printing Office, 1893), p. 6.

9. *Ibid.,* p. 203.

10. *Ibid.,* p. 165.

11. Tyler, p. 4.

12. *Ibid.,* pp. 4–5.

13. See, e.g., H. H. Giles, S. P. McCutchen, and A. N. Zechiel, *Exploring the Curriculum* (New York: Harper & Bros., 1942); V. T. Thayer, Caroline B. Zachry, and Ruth Kotinsky, *Reorganizing Secondary Education* (New York: Appleton Century, 1939). The former work was one of the volumes to come out of the Progressive Education Association's Eight-Year Study. Tyler was closely associated with that research. The latter volume was published under the auspices of the Progressive Education Association's Commission on Secondary School Curriculum. Tyler was also a member of the committee that prepared the NSSE yearbook on needs. Nelson B. Henry (ed.), *Adapting the Secondary School Program to the Needs of Youth,* Fifty-second Yearbook of the National Society for the Study of Education. Part 1 (Chicago: University of Chicago Press, 1953). An early statement of needs in relation to curriculum organization appeared in *The Development of the High-School Curriculum,* Sixth Yearbook of the Department of Superintendence (Washington, D.C.: Department of Superintendence, 1928). Needs as the basis for the curriculum in English was mentioned by E. L. Miller as early as 1922. North Central Association of Colleges and Secondary Schools, *Proceedings of the Twenty-seventh Annual Meeting of the North Central Association of Colleges and Secondary Schools* (Cedar Rapids, Iowa: Torch Press, 1922), p. 103.

14. Tyler, p. 6.

15. Franklin Bobbitt, *The Curriculum* (Boston: Houghton Mifflin Co., 1918), p. 45 ff.

16. Tyler, p. 10.

17. Reginald D. Archambault, "The Concept of Need and Its Relation to Certain Aspects of Educational Theory," *Harvard Educational Review* 27 (1957):51.

18. B. Paul Komisar, " 'Need' and the Needs Curriculum," in B. O. Smith and Robert H. Ennis (eds.), *Language and Concepts in Education* (Chicago: Rand McNally & Co., 1961), p. 37.

19. R. F. Dearden, " 'Needs' in Education," *British Journal of Educational Studies* 14 (1966):17.

20. Tyler, pp. 16—17.

21. Boyd H. Bode, *Modern Educational Theories* (New York: Macmillan Co., 1927), pp. 80—81.

22. Tyler, p. 13.

23. Franklin Bobbitt, *Curriculum-making in Los Angeles,* Supplementary Educational Monographs No. 20 (Chicago: University of Chicago, 1922), p. 7.

24. Tyler, p. 23.

25. Karl Popper, "Degree of Confirmation," *British Journal for the Philosophy of Science* 6 (1955):146 (original italics).

26. Tyler, p. 42.

27. *Ibid.,* p. 69.

28. Franklin Bobbitt, "The Objectives of Secondary Education," *School Review* 28 (1920):738—49.

29. John Dewey, *Human Nature and Conduct* (New York: Random House, 1922), p. 223. (Originally published by Henry Holt & Co.)

30. *Ibid.,* p. 227.

31. Robert K. Merton, "Manifest and Latent Functions," in *Social Theory and Social Structure* (Glencoe, Ill.: Free Press, 1957), pp. 19—84.

32. Lee J. Cronbach, "Evaluation for Course Improvement," in Robert W. Heath (ed.), *New Curricula* (New York: Harper & Row, 1964), p. 235 (original italics).

33. Robert F. Mager, *Preparing Instructional Objectives* (Palo Alto, Calif.: Fearon Publishers, 1962).

34. John I. Goodlad, "The Development of a Conceptual System for Dealing with Problems of Curriculum and Instruction," U.S. Department of Health, Education, and Welfare, Office of Education Cooperative Research Project No. 454 (Los Angeles: Institute for the Development of Educational Activities, UCLA, 1966), p. 5.

6. IMPLICATIONS OF PSYCHOLOGICAL THOUGHT FOR THE CURRICULUM

Dwayne Huebner[1]

Unraveling the relationship between psychological language and curriculum is no simple task, for we lack historical and philosophical perspective. Therefore I must begin with two items of the faith that guide my professional activities. The first is that if curriculum is a discipline, it is not a knowledge-producing discipline. It is an environment-producing discipline: disciplined praxis. If it is a discipline, it has a history that shapes the activity of the professional, and it has forms of criticism that can make it rational. As a discipline, then, it could be used to comment upon other disciplines and activities.

The second is that the discipline of curriculum, if it exists, has been led astray by an overdependency upon the category "learning." Clearly, this category must be one of the tools of the curriculum person. It is not, however, the major category. It is extremely unfortunate, for instance, that a writer could make the statement that "Education is for learning,"[2] rather than stating that "Learning is for education" or "Learning is a part of education." Our major category is "education." If the postulated concept "learning" is needed, it is but one of the conceptual tools by which the curriculum person builds his special world. In some ways the curriculum person has been introduced into a *cul de sac,* albeit a

---

SOURCE. In Glenys G. Unruh and Robert R. Leeper (eds.), *Influences in Curriculum Change* (Washington, D.C.: Association for Supervision and Curriculum Development, 1968), pp. 28–37.

fruitful one for the recent past and present, by the uncritical acceptance of the concept "learning."

By stating these two items of my professional faith, I wish to emphasize the point of view that the field of curriculum is not simply the mirror image of psychological knowledge, or of any behavioral science knowledge. In other words, neither psychological knowledge, nor the knowledge of other behavioral sciences serves as a template to stamp out curricular practices or actions. Knowledge within the behavioral sciences is but one tool, among many, that the curriculum specialist must use in building and caring for his special world. The problem then, in dealing with the relationship between psychological knowledge and the curriculum, is to seek clarification of the role of psychological thought in this possible discipline of curriculum—the discipline which builds or constructs situations and environments that educate.

Before undertaking this, it might be necessary to reaffirm my conviction that psychology, in-and-of itself, is an independent discipline, with its own *raison d'etre*. It is composed of its own "Society of Explorers," to use Polanyi's term;[3] explorers who search for truth, warranted assertions or theories to serve as policy guides for further experimentation. Psychological knowledge, as a product of a society of explorers, is self-correcting and has built-in forms of criticism which govern the use of the knowledge in man's future. However, when psychological knowledge is taken out of that society of explorers and used by other men in other occupations, it is yanked out of its self-correcting context and has the possibility of becoming dated and misused. The user risks reifying it, when all he meant to do was to make it an instrument.

Yet once a tool is objectified, sedimented out into the habits of a social group, it becomes difficult to uproot or difficult to discard for display in the museum of tools that once had their time and function. Within the society of explorers, psychological knowledge is validated by its truth value, however that value is assigned. Within a world or environment building discipline, psychological knowledge must be validated by its usefulness, and must compete in the market place of other useful knowledge tools.

CATEGORIES OF USEFULNESS

At least two categories of this usefulness can be identified. The first might be identified as its disclosure use; the second as its technological use. A definition of the technological use is relatively easy. It is the distinction which is made between the physical sciences and the fields of engineering. Knowledge produced within the society of explorers of the physical world is taken over and used by the engineers to make goods or to establish operations. In one sense, it might be said that the knowledge produced by the scientists is, through the work of the engineers, embodied into the ongoing world of things and processes.

Atomic theory is embodied in atomic bombs and nuclear reactors; cybernetic theory is embodied in computers and data storage and retrieval systems. In the same way, then, psychological theory or aspects of it can be said to be embodied in certain educational materials, and certain organized behavior patterns of the teachers. More of this later.

The disclosure use is perhaps more difficult to explicate. The term is borrowed directly from Ramsey's *Models and Mystery*,[4] in which he refers to the movement in science from picture models to analogue models. The first are scale replicas of processes or structures assumed to exist in nature; while the second make no such assumption but instead provide "insights" by which the "light dawns" or in which something new is disclosed. This sense of disclosure reflects Heidegger's definition of truth, an unveiling of that which was veiled. A disclosure model in the rigorous sciences, if it is a good one, is prolific in "generating deductions which are then open to experimental verification and falsification."[5]

However, in the human sciences the value of a disclosure model is not simply this ability to generate deductions, but what Ramsey calls the "empirical fit" in personal situations. The test of the empirical fit is "how stable the assertion is as an overall characterization of a complex, multi-varied pattern of behavior which is impossible in a particular case to specify deductively beforehand."[6] The use of a theory for disclosure, then, is to provide insight into a situation or person, an unveiling of what was there all the time, or a restructuring of perception so that new patterns of relationship or significance can appear.

Two lines of thought which follow from this idea of the disclosure use of scientific theories should be made explicit. The first relates Ramsey's notion to the distinction made by Thomas Kuhn in his *The Structure of Scientific Revolutions*.[7] He makes a distinction between normal science and revolutionary science. In normal science, the working scientists accept the prevailing paradigms which have been offered as the basic explanatory structures of the scientific community and try to fill in the many missing parts. However, a time comes when anomalies accumulate and a new explanatory paradigm is necessary. This involves an overthrow of the older paradigm and the establishment of a new tradition within the scientific community. It seems appropriate to refer to these new paradigms as new disclosure models, which open up a world previously unanticipated and which is rife with new exploratory possibilities. Whereas the older paradigms might serve as disclosure models for some people or in some situations, the new one is a cultural disclosure, an opening in the great mystery of being. Thus there are revolutionary changes in the worlds of science—the Copernican revolution, the Darwinian revolution, and the Einsteinian revolutions. It seems that there are also revolutions within the behavioral sciences and within psychology.

The other line of thought which this notion of disclosure suggests is that disclosure is not limited to scientific models. In fact, Ramsey refers to the possibility of disclosure models in theology. Disclosures come not only from the sciences, but from all of man's creative enterprises—his poetry, his philosophy, his drama, his religion, his art, and indeed his technology. In building his world, whether symbolically or physically, man projects a bit of himself into the world and thus unpeels another layer of the skin that encloses him. Is this not what McLuhan is saying in his *Understanding Media: the Extensions of Man:*[8] that by externalizing or extending his nervous system via the electric and electronic media man becomes aware of certain qualities of his being that have previously escaped notice?

Using these distinctions to discuss the relationship between psychology and the shaping of curriculum, it can be postulated that psychological knowledge serves first as one instrument of disclosure. It helps reveal to the curriculum person what it is to be a human being. But it is crucial to insist that it is but one instrument, not the only instrument. To shape a curriculum, all of man's viable disclosure models must be used—his sciences, his philosophies, his humanities and arts, and his theologies—for the student is too precious, indeed too sacred, to be entrusted to the disclosures of the behavioral sciences.

PSYCHOLOGY AND THE CURRICULUM

What are the implications of this for the shaping of the curriculum? First, that any psychological model might be used as a disclosure model for a teacher, supervisor, or curriculum builder. By wearing the spectacles of a particular psychological model for a time, the world of people might appear differently, and new possibilities for action, for feeling, and for thinking can appear. A distinction must be made whether we like it or not, between appearance and reality, between Kant's noumena and phenomena. We must recognize that the world as we learned to see it, ourselves, and others, is not necessarily the world as others see it, or as we might see it with different cognitive spectacles. Hence, any new psychological theory is a device for checking our accustomed world to be sure that we are not simply contemplating our navel in selfish self-repose.

These new psychological theories are not necessarily the revolutionary theories that Kuhn talks about. They are more apt to be the gradual filling out of the broad theoretical structures suggested by others long ago. Are we not still trying to come to terms with the Freudian revolution—that man's unconscious is a potent force in his behavior, however we define that unconscious and that force? Are we not still filling in the details, through normal psychological science, that man's behavior is influenced by the information that impinges upon him from the environment? This is an insight we associate with Thorndike but we should not forget Locke and Hume. Are we not still filling in the details that we associate with the near revolutionary theory of the Gestaltists, that man and his world are shaped by the way he perceives or cognizes his world? But this, too, might be more readily associated with Kant or Husserl than with Wertheimer or Koffka.

Again, we must insist upon disclosures from the other fields of man's great endeavor. The educator has been indoctrinated with the positivistic fallacy—that the world as it seems, or if you wish, as we know it, is the world as it is.[9] This leads us to the circular search, a tail-chasing activity whereby we study what man seems to be in order to understand him, and then use this knowledge to project the next steps. From this process comes the question of whether "ought" can be developed from "is," and of course the predominant opinion is that "ought" does not follow from what "is." The reverse of this is more apt to be true—that the "is" can follow from the "ought." By this statement, I intend that the world as it is known by the behavioral scientist need not be the world that is brought into the school. The knowledge discovered or constructed by the behavioral scientist can be used to help build this world, through its techno-logical instrumentality; but it need not, indeed should not, be used to specify the overall design of that world. The specification of the overall design must be made with the aid of the other great, indeed revolutionary disclosure models that have been projected by man.

Currently, it seems to me, some of these models center upon the spoken word. Man, Dasein, is the being-in-the-world who speaks. But his speech springs not simply from within. Rather, it is a result of two conditions. The first is that man is a being who hearkens to the world, a being who listens, a being whose life is a response to the call and summons of the world. The second condition is that the horizons of this world are temporal horizons—man is surrounded by his history. Man is embedded in this history which is his shell—his house. As Heidegger would say, language is man's house of being. I think that this image can be traced into the sources of the Judeo-Christian tradition; that it finds expression today in the works of Heidegger, Merleau-Ponty, and other existentially oriented philosophers and theologians; and that it could be used to examine the linguistic-analytic tradition of today. Obviously, I cannot go into these details in this paper. I can only suggest that the implication for curriculum is that we must design schools and educational environments which call forth responsible speech from our students. The word "responsible" is, of course, the catchword and by it I would suggest critical dialogue with people and with the environment.

To me, then, the "ought" for schools is derived from the great disclosure models devised by man. Existing behavioral sciences are no longer providing revolutionary disclosure models; they are currently operating within the realm of normal science—filling the gaps and building up the anomalies that might provide new revolutionary paradigms in the future. This is not to say that existing theories and newly emerging conceptions within psychology and the behavioral sciences cannot be disclosure models for individuals operating within schools, for frequently we remain unaware of our particular biases or orientations. In fact, even if aware, it does no harm to try on new spectacles for a change. It is simply to say that within our culture disclosure models now exist that are not being used to shape schools. Perhaps they are not being used because educators are not aware of their existence, or because these educators have accepted uncritically the bill of goods offered by the behavioral sciences. More probably they are not being used because we lack the means to implement them. It is in the creation of means that I believe the behavioral sciences can, and indeed are, making the greatest contribution to curriculum today. Through the technological fallout from psychological theories the educator can make possible the transformation of the "oughts" from the great revolutionary disclosure models into the "is" of school life.

ENVIRONMENTS THAT ENABLE

Let me assume for the sake of discussion that you accept my basic disclosure model—that the being, man, is known by his hearkening and speaking to the world in which he lives. The word "speaking" must, of course, be qualified to include all of his expressive modes. The task, then, and one not unbeknown to the curriculum designer, is to provide environments which make it possible for the individual to hearken to the world, to speak authentically from the center of his own being, and to engage in the ensuing conversation. In the past this has been impossible because of size of groups, insufficient or inadequate materials and media, or lack of organizational and pedagogical skill of school people. It seems to me that these are basically technological deficiencies and also, of course, economic problems. It is at this point of technology that psychological knowledge provides the necessary help. Psychological and other behavioral science knowledge can be used, technologically, to build the special conditions which realize the hearkening-speaking model. In other words, the revolutionary models identify openings into the fabric of man's being. Technology paves the roadway and builds the bridges so this opening, an "ought," can be entered, becoming an "is."

Examples are not too difficult to identify today. The development of programmed materials and computer-based instructional techniques can be considered an embodiment or, to use a more loaded word, an incarnation of learning theory, specifically reinforcement theory. We should rejoice in this, for it means that learning theory is now being used to help build the world, rather than being used to shape ideologies. It means that it is now possible to build into the environment those conditions by which certain skills can be learned, thus freeing the teachers and the students from organizational structures and demands that inhibit good education. Now that this component of the educational phenomenon is being embodied in the thing-world, the technological world, the curriculum person can return to his essential task of educating the student. This is the symbolic meaning of O. K. Moore's autotelic environment. This is the value of good computer-based simulation techniques. This is the significance of the good skill development auto-instructional materials that are being constructed. The process has been one of identifying certain characteristics of people in given situations, in this case, changes in behavior. These characteristics are used to build environmental conditions which increase the power of the individual to live in his world. By building these aspects into the world we free man to interact with man for the sake of conversation, not for the sake of control. By using learning theory to build educational environments we make it possible for the teacher to enter into significant dialogue with the student as a human being, not simply as a learner. This is the basis for my original distinction between learning and education. Now that the learning concerns can be taken care of through a technological environment, what can education become?

SETTING FOR LEARNING

Motivational theory serves a different function in the construction of the technological world which can help educate. The clue is taken from motivational research in industry and advertising. Motivational theory is used to help build the interface between the student and the technological environment and to determine the informational system to be used between them. In the past, motivational theory has been interpreted as a way to manipulate the student in order to interest him in something. A more realistic interpretation is that motivational theory is used to build the environment and to specify the communication system in such a way that the student will get involved. Hence, different interfaces must be provided for different kinds of students, just as different types of auto-instructional materials must be built for students with different learning styles. With a wide variety of materials with different interfaces, the teacher is further freed to enter into dialogue with the student—to hearken to his speaking.

Finally the studies in cognition and genetic epistemology offer the curriculum worker the tools for creating or making the scenes or stages within which education takes place. An example of this is the work of Educational Services, Incorporated, as illustrated by the examples that Bruner gives in his "Man: A Course of Study."[10] His theories of cognition are being used to select and build a variety of materials about tool making, social organization, and child rearing. The process is one of studying certain characteristics of people and using these characteristics to build educational materials. Learning theory is used to determine sequence and the responsiveness of the fabricated environment. Motivational theory is used to fabricate or construct the interfaces and informational system. Cognitive theory, however, is used to select those aspects of the world of others that are brought into the school.

There is great similarity here between some of the findings of, say, Berlyne[11] in his studies of directed thinking and the studies of Eisenstein[12] on film making. Eisenstein makes much of the montage which is made up of a variety of shots. He stresses the notion of conflict as essential in the construction of montage and even in filming individual shots. Interestingly enough, Berlyne expresses concern for the collative properties which lead to directed thinking, whereas Bruner[13] refers to the conflicts or, at least, lack of equilibrium among the enactive, iconic, and symbolic modes of representation as stimuli to cognitive movement. My point here is that if we consider cognitive theory not as something that explains what happens in the head of a student as the psychologist does, but as a way of designing the scenes or settings within which education occurs, then aspects of the curricular way of thinking will come close to the ways of thought that Eisenstein used to make his films. There could very well come a time when the category "concept" is no longer an effective or meaningful one for the psychologist. However, through technology, cognitive theory might well be embodied in the educational environments that we fabricate for students.

By considering psychological theories—whether learning theory, motivational theory, or cognitive theory—not as the psychologist does, i.e., as valid ways of explaining hidden processes within students, but as very powerful tools for constructing educational environments, we can return to the primary foci disclosed by the great revolutionary theories. Man is a hearkening-speaking being-in-the-world. Our task as curriculum people is to fabricate that educational environment which calls forth from the student authentic, poetic speech.

Our task is world building. Within that world, as teachers, we should be free to engage in conversation with the student about that which is called forth in him by the world we have created. If we see psychological theories as world-building tools rather than tools for understanding students, then we, too, are freed to live as hearkening-speaking beings in the world we build—not as people controllers or manipulators.

NOTES

1. Professor of Curriculum and Instruction, Department of Curriculum and Teaching, Teachers College, Columbia University, New York, New York.

2. Robert M. Gagné, "Educational Objectives and Human Performance," in J.D. Krumboltz (ed.), *Learning and the Educational Process* (Chicago: Rand McNally & Company, 1965), p. 4.

3. Michael Polanyi, *The Tacit Dimension* (New York: Doubleday & Company, Inc., 1966), pp. xi–108.

4. Ian T. Ramsey, *Models and Mystery* (London: Oxford University Press, 1964), pp. ix–74.

5. *Ibid.*, p. 14.

6. *Ibid.*, p. 38.

7. Thomas S. Kuhn, *The Structure of Scientific Revolutions* (Chicago: The University of Chicago Press, 1962), pp. xv–172.

8. Marshall McLuhan, *Understanding Media: the Extensions of Man* (New York: McGraw-Hill Book Company, Inc., 1964), pp. xiii−364.

9. Herbert Marcuse, *One-Dimensional Man* (Boston: Beacon Press, 1964), pp. xvii−260; *Reason and Revolution* (New York: Oxford University Press, 1941) and (Boston: Beacon Press, 1960), pp. xvi−431.

10. Jerome Bruner, *Toward a Theory of Instruction* (Cambridge, Massachusetts: The Belknap Press of Harvard University Press, 1966), pp. 73−101.

11. D. E. Berlyne, *Structure and Direction in Thinking* (New York: John Wiley & Sons, Inc., 1965), pp. xi−378.

12. Sergei Eisenstein, *Film Form and The Film Sense* (New York: The World Publishing Company, 1957). Originally published by Harcourt, Brace & World, Inc.: *Film Form,* 1949; *The Film Sense,* 1947.

13. Jerome Bruner *et al., Studies in Cognitive Growth* (New York: John Wiley & Sons, Inc., 1966).

7. THE CONTRIBUTION OF HISTORY TO THE STUDY OF THE CURRICULUM

Kenneth Charlton

There may be some among you who might ask, why would an historian be undertaking this subject? After all, the new star in the heavens which is called curriculum theory and development is very much concerned with the present and the future. Why call on an historian who is concerned with the past, a past which is dead and buried, or at the very least a past which cannot be known in the way the curriculum specialist knows about a curriculum?

And that may not be the only cause for doubt in your minds. Curriculum specialists nowadays talk in terms of models and theories, terms which historians rarely use. Some historians even deny them altogether. Again, curriculum theorists aim at generality and objectivity. Can history be general enough for curriculum theory? Can history be objective enough for curriculum theory? Paul Valery once described history as "the most dangerous poison distilled in the crucible of the human mind," and Matthew Arnold regarded it as "the vast Mississippi of falsehood." Henry Ford, of course, regarded it as "just bunk." The possibilities of a contribution seem remote!

But, even if the past is not dead and buried, even if history is not subject to these particular disabilities, in what possible way can it contribute to thinking about such an up-to-date matter as curriculum theory and development? Before we can begin to answer such a question, however, the historian has to ask some

SOURCE. In John F. Kerr (ed.), *Changing the Curriculum* (London: University of London Press, Ltd., 1968), pp. 63–78. Copyright 1968 by Kenneth Charlton.

questions of his own. To the curriculum theorist's question: "Can history contribute to curriculum theory and development?" the historian might well reply: "It depends, first of all, on what kind of theory you have in mind; and it depends, secondly, on what precisely it is you are theorizing about." For unless the historian is clear as to what is meant by "curriculum," and what kind of theory is considered appropriate for it, he would be hard pressed to know where to start. Herein, of course, lies the dilemma of meaning in intellectual discourse. If our terms are precisely defined they remain precise only if they are not widely used. If our terms are widely used they lose precision and produce confusion and misunderstanding rather than clarification, heat rather than light. And the problem is still further complicated when the plurality of knowledge (both in its content and in our means of achieving that content) is faced with the mono-lithicity implied in the term "curriculum theory."

As to the term "theory," I take it that our curriculum specialist does not have in mind the man in the street's view which equates theory with idle armchair speculation, divorced from the evidence of the real world; nor that he wants to equate theory with "doctrines" or "philosophies." Does he, then, insist that his curriculum theory is of the deductive-mathematical kind, a body of propositions consisting of postulates and theorems, where the postulates logically imply the theorems? Or is he happy to accept that such absolute logical rigor is inappropriate to his own study, and that theory is therefore to be thought of in terms of, say, a set of verified hypotheses, or of a conceptual framework which allows of and facilitates the systematic ordering of data. Has he in mind a structural model, or does he think of his theory as a set of prescriptive rules which lay down courses of action for given situations? Or does he prefer to accept B. O. Smith's enjoinder and consider his generalizing in terms of "strategies"[1] rather than theories of a scientific kind with claims to the usual consistency, comprehensiveness and parsimony?

Curriculum theorists have not made up their minds about the precise nature of their theorizing. It would be surprising (and dangerous) if they had. I stress the differences, however, merely to emphasize the difficulty facing the historian who is asked to consider curriculum theory from his limited standpoint. For example, if the curriculum theorist wants to do his curriculum theorizing deductively, as George and Elizabeth Maccia have done,[2] then history's contribution might be of one particular kind. If, on the other hand, the theorizing is to be done inductively, history obviously will have to contribute in a different way. Certainly the latter method is nearer to the professional historian's approach, despite the fact that some historians would deny that they theorize at all. A. J. P. Taylor, for example, has insisted, "I am not a philosophic historian; I have no system, no moral interpretation; I write to clear my mind, to discover how things happened and how men behaved." We would do well, however, to remember Pascal's dictum that "to reject philosophy is already to philosophize," and in the light of this to agree with Sir Keith Hancock that "those historians who have no theory fill the vacuum with their prejudices."[3]

As for the term curriculum, I take it that the curriculum specialist will want to think of it in extensive terms, and that his study (and therefore his theorizing) about it will take into account not only its content but also its methods, its objectives and even its evaluation. The question then becomes how can history contribute to decisionmaking and theorizing about these aspects of the curriculum, or, to put it in more familiar terms, how can an historian contribute to the curriculum theorist's attempts to generalize about the why and the what and the how of the curriculum.

But before these questions can be answered we have also to ask ourselves, "What is meant by history?" Or rather we have to ask the curriculum theorist to be clear what he means by history, and in what senses history is capable of offering a contribution. Does he have in mind that history can provide a deductive explanatory model? Or that history is an exercise of judgment? Does he think of history as a process of empathetic understanding? Or would he agree that history's model of narration is the model which most attracts him?

At one extreme end of a continuum history is thought of as a deductive model borrowed from the physical sciences and at the other extreme end history is regarded as an unrelated series of unique events. In this kind of context then, we have to ask: "Is history a different mode of experience from physical science, thus requiring a different method of investigation and explanation?" and we have to go on to ask: "In what senses are classification, induction, experimental techniques, statistical quantification and so on appropriate research tools for the historian, as for the curriculum theorist?"

In the context of this paper, however, and to bring the problem down to reasonable proportions, history can be thought of in two senses: In the first place it can be thought of as "the past," what we know about the past—something which can, perhaps, be used as data by the curriculum theorist, something which can provide the curriculum theorist with data from which he can learn "lessons," and something even which might offer precise precedents on which to act in the future. Whatever use is made of history, however, in this sense we are concerned with the *content* of history.

In the second sense, on the other hand, history may be thought of as the historian's *method* or the historian's *discipline*. We are thinking here of his basic concepts and the methods of enquiry which he considers to be peculiarly appropriate to his trade. We then have to ask: "How far are these concepts and methods likely to be of use in curriculum theorizing?"

Trying to answer the curriculum theorist's question, then, we can think of history as providing a model (of whatever kind), a model of procedure for curriculum building; or at the very least as contributing some small component of a model which might draw on several disciplines in its construction; or we can think of history as providing data from which a curriculum theory might be drawn, to explain which a curriculum theory might be formulated.

In a single paper one must perforce be selective, and perhaps arbitrarily so. I should like, therefore, to go on now to discuss (albeit all too briefly) four points which seem to me to be relevant to an historian's discussion of curriculum theory. I want to say something about models, about generality, about objectivity, and about tradition. First then, a word about models.

Curriculum theorists frequently discuss the use of models in their theorizing,[4] and yet the professional historian has traditionally been skeptical of this particular way of thought. H. A. L. Fisher, for example, reported that the more he sought a pattern in history, the less he was able to find one.[5] And those historians, or rather those writers, who claim to have found a pattern in history, are precisely the writers whom professional historians refuse to accept into the club. One has only to think of the reception of Arnold Toynbee's *Study of History*, or of those historians who seek to interpret Christian belief in their writing of history. The same kind of reception has been accorded to those writers who attempt to impose the model of evolution on the details of man's history. Palmerston, I imagine, was expressing a sentiment which many historians would echo sympathetically when he said, "Half the wrong conclusions at which man arrives are reached by the abuse of metaphors, and mistaking general resemblance or imaginary similarity for real identity."[6]

Yet, on the other hand, the historian makes use of a structural model the moment he assumes that the data he has assembled are ordered, or can be ordered and do not remain random. At the very least, he uses a narrative model, in accordance with which he arranges his data in chronological order, presumably on the assumption that this reflects a valid pattern and that at the same time it will enable him not merely to exhibit his data but also the better to offer an explanation of it.

Second, can history be general enough? The implication of this question is that curriculum theorizing can attain a level of generality similar to that of, say, the physical sciences, and assumes that the curriculum theorist is predominantly interested in universal laws or hypotheses which will enable him not simply to provide an explanation, at a high level of generality, of the data he collects, but also to predict from his formulated theory. Michael Oakeshott in his *Experience and its Modes* denies that the historian is concerned with generality at this level. The historian, he claims, is concerned with the description of particular events rather than the search for general laws which might govern these events: "the moment historical facts are regarded as instances of general laws history is dismissed."[7] To attempt to so regard them is to ignore a presupposition of historical enquiry, is to transform an historical way of investigating past events into a scientific one. For Oakeshott, the impossibility of explaining historical data on the scientific level is thus not simply an empirical one, a matter of mere practical difficulties. The difference is one of kind rather than of degree. And he is supported in his view by Sir Maurice Powicke who has proclaimed his adherence to "a view of history which insists that some things happen because men and women with thoughts make them happen. Historical events are not like movements caused by the law of gravitation, they cannot be separated from what we call mind."[8]

Even so, though the working historian does not as a rule search for general laws, he usually goes beyond Oakeshott's description of particular events. He goes beyond description to attempt also an explanation, and to do this he must go beyond the uniqueness of unique events in search of relationship between the events. As soon as he does this he raises the level of generality of his work, though without burning his fingers in the fire of prediction and prophecy.

Third, can history be objective enough? Once again the question implies a study objective enough for the curriculum theorist who wishes to take scientific objectivity as his model. The question is not (I take it) whether history is objective or not. Such a question is as unhelpful to the historian as it is to the scientist. Both would reply, "It depends how high you set your standards of objectivity."[9] My point here is not to set out a systematic argument to show that history may be thought of as sufficiently objective to enable it to contribute satisfactorily or appropriately to any consideration of curriculum theory. Here I can only assert that for the purpose of the curriculum theorist the content and discipline of history can be regarded as sufficiently objective to meet any requirements which he might insist upon.

It is true that, for Oakeshott, "history is the historian's experience. It is made by nobody save the historian; to write history is the only way of making it," and in the same way Collingwood has insisted, with Croce, that "all history is contemporary history."[10] It is, of course, all too short a step from such a stand-point to the "intrusion" of the historian and to the derogatory comments s·:ch as I mentioned at the beginning of this paper. But the study of history has gone a long way since the mid-nineteenth century when Positivism's influence on it was so strong. The relationship between knower and known is now recognized (by scientist and historian alike) to be much more complex than the Positivists supposed and insisted upon.[11]

In the same way, even though history does not share with science the search for general theories, it does demand the same kind of dedication, the same ruthlessness, the same passion for exactness as all the physical sciences. The historian binds himself by what is called his discipline, and in this sense he can claim an objectivity sufficient to persuade the curriculum theorist of his credentials, for I take it that neither the historian nor the curriculum theorist will claim for his study (or for the results of his study) an objectivity which will enable him to deduce conclusions from self-evident axioms.

Fourth, if we turn now from the method of history to its content we come right up against a concept in history which many theorists might well conclude would prevent history from contributing to curriculum theory. I refer here to the concept of tradition. For many a layman tradition has too easily been equated with the past, and has thus been considered to be a continual inhibiter of liberty, both of thought and of action, and therefore also of theorizing. Tradition, which imposes barriers on man's conduct and puts restrictions on his thought, is regarded as a despoiler of scrutiny, of disbelief, of skepticism, of receptiveness to the other point of view. Too often in the past we have seen the uncritical adulation of tradition, an adulation in which the past is always regarded as better than the present. It is this which has been the persistent enemy, it is claimed, of the liberal mind.[12] The dead hand of the past or the dead weight of tradition has suppressed individuality and selfhood. In this way, therefore, the past, equated with tradition, is regarded as being singularly unhelpful to an enterprise such as curriculum theory. On the other hand, the negative attitude to tradition which is expressed in a phrase such as "the dead hand of the past," or "the dead weight of tradition," reminds us that this absolute criticism of the past, as inevitably irrelevant and out-of-date, is equally destructive of practical decisionmaking. What is worse, both of these points of view are sustained by enthusiasms which themselves inhibit skeptical constructive scrutiny.

The concept of tradition is nevertheless one with which the curriculum theorist must concern himself, for he is already concerned with the curriculum of the past, either in a positive way, by doing some theorizing about it and perhaps bringing it up to date, or negatively by rejecting it altogether and building it anew. In one sense, however, the bedrock of the curriculum is that "funded capital of social experience" which in some way must be handed on to a growing generation. Few curriculum theorists, I imagine, would deny this as part of the exercise, but we are concerned here not simply with the knowledge of the past, what might be called traditional knowledge, but also with the attitudes of the past. In an age of rapid change it may very well be that these have only a marginal impact on curriculum renewal, but in fact it would be virtually impossible to reject them totally. For example, we continue to think of curriculum in traditional terms if we think of it in terms of why, how, and what? These are questions which have been useful to ask in the past in guiding curriculum planning and they presumably will continue to be so.

The present problem of curriculum planning is itself shot through with the past and with vestiges of the past, and future solutions however radical will inevitably carry something of the past with them. Some of these vestiges are physical, in the form of existing textbooks, and more important, though perhaps less obvious because more subtle, in terms of school architecture, which may inhibit change and facilitate adherence to past procedures, methods and attitudes. (The same is recognized as a problem by penal reformers, who find that prison architecture of the late nineteenth century determines, to a much greater degree than they would wish, the procedures of dealing with present day prisoners.)

But the vestiges are not simply physical. More importantly they are vestiges of mental attitudes and values,[13] and once again we come up against the point of view which insists that the mental attitudes and the values of the past are better by definition than those of the present. This, I would have thought, is to go too far, but at the same time one has to beware of rejecting tradition absolutely, for though tradition reduces the rate of change in a society, in so far as it allows of a moderate rate of change it also enhances the orderliness of change. In the same way we can refer to the stability of tradition and the sustaining nature of tradition, both of which might be considered necessary if change is not to become anarchy. What is to be avoided is a position at extreme ends of the continuum. At one end are to be found the traditionalists for whom anything which once existed is entirely sacred by virtue of its very connectedness with the past, a sacredness which is untouchable and unchangeable and is endowed with an unquestioned inevitability. At the other end of the continuum are the rebels, who reject everything simply because it was once observed. Both of these positions are, of course, tarred with the same brush of ideology and extremism, and both are hostile not only to liberty but to tradition itself. "The search for the usable past," as Edward Shils[14] has put it, is something which the curriculum theorist must be very much involved in.

The problem of tradition is, perhaps, even more crucial and even more complicated in curriculum theorizing in underdeveloped countries, where there is at one and the same time an even sharper wish to build anew (and to do so at a pace greatly exceeding that obtained by already developing nations) running alongside an even deeper pervasiveness of the past in both attitudes and practices, in which traditions are so hallowed as to be almost religious in character.[15] The situation is still further complicated by the fact that the society receiving (underdeveloped) and the society offering (developed) are differentially influenced by the past—in other words, have differential reactions to the past.

At all times, therefore, both the historian and the curriculum theorist have to remind themselves of the phenomenon of time-lag, or cultural time-lag, and this, too, is a matter of attitude as much as of practice. One has in mind here the lag between a set of values and social reality, a lag which was exemplified for example in the negative value judgments that were placed on usury at a time, in the fifteenth and sixteenth centuries, when interest paid on loans was an important and necessary feature of the expansion of credit. And we see it nearer at home in the continued use of the phrase "scholarship class" in junior schools, and in references to a high percentage of pupils in a particular school "getting through."

If curriculum theorizing takes place in a simple traditional society, then the role of history is relatively easily identified. That which was preferred in the past provides the indubitable content, method and purpose and even method of evaluation. In other words, that content which has been used in the past, which has been transmitted by methods used in the past and for purposes which have been designated as acceptable in the past, provides the norm for future action. And if such content and method continue to produce the kind of person, the kind of citizen, which has been preferred in the past, then they will be deemed to be successful. The problem becomes rather more complicated, however, if history is expected to play a part in curriculum theorizing for a dynamic rather than a static society; though, referring back to our opening doubts, paradoxically for some people "history" when invoked was considered as antipathetic to change. The way in which the youth of today refer to fashions and indeed attitudes as "ancient" is a good example of this.

Our model of curriculum theory must, then, include an element of time. It must include an awareness of the past, even if its purpose is to reject it, and an awareness of the future, even if only to recognize that some part of the past will remain to discolor its pristine newness. Furthermore, any curriculum which is devised as a result of the theorizing must include a component which helps sensitize a person first of all to his own past, and then to the past of others.

Our knowledge of the past should remind us, too, that though models with their various interconnected components are useful, they cease to remain so when the curriculum theorist imagines that component changes are uniform and regular, and happen at a predictable rate. In addition, we have to take into account not only the cultural time-lag to which I have referred, but we must also decide whether this is to be regarded as a good thing or a bad thing. Some people (and they need not be "traditionalists") would regard this phenomenon as an expression of man's wisdom, or at least a useful safety valve (whether consciously devised by man or not), or even a defense mechanism. We must remember that the song, "Fings ain't what they used to be," can evoke both hurrahs and boos. As Braithwaite reminds us, "The price of the employment of models is eternal vigilance,"[16] and in this case we have to make sure that the notion of change is both adequately represented and at the same time evaluated.

If the curriculum theorist thinks of his theory in tentative terms—that is, if he includes the factor of time in his model—he builds change into it, and his evidence for change is "the past." He thus builds a theory which is relevant to a particular kind of social situation, that is, not simply a situation which changes (for example, is expanding economically), but also one in which change is considered to be a good thing, for it is necessary in considering both of these points to remember that "social change" as a concept is neutral, but that it can be accorded a positive or negative value. As a result a theory will be constructed that presumably will be able to cope with change in society in the future, a society which is not only changing itself but which is also likely to subject the theory to critical scrutiny, to modification and even rejection.

It is important to remember, also, that debates about the curriculum themselves have their roots in past attitudes and past value judgments, and an awareness of this should increase one's sensitivity to the debate. These attitudes can be positive, though possibly unconscious, in their carry-over of the past into the present. They can also be negative, in the sense that they represent a reaction against an irrelevant, dead-and-buried past. The basic premise of the debate is that the previous curriculum has been overtaken by the course of events, that it is out of date and therefore is in need of renewal. The task is different, then, from one in which the main problem is conceived of in terms of making more efficient the methods of the past.

Now these vestiges of the past are powerful because their influence is implicit, rarely explicit, unconscious rather than conscious. On the other hand, when tradition is called into account then the problem becomes conscious and explicit (though attitudes to the word tradition can, of course, be either positive or negative). History, then, can help us to put into context not only curriculum theory itself but our attitudes both to theory and to the activity of theorizing, and the complexity of these attitudes should remind us that we ignore at our peril those philosophical, political, social, economic, religious and other factors which a theoretician might well ignore in trying to base his curriculum renewal on purely educational grounds.

But context, and its multi-dimensional nature, is of importance, too, in so far as education is concerned to help the pupil understand his situation—that is, to understand himself in a context of others and of the natural world. What *I am*, however, and what my context *is,* comprehends not only the present. It comprehends also the past, the past of myself and of others, dead and alive, a past which may be thought of in terms of how I and my context have come to be what they are. And at the same time it comprehends the future, what I hope to become and what I hope the context will become.

In linking the past with the present and the future, and in particular using the content of history, we have to beware of an amelioristic view of history which, for example, can say that "the history of education might well be written in terms of the moving frontier of social conscience."[17] This is unidimensional history which ignores the other forces at work in society, not simply those of politics, of religion, of economics and so on, but also those forces of indifference, apathy, ignorance and plain vested interest, all of which contribute to the shaping of institutions, attitudes and, of course, curricula. This is simply to say that the historian of education, say, is interested in the pathology of educational institutions, attitudes and curricula, as well as their ecology.

Even so, history can remind us that change is humanly possible, given the will and the opportunity for change. Without an awareness of the past we would be hard put to it to stand up and challenge arguments such as: "It's not possible, human nature being what it is . . ." and so on. History reminds us not only that things do change (for good or ill, depending on one's value system), but also that things can be changed, that we can change them. The achievement of political equality in the past has been a good example of this, and as Professor Simon has reminded us, "There is no more liberating influence than the knowledge that things have not always been as they are and need not remain so."[18]

The history of curriculum renewal itself is a good guide on this score, given the assumption that we can and do learn from past experience, and that this is not to be considered the same as prophecy and prediction. To say this, however, is to say very little. We have to go on to ask in what way do we learn? To what degree do we learn? How much do we learn? We can see curriculum renewal at work in the education of the governing class in sixteenth century England, a renewal which took place despite the unwillingness of the traditional institutions of education to change their curricula to suit new demands.[19] In the same way we can compare the way in which the Comenians of the seventeenth century laid down a particular set of criteria for curricular planning, both in content and method, for the ordinary child, and we can see a different set of criteria at work in the reaction of the eighteenth century and nineteenth century Naturalists.

In fact, this kind of consideration has to be put in the context of a history of the nature of knowledge, or rather a history of man's view of knowledge. For example, what was termed natural philosophy in the medieval period included what we now call the physical sciences as well as the science of mind, and of course, philosophy itself. The increase in knowledge in the modern world has resulted from a division of labor which has produced the various subjects into which natural philosophy has been divided, and this has served its purpose. In the twentieth century, however, there appears to be a move towards a synthesis of knowledge, and this may very well lead us by the end of the century to a quite different approach to the nature of knowledge, and therefore of the curriculum and curriculum theory. In fact, this is already happening in our present day schools, in the formulation of actual curricula which aim at integrating the various components of the curriculum, and in so doing reflect new views about the nature of knowledge. It is important, too, to remember that every discipline has its own history, as has knowledge and our classification of it, our ways of achieving it, our ways of defining it. It would be a brave (or incompetent) man who would claim that his own discipline owes nothing to the past. His more perceptive colleagues will recognize that it still retains something of the past in its assumptions, implicit, unspoken and even unrecognized as these may be for some of his less perceptive colleagues.

I have tried, in this paper, to emphasize that any attempt by an historian to answer the question, "How can history contribute to curriculum theory and development?" must first of all distinguish between the different views of history and the different views of curriculum theory which are current. Only then can he go on to deal with the substantive question, and this can be done in two ways. First of all he can consider the contribution which the structural disciplines of historical investigation, its concepts, its methods, can make, and secondly he can consider how far the content of history can be drawn on, not to provide particular and concrete answers or solutions to current problems, but to make us aware of the possibility of change, of the complexity of change, and of the carry over of the past into our present situation and future aspirations.

I can only hope that the points I have raised in this cautionary tale might be of help to those involved in theorizing about the curriculum of the past, present and future.

NOTES

1. B. O. Smith, "A Concept of Teaching," in B. O. Smith and R. H. Ennis (eds.) *Language and Concepts in Education* (Chicago: Rand McNally, 1961), p. 100.

2. E. S. Maccia, *Methodological Considerations in Curriculum Theory Building,* presented to A.S.C.D. Commission on Curriculum Theory, Chicago, 1965.

3. A. J. P. Taylor, *Englishmen and Others* (London: Hamish Hamilton, 1956), p. 27.

B. Pascal, *Pensées* i, 4.

W. K. Hancock, "Economic History at Oxford," in *Politics in Pitcairn and other Essays* (New York: Macmillan, 1947), p. 168.

4. Cf. E. S. Maccia and G. S. Maccia, "The Ways of Educational Theorizing through Models," *Occasional Paper 62−111,* Educational Theory Center, Ohio State University.

5. H. A. L. Fisher, *A History of Europe* (London: Eyre and Spottiswoode, 1935), preface.

6. Cited E. Leach, "Concepts: Models," *New Society* (14 May 1964), p. 22.

7. M. Oakeshott, *Experience and Its Modes* (Cambridge: Cambridge University Press, 1933), p. 154.

8. F. M. Powicke, *History, Freedom and Religion* (Oxford: Oxford University Press, 1938), p. 6.

9. Cf., for example, J. A. Passmore, "The Objectivity of History," *Philosophy* 33 (1958), pp. 97−116; and C. Blake, "Can History be Objective?" *Mind* 64 (1955), pp. 61−78.

10. Oakeshott, *op. cit.,* p. 99; and R. G. Collingwood, *The Idea of History* (Oxford: Oxford University Press, 1946), pp. 282 ff.

11. Cf. Michael Polanyi, *Personal Knowledge* (London: Routledge and Kegan Paul, 1958) and *The Study of Man* (London: Routledge and Kegan Paul, 1959), especially Lecture III, "Understanding History."

12. Cf. E. Shils, "Tradition and Liberty: Antinomy and Interdependence," *Ethics* 68 (No. 3, 1958), pp. 153−65.

13. K. Charlton, "Tradition and Change in Sixteenth and Seventeenth Century English Education," *Year Book of Education* (London: Evans Bros., 1958), pp. 54−65.

14. E. Shils, *loc. cit.,* p. 155.

15. Cf. A. Curle, "Tradition, Development and Planning," *Sociological Review* (New series) 8 (1960), pp. 223−38.

16. R. B. Braithwaite, *Scientific Explanation* (Cambridge: Cambridge University Press, 1953), p. 93.

17. H. L. Beales, *The Making of Social Policy* (Oxford: Oxford University Press, 1946), pp. 21–22.

18. B. Simon, "The History of Education," in J. W. Tibble (ed.), *The Study of Education* (London: Routledge and Kegan Paul, 1966), p. 92.

19. Cf. K. Charlton, *Education in Renaissance England.* Part Two (London: Routledge and Kegan Paul, 1965).

CHAPTER 2

What Purposes Should the Curriculum Serve?

It is clear that there should be legislation about education and that it should be conducted on a public system. But consideration must be given to the question, what constitutes education and what is the proper way to be educated. At present there are differences of opinion as to the proper tasks to be set; for all peoples do not agree as to the things that the young ought to learn, either with a view to virtue or with a view to the best life, nor is it clear whether their studies should be regulated more with regard to intellect or with regard to character. And confusing questions arise out of the education that actually prevails, and it is not at all clear whether the pupils should practice pursuits that are practically useful, or morally edifying, or higher accomplishments—for all these views have won the support of some judges; and nothing is agreed as regards the exercise conducive to virtue, for, to start with, all men do not honor the same virtue, so that they naturally hold different opinions in regard to training in virtue.

Aristotle
Politics VIII. 2

Given the practical nature of curriculum building, it is understandable that curriculum workers have traditionally been preoccupied with ancient but always relevant questions concerning the purposes and goals of an instructional program. Many people have argued that, without some clearly defined sense of direction, it seems hardly possible to make coherent and rational decisions about the selection and organization of curriculum content. While there appears to be general agreement on this score, competing social ideals, philosophical positions, and political ideologies inevitably come into play when the question of the purpose of schooling is raised.

Unfortunately, the question of how purposes are to be determined has often been reduced to a simplistic process of a political consensus achieved by appointing a committee or issuing a report. The reports frequently take the form of listing high-sounding goals like ethical character or self-realization. Sanctified by tradition, this approach to the question of educational purposes and goals has rarely been examined as to its impact (if any) on the curriculum and the instructional activities of teachers and students. Frequently, such goals are stated without any particular attention to those things that can be accomplished within a school context and without regard to the question of what is teachable. It seems likely that the issue of curriculum purposes would be better served by careful analysis of the nature of educational aims and by solid research on the institution of schooling in relation to those aims. Merely extending the lists of pious goals on which some consensus may be reached offers little by way of direction or substance to the process of curriculum development.

In the first article of the chapter (reading #8), a leading philosopher of education, Harry S. Broudy, makes a major attempt to clarify the conceptual confusion that frequently attends statements of goals and objectives. He analyzes the forms that these statements frequently take and comments on the functions they perform. In reading #9, Robert M. Gagné addresses the question of instructional objectives from the perspective of a behaviorist psychologist, Clearly, he sees the specification of objectives as a crucial first step in a systematic attack on curriculum planning. R. S. Peters, by contrast, raises questions about the usefulness and propriety of the practice in reading #10. Essentially, he sees goal setting as a misapplication of means-ends forms of reasoning. In the next article (reading #11), however, another prominent philosopher, William K. Frankena makes the case for educational aims in terms of "dispositions" drawn from principal philosophical traditions.

The last two articles in this chapter treat the educational aim of liberation as implied in the liberal arts curriculum. In reading #12, "Liberal Education and the Nature of Knowledge," Paul H. Hirst examines first the Greek ideal of what a liberal education should accomplish and then attempts to reconstruct that ideal in modern terms. In the last article (reading #13), the historian Arthur G. Wirth explores a major curriculum controversy in the early part of this century. As part of that controversy (in which John Dewey played a major role), the ideal of liberal education was being challenged by a reform-minded group of educators committed to education for vocational preparation and practical efficiency.

8. THE PHILOSOPHICAL FOUNDATIONS OF EDUCATIONAL OBJECTIVES[1]

Harry S. Broudy

The term "philosophical foundations" implies that there are other types of foundations from which the philosophical ones are to be distinguished. Accordingly, we commonly speak of historical, psychological, and sociological foundations of education as well as of philosophical ones. "Foundations," however, connotes a special relation between the parent disciplines (psychology, philosophy, etc.) and the study of educational problems. We probably would not speak of architecture or statistics as foundational to education, even though they are very useful to it. To get closer to the meaning of foundational in the sense that it will be used in this paper, it will be useful to dismiss the analogies with the building industry, funding agencies, and the art of corsetry that the word foundations suggests. About the only value these analogies have is that they convey a sense of priority and importance to foundational studies.

It would seem that a foundational discipline can contribute two sorts of things to the practice or study of education:

(1) Empirical theories which by translation into observational statements and rules of procedure yield prescriptions for practice. The behavioral sciences in principle can provide theory that could be "applied" to problems of educational practice. One well-known example is the theory of operant conditioning which has been turned into a strategy of teaching; another is John Dewey's description of the complete act of thought.

SOURCE. *Educational Theory* 20 (No. 1, Winter 1970), pp. 3–21.

(2) A set of concepts that furnishes a special context for the study of educational problems, but not necessarily a causal hypothesis that can be translated into procedures and techniques. For example, history furnishes a frame of reference for the discussion of education but not rules of practice. Political science and some forms of sociology are also foundational in the sense that they offer distinctive patterns of interpretation.

Philosophy would have to be classed with the interpretative foundational disciplines, and its value is to be estimated not by the rules of procedure it supplies for practice, but rather by the illumination it casts on problems of practice, i.e., whether or not it makes them more intelligible, and the discussions of them more orderly and precise. And the value of such intelligibility, one must suppose, is that the more completely we are aware of the context of a problem, the less likely are we to produce unwanted and unintended side effects in our practice.

The contextual material that philosophy contributes to the consideration of educational objectives is both substantive and critical. It is substantive as a source of ideas about man, society, and nature that figure in the prescriptions for the good life. It is critical by virtue of its concern with the nature of knowledge and the criteria of truth. Philosophy thus assumes jurisdiction over all types of knowledge claims. We shall expect, therefore, to find in the philosophical foundations of educational objectives: (1) references to ideas taken from metaphysics, epistemology (theory of knowledge), ethics, and aesthetics, and (2) analysis of discourse about educational objectives, including the discourse in (1) but not excluding discourse from other contexts and disciplines.

LEVELS OF CONCEPTUALIZATION IN EDUCATIONAL OBJECTIVES

The statement of educational objectives serves several functions. First of all, it may be used as a slogan to solicit support. "The aim of education is growth," for example, invites approbation from right-minded people in general and from those who are unhappy with rigid curricula in particular. Because slogans are often employed for their persuasive efficacy, it is not always profitable to scrutinize them for descriptive accuracy.[2]

Second, the statement of objectives is supposed to help guide the educative process, as a goal or target directs a journey or shot. Because it is believed that choice among ends in education is possible, it is felt that such choice is also necessary; for otherwise means, presumably, could not be selected for relevance and fitness, and failure in this respect would render the whole enterprise irrational, i.e., aimless or vacillating.

In the third place, a statement of objectives is held to be a test to be applied to the educative process. Thus a school with the announced objective of matriculating 75 percent of all its graduates in Ivy League colleges would be condemned out of its own mouth if it placed only 50 percent in such institutions.

To state educational objectives is therefore important. However, it becomes a problem because life, like a big country, offers a wide choice of destinations. Educational objectives may be broad, narrow; remote or proximate. They can be stated in terms of overt behavior, character traits, developmental tasks, life styles, learning products, learning processes, tendencies, dispositions, habits; school outcomes, test results, generic operations; attitudinal syndromes and learning strategies; national security, rates of juvenile and adult delinquency, church attendance, and credit ratings. In short, anything anyone regards as desirable can become an educational objective and, not infrequently, a school objective.

The situation is further complicated because educational objectives refer to (1) goals at which school systems do in fact aim and (2) goals a school system *ought* to aim at. Roughly, the first type is one for the behavioral sciences, sociology, anthropology, and perhaps political science to deal with. The second topic is usually taken to be in the province of philosophy, or that kind of philosophy which has to do with value—sometimes called axiology. A school system is constrained to deal with both questions at the same time, at all times. It may be appropriate to speculate a moment on why this is so, because it throws light on the mixed character of lists of objectives encountered in the educational literature. Such lists are compiled by school superintendents and every curriculum committee. Some have 10 items; some 50.

An examination of the history of education, or rather of educational litera- ture, will support the hypothesis that at any given time, in a fairly well developed culture, a system of instruction exists that purports to prepare its clients for success in that culture. The Egyptian schools at one time turned out scribes and accountants because desirable governmental jobs were available for them; the rhetorical schools of Greece and early Rome graduated men who became eminent because swaying the public was the way to political success. The medieval universities trained men to combine secular scholarship with Christian ideas and service in the ecclesiastical bureaucracy.

However, in every epoch some men criticized the success routes their con- temporaries were traveling, and they endorsed or proposed educational designs that would turn men into other routes on the ground that *real* success lay in following these directions. Thus Socrates paid with his life for not using the forensic skills that the Sophists had perfected, and in which he was no doubt adept himself. In arguing and dying for a vision of life in which a transcendental truth, and virtue based on it, were to be the "real success" routes, he was proposing a style of education quite at odds with that of the actual schools of his time. Montaigne, Locke, and others heaped scorn upon the sort of verbalism and pedantry in which the late vestiges of scholasticism and the aberrations of classicism abounded. In our own time there is no dearth of examples. Schools are criticized because they are too devoted to vocational preparation and to the achievement of middle-class values. Ideal schools and ideal people, the critics aver, would be more creative, more spontaneous, more exciting, more "caring," and more relevant, whatever these terms may be taken to mean. So in every age, the distinction has to be drawn between that at which schools do aim and that at which their critics say they ought to aim.

This is not to say that the schools uniformly produce the success to which they purport to be the routes. Curricula sometimes persist long after their utility is negated by changed circumstance. For example, the rhetorical curriculum in reduced form lived on long after oratory had ceased to be the road to political success. Today schools still make gestures toward a "liberal" education despite the fact that the Aristotelian notion of leisure, which was its rationale, is no longer—if it ever was—a valid premise for our culture, even for the upper classes. The liberal studies are listed in college catalogues, and some of them are required for undergraduate degrees, even though the liberal spirit—study for and only for the sake of self-cultivation—stipulated by Aristotle is hard to find in the American academic world.

And yet, if one examines the sentiments expressed by the schoolmasters in those diverse ages, one finds them professing ideals not very different from those of their critics. Isocrates, a most successful master of a most successful school of rhetoric, and Quintilian, another famous and successful schoolmaster, entertained high moral expectations for their pupils. The orator, said Quintilian, was the *good* man skilled in speaking and not merely a persuasive and eloquent pleader of causes. The school, however closely it is allied with the values of the dominant class of its time, no matter how tightly it hews to the success route of its day, is still an institution that embodies the professed ideals of the community. This internal division between the actual and the ideal within the school reflects the tension within individual men themselves.

The fact that lists of objectives contain aspirations as well as descriptions makes it impossible to comply with the demand that objectives always be stated in behavioral terms. In the first place, an aspiration aims at a situation that does not exist, and although "having the aspiration" does exist, translating it into behavioral terms presents problems. Second, some of the aspirational objectives are not behaviors at all, but rather dispositions to behaviors, and such dispositions are not easily tested by behaviors. Altruism, for example, is often listed as an outcome to be desired from a good education, but just what behavior is unequivocally and unmistakably a token or sign of altruism? In the third place, some school objectives, such as the formation of democratic attitudes, are not translatable into behavioral objectives because democratic attitudes are postures toward doing a wide variety of things. All of which does not mean that some educational objectives cannot and should not be stated in behavioral terms; rather it warns against mindless adherence to a dogma that has relevance only in a restricted domain of education, viz., some of the terminal products of a course of instruction.

We can understand also, considering the variety of things men regard as good, why there is such a bewildering plethora of taxonomies of educational objectives. The net effect of this abundance is that in order to preserve some semblance of clarity or sanity, discussion has to take place within one taxonomic system. Translation of taxonomies one into another is virtually impossible, and every attempt to bring them together into one overarching classification results in just one more taxonomy which no one besides its author feels obliged to consider, must less adopt.

Although there is no way at present of making different taxonomies of objectives comparable or translatable into each other, the chaos of every man with his own taxonomy may be mitigated by trying to sort them into types arranged at various levels of abstraction. After all, we do have to talk to each other about educational problems, and in doing so we cannot avoid talking about objectives. Meaningful communication in educational discourse depends on some uniformity in the connotation and denotation of terms. If A means by an "objective" something on the order of good citizenship and B means "critical thinking" while C means "ability to do problems in algebra," then it is fruitless for them to argue about problems of curriculum, methodology, and the organization of school systems. They pass each other as do vehicles on the multi-level clover-leafs of our modern expressways.

No less important are the consequences of the formulation of objectives for educational research. If objectives are stated as functions of numerous and elusive variables, e.g., good citizenship, growth, democratic living, mental health, then obviously they will resist empirical research. Furthermore, if objectives are too broad, educational research spills over into so many disciplines that it loses any distinctiveness it may claim; it gets lost in the sea of the behavioral sciences, and may have to be turned over to them. This may be desirable for all I know, but we had better be fully aware of the possibility.

There is also the risk that research may be irrelevant to educational problems unless communication about objectives among all educational workers is possible. Thus countless studies on animal learning and human rote learning, however relevant and fruitful they are for learning theory, may be of trivial import so far as producing school outcomes are concerned. Contrariwise, research on how school learnings are actually used in non-school situations may be stimulated, if objectives are formulated in terms of such uses, and if the different uses are distinguished both semantically and operationally. Time taken to conceptualize educational objectives carefully, critically, as precisely as possible is not wasted; casually, almost ritualistically, compiled lists of clichés are not only a waste of time, but a positive source of confusion and mystification.

LIFE OUTCOMES

Value Patterns as Objectives

Educational objectives are sometimes stated as value schema that are "borrowed" from metaphysics or ethics. Thus one might say that the goal of education is a life characterized by rationality, or virtue, or self-realization. Or with John Dewey it might be said that the aim of education is growth. In an important sense, however, it is not correct to say that education borrows these goals from philosophy, because a philosophical system that puts these characteristics at the top of its value hierarchy is already offering an educational prescription. Conversely, a set of educational aims stated at this level of generality is implicitly a philosophical position and needs only the explication of its arguments to become one. In other words, a general philosophical position does not *imply* a set of educational aims, it already *is* such a set. For such a position states criteria for the real and the true; and to say that one form of life is *more real* and *more true* than another is to say at the same time that it is *better* than another. As we shall have occasion to point out below, there is a school of philosophy that consigns all talk about Being, Substance, Perfection and other metaphysical notions to the limbo of a noncognitive misuse of language, but it is doubtful that this will really stop such talk either in philosophy or education.

The Platonic epistemology and metaphysics, for example, argue for a hierarchy of knowledge that is also a hierarchy of perfection. At the lowest rung is the knowledge we get by means of unstable images of things such as reflections in water or in shadows. Above it is the more stable, but still highly idiosyncratic, perception of individual objects that lies at the basis of belief. Higher on the ladder are the abstractions of science, and above them all are the Ideas themselves, the archetypes of reality apprehended by reason. The Eros, or the desiring element of the soul, follows the same ascending path from beautiful things and persons to the Idea of the Beautiful in itself.[3]

Clearly such a schema is a prescription for the good life, and insofar as education is concerned with such matters, Plato's philosophical position is relevant to it. Abstraction as the road to perfection is a profound and radical formula that determines the pecking order of academic life. Its potency is felt not only in the prestige hierarchy of the diverse intellectual disciplines, but also, I take it, in all verbal intelligence testing.

Forms of Society as Objectives

At a somewhat lower level of generality, one can ask: What sort of society, what social and institutional arrangements would be needed to educate individual human beings to achieve a certain pattern of value? Could Plato's good life pattern, for example, have been realized in a democracy? Could Dewey's good life be realized in a totalitarian state? The search for an answer is essentially the work of the social theorist and the political scientist. When an objective is phrased as the preservation of some form of the State or government, it creates demands for certain traits of character and behavior which, presumably, the educational system would either engender or reinforce. In a totalitarian State obedience clearly has a higher priority than in a democratic one; the tendency to be critical and individualistic will find more reinforcement in a democracy than in a totalitarian State. But when a given form of political organization is challenged, the arguments mount to the first level of objectives, i.e., to some theory about the nature and good of man; some theory of perfection in terms of which the societal form is justified or rejected. For this reason, a set of educational objectives that takes the social or governmental form as an axiom or postulate has to preclude calling that form into question.

We see examples of this whenever questioning of the virtues of democracy brings charges of disloyalty and treason. We are put into the awkward position of having to say either that the principle of democracy prevents calling the principle itself into question, or that there is really no rational way of defending democracy against its critics.

As examples of how justifications for a given form of society are carried to a more general level, let us take the Hegelian argument for the primacy of the state and Dewey's defense of democracy.

Roughly paraphrased, Hegel's argument goes something like this: every human individual is finite, i.e., limited in his power, and to that extent is dependent on other objects or persons to achieve his goals. And to the degree that one is dependent he is unfree, frustrated, and to that degree imperfect. The community is an entity that is more comprehensive, more self-sufficient, more powerful and therefore more real and more nearly perfect than the individuals who compose it. The individual becomes free, i.e., able to carry out his choices, if he joins his will to that of the community. The community's goals are more stable than those of the individual. By this line of reasoning, it does not take long to make out a case that true individuality is *really* achievable only in the most complete identification of self with the community or the State. The wisdom, the power, the glory, and the immortality of the State confer on each person who identifies with it genuine selfhood, genuine self-sufficiency, genuine individuality. One may quarrel with the argument, but there is sufficient truth in it to make it more than a verbal *tour de force*. Large numbers of men have accepted the doctrine and lived in Stated that exemplified it. I am not arguing the merits of the doctrine; it is simply an example of the point that one can take his ultimate stand on the preservation of the State and refuse to argue its merits, but if one does want to defend it rationally, it is to some metaphysical or ethical theory that one has to resort for concepts and arguments.[4]

The other example has to do with the way Dewey justifies democracy. In *Democracy and Education* he argues that the good society is the one which permits the maximum of sharing of experience. Sharing is a key concept for Dewey, because if we did not try to share experience, we would not have to objectify it for communication, and this objectification is at the heart of knowing; knowledge reduces a culture to communicable form. A band of robbers, Dewey notes, is bad not only because of the harm it inflicts, but also because the act of robbing and the organization of robbery are in the nature of the case exclusive. Sharing is also the antidote to conflict and discontinuity, and if there could be absolutes for Dewey, continuity and harmony might well be candidates for that status. So here once more the argument is not that something is good because it is democratic, but rather democratic is an honorific term precisely because it is the means to a more fundamental good—sharing.[5]

The societal type of objective is needed in any full statement of objectives, but it cannot be the final goal of the school. If it is left out, then the list invites the conclusion that any form of government would do equally well in achieving the good life. One cannot rule out this possiblity, but the evidence of history is even more against it than that a form of government guarantees the good life.

Even more important is the fact that the form of society conditions the ways in which the good life is achieved, so that to understand its workings, rationale, and one's relation to it is necessarily high on the school's agenda. Since the duties of citizenship are specific to the form of a society, they have to be taught with specific content, and the objectives should draw attention to this.

However, the greater danger is that already alluded to, viz., that the school so formulates its objectives that the form of society operates as if it were the final goal. It is one thing for a study to be prescribed because it is needed to exercise the functions of citizenship; it is quite another for the State to use its own welfare as a criterion of truth. Or to put it differently, it is defensible for the State to require that all pupils study the history of their country, but it is indefensible for the State to decide what constitutes "true" or "good" history. We need not recount the instances in which a State has decided what shall be good genetics, good art, and good literature. The danger lies not so much in whether the State makes good judgments in these matters, for conceivably it might make very good ones, but rather that for it to do so misconstrues the nature of knowledge and the criteria for judging the scholarship that produces it.

For there is no necessary connection between the political power of an idea or a theory and its truth. Ideas may be powerful if and because they are true, but their power is not the reason they are true. The existence of a criterion that is independent of political power, therefore, is essential if knowledge and truth are essential to the good life. The autonomy of the school as a social institution depends on its being able to appeal to the expertise of the scholar against the predilections of this or that group. For if anything can claim to transcend the cultural peculiarities of social groups, it is the tradition of intellectual inquiry.

The current demands of protestors on college campuses for a voice in the governance of the university illustrate the point at issue with sad but piercing clarity. As citizens in a democracy, the protestors have a right to demand a voice in the conduct of an institution that is sanctioned by the society of which they are members. All the rules of the game demand that political policies be settled by the weight of numbers translated into votes. That the students do not know enough to exercise this power is not a convincing excuse for withholding it. Citizens are not given achievement tests before they are allowed to cast their ballots for governors and presidents; why become so finicky in the case of college students wanting a voice in determining the policies of a university, especially a state university?

The proper retort, it seems, is that it depends on the policies under consideration. The limit of participatory democracy is reached when the content of courses and the qualifications of instructors are at issue. Being a student virtually implies lack of expertise in these domains. For these matters are not matters of opinion or desire or expediency in the sense that housing regulations, disciplinary rules, and the control of student organizations are. But if the ultimate criterion is voting power, there is no valid limit to its use, if the participants wish to have no limit. Only when theoretical room is left to question democracy or totalitarianism can there be a possible appeal from them. The autonomy of the school, therefore, is a prime concern when we evaluate educational objectives, and those who are content to derive them from some form of social organization should be quite clear about the price they are paying for it.

In this connection, it is interesting to note that the notions of natural law and natural rights—both metaphysical notions—are escape hatches from the tyranny of the State and the sovereign. In our own case, the Bill of Rights was promptly added to the Constitution for the purpose of enabling men to appeal beyond the law-making powers of the majority and the executive powers of officialdom. The Declaration of Independence speaks of unalienable rights, avowedly limiting the right of the sovereign power to alienate them. Natural law serves the same purpose.

It may not be amiss, therefore, to suggest to compilers of lists of educational objectives that before they commit their school systems to the ideals of the Declaration of Independence or the Bill of Rights they read carefully the textbooks to be used in the social studies. If they find—as they are likely to—that the authors of the texts deny the validity of natural law and natural rights, the objectives had better carry extensive footnotes to explain the sense in which the ideals are to be understood and taught.

Social Roles as Objectives

It is natural to follow the form of society as an objective with the question: What role is the student expected to play in each of the institutions that make up the society? When linked with the broader objective above it, the requirements of institutional roles become means for attaining that higher objective which, in turn, is supposed to be conducive to the realization of the good life.

In the literature, one not infrequently finds the total list of objectives stated in terms of what it would take for the citizen to play roles in the family, church, government, the economy, etc. In a complex culture some roles will be common to all members, e.g., being a member of a family, being a citizen, being a consumer, but some are specialized, e.g., that of a bank manager. By analyzing classes of tasks connected with these roles one finds the skills, knowledge, and attitudes they seem to require, and the school makes these its more immediate objectives and constructs the curriculum accordingly.

Sociologists of education, and perhaps social psychologists, typically undertake this type of analysis. Strictly speaking, at this level, the statement of objectives should be free from normative considerations. Presumably, the social scientists can specify objectively and dispassionately diverse roles and statuses and the obstacles thereto and facilitations thereof. Much more probable is the conjecture that these social scientists and their educational counterparts operate from an implicit vision of the ideal society and ideal life. The characteristics of the good life are taken as understood, just as the total form of the society is taken for granted. Without repeating the arguments in the previous section, it should be clear that taken as means to the higher objectives this approach makes sense; taken as the complete analysis of objectives it does not. Again it must be noted that institutional roles depend on the form of the good life for their validation, and not the other way around. Furthermore, the specialized roles within a society may change—the case of family roles and vocational roles are obvious examples of the school mistakenly assuming that they would remain constant. The rate of social change has produced an ever greater number of individual differentiations in life needs, but at the same time has made it more and more difficult to anticipate these needs by differentiated instruction. Paradoxically, the greater the variety of social roles and tasks, the greater may be the premium on general education, the sort that really is generalizable.

Life Styles as Objectives

Sometimes it is possible to combine the first three types of objectives in what might be called a life style. Given the form of society, an ideal of the good life value patterns, and the institutional roles of a given period, there emerges an image of something like the English country squire, the courtier of the Renaissance, the industrial tycoon, or the religious saint, or the rugged, individualistic, honest citizen of frontier days in this country.

In *The Republic* Plato described the degeneration of the State in terms of the aristocratic man (or his sons), characterized by a love of wisdom, turning into the timocratic man who is dominated by a love of honor, into the oligarchic man, the man whose main motive is wealth, to the democratic man who is in love with his desires, to the tyrannical man whose obsession with power and lust destroys him.[6] "Thus, when nature or habit or both have combined the traits of drunkenness, lust, and lunacy, then you have the perfect specimen of the despotic man."[7]

Aristotle does some similar character typing in the *Nichomachean Ethics* as examples of various combinations of excess and deficiency in the emotional life.[8] Thus the liberal man exemplifies the mean between stinginess and vulgarity in the matter of expenditures, and the brave man exhibits the mean between cowardice and rashness. Plutarch's *Lives* for centuries was a source of life styles as a basis for character education in the schools. When so described, life styles are objectives at a high level of abstraction, but when they are personified they become much more concrete. Leonardo da Vinci, for example, is more concrete as a model than the "Renaissance man"; St. Francis more than a "religious saint."

Educationally, the role of such models is not to be underestimated. Such personified images are among our most potent pedagogical resources if they seduce considerable proportions of the younger generation into imitating them. Horatio Alger heroes and Frank Merriwell were seductive models for an earlier generation; without such models, character education limps. To be sure, writers on education do not list "to be like Jackie (Kennedy) Onassis" or "to be like the Beatles" as educational objectives, but who doubts that in children as well as in their parents educational objectives take this form?

The objectives we have been discussing might be called life outcomes rather than school outcomes. The distinction is related to that between education taken in its broad sense and in its narrower sense of schooling or formal instruction. These differences are important not only because the latter is a relatively small part of the former, but also because they are qualitatively different. That is to say, the informal portion of education, in the broad sense of the word, is virtually the same as learning. It goes on with or without the awareness of the learner, and often there is no teacher other than the maze of interactions we call life. Formal education, on the other hand, is structured in terms of means and ends, and although some learning occurs outside of the teacher's plans or in spite of them, it is what one *means* to do that counts as the criteria of formal schooling.

In the broad sense, education goes on almost from cradle to the grave. The skein of factors that enter into it is a tangle that defies complete analysis. This type of learning is not, to any appreciable extent, within our control. Final estimates of its extent and worth are impossible so long as the subject is still alive—and learning. For these reasons a life style, a form of society, a value pattern are not school outcomes, nor can we fully identify and isolate the part that schooling will play in their development. Efforts to establish a tight correlation between school inputs and this sort of result are misguided precisely because the end result is the effect of so many causes over which we have no control, many of which we cannot even clearly identify, and of some of which we are totally unaware.

The slogan "Down with nonbehavioral objectives" has a twofold effect: first, of creating the illusion that if these life outcomes could be formulated in behavioral terms, we could fashion schooling so as to produce them more efficiently, e.g., if we could "behavioralize" democracy, our schools would produce it without straying from the path leading to the goal, as if our failure to render democracy triumphant is to be blamed on our inability to "point" to it.

In the second place, the slogan, taken literally and seriously, makes the school wary of all life outcomes, precisely because they resist translation into behavioral language, the language of observables. We may be able to avoid both of these consequences if we distinguish the role each type of objective plays in educational thinking.

Life outcomes such as have been described thus far in this paper are schema for the interpretation of life as a whole. They are patterns of action rather than aggregates of behaviors. Granted that for purposes of instruction these patterns need to be broken down into observable behaviors by the teacher, nevertheless the criterion for the success of the analysis is whether or not the total pattern has a certain quality or character. The satisfactory personality or the good looking face has a quality (a *Gestaltqualität*) that is a function of the way elements are put together and not merely the sum of these elements—something that Gestalt psychology insists upon and which ordinary experience supports. Life outcomes stress the relational features, and it is to these that philosophy, especially when done in a certain way, is specially relevant.

To sum up the discussion thus far, life outcomes are to be achieved and used during adult life and presumably to be retained throughout life. This means that they cannot, as they stand, be adopted as immediate objectives for schooling. For one thing, the school has no way of isolating its part in the result; for another, it has no way of checking out whether the result ever accrues. Nor is it clear as to what we shall regard as sufficient evidence for the presence or absence of the result. Metaphysical characteristics, social goals, generic roles, personality types and life style are ways of justifying *school* objectives and can be the matrix of them, but they are not to be mistaken for them. The aim of education as a whole, for example, can properly be said to be rational freedom or self-realization, but it is not the aim of any school. On the other hand, if a school is challenged to defend its objectives, it may have to end up with a commitment to self-realization or some equally general quality as its ultimate criterion of goodness.

SCHOOL OUTCOMES

School outcomes more properly refer to the terminal products of instruction. They are proximate rather than distant and usually do specify the knowledge, skill, or attitude that is supposed to accrue as a result of instruction. Presumably the school has considerable control over the inputs and the relations between them and the expected outputs. For example, if it is said that the aim of the arithmetic course is to enable the student to do decimals or multiply fractions, then presumably the relation between the instruction and the outcome has been established with a high degree of probability.

School outcomes can be arranged in a general-particular continuum in a number of ways. Thus a continuum could be constructed so that the particular end could be represented by content while the general end could be represented by operations, e.g., critical thinking, imagining, etc. Or contents could be sorted into those that have high or low degrees of generalizability, e.g., math, high; names of presidents, low. Or the goals could be stated in terms of the way in which learnings are to be used, e.g., by using them replicatively, i.e., as learned; associatively, as relatively undetermined responses to a class of stimuli; interpretively, as means of organizing stimuli by conceptual or other schemata; applicatively, to solve problems that have not been practiced during instruction.

There is a sense in which school objectives always claim implicitly that the outcomes will function beyond the period of instruction. Critical thinking, use of a subject matter for subsequent thinking or the solving of problems, and even attitudes toward learning or life tasks are supposed to manifest themselves after schooling. Hence the assumption is that there is a relation between doing the school task and performing the life task, such that if the school does something in its instruction, the life tasks will show its effects.

Two quite different problems are involved here, but I shall only mention them. One is establishing the causal connection, and this is, I suppose, the task of educational psychology, teaching methodology, and curriculum construction. The other is analysis of the logical and epistemic relations between a given piece of instruction and the life tasks to which it purports to be relevant. This is essentially a problem for the philosophy of education. For example, what constitutes a proper explanation, a definition, or inference is a philosophical question. It can be raised in the various subject matters of instruction and the uses of those subject matters in thinking about any kind of problem. Lacking full and facile awareness of the logical and the psychological nature of learning and teaching, the teacher has no way of distinguishing among responses symptomatic of rote learning, pseudo-understanding and of genuine ability to use learning in the applicative and interpretive modes.[9]

It is only after such philosophical and methodological questions are discussed, if not settled, that the objectives can be brought down to the more specific levels that we call course objectives, unit objectives, lesson objectives, and even objectives of episodes within the lesson. That we are far from agreement on the way school learnings are used in life tasks partly explains, to my way of thinking, why our taxonomies of educational objectives are so disparate and why lesson objectives and course objectives lack a credible relationship with the life outcomes to which they purport to be the means.

PHILOSOPHY AND EDUCATIONAL OBJECTIVES

As substantive, philosophy contributes to educational objectives certain ideas about reality, truth, and value as well as arguments for their justification; as critical, philosophy examines the validity of these arguments.

Philosophy has always been both substantive and critical, but in this country and Great Britain during the last half century professional philosophy has been primarily concerned with the critical side of the enterprise. This has taken two major forms: logical positivism and language analysis.

Logical positivism emanated from the Vienna Circle, a group of philosophers who gathered around Moritz Schlick in the Twenties. These men were interested in science and mathematics, and they hoped to develop by logical analysis a type of philosophizing that would itself be scientifically respectable. Influenced by Ludwig Wittgenstein's *Tractatus Logico-Philosophicus*[10] the Circle dedicated itself to (a) showing that all human knowledge is built up out of the data of experience, especially sense experience, (b) that propositions that could not be reduced to statements about observable items in experience were both literally and figuratively nonsense, i.e., meaningless, and (c) philosophy that talked about nonobservables was to be dismissed as disguised expressions of wishes rather than as description of anything.[11]

Ordinary language analysis grew out of the realization that if knowledge was to be restricted to scientific use of language, then most of life and discourse was not scientific. Accordingly, philosophers became curious about the meanings of nonscientific uses of language. Wittgenstein in his later work[12] argued that we used language in many ways. In addition to using it for describing states of affairs, we use it to command, interrogate, and to express feelings. There is no commonality to these uses; they are like games which have only a "family resemblance" to each other. No type of discourse is basic or privileged. Language "games," within which alone words have any meaning, are human activities carried on according to the rules of the particular game being played. The study of these language games, therefore, gives an insight to the culture which produced them.

It followed, therefore, that the task of philosophy was to explicate and clarify the meaning of propositions, exhibit the rules of the game being played, and to get rid of those notions which pretended to describe, but really were doing nothing of the sort. In other words, the substantive type of philosophy could be regarded as a form of language sickness which proper language analysis would diagnose and perhaps even cure. However, according to one writer, Wittgenstein's account of "previous philosophy as pathological does not seem to have been confirmed by much therapeutic success. The problems he aimed to dissolve have obstinately refused to stay dead."[13] This development of philosophy has had its counterpart in educational philosophy. Much of the current writing is in this vein of language analysis.[14]

Substantive views about the nature of reality, of truth, of goodness, and of beauty traditionally have been the concern of metaphysics, ethics, epistemology, and aesthetics. A fully developed philosophical system would have views in each of these departments, and the philosopher would take pains to make his epistemology, metaphysics, ethics, and aesthetics consistent with each other. We think of Plato, Aristotle, Descartes, St. Thomas Aquinas, Kant, Hegel, as examples of the systematic philosopher. Various names have been given to these systems: Platonic Realism, Moderate Realism, Idealism, Stoicism, Pragmatism, and a half hundred others. These names classify views by identifying them with a leading idea, or an approach, or a style of philosophizing, and like other forms of labeling are justified only by the time and thought they save.

These systematic theories—mixtures of observation, reflection, and speculation—were about the nature of man, his relation to nature, to other men, and to God. Ethics developed principles by which one defined, clarified, and justified what was worthwhile pursuing in life, what was to be judged right and wrong, and the conditions under which men could be held blameworthy and praiseworthy for what they did. For example, Plato could conceive of no better life than that which would result from the complete governance of life and society by Ideas, archetypes of absolute goodness, truth, and beauty. His guardians— the philosopher-statesmen—were to be men in whom a glimpse of these Ideas provided them and the State with sure touchstones for legislation and education.

One could list the systems of philosophy that have flourished in the world, but it is not the purpose of this paper to do so. The relevant point is that these ideas about life have been woven into the fabric of the human mind and consequently become operative when men set about formulating the objectives of education.

Philosophical ideas find their way into educational thinking in several ways. One likely route runs somewhat as follows: the convictions of the common man are subjected to reflective scrutiny by philosophers. The refined versions of these convictions, plus more or less of the reasoning behind them, find their way into the schooling of the educated classes; these produce and read materials that embody the ideas. As a result, the language and concepts of an age reflect these ideas. It has been argued, for example, that our ordinary way of saying that "The grass is green" assumes an Aristotelian metaphysics of a substance "grass" being able to take on the attributes "greenness." Or it may be, as others have charged, that Aristotle's metaphysics merely formalizes the grammatical structure of the Greek language. On either hypothesis, we can understand why analytic philosophers have felt that it was their duty to rid the language of these metaphysical ingredients.

I have already mentioned the deeply ingrained value syndrome that was made explicit in the metaphysics of Plato and Aristotle, viz., that the ladder of perfection paralleled the ladder of abstraction: the more theoretical the activity of man, the better the man. This value scale is still widely accepted, although it has repeatedly been challenged by those who believed that religious faith, strong will, and social action should rank higher than the contemplative life for which Plato and Aristotle reserved the highest rank. Today the dependence of our culture on science and science-based technology has made idea-power the basic and ultimate form of power. The intellectual has come into his own.

Another example is furnished by the influence on American thought and education by the philosophy of John Locke. Natural rights, constitutional law, separation of church and state, religious toleration, empiricism are among the notions that not only impressed the Founding Fathers but their descendants ever since. To be sure, today Locke is thought of as the arch defender of the middle class, but this tribe is far from extinct, and despite many reasons for believing that his liberalism with its emphasis on private property may no longer fit the requirements of a bureaucratic industrial state, his ideas are still influential, not only in political, but in educational circles.

Said Locke,

. . . I imagine you would think him a very foolish Fellow, that would not value a virtuous or a wise Man infinitely before a great Scholar. Not but that I think Learning a great Help to both in well-dispos-'d minds; but yet it must be confess'd also, that in others not so dispos'd, it helps them only to be the more foolish, or worse Men. I say this, that when you consider of the Breeding of your Son, and are looking out for a School-Master or a Tutor, you would not have (as is usual) Latin and Logick only in your Thoughts. Learning must be had, but in the second Place subservient only to greater Qualities. Seek out somebody that may know how discreetly to frame his Manners: Place him in Hands where you may, as much as possible, secure his Innocence, cherish and nurse up the good, and gently correct and weed out any bad Inclinations, and settle him in good Habits. This is the main Point, and this being provided for, Learning may be hand into the Bargain, and that, as I think, at a very easy rate, by Methods that may be thought on.[15]

The catalogue of the "good" small liberal arts college until recently reflected the objectives of education that were dear to Locke: virtue, wisdom, breeding, and learning. Scholarship, sheer intellectual activity, was put well below good breeding, and this, in turn, below virtue, which was closely tied to religious training, and wisdom, which consisted largely in managing one's affair with prudence. The advent of the high-powered intellectual onto the staff of this type of college has changed this emphasis, because Ph.D.'s tend to be of the same stripe as far as their evaluation of academic excellence is concerned. But the trustees and alumni of these colleges—many of them private—are reluctant to surrender the college to intellectuals. Virtue, wisdom, and breeding in their book, as in Locke's, are to be at the top; learning could be pursued in the graduate school.

Clearly not all philosophical systems have had equal impact on the formulation of educational objectives. Those philosophers who had things to say about education, naturally, were more likely to be read by schoolmasters and those who wrote for schoolmasters.

However, in the class of men who were both interested in formal philosophy and in problems of education, one would be inclined to mention Rousseau, Froebel, Herbart, and John Dewey as having the most direct and powerful impact on conceptions of education in modern times. By trying to say what education *really* is, i.e., how it should properly be conceived, they were, of course, proposing the life outcomes for which education ought to be responsible.

Bringing such materials to the prospective worker in education, to reiterate a point mentioned earlier, is the function of the philosophical foundations of education, but in addition it is also the function of such workers to formulate educational theories of their own that incorporate ideas from philosophy, and to carry on a critical examination of theories that do so. This criticism is undertaken in an attempt to test the adequacy of a theory in terms of its internal consistency and its systematic completeness. Those who make philosophy of education an academic specialty, therefore, not only teach courses to prospective workers in education—and of anyone else who might be interested—but also bring their scholarship to bear on the materials to be taught.

One might question the need for a specialized personnel in the philosophy of education. After all, schoolmen can read, and they, together with the bulk of classroom teachers, have a bachelor's degree or something approaching it. Surely in these encounters with general education they could have been expected to learn how to read the philosophers on their own, and to extract from them the ideas needed for discourse about education.

Unfortunately, in the first place, having attended a liberal arts college does not guarantee that the student has had formal work in philosophy, or more than the minimum required for graduation. In the second and more important place, general philosophers have only side glances for education, whereas what is called for is the reading of philosophy for its relevance to educational problems. Finally, as a result of the sins of omission and commission, the average school worker has acquired a collection of notions about education and life that exhibit little consistency, system, or completeness.

Currently, the substantive and the analytical contributions of philosophy to the formulation of educational objectives are being made by different sets of people, although there may be a few notable exceptions. This is true both in general and educational philosophy. One group talks about the problems of education or educational theory in terms of Idealism, Realism, Pragmatism, Existentialism, etc. This group is also likely to discourse in terms of ideas taken from metaphysics, epistemology, ethics, and social philosophy. The other group elucidates ideas, sorts them into logical types, and assays the meanings that can properly be attributed to them. Not the least part of their job is to convince their readers that much of what the substantive philosophers have had to say about education is either false or meaningless, and that many of the alleged "problems" in education are the results of the misuse of language.

As might be expected, the two groups do not regard each others' work with unrestricted enthusiasm. The substantive philosophers regard the analysts as playing language games that do not really generate any ideas for schooling while tearing down the ideas of others; the analysts regard the substantive philosohers as mixing up metaphysics with science, wishes with fact, and emotive use of language with the descriptive.

Without in any way attempting to settle this controversy or even to make peace between the parties, a few observations may help to clarify the issues:

1. Much is made by the analytical group of the argument that from traditional philosophical doctrines nothing can be deduced as to what ought to be done in the way of school policy or practice. For one thing a philosophical principle, e.g., education is self-realization, is so general that it tells us nothing about the proximate steps that have to be taken to bring self-realization about, nor does it provide a criterion for choosing one method over another. More important, however, is the principle that the way things are does not prove that they ought to be that way; usually they can stand improvement.

Both of these arguments are cogent, but their importance rests on a misunderstanding of the role that philosophical doctrines play in educational thought and practice. One can no more deduce a method of teaching children to read from the principle of self-realization than one can invent a new form of transportation by reciting Newton's laws of motion. One would have to consult the behavioral sciences for rules and principles that would give more specific guidance about what educational procedures would or would not produce self-realization. This does not mean that "self-realization" is useless or meaningless as an educational objective, but is is useful for interpretation rather than for application.

2. This brings us to the second objection, viz., that from the principle, for example, that all beings try to actualize their potentialities, one cannot conclude that they ought to. Perhaps they should not actualize their potentialities for cruelty and stupidity. But again, metaphysical "descriptions" are also descriptions of a value hierarchy; they purport to be value-facts and facts about value. One may reject these "descriptions" as unverifiable, but metaphysical statements do not claim empirical verifiability as the evidence for their truth. So it is difficult to see how peace can be achieved on this issue on theoretical grounds. But practically, education must get its value orientation somewhere, and if it does not get them from philosophical doctrines, it has to take them from the *mores* of the group or the customs of the culture. The difficulties of defending

such a procedure have already been touched upon; it precludes the possibility of subjecting the basic values of a school system to rational scrutiny. Once put to such a scrutiny, appeal would have to be made to a higher principle of value determination, and one would be back into metaphysical questions once more.

The educational enterprise can utilize both types of philosophizing, and each group would contribute more if it did "its own thing," so to speak, without spending so much time in denigrating what the other was doing. Examples of tasks that the analytical philosophers can help with are sharpening distinctions between teaching and learning, the analysis of subject matters in terms of differential cognitive operations, the adequacy of various psychological theories for educational theory.[16]

SUMMARY

This paper has tried to identify, exemplify, and justify the role of philosophy in the formulation and discussion of educational objectives. It was thought advisable to do this by first exhibiting the various levels of generality at which objectives could be conceptualized, the relations between them and the way in which philosophical materials and approaches made their contribution to the objectives at the various levels. It was concluded that (1) substantive philosophy makes its contribution to objectives at their most general level by providing value hierarchies or value schemata that are either made explicit or are implicit in systematic positions on metaphysics, epistemology, and ethics. (2) Analytical philosophy makes its major contribution by clarifying ideas and evaluating their logical and linguistic adequacy in educational discourse. Generally this applies more directly to the lower-level objectives, but all levels of educational discourse are subject to critical analysis. (3) Although the two types of philosophizing tend to be done by different personnel within educational philosophy, both are needed. (4) Because philosophy's contribution to educational objectives is complex, and because it comes into educational literature in so many ways, there is a need for people trained in philosophy of education to do scholarly work in making sure that the ideas and procedures taken from philosophy are used with precision and with some concern for internal consistency and systematic adequacy. (5) Finally, such scholarly work should have a salutary effect in selecting and organizing the materials taught to prospective workers in education.

NOTES

1. This article was originally prepared at the request of the U.S. Office of Education.
2. B. Paul Komisar and James E. McClellan, "The Logic of Slogans," in B. O. Smith and R. H. Ennis (eds.) *Language and Concepts in Education* (Chicago: Rand McNally, 1961).
3. *The Republic* 509 D−511 E.

4. Georg W. F. Hegel, *Philosophy of Right,* translated by T. M. Knox (Oxford: Clarendon Press, 1942).

5. John Dewey, *Democracy and Education* (New York: The Macmillan Co., 1961), chap. VII.

6. 543 E—588 A.

7. IX, 572

8. III, 6—V, 11.

9. In this connection, see Robert H. Ennis, *Logic in Teaching* (Englewood Cliffs, N.J.: Prentice-Hall, Inc., 1969).

10. London, 1921. Translated, London, 1922.

11. *The Vienna Circle: Its Scientific World-Conception,* 1929.

12. *Philosophical Investigations* (London: Oxford, 1953).

13. M. Quinton, "Contemporary British Philosophy," in D. J. O'Connor (ed.) *A Critical History of Western Philosophy* (Glencoe, Ill.: The Free Press, 1964), p. 543.

14. For a recent bibliography on this approach, see H. S. Broudy, M. J. Parsons, I. A. Snook, and R. D. Szoke, *Philosophy of Education: An Organization of Topics and Selected Sources* (Urbana: University of Illinois Press, 1967).

15. *Some Thoughts Concerning Education,* paragraph 147.

16. Cf. Smith and Ennis (eds.), *Language and Concepts in Education, passim.*

9. THE IMPLICATIONS OF INSTRUCTIONAL OBJECTIVES FOR LEARNING

Robert M. Gagné

The importance of defining instructional objectives as an initial step in the planning of instruction was emphasized a number of years ago by Tyler (1949). There can be little doubt that the activity that was stimulated by this initial formulation has been tremendously productive in the design of achievement tests in many colleges, the conduct of evaluation programs, as well as the broader enterprises of course and curriculum planning. A number of these efforts and their results have been reported in volumes edited by Dressel (1954). One can judge from reading these reports that many college and university teachers have derived great benefits from the discipline of thought about teaching and testing that has been generated by their own attempts to define the objectives of instruction.

It should also be mentioned, perhaps, that one can now identify at least two additional areas of instruction in which the importance of specifying objectives has been explicitly recognized. While it is not clear that these ideas have arisen entirely independently, it is at least noteworthy that such a need has been arrived at via a somewhat different route in each case. The first of these areas is technical training in the military services, in connection with which the terms *task description* and *task analysis* have been employed. Basically, these terms

SOURCE. In C. M. Lindvall (ed.), *Defining Educational Objectives* (Pittsburgh, Penn.: University of Pittsburgh Press, 1964), pp. 37–46. Reprinted by permission of the University of Pittsburgh Press. Copyright © 1964 by the University of Pittsburgh Press.

reflected a recognition of the importance of specifying what the *outcomes* of training needed to be before the training was planned. The necessity for such specification was particularly evident in the case of military training because there is such an immediate relation between the intentions of training itself and the performance of the trained man on the job. Miller (1953) was a pioneering thinker in this area, but others also contributed important ideas. There is little formal difference, however, between what is called task description and the definition of instructional objectives.

The second additional source of writing about instructional objectives, a more recent one, comes from the work on programmed instruction. Scarcely any writer or systematist in this field has failed to state that the specifying of instructional objectives is an important first step in planning the instructional program as well as the assessment which will follow it. An important chapter in the volume by Taber, Glaser and Schaefer (1962) draws out some of the parallels between the approaches suggested by task analysis in military training and the more recently formulated requirements of programmed instruction. A delightful book by Mager (1961) gives a very clear account of what is meant by preparing objectives for programmed instruction, and a description of the implications of this effort for the success of such instruction. Another writer in this field who has dealt explicitly with this problem is Gilbert (1962); his mathetics approach is characterized by painstaking attention to the defining of objectives.

Besides these research areas just mentioned, there has been a constantly growing emphasis in educational circles generally upon the essentiality of specifying instructional objectives for planning purposes. Even the modern curriculum builders in science and mathematics have not been able to ignore entirely the voices of those who forcefully insist on the definition of objectives, often in opposition to those scientists who vigorously uphold the point of view that one cannot think about human behavior objectively, at least not in an educational setting.

These recent trends have tended to place increasing emphasis upon the use of specified objectives in drawing inferences about the *tactics of instruction*. This kind of use was recognized by Tyler, and discussed rather briefly in his earlier work. He points out that the task of planning a course, beginning with the definition of objectives, proceeds by inferring from these descriptions the kinds of learning experiences which can be expected best to produce the required outcomes. But this trend of thought has not been developed by those who have followed in this tradition. Bloom's book (1956) on a taxonomy of objectives, for example, describes six categories of objectives, which are considered to constitute a hierarchy, in the sense that the later classes of objectives build upon the earlier ones. The categories are: knowledge, comprehension, application, analysis, synthesis and evaluation.

These categories provide a highly informative picture of the variety of kinds of human performances which may reasonably be expected in an educational setting. Yet it cannot be said that they serve clearly to distinguish a similar variety of learning experiences, or a set of tactics for optimal instruction. In particular, some of the members of these categories (as exemplified by test items) are distinct from each other only in terms of their specific content, rather than in terms of formal characteristics which affect their conditions of learning. "Knowledge of terminology," for example, is difficult to distinguish from "knowledge of classifications and categories"; likewise, "knowledge of generalizations" does not appear to be very different from "comprehension," and neither of these from "comprehending the interrelationships of ideas." Beginning with the test items themselves (rather than the names assigned to them) it seems quite possible that a set of inferences might be drawn which would in fact suggest differential training implications. But currently, this task awaits the doing.

Is it in fact possible to divide objectives into categories which differ in their implications for learning? To do this, one has to put together a selected set of learning conditions, on the one hand, and an abstracted set of characteristics of human tasks, on the other. This is the kind of effort which has been called *task analysis*. Its objective is to distinguish, not the tasks themselves (which are infinitely variable), but the *inferred behaviors* which presumably require different conditions of learning. Such behavior categories can be distinguished by means of several different kinds of criteria, which in an ultimate sense should be completely compatible with each other. What I should like to try to do here, however, is to use one particular set of criteria, which pertain to the question of "What is learned?"

In a general sense, what is learned is a *capability*. Furthermore, it is a capability of exhibiting certain performances which could not be exhibited before the learning was undertaken. Is it possible to describe such learned capabilities in terms which will permit distinctions to be made among them? This is the sort of attempt to be made in the following paragraphs.

THE CAPABILITIES ESTABLISHED BY LEARNING

When one sets out to identify capabilities, the suggestion made by the evidence, early in the game, is that these capabilities are arranged in a hierarchy. One depends upon another, in the sense that learning any one capability usually depends upon the previous learning of some other, simpler one. In fact, this may be one of the most important generalizations one can make about human learning.

As a consequence, if one begins at the bottom of such a hierarchy, one must begin with extremely simple forms of behavior. While such simple forms are clearly learned, it is nevertheless difficult to find actual human tasks in which they occur in a pure and uncombined form. In other words, one's credulity would be strained a bit were it to be claimed that these simple forms of behavior often occur, by themselves, as objectives of instruction. They do occur, but rather infrequently. Their importance, however, lies in the fact that they do underlie and support other capabilities which are higher in the hierarchy. For the learning of each of these higher capabilities requires that one or more subordinate capabilities must already have been acquired. The most important condition of learning, it is suggested here, is the specification of what must have been previously learned.

Accordingly, we shall start our description of the varieties of learned capabilities with quite simple forms of behavior, whose usefulness will become fully apparent only when we have proceeded to describe more complex forms.

1. *Response learning*. A very basic form of behavior is called response learning, or is sometimes given other names, such as "echoic behavior" (Skinner, 1957). The individual learns to respond to a stimulus which is essentially the same as that produced by the response itself. In a child, the mother's spoken word "doll" calls out the response "doll" on the part of the child. Naturally, this kind of learning is particularly evident in instructional objectives applicable to children. In adults, one finds it in the learning of new sounds in a foreign language, as well as in new types of motor acts. Modern language scholars seem to be in pretty good agreement that response learning is basic to other learning in foreign languages.

2. *Identification learning (multiple discrimination)*. In this form of behavior, the individual acquires the capability of making different responses to a number of different stimuli. Of course, he does this when he identifies colors, or late model cars, or numerals, or any of a great variety of specific stimuli. By "specific" I mean stimuli that within a given setting, retain a more or less constant physical appearance. Multiple discriminations are also widespread within the domain of things to be learned. Words like *faim* have to be discriminated from *femme* in order that they can really be pronounced differently. Within a given algebraic expression, a coefficient must be distinguished from an exponent, and both from a subscript (again, in appearance, and whether or not they can be "named"). Such learning *presupposes* response learning, so that if the stimuli concerned must be identified by having the learner construct them on paper, he must already have learned how to do this.

3. *Chains or sequences*. Long chains of responses can most readily be identified in motor acts of various sorts. But there are many kinds of *short* sequences which are very important to the individual's performance. One of the most prominent is a chain of two acts the first of which is an *observing response*. If one is concerned, for example, with getting someone to "put 17 in the numerator," this act has two main parts: (1) finding the location of the numerator

(an observing response), and (2) writing in that place the numeral 17. In establishing such behavior as part of a larger and more complex performance like simplifying fractions, one has to see to it that such a chain is learned. How this is done is a bit more complicated than it seems at first glance. Again, however, the most important consideration is that certain things be *previously learned*. The location of the numerator must previously have been discriminated from other locations, and 17 must have been discriminated from other numerals. Furthermore, the basic responses required must also have been acquired.

4. *Association.* For many years, psychologists appeared to be considering this the most basic form of learning, but such is no longer the case. It is now fairly generally agreed, and supported by a good deal of evidence (McGuire, 1961), that the learning of associations involves more than an S-R connection. Instead, an association is perhaps best considered as a three-step chain, containing in order (1) an observing response which distinguishes the stimulus, (2) a *coding* response which usually is implicit, and (3) the response which is to be expected as the outcome of the association. Associations are of course widely prevalent in instruction, and sometimes can be considered important instructional objectives. Learning English equivalents for foreign words has usually been considered the classic example of association learning. There is a great deal of evidence to show that such learning has prerequisites of prior learning as one of its most important conditions. Response learning must have been completed (for optimal results), as the work of Underwood and Scholz (1960) emphasizes. Multiple discrimination learning must previously have been accomplished in order for the stimuli to be distinctive—*echt* must be observed differently from *acht*. Finally, a chain must previously have been acquired linking the code with the desired response, so that if the association *lady—die Dame* is to be acquired, something like "dame" can provide the link.

Up to this point, it may be said that I have not talked about the kinds of learned activities that are often very important objectives in instruction. This is quite true, although I have tried to show that sometimes even these simple kinds of behavior may be legitimate objectives. Mainly, though, these kinds of learned capabilities may be considered *subordinate objectives* of instruction. They are the kinds of activities which are only infrequently to be measured by achievement tests. There is no reason why one should expect to find them in Bloom's book, for example, Nevertheless, they are distinguishable kinds of learned capabilities, which appear to depend upon each other for establishment in the order given. But their most important characteristic, by all odds, lies in the fact that they support all the varieties of more complex learning. In attempting to specify the conditions of learning that attend more complex capabilities, one cannot neglect these simpler forms of behavior. This is because the more complex forms depend in a crucial fashion on the simpler forms, in this way: if one tries to establish more complex behavior without the requisite simpler forms having been learned, the learning attempt will be markedly ineffective.

But let us now consider these more complex forms which frequently occur in lists of instructional objectives.

CONCEPTS

A concept is acquired when a set of objectives or events *differing* in physical appearance is identified as a class. The class names for common objects like chairs, houses, hats, are the most familiar examples. Even clearer, however, are such categories as "round," "square," "tall," "middle" and others which are so clearly independent of physical appearance. Concept achievement is observed when the subject becomes capable of responding to different physical objects as if he were placing them in one or more classes, like "round," or "square and large." In other words, the subject is now performing a task which is not defined in terms of specific stimuli. The particular physical characteristics of these objects, pictures, or what not, do not have to remain fixed in physical appearance in order to define the task. They must, however, be capable of being classified by the experimenter into the abstract categories he wants the subject to work with.

In addition, the task of identifying concepts cannot be defined in terms of specific responses. In contrast to paired-associate learning, one does not demand a particular response in order to consider the behavior correct. We may require the subject to *point* to a round object, to *draw* a round object, to *say* the word round, or any of a variety of other things. All that we insist upon is that these responses reliably identify the class "round."

The most important conditions for learning a concept appear to be the pre-learning that must have taken place. If there has not been previous identification of the object, the learner will be unable to acquire the concept. Similarly, he will not be able to learn a concept if he does not have an available response. Suppose a learner is shown an object to which he doesn't have the label "round." Can he then learn the required classification? The prediction is clearly negative. Or suppose, on the other hand, one asks the learner to make a classification the response for which he has not previously learned, like "rhomboid." Can he acquire the concept? Again the prediction is clearly "no." What must be done, if one is interested in concept acquisition *per se*, is to insure that the learner has previously learned all the necessary labels, and has previously acquired all the necessary responses, that he is going to be asked to make. In other words, association learning, stimulus discrimination learning, and response learning are all pre-conditions of concept learning.

If one can assume these more basic forms as having been acquired, then the procedure of concept learning is fairly simple. It consists mainly in establishing associations in which the variety of specific stimuli that make up the class to be acquired are represented. One cannot do this by presenting all of them, of course; accordingly, this is usually done by presenting a suitable variety of objects and seeing to it that they are connected with the desired response. If the concept is *cell*, in biology, obviously one must use a sufficient variety of cells having different physical appearances in order to establish the required classification.

PRINCIPLES

The next more complex form of learning pertains to the acquisition of principles. One can consider these, in their basic form, as a chain of concepts of the form "If A, then B." The learning of principles does not appear to have been studied in an analytic fashion. Yet it is not difficult to imagine an experimental situation in which their acquisition could be observed and measured. Suppose the individual has learned to classify an array of stimuli as "round" or "square," and another array as "the odd one" or "not the odd one." What would be studied in this situation are the conditions leading to the use of the principle "When round, choose the odd one." The stimulus situation would consist of presentations of the two arrays of stimuli (in suitable variety of physical dimensions) simultaneously. Undoubtedly, one could simply present such a situation in repeated trials, and observe the errors made or the number of trials required to attain the rule. But this is not the only kind of learning situation one thinks of, particularly if the question "how could such a principle be most rapidly achieved" is of interest. In a sense, *principle learning* appears to be a simple form of what has been called problem solving.

Let me be as clear as I can about what the task is. It is one in which the individual uses a concept describing one class of objects (or events) to identify another concept describing another class of objects and events. Now whether he can *say* what he is doing is not a necessary criterion of whether he has acquired a principle. But he must have the capability of performing correctly a task of the sort "If A, then B," where A and B are concepts defined by the experimenter.

Of course this is a very important kind of learning. Think how much of what we call knowledge is really this kind of thing! "When a liquid is heated, it changes to a gas"; "if force is increased, acceleration increases"; "if temperature is raised, pressure goes up"; "if the rods are placed in darkness, their sensitivity increases"; and so on. Of course I am not suggesting that all principles are this simple. But I *am* suggesting that most knowledge is principles.

Again it is evident that the important set of conditions necessary for principle learning is previous learning, this time of the concepts which make up the principle. One either assumes that the learner already knows the concepts "liquid," "heating" and "gas," in acquiring the principle, or else they must first be learned. This does not mean, of course, that the attempt cannot be made to undertake everything at once—to teach the concepts and the principle all at one time. But it does mean that the optimal conditions for learning cannot be clearly seen to operate in such a situation. A teacher may find that certain members of his class have not learned the principle "When a liquid is heated, it changes to a gas" because they have never learned to identify the concept "liquid"! But when one can truly assume that concept learning has previously been completed, the conditions for principle learning become clear. The proper chain of events is presented by means of particular objects representing the concepts making up the chain; for example, a container of water may be heated with a flame and the steam collected in another container.

PROBLEM SOLVING

Problem solving is a kind of learning by means of which principles are put together in chains to form what may be called "higher-order principles." Again, this is a form of learning of widespread occurrence in education. Typically, the "higher-order principles" are induced from sets of events presented to the learner in instruction. If carried out properly, these become the generalizations which enable the student to think about an ever-broadening set of new problems.

It may be worthwhile to consider for a moment what the nature of the problem-solving task is, as exhibited by experimental investigations. What can the individual do after he has solved the problem? Suppose it is Maier's (1933) Candle Problem. We say of the learner that he has achieved problem solution, but what does this mean? It would appear that what Maier and others think it means (without having tested it directly) is this: Having solved the specific problem, the subject is able to solve a whole range of problems similar to it, regardless of variations in the room, the distance involved, the type of candle, the size of tapes, clamps and sticks. The phrase "similar to it" means something in particular, that is, that the subject can achieve correct solutions to an *entire class* of problems which can readily be identified as a class by the experimenter, if not by the subject himself. In this instance, the class of tasks may be roughly described as "using segments of rigid and flexible tubing to construct a long tube capable of conducting air, which can then be made rigid by clamping it to rigid structures like sticks of wood." Notice that it is not necessarily intended that the subject can necessarily *say* a sentence like this when he has solved the problem. But he should be able to *do* it, and it would be helpful if the experimenter were able to say it.

Problem solving begins with the assumption (or the establishment) of pre-available principles. It ends with the demonstration that the individual has acquired a new "higher-order rule," the capability of solving a new kind of problem. A beginning student of algebra is set the problem: "Multiply X^2 and X^3," which he has not seen before at all. First of all, it is clear that he must previously have acquired certain *concepts,* namely, the concepts of variable and exponent (in the sense that he must be able to recognize these stimulus objects as "variables with exponents"). Second, he must previously have acquired some *principles.* One is a rule for multiplication, approximately stated as "multiplying a number by *n* means adding the number *n* times." Another is a rule for exponents, roughly, "an exponent *r* means multiplying the number by itself *r* times." Can the student solve this problem? Perhaps he will need to be reminded that he knows these subordinate rules. Perhaps he will need some *guidance* or "direction" for his thinking. Whatever may be required to achieve it, what is wanted in solution is the discovery of a new and more inclusive rule to this effect: "Multiplying identical variables with exponents is done by multiplying the variable by itself the number of times represented by the *sum* of the two exponents." The attainment of such a higher-order rule can, under proper circumstances, be inferred by the correct answer X^5, as well as by correct answers to any and all other tasks belonging to the class "multiplying variables with exponents."

STRATEGIES

Are there forms of behavior which are more complex than principles, or than the "higher-order principles" acquired in problem solving? Some authors seem to imply another *form* of learned organization in the strategies with which an individual approaches a problem (Bruner, 1961). There can be little doubt as to the existence of such strategies in problem solving (Bruner, 1956). It may be that strategies are *mediating principles* which do not appear directly in the performance of the task set to the individual, but which may nevertheless affect the speed or excellence of that performance. Accordingly, one may have to use rather special methods to uncover these strategies, which implies that the job of achievement testing may be a difficult one.

But it is possible to conceive of strategies as being principles in their fundamental nature, and of being made up of chains of concepts. Such strategies as "choose the odd, except when the light is on the right," or "choose the alternate keys in order," are the kind that occur in experimental studies. In education, presumably, there are strategies pertaining to the appreciation of poetry, the understanding of history or the pursuit of scientific inquiry.

If strategies are really a kind of "higher-order" principle, then they obviously can be learned in the same way as other principles. If an individual is going to be able to learn the strategy "first match the internal figures in triangularity," he must already have mastered the concepts "internal figures" and "triangle." If he has previously acquired these concepts, the learning will be fairly easy. If he has not, then it is difficult to say what is happening, since the concepts will have to be learned at the same time as the principle (or strategy). It would appear, therefore, that even in the case of strategies one needs to assume the pre-learning of concepts and principles as a condition of learning of major importance.

BEHAVIOR CATEGORIES AND THE PRE-CONDITIONS OF LEARNING

What has been described in the previous sections are eight major categories of behavior which differ from each other, it is proposed, in terms of the conditions required to make learning occur with optimal effectiveness. Four of these forms of capability are simple ones which occur only rarely as distinct instructional objectives in the higher levels of the educative process. They appear more frequently as objectives in connection with the instruction of young children. Their importance, however, lies in the fact that they underlie the learning of other more complex forms of behavior which are typical of later years. Occasionally, too, it may be necessary to remind ourselves that these simpler forms are really there all the time. If we cannot assume that such learning has occurred, then provisions must be made to make it occur before the more complex varieties can be undertaken with efficacy. An example is the apparent need for response learning of unfamiliar foreign words as a first step in language learning.

These forms of behavior may be arranged in a hierarchy from simple to complex. The major reason for doing this is to indicate that the *learning conditions* for the more complex forms may be described most clearly if the *pre-conditions* are first identified. In fact, these pre-conditions constitute one of the most important things that can be said about the learning of these kinds of behaviors. The hierarchy of behaviors has this appearance:

The learning of

Problem Solving and *Strategy-Using*

require the pre-learning of:

Principles

which require the pre-learning of:

Concepts

which require the pre-learning of:

Associations

which require the pre-learning of:

Chains

which require the pre-learning of:

Identifications

which require the pre-learning of:

Responses

Of course, there are other conditions for learning than the ones implied by this hierarchy. But it is difficult to determine how important they are mainly because they seem so obvious. *Reinforcement,* for example, as it is defined by Skinner (1950) is a condition which one is inclined to assume is present, while admitting that learning cannot occur without it. A new act, we are told, can always be attached by learning to an old act, so long as the latter is the stronger. The implication appears to be, then, that the problem of finding proper conditions of learning reduces to one of finding the right sequences for events in the instructional situation. This is implied by the work of Gilbert (1962) in his discussion of the tactics of learning. *Contiguity* is surely an important condition, too, since these sequences of events must occur within certain limited time spans in order for learning to occur. But contiguity is also a fairly obvious condition to the teacher if the student is to learn the name of an unfamiliar object, the name and his response must somehow be made to occur together within a short time span.

The implications of these categories for achievement testing are clear up to a point, but knowledge is limited beyond that point. Certainly the four fundamental categories can be measured, since experimental psychologists have been measuring them for many years. To describe how the more complex forms can be assessed would go beyond the scope of this paper. It is apparent, though, that there are many available techniques in the field of achievement testing for this purpose. The major implication is that these are the categories of objectives to be distinguished, if one approaches the job from the standpoint of differential sets of conditions for optimal learning.

REFERENCES

Bloom, B. S. (ed.) *Taxonomy of Educational Objectives* (New York: Longmans, Green, 1956).

Bruner, J. S., Goodnow, J. J., and Austin, G. A. *A Study of Thinking* (New York: Wiley, 1956).

Bruner, J. S. "The Art of Discovery." *Harvard Educational Review* 31 (1961): 21–32.

Dressel, P. L. (ed.) *Evaluation in General Education* (Dubuque, Iowa: Wm. C. Brown Co., 1954).

Gilbert, E. T. "Mathetics: The Technology of Education." *J. Mathetics* 1 (1962): 7–73.

McGuire, W. J. "A Multiprocess Model for Paired-Associate Learning." *Journal of Experimental Psychology* 62 (1961): 335–347.

Mager, R. F. "A Method for Preparing Auto-Instructional Programs." *I.R.E. Trans. on Educ.*, 1961.

Maier, N. R. F. "An Aspect of Human Reasoning." *British Journal of Psychology* 24 (1933): 144–155.

Miller, R. B. "A Method for Man-Machine Task Analysis." *Wright Air Development Center Technical Report* 53–137, 1953.

Skinner, B. F. "Are Theories of Learning Necessary?" *Psychol. Review* 57 (1950): 193–216.

Skinner, B. F. *Verbal Behavior* (New York: Appleton-Century-Crofts, 1957).

Taber, J. I., Glaser, R., and Schaefer, H. H. *A Guide to the Preparation of Programmed Instructional Material* (Pittsburgh: Department of Psychology, University of Pittsburgh, 1962).

Tyler, R. W. "Achievement Testing and Curriculum Construction." In E. G. Williamson (ed.) *Trends in Student Personnel Work* (Minneapolis: University of Minnesota Press, 1949), pp. 391–407.

Underwood, B. J., and Scholz, R. W. *Meaningfulness and Verbal Learning* (Chicago: Lippincott, 1960).

10. MUST AN EDUCATOR HAVE AN AIM?

Richard Peters

Many in recent times have blamed philosophers for neglecting their traditional task in relation to education. For, in the old days, it is argued, philosophers explained what the good life and the good society were; and this provided aims for educationists. But nowadays, as Sir Richard Livingstone put it, we are lacking in a knowledge of the "science of good and evil." I think that most modern philosophers would claim that, in this respect, they had advisedly neglected their traditional task, for the very good reason that they have become clearer about what their task as philosophers is. The so-called "revolution in philosophy" of the twentieth century has been largely a matter of becoming clearer about what philosophy is and is not. And one of the conclusions that has emerged is that it is not a sort of super-science of good and evil.

However, this newly found modesty about providing blueprints for the good life does not altogether either excuse or explain the neglect by modern philosophers of philosophical problems connected with education. I do not think that this neglect springs from the conviction that there *are* no such philosophical problems. Rather it is because philosophers have been so concerned with their "revolution" that they have concentrated more on the central problems of

SOURCE. *Authority, Responsibility and Education* (London: George Allen & Unwin Ltd., 1959), pp. 83−95. Copyright © by George Allen & Unwin Ltd., 1959. Third edition © by George Allen & Unwin Ltd., 1973. Published in the U.S.A. by Paul S. Eriksson, Inc.

123

philosophy—those connected with knowledge and belief, appearance and reality, free will and determinism, mind and body, space and time. Peripheral problems connected with concepts like "education," "authority," and "character" have been crowded out, as Hobbes put it, "no otherwise than the sun deprives the rest of the stars of light, not by hindering their action, but by obscuring and hiding them with his excess of brightness." It is time that philosophers supplemented their sun-worship by a bit of star-gazing—but this, as I shall try to show, does not mean trying to return to the old task of constructing a horoscope of educational aims.

I suppose the conviction that an educator must have aims is generated by the concept of "education" itself; for it is a concept that has a standard or norm, as it were, built into it. To speak of "education," even in contexts quite remote from that of the classroom, is to commit oneself, by implication, to a judgment of value. One might say, for instance, that it was a "real education" for compilers of the Wolfenden Report to wander round Piccadilly at night-time. Some state of mind is here presupposed which is regarded as commendable, and some particular experiences are regarded as leading on to or contributing to it. There is thus a wide sense of "education" in which almost anything could be regarded as being part of one's education. Rousseau said that "education comes to us from nature, from men, and from things." And of course he was right; for the concept works in as wide a way as this. But there is a narrower and more usual sense of "education" in which *men* are very much to the fore. For we usually speak of education in contexts where we consciously put ourselves or others in such improving situations.

Given that "education" implies, first, some commendable state of mind and, secondly, some experience that is thought to lead up to or to contribute to it, and given also that people are usually deliberately put in the way of such experiences, it is only too easy to think of the whole business in terms of models like that of building a bridge or going on a journey. The commendable state of mind is thought of as an end to be aimed at, and the experiences which lead up to it are regarded as means to its attainment. For this model of adopting means to premeditated ends if one that haunts all our thinking about the promotion of what is valuable. In the educational sphere we therefore tend to look round for the equivalent of bridges to be built or ports to be steered to. Hence the complaints of lack of direction when obvious candidates do not appear to fill the bill.

It is my conviction that this model misleads us in the sphere of education. We have got the wrong picture of the way in which values must enter into education; and this is what occasions the disillusioned muttering about the absence of agreed aims. But to bring out how we are misled we must look at the contexts where the means-end model *is* appropriate. There is, first of all, that of plans and purposes where we do things in order to put ourselves in the way of other things. We get on a bus in order to get to work; we fill up a form in order to get some spectacles.

Our life is not just doing one thing after another; we impose plans and schedules on what we do by treating some as instrumental to others. Some of these we regard as more commendable than others, and what we call our scale of values bears witness to such choices. The second means-end context is that of making or producing things. We mix the flour in order to make a cake or weld steel in order to make a bridge. We speak of the end-product in a factory and of the means of production in an economic system.

In both these contexts we might well ask a person what he was aiming at, what his objective was. But in both cases the answer would usually be in terms of something pretty concrete. He might say something like ''getting a better job'' or ''marrying the girl'' in the first context; or something like ''producing a soundless aeroplane'' in the second. Similarly if a teacher was asked what he was aiming at, he might state a limited objective like ''getting at least six children through the eleven-plus.'' But he might, as it were, lift his eyes a bit from the scene of battle and commit himself to one of the more general aims of education—elusive things like ''the self-realization of the individual,'' ''character,'' ''wisdom,'' or ''citizenship.'' But here the trouble starts; for going to school is not a *means* to these in the way in which getting on a bus is a means to getting to work; and they are not made or produced out of the material of the mind in the way in which a penny is produced out of copper. These very general aims are neither goals nor are they end-products. Like ''happiness'' they are high-sounding ways of talking about doing some things rather than others and doing them in a certain manner.

It might be objected that education is an art like medicine and that in medicine there is a commonly accepted end-product—physical health. Why should there not be a similar one for education—mental health, for instance? The answer is fairly obvious. Doctors deal mainly with the body and if they agree about what constitutes physical health it is because it can be defined in terms of physical criteria like temperature level and metabolism rate. Also there is little objection to manipulating and tinkering with the body in order to bring about the required result.

In the case of education, however, there are no agreed criteria for defining mental health; for either it designates something purely negative like the absence of unconscious conflicts, or, in so far as it is a positive concept, it has highly disputable personal and social preferences written into it. Also education is not, like medicine or psychiatry, a remedial business. When we are concerned with the minds of men there are objections to bringing about positive results in certain sorts of ways. People make moral objections to pre-frontal leucotomy even as a remedial measure. How much more objectionable would it be to promote some more positive state of mind, like a love of peace, in all men by giving them drugs or operating on everyone at birth? Indeed, in my view, disputes between educationists, which take the form of disputes about aims, have largely been disputes about the desirability of a variety of principles involved in such procedures. Values are involved in education not so much as goals or end-products, but as principles implicit in different manners of proceeding or producing.

Of course there can be considerable disagreement about the value of what is to be passed on as well as about the manner of passing it on. At the moment, for instance, there is much disagreement as to whether education should be liberal, technical, or vocational. And this reflects different assessments about the value of what is to be passed on, which is a matter of governmental policies as well as of personal preferences. An educator has an important social function in a community and, however idiosyncratic his individual aims may be, he cannot be completely indifferent to the pressing needs of the community, especially if he is paid by the state. Different weight is attached by different educators to the needs of the community as distinct from those of the individual child. Indeed those who stress "mental health" as an educational aim may well be protesting against the effects of collective pressure on the individual. Instead of trying to interpret this aim positively we might regard it as a timely warning against pushing the individual into socially approved tasks at too great a cost to his stability. It is as if a teacher was insisting that, whilst he was fulfilling his essential social function of passing on information and skills and preparing children for different jobs, it should never be forgotten that children may become unhappy and neurotic, isolates from their group, or sexually unbalanced. And the educator should not disregard these other things that go to make up "the whole man." In the old days talk of "character-training" used to serve as a corrective to undue academic or vocational pressure; or religious ideals were appealed to. But nowadays such a corrective must seem to have scientific authority. So "mental health" enters the field of education—the old Aristotelian "harmony of the soul" in respectable trappings.

But those who stress the importance of a "liberal" education are not merely voicing a protest against an academic or vocational emphasis in education which neglects the individual needs of children. Neither are they claiming merely that there should be arts subjects in the curriculum as well as science and typewriting. Their protest relates to the manner as well as to the matter of education. For both science and arts subjects can be passed on by liberal or illiberal procedures. Literature and science can both be treated as "subjects" and, as it were, stamped in to a student. Or they can be treated as living disciples of critical thought and of the imagination, in which the student can be trained on an apprenticeship system. "Liberal" is a term used of certain types of principles and procedures such as respect for persons and facts, toleration, and deciding matters by discussion rather than by dictate. Its association with the *content* of courses is derivative from the belief that some subjects foster such principles more than others. But this is a naïve view—rather like the strange belief that technical colleges can be made more "liberal" if a certain amount of time is devoted to teaching "the humanities" to supplement science subjects. For it is surely the *manner* in which any course is presented rather than its matter which is crucial in developing a liberal attitude of mind.

To illustrate more clearly the distinction which I am drawing between "aims" and "principles of procedure," let me take a parallel from politics. A man who believes in equality, might, like Godwin, be lured by a positive picture of a society in which differences between people would be minimized. He might want to get rid of differences in wealth and rank, even to breed people in the attempt to iron out innate differences. He might even go so far as to advocate the abolition of institutions like the army or the Church in which some men were given opportunities of lording it over others. Another social reformer, however, might employ the principle of equality in a much more negative sense without any concrete picture to lure him on his journey. He might insist, merely, that whatever social changes were introduced, no one should be treated differently from anyone else unless a good reason could be produced to justify such unequal treatment. The Godwin type of man would rightly be regarded as pursuing equality as a very general aim; the more cautious Liberal would have no particular aim connected with equality. He would merely insist that whatever schemes were put forward must not be introduced in a way which would infringe his procedural principle.

I think that this is an illuminating parallel to the point I am trying to make about the aims of education. For, in my view, many disputes about the aims of education are disputes about principles of procedure rather than about "aims" in the sense of objectives to be arrived at by taking appropriate means. The so-called "aims" in part pick out the different valuations which are built into the different procedures like training, conditioning, the use of authority, teaching by example and rational explanation, all of which fall under the general concept of "education."

Consider, for instance, the classic dispute about the aims of education which is so often connected with an argument about the derivation of the word "education." There were those like Sir Percy Nunn who stressed the connection with *educere*—to lead out. For them the aim of education must therefore be the development or realization of individual potentialities. Others, like Sir John Adams, stressed the derivation from *educare*—to train, or mould according to some specification. They might be regarded as people who in fact believed in aims in a proper sense, in moulding boys into Christian gentlemen, for instance. The progressive who protests against this conception of education is not simply jibbing at the end-product of a Christian gentleman. He is also jibbing at the assimilation of education to an art where something is produced out of material. Rousseau, for instance, protested vociferously against treating children as little mannikins, as material to be poured into an adult mould. A child, he argued, should be treated with respect as a person. The progressive, therefore, like

Dewey or Kilpatrick, presents another picture of the educational process. The child's interest must be awakened and he must be put into situations where the task rather than the man exerts the discipline. He will thus acquire habits and skills that are useful to him, and, by co-operating with others in common tasks, will develop respect for others and for himself. In the eyes of the progressive the use of authority as a principle of procedure is not only an inefficient way to pass on skills and information; it is also an immoral way to treat a child. It is made even worse in both respects by techniques like the use of reward and punishment.

So at the one end of the family tree generated by the concept of "education" there are procedures involving the use of authority in which the voice and the cane are used to produce a desirable end-product. Education is here thought of after the model of means to ends in the arts. At the other end the model of purpose and planning is stressed; but it is the purpose and planning of the child, not of the adult. As Rousseau put it: "By attempting nothing in the beginning you would have produced an educational prodigy."

But, as any educationist must know, if he reflects on the matter, these are only a limited selection of the procedures that are in fact employed. There is, for instance, the influence exerted by one person on another in some sort of apprenticeship system, when the teacher guides rather than goads. We learn carpentry by doing it with someone who is a bit better at carpentry; we learn to think clearly by talking with someone who thinks a bit more clearly than we do. And this other person need not be a charismatic figure so beloved by the advocates of "impressionism" in the public schools or Boy Scout movement. It may be a person who is not only skilled but who has the additional ability of being able to explain and give an account of what he is up to. Progressives often object to talk and chalk and confuse the use of the voice with one way in which it is used—the authoritative way. But most good teachers use their voices to excite and to explain, not simply to instruct, command, or drill.

My guess is that most of the important things in education are passed on in this manner—by example and explanation. An attitude, a skill, is caught; sensitivity, a critical mind, respect for people and facts develop where an articulate and intelligent exponent is on the job. Yet the model of means to ends is not remotely applicable to the transaction that is taking place. Values, of course, are involved in the transaction; if they were not it would not be called "education." Yet they are not end-products or terminating points of the process. They reside both in the skills and cultural traditions that are passed on and in the procedure for passing them on. As Aristotle put the matter long ago:

> For the things we have to learn before we can do them, we learn by doing them, e.g. men become builders by building, and lyre-players by playing the lyre; so too we become just by doing just acts, temperate by doing temperate acts . . . but it is not the man who does these that is just and temperate, but the man who does them *as* just and temperate men do them.

And how can this happen unless we learn them in the company of experienced practitioners—who understand what they are doing and who can explain it to others?

There are all sorts of things that can be passed on that are valuable. Almost anything, as I started off by saying, can be regarded as being of educational value. And, to a large extent, those who favor one type of procedure rather than another choose examples that suit themselves and advocate the practice of things that can be passed on best in accordance with their favorite model. The man who advocates authority and drill is most at home with things like Latin and arithmetic where rules have simply to be learnt defining what is right or wrong and where, in the early stages at any rate, there is little scope for rational explanation or learning by experience. The progressive is most at home with things like art, drama, and environmental studies where projects can develop without too much artificiality. And the man who believes in rational instruction is usually inclined towards things like science, history, and geometry. An intelligent teacher, I suppose, will always first try to interest his pupils. As Whitehead put it, romance must precede precision. But, given the interest, he will adapt his procedure to what he is trying to teach.

In society generally there are those who are prone to view life not as a stream of experience to be enjoyed nor as a series of predicaments to be lived through but as a chain of obstacles to be overcome in the pursuit of goals that stretch out like a chain of oases in a desert, or as recalcitrant material to be moulded into some pleasing social or personal pattern. And, of course, many of the things which we do can be regarded as ways of implementing concrete and limited objectives. But this picture of the pursuit of aims is often exalted into grandiose talk about the purpose of life or the purpose of political activity. Self-realization, the greatest happiness of the greatest number, and the classless society act as lures to provide a distant destination for the great journey of life.

Such general aims are not just harmless extravagances due to the overworking of a limited model of means to ends, a sort of metaphysical whistle in the dark. For men will do terrible things to other men in order to implement aims like racial purity which are both idiotic and illusory. The crucial question to ask, when men wax enthusiastic on the subject of their aims, is what *procedures* are to be adopted in order to implement them. We then get down to moral brass tacks. Do they in fact favor the model of implementing aims taken from the arts and from technology? There are those who favor the maximum of authoritative regulation such as is necessary in an army; there are those who use other people and mould them for their own purposes; there are those who are determined to live according to rational principles and to extend the maximum of toleration to others who disagree with them; there are those whose preoccupation is the pursuit of private good for whom hell is the other fellow.

These differences of procedure are writ large in the family, in economic affairs, and in political life. In education they are accentuated because the impact of man upon man is more conscious and because people are put into positions of authority where there is great scope for adopting their favored procedures. My point is that arguments about the aims of education reflect these basic differences in principles of procedure. The Puritan and the Catholic both thought they were promoting God's kingdom, but they thought it had to be promoted in a different manner. And the different manner made it quite a different kingdom.

Of course arguments about general aims do not reflect *only* differences in principles of procedure or disagreements about the relative importance of public needs and individual development. Equally important are valuations of content where the merits of, e.g., art as distinct from those of science or history are under discussion. But the real issues involved in such comparisons are obscured by talk about self-realization, life, happiness, and so on. For what sort of self is to be realized? What quality of life is worth perpetuating? Teachers surely care whether or not poetry rather than push-pin is perpetuated, to use a time-honored example. The problem of justifying such "higher" activities is one of the most difficult and persistent problems in ethics. But talk about self-realization and other such omnibus "ends" does more than obscure it; it also encourages an *instrumental* way of looking at the problem of justification. For a nebulous end is invented which such activities are supposed to lead up to, because it is erroneously assumed that education must be justified by reference to an end which is extrinsic to it. The truth is much more that there is a quality of life embedded in the activities which constitute education, and that "self-realization" can be explicated only by reference to such activities. Thus, if by "life" is meant what goes on outside schools and universities, there is an important sense in which "life" must be for the sake of education, not education for life.

11. EDUCATIONAL VALUES AND GOALS: SOME DISPOSITIONS TO BE FOSTERED*

William K. Frankena

There has been much impatience with what R. S. Peters calls "the endless talk about the aims of education," but this talk continues to go on, and we are invited to add to it on this happy occasion. Indeed, those who deny that education has ends or that educators must have aims seem always to end up talking about much the same thing in a slightly different idiom. At any rate, I am quite ready, at least on this occasion, to assume that there are values or goals which it is the business of education to promote, whether they are external, imposed, and far-off, or internal, autonomous, and nearby. I shall also assume that the values or goals which education is to promote consist of certain abilities, dispositions, habits, or traits. To have a single term for them I shall call them "dispositions," taking this word, not in the narrower ordinary "sunny disposition" sense, but in the wider one common among philosophers.[1] So far as I am aware, there is really only one view that might reject the concept of dispositions in this sense, namely existentialism,[2] and, as we shall see, even it seems to advocate our developing certain dispositions or, if you prefer, choosing certain postures.

SOURCE. *The Monist* 52 (January 1968), pp. 1–10. Reprinted by permission of The Open Court Publishing Company, La Salle, Illinois. Copyright © 1968 by the Edward C. Hegeler Foundation, La Salle, Illinois.

*Read at Fiftieth Anniversary Celebration, Graduate School of Education, University of Pennsylvania, Jan. 21, 1966.

Which dispositions is education to foster, then? Desirable ones, of course, since we do not call the formation of undesirable dispositions education or learning, but which ones are these? One answer is that the task of education is to foster the dispositions desired or regarded as desirable by the society doing (or paying for) the educating. This answer has a certain practical realism about it, but it is hardly a philosophical one, since it equates the desirable with what is desired or thought to be desirable. A properly philosophical reply would say that the desirable dispositions are those required either for the moral life, the life of right action, or for the good life, a life of intrinsically worthwhile activities. I shall not try now, however, to present even an outline of the content of the good life, of the requirements of the moral life, or of the dispositions to be fostered in view of them. Instead, I shall take a somewhat different approach, also philosophical in a sense, which strikes me as interesting. I shall look at the three main movements in recent philosophy to see what dispositions they advocate our fostering. What interests me is that, different as they are, these three movements seem to offer us, not indeed the same, but *supplementary* lists of dispositions, which we may combine, perhaps with certain corrections and additions.

In doing this I do not mean to aid and abet the tendency toward eclecticism already too far advanced in so-called philosophy of education, which I join Reginald Archambault and others in decrying.[3] I should hope and maintain that the promotion of the dispositions to be mentioned can be defended on a properly philosophical basis and must be eschewed if it cannot be. On the other hand, I think that it can be defended on more than one philosophical basis, and that we may agree on the following lists of dispositions even though we start from different philosophical premises. This is one reason why I am taking the approach I do. Each of us must have a philosophy of his own which serves as the basis of his thoughts on education, not just an eclectical synthesis of philosophical phrases and social science jargon, but, at least in the area of public education, formal or informal, we must manage some kind of agreement in our working conclusions about the dispositions to be promoted.

In what I shall say I can, of course, only be rough and suggestive, rather than accurate or complete.

II

The three movements I refer to are (1) Deweyan experimentalism, instrumentalism, or pragmatism, (2) analytical philosophy, and (3) existentialism (*cum* phenomenology). These, apart from Thomism and Marxism, are the main currents in western philosophy today. Let us consider first Deweyanism, the philosophical movement most familiar to American educators. What is characteristic here, so far as education is concerned, is its emphasis on what Sidney Hook calls "the centrality of method," the method of reflective thinking, scientific intelligence, or experimental inquiry. The concept of the method, with its five stages, is well-known. It is thought of as *the* method of thinking, and the main task of education is regarded as that of fostering the habit of thinking in this way in all areas of thought and action. Get the power of thinking thus, Dewey virtually said, and all other things will be added unto you. What interests me now is the fact that this habit of thought is conceived of as involving a whole family of dispositions: curiosity, sensitivity to problems, observational perceptiveness, regard for empirical fact and verification, imaginative skill at thinking up hypotheses, persistence, flexibility, open-mindedness, acceptance of responsibility for consequences, and the like. Being associated with thinking, these dispositions have a strongly intellectual cast, though Deweyans reject the distinction between intellectual and moral dispositions, and think of them as at least quasi-moral—and sometimes stress this practical aspect of them so much as to be charged with *anti*-intellectualism. They are dispositions whose matrix is the practice of empirical science. If we assume that this practice is one of the things human beings must be good at, then we may take this family of dispositions as among those to be fostered, even if we do not conceive of them exactly as Dewey did.

Analytical philosophy comes in various styles and must not be identified with either the logical positivism and therapeutic logico-analysis of yesteryear or the ordinary language philosophy of today. In one style or another it has become more or less dominant in British and American philosophy, and is beginning to be influential in the philosophy of education.[4] Now, analytical philosophers of all sorts have tended to abjure the actual making or propounding of ethical, normative, or value judgments, and to be chary about laying down aims or principles for education and about making educational recommendations. They tend to limit philosophy to conceptual and linguistic analysis and methodological clarification. This attitude has been relaxing lately, but, in any case, there is a set of dispositions which are held dear by all analytical philosophers, no matter how purist: clarity, consistency, rigor of thought, concern for semantic meaningfulness, methodological awareness, consciousness of assumptions, and so on. These dispositions have been nicely characterized as "logical values" or "values in speaking [and thinking]" by J. N. Findlay.[5] Typically, analytical philosophers think, with some justice, that these values have been neglected both in theory and practice by Deweyans and existentialists, as well as by speculative philosophers, Hegelian, Whiteheadian, etc.—and especially by nonanalytical philosophers of education. Whether they are right or wrong in this, it does seem clear that their values should be among our goals of education at all levels. The title of a recent book proclaims that clarity is not enough,[6] and perhaps it is not, but it is nevertheless something desirable, and even imperative, both in our thinking about education·and in our thinking about other things.

Existentialism is characteristically opposed both to analytical philosophy (though there are now some attempts at a rapprochement between these two movements) and to pragmatic empiricism. It is suspicious, among other things, of the "objectivity" so much prized, in different ways, by these other two movements. The implications of existentialism for education have begun to get attention from O. F. Bollnow and others,[7] but this is not what concerns me now. What interests me is that existentialism presents us with a third family of dispositions to be fostered: authenticity, decision, commitment, autonomy, individuality, fidelity, responsibility, etc. These are definitely moral (or, at any rate, "practical") dispositions as compared with the more intellectual, logical, or scientific ones stressed by Deweyan and analytical philosophers; but they are moral or practical dispositions that relate to the *manner* of life rather than to its *content*—not to *what* we do so much as to *how* we do it. To quote a recent writer: "Existential morality is notorious for its lack of content. But it does not cease for that reason to be morality. Everything is in the manner, as its sponsors would, and do, say."

As one of these sponsors does say:

Value lies not so much in what we do as in how we exist and maintain ourselves in time . . . words like *authentic, genuine, real,* and *really* . . . express those more basic "existential values," as we may call them, which underlie all the valuable things that we do or say. Since they characterize our ways of existing in the world, they are universal in scope, and apply to every phrase and region of our care. There is nothing that we say, or think, or do that may not be done either authentically . . . or unauthentically. . . . They are not "values" at all, in the traditional sense of this term, for they cannot be understood apart . . . . They are patterns of our lived existence in the world.[8]

I do not wish to suggest that an "existential" manner or posture is enough, and certainly not that we should be in a state of "anxiety" all the time, but it does seem plausible to maintain that there is a place in education for the development of such "existential" virtues along with others supplementing or even modifying them. There is at least *some* point in "the underground man's" remark in Dostoevsky's *Notes,* "perhaps, after all there is more 'life' in me than in you."

III

Thus we see that, even though representatives of all three of our philosophical movements are typically reluctant to "talk about the aims of education," each movement itself enshrines or espouses certain dispositions that may well be included among the aims of education by those of us who do not mind such talk. The three philosophies are in general opposed to one another, and one cannot simply combine them, but the dispositions they value may be combined and included in our list of those to be cultivated in education, though perhaps not without some pulling and hauling. This is the main point I wish to make. I should like, however, to subjoin a few further points.

(1) Of course, we can espouse the Deweyan list of dispositions, even if we do not conceive them exactly as he does, only if we assume that empirical inquiry of a scientific kind is a good thing—sufficient, necessary, or at least helpful to the good or the moral life. This, however, is an assumption that would be denied only by certain extreme kinds of rationalism, irrationalism, and otherworldliness. In the same way, an adoption of the analytical philosopher's list of dispositions as among those to be cultivated involves assigning at least a considerable value to clarity, rigor, etc., an assignment which only an extreme irrationalist could refuse to make, though, of course, those who do make it will not all have the same conception of clarity or rigor. As for the existential virtues—it looks as if they can and must be accepted in some form by almost anyone who takes morality or religion seriously, that is, by anyone whose approach is not purely aesthetic, conventional, legalistic, or spectatorial.

(2) It seems to me that existentialism and its sisters and its cousins and its aunts do not put sufficient store on rationality, meaning by this roughly the set of dispositions prized by the Deweyans and the analytical philosophers taken together. Indeed, they tend to suspect and impugn it. Yet, even if we confine ourselves to the *how* of our approach to life, and let the *what* take care of itself, it seems at least irrational to neglect the virtues of logic and science. To quote Israel Scheffler,

We are . . . faced by important challenges from within and without . . . whatever we do, we ought, I believe, to keep uppermost the ideal of rationality, and its emphasis on the critical, questioning, responsible, free mind.[9]

(3) Even so, the existentialists (and their sisters and their cousins and their aunts) are perhaps right in feeling that the values of rationality must at least be supplemented by those of commitment and engagement, as S. T. Kimball and J. E. McClellan have argued,[10] along with many others who think that our western culture is in danger of being overcome by its "committed" opponents. (In this perspective it is a bit ironical that our "uncommitted" are precisely those who are most attracted by existentialism.) (4) Of course, if we try to combine rationality and commitment—the first without the second being empty and the second without the first blind—we must find some teachable kind of union of open-mindedness and belief, of objectivity and decision. This is one of the crucial problems of our culture, as has often been pointed out.

(5) In my opinion, none of the three families of dispositions includes enough emphasis on sheer (not "mere") knowledge, the intellectual virtue so esteemed by Aristotelians—not just knowing *how* (which was given a big boost by Gilbert Ryle) but knowing *that,* the kind of knowledge contained in the findings of

history, science, and other cognitive studies (including knowing *why*). One reads, for example, that a college education must have as its goals "intellectual initiative and mature self-reliance," a statement which roughly synthesizes Dewey and existentialism, but there is enough "formalism" in me to make me convinced that education ought to promote, not only certain "qualities of mind [and character]," but also certain "forms of knowledge," even if the knowledge must sometimes be second-hand and not acquired "by doing."[11] To parody Bertrand Russell, the good life, moral and otherwise, is a life inspired by certain qualities of mind and character and guided by knowledge. Actually possessed knowledge *that* is important both for the guidance of action and for the content of the good life. I therefore feel some agreement with Maritain when he writes that contemporary education has too much substituted "training-value for knowledge-value . . . mental gymnastics for truth, and being in fine fettle, for wisdom."[12] As Jerome Bruner puts it:

Surely, knowledge of the natural world, knowledge of the human condition, knowledge of the nature and dynamics of society, knowledge of the past so that it may be used in experiencing the present and aspiring to the future—all of these . . . are essential to an educated man. To these may be added another: knowledge of the products of our artistic heritage . . . .[13]

John Stuart Mill was, no doubt, right in attacking education that is "all *cram*" and does not provide "exercises to form the thinking faculty itself," but he went too far in adding, ". . . the end of education is not to *teach,* but to fit the mind for learning from its own consciousness and observations. . . . Let all *cram* be ruthlessly discarded." For Mill himself goes on to insist that each person must be "made to feel that . . . in the line of his peculiar duty, and in the line of the duties common to all men, it is his business to *know*."[14] It seems to me to follow that there is place in education for some "teaching" and even some "cram." I grant it may be that, if we seek first to form the thinking faculty itself (i.e., certain qualities of mind), then all other things will eventually be added unto us, including knowledge. But must we wait until after school is over for them to be added? *Can* we?

A recent cartoon about education has a father saying to his child sitting in a high chair with his food before him, "Think. Assimilate. Evaluate. Grow." It seems to me that this is to the point as a spoof of a certain conception of education, since the word "Grow" does not add anything, and that a more sensible view would say, "Think. Assimilate. Evaluate. Know."

(6) There are, of course, certain other sorts of dispositions that must be added to the three families indicated above as goals of education. There are, first, moral dispositions relating to *what* we do and not merely to *how* we do it, e.g., benevolence and justice (i.e., knowing *what* to do and being disposed to do it), second, the dispositions involved in aesthetic appreciation, creation, and

judgment (not just "knowledge of the products of our artistic heritage"), and, third, the dispositions required by the democratic way of life, so far as these are not already covered.

(7) In what I have said thus far, I have had *public* education primarily in mind. *Private* education, formal and informal, may add still another group of dispositions, namely, those involved in religious faith, hope, love, and worship. However, some care is needed, perhaps even some reconstruction, if one proposes to combine a Deweyan emphasis on scientific intelligence or an analytical philosopher's emphasis on clarity and rigor with anything like a traditional theistic faith. If one proposes to foster such a faith, one must at least give up trying to cultivate also a disposition to rely on logic and science *alone* as a basis of belief and action. If one wishes to insist on the necessity of the latter disposition, one must reconstruct the traditional conception of religion and God—as Dewey did in *A Common Faith*. Of course, if one means by religion merely some kind of basic commitment or other, or any kind of ultimate belief about the world whatsoever, or a vague "duty and reverence" (as Whitehead does),[15] or simply whatever an individual does with his solitude (Whitehead again), then all education is and must be religious (as Whitehead says), even an atheistic or militantly anti-religious one. Then "the Galilean" has indeed conquered, but then he has also become very, very pale—so pale as to be indistinguishable from or to his opponents. For, even if one has a "religious" belief in this wide sense, one may still also believe that

> . . . beyond the extreme sea-wall, and
> between the remote sea-gates,
> Waste water washes, and tall ships founder,
> and deep death waits . . .

as Swinburne did.[16] I say this because of what one finds in some discussions of the place of religion in public schools, where, from the premise that every ultimate belief is a religion, the conclusions are drawn, first, that religion both is and should be taught in public schools, and, second, that therefore theism (or Catholicism, Protestantism, and Judaism) may and should be taught there. As for private schools and colleges—whether they should in fact foster religious dispositions in a narrower theistic sense is too large a question to treat here; the answer, I suppose, assuming that there should be private schools and colleges at all, is that it depends on the purposes for which they exist.

NOTES

1. Dewey prefers the word "habit," but uses "disposition" also. See the end of Pt. I, Section I in John Dewey, *Human Nature and Conduct* (New York: Modern Library, 1930); *Democracy and Education* (Macmillan Paperback edition), p. 238.

2. See O. F. Bollnow, *Existenzphilosophie und Pädagogik* (Stuttgart: W. Kohlhammer Verlag, 1962), pp. 14 ff.

3. R. Archambault (ed.), *Philosophical Analysis and Education* (London: Routledge & Kegan Paul Ltd., 1965), p. 3.

4. See *ibid.*, pp. 6, 13.

5. See J. N. Findlay, *Language, Mind and Value* (London, 1963), pp. 105–27.

6. H. D. Lewis (ed.), *Clarity is not Enough* (London, 1963).

7. Cf. Bollnow, *op. cit.;* G. F. Kneller, *Existentialism and Education* (New York: Wiley, 1958); Van Cleve Morris, *Existentialism in Education* (New York, 1965).

8. See, respectively, C. Smith, *Contemporary French Philosophy* (London, 1964), p. 229; J. D. Wild, *Existence and the World of Freedom* (Englewood Cliffs, N. J.: Prentice-Hall, 1963), pp. 161–65. See also Whitehead's remarks on "style" in *Aims of Education* (Mentor Books, 1949), p. 24.

9. Israel Scheffler, "Concepts of Education: Some Philosophical Reflections on the Current Scene," in E. Landy and P. A. Berry (eds.), *Guidance in American Education* (Cambridge, Mass.: Harvard University Press, 1964), p. 26.

10. S. T. Kimball and J. E. McClellan, *Education and the New America* (New York, 1962).

11. See P. H. Hirst in R. Archambault, *Philosophical Analysis, op. cit.,* pp. 117 f., for a discussion on this point.

12. J. Maritain, *Education at the Crossroads* (Yale Paperback edition), p. 55; cf. Aquinas' remark that: "The first thing that is required of an active man is that he know."

13. Jerome Bruner, *On Knowing* (New York: Atheneum, 1965), p. 122.

14. See his essay "On Genius" in K. Price, *Education and Philosophical Thought* (Boston, 1962), pp. 455 f.

15. A. N. Whitehead, *Aims of Education* (Mentor Books), p. 26.

16. C. Swinburne, "Hymn to Proserpine." Or as B. Russell did in "A Free Man's Worship."

12. LIBERAL EDUCATION AND THE NATURE OF KNOWLEDGE

Paul H. Hirst

The phrase "liberal education" has today become something of a slogan which takes on different meanings according to its immediate context. It usually labels a form of education of which the author approves, but beyond that its meaning is often entirely negatively derived. Whatever else a liberal education is, it is *not* a vocational education, *not* an exclusively scientific education, or *not* a specialist education in any sense. The frequency with which the term is employed in this way certainly highlights the inadequacies of these other concepts and the need for a wider and, in the long run, more worthwhile form of education. But as long as the concept is merely negative in what it intimates, it has little more than debating value. Only when it is given explicit positive content can it be of use in the serious business of educational planning. It is my contention in this paper that whatever vagaries there have been in the use of the term, it is the appropriate label for a positive concept, that of an education based fairly and squarely on the nature of knowledge itself, a concept central to the discussion of education at any level.

SOURCE. In Reginald D. Archambault (ed.), *Philosophical Analysis and Education* (London: Routledge & Kegan Paul Ltd., 1965), pp. 113−138. American edition published by Humanities Press, Inc., Atlantic Highlands, New Jersey, 1972. Also in Paul H. Hirst, *Knowledge and the Curriculum* (London: Routledge & Kegan Paul Ltd., 1974), pp. 30−53.

THE GREEK NOTION OF LIBERAL EDUCATION

The fully developed Greek notion of liberal education was rooted in a number of related philosophical doctrines; first about the significance of knowledge for the mind, and secondly about the relationship between knowledge and reality. In the first category there was the doctrine that it is the peculiar and distinctive activity of the mind, because of its very nature, to pursue knowledge. The achievement of knowledge satisfies and fulfills the mind which thereby attains its own appropriate end. The pursuit of knowledge is thus the pursuit of the good of the mind and, therefore, an essential element in the good life. In addition, it was held that the achievement of knowledge is not only the attainment of the good of the mind itself, but also the chief means whereby the good life as a whole is to be found. Man is more than pure mind, yet mind is his essential distinguishing characteristic, and it is in terms of knowledge that his whole life is rightly directed.

That knowledge is equal to its task was guaranteed by the second group of doctrines. These asserted that the mind, in the right use of reason, comes to know the essential nature of things and can apprehend what is ultimately real and immutable. Consequently, man no longer needs to live in terms of deceptive appearances and doubtful opinions and beliefs. All his experiences, life and thought can be given shape and perspective by what is finally true, by knowledge that corresponds to what is ultimately real. Further, the particular way in which reason is here represented as attaining knowledge, results in a view of the whole of man's understanding as hierarchically structured in various levels. From the knowledge of mere particulars to that of pure being, all knowledge has its place in a comprehensive and harmonious scheme, the pattern of which is formed as knowledge is developed in apprehending reality in its many different manifestations.

From these doctrines there emerged the idea of liberal education as a process concerned simply and directly with the pursuit of knowledge. But the doctrines give to this general idea particular meaning and significance; for they lead to a clear definition of its scope and content, and to a clear justification for education in these terms. The definition is clear, because education is determined objectively in range, in structure and in content by the forms of knowledge itself and their harmonious, hierarchical interrelations. There is here no thought of defining education in terms of knowledge and skills that may be useful, or in terms of moral virtues and qualities of mind that may be considered desirable. The definition is stated strictly in terms of man's knowledge of what is the case. The development of the mind to which it leads, be it in skills, virtues or other characteristics, is thought to be necessarily its greatest good.

The justification that the doctrines lend to this concept of education is threefold. First, such an education is based on what is true and not on uncertain opinions and beliefs or temporary values. It therefore has a finality which no other form of education has. Secondly, knowledge itself being a distinctive human virtue, liberal education has a value for the person as the fulfillment of the mind, a value which has nothing to do with utilitarian or vocational considerations. Thirdly, because of the significance of knowledge in the determination of the good life as a whole, liberal education is essential to man's understanding of how he ought to live, both individually and socially.

Here, then, the Greeks attained the concept of an education that was "liberal" not simply because it was the education of free men rather than slaves, but also because they saw it as freeing the mind to function according to its true nature, freeing reason from error and illusion and freeing man's conduct from wrong. And ever since Greek times this idea of education has had its place. Sometimes it has been modified or extended in detail to accommodate within its scheme new forms of knowledge: for instance Christian doctrines and the various branches of modern science. Sometimes the concept has been misinterpreted: as in Renaissance humanism when classical learning was equated with liberal education. Sometimes it has been strongly opposed on philosophical grounds: as by Dewey and the pragmatists. Yet at crucial points in the history of education the concept has constantly reappeared. It is not hard to understand why this should be so.

Education, being a deliberate, purposeful activity directed to the development of individuals, necessarily involves considerations of value. Where are these values to be found? What is to be their content? How are they to be justified? They can be, and often are, values that reflect the interests of a minority group in the society. They may be religious, political or utilitarian in character. They are always open to debate and detailed criticism, and are always in need of particular justification. Is there not perhaps a more ultimate basis for the values that should determine education, some more objective ground? That final ground has, ever since the Greeks, been repeatedly located in man's conception of the diverse forms of knowledge he has achieved. And there has thus arisen the demand for an education whose definition and justification are based on the nature and significance of knowledge itself, and not on the predilections of pupils, the demands of society, or the whims of politicians. Precisely this demand was behind the development by the Greeks of an education in the seven liberal arts, an introduction to and a pursuit of the forms of knowledge as they were then conceived. It was precisely this demand that prompted Newman and Arnold in the nineteenth century to call for an education that aimed at the cultivation and development of the mind in the full range of man's understanding. It is the same demand that today motivates such classical realists as Maritain and R. M. Hutchins.

A TYPICAL MODERN STATEMENT: THE HARVARD REPORT

It may well be asked, however, whether those who do not hold the doctrines of metaphysical and epistemological realism can legitimately subscribe to a concept of education of this kind. Historically it seems to have had positive force only when presented in this particular philosophical framework. But historical association must be distinguished from logical connection and it is not by any means obvious that all the characteristic features of the concept are dependent on such philosophical realism. If the doctrines about mind, knowledge and reality mentioned at the beginning of this paper are regarded as at best too speculative a basis for educational planning, as well they may be, the possibility of an education defined and justified entirely in terms of the scope and character of knowledge needs re-examination. The significance of the concept originally came directly from the place the basic doctrines give to knowledge in a unified picture of the mind and its relation to reality. Knowledge is achieved when the mind attains its own satisfaction or good by corresponding to objective reality. A liberal education in the pursuit of knowledge is, therefore, seeking the development of the mind according to what is quite external to it, the structure and pattern of reality. But if once there is any serious questioning of this relationship between mind, knowledge and reality, the whole harmonious structure is liable to disintegrate. First there arise inevitably problems of definition. A liberal education defined in terms of knowledge alone is acceptable as long as knowledge is thought to be necessarily developing the mind in desirable ways, and hence promoting the good life. But if doubt is cast on these functions of knowledge, must not liberal education be redefined stating explicitly the qualities of mind and the moral virtues to which it is directed? And if knowledge is no longer seen as the understanding of reality but merely as the understanding of experience, what is to replace the harmonious, hierarchical scheme of knowledge that gave pattern and order to the education? Secondly there are equally serious problems of justification. For if knowledge is no longer thought to be rooted in some reality, or if its significance for the mind and the good life is questioned, what can be the justification for an education defined in terms of knowledge alone?

Difficulties of both kinds, but particularly those of definition, can be seen in the well-known Harvard Committee Report: *General Education in a Free Society*.[1] (In the Committee's terminology the aims of a "liberal" and a "general" education are identical.) Though certain of the doctrines that originally supported the concept of a liberal education are implicit in this work, the classical view of the significance of knowledge for the mind is considerably weakened, and the belief that in metaphysics man has knowledge of ultimate reality is ignored, if not rejected. The result is an ambiguous and unsatisfactory treatment of the problem of definition and a limited and debatable treatment of the question of justification. Some examination of the Report on both these scores, particularly the former, will serve to show that adequate definition and justification are not only not dependent on the classical doctrines, but can in fact be based directly on an explication of the concepts of "mind" and "knowledge" and their relationship.

The Report attempts the definition of a liberal education in two distinct ways: in terms of the qualities of mind it ought to produce and the forms of knowledge with which it ought to be concerned. What the precise relationship is between these two is not clear. It is asserted that they are "images of each other," yet that there is no escape from "describing general education at one time looking to the good man in society and at another time as dictated by the nature of knowledge itself."[2] Which of the forms of description is to be given pride of place soon emerges, however. First, three areas of knowledge are distinguished, primarily by their distinctive methods: the natural sciences, the humanities and social studies. But it is made plain that "the cultivation of certain aptitudes and attitudes of mind" is being aimed at, the elements of knowledge being the means for developing these. Liberal education is therefore best understood in terms of the characteristics of mind to which it leads. "By characteristics we mean aims so important as to prescribe how general education should be carried out and which abilities ought to be sought above all others in every part of it. These abilities in our opinion are: to think effectively, to communicate thought, to make relevant judgments, to discriminate among values."[3] The meaning of each of these four is elaborated at some length. Amongst the many things detailed of "effective thinking" it is first said to be logical thinking of a kind that is applicable to such practical matters as deciding who to vote for and what wife to choose: it is the ability to extract universal truths from particular cases and to infer particulars from general laws: it is the ability to analyze a problem and to recombine the elements by the use of imagination. This thinking goes further than mere logic, however. It includes the relational thinking of everyday life, the ability to think at a level appropriate to a problem whatever its character. It includes too the imaginative thinking of the poet, the inventor, and the revolutionary. "Communication," though "obviously inseparable from effective thinking," is said to involve another group of skills, those of speaking and listening, writing and reading. It includes certain moral qualities such as candor, it covers certain vital aspects of social and political life and even the high art of conversation. "The making of relevant value judgments" involves "the ability of the student to bring to bear the whole range of ideas upon the area of experience," it is the art of effectively relating theory to practice, of abstractions to facts, of thought to action. Finally there is "discrimination among values." This includes the distinction of various kinds of value and their relative importance, an awareness of the values of character like fair play and self-control, intellectual values like the love of truth and aesthetic values like good taste, and, in addition, a commitment to such values in the conduct of life.[4]

As to how exactly these abilities come to be those developed by the three types of knowledge, little is said. It is noted that "the three phases of effective thinking, logical, relational, and imaginative, correspond roughly to the three divisions of learning, the natural sciences, the social studies, and the humanities, respectively."[5] The difficult connection between education in the making of value judgments and the formation of moral character is noted. Otherwise the remarks are of a general nature, emphasizing that these abilities must be consciously developed in all studies and generalized as far as possible.

This double, if one-sided, characterization of liberal education seems to me unsatisfactory and seriously misleading if what is said of the four abilities is examined more closely. In the first place, the notion that a liberal education can be directly characterized in terms of mental abilities and independently of fully specifying the forms of knowledge involved, is I think false. It is the result of a misunderstanding of the way in which mental abilities are in fact distinguishable. From what is said of "effective thinking," it is perfectly plain that the phrase is being used as a label for mental activity which results in an achievement of some sort, an achievement that is, at least in principle, both publicly describable and publicly testable—the solving of a mathematical problem, responsibly deciding who to vote for, satisfactorily analyzing a work of art. Indeed there can be effective thinking only when the outcome of mental activity can be recognized and judged by those who have the appropriate skills and knowledge, for otherwise the phrase has no significant application. Thus although the phrase labels a form of mental activity, and such mental processes may well be directly accessible only to the person whose processes they are, its description and evaluation must be in public terms occurring in public language. Terms which, like "effective thinking," describe activities involving achievements of some sort, must have public criteria to mark them. But in that case, none of the four abilities can in fact be delineated except by means of their detailed public features. Such characterization is in fact forced on the Committee when they come to amplify what they mean. But their approach is simply illustrative, as if the abilities are directly intelligible in themselves, and the items and features of knowledge they give merely examples of areas where the abilities can be seen. If the public terms and criteria are logically necessary to specifying what the abilities are, however, then no adequate account of liberal education in terms of these can be given without a full account in terms of the public features of the forms of knowledge with which it is concerned. Indeed the latter is logically prior and the former secondary and derivative.

In the second place, the use of broad, general terms for these abilities serves in fact to unify misleadingly quite disparate achievements. For the public criteria whereby the exercise of any one of these abilities is to be judged are not all of a piece. Those that under the banner of "effective thinking" are appropriate in, say, aesthetic appreciation are, apart from certain very general considerations, inappropriate in, say, mathematical thinking. In each case the criteria are peculiar to the particular area of knowledge concerned. Similarly, for instance, "communication" in the sciences has only certain very basic features in common with "communication" in poetic terms. It is only when the abilities are fully divided out, as it were, into the various domains and we see what they refer to in public terms that it is at all clear what is involved in developing them. To talk of developing "effective thinking" is like talking of developing "successful games playing." Plainly that unifying label is thoroughly misleading when what constitutes playing cricket has practically nothing in common with what constitutes playing tiddly-winks. The implications of the term are not at all appreciated until what is wanted is given detailed specification. It is vitally important to realize the very real objective differences that there are in forms of knowledge, and therefore in our understanding of mental processes that are related to these. Maybe this unfortunate desire to use unifying concepts is a relic of the time when all forms of knowledge were thought to be similar, if not identical in logical structure and that the "laws of logic" reflected the precise psychological operations involved in valid thinking. Be that as it may, the general terms used in the Report are liable both to blur essential distinctions and to direct the attention of educational planners into unprofitable descriptions of what they are after.

Thirdly, in spite of any protestations to the contrary, the impression is created by this terminology that it is possible to develop general unitary abilities of the stated kind. The extent to which this is true is a matter for empirical investigation into the transfer of training. Nevertheless such abilities must necessarily be characterized in terms of the public features of knowledge, and whatever general abilities there may be, the particular criteria for their application in diverse fields are vital to their significance for liberal education. But to think in these terms is to be in danger of looking for transfer of skills where none is discernible. We must not assume that skill at tiddly-winks will get us very far at cricket, or that if the skills have much in common, as in say squash and tennis, then the rules for one activity will do as the rules for the other.

Failure to appreciate these points leads all too readily to programs of education for which quite unwarranted claims are made. It is sometimes said, for instance, that the study of one major science can in itself provide the elements of a liberal education—that it can lead to the development of such abilities as effective thinking, communication, the making of relevant judgments, and even to some extent, discrimination among values. But this facile view is seen to be quite untenable if it is once understood how these abilities are defined, and how any one form of knowledge is related to them. Much more plausible and much more common is the attempt to relate directly the study of particular subjects to the development of particular unitary abilities. The Harvard Committee do this with subdivisions of "effective thinking" when they suggest that, roughly speaking, logical thinking is developed by the sciences, relational thinking by social studies, and imaginative thinking by the humanities. This, of course, could be said to be true by definition if logical thinking were taken to be just that kind of thinking that is developed by the study of the sciences. But such a straight and limited connection is not at all what is indicated in the Report. The forms of thinking there are much more generalized. It follows then that logical, relational and imaginative thinking must be independently defined. Because of the vagueness of the terms it might appear that this would be simple enough. But in fact this very vagueness makes the task almost impossible, for any one of the three terms might, with considerable justice, be applied to almost any example of thinking. (And the appropriateness of using such a term as ''imaginative'' to describe a distinct type of thinking rather than its manner or style is very debatable.) Even if this most serious difficulty were overcome somehow, there would remain the problem of establishing empirical evidence, for asserting both the existence of such an ability, and that a particular study leads to its development. Generally speaking there is little such evidence. What there is on transfer of training suggests that it occurs only where there is marked logical similarity in the elements studied.[6]

Finally the characterization of a liberal education in these terms is misleading owing to the tendency for the concept to be broadened so that it is concerned not only with the development of the mind that results from the pursuit of knowledge, but also with other aspects of personal development, particularly emotional and moral, that may or may not be judged desirable. This tendency can be clearly seen in the Report's comments on the abilities of communication, making relevant judgments and discriminating among values. Stretching the edges of the concept in these ways leads to a much wider, more generalized notion of education. It then ceases to be one defined directly in terms of the pursuit of knowledge as liberal education originally was, and thus cannot be justified by justifying that pursuit. But this is surely to give up the concept in favor of another one that needs independent justification. The analysis of such a concept is beyond our present concern.

A REASSERTION AND A REINTERPRETATION

On logical grounds, then, it would seem that a consistent concept of liberal education must be worked out fully in terms of the forms of knowledge. By these is meant, of course, not collections of information, but the complex ways of understanding experience which man has achieved, which are publicly specifiable and which are gained through learning. An education in these terms does indeed develop its related abilities and qualities of mind, for the mind will be characterized to a greater or less degree by the features of the understanding it seeks. Each form of knowledge, if it is to be acquired beyond a general and superficial level, involves the development of creative imagination, judgment, thinking, communicative skills, etc., in ways that are peculiar to itself as a way of understanding experience. To list these elements, picking them out, as it were, across the forms of knowledge of which they are part and in each of which they have a different stamp, draws attention to many features that a liberal education must of course include. But it draws attention to them at the expense of the differences among them as they occur in the different areas. And of itself such listing contributes nothing to the basic determination of what a liberal education is. To be told that it is the development of effective thinking is of no value until this is explicated in terms of the forms of knowledge which give it meaning: for example in terms of the solving of problems in Euclidean geometry or coming to understand the poems of John Donne. To be told instead that it is concerned with certain specified forms of knowledge, the essential characteristics of which are then detailed explicitly as far as possible, is to be given a clear understanding of the concept and one which is unambiguous as to the forms of thinking, judgment, imagination and communication it involves.

In his Gulbenkian Foundation Report: *Arts and Science Sides in the Sixth Form*, Mr. A. D. C. Peterson comes considerably nearer than the Harvard Committee to the definition of a liberal education (once more termed here a "general education") by proceeding in just this fashion. Being concerned that this should not be worked out in terms of information, he shies away from any direct use of the term "knowledge" and defines the concept modestly as one that "develops the intellect in as many as possible of the main modes of thinking."[7] These are then listed as the logical, the empirical, the moral and the aesthetic. The phrase "modes of thinking," it is true, refers directly to forms of mental activity, and Mr. Peterson's alternatives for it, "modes of human experience," "categories of mental experience" and (elsewhere) "types of judgment," all look in the same direction. Yet the "modes" are not different aspects of mind that cut across the forms that human knowledge takes, as the Harvard Report's "abilities" are. They are, rather, four parallel forms of mental development. To complete this treatment so that there is no ambiguity, however, it must be made clear in a way that Mr. Peterson does not make it clear, that the four forms can only be distinguished, in the last analysis, in terms of the public features that demarcate the areas of knowledge on which they stand. Logical, empirical, moral and aesthetic forms of understanding are distinguishable from each other only by their distinctive concepts and expressions and their criteria for distinguishing the true from the false, the good from the bad. If Mr. Peterson's "modes" are strictly explicated on the basis of these features of knowledge, then his concept of education becomes one concerned with the development of the mind as that is determined by certain forms of knowledge. This is to be in sight of a modern equivalent of the traditional conception of liberal education.

But the reassertion of this concept implies that there is once more the acceptance of some kind of "harmony" between knowledge and the mind. This is, however, not now being maintained on metaphysical grounds. What is being suggested, rather, is that the "harmony" is a matter of the logical relationship between the concept of "mind" and the concept of "knowledge," from which it follows that the achievement of knowledge is necessarily the development of mind—that is, the self-conscious rational mind of man—in its most fundamental aspect.

Whatever else is implied in the phrase, to have "a rational mind" certainly implies experience structured under some form of conceptual scheme. The various manifestations of consciousness, in, for instance, different sense perceptions, different emotions, or different elements of intellectual understanding, are intelligible only by virtue of the conceptual apparatus by which they are articulated. Further, whatever private forms of awareness there may be, it is by means of symbols, particularly in language, that conceptual articulation becomes objectified, for the symbols give public embodiment to the concepts. The result of this is that men are able to come to understand both the external world and their own private states of mind in common ways, sharing the same conceptual schema by learning to use symbols in the same manner. The objectification of understanding is possible because commonly accepted criteria for using the terms are recognized even if these are never explicitly expressed. But further as the symbols derived from experience can be used to examine subsequent experience, assertions are possible which are testable as true or false, valid or invalid. There are thus also public criteria whereby certain forms of expression are assessable against experience. Whether the "objects" concerned are themselves private to the individual like mental processes, or publicly accessible like temperature readings, there are here tests for the assertions which are themselves publicly agreed and accepted.

It is by the use of such tests that we have come to have the whole domain of knowledge. The formulating and testing of symbolic expressions has enabled man to probe his experience for ever more complex relations and for finer and finer distinctions, these being fixed and held for public sharing in the symbolic systems that have been evolved. But it is important to realize that this progressive attainment of a cognitive framework with public criteria has significance not merely for knowledge itself, for it is by its terms that the life of man in every particular is patterned and ordered. Without its structure all other forms of consciousness, including, for example, emotional experiences, or mental attitudes and beliefs, would seem to be unintelligible. For the analysis of them reveals that they lack independent intelligible structure of themselves. Essentially private though they may be in many or all of their aspects, their characteristic forms are explicable only by means of the publicly rooted conceptual organizations we have achieved. They can be understood only by means of the objective features with which they are associated, round which they come to be organized and built. The forms of knowledge are thus the basic articulations whereby the whole of experience has become intelligible to man, they are the fundamental achievement of mind.

Knowledge, however, must never be thought of merely as vast bodies of tested symbolic expressions. These are only the public aspects of the ways in which human experience has come to have shape. They are significant because they are themselves the objective elements round which the development of mind has taken place. To acquire knowledge is to become aware of experience as structured, organized and made meaningful in some quite specific way, and the varieties of human knowledge constitute the highly developed forms in which man has found this possible. To acquire knowledge is to learn to see, to experience the world in a way otherwise unknown, and thereby come to have a mind in a fuller sense. It is not that the mind is some kind of organ or muscle with its own inbuilt forms of operation, which if somehow developed, naturally lead to different kinds of knowledge. It is not that the mind has predetermined patterns of functioning. Nor is it that the mind is an entity which suitably directed by knowledge comes to take on the pattern of, is conformed to, some external reality. It is rather that to have a mind basically involves coming to have experience articulated by means of various conceptual schema. It is only because man has over millennia objectified and progressively developed these that he has achieved the forms of human knowledge, and the possibility of the development of mind as we know it is open to us today.

A liberal education is, then, one that, determined in scope and content by knowledge itself, is thereby concerned with the development of mind. The concept is thus once more clearly and objectively defined in precisely the same way as the original concept. It is however no longer supported by epistemological and metaphysical doctrines that result in a hierarchical organization of the various forms of knowledge. The detailed working out of the education will therefore be markedly different in certain respects. The distinctions between the various forms of knowledge which will principally govern the scheme of education will now be based entirely on analyses of their particular conceptual, logical and methodological features. The comprehensive character of the education will of course remain, since this is essentially part of the definition of the concept, but any question of the harmonious organization of its various elements will depend on the relationships between them that are revealed by these analyses.

But if the concept is reasserted in these terms, what now of the question of its justification? The justification of a liberal education as supported by the doctrines of classical realism was based on the ultimacy of knowledge as ordered and determined by reality, and the significance of knowledge for the mind and for the good life. Having weakened these doctrines, the Harvard Committee's justification of their concept ignores the question of the relationship between knowledge and reality, and there is a specific rejection of the view that knowledge is in itself the good of the mind. They assert, however, the supreme significance of knowledge in the determination of all human activity, and supplement this, as is certainly necessary because of the extended nature of their concept, by general considerations of the desirability of their suggestions. When once more the concept is strictly confined so as to be determined by the forms of knowledge, the return to a justification of it without reference to what is generally thought desirable on social or similar grounds become possible. And such justification for the concept is essential if the education it delineates is to have the ultimate significance that, as was earlier suggested, is part of its raison d'être. This justification must now however stem from what has already been said of the nature of knowledge as no metaphysical doctrine of the connection between knowledge and reality is any longer being invoked.

If the achievement of knowledge is necessarily the development of mind in its most basic sense, then it can be readily seen that to ask for a justification for the pursuit of knowledge is not at all the same thing as to ask for the justification for, say, teaching all children a foreign language or making them orderly and punctual in their behavior. It is in fact a peculiar question asking for justification for any development of the rational mind at all. To ask for the justification of any form of activity is significant only if one is in fact committed already to seeking rational knowledge. To ask for a justification of the pursuit of rational knowledge itself therefore presupposes some form of commitment to what one is seeking to justify. Justification is possible only if what is being justified is both intelligible under publicly rooted concepts and is assessable according to accepted criteria. It assumes a commitment to these two principles. But these very principles are in fact fundamental to the pursuit of knowledge in all its forms, be it, for instance, empirical knowledge or understanding in the arts. The forms of knowledge are in a sense simply the working out of these general principles in particular ways. To give justification of any kind of knowledge therefore involves using the principles in one specific form to assess their use in another. Any particular activity can be examined for its rational character, for its adherence to these principles, and thus justified on the assumption of them. Indeed in so far as activities are rational this will be possible. It is commitment to them that characterizes any rational activity as such. But the principles themselves have no such assessable status, for justification outside the use of the principles is not logically possible. This does not mean that rational pursuits in the end lack justification, for they could equally well be said to have their justification written into them. Nor is any form of viciously circular justification involved by assuming in the procedure what is being looked for. The situation is that we have here reached the ultimate point where the question of justification ceases to be significantly applicable. The apparent circularity is the result of the interrelation between the concepts of rational justification and the pursuit of knowledge.

Perhaps the finality of these principles can be brought out further by noting a negative form of the same argument. From this point of view, to question the pursuit of any kind of rational knowledge is in the end self-defeating, for the questioning itself depends on accepting the very principles whose use is finally being called in question.

It is because it is based on these ultimate principles that characterize knowledge itself and not merely on lower level forms of justification that a liberal education is in a very real sense the ultimate form of education. In spite of the absence of any metaphysical doctrine about reality this idea of liberal education has a significance parallel to that of the original Greek concept. It is an education concerned directly with the development of the mind in rational knowledge, whatever form that freely takes. This parallels the original concept in that according to the doctrine of function liberal education was the freeing of the mind to achieve its own good in knowledge. In each case it is a form of education knowing no limits other than those necessarily imposed by the nature of rational knowledge and thereby itself developing in man the final court of appeal in all human affairs.

As here reformulated the concept has, again like the original, objectivity, though this is no longer backed by metaphysical realism. For it is a necessary feature of knowledge as such that there be public criteria whereby the true is distinguishable from the false, the good from the bad, the right from the wrong. It is the existence of these criteria which gives objectivity to knowledge; and this in its turn gives objectivity to the concept of liberal education. A parallel to another form of justification thus remains, and the concept continues to warrant its label as that of an education that frees the mind from error and illusion. Further, as the determination of the good life is now considered to be itself the pursuit of a particular form of rational knowledge, that in which what ought to be done is justified by the giving of reasons, this is seen as a necessary part of a liberal education. And as all other forms of knowledge contribute in their way to moral understanding, the concept as a whole is once more given a kind of justification in its importance for the moral life. But this justification, like that of objectivity, no longer has the distinct significance which it once had, for it is again simply a necessary consequence of what the pursuit of knowledge entails. Nevertheless, liberal education remains basic to the freeing of human conduct from wrong.

CERTAIN BASIC PHILOSOPHICAL CONSIDERATIONS

Having attempted a reinstatement of the concept without its original philosophical backing, what of the implications of this for the practical conduct of education? In working these out it is necessary first to try to distinguish the various forms of knowledge and then to relate them in some way to the organization of the school or college curriculum. The first of these is a strictly philosophical task. The second is a matter of practical planning that involves many considerations other than the purely philosophical, and to this I will return when certain broad distinctions between forms of knowledge have been outlined.

As stated earlier, by a form of knowledge is meant a distinct way in which our experience becomes structured round the use of accepted public symbols. The symbols thus having public meaning, their use is in some way testable against experience and there is the progressive development of series of tested symbolic expressions. In this way experience has been probed further and further by extending and elaborating the use of the symbols and by means of these it has become possible for the personal experience of individuals to become more fully structured, more fully understood. The various forms of knowledge can be seen in low level developments within the common area of our knowledge of the everyday world. From this there branch out the developed forms which, taking certain elements in our common knowledge as a basis, have grown in distinctive ways. In the developed forms of knowledge the following related distinguishing features can be seen:

(1) They each involve certain central concepts that are peculiar in character to the form. For example, those of gravity, acceleration, hydrogen, and photosynthesis characteristic of the sciences; number, integral and matrix in mathematics; God, sin and predestination in religion; ought, good and wrong in moral knowledge.

(2) In a given form of knowledge these and other concepts that denote, if perhaps in a very complex way, certain aspects of experience, form a network of possible relationships in which experience can be understood. As a result the form has a distinctive logical structure. For example, the terms and statements of mechanics can be meaningfully related in certain strictly limited ways only, and the same is true of historical explanation.

(3) The form, by virtue of its particular terms and logic, has expressions or statements (possibly answering a distinctive type of question) that in some way or other, however indirect it may be, are testable against experience. This is the case in scientific knowledge, moral knowledge, and in the arts, though in the arts no questions are explicit and the criteria for the tests are only partially expressible in words. Each form, then, has distinctive expressions that are testable against experience in accordance with particular criteria that are peculiar to the form.

(4) The forms have developed particular techniques and skills for exploring experience and testing their distinctive expressions, for instance the techniques of the sciences and those of the various literary arts. The result has been the amassing of all the symbolically expressed knowledge that we now have in the arts and the sciences.

Though the various forms of knowledge are distinguishable in these ways it must not be assumed that all there is to them can be made clear and explicit by these means. All knowledge involves the use of symbols and the making of judgments in ways that cannot be expressed in words and can only be learnt in a tradition. The art of scientific investigation and the development of appropriate experimental tests, the forming of an historical explanation and the assessment of its truth, the appreciation of a poem: all of these activities are high arts that are not in themselves communicable simply by words. Acquiring knowledge of any form is therefore to a greater or less extent something that cannot be done simply by solitary study of the symbolic expressions of knowledge, it must be learnt from a master on the job. No doubt it is because the forms require particular training of this kind in distinct worlds of discourse, because they necessitate the development of high critical standards according to complex criteria, because they involve our coming to look at experience in particular ways, that we refer to them as disciplines. They are indeed disciplines that form the mind.

Yet the dividing lines that can be drawn between different disciplines by means of the four suggested distinguishing marks are neither clear enough nor sufficient for demarcating the whole world of modern knowledge as we know it. · The central feature to which they point is that the major forms of knowledge, or disciplines, can each be distinguished by their dependence on some particular kind of test against experience for their distinctive expressions. On this ground alone however certain broad divisions are apparent. The sciences depend crucially on empirical experimental and observational tests, mathematics depends on deductive demonstrations from certain sets of axioms. Similarly moral knowledge and the arts involve distinct forms of critical tests though in these cases both what the tests are and the ways in which they are applied are only partially statable. (Some would in fact dispute the status of the arts as forms of knowledge for this very reason.) Because of their particular logical features it seems to me necessary to distinguish also as separate disciplines both historical and religious knowledge, and there is perhaps an equally good case, because of the nature of their empirical concepts, for regarding the human sciences separately from the physical sciences. But within these areas further distinctions must be made. These are usually the result of the grouping of knowledge round a number of related concepts, or round particular skills or techniques. The various sciences and the various arts can be demarcated within the larger units of which they are in varying degrees representative in their structure, by these means.

But three other important classifications of knowledge must in addition be recognized. First there are those organizations which are not themselves disciplines or subdivisions of any discipline. They are formed by building together round specific objects, or phenomena, or practical pursuits, knowledge that is characteristically rooted elsewhere in more than one discipline. It is not just that these organizations make use of several forms of knowledge, for after all the sciences use mathematics, the arts use historical knowledge and so on. Many of the disciplines borrow from each other. But these organizations are not concerned, as the disciplines are, to validate any one logically distinct form of expression. They are not concerned with developing a particular structuring of experience. They are held together simply by their subject matter, drawing on all forms of knowledge that can contribute to them. Geography, as the study of man in relation to his environment, is an example of a theoretical study of this kind, engineering an example of a practical nature. I see no reason why such organizations of knowledge, which I shall refer to as "fields," should not be endlessly constructed according to particular theoretical or practical interests. Secondly, whilst moral knowledge is a distinct form, concerned with answering questions as to what ought to be done in practical affairs, no specialized subdivisions of this have been developed. In practical affairs, moral questions, because of their character, naturally arise alongside questions of fact and technique, so that there have been formed "fields" of practical knowledge that include distinct moral elements within them, rather than the subdivisions of a particular discipline. Political, legal and educational theory are perhaps the clearest examples of fields where moral knowledge of a developed kind is to be found. Thirdly, there are certain second order forms of knowledge which are dependent for their existence on the other primary areas. On the one hand there are the essentially scientific studies of language and symbolism as in grammar and philology. On the other hand there are the logical and philosophical studies of meaning and justification. These would seem to constitute a distinct discipline by virtue of their particular concepts and criteria of judgment.

In summary, then, it is suggested that the forms of knowledge as we have them can be classified as follows:

(I)   Distinct disciplines or forms of knowledge (subdivisible): mathematics, physical sciences, human sciences, history, religion, literature and the fine arts, philosophy.

(II)   Fields of knowledge: theoretical, practical (these may or may not include elements of moral knowledge).

It is the distinct disciplines that basically constitute the range of unique ways we have of understanding experience if to these is added the category of moral knowledge.

THE PLANNING AND PRACTICAL CONDUCT OF LIBERAL EDUCATION

Turning now to the bearing of this discussion on the planning and conduct of a liberal education, certain very general comments about its characteristic features can be made though detailed treatment would involve psychological and other considerations that are quite beyond the scope of this paper.

In the first place, as liberal education is concerned with the comprehensive development of the mind in acquiring knowledge, it is aimed at achieving an understanding of experience in many different ways. This means the acquisition by critical training and discipline not only of facts but also of complex conceptual schemes and of the arts and techniques of different types of reasoning and judgment. Syllabuses and curricula cannot therefore be constructed simply in terms of information and isolated skills. They must be constructed so as to introduce pupils as far as possible into the interrelated aspects of each of the basic forms of knowledge, each of the several disciplines. And they must be constructed to cover at least in some measure the range of knowledge as a whole.

In a program of liberal education that is based directly on the study of the specific disciplines, examples of each of the different areas must of course be chosen. Selection of this kind is not however simply an inevitable practical consequence of the vast growth of knowledge. It is equaly in keeping with what a liberal education is aiming at. Though its aim is comprehensive it is not after the acquisition of encyclopedic information. Nor is it after the specialist knowledge of the person fully trained in all the particular details of a branch of knowledge. Such a specialist can not only accurately employ the concepts, logic and criteria of a domain but also knows the skills and techniques involved in the pursuit of knowledge quite beyond the immediate areas of common human experience. Nor is liberal education concerned with the technician's knowledge of the detailed application of the disciplines in practical and theoretical fields. What is being sought is, first, sufficient immersion in the concepts, logic and criteria of the discipline for a person to come to know the distinctive way in which it "works" by pursuing these in particular cases; and then sufficient generalization of these over the whole range of the discipline so that his experience begins to be widely structured in this distinctive manner. It is this coming to look at things in a certain way that is being aimed at, not the ability to work out in minute particulars all the details that can in fact be discerned. It is the ability to recognize empirical assertions or aesthetic judgments for what they are, and to know the kind of considerations on which their validity will depend, that matters. Beyond this an outline of the major achievements in each area provides some grasp of the range and scope of experience that has thus become intelligible. Perhaps this kind of understanding is in fact most readily distinguishable in the literary arts as critical appreciation in contrast to the achievement of the creative writer or the literary hack. But the distinction is surely applicable to other forms of knowledge as well.

This is not to assert that "critical appreciation" in any form of knowledge can be adequately achieved without some development of the understanding of the specialist or technician. Nor is it to imply that this understanding in the sciences, the arts or moral issues can be had without participation in many relevant creative and practical pursuits. The extent to which this is true will vary from discipline to discipline and is in fact in need of much investigation, particularly because of its importance for moral and aesthetic education. But it is to say that the aim of the study of a discipline in liberal education is not that of its study in a specialist or technical course. The first is concerned with developing a person's ways of understanding experience, the others are concerned with mastering the details of knowledge, how it is established, and the use of it in other enterprises, particularly those of a practical nature. It is of course perfectly possible for a course in physics, for example, to be devoted to a double purpose if it is deliberately so designed. It may provide both a specialist knowledge of the subject and at the same time a genuine introduction to the form of scientific knowledge. But the two purposes are quite distinct and there is no reason to suppose that by aiming at one the other can automatically be achieved as well. Yet it would seem to be true that some specialist study within a discipline, if it is at all typical of the discipline, is necessary to understanding the form of knowledge in any developed sense. The study of a discipline as part of liberal education, however, contributes practically nothing directly to any specialist study of it, though it does serve to put the specialism into a much wider context.

A liberal education approached directly in terms of the disciplines will thus be composed of the study of at least paradigm examples of all the various forms of knowledge. Thus study will be sufficiently detailed and sustained to give genuine insight so that pupils come to think in these terms, using the concepts, logic and criteria accurately in the different domains. It will then include generalization of the particular examples used so as to show the range of understanding in the various forms. It will also include some indication of the relations between the forms where these overlap and their significance in the major fields of knowledge, particularly the practical fields, that have been developed. This is particularly important for moral education, as moral questions can frequently be solved only by calling on the widest possible range of human understanding. As there is in fact no developed discipline of moral knowledge, education in moral understanding must necessarily be approached in a rather different way. For if it is to cover more than everyday personal matters this has to be by the study of issues that occur in certain particular fields of knowledge. The major difficulty this presents will be referred to briefly later. The important point here is that though moral understanding has to be pursued in contexts where it is not the only dominant interest, the aim of its pursuit is precisely the same as for all other elements in a liberal education, the understanding of experience in a unique way. What is wanted (just as in the study of the disciplines *per se*) is, basically, the use of the appropriate concepts, logic, and criteria, and the appreciation of the range of understanding in this form.

It is perhaps important to stress the fact that this education will be one in the forms of knowledge themselves and not merely a self-conscious philosophical treatment of their characteristics. Scientific and historical knowledge are wanted, not knowledge of the philosophy of science and the philosophy of history as substitutes. A liberal education can only be planned if distinctions in the forms of knowledge are clearly understood, and that is a philosophical matter. But the education itself is only partly in philosophy, and that is only possible when pupils have some grasp of the other disciplines themselves.

Precisely what sections of the various disciplines are best suited to the aims of liberal education cannot be gone into here. It is apparent that on philosophical grounds alone some branches of the sciences, for instance, would seem to be much more satisfactory as paradigms of scientific thinking than others. Many sections of physics are probably more comprehensive and clear in logical character, more typical of the well developed physical sciences than, say, botany. If so, they would, all other things being equal, serve better as an introduction to scientific knowledge. Perhaps in literature and the fine arts the paradigm principle is less easy to apply though probably many would favor a course in literature to any one other. But whatever the discipline, in practice all other things are not in fact equal and decisions about the content of courses cannot be taken without careful regard to the abilities and interests of the students for whom they are designed.

Yet hovering round such decisions and questions of syllabus planning there is frequently found the belief that the inherent logical structure of a discipline, or a branch of a discipline necessarily determines exactly what and exactly how the subject is to be taught and learnt. The small amount of truth and the large amount of error in this belief can only be distinguished by clarifying what the logic of a subject is. It is not a series of intellectual steps that must be climbed in strict order. It is not a specific psychological channel along which the mind must travel if there is to be understanding. This is to confuse logical characteristics with psychological processes. The logic of a form of knowledge shows the meaningful and valid ways in which its terms and criteria are used. It constitutes the publicly accepted framework of knowledge. The psychological activities of the individual when concerned with this knowledge are not in general prescribed in any temporal order and the mind, as it were, plays freely within and around the framework. It is simply that the framework lays down the general formal relations of the concepts if there is to be knowledge. The logic as publicly expressed consists of the general and formal principles to which the terms must conform in knowledge. Coming to understand a form of knowledge involves coming to think in relations that satisfy the public criteria. How the mind plays round and within these is not itself being laid down at all, there is no dragooning of psychological processes, only a marking out of the territory in which the mind can wander more or less at will. Indeed understanding a form of knowledge is far more like coming to know a country than climbing a ladder. Some places in a territory may only be get-at-able by a single specified route and some forms of knowledge may have concepts and relations that cannot be understood without first understanding certain others. But that countries are explorable only in one way is in general false, and even in mathematics, the most strictly sequential form of knowledge we have, many ways of coming to know the territory are possible. The logic of a subject is relevant to what is being taught, for its patterns must be accepted as essential to the form of knowledge. But how those patterns are best discerned is a matter for empirical investigation.

School subjects in the disciplines as we at present have them are in no way sacrosanct on either logical or psychological grounds. They are necessarily selections from the forms of knowledge that we have and may or may not be good as introductions for the purposes of liberal education. In most cases they have developed under a number of diverse influences. The historical growth of the subjects has sometimes dominated the programs. The usefulness of certain elements, the demands of higher specialist education, certain general "psychological" principles such as progressing from the simple to the complex, from the particular to the general, the concrete to the abstract, all these factors and many others have left their marks. This being so, many well established courses need to be critically re-examined both philosophically and psychologically before they can be accepted as suitable for liberal education. Superficially at least most of them would seem to be quite inappropriate for this purpose.

Though a liberal education is most usually approached directly in the study of various branches of the disciplines, I see no reason to think that this must necessarily be so. It is surely possible to construct programs that are in the first place organized round certain fields of knowledge either theoretical or practical. The study of aspects of power, natural as well as social and political, might for instance be one element in such a scheme: or a regional study that introduces historical, geographical, industrial and social considerations: or a practical project of design and building involving the sciences, mathematics and visual arts. In this case, however, it must be recognized that the fields are chosen because together they can be used to develop understanding of all the various forms of knowledge, and explicit steps must be taken to see that this end is achieved. There will necessarily be the strongest tendency for liberal education to be lost sight of and for the fields to be pursued in their own right developing the techniques and skills which they need. These may be valuable and useful in many ways, and perhaps essential in many a person's whole education. (Certainly liberal education as is here being understood is only one part of the education a person ought to have, for it omits quite deliberately for instance specialist education, physical education and character training.) But a course in various fields of knowledge will not in fact be a liberal education unless that aim is kept absolutely clear and every opportunity is taken to lead to a fuller grasp of the disciplines. Again some fields of study will be better for this purpose than others but all will demand the highest skill from the teacher, who must be under no misapprehension as to what the object of the exercise really is. Yet it is difficult to see how this kind of approach can be fully adequate if it does not in the end lead to a certain amount of study of the distinct disciplines themselves. For whatever ground may have been covered indirectly, a satisfactory understanding of the characteristically distinct approaches of the different forms is hardly possible without some direct gathering together of the elements of the disciplines that have been implicit in all that has been done.

Whatever the pattern of a liberal education in its later stages, it must not be forgotten that there is being presupposed a broad basic education in the common area of everyday knowledge where the various disciplines can be seen in embryo and from which they branch out as distinct units. In such a basic primary education, the ever growing range of a child's experience and the increasing use of linguistic and symbolic forms lays the foundation for the various modes of understanding, scientific, historical, religious, moral, and so on. Out of this general pool of knowledge the disciplines have slowly become ever more differentiated and it is this that the student must come to understand, not confusing the forms of knowledge but appreciating them for what they are in themselves, and recognizing their necessary limitations.

But is then the outcome of a liberal education to be simply the achievement of a series of discreet ways of understanding experience? In a very real sense yes, but in another sense not entirely. For one thing, we have as yet not begun to understand the complex interrelations of the different forms of knowledge themselves, for they do not only have unique features but common features too, and in addition one discipline often makes extensive use of the achievements of another. But we must also not forget that the various forms are firmly rooted in that common world of persons and things which we all share, and into this they take back in subtle as well as simple ways the understanding they have achieved. The outcome of a liberal education must therefore not be thought of as producing ever greater disintegration of the mind but rather the growth of ever clearer and finer distinctions in our experience. If the result is not some quasi-aesthetic unity of the mind neither is it in any sense chaos. Perhaps the most suggestive picture of the outcome is that used by Professor Michael Oakeshott, though for him it has more literal truth than is here intended. In this the various forms of knowledge are seen as voices in a conversation, a conversation to which they each contribute in a distinctive way. If taken figuratively, his words express more succinctly than mine can precisely what it seems to me a liberal education is and what its outcome will be.

As civilized human beings, we are the inheritors, neither of an inquiry about ourselves and the world, nor of an accumulating body of information, but of a conversation, begun in the primeval forests and extended and made more articulate in the course of centuries. It is a conversation which goes on both in public and within each of ourselves. Of course there is argument and inquiry and information, but wherever these are profitable they are to be recognized as passages in this conversation, and perhaps they are not the most captivating of the passages. . . . Conversation is not an enterprise designed to yield an extrinsic profit, a contest where a winner gets a prize, nor is it an activity of exegesis; it is an unrehearsed intellectual adventure. . . . Education, properly speaking, is an initiation into the skill and partnership of this conversation in which we learn to recognize the voices, to distinguish the proper occasions of utterance, and in which we acquire the intellectual and moral habits appropriate to conversation. And it is this conversation which, in the end, gives place and character to every human activity and utterance.[8]

NOTES

1. *General Education in a Free Society.* Report of the Harvard Committee (London: Oxford University Press, 1946).

2. *Ibid.,* p. 58.

3. *Ibid.,* pp. 64–65.

4. *Ibid.,* pp. 65–73.

5. *Ibid.,* p. 67.

6. Precisely the same criticisms might be made of some remarks by Professor P. H. Nowell-Smith in his inaugural lecture, *Education in a University* (Leicester University Press, 1958), pp. 6–11. In these he suggests that the prime purpose of the study of literature, history and philosophy is that each develops one of the central powers of the mind—creative imagination, practical wisdom, and logical thought. Once more we are up against the question of the definition of these "powers" and if that problem can be solved, the question of sheer evidence for them and the way they can be developed.

7. *Arts and Science Sides in the Sixth Form.* Gulbenkian Foundation Report (Oxford University Department of Education, 1960), p. 15.

8. Michael Oakeshott, *Rationalism in Politics and Other Essays* (London: Methuen, 1962), pp. 198–99.

13. PHILOSOPHICAL ISSUES IN THE VOCATIONAL-LIBERAL STUDIES CONTROVERSY (1900−1917): JOHN DEWEY vs. THE SOCIAL EFFICIENCY PHILOSOPHERS[1]

Arthur G. Wirth

The question is whether or not our beautiful, libertarian, pluralist and populist experiment is viable in modern conditions.

Paul Goodman*

By looking at the set of forces in contention in the vocational education movement (1900−1917), we can see more than how technology acts as a pressure for institutional change. We can see something about the conflict of the two Americas we, in fact, have become in the hundred years since the Civil War: the America which defines its aspirations in terms of the blind drive for an increase in material goods, and that other America which Paul Goodman has described as the "libertarian, pluralist and populist experiment."

To be blunt and to oversimplify, the choice then and now is whether schools are to become servants of technocratic efficiency needs, or whether they can act to help men humanize life under technology.

In the liberal-vocational studies debate prior to Smith-Hughes, the technocratic drives of what Paul Goodman calls the Empty Society of mindless pro-

SOURCE. *Studies in Philosophy and Education* 8 (No. 3, 1974), pp. 169—82. Reprinted by permission of *Studies in Philosophy and Education,* Southern Illinois University, Edwardsville, Illinois.

People or Personnel and *Like a Conquered Province* (New York: Alfred A. Knopf, Vintage Books, 1968), p. 274.

ductivity showed in the social efficiency philosophy of David Snedden and Charles Prosser. On the other hand, John Dewey tried to define an approach that would combine democratic and humanistic values with science and industry. This paper aims to compare the two philosophical models which grew out of that debate.[2]

First, a word about the vocational or industrial education movement. In the loose sense it refers to the various pressures on schools to introduce offerings to meet complex skill needs of an industrial America including phenomena like manual training, commercial and agricultural education, home economics, and trade-training courses. In a narrower sense it refers to the drive to win federal support for vocational education in the period 1906–1917. This movement began with two events: the Massachusetts report of Governor Douglas's Commission on Vocational Education, and the founding of the National Society for the Promotion of Industrial Education. It culminated in the passage of the Smith-Hughes Act (1917). By the end of the second decade of the twentieth century we had enacted federal legislation to support vocational training programs—and this innovation was made possible by the coordinated support of interest groups as diverse as the National Association of Manufacturers, the Chamber of Commerce, the American Federation of Labor, major farm organizations, and the Settlement House leaders.

Spokesmen for the social efficiency philosophy played leading roles in this development. David Snedden[3] left a professorship at Teachers College Columbia University to become Commissioner of Education under Governor Douglas in Massachusetts. His major role was to introduce a separate system of vocational education. He appointed his colleague Charles Prosser as his deputy to create and administer the new vocational programs. Snedden was a voluminous writer and one of the founders of the new discipline of educational sociology. He was listed by Norman Woelfel as one of the seventeen leaders in American education who were "Molders of the American Mind," and he was the first editor of *The American Vocational Journal*.

Charles Prosser[4] became Executive Secretary of the National Society for the Promotion of Industrial Education (N.S.P.I.E.) in 1912 and had the organizational genius to bring together the coalition of groups to make possible the enactment of the Smith-Hughes Act. He was, in fact, the effective author of the act. (His son, in an interview in St. Louis, remembered seeing his father write the first draft of Smith-Hughes at the table in their dining room.) He became Director of the famous Dunwoody Institute of Vocational Training in Minneapolis and was the first Executive Director of the Federal Board of Vocational Education. In 1945 he was author of the Prosser Life-Adjustment Resolution, which launched the ill-fated movement bearing that name.

THE SOCIAL EFFICIENCY PHILOSOPHERS

Beginning in the late 90s the National Association of Manufacturers became a powerful force advocating the addition of a vocational component to the school system. The Association had formed as a result of the 1893 depression. Its members soon identified as the cause of their problems a serious overproduction which had accompanied frenzied post-Civil War industrial expansion. Catastrophe, they felt, would be their lot if they limited themselves to the demands of the domestic market. New opportunities lay overseas in Latin America and Asia. Their salvation lay in entering the international economic arena. As they ventured out they found tough competition from aggressive German businessmen. Soon they sent emissaries to Germany to assess the source of German effectiveness. Their analysts reported that one critical source of German advantage was the existence of a powerful set of carefully-designed skill-training programs. There were, for example, twenty-one different schools for the building trades alone; there were *Werkmeisterschulen* for foremen and research-oriented *Technische Hochschulen* for engineers at the top. This finely-graded set of training programs was neatly meshed to the hierarchical skill needs of the technological system. It was administered by the Ministry of Commerce rather than Education so that it could be run by practical men rather than fuzzy-minded educators. American manufacturers became convinced that they could compete successfully only if the American school system introduced a set of separate vocational schools patterned after the German model.

David Snedden and Charles Prosser in their work and writings developed the theoretical rationale for the technocratic model. It was marked by a conservative social philosophy, a methodology of specific training operations based on principles of S-R psychology, a curriculum designed according to a job analysis of the needs of industry, and by a preference for a separately-administered set of vocational schools.

Snedden shared the basic faith of Herbert Spencer and the conservative Social Darwinists that the emergence of scientific-corporate capitalism was the cosmic instrument for progress. He accepted the basic proposition of the manufacturers that what was good for business was good for America. In order to help more Americans enjoy progress, the task of education was to aid the economy to function as efficiently as possible—"To make each child a better socius," a more fit member of a complex society.

His social philosophy was reflected in his recommendation for the teaching of history. The job was to define the kind of citizen we wanted for the well-functioning society, then extrapolate the specific forms of training which would produce this type. The history teacher, he said, has a heavy obligation to present the opinions of the controlling majority—or withdraw from teaching. If a teacher held minority views he should suppress them and express the position of the majority.

Snedden worked from an assumption about the nature of social life which he borrowed from his sociology teacher Franklin Giddings:

Society, like the material world . . . passes from homogeneity and indefiniteness of non-organization to the heterogeneity and definiteness of organization. The process of selection *is based upon the differences growing out of the unequal conditions of both heredity and nurture to which man is born.* Inequality—physical, mental, and moral—is an inevitable characteristic of the social population.[5]

Snedden put the same idea in his own words in the 1920s when he likened the good society to a winning "team group." A team is made stronger by specialization of functions. Some, like the officers on a submarine crew, would be trained to lead and coordinate; others would be trained for their special functions in the ranks.[6]

Snedden argued that the ultimate aim of education was "the greatest degree of efficiency." We could afford to permit the universities to continue to provide inadequate education for the professionals and the leadership class, he said; but we could not tolerate the failure of lower schools to provide for "those who do duty in the ranks . . . who will follow, not lead." Efficiency for "the rank and file" meant "not only training for culture's sake, but that utilitarian training which looks to individual efficiency in the world of work." Training in the trades and business, Snedden said, was a legitimate obligation of public education. The "old educator" relied on Greek, Latin, and mathematics. This curriculum, more than poverty or the lure of employment, was what drove children from school. The "new education," he predicted, would be an elective program that included both a variety of child interests and a regimen designed to fit the child to his place in society. It would lead the child "toward the realities of present life"; and when the child was properly "fitted," he would possess "such an intelligent understanding or authority as (to) make the exercise of arbitrary authority unnecessary."[7]

Fortunately, as Snedden saw it, human beings fall into ability levels which parallel the hierarchical work requirements of modern society. New scientific testing instruments combined with vocational guidance would make it possible for schools to do what Charles Eliot had suggested in 1907—differentiate children into programs according to their "probable destinies" based on heredity plus economic and social factors. The new junior high schools would perform the task of sorting students into differentiated courses: prevocational offerings in commercial subjects, industrial arts, and agricultural or household arts for those "who most incline to them or have need of them."[8]

Frederick Fish, President of AT&T and Chairman of the Massachusetts Board of Education, was impressed by the vision of his Commissioner of Education. In 1910 Fish echoed Snedden in calling the schools to revise their values by providing training to meet "the practical needs of life" for "the rank and file."[9]

The Snedden-Fish regime was prepared to act as well as talk. Snedden appointed his Teachers College colleague Charles Prosser to develop a system of vocational schools for the major industrial centers of the state.

By 1912, when Prosser became Executive Secretary of The National Society for the Promotion of Industrial Education (N.S.P.I.E.), he had clarified his goal: to reject the impractical manual training of the general educators and replace it with "real vocational education," by which he meant training for useful employment—train the person to get a job, train him so he could hold it and advance to a better job.[10]

Prosser insisted that all of vocational content must be specific and that its source was to be found "in the experience of those who have mastered the occupation." Throughout his long career, Prosser repeated endlessly the arguments for his position. Traditional scholastic education, he maintained, aimed to prepare the citizen for the worthy use of leisure time. Traditional schoolmen, committed to the task of fostering "leisure culture," operated from the discredited psychological tradition of faculty psychology and formal discipline. There were several clear reasons why new programs of vocational training could not be entrusted to such men. "Culturists" were cut off from the practical world of work, and their outmoded theory of learning made them incapable of managing genuine skill-training programs. "Vocational education," Prosser argued, "only functions in proportion as it will enable an individual actually to do a job. . . . Vocational education must establish habits: habits of correct thinking and of correct doing. Hence, its fundamental theory must be that of habit psychology."[11] The new scientific psychology pioneered by Edward Thorndike, said Prosser, assumed that the mind is a habit-forming machine. There was an obvious fit between this psychological theory and vocational education when the latter was conceived as "essentially a matter of establishing certain habits through repetitive training both in thinking and doing."[12] In contrast to the theory of general mind-training, Thorndike's theory taught that "all habits of doing and thinking are developed in specific situations." Prosser deduced correlatively that the content of vocational training should be determined by "the actual functioning content" of a given occupation. "If you want to train a youth to be an efficient plumber, you must select the actual experiences in the practice of the plumbing trade that he should have and see that he gets these in a real instead of a pseudo way."[13] Furthermore, general studies like mathematics or science should be broken into short units which would bear "directly on specific needs of workers in the performance of specific tasks or operations." They should, when possible, be taught by the craftsman-teacher skilled in the task, rather than by general mathematics or science teachers.

A prototype of the plan favored by Prosser was established in the short unit courses which he developed while Director of the Dunwoody Institute in Minneapolis. "In garment making, one unit might deal with kimonos, one with underwear, and another with house dresses."[14] At the Dunwoody Institute, units were programmed in great detail to lead students step-by-step through the skill development cycle. Students punched in on time clocks, and instructors behaved like shop foremen rather than public school teachers. A no-nonsense attitude prevailed. If students were not punctual, orderly, and efficient, they were asked to leave.

If this brief description of Dunwoody conveys a feeling of Prosser's orientation, some of the features he wrote into Smith-Hughes can readily be understood. Approved programs had to meet the criterion of "fitting for useful employment" persons over fourteen but under college age who were preparing for work on farms, in trades, in industrial pursuits, and the like. Federal funds were given only for support of vocational training classes. General education costs were to be borne by the states and local school districts. At least fifty percent of subsidized instruction had to be devoted to "practical work on a useful or productive basis." Funds for the training of teachers were restricted to those who "have had adequate vocational experience or contact in the line of work for which they are preparing."[15]

Since his rationale excluded general educators from the management of vocational training, Prosser fought as long as possible for a separately-administered type of vocational education. In the final politicking prior to 1917, he had to make some concessions; but, in the main, he created a framework which permitted vocational programs to stand apart. The Smith-Hughes Act did establish a Federal Board for Vocational Education, separate from the United States Office of Education and responsible only to Congress. The seven-member Board consisted of the Secretaries of Labor, Commerce, and Agriculture and three citizens representing labor, agriculture, and manufacturing. The Commissioner of Education was added to allay the anxieties of the N.E.A.[16]

Prosser was immediately appointed Executive Director of the Federal Board and served in that office in its first two crucial years. He established the initial tone of administration. States were given the option of setting up separate boards, or of administering vocational education under the aegis of their general boards of education. In actuality, both the language of Smith-Hughes and the administrative style of Dr. Prosser assured that vocational education would function as a separate aspect of education within the states. The genius of Charles Prosser lay in his capacity to create well-tooled manpower training programs. Somewhere in a technological society that task must be done.

DEWEY'S POSITION

Snedden, Prosser and Dewey were part of a general reform movement which assumed that traditional schooling would have to give way to approaches more relevant to new social-economic conditions. On the surface there were points of agreement. They all condemned "sterile, bookish education." All were convinced that city schools were isolated from the life-concerns of urban children. All three wanted to broaden the curriculum to include studies appropriate to a technological era. Just below the surface, however, there were profound differences. Dewey was quite aware of the disagreements, but Snedden was hurt and bewildered when Dewey lashed out at him for his advocacy of separate vocational schools. Snedden expressed his sense of betrayal in a letter to *The New Republic* in which he said that those who had been seeking sound vocational education had become accustomed to opposition from the academic brethren. "But to find Dr. Dewey apparently giving aid and comfort to opponents of a broader, richer, and more effective program of education . . . is discouraging."[17]

If Snedden expected Dewey to relent, he was in for disappointment. Dewey replied sharply that his differences with Snedden were profoundly social and political as well as educational.

The kind of vocational education in which I am interested in is not one which will "adapt" workers to the existing industrial regime; I am not sufficiently in love with the regime for that. It seems to me that the business of all who would not be educational time-savers is to resist every move in this direction, and to strive for a kind of vocational education which will first alter the existing industrial system, and ultimately transform it.[18]

Furthermore, Dewey charged that Snedden had failed to meet the heart of his argument on pedagogical matters: "I argued that a separation of trade education and general education of youth has the inevitable tendency to make both kinds of training narrower and less significant than the schooling in which the traditional education is reorganized to utilize the subject matter—active, scientific, and social of the present day environment."[19]

Dewey was right—the differences were profoundly social and political as well as educational. Snedden and Prosser, operating from Social Darwinist assumptions, viewed individuals as isolated units with varying capacities and potentials; if each pursued his own advantage, a rough sorting out would take place which would coincide with the skill and status needs of a hierarchically-organized work world. The schools could aid the process by scientific counseling. Differentiated skill-training programs, designed in terms of emerging needs of industry and business, would provide the kind of trained manpower required by the corporate system. The emerging American industrial democracy would provide opportunity for everyone to have an equal chance to run for the prizes—and all could have a share in an ever-growing material prosperity. If that was not what the "American dream" was all about, then what was it? Snedden and Prosser were simply mystified by those who were so astigmatic as to look at the new scene and come away with doubts and misgivings—or with fear and trembling.

Dewey, of course, had a very different conception of the nature of the person and the problems of democratic traditions in the technological society. He rejected the image of isolated individuals moved by the play of natural forces in the marketplace. He operated from the social psychology position of his colleague George H. Mead—with its self-other concept of personality. The self was seen as emerging from both the patterning of culture plus the value choices of the individual. The premise held that, if you wanted persons with qualities capable of sustaining democratic values, they had to be nourished in communities marked by such values. The problem as Dewey saw it was whether democratic values of meaningful participation and respect for persons could be sustained under urban-corporate conditions. People were beginning to repeat the rhetoric of democratic values while living in daily contradiction of them. This produced individuals wasted by neurotic conflicts, incapable of sustaining meaningful freedoms.

The task of overcoming the contradictions, as Dewey defined it, was to develop strategies for bringing qualities of the democratic ethos into institutions being transformed by science, technology and corporatism. Dewey rejected elitist answers. His general strategy was to seek means by which the qualities of mind, required to reform institutions, could be made available across the entire population.

In his design the schools were assigned a critical role: they could help the young gain insights as to how human experience was being transformed by science, technology, and economic corporatism; they could teach the hypothetical mode of thought required to handle complex problems; the schools themselves could be turned into communities where the young in living and learning would experience the life qualities exemplified in the creative work of scientists and artists. By spending the years of childhood and youth in such learning communities, the young might become the kind of persons who could change institutional life styles so they would serve to liberate persons rather than manipulate them as functionaries.

While Dewey and the progressives no doubt had exaggerated hopes for schools as agents of reform, it is not true that Dewey expected the school to do it single-handedly. The meliorist philosophy assumed that institutional reform would have to go on across the board. For example, the critical, evaluative quality would manifest itself in muckraking journalism and scholarship; the formation of unions would counter the helplessness of individual workers and create union bases of power and criticism to make changes in the quality of work-life and product (a hope at odds with the later myopic quality of some unions who became content to collaborate with employers in simply milking consumers).

The move would be in the direction of creating persons capable of producing "the planning society" in which each institution would be evaluated by whether modes of operating contributed to the growth of persons. This was to take the place of an exploitative economic system which let all consequences flow from a senseless pursuit of profits.

With concerns like these why would Dewey get seriously involved with the vocational education movement? The importance Dewey attached to the relation of vocational to liberal studies is evidenced by a generally-overlooked passage in *Democracy and Education:* "At the present time the conflict of philosophic theories focuses in the discussion of the proper place and function of vocational factors in education . . . *significant differences in fundamental philosophical concepts find their chief issue in connection with this point.*"[20]

I shall note only several examples of Dewey's complex argument that new integrations of technological or vocational studies with liberal studies could serve to revitalize school learning and eventually aid in social transformation.

First, he worked from a premise rooted in the new sociology and economics, namely, that the basic mode employed in producing life-necessities had a pervasive effect on all social institutions and on qualities of selfhood. Thus, when there were shifts from a hunting-and-gathering to a pastoral or to agricultural economies, then modes of governing, defending and educating would change. New expressions in the arts, religion and philosophy were inevitable. As men entered the twentieth century they were well into one of the great transition periods—with expansion of scientific thought and technique as the great change factor. A distinctive feature of Dewey's philosophy was his conviction that human renewal might be engendered from within the very culture of science, which also posed major threats. (This aspect of Dewey's thought is generally scorned today, but it continues to be shared by radicals like Paul Goodman and George Dennison.)[21]

Pedagogically Dewey placed the occupations at the heart of the program of his Laboratory School. Children, for example, could get the feeling of how science and technology had affected such a basic process as the turning of raw wool into clothing by first trying the process by hand and then observing factory methods. They could study also what the social and human effects were when men moved from handicraft to corporate industrial modes of production. The doing and the intellectualizing phases of such projects should be conducted so that children would get the feel of the scientific mode of inquiry that underlay the process—the hypothetical style of holding ideas, and reporting and testing them in a climate of openness.

Secondly, he argued that chances to take part in the "doing" aspects of such studies would offer an alternative to the ancient tradition of equating education with lesson-saying in classrooms. In his Laboratory School children worked at weaving, cooking, constructing, gardening. Studies in the sciences, history, language, mathematics and the arts were related to these activities. As students grew older activities and studies could be extended to the out-of-school community. Thus Dewey developed an interest in the Gary Plan, where children combined science study with experiences in the school steam plant or in the steel mills of the town. Dewey was drawn, too, to the polytechnical education concepts in the U.S.S.R. in the 20s and the reforms of rural education in the *escuelas de acción* of the Mexican Revolution. Currently such programs as the New Jersey Technology for Children Project, the work of the Center for Technological Education in the San Francisco Bay Area, the Parkway Plan in Philadelphia, and the University Without Walls experiments would contain features related to Dewey's rationale.

Thirdly, there was the valuational aspect. In *Individualism Old and New* and elsewhere he made his economic critique in which he argued that the single-minded pursuit of profit of a laissez-faire economy involved a tragic misuse of the power of science and technology. Children and the young had to be educated so as to learn how to examine the consequences of technology. He stated the criterion they should learn to employ in an often-quoted statement in *Reconstruction in Philosophy:*

All social institutions have a meaning, a purpose. That purpose is to set free and to develop the capacities of human individuals without respect to race, sex, class or economic status. . . . (The) test of their value is the extent to which they educate every individual into the full stature of his possibility. Democracy has many meanings, but if it has a moral meaning, it is found in resolving that *the supreme test of all political institutions and industrial arrangements shall be the contribution they make to the all-around growth of every member of a society.*[22]

The goal was to develop a populace who would take that criterion seriously and apply it to all institutions.

With a rationale like this Dewey joined those who resisted the pressures for a dual system in the vocational education movement. The only defensible approach, Dewey argued, was to incorporate a new kind of industrial education—as part of general education reform—whose aim would be to cultivate "industrial intelligence" throughout the population.

A general education designed to promote industrial intelligence would provide a genuine alternative to German dualism:

Instead of trying to split schools into two kinds, one of a trade type for children whom it is assumed are to be employees and one of a liberal type for the children of the well-to-do, it will aim at such a reorganization of existing schools as will give all pupils a genuine respect for useful work, an ability to render service, and a contempt for social parasites whether they are called tramps or leaders of "society". . . . It will indeed make much of developing motor and manual skill, but not of a routine or automatic type. It will rather utilize active and manual pursuits as the means of developing constructive, inventive and creative power of mind. It will select the materials and the technique of the trades not for the sake of producing skilled workers for hire in definite trades, but for the sake of securing industrial intelligence—a knowledge of the conditions and processes of present manufacturing, transportation and commerce so that the individual may be able to make his own choices and his own adjustments, and be master, so far as in him lies, of his own economic fate. It will be recognized that, for this purpose, a broad acquaintance with science and skill in the laboratory control of materials and processes is more important than skill in trade operations. It will remember that the future employee is a consumer as well as a producer, that the whole tendency of society, so far as it is intelligent and wholesome, is to an increase of the hours of leisure, and that an education which does nothing to enable individuals to consume wisely and to utilize leisure wisely is a fraud on democracy. So far as method is concerned, such a conception of industrial education will prize freedom more than docility; initiative more than automatic skill; insight and understanding more than capacity to recite lessons or to execute tasks under the direction of others.[23]

Neither Congress nor the people were of a mind to heed such talk. By 1917, the urgent need to increase military production provided the special motivation required to spur federal action. Congress and the President gave Charles Prosser and his colleagues the measure for which they had worked so long and hard.

As we approach the last decades of the twentieth century a major challenge for all societies is to create life styles which will overcome the divorce of technology from humanistic concerns. If we make it, educational reform and social renewal will go on together. The emergence of educational experiments aimed at providing humanizing experiences with technology will be one kind of sign. The flourishing of bland, well-engineered school efforts to serve narrow technocratic efficiency needs will be a counterindication. The inner conflict over which kind of society Americans want to create with the power of science and technology continues—only the stakes are getting higher.

NOTES

1. The material for this article came from research originally sponsored by the U.S. Office of Education and which I subsequently rewrote for publication in *Education in the Technological Society: The Vocational-Liberal Studies Controversy in the Early Twentieth Century* (New York: Intext Educational Publishers, 1972).

2. I have tried a more complete account of this story, in Arthur G. Wirth, *Education in the Technological Society* (Scranton, Pa.: The International Textbook Co., 1972). This study was based on a report for the U.S. Office of Education, *The Vocational-Liberal Studies Controversy between John Dewey and Others* [1906–1917], 1971.

3. Snedden's biography has been ably written by Walter Drost, *David Snedden and Education for Social Efficiency* (Madison, Wis.: University of Wisconsin Press, 1967).

4. See John Gadell, "Charles Allen Prosser: His Work in Vocational and General Education," Ph.D. dissertation, Washington University, St. Louis, 1972.

5. Franklin Giddings, *Principles of Sociology* (New York: The Macmillan Co., 1896), p. 9.

6. David Snedden, "Education for a World of Team Players and Team Workers," *School and Society* 20 (1 November 1924): 554—56.

7. See Drost, *David Snedden,* pp. 42—45.

8. David Snedden, "Differences among Varying Groups of Children Should Be Recognized," *N.E.A. Addresses and Proceedings,* 29 June-3 July 1908, p. 753.

9. Frederick P. Fish, "The Vocational and Industrial School," *N.E.A. Proceedings,* 1910, pp. 367—68.

10. Charles A. Prosser and Thomas H. Quigley, *Vocational Education in a Democracy.* Rev. ed. (Chicago: American Technical Society, 1950), pp.454—55.

11. *Ibid.,* pp. 215—20 *et passim.*

12. *Ibid.,* p. 216.

13. *Ibid.,* p. 228.

14. *Ibid.,* p. 291.

15. *Smith-Hughes Act of 1917,* in U.S. *Statutes at Large,* XXXIX, Part I, pp. 929—36.

16. Melvin Barlow, *History of Industrial Education in the United States* (Peoria, Ill.: Charles A. Bennett Co., 1967), pp. 114—15.

17. David Snedden in *The New Republic* 3 (5 May 1915), p. 40.

18. John Dewey in *The New Republic* 3 (5 May 1915), p. 42.

19. *Ibid.*

20. John Dewey, *Democracy and Education* (New York: The Macmillan Co., 1916), p. 358 (italics mine).

21. See, for example, Paul Goodman, "Can Technology Be Humane?" *The New York Review of Books* (20 November 1969): 27—34, and *Like a Conquered Province* (New York: Random House, Vintage Books, 1968). Also George Dennison, *Lives of Children* (New York: Random House, 1969), pp. 267—70.

22. John Dewey, *Reconstruction in Philosophy* (New York: The American Library, Mentor Books, 1950), p. 147 (italics mine).

23. John Dewey, "Learning to Earn," in *Education Today* (New York: G. P. Putnam's Sons, 1940), pp. 131—32.

CHAPTER **3**

How Should Knowledge Be Selected and Organized for the Curriculum?

I have said that all branches of knowledge are connected together, because the subject matter of knowledge is intimately united in itself, as being the acts and the work of the Creator. Hence, it is that the sciences, into which our knowledge may be said to be cast, have multiplied bearings one on another, and an internal sympathy, and admit, or rather demand, comparison and adjustment. They complete, correct, balance each other. This consideration, if well founded, must be taken into account, not only as regards the attainment of truth, which is their common end, but as regards the influence which they exercise upon those whose education consists in the study of them.

John Henry Cardinal Newman
Discourse V, Knowledge Its Own End

It is generally recognized by educators and laymen alike that knowledge is the stock-in-trade of the school. While there is almost universal agreement on this basic proposition, there is little consensus on such perennial questions as what constitutes knowledge, what knowledge should be made available to all students, and what specialized knowledge should be taught to selected groups of students. Furthermore, there are conflicting viewpoints as to how knowledge selected for the curriculum should be organized for teaching, for example, whether the required program should be based on the academic disciplines traditionally defined on the university level or built around practical topics and problems of everyday living. And to complicate the situation even further, questions regarding the distinctive roles of students, professional educators, and patrons of the school in selecting content are raised, debated at length, and yet remain unclarified.

173

The major purpose of this chapter is not to resolve once and for all the epistemological or sociological issues on which curriculum decisions of selection and organization rest, but to convey something of the range of controversy that characterizes this question. Behind every school curriculum, written and unwritten, there lies a basic assumption as to what is worth knowing. Too often, these assumptions remain submerged or are treated only superficially. To some extent, then, this chapter is intended to reflect the controversies that inevitably arise when questions of what is worth knowing and what knowledge gets distributed to whom are raised to the level of conscious examination.

The first article in this chapter (reading #14) is probably the best known on the subject of curriculum and certainly one of the most profound. In it, John Dewey sets forth the principal components in educational theory and how their relationship to one another is often misconceived and misinterpreted. In reading #15, Joseph Schwab addresses the complex question of how the structures of the disciplines may be used as a basis for curriculum organization. A different basis for curriculum is then presented in reading #16 by Florence Stratemeyer reflecting a curriculum organized around "persistent life situations." The Schwab and the Stratemeyer positions are representative of two contrasting schools of thought on the question of knowledge and curriculum organization. In the following article (reading #17), Arno Bellack examines the two fundamentally different positions and offers a proposal that combines elements of each.

In reading #18 Maxine Greene draws from literary criticism and the work of phenomenologists like Merleau-Ponty to bring new insights into the relationship between knowledge and the curriculum, particularly with respect to how the learner commits himself to act upon the world. The two articles that follow approach the question of knowledge and the curriculum from a sociology of knowledge framework. In reading #19, the English sociologist Michael F. D. Young analyzes the work of certain major sociologists as it relates to central curriculum questions, espcially the social organization of knowledge implied in the curriculum. The final article in this chapter, reading #20 by Nell Keddie, considers the process by which knowledge becomes selectively accessible through curricula differentiated for different groups. Her study is notable for its substantiation of theoretical insights through classroom observation and analysis.

14. THE CHILD AND THE CURRICULUM

John Dewey

In 1894, John Dewey decided to leave his post at the University of Michigan in order to accept the position of head of the Department of Philosophy, Psychology, and Pedagogy at the University of Chicago. According to an account by his daughter, Jane, the inclusion of pedagogy in the Department of Philosophy and Psychology was an important factor in Dewey's decision. By 1896, Dewey and a group of parents involved with the Illinois Society for Child Study decided to establish the Laboratory School. For Dewey, it was a vehicle for testing and developing his educational ideas. He sought to organize the curriculum primarily around areas of social activity, which he called "occupations," rather than around conventional subject matter. Dewey was, in a sense, testing the thesis that not just the skills of writing, reading, and arithmetic, but all knowledge is derived essentially from engaging in fundamental human activities such as those involved in growing and preparing food and in making clothing. The following essay was written by Dewey as an explication of his theory of curriculum while the Laboratory School was still in operation.

In 1904, Dewey resigned his position at the University of Chicago in order to accept a new appointment as professor of philosophy at Columbia University, and the Laboratory School was discontinued. In his last book on education, Experience and Education, *written in 1938, Dewey reaffirmed the position he took in 1902, particularly in the chapter, "Progressive Organization of Subject-Matter."*

Profound differences in theory are never gratuitous or invented. They grow out of conflicting elements in a genuine problem—a problem which is genuine just because the elements, taken as they stand, are conflicting. Any significant problem involves conditions that for the moment contradict each other. Solution comes only by getting away from the meaning of terms that is already fixed upon and coming to see the conditions from another point of view, and hence in a fresh light. But this reconstruction means travail of thought. Easier than thinking with

SOURCE: *The Child and the Curriculum* (Chicago: The University of Chicago Press, 1902). Copyright 1902 by the University of Chicago.

surrender of already formed ideas and detachment from facts already learned, is just to stick by what is already said, looking about for something with which to buttress it against attack.

Thus sects arise; schools of opinion. Each selects that set of conditions that appeal to it; and then erects them into a complete and independent truth, instead of treating them as a factor in a problem, needing adjustment.

The fundamental factors in the educative process are an immature, undeveloped being; and certain social aims, meanings, values incarnate in the matured experience of the adult. The educative process is the due interaction of these forces. Such a conception of each in relation to the other as facilitates completest and freest interaction is the essence of educational theory.

But here comes the effort of thought. It is easier to see the conditions in their separateness, to insist upon one at the expense of the other, to make antagonists of them, than to discover a reality to which each belongs. The easy thing is to seize upon something in the nature of the child, or upon something in the developed consciousness of the adult, and insist upon *that* as the key to the whole problem. When this happens a really serious practical problem—that of interaction—is transformed into an unreal, and hence insoluble, theoretic problem. Instead of seeing the educative steadily and as a whole, we see conflicting terms. We get the case of the child *vs.* the curriculum; of the individual nature *vs.* social culture. Below all other divisions in pedagogic opinion lies this opposition.

The child lives in a somewhat narrow world of personal contacts. Things hardly come within his experience unless they touch, intimately and obviously, his own well-being, or that of his family and friends. His world is a world of persons with their personal interests, rather than a realm of facts and laws. Not truth, in the sense of conformity to external fact, but affection and sympathy, is its keynote. As against this, the course of study met in the school presents material stretching back indefinitely in time, and extending outward indefinitely into space. The child is taken out of his familiar physical environment, hardly more than a square mile or so in area, into the wide world—yes, and even to the bounds of the solar system. His little span of personal memory and tradition is overlaid with the long centuries of the history of all peoples.

Again, the child's life is an integral, a total one. He passes quickly and readily from one topic to another, as from one spot to another, but is not conscious of transition or break. There is no conscious isolation, hardly conscious distinction. The things that occupy him are held together by the unity of the personal and social interests which his life carries along. Whatever is uppermost in his mind constitutes to him, for the time being, the whole universe. That universe is fluid and fluent; its contents dissolve and re-form with amazing rapidity. But, after all, it is the child's own world. It has the unity and completeness of his own life. He goes to school, and various studies divide and fractionize the world for him. Geography selects, it abstracts and analyzes one set of facts, and from one particular point of view. Arithmetic is another division, grammar another department, and so on indefinitely.

Again, in school each of these subjects is classified. Facts are torn away from their original place in experience and rearranged with reference to some general principle. Classification is not a matter of child experience; things do not come to the individual pigeonholed. The vital ties of affection, the connecting bonds of activity, hold together the variety of his personal experiences. The adult mind is so familiar with the notion of logically ordered facts that it does not recognize—it cannot realize—the amount of separating and reformulating which the facts of direct experience have to undergo before they can appear as a "study," or branch of learning. A principle, for the intellect, has had to be distinguished and defined; facts have had to be interpreted in relation to this principle, not as they are in themselves. They have had to be regathered about a new center which is wholly abstract and ideal. All this means a development of a special intellectual interest. It means ability to view facts impartially and objectively; that is, without reference to their place and meaning in one's own experience. It means capacity to analyze and to synthesize. It means highly matured intellectual habits and the command of a definite technique and apparatus of scientific inquiry. The studies as classified are the product, in a word, of the science of the ages, not of the experience of the child.

These apparent deviations and differences between child and curriculum might be almost indefinitely widened. But we have here sufficiently fundamental divergences: first, the narrow but personal world of the child against the impersonal but infinitely extended world of space and time; second, the unity, the single whole-heartedness of the child's life, and the specializations and divisions of the curriculum; third, an abstract principle of logical classification and arrangement, and the practical and emotional bonds of child life.

From these elements of conflict grow up different educational sects. C·ie school fixes its attention upon the importance of the subject matter of the curriculum as compared with the contents of the child's own experience. It is as if they said: Is life petty, narrow, and crude? Then studies reveal the great, wide universe with all its fullness and complexity of meaning. Is the life of the child egoistic, self-centered, impulsive? Then in these studies is found an objective universe of truth, law, and order. Is his experience confused, vague, uncertain, at the mercy of the moment's caprice and circumstance? Then studies introduce a world arranged on the basis of eternal and general truth; a world where all is measured and defined. Hence the moral: ignore and minimize the child's individual peculiarities, whims, and experiences. They are what we need to get away from. They are to be obscured or eliminated. As educators our work is precisely to substitute for these superficial and casual affairs stable and well-ordered realities; and these are found in studies and lessons.

Subdivide each topic into studies; each study into lessons; each lesson into specific facts and formulae. Let the child proceed step by step to master each one of these separate parts, and at last he will have covered the entire ground. The road which looks so long when viewed in its entirety, is easily traveled, considered as a series of particular steps. Thus emphasis is put upon the logical subdivisions and consecutions of the subject matter. Problems of instruction are problems of procuring texts giving logical parts and sequences, and of presenting these portions in class in a similar definite and graded way. Subject matter furnishes the end, and it determines method. The child is simply the immature being who is to be matured; he is the superficial being who is to be deepened; his is narrow experience which is to be widened. It is his to receive, to accept. His part is fulfilled when he is ductile and docile.

Not so, says the other sect. The child is the starting point, the center, and the end. His development, his growth, is the ideal. It alone furnishes the standard. To the growth of the child all studies are subservient; they are instruments valued as they serve the needs of growth. Personality, character, is more than subject matter. Not knowledge or information, but self-realization, is the goal. To possess all the world of knowledge and lose one's own self is as awful a fate in education as in religion. Moreover, subject matter never can be got into the child from without. Learning is active. It involves reaching out of the mind. It involves organic assimilation starting from within. Literally, we must take our stand with the child and our departure from him. It is he and not the subject matter which determines both quality and quantity of learning.

The only significant method is the method of the mind as it reaches out and assimilates. Subject matter is but spiritual food, possible nutritive material. It cannot digest itself; it cannot of its own accord turn into bone and muscle and blood. The source of whatever is dead, mechanical, and formal in schools is found precisely in the subordination of the life and experience of the child to the curriculum. It is because of this that "study" has become a synonym for what is irksome, and a lesson identical with a task.

This fundamental opposition of child and curriculum set up by these two modes of doctrine can be duplicated in a series of other terms. "Discipline" is the watchword of those who magnify the course of study; "interest" that of those who blazon "The Child" upon their banner. The standpoint of the former is logical; that of the latter psychological. The first emphasizes the necessity of adequate training and scholarship on the part of the teacher; the latter that of need of sympathy with the child, and knowledge of his natural instincts. "Guidance and control" are the catchwords of one school; "freedom and initiative" of the other. Law is asserted here; spontaneity proclaimed there. The old, the conservation of what has been achieved in the pain and toil of the ages, is dear to the one; the new, change, progress, wins the affection of the other. Inertness and routine, chaos and anarchism, are accusations bandied back and forth. Neglect of the sacred authority of duty is charged by one side, only to be met by counter-charges of suppression of individuality through tyrannical despotism.

Such oppositions are rarely carried to their logical conclusion. Common sense recoils at the extreme character of these results. They are left to theorists, while common sense vibrates back and forward in a maze of inconsistent compromise. The need of getting theory and practical common sense into closer connection suggests a return to our original thesis: that we have here conditions which are necessarily related to each other in the educative process, since this is precisely one of interaction and adjustment.

What, then, is the problem? It is just to get rid of the prejudicial notion that there is some gap in kind (as distinct from degree) between the child's experience and the various forms of subject matter that make up the course of study. From the side of the child, it is a question of seeing how his experience already contains within itself elements—facts and truths—of just the same sort as those entering into the formulated study; and, what is of more importance, of how it contains within itself the attitudes, the motives, and the interests which have operated in developing and organizing the subject matter to the plane which it now occupies. From the side of the studies, it is a question of interpreting them as outgrowths of forces operating in the child's life, and of discovering the steps that intervene between the child's present experience and their richer maturity.

Abandon the notion of subject matter as something fixed and ready-made in itself, outside the child's experience; cease thinking of the child's experience as also something hard and fast; see it as something fluent, embryonic, vital; and we realize that the child and the curriculum are simply two limits which define a single process. Just as two points define a straight line, so the present standpoint of the child and the facts and truths of studies define instruction. It is continuous reconstruction, moving from the child's present experience out into that represented by the organized bodies of truth that we call studies.

On the face of it, the various studies, arithmetic, geography, language, botany, etc., are themselves experience—they are that of the race. They embody the cumulative outcome of the efforts, the strivings, and successes of the human race generation after generation. They present this, not as a mere accumulation, not as a miscellaneous heap of separate bits of experience, but in some organized and systematized way—that is, as reflectively formulated.

Hence, the facts and truths that enter into the child's present experience, and those contained in the subject matter of studies, are the initial and final terms of one reality. To oppose one to the other is to oppose the infancy and maturity of the same growing life; it is to set the moving tendency and the final result of the same process over against each other; it is to hold that the nature and the destiny of the child war with each other.

If such be the case, the problem of the relation of the child and the curriculum presents itself in this guise: Of what use, educationally speaking, is it to be able to see the end in the beginning? How does it assist us in dealing with the early stages of growth to be able to anticipate its later phases? The studies, as we have agreed, represent the possibilities of development inherent in the child's immediate crude experience. But, after all, they are not parts of that present and immediate life. Why, then, or how, make account of them?

Asking such a question suggests its own answer. To see the outcome is to know in what direction the present experience is moving, provided it moves normally and soundly. The faraway point, which is of no significance to us simply as far away, becomes of huge importance the moment we take it as defining a present direction of movement. Taken in this way it is no remote and distant result to be achieved, but a guiding method in dealing with the present, The systematized and defined experience of the adult mind, in other words, is of value to us in interpreting the child's life as it immediately shows itself, and in passing on to guidance or direction.

Let us look for a moment at these two ideas: interpretation and guidance. The child's present experience is in no way self-explanatory. It is not final, but transitional. It is nothing complete in itself, but just a sign or index of certain growth tendencies. As long as we confine our gaze to what the child here and now puts forth, we are confused and misled. We cannot read its meaning. Extreme depreciations of the child morally and intellectually, and sentimental idealizations of him, have their root in a common fallacy. Both spring from taking stages of a growth or movement as something cut off and fixed. The first fails to see the promise contained in feelings and deeds which, taken by themselves, are unpromising and repellant; the second fails to see that even the most pleasing and beautiful exhibitions are but signs, and that they begin to spoil and rot the moment they are treated as achievements.

What we need is something which will enable us to interpret, to appraise, the elements in the child's present puttings forth and fallings away, his exhibitions of power and weakness, in the light of some larger growth process in which they have their place. Only in this way can we discriminate. If we isolate the child's present inclinations, purposes, and experiences from the place they occupy and the part they have to perform in a developing experience, all stand upon the same level; all alike are equally good and equally bad. But in the movement of life different elements stand upon different planes of value. Some of the child's deeds are symptoms of a waning tendency; they are survivals in functioning of an organ which has done its part and is passing out of vital use. To give positive attention to such qualities is to arrest development upon a lower level.It is systematically to maintain a rudimentary phase of growth. Other activities are signs of a culminating power and interest; to them applies the maxim of striking while the iron is hot. As regards them, it is perhaps a matter of now or never. Selected, utilized, emphasized, they may mark a turning-point for good in the child's whole career; neglected, an opportunity goes, never to be recalled. Other acts and feelings are prophetic; they represent the dawning of flickering light that will shine steadily only in the far future. As regards them there is little at present to do but give them fair and full chance, waiting for the future for definite direction.

Just as, upon the whole, it was the weakness of the "old education" that it made invidious comparisons between the immaturity of the child and the maturity of the adult, regarding the former as something to be got away from as soon as possible and as much as possible; so it is the danger of the "new education" that it regard the child's present powers and interests as something finally significant in themselves. In truth, his learnings and achievements are fluid and moving. They change from day to day and from hour to hour.

It will do harm if child-study leave in the popular mind the impression that a child of a given age has a positive equipment of purposes and interests to be cultivated just as they stand. Interests in reality are but attitudes toward possible experiences; they are not achievements; their worth is in the leverage they afford, not in the accomplishment they represent. To take the phenomena presented at a given age as in any way self-explanatory or self-contained is inevitably to result in indulgence and spoiling. Any power, whether of child or adult, is indulged when it is taken on its given and present level in consciousness. Its genuine meaning is in the propulsion it affords toward a higher level. It is just something to do with. Appealing to the interest upon the present plane means excitation; it means playing with a power so as continually to stir it up without directing it toward definite achievement. Continuous initiation, continuous starting of activities that do not arrive, is, for all practical purposes, as bad as the continual repression of initiative in conformity with supposed interests of some more perfect thought or will. It is as if the child were forever tasting and never eating; always having his palate tickled upon the emotional side, but never getting the organic satisfaction that comes only with the digestion of food and transformation of it into working power.

As against such a view, the subject matter of science and history and art serves to reveal the real child to us. We do not know the meaning either of his tendencies or of his performances excepting as we take them as germinating seed, or opening bud, of some fruit to be borne. The whole world of visual nature is all too small an answer to the problem of the meaning of the child's instinct for light and form. The entire science of physics is none too much to interpret adequately to us what is involved in some simple demand of the child for explanation of some casual change that has attracted his attention. The art of Rafael or of Corot is none too much to enable us to value the impulses stirring in the child when he draws and daubs.

So much for the use of the subject matter in interpretation. Its further employment in direction or guidance is but an expansion of the same thought. To interpret the fact is to see it in its vital movement, to see it in its relation to growth. But to view it as a part of a normal growth is to secure the basis for guiding it. Guidance is not external imposition. *It is freeing the life-process for its own most adequate fulfillment.* What was said about disregard of the child's present experience because of its remoteness from mature experience; and of the sentimental idealization of the child's naïve caprices and performances, may be repeated here with slightly altered phrase. There are those who see no alternative between forcing the child from without, or leaving him entirely alone. Seeing no alternative, some choose one mode, some another. Both fall into the same fundamental error. Both fail to see that development is a definite process, having its own law which can be fulfilled only when adequate and normal conditions are provided. Really to interpret the child's present crude impulses in counting, measuring, and arranging things in rhythmic series, involves mathematical scholarship—a knowledge of the mathematical formulae and relations which have, in the history of the race, grown out of just such crude beginnings. To see the whole history of development which intervenes between these two terms is simply to see what step the child needs to take just here and now; to what use he needs to put his blind impulse in order that it may get clarity and gain force.

If, once more, the "old education" tended to ignore the dynamic quality, the developing force inherent in the child's present experience, and therefore to assume that direction and control were just matters of arbitrarily putting the child in a given path and compelling him to walk there, the "new education" is in danger of taking the idea of development in altogether too formal and empty a way. The child is expected to "develop" this or that fact or truth out of his own mind. He is told to think things out, or work things out for himself, without being supplied any of the environing conditions which are requisite to start and guide thought. Nothing can be developed from nothing; nothing but the crude can be developed out of the crude—and this is what surely happens when we throw the child back upon his achieved self as a finality, and invite him to spin new truths of nature or of conduct out of that. It is certainly as futile to expect a child to evolve a universe out of his own mere mind as it is for a philosopher to attempt that task. Development does not mean just getting something out of the mind. It is a development of experience and into experience that is really wanted. And this is impossible save as just that educative medium is provided which will enable the powers and interests that have been selected as valuable to function. They must operate, and how they operate will depend almost entirely upon the stimuli which surround them, and the material upon which they exercise themselves. The problem of direction is thus the problem of selecting appropriate stimuli for instincts and impulses which it is desired to employ in the gaining of new experience. What new experiences are desirable, and thus what stimuli are needed, it is impossible to tell except as there is some comprehension of the development which is aimed at; except, in a word, as the adult knowledge is drawn upon as revealing the possible career open to the child.

It may be of use to distinguish and to relate to each other the logical and the psychological aspects of experience—the former standing for subject matter in itself, the latter for it in relation to the child. A psychological statement of experience follows its actual growth; it is historic; it notes steps actually taken, the uncertain and tortuous, as well as the efficient and successful. The logical point of view, on the other hand, assumes that the development has reached a certain positive stage of fulfillment. It neglects the process and considers the outcome. It summarizes and arranges, and thus separates the achieved results from the actual steps by which they were forthcoming in the first instance. We may compare the difference between the logical and the psychological to the difference between the notes which an explorer makes in a new country, blazing a trail and finding his way along as best he may, and the finished map that is constructed after the country has been thoroughly explored. The two are mutually dependent. Without the more or less accidental and devious paths traced by the explorer there would be no facts which could be utilized in the making of the complete and related chart. But no one would get the benefit of the explorer's trip if it was not compared and checked up with similar wanderings undertaken by others; unless the new geographical facts learned, the streams crossed, the mountains climbed, etc., were viewed, not as mere incidents in the journey of the particular traveler, but (quite apart from the individual explorer's life) in relation to other similar facts already known. The map orders individual experiences, connecting them with one another irrespective of the local and temporal circumstances and accidents of their original discovery.

Of what use is this formulated statement of experience? Of what use is the map?

Well, we may first tell what the map is not. The map is not a substitute for a personal experience. The map does not take the place of an actual journey. The logically formulated material of a science or branch of learning, of a study, is no substitute for the having of individual experiences. The mathematical formula for a falling body does not take the place of personal contact and immediate individual experience with the falling thing. But the map, a summary, an arranged and orderly view of previous experiences, serves as a guide to future experience; it gives direction; it facilitates control; it economizes effort, preventing useless wandering, and pointing out the paths which lead most quickly and most certainly to a desired result. Through the map every new traveler may get for his own journey the benefits of the results of others' explorations without the waste of energy and loss of time involved in their wanderings—wanderings which he himself would be obliged to repeat were it not for just the assistance of the objective and generalized record of their performances. That which we call a science or study puts the net product of past experience in the form which makes it most available for the future. It represents a capitalization which may at once be turned to interest. It economizes the workings of the mind in every way. Memory is less taxed because the facts are grouped together about some common principle, instead of being connected solely with the varying incidents of their original discovery. Observation is assisted; we know what to look for and where to look. It is the difference between looking for a needle in a haystack, and searching for a given paper in a well-arranged cabinet. Reasoning is directed, because there is a certain general path or line laid out along which ideas naturally march, instead of moving from one chance association to another.

There is, then, nothing final about a logical rendering of experience. Its value is not contained in itself; its significance is that of standpoint, outlook, method. It intervenes between the more casual, tentative, and roundabout experiences of the past, and more controlled and orderly experiences of the future. It gives past experience in that net form which renders it most available and most significant, most fecund for future experience. The abstractions, generalizations, and classifications which it introduces all have prospective meaning.

The formulated result is then not to be opposed to the process of growth. The logical is not set over against the psychological. The surveyed and arranged result occupies a critical position in the process of growth. It marks a turning-point. It shows how we may get the benefit of past effort in controlling future endeavor. In the largest sense the logical standpoint is itself psychological; it has its meaning as a point in the development of experience, and its justification is in its functioning in the future growth which it insures.

Hence the need of reinstating into experience the subject matter of the studies, or branches of learning. It must be restored to the experience from which it has been abstracted. It needs to be *psychologized*; turned over, translated into the immediate and individual experiencing within which it has its origin and significance.

Every study or subject thus has two aspects: one for the scientist as a scientist; the other for the teacher as a teacher. These two aspects are in no sense opposed or conflicting. But neither are they immediately identical. For the scientist, the subject matter represents simply a given body of truth to be employed in locating new problems, instituting new researches, and carrying them through to a verified outcome. To him the subject matter of the science is self-contained. He refers various portions of it to each other; he connects new facts with it. He is not, as a scientist, called upon to travel outside its particular bounds; if he does, it is only to get more facts of the same general sort. The problem of the teacher is a different one. As a teacher he is not concerned with adding new facts to the science he teaches; in propounding new hypotheses or in verifying them. He is concerned with the subject matter of the science as *representing a given stage and phase of the development of experience*. His problem is that of inducing a vital and personal experiencing. Hence, what concerns him, as teacher, is the ways in which that subject may become a part of experience; what there is in the child's present that is usable with reference to it; how such elements are to be used; how his own knowledge of the subject matter may assist in interpreting the child's needs and doings, and determine the medium in which the child should be placed in order that his growth may be properly directed. He is concerned, not with the subject matter as such, but with the subject matter as a related factor in a total and growing experience. Thus to see it is to psychologize it.

It is the failure to keep in mind the double aspect of subject matter which causes the curriculum and child to be set over against each other as described in our early pages. The subject matter, just as it is for the scientist, has no direct relationship to the child's present experience. It stands outside of it. The danger here is not a merely theoretical one. We are practically threatened on all sides. Textbook and teacher vie with each other in presenting to the child the subject matter as it stands to the specialist. Such modification and revision as it undergoes are a mere elimination of certain scientific difficulties, and the general reduction to a lower intellectual level. The material is not translated into life-terms, but is directly offered as a substitute for, or an external annex to, the child's present life.

Three typical evils result: In the first place, the lack of any organic connection with what the child has already seen and felt and loved makes the material purely formal and symbolic. There is a sense in which it is impossible to value too highly the formal and the symbolic. The genuine form, the real symbol, serve as methods in the holding and discovery of truth. They are tools by which the individual pushes out most surely and widely into unexplored areas. They are means by which he brings to bear whatever of reality he has succeeded in gaining in past searchings. But this happens only when the symbol really symbolizes— when it stands for and sums up in shorthand actual experiences which the individual has already gone through. A symbol which is induced from without, which has not been led up to in preliminary activities, is, as we say, a *bare* or *mere* symbol; it is dead and barren. Now, any fact, whether of arithmetic, or geography, or grammar, which is not led up to and into out of something which has previously occupied a significant position in the child's life for its own sake, is forced into this position. It is not a reality, but just the sign of a reality which *might* be experienced if certain conditions were fulfilled. But the abrupt presentation of the fact as something known by others, and requiring only to be studied and learned by the child, rules out such conditions of fulfillment. It condemns the fact to be hieroglyph: it would mean something if one only had the key. The clue being lacking, it remains an idle curiosity, to fret and obstruct the mind, a dead weight to burden it.

The second evil in this external presentation is lack of motivation. There are not only no facts or truths which have been previously felt as such with which to appropriate and assimilate the new but there is no craving, no need, no demand. When the subject matter has been psychologized, that is, viewed as an outgrowth of present tendencies and activities, it is easy to locate in the present some obstacle, intellectual, practical, or ethical, which can be handled more adequately if the truth in question be mastered. This need supplies motive for the learning. An end which is the child's own carries him on to possess the means of its accomplishment. But when material is directly supplied in the form of a lesson to be learned as a lesson, the connecting links of need and aim are conspicuous for their absence. What we mean by the mechanical and dead in instruction is a result of this lack of motivation. The organic and vital mean interaction—they mean play of mental demand and material supply.

The third evil is that even the most scientific matter, arranged in most logical fashion, loses this quality, when presented in external, ready-made fashion, by the time it gets to the child. It has to undergo some modification in order to shut out some phases too hard to grasp, and to reduce some of the attendant difficulties. What happens? Those things which are most significant to the scientific man, and most valuable in the logic of actual inquiry and classification, drop out. The really thought-provoking character is obscured, and the organizing function disappears. Or, as we commonly say, the child's reasoning powers, the faculty of abstraction and generalization, are not adequately developed. So the subject matter is evacuated of its logical value, and, though it is what it is only from the logical standpoint, is presented as stuff only for "memory." This is the contradiction: the child gets the advantage neither of the adult logical formulation, nor of his own native competencies of apprehension and response. Hence the logic of the child is hampered and mortified, and we are almost fortunate if he does not get actual non-science, flat and commonplace residua of what was gaining scientific vitality a generation or two ago—degenerate reminiscence of what someone else once formulated on the basis of the experience that some further person had, once upon a time, experienced.

The train of evils does not cease. It is all too common for opposed erroneous theories to play straight into each other's hands. Psychological considerations may be slurred or shoved to one side; they cannot be crowded out. Put out of the door, they come back through the window. Somehow and somewhere motive must be appealed to, connection must be established between the mind and its material. There is no question of getting along without this bond of connection; the only question is whether it be such as grows out of the material itself in relation to the mind, or be imported and hitched on from some outside source. If the subject matter of the lessons be such as to have an appropriate place within the expanding consciousness of the child, if it grows out of his own past doings, thinkings, and sufferings, and grows into application in further achievements and receptivities, then no device or trick of method has to be resorted to in order to enlist "interest." The psychologized *is* of interest—that is, it is placed in the whole of conscious life so that it shares the worth of that life. But the externally presented material, that, conceived and generated in standpoints and attitudes remote from the child, and developed in motives alien to him, has no such place of its own. Hence the recourse to adventitious leverage to push it in, to factitious drill to drive it in, to artificial bribe to lure it in.

Three aspects of this recourse to outside ways for giving the subject matter some psychological meaning may be worth mentioning. Familiarity breeds contempt, but it also breeds something like affection. We get used to the chains we wear, and we miss them when removed. 'Tis an old story that through custom we finally embrace what at first wore a hideous mien. Unpleasant, because meaningless, activities may get agreeable if long enough persisted in. *It is possible for the mind to develop interest in a routine or mechanical procedure, if conditions are continually supplied which demand that mode of operation and preclude any other sort.* I frequently hear dulling devices and empty exercises defended and extolled because "the children take such an 'interest' in them." Yes, that is the worst of it; the mind, shut out from worthy employ and missing the taste of adequate performance, comes down to the level of that which is left to it to know and do, and perforce takes an interest in a cabined and cramped experience. To find satisfaction in its own exercise is the normal law of mind, and if large and meaningful business for the mind be denied, it tries to content itself with the formal movements that remain to it—and too often succeeds, save in those cases of more intense activity which cannot accommodate themselves, and that make up the unruly and *declassé* of our school product. An interest in the formal apprehension of symbols and in their memorized reproduction becomes in many pupils a substitute for the original and vital interest in reality; and all because, the subject matter of the course of study being out of relation to the concrete mind of the individual, some substitute bond to hold it in some kind of working relation to the mind must be discovered and elaborated.

The second substitute for living motivation in the subject matter is that of contrast-effects; the material of the lesson is rendered interesting, if not in itself, at least in contrast with some alternative experience. To learn the lesson is more interesting than to take a scolding, be held up to general ridicule, stay after school, receive degradingly low marks, or fail to be promoted. And very much of what goes by the name of "discipline," and prides itself upon opposing the doctrines of a soft pedagogy and upon upholding the banner of effort and duty, is nothing more or less than just this appeal to "interest" in its obverse aspect—to fear, to dislike of various kinds of physical, social, and personal pain. The subject matter does not appeal; it cannot appeal; it lacks origin and bearing in a growing experience. So the appeal is to the thousand and one outside and irrelevant agencies which may serve to throw, by sheer rebuff and rebound, the mind back upon the material from which it is constantly wandering.

Human nature being what it is, however, it tends to seek its motivation in the agreeable rather than in the disagreeable, in direct pleasure rather than in alternative pain. And so has come up the modern theory and practice of the "interesting," in the false sense of that term. The material is still left; so far as its own characteristics are concerned, just material externally selected and formulated. It is still just so much geography and arithmetic and grammar study; not so much potentiality of child-experience with regard to language, earth, and numbered and measured reality. Hence the difficulty of bringing the mind to bear upon it; hence its repulsiveness; the tendency for attention to wander; for other acts and images to crowd in and expel the lesson. The legitimate way out is to transform the material; to psychologize it—that is, once more, to take it and to develop it within the range and scope of the child's life. But it is easier and simpler to leave it as it is, and then by trick of method to *arouse* interest, to *make* it *interesting*; to cover it with sugar-coating; to conceal its barrenness by intermediate and unrelated material and finally, as it were, to get the child to swallow and digest the unpalatable morsel while he is enjoying tasting something quite different. But alas for the analogy! Mental assimilation is a matter of consciousness; and if the attention has not been playing upon the actual material, that has not been apprehended, nor worked into faculty.

How, then, stands the case of Child *vs.* Curriculum? What shall the verdict be? The radical fallacy in the original pleadings with which we set out is the supposition that we have no choice save either to leave the child to his own unguided spontaneity or to inspire direction upon him from without. Action is response; it is adaptation, adjustment. There is no such thing as sheer self-activity possible—because all activity takes place in a medium, in a situation, and with reference to its conditions. But, again, no such thing as imposition of truth from without, as insertion of truth from without, is possible. All depends upon the activity which the mind itself undergoes in responding to what is presented from without. Now, the value of the formulated wealth of knowledge that makes up the course of study is that it may enable the educator *to determine the environment of the child,* and thus by indirection to direct. Its primary value, its primary indication, is for the teacher, not for the child. It says to the teacher: Such and such are the capacities, the fulfillments, in truth and beauty and behavior, open to these children. Now see to it that day by day the conditions are such that *their own activities* move inevitably in this direction, toward such culmination of themselves. Let the child's nature fulfill its own destiny, revealed to you in whatever of science and art and industry the world now holds as its own.

The case is of Child. It is his present powers which are to assert themselves; his present capacities which are to be exercised; his present attitudes which are to be realized. But save as the teacher knows, knows wisely and thoroughly, the race-experience which is embodied in that thing we call the Curriculum, the teacher knows neither what the present power, capacity, or attitude is, nor yet how it is to be asserted, exercised, and realized.

15. STRUCTURE OF THE DISCIPLINES: MEANINGS AND SIGNIFICANCES

Joseph J. Schwab

We embark here on an exploration of one of the most difficult of terrains: investigation of the nature, variety, and extent of human knowledge; and the attempt to determine what that nature, variety, and extent have to tell us about teaching and learning. My share of this task is a specialized one and a preliminary one. It is simply to map that terrain. Later papers will explore the land itself.

What is meant by the structure of the disciplines? It means three things, three distinct but related sets of problems. Let us take a foretaste of all three together without discriminating them by name.

It has been widely supposed that there are indubitable grounds for recognizing basically different orders of phenomena, each requiring a different discipline for its investigation because of the differences in the character of the phenomena.

There are many different views based on such a premise. For example, many philosophers have insisted on a fundamental distinction between living phenomena and nonliving, thus generating the notion that there are two fundamentally different sciences, the biological and the physiochemical. These two sciences were supposed to differ in method, in guiding conceptions, in the kind of knowledge produced, and in degree of certainty, differing to precisely the same extent that their subject matters were supposed to differ.

SOURCE. In G. W. Ford and Lawrence Pugno (eds.), *The Structure of Knowledge and the Curriculum* (Chicago: Rand McNally & Company, 1964), pp. 1–30. Copyright © 1964 by Joseph J. Schwab. All rights reserved.

Another such view is generated by a distinction between man and nature, a distinction in which nature is conceived as bound by inexorable laws while men are in some sense and in some degree free. In this view, two major areas of investigation are again discriminated: on the one hand, science, concerned with the inexorable laws that nature presumably obeys; and on the other hand, a discipline in the neighborhood of ethics and politics, which would investigate the freedom that man has and the ways in which men make their choices.

There is also a view that emphasizes the vast difference between the generality of "natural" phenomena (i.e., their predictability, the tendency of "natural" things to behave or be the same in instance after instance) and the particularity of human events (the essentially unique and nonrepeating character of acts notable in the behavior of man). Again, two widely different bodies of investigation and study are generated: science on the one hand and history on the other. Science, in this view, would seek the general laws that characterize the repeating behavior of natural things, while history would seek to determine the precise, unique events that characterized each life, each era, each civilization or culture that it studied. Hence, again, there would be two basically different curriculum components, differing in method, principle, and warrantability.

There have been similar separations of other disciplines, notably mathematics and logic. Mathematics was long ago seen to differ radically from other disciplines, including the sciences, in that its subject matter appeared to have no material existence. The objects of physical or biological enquiry could be seen, touched, smelled, tasted. The objects of mathematics could not. The plane, the line, the point, unity, number, etc. existed in some way which was not material or did not exist at all. This peculiarity of mathematical objects continues to be a puzzle. No one view of the nature of mathematics has been developed which is satisfactory to all concerned, though most moderns are agreed that mathematics differs radically from the other sciences.

Logic has been set apart because of its unique relationship to other disciplines rather than because of something peculiar about its subject matter. To one degree or another, all other disciplines test the reliability of their conclusions by appealing to canons of reasoning and of evidence which are developed in the first place by the discipline of logic. Since logic is responsible for developing these canons, it cannot itself use them to check its own work. Logic thus stands as a sort of "queen of the sciences," dictating their rules but having for itself rules of some other and puzzling sort. Unlike the case of mathematics, this peculiarity of logic is no longer universally recognized. In some quarters, for example, it is held that logic does no more than formulate the methods and the canons of reasoning and of evidence which other sciences have developed, used, and bear witness to by their effectiveness. In this view, logic is not so much the queen of the sciences as their handmaiden.

Let us continue our foretaste of the problems of the structures of the disciplines by noting a peculiarity of the distinctions we have described. The peculiarity is that the differences among phenomena which appear at one period in the history of the disciplines to be radical and self-evident may at a later date disappear or become inconsequential as bases for differentiating disciplines. Take, for example, the differentiation of biology from the physical-chemical sciences. In early times and through the eighteenth century, fundamental differences between the living and the nonliving could not be evaded. The living thing was "self-moving"; no other object was. The living thing reproduced itself; the living thing developed, had a personal history which no nonliving thing could duplicate. Then, in the middle to late nineteenth century, some of these differences ceased to be notable, others disappeared entirely from human recognition. In this altered climate, the physiologist Claude Bernard pleaded for a study of living things strictly in terms of physics and chemistry. Since then, such an approach to living things has been so fruitful that it is now safe to say that it will be only a brief time before we shall synthesize living molecules in the laboratory. In recent years a still further shift in outlook has taken place: we now hear pleas from some physicists that certain physical phenomena be treated in much the way that living things were investigated *before* Bernard.

A similar shift is visible on a smaller scale in the history of the science of mechanics. Three hundred years ago the behavior of celestial bodies (the planets and the stars) and the behavior of terrestrial bodies in motion (things rolling on the surface of the earth and things thrown or propelled through the air) appeared to be radically different. Terrestrial bodies inevitably came to rest and fell to earth; celestial bodies inevitably continued in their regular motion without stop. Then, with Newton, these differences, though still visible, became entirely unimportant.

In brief, what we see of and in things changes from epoch to epoch. Differences that once appeared to be radical are seen later to be illusory or trivial; then, at another period, some of these differences reappear in a new guise. What can account for such changes in what appears to be objectively perceived? The answer is most easily exemplified in the case of mechanics, where in our own day the once radical difference between terrestrial and celestial bodies continues to be treated as illusory.

Granted that this difference was an illusion, what made the illusion disappear? The answer is this: Newton conceived an idea called universal gravitation. In the light of this idea, it became desirable and possible to examine the motion of the celestial bodies (in Newton's case, the moon) in a new way. Specifically, it became desirable and possible to measure the changing directions and changing velocities of the moon in such a fashion that it could be described as continually falling toward earth, while, at the same time, continually moving in a straight line at an angle to its fall. Thus its continuous orbit of the earth could be understood as the resultant of these two motions. In the same way it became possible to conceive of a terrestrial missile as falling to earth and coming to rest there only because its initial velocity in a straight line was not great enough to carry it straight forward beyond the bend of the earth before its fall brought it into contact with the earth. One could then see that as the initial velocity of a missile became greater and greater, it would not only go farther before it fell to earth, but at some point the increased velocity would be so great that the fall of the missile would be compensated by the falling away of the spherical surface of the earth. Such a missile would then become a satellite of the earth precisely like the moon. In brief, a new conception dictating new studies and a new way to interpret the data exhibited the movement of celestial bodies as nothing more than an extreme case of the motions of familiar terrestrial bodies moving at lower velocities.

In general, two collections of phenomena appear to be vastly different because we have used separate and distinct bodies of conceptions in studying them and discovering knowledge about them. Each such body of conceptions dictates what data we think we should seek, what experiments to perform, and what to make of our data by way of knowledge. If widely different conceptions are used to guide enquiries on two different collections of phenomena, we end inevitably with bodies of knowledge which exhibit few similarities and many differences. It is through the limiting or distorting lenses of these bodies of knowledge that we look at things. Hence, if the lenses distort or limit in different ways, we see things as different. The differences we see disappear if, but only if, a new conception is given birth which permits the study of both collections of phenomena in one set of terms and therefore makes for unity where diversity existed before.

Before we discriminate the problems of the structure of the disciplines, let us take note of a *caveat*. It is this: the integration of previously separate bodies of knowledge by new and unifying conceptions should not blind us to the possibility that some of the differences we recognize among phenomena may be genuine; some differentiation of disciplines may be perennial. There really may be joints in nature, a forearm, then an elbow, and then an upper arm. Science, ethics, and aesthetics may indeed represent three widely variant objects of enquiry. The doctrine of the unity of science, which insists on a unification of all knowledge, is either a dogma or a hope but not a fact. There are no data from which to conclude decisively that eventually all the disciplines will become or should become one.

Now let us step back and identify in this foretaste of knowledge and knowledge-seeking the three major but related sets of problems which define the area called structure of the disciplines.

Recall first our brief review of efforts to discriminate life from nonlife, science from history, and so on. These efforts illustrate the first problem of the structure of the disciplines. It is the problem of determining the membership and organization of the disciplines, of identifying the significantly different disciplines, and of locating their relations to one another.

This set of problems is illustrated by the following questions. *Is* mathematical knowledge significantly different from knowledge of physical things? If so, how are the behaviors of mathematical objects related to the behaviors of physical objects? That is, how must we account for the extraordinary usefulness of mathematics to the sciences? Is it because we impose mathematical forms on our observation of physical things, or is it because, in some mysterious way, the objects of the external world behave according to patterns that we discover through mathematical enquiry into our own intellects? Similarly, we might raise questions about practical knowledge and scientific or theoretical knowledge. Are they much the same or truly different? Is practical knowledge merely the application of science? Or does science take hold of ideal objects extrapolated from experience of things while practical knowledge must supply the bridge for return from scientific knowledge of such ideal objects to the actual and practicable? This set of problems may properly be called a problem of the structure of the disciplines, if we keep in mind that by the plural "disciplines" we refer to them collectively rather than distributively, while "structure" is singular and refers to the organization of the disciplines *inter se.*

The significance of this set of problems to education is obvious enough. To identify the disciplines that constitute contemporary knowledge and mastery of the world, is to identify the subject matter of education, the material that constitutes both its resources and its obligations. To locate the relations of these disciplines to one another is to determine what may be joined together for purposes of instruction and what should be held apart; these same relations will also weigh heavily in determining our decisions about the sequence of instruction, for it will tell us what must come before what, or what is most desirable placed first, or second, or third.

The second set of problems of the structure of the disciplines is exemplified by the tremendous role of the concept of universal gravitation in supplying us with a more nearly universal mechanics. A similar role is played by other conceptions in the attainment and formulation of all scientific knowledge. Embedded in the knowledge we have of the workings of the human body lies one or another concept of the nature of an organism, of the character of the parts of such an organism and how they relate to one another. Back of our knowledge of heredity lies a conception of particles behaving as do the terms in the expansion of a binominal to the second or higher powers. Back of our ability to make decisions in playing games lie similar conceptions. Again, the conceptions happen to be mathematical: the expansion of the binominal or a more complex mathematical structure derived by taking the expansion of the binominal to its limit. These mathematical conceptions provide us with a body of probability theory with which we play poker, determine tactics in battle, plan the production and sale of the products of our industries. Similarly, knowledge of human behavior, both individual and social, has arisen only as the men concerned with enquiry in psychology, sociology, and anthropology have developed conceptions that have enabled them to plan their researches.

In general then, enquiry has its origin in a conceptual structure, often mathematical, but not necessarily so. It is this conceptual structure through which we are able to formulate a telling question. It is through the telling question that we know what data to seek and what experiments to perform to get those data. Once the data are in hand, the same conceptual structure tells us how to interpret them, what to make of them by way of knowledge. Finally, the knowledge itself is formulated in the terms provided by the same conception. Thus we formulate and convey some of the knowledge we discover about the body in terms of organs and functions; we formulate and communicate our knowledge of atomic structure in terms of a concept of particles and waves; we formulate some of our knowledge of human personality in terms of physic organs and their functions and other portions of it in terms of interpersonal relations.

In each science and in many arts such conceptual structures prevail. The second problem of the structure of the disciplines is to identify these structures and understand the powers and limits of the enquiries that take place under the guidance. Let us call this set of problems the problem of the *substantive* structures of each discipline.

Again, the significance of this problem of the structure of the disciplines to education is obvious enough—or at least one part of it is. For to know what structures underlie a given body of knowledge is to know what problems we shall face in imparting this knowledge. Perhaps the conceptual structure is no more complex than that involved in the discrimination of two classes of things by a single criterion, such as color or shape. In that case, we may suppose that little difficulty would be encountered in teaching this body of knowledge even to the very young. Perhaps the conceptual structure is more complex but so firmly embedded in commonsense knowledge of things that the child at some early, given age will already have encountered it and become familiar with it. In that case, we should, again, have little difficulty in imparting our knowledge, provided that we impart it at the right time in the development of the child in our culture. However, suppose the conceptual structure is both complex and largely unused in commonsense knowledge? This would be the case at the moment for the physical conception of a wave-like particle. In such a case, to locate and identify the conception is to locate and identify a difficult problem of instruction requiring much experiment and study.

A second curricular significance of the problem of the substantive structures of each discipline is less obvious. It concerns a peculiar consequence of the role of conceptual structures on our knowledge, a consequence little noted until recently. The dependence of knowledge on a conceptual structure means that any body of knowledge is likely to be of only temporary significance. For the knowledge which develops from the use of a given concept usually discloses new complexities of the subject matter which call forth new concepts. These new concepts in turn give rise to new bodies of enquiry and, therefore, to new and more complete bodies of knowledge stated in new terms. The significance of this ephemeral character of knowledge to education consists in the fact that it exhibits the desirability if not the necessity for so teaching what we teach that students understanding that the knowledge we possess is not mere literal, factual truth but a kind of knowledge which is true in a more complex sense. This in turn means that we must clarify for students the role of concepts in making knowledge possible (and limiting its validity) and impart to them some idea of the particular concepts that underlie present knowledge of each subject matter, together with the reasons for the appropriateness of these concepts and some hint of their limitations.*

The third problem of the structure of the disciplines we shall call the problem of the *syntactical* structure of the disciplines. This problem is hidden in the fact that if different sciences pursue knowledge of their respective subject matters by means of different conceptual frames, it is very likely that there will be major differences between one discipline and another in the way and in the extent to which it can verify its knowledge. There is, then, the problem of determining for each discipline what it does by way of discovery and proof, what criteria it uses for measuring the quality of its data, how strictly it can apply canons of evidence, and in general, of determining the route or pathway by which the discipline moves from its raw data through a longer or shorter process of interpretation to its conclusion.

Again, certain obvious consequences to education accrue from such a study. For, unless we intend to treat all knowledge as literal, true dogma, and thereby treat students as mere passive, obedient servants of our current culture, we want our students to know, concerning each body of knowledge learned, how sound, how dependable it is.

In summary then, three different sets of problems constitute the general problem of the structure of the disciplines. First there is the problem of the organization of the disciplines: how many there are; what they are; and how they relate to one another. Second, there is the problem of the substantive conceptual structures used by each discipline. Third, there is the problem of the syntax of each discipline: what its canons of evidence and proof are and how well they can be applied. Let us turn now to a brief investigation of each of these problems.

---

*See Joseph J. Schwab, "Enquiry, the Science Teacher, and the Educator," *School Review* 68 (Summer 1960), for an elaboration of this point.

THE PROBLEM OF THE ORGANIZATION OF THE DISCIPLINES

With the problem of the organization of the disciplines we must face at once one of the inevitable complexities of this terrain, the fact that it does not and cannot supply a single, authoritative answer to the question of what disciplines there are, how many there are, and how they are related to one another. The reason for this complexity is fairly obvious. The problem of organization is a problem of classification primarily. If we classify any group of complex things, we are faced with a wide choice of bases of classification. (Even with postage stamps, we could classify by country of origin, by color, by shape or size, or by some combination of two or more of these.) Disciplines are very complex, hence the diversity and variety of available modes of classification are great. Consequently, depending on what one emphasizes about the disciplines, one or another or still a third or a fifth or a tenth classification of them is generated.

Four bases of classification of disciplines have always demanded attention: (1) their subject matter, what they aim to investigate, or work upon; (2) their practitioners, what competences and habits are required to carry on their work; (3) their methods (syntax), and modes of enquiry by which the enquirer brings himself to bear on the subject matter; (4) their ends, the kinds of knowledge or other outcomes at which they aim. Let us, then, examine a few organizations of the disciplines which use one or more of these, choosing them for the light they may throw on current curriculum problems.

The basic organization of the sciences proposed by Aristotle is worth taking a brief look at nowadays because we have tended to forget what it emphasizes. In this organization, Aristotle made most use of the end or aim of the disciplines together with the character of the materials they work on, the subject matter. Using these two as bases of classification, Aristotle distinguished three major groups of disciplines, the names of which have survived even in our current commonsense knowledge of the disciplines—though the significance assigned them has altered or been lost. The three basic divisions are the *Theoretical,* the *Practical,* and the *Productive.*

The theoretical disciplines are those whose aim is to know. For Aristotle, "to know" meant to know indubitably. Therefore, the theoretical disciplines included only those whose subject matters exhibited such inexorable regularity that they could be considered proper objects of "knowing" enquiry. Aristotle thought there were three such "knowing" or theoretical disciplines: physics, mathematics, and metaphysics. Today, though we would be very doubtful about the possibility of indubitable knowledge, we would, nevertheless, recognize a group of "theoretical" disciplines whose aim was to know and whose subject matters were such that the knowledge these disciplines sought was as nearly stable as knowledge can be. We would include the physical and biological sciences in this group. We would include substantial portions of the social sciences. We would exclude metaphysics as doubtful indeed. We would exclude mathematics, not because it is doubtful, but because we would consider it very special.

The practical disciplines, for Aristotle, included those concerned with choice, decision, and action based on deliberate decision. Precisely because its aim was to do, and therefore to alter the course of things, its subject matter had to have the property that was exactly opposite to the property required for the theoretical sciences. The subject matters of the practical sciences by necessity, must be not inexorable in their behavior, but capable of alteration, not fixed and stable but changeable.

It is exceedingly important, if we are to appreciate the bearing of this Aristotelian classification on modern problems, that we realize that "deliberate action" meant for Aristotle actions undertaken for their *own sakes* and not actions undertaken merely as the necessary preliminaries to some other end. Such actions, undertaken for their own sakes, constitute, then, what we mean by "a good life." They are the activities that stem from and express the best of which each man is capable. The practical sciences were (and are) therefore, ethics and politics. For us in modern times, ethics and politics would include not only each individual effort to lead and examine a deliberate life and the governing and policymaking in high places, but also the difficult and terrifying business of being parents, of being teachers *deliberately* and not as automatons, and the responsible work of administration and policymaking at all levels, together with those parts of the social sciences which contribute to such activities. I need not add that of all the things the schools might do, they do least of this. A few nursery schools, a very few teachers at the elementary level, and some few men and women at the college level give thought and time and energy toward evoking in their students the competencies and habits that lead to the making of good choices and good decisions and help the person to act in ways commensurate with his decisions. But by and large, the time, the energy, and the resources of our public schools ignore the very existence of practical disciplines in the Aristotelian sense.

The productive disciplines in the Aristotelian scheme are what the word "productive" suggests. They are the disciplines devoted to *making*: the fine arts, the applied arts, engineering. In connection with the significance of the Aristotelian productive disciplines for modern curriculum problems, let us note a principal characteristic of the entire Aristotelian organization: it emphasizes the sharp differences among the three groups of disciplines. The theoretical disciplines, devoted to knowing, concern themselves with those aspects of things which are fixed, stable, enduring. Hence, the theoretical disciplines are concerned with precisely these aspects of things which we cannot alter by making or make use of by doing. The productive disciplines are concerned with what is malleable, capable of being changed. The practical disciplines are concerned with another sort of malleability of human character, its ability to deliberate on its future and (within limits) to do as it sees fit.

We, on the other hand, have tended to fall into the habit of treating all disciplines proper to the schools as if they were theoretical. We manage to maintain this preoccupation in the case of the practical disciplines by ignoring them. In the case of the productive disciplines, we ignore them in some cases and in others resort to the trick of treating them as if they were theoretical. Music appreciation is taught as if its purpose were to recognize obvious themes of symphonies or concertos and proudly announce the opus number and the composer's name. Performing music is taught as if the aim were merely to follow the notes and obey the teacher's instructions about the score. Literature is taught as if dramas and novels were windows looking out on life, or worse, as if, as in the case of music appreciation, the object of the game were to know choice tidbits about the character, the life, or the times of the author. Art is taught, like literature, as if its aim were to provide a true, a faithful photograph of life. Happily, the exceptions to these strictures are increasing. Music appreciation is more and more being taught as a mastery of those arts by which the ear and the mind creatively take in the form and content of music. Performing music is more and more being taught in such a way that the students learn the grounds by which to discover and select from alternative interpretations of the score. Poetry, literature, and drama are more and more the objects of the kind of scrutiny which permits their appreciation as works of art rather than as sources of vicarious experience. More and more teachers of art permit their students the freedom for creation which society has long since accorded the professional artist. Nevertheless, the theoretizing of the productive disciplines is still prevalent enough to render this warning relevant.

Let us turn to another organization of the sciences, notable in that one version of it is reborn with every undergraduate generation. This is Auguste Comte's positive hierarchy of the sciences. This scheme is based on the view that subject matter, and only subject matter, should provide the basis for classification. It takes the further view that subject matters should be ordered in terms of *their* subject matters; that is, Comte maintains that orders of phenomena can be discerned, each order consisting of members of the next lower order organized into more complex structures. Using this Chinese box conception of the world, Comte locates physical things as the simplest of all orders (presumably something like our modern fundamental particles). Chemicals come next, as consisting of physicals organized in a new way. Then come biologicals as still higher organizations of chemicals. Finally, at the top, come socials as organizations of biologicals. Thus the Comtian hierarchy of the sciences runs: physics, chemistry, biology, the social sciences. Then Comte adds one last factor. At the bottom of the entire structure he places another ''science''—mathematics, mathematics conceived as a kind of natural logic governing the study of all the sciences above it.

Perhaps because of its simplicity and its tendency to be reborn in every generation, this particular organization of the disciplines has been one of the most tyrannical and unexamined curriculum principles in our time. It has dictated, I suspect, at least thirty-five percent of all the sequences and orders of study of the sciences at the high school and college level in the country. The biologist tries to make his task easier by insisting that chemistry precede his subject field. In turn, the chemist demands that physics precede his. The physicist demands that mathematics precede physics. And each appeals to the Comtian hierarchy as the principal reason for his demand.

There is some justice in this view but there is injustice too. For it is quite possible to read the Comtian hierarchy the other way around. The inverted reading can, indeed, be done without departing from Comte's own principles, as Comte himself well knew. The principle in question requires that each science in the hierarchy shall be well developed before the one above it can be developed. Thus an adequate sociology must wait upon a thoroughly adequate biology; biology, in turn, cannot become complete until chemistry is complete, and so on. This *seems* to suggest that physics ought to be developed by a study simply of physical things, postponing chemistry until the study of physicals is complete; in the same way chemistry would be developed by a study of chemicals, postponing biology until the chemistry is complete. However, if we look closely at the basic Comtian principles, we realize that a complete, positive knowledge of the constituents and the organization of chemicals can be developed only if we have sought out and identified all the behaviors of which chemicals are capable. At this point arises the startling corollary that leads to an inverted reading of the Comtian hierarchy. For, clearly, if biologicals are organizations of chemicals, biologicals constitute the place in which some large array of chemical potentialities becomes real and can be seen. It follows, then, that a study of biologicals must precede any completion of chemistry; a study of socials must, in the same way, precede complete knowledge of biologicals, and so on.

The developments of science since the days of Comte most certainly bear out this reading of his hierarchy. Organic chemistry has developed only as we have studied the complex chemistry of the living organism. The behavior of the human individual has become better understood as we have studied human culture and society. The development by physicists of adequate theories of atomic structure rests upon knowledge of chemicals. Thus we see that it is just as plausible to read the Comtian hierarchy downward from sociology through biology, chemistry, and physics to mathematics, as it is to read it upward from mathematics to physics, to chemistry, to biology, and finally to social science.

We cannot, then, rest our arguments for mathematics as prerequisite to physics, physics prerequisite to chemistry, and so on, on the assumption that the upward reading of the Comtian hierarchy constitutes an unequivocal curriculum principle. Rather, we might well argue that bits and portions of each of these alleged prerequisites should be taught as the need arises during the study of the higher sciences. For example, physics might well be taught by examining the obvious behaviors of physical things up to the point where it becomes clear to student and teacher alike that further progress in the physics requires mastery of certain mathematical conceptions or operations. At this point, the class would turn to the mastery of the mathematics required by the physics under study. In the same way, the complex study of the microchemistry of the living cell would not be taught as a prerequisite to study of the organism and its larger parts and functions; rather, the visible behaviors of the organism, of its organ systems and gross organs might well come first, with the biochemical materials so placed as to be meaningful to the students as the physiochemical basis for the behaviors already known.

The curriculum sequence of prerequisites based on the upward reading of the Comtian hierarchy (i.e., mathematics to physics to chemistry, etc.) is often referred to as the "logical order" of instruction. The fact that the Comtian hierarchy can be read plausibly in either direction requires us to realize, however, that the phrase "logical order" applied only to one of them is a special pleading. Either order is "logical." The upward order from mathematics to the social sciences we might well call the dogmatic order, i.e., the order that runs from the current explanation to that which is explained. The downward order from, say, biology to chemistry, we might call the order of enquiry, i.e., the order that runs from a display of phenomena calling for explanation to the explanation the science has developed. A curriculum choice between the order of enquiry and the dogmatic order cannot be made on subject-matter criteria alone. Rather, we must look to the capacities of our students, to knowledge of ways in which learning takes place, and to our objectives, what we hope our students will achieve, in order to make our decision.

THE PROBLEM OF THE SYNTAX OF THE DISCIPLINES

If all disciplines sought only to know and if the knowledge they sought were merely the simple facts, the syntax of the disciplines would be no problem. As we have seen, the disciplines are not this simple. Many are not, in the Aristotelian sense, theoretical at all: they seek ends that are not knowledge but something else—making, the appreciation of what is made, the arts and habits of deliberation, choice, and action. Those that are theoretical seek knowledge of different kinds (commensurate to their subject matters), hence use different methods and different canons of evidence and warrantability. For example, science seeks very general or even universal knowledge, while much history seeks the most detailed and particular knowledge. Each of these objects of enquiry poses problems peculiar to itself. Hence knowledge of each of them is sought in different ways. Even within the sciences there is much variability.

Biologists find it necessary or desirable to seek knowledge in bits and pieces while physicists, at the other extreme, work hard to develop broad, comprehensive theories which embrace vast ranges of subject matter. The evidence that justifies the acceptance of an isolated bit of knowledge and the evidence that justifies the acceptance of a broad, comprehensive theory are of different sorts. There is a problem, therefore, of determining for each discipline or for small groups of disciplines what pathway of enquiry they use, what they mean by verified knowledge and how they go about this verification.

To illustrate this diversity, let us take three "things" that are asserted to exist and to have certain defining properties and behaviors. Let us take, first, an automobile, second, an electron, third, a neutrino. Let the three statements read as follows:

The automobile in front of the house is black.
The electron is a particle with a small mass and a negative electrical charge.
The neutrino is a particle with neither charge nor rest mass.

All three statements, let us suppose, are "true." That they are "true" in different senses becomes plain when we consider the following points. We say that the car in front of the house is black and say it with confidence on two bases. First, we look at the car and its neighborhood and report what we saw; our colleague nods agreement. This, then, is a very simple syntax of discovery, requiring only a naive, private experience of the objects we propose to make statements about plus a transaction between ourself, another enquirer, and the same objects.

By contrast, the syntax that leads us to assert that the electron is a particle with a small mass and a negative electrical charge is far more complex. The statement most certainly does not rest on the fact that I have looked at an electron and that my colleague has also looked and nodded agreement. It cannot arise from such a syntax because the electron is not visible. It rests, rather, on a syntax that involves looking at quite different things, seeking agreement about them, and then adding two further steps. We note certain phenomena; others note the same; then we seek an *explanation* for what we have seen. For explanation we conceive the existence of a minute particle. To it, we assign precisely the mass and precisely the magnitude and kind of charge which would permit this particle—if it existed—to give rise to the phenomena we have observed. The two additional steps are hidden in the additional process of seeking explanation. First, we conceive of something that would account for the phenomena we are concerned about. However, we are not satisfied to use just any conception that will account for it. Rather, we demand that the conception fulfill a second condition: that it fit in with, be coherent with, the rest of the body of knowledge that constitutes our science. In the case of our electron we meet this condition by choosing a particular mass and a particular charge as its important properties. The choice of a particular mass ties our electron to the entire body of physical knowledge called gravitational dynamics. The assignment of a certain electrical charge ties our particle to our knowledge of electricity and its dynamical laws.

The assertion about the neutrino rests on still a third kind of syntactical structure. For not only are neutrinos invisible by definition but they have been assigned a *lack* of such properties as charge and rest mass which characterize the electron. The assigned lack of such properties means that in the ordinary course of events the behavior of neutrinos would have no detectable consequences, would give rise to no phenomena such as we observed and accounted for by positing the existence of the electron. Instead, the ground for positing the existence of the neutrino was roughly as follows: certain effects were found in a phenomenon called beta decay which appeared to be exceptions to certain of the so-called conservation laws, laws that formed part of the very foundation of the body of physical knowledge. One way to account for these beta decay phenomena would be to treat them as "disproofs" of these conservation laws. Another way would have been to treat the decay phenomena as exceptions to the conservation laws and then to dream up an ad hoc explanation for the exception. Physicists preferred, however (for reasons I shall not go into now), to keep the conservation laws intact and universal, and the only conceived alternative enabling them to retain these laws was to suppose the existence of a well-nigh undetectable particle that carried off the quantities whose disappearance would otherwise have called the conservation laws into question.

We have here, then, three different senses in which statements are said to be "true" or warranted, differences of sense not revealed by the statements themselves. The statements are all of the same form—the automobile is black, the neutrino is such and such, the electron is something else. Only the context, the structure of problem, evidence, inference, and interpretation which constitutes the syntax of discovery behind each statement would reveal to us the different senses in which each is true.

The significance of this variety of modes of enquiry, of patterns of discovery and verification, lies in this: most statements of most disciplines are like the single words of a sentence. They take their most telling meanings, not from their dictionary sense, not from their sense in isolation, but from their context, their place in the syntax. The meaning of F = MA or of free fall, of electron or neutrino, is understood properly only in the context of the enquiry that produced them.

This need for context of enquiry wherewith to make teaching and learning clear has been almost universally overlooked because of a singular failure in the subject-matter preparation of teachers. They have been permitted to assume, or, indeed, have been flatly told, that "induction" or "scientific method" stands for something simple, single, and well defined. Quite the contrary is true: "induction" is not the name for some single, definite process but merely an honorific word attached by various philosophers to whatever mode of enquiry they favor. To a few philosophers, "induction" means the process of simple enumeration of a large number of instances of something or other by which we try to discern what is common among them. In this view, the outcome of "induction" is "generalization." To other philosophers, "induction" means the analysis of phenomena into unit events and the attempt to find out which events invariably precede which others. To still others, "induction" means the attempt to conceive ideas, however remote they may be from the possibility of direct verification, which will "explain," "account for," "embrace," the largest possible variety of phenomena with the greatest economy.

THE PROBLEM OF THE SUBSTANTIVE STRUCTURES OF THE DISCIPLINES

Let us first redevelop the idea of substantive structures and their role in enquiry as sketched in our introduction.

The fact that we propose to investigate a given subject is to admit that we are, in large part, ignorant of it. We may have some superficial knowledge: we may have dealt with the subject matter as part of our round of practical problems; but the very fact that we propose to investigate the subject means that we mistrust our knowledge or consider it entirely inadequate. Thus, enquiry begins in virtual ignorance. Ignorance however, cannot originate an enquiry. Subjects complex enough to demand enquiry are subjects that confound us by the great variety of characteristics, qualities, behaviors, and interactions they present to our view. This richness paralyzes enquiry, for it is far too much to handle all at once and, in our ignorance, we have no way of discerning the greater from the lesser fact; we cannot discriminate the facts that are most "telling" about our subject matter from those that are trivial. In short, if data are to be collected, we must have some sort of guide to relevance and irrelevance, importance and unimportance.

This role of guide to the enquiry is played by a conception borrowed or invented by the enquirer. These conceptions constitute the substantive structures of a discipline.

Let us take, as an example of a primitive beginning of enquiry, the situation that prevailed in the study of animal behavior some sixty years ago. Our knowledge of the behavior of small aquatic animals at that time was no greater than might have been possessed by an alert, small boy who had watched the darting of fish, the play of tadpoles, and the movements of insect larvae in the ponds and streams of his farm. What, then, should we investigate about these dartings, movements, and plays? Should we ask what needs they serve? Perhaps. Yet we do not even know that needs are involved. Shall we ask what purposes the animals have in mind? We do not know whether they have purposes or not. Shall we then try to discover the patterns of these motions, the order in which they occur? The trouble with this is that when a vast number of movements are involved, we must suppose, by analogy to ourselves, that they do not all belong together. Hence the overall order of them would be meaningless. Yet we cannot discern each coherent subgroup of motions because we do not yet know either the beginnings ("wants," "needs," "stimuli") or their terminations ("goals," "needs satisfied," "terminal response").

This frustration of enquiry was resolved by appealing to the then popular view that all things, including living things, were no more than simple machines, the pattern of which was the simple one known to nineteenth-century physics. This idea of a simple machine was applied to the study of behavior by supposing that every movement through space of an animal was a response to some single, specific, stimulating factor in the environment. It was further supposed that each such stimulated response could be one of only two possible kinds—a movement toward the stimulus or a movement away from it. Such a movement was dubbed a "tropism," "taxis"; movements toward the stimulus being called positive, those away from the stimulus, negative.

This naive and now obsolete conception removed the frustration of enquiry by giving us questions to ask. We were to determine for each organism what stimuli it responded to and whether it responded in the positive or negative sense. These identified questions in turn determined the pattern of experiment. We were to place our aquatic organism in a tank of water, make sure that all physical stimuli but one were uniform throughout the tank, let one stimulus, light, for example, be of high intensity at one end of the tank and low intensity at the other, and then note, as our important datum, which way the animal went. Then our knowledge of animal behavior was to be summed up in a catalogue of negative and positive tropisms characteristic of each species investigated.

Similar naive conceptions enabled us to begin enquiry in other complex fields. Chemistry was able to make great advances in the study of the array of substances of the world by imposing on them the notion of "element." By "element" was meant a substance of ultimate simplicity, a substance made only of itself and incapable of being changed into another such simple substance. This conception dictated the questions to be asked of matter by chemists and the patterns of experiment. The fundamental question was: into what simpler substance can this substance be decomposed? Hence the patterns of experiment were analysis and synthesis. Similar "elements" were devised to guide our earliest enquiries into human personality. We conceived of each human person as consisting of a greater or lesser quantity of each of a number of "traits." Like the chemical elements, each such "trait" (such as courage, imagination, logical reasoning, assiduity) was supposed to be simple (made of no further subtraits) and independent of all other traits.

The substantive principles chosen to guide enquiry are controlled by two opposing criteria. One of these I shall call reliability. Reliability requires that the guiding principle be free of vagueness and ambiguity, that the referents of its terms have unequivocal location and limit, and that the measurements or manipulations of these referents can be made precisely and can be repeated within uniform results. The substantive structures cited as examples above meet this criterion as well as could be expected.

They do not, however, satisfactorily fulfill the second criterion, which I shall call validity. Note the failure in each case which illustrates the lack of adequate validity. Animal behavior is reduced to a catalogue of independent responses to independently acting stimuli. Yet our knowledge of ourselves and of higher animals makes it highly unlikely that any animal's behavior will be a repertory of separate and independent responses to stimuli. It is much more likely (we suspect) that previous responses modify later ones and that the response to two stimuli presented simultaneously will *not* be the algebraic sum of the responses to each when presented separately. The idea of simple and independent traits, which enabled us to make a start on a study of human personality, is similarly questionable. It is entirely likely that traits are not independent at all but, rather, affect one another. Further, traits may not be fixed quantities but products of experience, changing as our experience grows and changes. Indeed, it may be that a much richer and more complete understanding of human personality could be achieved by doing away entirely with a notion of traits in any form. The notion of chemical element and compound in its most primitive form we may also suspect to be highly incomplete. It supposes that the properties of a compound arise simply by juxtaposition or union of two or more elements. Yet our experience in art, architecture, and engineering tells us that it is not only the constituents of a compound which confer properties on the compound but the organization of these constituents as well.

In short, the criterion of validity asks that the data we use be not only reliable but representative. It asks that the substantive structure that points to these data as the appropriate data of enquiry reflect as much as possible of the richness and complexity of the subject matter to which it is applied.

The existence of these two criteria is important to us because they lead to two characteristics of knowledge which, in turn, have important implications for curriculum. In the first place, the play of these two criteria confer on scientific knowledge a distinctly revisionary character. In the second place, in some sciences the same interplay leads to the concurrent development of a number of bodies of knowledge of the same subject matter.

The revisionary character of scientific knowledge accrues from the continuing assessment and modification of substantive structures. As investigations proceed under the guidance of an early, naive structure, we begin to detect inconsistencies in our data and disparities between our conclusions and the behavior of our subject. These inconsistencies and disparities help us identify the invalidities in our conception. Meanwhile, the naive structure has enabled us nevertheless to gain some knowledge of our subject and to sharpen our techniques for study. Our new knowledge of the subject, our improved techniques, and our sharpened awareness of inadequacies in our substantive structures enable us to conceive new structures more complex than the old, more adequate to the richness of the subject matter. With the advent of a new structure, the knowledge contained in the older conceptions, though "right" enough in its own terms, is rendered obsolete and replaced by a new formulation which puts old facts and new ones together in more revealing ways.

While different substantive structures tend to succeed one another in physics, chemistry, and biology, other disciplines are characterized by the concurrent utilization of several sets of structures. In the recent study of human personality, for example, two bodies of knowledge competed in the market place at the same time. One body of knowledge had been developed by conceiving personality, after the analogy of the body, as consisting of psychic organs. The other body of knowledge had been developed by conceiving of personalities as arising from the need of persons for one another, as developing, for better or for worse, out of the experience of self and of others. Personality, this body of knowledge held, is best described in terms of the various relations the self can establish with others.

Such a pluralism of substantive structures and of bodies of knowledge is characteristic of the social sciences generally and of many humane studies. There is more than one body of economic knowledge; different anthropologists and different sociologists tackle their problems in different terms and in different ways; different critics use widely different conceptions of the art object in the analysis and evaluation of drama, poetry, music, and painting.

The curricular significances of the revisionary character of knowledge and the plural character of knowledge are too numerous to develop fully here. Let us be satisfied with three.

In the first place, both characteristics point to the danger of a purely dogmatic, inculcative curriculum. If we dogmatically select one of several bodies of theory in a given field and dogmatically teach this as the truth about its subject matter, we shall create division and failure of communication among our citizens. Students of different school systems in different regions who are dogmatically taught different histories of crucial moments in our nation's development are an obvious case in point. It is no less divisive, however, if our future citizens are barred from sharing enjoyment of literature and the arts by having been the victims of different dogmas, or barred from understanding each other by having been inculcated with different dogmatic views of the roots of human action or the origins of culture and civilization. The alternative is to avoid indoctrination. We may, if we like, choose but one of several pluralities of bodies of knowledge. But if we do, let it be taught in such a way that the student learns what substantive structures gave rise to the chosen body of knowledge, what the strengths and limitations of these structures are, and what some of the alternative structures are which give rise to alternative bodies of knowledge.

The revisionary character of knowledge assumes curriculum significance because revisions now take place so rapidly that they will probably occur not once but several times in the lives of our students. If they have been taught their physics, chemistry, or biology dogmatically, their discovery that revision has occurred can lead only to bewilderment and disaffection. Again, the alternative is the teaching of scientific knowledge in the light of the enquiry that produced it. If students discover how one body of knowledge succeeds another, if they are aware of the substantive structures that underlie our current knowledge, if they are given a little freedom to speculate on the possible changes in structures which the future may bring, they will not only be prepared to meet future revisions with intelligence but will better understand the knowledge they are currently being taught.

16. DEVELOPING A CURRICULUM FOR MODERN LIVING

Florence Stratemeyer

In the curriculum focused on learner's interests and the persistent life situations which are a part of those concerns, the nature of society, the nature of the learner, and the way in which learning takes place are viewed as central in curriculum development. Society provides the framework within which children and youth live and learn, and inevitably affects what they bring to school and the ways in which they put their school experiences to work. The kind of society from which learners come gives direction to the values they seek to achieve as they share with others the task of building their country and their world. If that task is to be prosecuted constructively a curriculum proposal must take into account the capacities of the individual, how he matures, and the way he learns. Not to do so risks wasting valuable hours of child and teacher time on concepts or skills that could be acquired much more effectively at another stage of develop-

SOURCE. In Ronald T. Hyman (ed.), *Approaches in Curriculum* (Englewood Cliffs, N.J.: Prentice-Hall, Inc., 1973), pp. 53–72. Copyright © 1973. Reprinted by permission of Prentice-Hall, Inc. Adapted by the author with the permission of the publisher from Florence Stratemeyer, Hamden L. Forkner, Margaret G. McKim, and A. Harry Passow, ''A Proposal for Designing a Curriculum for Living in Our Time,'' in *Developing a Curriculum for Modern Living* (New York: Teachers College Press, 1957), chapter 5.

208

ment. More serious is the possibility of "teaching" skills, concepts, and facts that do not make their anticipated contribution to effective living.

THE EVERYDAY CONCERNS OF THE LEARNER ARE THE STARTING POINT

Children and youth develop at different rates, have widely differing backgrounds, and come to school with varying interests. Their concerns are many— how to make a model airplane fly, what to feed a pet turtle, whom to elect as captain of the baseball team, why paints dry out, how to interpret the headlines in the daily paper, how to get a bicycle license, what it means to fly faster than sound, whether to complete a committee assignment or go out with the "gang," how to build a "ham" radio station, which college to attend, what part to take in a community clean-up campaign.

In some cases the problems and interests are those of individuals; in others they are group concerns. In some situations the learners have clearly formulated purposes; in others they are inarticulate. In some cases learners may be unaware of situations in the immediate community or the larger national or world setting that could have much meaning if only their attention were drawn to them. They may not sense sources of aesthetic expression in which they could find lasting satisfactions if they were given opportunity to explore. They may not respond to wonders in the natural or technological world in which deep and abiding interests might develop if these worlds were opened to them.

These everyday concerns of learners are the sources of situations which have meaning for them in the light of their maturity and experience and which provide strong motivation for learning. Expressed or unexpressed, these immediate problems, concerns, and interests need to be the starting points around which classroom experiences are developed. This is a concept of the curriculum which . . .

recognizes the worth of each individual and allows for his uniqueness— in needs, concerns, talents, interests

helps the learner face the world at his level of understanding

recognizes the nature of his growth and utilizes the meanings experiences have for him

values the learner's daily living at any stage of his development as important to the society of which he is a member

relates his in-school and out-of-school experiences

A curriculum which has maximum meaning for learners develops as learners and their teacher work together on the problems and interests of everyday living.

EVERYDAY CONCERNS ARE RELATED TO PERSISTENT LIFE SITUATIONS

Present concerns of learners must be dealt with in such a way as to provide sound bases for future action. This will happen when present concerns, or situations of everyday living, are seen in the light of *persistent life situations*. These are the situations that recur in the life of the individual in many different ways as he grows from infancy to maturity. Every individual is concerned to some degree with such fundamentals as keeping well, understanding himself, making a living, getting along with others, adjusting to the natural environment, dealing with social and political structures and forces, developing a sustaining philosophy or set of values. These and other concerns tend to persist throughout life, although the circumstances through which they are met vary with the individual's background and maturity.

> *Getting along with others* is a persistent life situation that occurs in effectively coping with a brother's teasing, in being an accepted member of a peer group, in attending committee meetings, in working in the councils of nations.
>
> *Intergroup cooperation* is a persistent life situation that is involved in relationships between members of one peer group and another, among various committees in a class, among class groups in a school, between labor and management, among different racial, religious, national, and political groups.

A curriculum in which the learner and society are brought into relationship is one in which the everyday concerns of children and youth are seen as aspects of persistent life situations with which all members of society must be able to deal.

Teachers who try to help children and youth deal with their everyday concerns in ways that will enable them to cope with the situations that recur throughout life identify five *characteristics of persistent life situations* as significant in guiding learning.

Persistent Life Situations Recur Throughout the Life of the Individual

The same persistent situation reappears again and again in the everyday concerns of the individual at different stages of his development. *Therefore, the child or youth who is helped to see that similar situations recur in his everyday living can apply what he has learned in one situation to another and can test in experience the worth of his former learning.*

Managing money is a life situation that recurs again and again.

> A *five- or six-year-old* manages money as he goes on an errand to a neighborhood store, and as he decides how much of his allowance to spend on candy, put aside for Sunday School, or save in his bank.

At *eight or ten* the child also meets the same persistent life situation when he buys at the store, shares in decisions about spending family funds, puts money in the local or school bank, repays money borrowed from parents.

At *fifteen* the young person also buys at the store. He decides where to buy so that he can get the best merchandise for his money, what the price differences are on similar materials, what labels on materials mean. His everyday concerns may include budgeting his allowance, deciding whether to ask for a larger allowance, seeking jobs to supplement his allowance so that he can satisfy his needs.

The *adult* also deals with problems of money management in making purchases and he meets many of the same everyday concerns faced by the adolescent. He deals with larger amounts of money and more complicated situations—deciding when to purchase commodities wholesale, getting information from various agencies for consumer protection, financing a home or a business, providing funds for the education of offspring, providing security for later life.

Persistent Life Situations Take On New Meaning as the Individual Matures

Different aspects of persistent life situations become meaningful to the individual as he matures. *Therefore, the child or youth who is helped to deal with persistent life situations as they reappear in more complex form grows in insight into the problems he faces and widens and extends his understandings and concepts.*

Being accepted in a group is a persistent life situation that all individuals face, but acceptance has different meanings at different ages.

For the *six-year-old* being accepted in a group may mean getting others to play with him, knowing when and how to share his toys and other possessions, being allowed to use the toys of other children, being chosen by his group to do certain jobs. The six-year-old wants everyone to like him, but on his own terms.

The *ten-year-old* has some understanding of the feelings and wishes of others. He is willing for others to be considered, provided his wishes are not neglected. He is willing to have his friend made captain of the team if he himself is chosen to be on the team. Special problems of acceptance arise in working on teams or committees with members of the opposite sex.

For a *fifteen-year-old* both social customs and taboos must be carefully observed to gain acceptance in a peer group. Acceptance for the adolescent also means maintaining the security of close family ties while achieving acceptance by the new groups that are becoming a part of his developing independence. Among the everyday situations that he faces as he seeks to establish himself in his group are deciding when to break with community customs, resolving conflicts between the values of family and of friends, deciding whether to seek a class office, and deciding how long to observe a code not accepted by others in the group.

An *adult* continues to face the persistent life situation of being an accepted member of groups. He must learn how to make a constructive contribution to a community group; how to develop satisfactory group membership in church, club, or business when there are differences in race, religious affiliation, socio-economic status; how to relate himself to his family group; how to help his children make a positive contribution to the family group.

Many Persistent Life Situations May Be Involved In A Given Immediate Situation

Almost any everyday concern includes more than one persistent life situation. The number of persistent life situations included will vary from one immediate concern to another. *Therefore, the child or youth who is helped to give direct attention to the various persistent life situations involved in an activity will grow in ability to cope with the range of persistent life situations. Which one or ones of the several persistent life situations will receive the greatest attention depends on the needs of the learner.*

The *first grader* building a boat may deal with such persistent life situations as *measuring, using appropriate resources* (choosing suitable materials), *using common tools correctly, establishing effective working relations with others* (with other children who want to use the workbench and tools). For some first graders there will be the added problem of experimenting with color as a *means of aesthetic expression* as they choose the color to paint finished boats.

The *adolescent* buying his lunch in the school cafeteria may be dealing with the persistent problems of *meeting food needs* (selecting a balanced meal in terms of individual needs), *managing money* (buying within a fixed allowance and budgeting funds), *achieving status in a group* (which may involve buying extra desserts to secure the favor of friends or buying foods in keeping with the mores of the "gang").

The *adult* buying food in the local market may deal with such persistent life situations as *meeting food needs* as he selects in terms of a balanced meal, *determining the quality of goods, managing money*, and *determining a fair price for goods*. For some adults the everyday experience of purchasing food may also involve dealing with such added persistent life situations as *using sound bases for interpreting information* when reading advertisements or labels, *using systems of credit buying* if the goods are not to be paid for immediately, and on occasion the additional persistent situation of *respecting property rights* as one is tempted to handle or sample merchandise.

The Same Persistent Life Situation May Be Met and Coped with Through Very Different Experiences

Because of differences in abilities, interests, and associations learners of essentially the same maturity learn to cope with the same persistent life situations through widely varied everyday experiences. *Therefore, children and youth who are helped to deal with persistent life situations through experiences growing out of their own backgrounds and the associations which have meaning for them, have a flexible curriculum adjusted to individual and local situations. At the same time opportunity for growth in ability to deal with common and universal problems is provided.*

The possibility of helping learners grow in ability to cope with the same persistent life situations—to arrive at essentially the same basic understandings and ways of behaving—through a variety of experiences is significant for the teacher who recognizes the range of individual interests within a group. Individual needs and interests can be provided for through work on different aspects of a persistent life situation, through different approaches and ways of working, through recognition of the right of individuals to bring different purposes to a common experience, through provision for individual as well as group experiences.

Using tools, machines, and equipment is a persistent life situation met under different conditions in different communities.

In a *tenement* area where cooking is done on a small plate, where illumination comes from one outlet in the center of the room, and where there is no mechanical refrigeration, children and youth may "use tools, machines, and equipment" in regulating the gas burner on the stove while preparing a meal, and in building a window box for keeping food cool. These children may use simple tools in mending or building furniture, rigging a pulley clothesline, repairing toys, or carving wooden figures as a hobby.

In a *suburban home,* equipped with central heating, home freezer, numerous electrical outlets, vacuum cleaner and washing machine, and having lawn and garden plots, children and youth may use different tools and equipment as they read the heating thermostat, care for the bicycle which takes them to and from school, manage a part of the family garden, mow the lawn, or rake leaves. But they use many of the same tools as children of the tenement area as they put up screens, repair toys, build a birdhouse, or carve wooden figures as a hobby.

The two groups have a different orientation and different experiences. Whatever orientation or insight into the use, production, and distribution of tools and equipment will have meaning must grow out of the learner's own experience.

Working with different racial and religious groups is another persistent life situation that learners meet in a variety of ways. The meaning of this situation may differ in homogeneous and heterogeneous groups.

In a *heterogeneous population* the problem of religious differences may arise when certain children are absent from school because of special religious holidays or when they observe or comment on food practices. Or the immediate circumstances might be a reference to special religious schools. Whatever the everyday concern, its meaning to the learner who is a member of the minority group involved is quite different from its meaning to members of the majority group.

In a *homogeneous population,* where children have similar racial, national, religious, and economic backgrounds, understandings of differences among groups will come about differently. Within such groups many situations will arise which call for consideration and understanding of other racial, religious, social, and economic groups. There will be situations such as those created by radio, television, and news comments on federal aid to religious schools, reports on cases of racial discrimination, a local election issue relating to legislation in the interest of minority groups.

Persistent Life Situations Are a Part of All Aspects of the Learner's Daily Life

Persistent life situations are faced by the learner at home, at school, in the neighborhood, at church, at the movies, at camp, and in the host of other places where he works and plays. The same persistent life situation may be a part of several experiences which a learner has in any one day. *Therefore, children and youth who are helped to relate and integrate experiences—to see the same persistent life situation in everyday activities in the school, home, and community . . .*

> *will develop consistent ways of behaving as learnings gained in one situation are used in another*
>
> *will find in-school learning functionally useful out of school and vice versa*

Maximum growth is possible only when the dominant agencies guiding the learner's activities—home, school, church, community—coordinate their efforts. The school must view the learner's total experience and the curriculum must be responsive to the contributions of other agencies and learning experiences.

Using safety measures is a persistent life situation that occurs:

In the *home* when deciding where to keep playthings and tools, when using tools and machines, when using matches or caring for fires, when repairing household appliances, when deciding where to play, when deciding where to keep medicines.

In the *school* when using tools and equipment, when deciding where to keep tools and how to use them, when participating in fire drills, when working with traffic patrol, when participating in active sports.

In the *community* when riding a bicycle or driving a car, when crossing streets, when swimming, when picnicking in woods, when taking action on legislation regarding safety measures.

Dealing with success and failure is a persistent life situation that occurs:

In the *home* when a favorite toy breaks or a pet dies, when parental restrictions upset plans, when brothers or sisters tease, when parents praise a job well done, when report cards come home, when constructing a playhouse or taking a paper route.

In the *neighborhood* when participating in such social gatherings as dances at the community center and birthday parties; when taking part in recreational activities such as playing ball, tennis, and card games; when participating in club activities through voluntary effort—serving as chairman, officer, or committee member.

In the *school* when representing a class in making an announcement in assembly; when making a report, responding to a question, taking an examination; when participating in a class play, playing on the basketball team, acting as a member of the newspaper staff, serving on the student council, nutrition committee, or safety patrol.

Persistent Life Situations Call for Competencies that Require Growth in:

Individual Capacities—Including physical and mental health, intellectual power, manipulative skills, moral choice, aesthetic expression and appreciation

Social Relationships—Including person-to-person, person-to-group, and group-to-group relationships

Control of Environmental Factors and Forces—Including control of natural, technological, economic, social, and political forces and structures

In almost every situation of daily living individual capacities are called into play, and nearly always social relationships are present. The surrounding environment—natural, technological, or socio-economic-political—is a part of every situation. Growth in individual capacities, social relationships, and control of the environment is clearly interrelated, and the quality of development in one may influence the competence that can be attained in another. *Therefore, the child or youth who is helped to develop individual capacities, social relationships, and ability to control environmental factors and forces as he copes with persistent life situations is assured balanced growth.*

Writing a letter involves the persistent life situation of *expressing ideas in written form.* This requires primarily *individual capacity* to use correct words and sentence structure and to spell accurately, as well as capacity to deal with ideas, so that the letter will be understood. But writing a letter also involves the persistent life situation of *making appropriate responses to others* in *social relationships.* Further, it requires control of *environmental factors* as the individual copes with the persistent life situation of *using common tools and equipment correctly* as he employs pen or typewriter, and adjusts lighting facilities, table, and chair.

Deciding on the person for whom one will vote in an election is an immediate concern which involves *social relationships* and deals with the persistent life situation of *selecting leaders.* But *individual capacities* are also developed as the individual faces the persistent problems of *following and evaluating oral presentations and discussions, using sound bases for interpreting information, using appropriate resources* as he reads and listens to campaign speeches. *Environmental factors and forces* are a part of the experience as the individual deals with the persistent situation of *using instruments of communication* as he adjusts the radio or television and uses the voting machine, as well as the recurring problem of *electing governmental or other representatives* as he casts his vote.

CHARACTERISTICS OF THE CURRICULUM IN WHICH EVERYDAY CONCERNS ARE RELATED TO PERSISTENT LIFE SITUATIONS

In the range of the persistent life situations with which all individuals must deal, the teacher finds his guides for balanced development. In the ways in which they recur from childhood through adulthood he finds his cues for deciding how to help his group explore their concerns and assures continuous growth. This is a concept of the curriculum in which . . .

the basic problems and situations which are central in life itself are central in education

the *scope* lies in the range of persistent life situations with which every individual deals in some measure, and provides the guide to balanced development

the *content* of the curriculum consists of the experiences engaged in while dealing with everyday concerns as they are related to persistent life situations

continuity is achieved because persistent life situations are a continuing thread, appearing again and again in different combinations and circumstances as the learner moves from childhood through adulthood. Continuity also lies in the extension and widening of concepts/generalizations as new aspects of persistent life situations are dealt with. A curriculum which helps learners to deal with varied aspects of the same persistent life situation recognizes that . . .

children and youth seek to learn those things that their maturity and experience make meaningful to them

an optimal moment of learning for one person may not be the same as that for another

in meeting new situations the individual draws upon the generalizations which have emerged from previous experience

sequence is determined by the changing aspects of persistent life situations as the learner moves from childhood into the full responsibiities of adulthood.

school and community experiences *are related* because the same persistent life situations are faced in the home, at schol, in the neighborhood, at church, and in the varied other places where the learner works and plays. A curriculum built with regard for the fact that the same persistent life situation is met in both in-school and out-of-school activities of children and youth recognizes that the school as the delegated educational agency must . . .

consider the total educational program needed by learners in the given community be keenly aware of those things which other agencies are helping him to learn

vary its own leadership to recognize the best use of community resources

useful *facts, generalizations, skills,* and *attitudes are learned.* The curriculum which helps individuals deal with the same persistent life situation as it is faced in different forms and under different circumstances affords maximum opportunity to generalize and build skills and attitudes to use in recurring situations. Understandings, skills, and attitudes expand as persistent life situations are met in new experiences.

A SUMMARY LOOK

A curriculum which helps learners to deal with varied aspects of the same persistent life situation and with the range of these recurring situations builds on knowledge of the learner and the learning process.

Children and youth learn those things that are related to their purposes. The proposed curriculum, therefore, . . .

starts with the everyday concerns and experiences of learners

deals with those aspects of persistent life situations appropriate to the learners' background and maturity

helps learners deal with the one or more persistent situations which are a part of the immediate situation and most closely related to their needs.

provides opportunities for learners to share in the selection and development of experiences

Individuals differ in interests, needs, abilities, and growth patterns. The proposed curriculum, therefore, . . .

provides varied experiences for individuals and for groups from one year to another

helps individuals work on different aspects of the same persistent life situation which is a part of a group concern

helps individuals work on different persistent life situations which are a part of the group's immediate problem

gives recognition to the right of individuals to bring different purposes to a common experience and to use different ways of working takes into account the fact that learners will attain different levels of growth in dealing with a given situation, growth that will be further developed as the persistent situations recur

Physical, mental, emotional, and social development are related and take place simultaneously; learning is affected by the interrelations among these areas of growth. Therefore, the proposed curriculum . . .

helps learners deal with the several persistent life situations that make up an immediate situation

helps learners see interrelationships among areas of experience as they deal with the various persistent life situations which must be considered in dealing with the immediate concern

provides for rounded and balanced development through helping children and youth deal with the range of persistent life situations

fosters growth in individual capacities, social relationships, and control of environmental factors and forces needed in dealing with persistent life situations

Something is learned only when the individual can and will act on his new insights, skills, and understandings. Thus, the proposed curriculum . . .

help learners deal with persistent life situations as they appear at home, in the neighborhood, at church, at work, at play

helps individuals use their learnings—understandings, generalizations, skills—as guides in dealing with the same persistent life situations when they recur

helps learners develop consistent ways of behaving as learnings gained in one situation are used in another

The concept of Persistent Life Situations provides the key to relating the learner and society.

Because persistent life situations are a part of all aspects of life . . .

balanced or rounded development can be defined by the range and variety of situations with which all persons inevitably deal and in which all need to develop competence no experience, however transitory or specific, need be trivial if the learner is helped to see and deal with the recurring situations or problems which are a part of that experience

children and youth can be helped to see the same persistent life situation in everyday activities in home, school, and community

children and youth can be helped to develop consistent ways of behaving by using learnings from one situation in another

children and youth will find in-school learnings functionally useful out of school and vice versa

Because persistent life situations recur and take on new meanings as the individual matures . . .

the child or youth who is helped to see that similar situations recur in his everyday living can apply what he has learned in one situation to another and can test in experience the worth of his former learning

the child or youth who is helped to deal with these problems as they appear in more complex form grows in the ability to meet the problems he faces and extends his understandings, insights, and skills

maximum opportunity is provided for the learner to organize facts, concepts, and generalizations which are his cultural heritage for use in coping with the actual problems of life

continuity lies within the learner, not in external logic, and is achieved because life itself has continuity

Because the same persistent life situation may be a part of very different experiences . . .

the curriculum can be responsive to the interests and abilities of individual learners through all-class, small-group, and individual activities

the curriculum can be developed in terms of the particular situations of most concern to individuals and still enable them to grow in skills, understandings, and competencies needed by all persons

both a flexible curriculum and one which provides for growth in ability to deal with common and universal problems can be provided

Because many persistent life situations may be involved in an immediate situation . . .

> such situations can be used to develop a variety of skills and competencies
>
> individual needs and interests can be provided for through work on group problems
>
> emphases can be adjusted so that the needs and abilities of the individual learner will determine which of the several persistent life situations will receive the greatest attention
>
> children and youth can be helped to understand interrelationships among persistent life situations

Because dealing with persistent life situations calls for action based on understanding . . .

> maximum opportunity can be afforded to generalize and to use basic understandings and accepted values in new situations
>
> learners can be helped to acquire knowledge, concepts, and skills under circumstances which provide optimum encouragement to use these learnings
>
> learnings tend to remain at a high level of competence, since recurring situations call for their repeated use
>
> learners can be helped to acquire problem-solving skills essential in a world of change

Those who accept this approach to curriculum development are committed to deal with each situation as precisely and thoroughly as the maturity of the pupils permits. It is unnecessary to study all aspects of a problem when it is first considered. To do so might well mean dealing with concepts beyond both the concern and the ability of the learner. Because it is a persistent life situation, it will be met again. When it is, the learner's increased maturity will provide readiness for looking at it in new ways and with greater depth. The very fact that the situation will recur in more complex settings as the learner matures, together with the fact that the maturing individual will be able to see its new facets even in the same everyday experiences, provides a fundamental safeguard against a curriculum which leads to a smattering of knowledge or a meager understanding of many things.

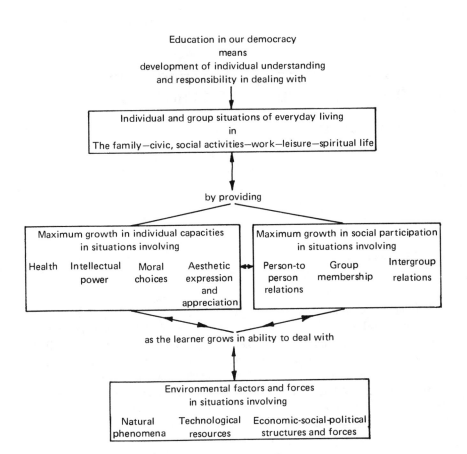

Education in our democracy
means
development of individual understanding
and responsibility in dealing with

Individual and group situations of everyday living
in
The family—civic, social activities—work—leisure—spiritual life

by providing

Maximum growth in individual capacities
in situations involving

Health   Intellectual   Moral   Aesthetic
         power   choices expression
                                and
                                appreciation

Maximum growth in social participation
in situations involving

Person-to   Group   Intergroup
person   membership   relations
relations

as the learner grows in ability to deal with

Environmental factors and forces
in situations involving

Natural   Technological   Economic-social-political
phenomena   resources   structures and forces

FIGURE 1

A Summary View

17. THE STRUCTURE OF KNOWLEDGE AND THE STRUCTURE OF THE CURRICULUM

Arno A. Bellack

During the current period of curriculum reform, most of the debate hinges on an old and familiar question: "What shall the schools teach?" This is a perennial question, one that apparently every generation has to solve over again for itself in the light of changing conditions and changing needs. And it is a question that can be answered only by reference to one's view of the nature of knowledge, for by universal agreement knowledge is the stock-in-trade of the school. Few would deny that the fields of organized inquiry are significant aspects of our culture that the school is uniquely equipped to introduce to students.

But there is also general agreement that the school's responsibility extends beyond teaching the organized fields of learning and inquiry; the school must also serve a multitude of ends and needs created by our society and our culture. At different times in the history of our schools widely different views have been held regarding the way in which knowledge should be organized and taught to meet these ends and needs. The traditionalists, for example, taught the time-honored subjects as anthologies of separate topics, with the hope that the bits and pieces of information would somehow or other turn out to be useful in the lives of their students. History became a recital of "one damned thing after another" (the phrase is Toynbee's), civics turned out to be a collection of miscellaneous information about government, and geography was nothing more than a catalogue of facts about places scattered over the globe.

SOURCE. In Dwayne Huebner (ed.), *A Reassessment of the Curriculum* (New York: Teachers College Press, 1964), pp. 25–40. Copyright 1964 by Teachers College, Columbia University.

Convinced that this kind of teaching would not prepare students to face the increasingly complex problems of their society, the progressive reformers of the 1930's and '40's proposed a new curriculum—one centered on the personal and social problems of youth and drawing on the academic disciplines as they became relevant to the problems under study. The disciplines were viewed as reservoirs from which facts and ideas could be drawn as needed; emphasis was on the *practical* ordering of knowledge with reference to problems to be solved.

Contemporary efforts to redefine the role of knowledge in the curriculum place emphasis on the *logical* order inherent in knowledge itself, on the structure of concepts and principles of inquiry that characterize the various fields of learning. Whereas formerly factual and descriptive content was stressed, now the emphasis is on basic concepts and methods which scholars use as intellectual tools to analyze and order their data.

Several claims are made for teaching the fundamental structures of the disciplines, two of which are of central importance and are worth considering here. The first is that understanding of fundamental ideas is the main road to adequate transfer of training. Professor Bruner, who is largely responsible for introducing the concept of structure into educational discourse, observes that

knowledge is a model we construct to give meaning and structure to regularities in experience. The organizing ideas of any body of knowledge are inventions for rendering experience economical and connected. We invent concepts such as force in physics, the bond in chemistry, motives in psychology, style in literature as means to the end of comprehension . . . . The power of great organizing concepts is in large part that they permit us to understand and sometimes to predict or change the world in which we live. But their power lies also in the fact that ideas provide instruments for experience.

Therefore, he contends, "the structure of knowledge—its connectedness and its derivations that make one idea follow another—is the proper emphasis in education."[1]

The second important claim for emphasis on structure is that by constantly re-examining material taught in the schools for its fundamental patterns of organization, the schools will be able to narrow the gap between "advanced" knowledge and "elementary" knowledge. Since scholars at the forefront of their disciplines are able to make the greatest contribution to the substantive reorganization of their fields, current curriculum projects place great emphasis on the participation of university researchers in continuing revision of the program of studies. Scholars in the various disciplines and their professional organizations have in recent years made proposals for revamping the curriculum in elementary and secondary schools—first in mathematics, physics, chemistry, and biology; then in English; and recently and belatedly in economics, geography, anthropology, and history.

The focus of attention in each of these projects is an individual discipline.

Little or no attention is given to the relationships of the individual fields to each other or to the program of studies within which they must find their place. National committees in the fields of chemistry, physics, and biology have proceeded independently of each other. The projects in economics, geography, and anthropology are unrelated to one another or to the other social sciences. Only in mathematics has there been a disposition to view the field as a whole, but this is a reflection of developments within the discipline of mathematics at the higher levels of scholarship.

The situation developing in the elementary and secondary schools thus begins to reflect, at least to some degree, the state of affairs in the universities with respect to the development and organization of knowledge, which Professor John Randall has described in this way:

> As reflected in the microcosm of the modern university, the world of knowledge has today become radically plural. It is a world of many different knowledges, pursued in varied ways to diverse ends. These many inquiries are normally carried on with little thought for their relation to each other. The student of John Donne's poetry, the student of the structure of the atom—each gives little enough attention to what the others are doing, and none at all to any total picture of anything. Each has his own goals, his own methods, his own language for talking about what he is doing and what he has discovered. Each seems happiest when left to his own devices, glad indeed if he can keep others from treading on his toes. Each is convinced that what he himself is doing is worth while. But none has too much respect for the others, though he is willing enough to tolerate them. They have all little understanding of each other's pursuits—what they are trying to do, how they are doing it, and what they really mean when they talk about it.[2]

I emphasize this pluralism in the academic world not to deplore it but to call attention to the problem that it presents for those who are concerned with the organization of the entire curriculum. For the curriculum builder is concerned not only with the structures of the individual disciplines, but also with the structure of the instructional program within which the fields of knowledge find their place. The problem can be very simply stated, if not easily solved: What general structure of the curriculum can be developed so that autonomy of the parts does not result in anarchy in the program as a whole? This is the question I propose to discuss briefly here.

When one looks beyond the structure of the individual disciplines and asks about the structure of the curriculum, attention is focused on *relationships* among the various fields that comprise the program of studies. For just as relationships among ideas are at the heart of the concept of structure as applied to the individual disciplines, so relationships among the disciplines are at the heart of the notion of structure as applied to the curriculum as a whole.

The mathematics teacher, the science teacher, the music teacher, and so on through the list of specialized functionaries in the school—each tends typically to interpret the entire program of the school through his own specialized teaching field. This is probably inevitable, and it would not be undesirable except for one stubborn fact: each of the specialized aspects of the program deals with human beings, and since human beings are not infinitely plastic in adapting to particular situations, it follows that what goes on at one place in the system sets limiting conditions for the accomplishments of purposes elsewhere in the system. Hence the importance of giving attention not only to connections between ideas in an individual field, but also to relationships among the fields of knowledge included in the curriculum.

There are many ways in which one can conceive of these inter-connections. I should like to focus attention on three types of relationships that obtain (or *ought* to obtain) among the teaching fields that comprise the curriculum:

(1) *Relationships among cognate or allied disciplines that deal with similar problems or phenomena.* Here I have in mind, for example, relations among the social sciences, whose common objective is to describe and explain the social and cultural behavior of man; and connections among the natural sciences, whose common aim is to describe and explain physical and biological phenomena.

(2) *Relationships among the broad areas of knowledge—the sciences and mathematics on the one hand, and the humanities on the other.* Call to mind the problem raised by C. P. Snow in his *The Two Cultures and the Scientific Revolution,* the great gulf that lies between the literary world and the scientific world. Snow insists that the only way to close the gap between the two cultures is by rethinking our education.

(3) *Relationships of knowledge to human affairs.* Given the current emphasis on the role of organized knowledge in the curriculum, we do well to remind ourselves that the goal of general education is not to train students as specialists in mathematics, geography, biology, or whatever other subjects they might study. Rather, the goal is to make available to students the intellectual and aesthetic resources of their culture in such a way that they become guides for intelligent action and help students create meaning and order out of the complex world in which they find themselves.

Let us briefly examine these three types of relationships.

RELATIONSHIPS AMONG ALLIED DISCIPLINES

According to long and honorable tradition, knowledge is grouped for pedagogical purposes in four major categories—the natural sciences, the social sciences, mathematics, and the humanities (the latter an omnibus term that includes art, literature, philosophy, and music). These broad groupings of organized disciplines are generally recognized as basic cultural interests of our society which constitute both the resources and the obligations of the schools. Each major field represents distinctive methods and conceptual schemes in which the world and man are viewed from quite different vantage points. Instruction in these areas has as its primary goal equipping students with key concepts and methods that inform and sustain intelligent choice in human affairs.

Although the four major areas of knowledge are generally recognized as important components of the curriculum, they are not currently used as the context or framework for curriculum building. Instead, as we have already noted, recent curriculum projects have focused attention on individual disciplines without concern for their relationships to allied fields. Thus the economists, the geographers, and the anthropologists have proceeded independently of each other, as have the biologists, chemists, and physicists. To be sure, economists suggest ways in which economic ideas can be taught in history; and anthropologists show how some of their generalizations can be woven into courses in geography. This is all to the good; it even seems to suggest that integration of a limited variety might be appropriate for teaching purposes. But scant attention is given to building a curriculum design within which the individual fields might find their place.

It is my contention that this approach has certain inherent shortcomings and that we would do well to shift the context for curriculum planning from the individual disciplines, as is now the vogue, to the broad groupings of knowledge represented by the natural sciences, the social sciences, mathematics, and the humanities. Let us briefly consider some of the problems involved in curriculum building in the social sciences to show why this proposed shift is desirable and necessary.

The social sciences—economics, social psychology, political science, sociology, anthropology, geography, and history—are all seeking explanations of the same phenomenon, man's social life. This common goal is what makes it reasonable to group them together as the *social* sciences. All of them have grown out of man's attempt to interpret, understand, and control the social environment. But each field formulates its own questions about this subject matter and develops its own system of concepts to guide its research. The economist is preoccupied with the concept of scarcity, the political scientist with the concepts of power and authority, the anthropologist with the notion of culture, and the sociologist with social functions and social systems. Each science is thus abstract, dealing with only certain facets of actual social relationships and institutions—facets that do not permit of physical separation but only of analytical separation.

Man's social life as it is actually lived is therefore far more complex than the limited image of it reflected in the concepts and generalizations of any one of the social disciplines. It follows then, as Professor Kingsley Davis has suggested, that "in so far as the prediction of actual events is concerned, the various social sciences are mutually interdependent, because only by combining their various points of view can anything approaching a complete anticipation of future occurrences be achieved."[3] Policies that are proposed and actions that are taken to deal with problems in social affairs are of necessity interdisciplinary, for concrete social reality is not mirrored in the findings of any one discipline.

Now this is a matter of central importance to those whose job it is to plan and organize the social studies curriculum. To focus exclusive attention on certain aspects of the social world as seen through the eyes of one or two of the social sciences is to give students a myopic vision of man's social behavior and his institutions. To shape children's conceptions of the social world through exclusive emphasis on the language of the economist, for example, to the exclusion of the language of the sociologist, political scientist, anthropologist, and historian is to determine that they shall interpret human affairs principally in terms which the economist uses to view reality—in terms of supply, demand, scarcity, production, and consumption.

Students must be helped to see the limitations as well as the uses of a single discipline in interpreting events as they actually occur. And for anything approaching a comprehensive view of man's functioning in society, the specialized perspectives of all the social sciences are needed. Curriculum builders in the social studies have the enormously difficult job of providing a place in their programs for all the social sciences, each of which contributes its distinctive perspective on human institutions and human behavior.

It is clear that such a program can be developed only on the basis of collaboration among the various social sciences. Such collaboration does not presuppose a "unified social science" as the basis for planning the elementary and secondary school curriculum. Quite the opposite is the case. For the social disciplines today are characterized by a plurality of methods and conceptual schemes developed by social scientists to deal with problems within their individual spheres. Instead of a unity of method or a single universe of discourse, we find a vast confederation of separate areas of study. Modes of thinking and analysis differ from field to field, and even from problem to problem within the same field. In time, a Bacon of the sciences that bear on the social and cultural behavior of man may emerge, but that time is not yet.

At the same time, in spite of increasing specialization and internal differentiation, there are interconnections among the social sciences that curriculum planning for the schools should take into account. For example, the various social sciences borrow rather handily from each other when it comes to both concepts and methods. Historians make use of concepts from all the other social sciences. Political scientists interested in political socialization get their methods from behavioral scientists and seem in many respects more closely related to sociologists and social psychologists than to fellow political scientists. Certain anthropologists have utilized the Freudian view of human development in analyzing patterns of various cultures. Geographers make extensive use of the perspectives of history and concepts developed by all the behavioral sciences.

Furthermore, we find not only interchange of concepts and methods but growing collaboration among specialists. For example, studies of the nature and function of "authority" are now undertaken jointly by political scientists and sociologists, and there have been recent studies conducted by economists in collaboration with anthropologists to determine whether certain economic theories hold for different types of economic systems. The convergence of social scientists upon the same problems has given rise to what Professor Robert Merton calls "interdisciplines," such as social biology, political sociology, and sociological history.

The picture that emerges from this cursory review of the current state of affairs in the social sciences is one of great diversity. Given this mosaic of disciplines and interdisciplines, each characterized by multiple conceptual schemes and methods, the curriculum builder is faced with the problem of developing structures for teaching that relate the social sciences to each other in meaningful ways and avoid undue fragmentation of knowledge.

What has been said about the social sciences applies in principle to the natural sciences, mathematics, and the humanities. The significant point is that there is a need for a broader context for curriculum planning than the separate disciplines, and the broad fields of knowledge furnish a useful framework for this purpose. I am not calling for indiscriminate scrambling of superficial knowledge. Indeed, at this point we would do well to suspend judgment as to when in the school program teaching should be organized around the individual disciplines, and when around the broad groupings of the disciplines. In all likelihood, different patterns of organization will be found to be appropriate for different levels of the school program. Dewey's notion of the "progressive organization of knowledge," long ignored by most of his interpreters, might serve as a guiding hypothesis in planning the sequence of the program through the elementary and secondary school years.

In sum, scholars in the natural sciences, the social sciences, mathematics, and the humanities should now be invited to join in the search for new structures for teaching—structures that respect the integrity of the individual fields and at the same time help these fields find their place in a pattern of studies that provides a substantial measure of coherence and relatedness for the program as a whole.

RELATIONSHIPS AMONG BROAD FIELDS OF KNOWLEDGE

There is not only the question of relationships among disciplines that deal with similar problems or phenomena, but also the question of the relationships among the broad areas of knowledge—the sciences and mathematics on the one hand, and the humanities on the other. The growing separation and lack of effective communication between the arts and sciences have been widely noted and greatly deplored. C. P. Snow's analysis of this situation in terms of the two cultures of the literary intellectuals and the scientists is well known to all of us. That this state of affairs should somehow be remedied is the theme of many earnest discussions. The upshot of the discussion is usually that there is one way out of all this: it is, as Snow suggests, by rethinking our education.

But how shall the school go about bridging the gulf between the literary and aesthetic and the scientific studies? It seems reasonable to inquire first of all if human knowledge in its many dimensions forms a recognized unity within which the fields of inquiry and creativity fall neatly into place. Is there a sense in which all knowledge is one, with the arts and the sciences having a place in a unity of fundamental principles or basic methods of inquiry?

The progressives, taking their cue from Dewey, found for themselves, such a unity in the "scientific method" (or the "method of intelligence," as it was frequently labeled) that was assumed to characterize all types of rational, intelligent activity in academic pursuit and in artistic and practical affairs as well. The problem-solving method came to be viewed as the basic ingredient in programs of general education.

But by no means is there agreement among scientists that there is a single all-encompassing set of procedures, even in the natural sciences, as assumed by those who talk about *the* scientific method. There seems to be little warrant for assuming that there is one overarching method sufficiently flexible and inclusive to deal with problems in the various scientific fields, to say nothing of the arts, crafts, and applied areas. Indeed, as we have already noted, the intellectual world today is characterized by a plurality of methods and conceptual schemes developed by the disciplines to deal with problems within their individual spheres. Analysis of the various disciplines reveals a wide range of organizations and intellectual methods associated with them. Instead of a unity of method or a single universe of discourse, we are confronted with a vast confederation of separate areas of study. Modes of analysis differ from field to field, and even from problem to problem within the same field.

The heterogeneous character of the intellectual resources that are a part of the culture is a fact of major significance for the curriculum builder. We would do well frankly to recognize this and make a place in our programs for the variety of logical orders that characterize the fields of knowledge on which we draw in building the curriculum.

But what then of the relationships among the various fields of creativity and inquiry? Is it perhaps possible, in spite of the variety of logical orders characteristic of knowledge in its various branches, to identify the principal kinds of cognitive operations or modes of thinking that characterize man's intellectual activities?

A proposal to facilitate students' insight into relationships among the various fields of knowlege by introducing them to the "principal modes of intellectual activity" comes from Professor Peterson of Oxford University. In making suggestions for the reform of secondary education in Britain, Peterson urges educators to stop thinking of general education in terms of "general knowledge":

> It is not a sign that a man lacks general education if he does not know the date of The Treaty of Utrecht, the latitude of Singapore, the formula for nitro-glycerine or the author of the *Four Quarters*. It does denote a lack of general education if he cares nothing for any of the arts, confuses a moral judgment with an aesthetic judgment, interprets the actions of Asian political leaders in terms of nineteenth century English parliamentarianism or believes that the existence of God has been scientifically disproved.[4]

Peterson urges therefore that the British secondary schools devise programs of general education not in terms of wide general knowledge, but in terms of development in the main modes of intellectual activity, of which he identifies four: the logical (or the analytic), the empirical, the moral, the aesthetic. These different modes of thought are associated with different uses of language. For example, the empirical mode has to do with statements about the world based on our experience of it. The analytic mode has to do with statements that do not describe the world of fact, but rather tell us how the meanings of symbols are related to one another logically. (A definition is a special case of analytic sentences.) The moral and the aesthetic modes are concerned with statements of preferences, evaluations, and judgments of the good and the evil, the beautiful and the ugly, the desirable and the undesirable.

Any one discipline gives opportunity for the development of more than one mode of thought, and each mode can be developed through more than one of the disciplines. For example, literature can contribute to the development of both moral and aesthetic judgment. Mathematics and philosophy both contribute to the development of the analytic mode. History has probably the widest range of any discipline, for the historian employs all four modes in constructing his comprehensive interpretation of what happened in the past.

If students are to gain understanding of the similarities and differences among the fields of knowledge, the different modes of mental activity must be made explicit to them:

> They must have time and guidance in which to see that what is a proof in the Mathematics they pursue on Tuesday is not the same kind of thing as a proof in History, which follows on Wednesday; that the truth of George Eliot or Joseph Conrad is not the same thing as the truths of Mendel or Max Plank; and yet that there are similarities as well as differences.[5]

Peterson accordingly suggests that in addition to giving attention to these varying modes of thought in the subject fields, the secondary program include a special course in which these ways of thinking are the object of study. One important aspect of such teaching has to do with ways in which these modes of thought are verified. Verification is particularly significant in that it is the guide to meaning of the various types of thought. For example, empirical statements are verified by tests conducted in terms of experience, whereas moral statements are verified by reference to criteria or principles of judgment. On the other hand, analytic statements depend for their truth on an agreed upon set of rules, and follow logically from accepted definitions.

Thus far I have suggested that in structuring the curriculum with due regard for the relationships among the fields of knowledge we view knowledge from two complementary perspectives. In the first, emphasis is on the conceptual schemes and methods of inquiry associated with the broad fields of knowledge, the natural sciences, the social sciences, mathematics, and the humanities. In the second, attention is focused on modes of thought—the analytic, the empirical, the aesthetic, and the moral—that transcend the boundaries of the individual fields. These two views thus represent mutually reinforcing conceptions of knowledge that serve well as the basis for curriculum planning.

Professor Toulmin has coined two terms that might be helpful in clarifying the relationships between these two views of knowledge. He distinguishes between "participant's language" and "onlooker's language."[6] Participant's language is the language used by members of a professional group or discipline as they carry on their work in their specialized field. Hence we talk today about the language of science, the language of psychology, the language of mathematics, and even the language of education. In the context of our discussion, participant's language has to do with the language systems that are the distinguishing characteristics of the various disciplined areas of study such as the sciences, mathematics, and the humanities.

Now if we want to examine or talk about the language we use in any one of these fields, we must use another level of discourse. We must, in Toulmin's terms, use onlooker's language. For example, it was suggested that students need help in understanding that a proof in mathematics is not the same as a proof in science or that the "truth" of a scientist is not the same as the "truth" of the poet or novelist. To make these comparisons and contrasts we need a language system that enables us to look at these various areas of study from the outside, as it were. The principal modes of thought—the analytic, the empirical, the moral, and the aesthetic—furnish us with language tools that are useful for this purpose. Hence their importance in teaching.

RELATIONSHIPS OF KNOWLEDGE TO HUMAN AFFAIRS

That the schools ought to provide students with the means for intelligent action is not a new or controversial idea. When, however, it comes to deciding what to teach and how to teach to accomplish this goal, we find marked differences of opinion.

Is it sufficient in general education, for example, to have students learn how to think like physicists, historians, or economists? I think not. For the economist *as* economist (to mention just one field) is in no position to prescribe courses of action regarding the host of public policy issues we face, and questions of public policy and decision loom large in general education. To be sure, economics does provide us with a body of theory that is essential in examining the probable consequences of alternative economic policies, and a good many of these analytical tools ought to become part of the intellectual equipment of all students. Economists are able to tell us what the probable consequences will be if the supply of money is increased, or if the interest rates are lowered; but they cannot *as* economists tell us whether or not we ought to take either of these two courses of action. Decisions regarding these alternative courses of action involve technical economic analysis *and* weighing of values.

It is therefore clear that both values and economic theory are involved in deciding courses of action in economic affairs, and both must find their place in social studies teaching. Here the different modes of thought come prominently into play. Technical economic analysis involves the empirical mode of thinking (that is, it is concerned with matters of fact and theory), while considering alternative values involves the moral mode (that is, it is concerned with criteria of what is desirable or undesirable). The teacher's job is to help students learn to make these necessary distinctions, so that they recognize when questions of fact and analysis are under consideration and when questions of value are at stake.[7] This would of course hold as well for instruction in fields of study other than economics.

Thus far we have been talking about problems associated with a single field. But problems in the world of human affairs do not come neatly labeled "historical," "economic," or "political." They come as decisions to be made and force us to call upon all we know and make us wish we knew more. It was concern for broad cultural and moral questions that go beyond the boundaries of any one discipline that led the progressives to urge that students have the opportunity to deal with them in all their complexity. They proposed a new curriculum, one centered on the problems of youth and broad social issues and drawing upon the academic disciplines as they become relevant to the problems under study. This idea became the hallmark of progressivism in curriculum building. It gained wide acceptance among educators and found expression in many influential statements of policy and opinion during the 1920's, '30's, and '40's. Attempted applications of this viewpoint were made in courses labeled core, common learnings, and the like.

Difficulties in this approach soon became apparent, not the least of which was the students' lack of first-hand acquaintance with the disciplines that were the source of the concepts and ideas essential to structuring problems under study. Without adequate understanding of the various fields of knowledge, students had no way of knowing which fields were relevant to problems of concern to them. Indeed, without knowledge of the organized fields it was difficult for them to ask the kinds of questions about their problems that the various disciplines could help them answer.

Giving students an opportunity to grapple with broad social and cultural problems was basically a promising innovation. But at the same time one is forced to recognize that problem solving on such a broad base cannot be pursued successfully without growing understanding of the fields of knowledge on which the problem solver must draw.

Recognizing then the value in systematic study of the fields of knowledge and the importance of developing competence in dealing with problems and issues that are broader than those of any one field, the question arises of why opportunities for both types of activities should not be included in the program for all students. One might envision a general education program that would include basic instruction in the major fields defined earlier in this paper (the natural sciences, the physical sciences, mathematics, and the humanities), together with a coordinating seminar in which students deal with problems ''in the round'' and in which special effort is made to show the intimate relationships between the fields of study as concepts from those fields are brought to bear on these problems. Such a seminar would also furnish excellent opportunities to help students become aware of the different modes of thought and various types of language usage involved in dealing with problematic situations and the necessity for making clear distinctions among them.

This is not a new proposal. I am here dusting off an old idea first set forth in the 1956 ASCD Yearbook, *What Shall the High Schools Teach?* In making this suggestion, we were much influenced by Dewey's contention that

The aim of education should be to secure a balanced interaction of the two types of mental attitude (the practical and the theoretical), having sufficient regard to the disposition of the individual not to hamper and cripple whatever powers are naturally strong in him. The narrowness of individuals of strong concrete bent needs to be liberalized. Every opportunity that occurs within practical activities for developing curiosity and susceptibility to intellectual problems should be seized. Violence is not done to natural disposition; rather, the latter is broadened. Otherwise, the concrete becomes narrowing and deadening. As regards the smaller number of those who have a taste for abstract, purely intellectual topics, pains should be taken to multiply opportunities and demands for the application of ideas, for translating symbolic truths into terms of everyday and social life. Every human being has both capabilities, and every individual will be more effective and happier if both powers are developed in easy and close interaction with each other.[8]

Let it be recognized that the difficulties in building a curriculum that takes account of the relationships among the various fields of inquiry and creativity are overwhelming. The greatest difficulty is that the job involves the collaboration of specialists—in the various disciplines, in curriculum development, and in teaching. In such collaborative efforts it would seem that curriculum specialists, concerned as they are with the instructional program as a whole, have a crucial role to play. But in all frankness it must be recognized that they do not play a central crucial role in curriculum revision projects now underway. Whether they will be able to do so in the future is another matter. And I suspect that whether they will indeed make the contribution one might reasonably expect them to make will depend, first of all, on their ability to work effectively with representatives of the various fields of knowledge to identify important relationships among these fields and to fashion programs of instruction that take due account of these relationships and connections; and secondly, on their ability to build curricula that help students see the relevance of the intellectual resources of the culture for their own lives as productive workers, as citizens, and as individuals. For as Professor Bestor, who scarcely qualifies as an advocate of education for life adjustment, has reminded us, "The basic argument of the intellectual disciplines in education is not that they lift a man's spirits above the world, but that they equip his mind to enter the world and perform its tasks."[9]

NOTES

1. Jerome Bruner, *On Knowing* (Cambridge, Mass.: Harvard University Press, 1962), p. 120.

2. John H. Randall, Jr., "The World to be Unified," in Lewis Leary (ed.), *The Unity of Knowledge* (Garden City, N.Y.: Doubleday and Company, 1955), p. 63.

3. Kingsley Davis, *Human Society* (New York: The Macmillan Company, 1948), p. 8.

4. Oxford University Department of Education, *Arts and Sciences Sides in the Sixth Form* (Abingdon-Berkshire, The Abbey Press, 1960), p. 13.

5. *Ibid.*, p. 18.

6. Stephen Toulmin, *Philosophy of Science* (London: Hutchinson University Library, 1953), p. 13.

7. See *Economic Education in the Schools*. Report of the National Task Force on Economic Education, 1961.

8. John Dewey, *How We Think* (Boston: D.C. Heath and Co., 1933), pp. 228–29.

9. Arthur E. Bestor, *Educational Wastelands* (Urbana, Ill.: University of Illinois Press, 1953), p. 15.

BIBLIOGRAPHY

American Council of Learned Societies and the National Council for the Social Studies. *The Social Studies and the Social Sciences* (New York: Harcourt, Brace and World, 1962).

Arts and Sciences Sides in the Sixth Form. Oxford University Department of Education (Abingdon-Berkshire: The Abbey Press, 1960).

Bellack, Arno A. "Selection and Organization of Curriculum Content: An Analysis." *What Shall the High Schools Teach?* 1956 Yearbook of the Association for Supervision and Curriculum Development (Washington, D.C.: The Association, 1956), pp. 97–126.

Bestor, Arthur E. *Educational Wastelands* (Urbana, Illinois: University of Illinois Press, 1953).

Bode, Boyd H. "Logical and Psychological Organization of Subject Matter." In *Modern Educational Theories* (New York: Vintage Books), pp. 43–72. (First published in 1927 by the Macmillan Company.)

Brodbeck, May. "Toward a Fabric of Knowledge." *Educational Record* 43 (July 1962): 217–22.

Bruner, Jerome S. *On Knowing* (Cambridge, Mass.: The Belknap Press of Harvard University, 1962).

————. *The Process of Education* (Cambridge, Mass.: Harvard University Press, 1960).

Conant, James B. *Education in a Divided World* (Cambridge, Mass.: Harvard University Press, 1949).

Davis, Kingsley. *Human Society* (New York: The Macmillan Company, 1948).

Deciding What To Teach. Project on the Instructional Program of the Public Schools (Washington, D.C.: National Education Association, 1963).

Dewey, John. "The Child and the Curriculum." In Martin S Dworkin (ed.), *Dewey on Education.* Classics in Education No. 3 (New York: Bureau of Publications, Teachers College, Columbia University, 1959), pp. 91–111.

————. *Experience and Education* (New York: The Macmillan Company, 1938).

————. *How We Think* (Lexington, Mass.: D. C. Heath and Company, 1933).

Economic Education in the Schools. Report of the National Task Force on Economic Education (New York: Committee for Economic Development, 1961).

Eisner, Elliot W. "Knowledge, Knowing and the Visual Arts." *Harvard Educational Review* 33 (Spring 1963): 208–18.

Fraser, Dorothy M. *Current Curriculum Studies in Academic Subjects* (Washington, D.C.: National Education Association, 1962).

High School Studies Perspectives (Boston: Houghton Mifflin Company, 1962).

Jenkins, William A. (ed.) *The Nature of Knowledge* (Milwaukee: University of Wisconsin, 1961).

Jones, Howard Mumford. *One Great Society* (New York: Harcourt, Brace and Company, 1959).

McClellan, James E. "Knowledge and the Curriculum." *Teachers College Record* 57 (March 1956): 410–18.

Miel, Alice. "Knowledge and The Curriculum." In Alexander Frazier (ed.) *New Insights And The Curriculum.* 1963 Yearbook of the Association for Supervision and Curriculum Development (Washington, D.C.: The Association, 1963), pp. 71–104.

Nagel, Ernest. "The Methods of Science: What Are They? Can They Be Taught? In

Israel Scheffler (ed.) *Philosophy and Education* (Boston: Allyn and Bacon, Inc., 1958), pp. 146–53.

Phenix, Philip H. "The Disciplines as Curriculum Content." In A. Harry Passow (ed.) *Curriculum Crossroads* (New York: Bureau of Publications, Teachers College, Columbia University, 1962), pp. 57–65.

———. "Key Concepts and the Crisis in Learning." *Teachers College Record* 58 (December 1956): 137–43.

Randall, John H. "The World to Be Unified." In Lewis Leary (ed.) *The Unity of Knowledge* (Garden City, New York: Doubleday and Company, 1955).

Rosenbloom, Paul C. (ed.) *Modern Viewpoints in the Curriculum* (New York: McGraw-Hill Book Company, 1964).

The Scholars Look at the Schools (Washington, D.C.: National Education Association, 1962).

Schwab, Joseph J. "The Concept of the Structure of a Discipline." *Educational Record* 43 (July 1962): 197–205.

Smith, B. Othanel, and Robert H. Ennis (eds.) *Language and Concepts in Education* (Chicago: Rand McNally and Company, 1961).

Snow, C. P. *The Two Cultures and the Scientific Revolution* (Cambridge, England: Cambridge University Press, 1959).

Toulmin, Stephen. *Philosophy of Science* (New York: Harper Torchbooks, The Science Library, Harper and Brothers).

"What Shall The Schools Teach?" *Teachers College Record* 60 (February 1959): 239–96. Entire issue.

Wilson, John Boyd. *Language and the Pursuit of Truth* (Cambridge, England: University Press, 1958).

18. CURRICULUM AND CONSCIOUSNESS

Maxine Greene

Curriculum, from the learner's standpoint, ordinarily represents little more than an arrangement of subjects, a structure of socially prescribed knowledge, or a complex system of meanings which may or may not fall within his grasp. Rarely does it signify possibility for him as an existing person, mainly concerned with making sense of his own life-world. Rarely does it promise occasions for ordering the materials of that world, for imposing "configurations"[1] by means of experiences and perspectives made available for personally conducted cognitive action. Sartre says that "knowing is a moment of *praxis*," opening into "what has not yet been."[2] Preoccupied with priorities, purposes, programs of "intended learning"[3] and intended (or unintended) manipulation, we pay too little attention to the individual in quest of his own future, bent on surpassing what is merely "given," on breaking through the everyday. We are still too prone to dichotomize: to think of "disciplines" or "public traditions" or "accumulated wisdom" or "common culture" (individualization despite) as objectively existent, external to the knower—there to be discovered, mastered, learned.

Quite aware that this may evoke Dewey's argument in *The Child and the Curriculum*, aware of how times have changed since 1902, I have gone in search of contemporary analogies to shed light on what I mean. ("Solution comes," Dewey wrote, "only by getting away from the meaning of terms that is already fixed upon and coming to see the conditions from another point of view, and

SOURCE. *Teachers College Record* 73 (No. 2, December 1971), pp. 253–69.

237

hence in a fresh light."')[4] My other point of view is that of literary criticism, or more properly philosophy of criticism, which attempts to explicate the modes of explanation, description, interpretation, and evaluation involved in particular critical approaches. There is presently an emerging philosophic controversy between two such approaches, one associated with England and the United States, the other with the Continent, primarily France and Switzerland; and it is in the differences in orientation that I have found some clues.

These differences are, it will be evident, closely connected to those separating what is known as analytic or language philosophy from existentialism and phenomenology. The dominant tendency in British and American literary criticism has been to conceive literary works as objects or artifacts, best understood in relative isolation from the writer's personal biography and undistorted by associations brought to the work from the reader's own daily life. The new critics on the Continent have been called "critics of consciousness."[5] They are breaking with the notion that a literary work can be dealt with objectively, divorced from experience. In fact, they treat each work as a manifestation of an individual writer's experience, a gradual growth of consciousness into expression. This is in sharp contrast to such a view as T. S. Eliot's emphasizing the autonomy and the "impersonality" of literary art. "We can only say," he wrote in an introduction to *The Sacred Wood*, "that a poem, in some sense, has its own life; that its parts form something quite different from a body of neatly ordered biographical data; that the feeling, or emotion, or vision resulting from the poem is something different from the feeling or emotion or vision in the mind of the poet."[6] Those who take this approach or an approach to a work of art as "a self-enclosed isolated structure"[7] are likely to prescribe that purely aesthetic values are to be found in literature, the values associated with "significant form"[8] or, at most, with the contemplation of an "intrinsically interesting possible."[9] M. H. Abrams has called this an "austere dedication to the poem *per se*,"[10] for all the enlightening analysis and explication it has produced. "But it threatens also to commit us," he wrote, "to the concept of a poem as a language game, or as a floating Laputa, insulated from life and essential human concerns in a way that accords poorly with our experience in reading a great work of literature."

For the critic of consciousness, literature is viewed as a genesis, a conscious effort on the part of an individual artist to understand his own experience by framing it in language. The reader who encounters the work must recreate it in terms of *his* consciousness. In order to penetrate it, to experience it existentially and empathetically, he must try to place himself within the "interior space"[11] of the writer's mind as it is slowly revealed in the course of his work. Clearly, the reader requires a variety of cues if he is to situate himself in this way; and these are ostensibly provided by the expressions and attitudes he finds in the book, devices which he must accept as orientations and indications—"norms," perhaps, to govern his recreation. *His* subjectivity is the substance of the literary object; but, if he is to perceive the identity emerging through the enactments of the book, he must subordinate his own personality as he brackets out his everyday, "natural" world.[12] His objective in doing so, however, is not to analyze or explicate or evaluate; it is to extract the experience made manifest by means of the work. Sartre says this more concretely:

> Reading seems, in fact, to be the synthesis of perception and creation. . . . The object is essential because it is strictly transcendent, because it imposes its own structures, and because one must wait for it and observe it; but the subject is also essential because it is required not only to disclose the object (that is, to make *there be* an object) but also that this object might *be* (that is, to produce it). In a word, the reader is conscious of disclosing in creating, of creating by disclosing. . . . If he is inattentive, tired, stupid, or thoughtless most of the relations will escape him. He will never manage to "catch on" to the object (in the sense in which we see that fire "catches" or "doesn't catch"). He will draw some phrases out of the shadow, but they will appear as random strokes. If he is at his best, he will project beyond the words a synthetic form, each phrase of which will be no more than a partial function: the "theme," the "subject," or the "meaning."[13]

There must be, he is suggesting, continual reconstructions if a work of literature is to become meaningful. The structures involved are generated over a period of time, depending upon the perceptiveness and attentiveness of the reader. The reader, however, does not simply regenerate what the artist intended. His imagination can move him beyond the artist's traces, "to project beyond the words a synthetic form," to constitute a new totality. The autonomy of the art object is sacrificed in this orientation; the reader, conscious of lending his own life to the book, discovers deeper and more complex levels than the level of "significant form." (Sartre says, for instance, that "Raskolnikov's waiting is *my* waiting, which I lend him. Without this impatience of the reader he would remain only a collection of signs. His hatred of the police magistrate who questions him is my hatred which has been solicited and wheedled out of me by signs, and the police magistrate himself would not exist without the hatred I have for him via Raskolnikov.")[14]

DISCLOSURE, RECONSTRUCTION, GENERATION

The reader, using his imagination, must move within his own subjectivity and break with the common sense world he normally takes for granted. If he could not suspend his ordinary ways of perceiving, if he could not allow for the possibility that the horizons of daily life are not inalterable, he would not be able to engage with literature at all. As Dewey put it: "There is work done on the part of the percipient as there is on the part of the artist. The one who is too lazy, idle, or indurated in convention to perform this work will not see or hear. His 'appreciation' will be a mixture of scraps of learning with conformity to norms of conventional admiration and with a confused, even if genuine, emotional excitation."[15] The "work" with which we are here concerned is one of disclosure, reconstruction, generation. It is a work which culminates in a bringing something into being by the reader—in a "going beyond" what he has been.[16]

Although I am going to claim that learning, to be meaningful, must involve such a "going beyond," I am not going to claim that it must also be in the imaginative mode. Nor am I going to assert that, in order to surpass the "given," the individual is required to move into and remain within a sealed subjectivity. What I find suggestive in the criticism of consciousness is the stress on the gradual disclosure of structures by the reader. The process is, as I have said, governed by certain cues or norms perceived in the course of reading. These demand, if they are to be perceived, what Jean Piaget has called a "continual 'decentering' without which [the individual subject] cannot become free from his intellectual egocentricity."[17]

The difference between Piaget and those interested in consciousness is, of course, considerable. For one thing, he counts himself among those who prefer not to characterize the subject in terms of its "lived experience." For another thing, he says categorically that "the 'lived' can only have a very minor role in the construction of cognitive structures, for these do not belong to the subject's *consciousness* but to his operational *behavior*, which is something quite different."[18] I am not convinced that they are as different as he conceives them to be. Moreover, I think his differentiation between the "individual subject" and what he calls "the epistemic subject, that cognitive nucleus which is common to all subjects at the same level,"[19] is useful and may well shed light on the problem of curriculum, viewed from the vantage point of consciousness. Piaget is aware that his stress on the "epistemic subject" looks as if he were subsuming the individual under some impersonal abstraction;[20] but his discussion is not far removed from those of Sartre and the critics of consciousness, particularly when they talk of the subject entering into a process of generating structures whose being (like the structures Piaget has in mind) consists in their "coming to be."

Merleau-Ponty, as concerned as Piaget with the achievement of rationality, believes that there is a primary reality which must be taken into account if the growth of "intellectual consciousness" is to be understood. This primary reality is a perceived life-world; and the structures of the "perceptual consciousness"[21] through which the child first comes in contact with his environment underlie all the higher level structures which develop later in his life. In the prereflective, infantile stage of life he is obviously incapable of generating cognitive structures. The stage is characterized by what Merleau-Ponty calls "egocentrism" because the "me" is part of an anonymous collectivity, unaware of itself, capable of living "as easily in others as it does in itself."[22] Nevertheless, even then, before meanings and configurations are imposed, there is an original world, a natural and social world in which the child is involved corporeally and affectively.

Perceiving that world, he effects certain relations within his experience. He organizes and "informs" it before he is capable of logical and predicative thought. This means for Merleau-Ponty that consciousness exists primordially—the ground of all knowledge and rationality.

The growing child assimilates a language system and becomes habituated to using language as "an open system of expression" which is capable of expressing "an indeterminate number of cognitions or ideas to come."[23] His acts of naming and expression take place, however, around a core of primary meaning found in "the silence of primary consciousness." This silence may be understood as the fundamental awareness of being present in the world. It resembles what Paulo Freire calls "background awareness"[24] of an existential situation, a situation actually lived before the codifications which make new perceptions possible. Talking about the effort to help peasants perceive their own reality differently (to enable them, in other words, to learn), Freire says they must somehow make explicit their "real consciousness" of their worlds, or what they experienced while living through situations they later learn to codify.

The point is that the world is constituted for the child (by means of the behavior called perception) prior to the "construction of cognitive structures." This does not imply that he lives his life primarily in that world. He moves outward into diverse realms of experience in his search for meaning. When he confronts and engages with the apparently independent structures associated with rationality, the so-called cognitive structures, it is likely that he does so as an "epistemic subject," bracketing out for the time his subjectivity, even his presence to himself.[25] But the awareness remains in the background; the original perceptual reality continues as the ground of rationality, the base from which the leap to the theoretical is taken.

Merleau-Ponty, recognizing that psychologists treat consciousness as "an object to be studied," writes that it is simply not accessible to mere factual observation:

The psychologist always tends to make consciousness into just such an object of observation. But all the factual truths to which psychology has access can be applied to the concrete subject only after a philosophical correction. Psychology, like physics and the other sciences of nature, uses the method of induction, which starts from facts and then assembles them. But it is very evident that this induction will remain blind if we do not know in some other way, and indeed from the inside of consciousness itself, what this induction is dealing with.[26]

Induction must be combined "with the reflective knowledge that we can obtain from ourselves as conscious objects." This is not a recommendation that the individual engage in introspection. Consciousness, being intentional, throws itself outward *towards* the world. It is always consciousness *of* something—a phenomenon, another person, an object in the world. Reflecting upon himself as a conscious object, the individual—the learner, perhaps—reflects upon his relation to the world, his manner of comporting himself with respect to it, the changing perspectives through which the world presents itself to him. Merleau-Ponty talks about the need continually to rediscover "my actual presence to myself, the fact of my consciousness which is in the last resort what the word and the concept of consciousness mean."[27] This means remaining in contact with one's own perceptions, one's own experiences, and striving to constitute their meanings. It means achieving a state of what Schutz calls "wide-awakeness . . . a plane of consciousness of highest tension originating in an attitude of full attention to life and its requirements."[28] Like Sartre, Schutz emphasizes the importance of attentiveness for arriving at new perceptions, for carrying out cognitive projects. All this seems to me to be highly suggestive for a conception of a learner who is "open to the world,"[29] eager, indeed *condemned* to give meaning to it—and, in the process of doing so, recreating or generating the materials of a curriculum in terms of his own consciousness.

SOME ALTERNATIVE VIEWS

There are, of course, alternative views of consequence for education today. R. S. Peters, agreeing with his philosophic precursors that consciousness is the hallmark of mind and always "related in its different modes to objects," asserts that the "objects of consciousness are first and foremost objects in a public world that are marked out and differentiated by a public language into which the individual is initiated."[30] (It should be said that Peters is, *par excellence,* the exponent of an "objective" or "analytic" approach to curriculum, closely related to the objective approach to literary criticism.) He grants that the individual "represents a unique and unrepeatable viewpoint on this public world"; but his primary stress is placed upon the way in which the learning of language is linked to the discovery of that separately existing world of "objects in space and time." Consciousness, for Peters, cannot be explained except in connection with the demarcations of the public world which meaning makes possible. It becomes contingent upon initiation into public traditions, into (it turns out) the academic disciplines. Since such an initiation is required if modes of consciousness are to be effectively differentiated, the mind must finally be understood as a "product" of such initiation. The individual must be enabled to achieve a state of mind characterized by "a mastery of and care for the worthwhile things that have been transmitted, which are viewed in some kind of cognitive perspective."[31]

Philip H. Phenix argues similarly that "the curriculum should consist entirely of knowledge which comes from the disciplines, for the reason that the disciplines reveal knowledge in its teachable forms."[32] He, however, pays more heed to what he calls "the experience of reflective self-consciousness,"[33] which he associates specifically with ''concrete existence in direct personal encounter.''[34] The meanings arising out of such encounter are expressed, for him, in existential philosophy, religion, psychology, and certain dimensions of imaginative literature. They are, thus, to be considered as one of the six ''realms of meaning'' through mastery of which man is enabled to achieve self-transcendence. Self-transcendence, for Phenix, involves a duality which enables the learner to feel himself to be agent and knower, and at once to identify with what he comes to know. Self-transcendence is the ground of meaning; but it culminates in the engendering of a range of ''essential meanings,'' the achievement of a hierarchy in which all fundamental patterns of meaning are related and through which human existence can be fulfilled. The inner life of generic man is clearly encompassed by this scheme; but what is excluded, I believe, is what has been called the ''subjectivity of the actor,'' the *individual* actor ineluctably present to himself. What is excluded is the feeling of separateness, of strangeness when such a person is confronted with the articulated curriculum intended to counteract meaninglessness.

Schutz writes:

When a stranger comes to the town, he has to learn to orientate in it and to know it. Nothing is self-explanatory for him and he has to ask an expert . . . to learn how to get from one point to another. He may, of course, refer to a map of the town, but even to use the map successfully he must know the meaning of the signs on the map, the exact point within the town where he stands and its correlative on the map, and at least one more point in order correctly to relate the signs on the map to the real objects in the city.[35]

The prestructured curriculum resembles such a map; the learner, the stranger just arrived in town. For the cartographer, the town is an ''object of his science,'' a science which has developed standards of operation and rules for the correct drawing of maps. In the case of the curriculum-maker, the public tradition or the natural order of things is ''the object'' of his design activities. Here too there are standards of operation: the subject matter organized into disciplines must be communicable; it must be appropriate to whatever are conceived as educational aims. Phenix has written that education should be understood as ''a guided recapitulation of the processes of inquiry which gave rise to the fruitful bodies of organized knowledge comprising the disciplines.''[36] Using the metaphor of the map, we might say that this is like asking a newcomer in search of direction to recapitulate the complex processes by which the cartographer made his map. The map may represent a fairly complete charting of the town; and it may ultimately be extremely useful for the individual to be able to take a cartographer's perspective. When that individual first arrives, however, his peculiar plight ought not to be overlooked: his ''background awareness'' of being alive in an unstable world; his reasons for consulting the map; the interests he is pursuing as he attempts to orient himself when he can no longer proceed by rule of thumb. He himself may recognize that he will have to come to understand the signs on the map if he is to make use of it. Certainly he will have to decipher the relationship between those signs and "real objects in the city." But his initial concern will be conditioned by the "objects" he wants to bring into visibility, by the landmarks he needs to identify if he is to proceed on his way.

LEARNING—A MODE OF ORIENTATION

Turning from newcomer to learner (contemporary learner, in our particular world), I am suggesting that his focal concern is with ordering the materials of his own life-world when dislocations occur, when what was once familiar abruptly appears strange. This may come about on an occasion when "future shock" is experienced, as it so frequently is today. Anyone who has lived through a campus disruption, a teachers' strike, a guerilla theatre production, a sit-in (or a be-in, or a feel-in) knows full well what Alvin Toffler means when he writes about the acceleration of change. "We no longer 'feel' life as men did in the past," he says. "And this is the ultimate difference, the distinction that separates the truly contemporary man from all others. For this acceleration lies behind the impermanence—the transience—that penetrates and tinctures our consciousness, radically affecting the way we relate to other people, to things, to the entire universe of ideas, art and values."[37] Obviously, this does not happen in everyone's life; but it is far more likely to occur than ever before in history, if it is indeed the case that change has speeded up and that forces are being released which we have not yet learned to control. My point is that the contemporary learner is more likely than his predecessors to experience moments of strangeness, moments when the recipes he has inherited for the solution of typical problems no longer seem to work. If Merleau-Ponty is right and the search for rationality is indeed grounded in a primary or perceptual consciousness, the individual may be fundamentally aware that the structures of "reality" are contingent upon the perspective taken and that most achieved orders are therefore precarious.

The stage sets are always likely to collapse.[38] Someone is always likely to ask unexpectedly, as in Pinter's *The Dumb Waiter*, "Who cleans up after we're gone?"[39] Someone is equally likely to cry out, "You seem to have no conception of where we stand! You won't find the answer written down for you in the bowl of a compass—I can tell you that."[40] Disorder, in other words, is continually breaking in; meaninglessness is recurrently overcoming landscapes which once were demarcated, meaningful. It is at moments like these that the individual reaches out to reconstitute meaning, to close the gaps, to make sense once again. It is at moments like these that he will be moved to pore over maps, to disclose or generate structures of knowledge which may provide him unifying perspectives and thus enable him to restore order once again. His learning, I am saying, is a mode of orientation—or reorientation—in a place suddenly become unfamiliar. And "place" is a metaphor, in this context, for a domain of consciousness, intending, forever thrusting outward, "open to the world." The curriculum, the structures of knowledge, must be presented to such a consciousness as possibility. Like the work of literature in Sartre's viewing, it requires a subject if it is to be disclosed; it can only *be* disclosed if the learner, himself engaged in generating the structures, lends the curriculum his life. If the curriculum, on the other hand, is seen as external to the search for meaning, it becomes an alien and an alienating edifice, a kind of "Crystal Palace" of ideas.[41]

There is, then, a kind of resemblance between the ways in which a learner confronts socially prescribed knowledge and the ways in which a stranger looks at a map when he is trying to determine where he is in relation to where he wants to go. In Kafka's novel, *Amerika,* I find a peculiarly suggestive description of the predicament of someone who is at once a stranger and a potential learner (although, it eventually turns out, he never succeeds in being taught). He is Karl Rossmann, who has been "packed off to America" by his parents and who likes to stand on a balcony at his Uncle Jacob's house in New York and look down on the busy street:

From morning to evening and far into the dreaming night that street was a channel for the constant stream of traffic which, seen from above, looked like an inextricable confusion, forever newly improvised, of foreshortened human figures and the roofs of all kinds of vehicles, sending into the upper air another confusion, more riotous and complicated, of noises, dusts and smells, all of it enveloped and penetrated by a flood of light which the multitudinous objects in the street scattered, carried off and again busily brought back, with an effect as palpable to the dazzled eye as if a glass roof stretched over the street were being violently smashed into fragments at every moment.[42]

Karl's uncle tells him that the indulgence of idly gazing at the busy life of the city might be permissible if Karl were traveling for pleasure; "but for one who intended to remain in the States it was sheer ruination." He is going to have to make judgments which will shape his future life; he will have, in effect, to be reborn. This being so, it is not enough for him to treat the unfamiliar landscape as something to admire and wonder at (as if it were a cubist construction or a kaleidoscope). Karl's habitual interpretations (learned far away in Prague) do not suffice to clarify what he sees. If he is to learn, he must identify what is questionable, try to break through what is obscure. Action is required of him, not mere gazing; *praxis,* not mere reverie.

If he is to undertake action, however, he must do so against the background of his original perceptions, with a clear sense of being present to himself. He must do so, too, against the background of his European experience, of the experience of rejection, of being "packed off" for reasons never quite understood. Only with that sort of awareness will he be capable of the attentiveness and commitment needed to engage with the world and make it meaningful. Only with the ability to be reflective about what he is doing will he be brave enough to incorporate his past into the present, to link the present to a future. All this will demand a conscious appropriation of new perspectives on his experience and a continual reordering of that experience as new horizons of the "Amerika" become visible, as new problems arise. The point is that Karl Rossmann, an immigrant in an already structured and charted world, must be conscious enough of himself to strive towards rationality; only if he achieves rationality will he avoid humiliations and survive.

As Kafka tells it, he never does attain that rationality; and so he is continually manipulated by forces without and within. He never learns, for example, that there can be no justice if there is no good will, even though he repeatedly and sometimes eloquently asks for justice from the authorities—always to no avail. The ship captains and pursers, the business men, the head waiters and porters all function according to official codes of discipline which are beyond his comprehension. He has been plunged into a public world with its own intricate prescriptions, idiosyncratic structures, and hierarchies; but he has no way of appropriating it or of constituting meanings. Throughout most of the novel, he clings to his symbolic box (with the photograph of his parents, the memorabilia of childhood and home). The box may be egocentrism; it may signify his incapacity to embark upon the "decentering" required if he is to begin generating for himself the structures of what surrounds.

In his case (and, I would say, in the case of many other people) the "decentering" that is necessary is not solely a cognitive affair, as Piaget insists it is. Merleau-Ponty speaks of a "lived decentering,"[43] exemplified by a child's learning "to relativise the notions of the youngest and the eldest" (to learn, e.g., to become the eldest in relation to the newborn child) or by his learning to think in terms of reciprocity. This happens, as it would have to happen to Karl, through actions undertaken within the "vital order," not merely through intellectual categorization. It does not exclude the possibility that a phenomenon analogous to Piaget's "epistemic subject" emerges, although there appears to be no reason (except, perhaps, from the viewpoint of empirical psychology) for separating it off from the "individual subject." (In fact, the apparent difference between Piaget and those who talk of "lived experience" may turn upon a definition of "consciousness." Piaget, as has been noted,[44] distinguishes between "consciousness" and "operational behavior," as if consciousness did *not* involve a turning outward to things, a continuing reflection upon situationality, a generation of cognitive structures.) In any case, every individual who consciously seeks out meaning is involved in asking questions which demand essentially epistemic responses.[45] These responses, even if incomplete, are knowledge claims; and, as more and more questions are asked, there is an increasing "sedimentation" of meanings which result from the interpretation of past experiences looked at from the vantage point of the present. Meanings do not inhere in the experiences that emerge; they have to be constituted, and they can only be constituted through cognitive action.

Returning to Karl Rossmann and his inability to take such action, I have been suggesting that he *cannot* make his own "primary consciousness" background so long as he clings to his box; nor can he actively interpret his past experience. He cannot (to stretch Piaget's point somewhat) become or will himself to be an "epistemic subject." He is, as Freire puts it, submerged in a "dense, enveloping reality or a tormenting blind alley" and will be unless he can "perceive it as an objective-problematic situation."[46] Only then will he be able to intervene in his own reality with attentiveness, with awareness—to act upon his situation and make sense.

It would help if the looming structures which are so incomprehensible to Karl were somehow rendered cognitively available to him. Karl might then (with the help of a teacher willing to engage in dialogue with him, to help him pose his problems) reach out to question in terms of what he feels is thematically relevant or "worth questioning."[47] Because the stock of knowledge he carries with him does not suffice for a definition of situations in which porters manhandle him and women degrade him, in which he is penalized for every spontaneous action, he cannot easily refer to previous situations for clues. In order to cope with this, he needs to single out a single relevant element at first (from all the elements in what is happening) to transmute into a theme for his "knowing consciousness." There is the cruel treatment meted out to him, for example, by the Head Porter who feels it his duty "to attend to things that other people neglect." (He adds that, since he is in charge of all the doors of the hotel [including the "doorless exits"], he is "in a sense placed over everyone," and everyone has to obey him absolutely. If it were not for his repairing the omissions of the Head Waiter in the name of the hotel management, he believes, "such a great organization would be unthinkable.")[48] The porter's violence against Karl might well become the relevant element, the origin of a theme.

MAKING CONNECTIONS

"What makes the theme to be a theme," Schutz writes, "is determined by motivationally relevant interest-situations and spheres of problems. The theme which thus has become relevant has now, however, become a problem to which a solution, practical, theoretical, or emotional, must be given."[49] The problem for Karl, like relevant problems facing any individual, is connected with and a consequence of a great number of other perplexities, other dislocations in his life. If he had not been so badly exploited by authority figures in time past, if he were not so childishly given to blind trust in adults, if he were not so likely to follow impulse at inappropriate moments, he would never have been assaulted by the Head Porter. At this point, however, once the specific problem (the assault) has been determined to be thematically relevant for him, it can be detached from the motivational context out of which it derived. The meshwork of related perplexities remains, however, as an outer horizon waiting to be explored or questioned when necessary. The thematically relevant element can then be made interesting in its own right and worth questioning. In the foreground, as it were, the focus of concern, it can be defined against the background of the total situation. The situation is not in any sense obliterated or forgotten. It is *there,* at the fringe of Karl's attention while the focal problem is being solved; but it is, to an extent, "bracketed out." With this bracketing out and this foreground focusing, Karl may be for the first time in a condition of wide-awakeness, ready to pay active attention to what has become so questionable and so troubling, ready to take the kind of action which will move him ahead into a future as it gives him perspective on his past.

The action he might take involves more than what is understood as problem-solving. He has, after all, had some rudimentary knowledge of the Head Porter's role, a knowledge conditioned by certain typifications effected in the prepredicative days of early childhood. At that point in time, he did not articulate his experience in terms of sense data or even in terms of individual figures standing out against a background. He saw typical structures according to particular zones of relevancy. This means that he probably saw his father, or the man who was father, not only as bearded face next to his mother, not only as large figure in the doorway, but as over-bearing, threatening, incomprehensible Authority who was "placed over everyone" and had the right to inflict pain. Enabled, years later, to confront something thematically relevant, the boy may be solicited to recognize his present knowledge of the porter as the sendiment of previous mental processes.[50] The knowledge of the porter, therefore, has a history beginning in primordial perceptions; and the boy may succeed in moving back from what is seemingly "given" through the diverse mental processes which constituted the porter over time. Doing so, he will be exploring both the inner and outer horizons of the problem, making connections within the field of his consciousness, interpreting his own past as it bears on his present, reflecting upon his own knowing.

And that is not all. Having made such connections between the relevant theme and other dimensions of his experience, he may be ready to solve his problem; he may even feel that the problem is solved. This, however, puts him into position to move out of his own inner time (in which all acts are somehow continuous and bound together) into the intersubjective world where he can function as an epistemic subject. Having engaged in a reflexive consideration of the activity of his own consciousness, he can now shift his attention back to the life-world which had been rendered so unrecognizable by the Head Porter's assault. Here too, meanings must be constituted; the "great organization" must be understood, so that Karl can orient himself once again in the everyday. Bracketing out his subjectivity for the time, he may find many ways of engaging as a theoretical inquirer with the problem of authority in hotels and the multiple socioeconomic problems connected with that. He will voluntarily become, when inquiring in this way, a partial self, an inquirer deliberately acting a role in a community of inquirers. I am suggesting that he could not do so as effectively or as authentically if he had not first synthesized the materials within his inner time, constituted meaning in his world.

The analogy to the curriculum question, I hope, is clear. Treating Karl as a potential learner, I have considered the hotels and the other structured organizations in his world as analogous to the structures of prescribed knowledge—or to the curriculum. I have suggested that the individual, in our case the student, will only be in a position to learn when he is committed to act upon his world. If he is content to admire it or simply accept it as given, if he is incapable of breaking with egocentrism, he will remain alienated from himself and his own possibilities; he will wander lost and victimized upon the road; he will be unable to learn. He may be conditioned; he may be trained. He may even have some rote memory of certain elements of the curriculum; but no matter how well devised is that curriculum, no matter how well adapted to the stages of his growth, learning (as disclosure, as generating structures, as engendering meanings, as achieving mastery) will not occur.

At once, I have tried to say that unease and disorder are increasingly endemic in contemporary life, and that more and more persons are finding the recipes they habitually use inadequate for sense-making in a changing world. This puts them, more and more frequently, in the position of strangers or immigrants trying to orient themselves in an unfamiliar town. The desire, indeed the *need*, for orientation is equivalent to the desire to constitute meanings, all sorts of meanings, in the many dimensions of existence. But this desire, I have suggested, is not satisfied by the authoritative confrontation of student with knowledge structures (no matter how "teachable" the forms in which the knowledge is revealed). It is surely not satisfied when the instructional situation is conceived to be, as G. K. Plochmann has written, one in which the teacher is endeavoring "with respect to his subject matter, to bring the understanding of the learner in equality with his own understanding."[51] Described in that fashion, with "learner" conceived generically and the "system" to be taught conceived as preexistent and objectively real, the instructional situation seems to me to be one that alienates because of the way it ignores both existential predicament and primordial consciousness. Like the approach to literary criticism Abrams describes, the view appears to commit us to a concept of curriculum "as a floating Laputa, insulated from life and essential human concerns. . . ."[52]

The cries of "irrelevance" are still too audible for us to content ourselves with this. So are the complaints about depersonalization, processing, and compulsory socialization into a corporate, inhuman world. Michael Novak, expressing some of this, writes that what our institutions "decide is real is enforced as real." He calls parents, teachers, and psychiatrists (like policemen and soldiers) "the enforcers of reality"; then he goes on to say:

When a young person is being initiated into society, existing norms determine what is to be considered real and what is to be annihilated by silence and disregard. The good, docile student accepts the norms; the recalcitrant student may lack the intelligence—or have too much; may lack maturity—or insist upon being his own man.[53]

I have responses like this in mind when I consult the phenomenologists for an approach to curriculum in the present day. For one thing, they remind us of what it means for an individual to be present to himself; for another, they suggest to us the origins of significant quests for meaning, origins which ought to be held in mind by those willing to enable students to be themselves.

If the existence of a primordial consciousness is taken seriously, it will be recognized that awareness begins perspectively, that our experience is always incomplete. It is true that we have what Merleau-Ponty calls a "prejudice" in favor of a world of solid, determinate objects, quite independent of our perceptions. Consciousness does, however, have the capacity to return to the precognitive, the primordial, by "bracketing out" objects as customarily seen. The individual can release himself into his own inner time and rediscover the ways in which objects arise, the ways in which experience develops. In discussing the possibility of Karl Rossmann exploring his own past, I have tried to show what this sort of interior journey can mean. Not only may it result in the effecting of new syntheses within experience; it may result in an awareness of the process of knowing, of believing, of perceiving. It may even result in an understanding of the ways in which meanings have been sedimented in an individual's own personal history. I can think of no more potent mode of combatting those conceived to be "enforcers of the real," including the curriculum designers.

But then there opens up the possibility of presenting curriculum in such a way that it does not impose or enforce. If the student is enabled to recognize that reason and order may represent the culminating step in his constitution of a world, if he can be enabled to see that what Schutz calls the attainment of a "reciprocity of perspectives"[54] signifies the achievement of rationality, he may realize what it is to generate the structures of the disciplines on his own initiative, against his own "background awareness." Moreover, he may realize that he is projecting beyond his present horizons each time he shifts his attention and takes another perspective on his world. "To say there exists rationality," writes Merleau-Ponty, "is to say that perspectives blend, perceptions confirm each other, a meaning emerges."[55] He points out that we witness at every moment "the miracles of related experiences, and yet nobody knows better than we do how this miracle is worked, for we are ourselves this network of relationships.'' Curriculum can offer the possibility for students to be the makers of such networks. The problem for their teachers is to stimulate an awareness of the questionable, to aid in the identification of the thematically relevant, to beckon beyond the everyday.

I am a psychological and historical structure, and have received, with existence, a manner of existence, a style. All my actions and thoughts stand in a relationship to this structure, and even a philosopher's thought is merely a way of making explicit his hold on the world, and what he is. The fact remains that I am free, not in spite of, or on the hither side of these motivations, but by means of them. For this significant life, this certain significance of nature and history which I am, does not limit my access to the world, but on the contrary is my means of entering into communication with it. It is by being unrestrictedly and unreservedly what I am at present that I have a chance of moving forward; it is by living my time that I am able to understand other times, by plunging into the present and the world by taking on deliberately what I am fortuitously, by willing what I will and doing what I do, that I can go further.[56]

To plunge in; to choose; to disclose; to move: this is the road, it seems to me, to mastery.

NOTES

1. Maurice Merleau-Ponty, *The Primacy of Perception,* edited by James M. Edie (Evanston, Ill.: Northwestern University Press, 1964), p. 99.
2. Jean-Paul Sartre, *Search for a Method* (New York: Alfred A. Knopf, 1963), p. 92.
3. Ryland W. Crary, *Humanizing the School: Curriculum Development and Theory* (New York: Alfred A. Knopf, 1969), p. 13.
4. John Dewey, ''The Child and the Curriculum,'' in Martin S. Dworkin (ed.), *Dewey on Education* (New York: Teachers College Bureau of Publications, 1959), p. 91.
5. Sarah Lawall, *Critics of Consciousness* (Cambridge, Mass.: Harvard University Press, 1968).
6. T. S. Eliot, *The Sacred Wood* (New York: Barnes & Noble University Paperbacks, 1960), p. x.
7. Dorothy Walsh, ''The Cognitive Content of Art,'' in Francis J. Coleman (ed.), *Aesthetics* (New York: McGraw-Hill, 1968), p. 297.
8. Clive Bell, *Art* (London: Chatto & Windus, 1914).
9. Walsh, *op. cit.*
10. M. H. Abrams, ''Belief and the Suspension of Belief,'' in M. H. Abrams (ed.), *Literature and Belief* (New York: Columbia University Press, 1957), p. 9.
11. Maurice Blanchot, *L'Espace littéraire* (Paris: Gallimard, 1955).
12. See, e.g., Alfred Schutz, ''Some Leading Concepts of Phenomenology,'' in

Maurice Natanson (ed.), *Collected Papers* I (The Hague: Martinus Nijhoff, 1967), pp. 104–5.

13. Jean-Paul Sartre, *Literature and Existentialism*. 3rd ed. (New York: The Citadel Press, 1965), p. 43.

14. *Ibid.*, p. 45.

15. John Dewey, *Art as Experience* (New York: Minton, Balch & Company, 1934), p. 54.

16. Sartre, *Search for a Method, op. cit.*, p. 91.

17. Jean Piaget, *Structuralism* (New York: Basic Books, 1970), p. 139.

18. *Ibid.*, p. 68.

19. *Ibid.*, p. 139.

20. *Ibid.*

21. Maurice Merleau-Ponty, *Phenomenology of Perception* (London: Routledge & Kegan Paul Ltd., 1962).

22. Merleau-Ponty, *The Primacy of Perception, op. cit.*, p. 119.

23. *Ibid.*, p. 99.

24. Paulo Freire, *Pedagogy of the Oppressed* (New York: Herder and Herder, 1970), p. 108.

25. Schutz, "On Multiple Realities," *op. cit.*, p. 248.

26. Merleau-Ponty, *The Primacy of Perception, op. cit.*, p. 58.

27. Merleau-Ponty, *Phenomenology of Perception, op. cit.*, p. xvii.

28. Schutz, "On Multiple Realities," *op. cit.*

29. Merleau-Ponty, *Phenomenology of Perception, op. cit.*, p. xvii.

30. R. S. Peters, *Ethics and Education* (London: George Allen and Unwin, 1966), p. 50.

31. R. S. Peters, *Ethics and Education* (Glenview, Ill.: Scott Foresman and Co., 1967), p. 12.

32. Philip H. Phenix, "The Uses of the Disciplines as Curriculum Content," in Donald Vandenberg (ed.), *Theory of Knowledge and Problems of Education* (Urbana, Ill.: University of Illinois Press, 1969), p. 195.

33. Philip H. Phenix, *Realms of Meaning* (New York: McGraw-Hill, 1964), p. 25.

34. *Ibid.*

35. Schutz, "Problem of Rationality in the Social World," in Maurice Natanson (ed.), *Collected Papers* II (The Hague: Martinus Nijhoff, 1967), p. 66.

36. Phenix, "The Uses of the Disciplines as Curriculum Content," *op. cit.*, p. 195.

37. Alvin Toffler, *Future Shock* (New York: Random House, 1970), p. 18.

38. Albert Camus, *The Myth of Sisyphus* (New York: Alfred A. Knopf, 1955), p. 72.

39. Harold Pinter, *The Dumb Waiter* (New York: Grove Press, 1961), p. 103.

40. Tom Stoppard, *Rosencrantz and Guildenstern are Dead* (New York: Grove Press, 1967), pp. 58–59.

41. Cf. Fyodor Dostoevsky, *Notes from Underground,* in *The Short Novels of Dostoevsky* (New York: Dial Press, 1945). "You believe in a palace of crystal that can never be destroyed . . . a palace at which one will not be able to put out one's tongue or make a long nose on the sly." p. 152.

42. Franz Kafka, *Amerika* (Garden City, N.Y.: Doubleday Anchor Books, 1946), p. 38.

43. Merleau-Ponty, *The Primacy of Perception, op. cit.,* p. 110.

44. Piaget, *op. cit.*

45. Richard M. Zaner, *The Way of Phenomenology* (New York: Pegasus Books, 1970), p. 27.

46. Freire, *op. cit.,* p. 100.

47. Schutz, "The Life-World," in Maurice Natanson (ed.), *Collected Papers* III (The Hague: Martinus Nijhoff, 1967), p. 125.

48. Kafka, *op. cit.,* p. 201.

49. Schutz, "The Life-World," *op. cit.,* p. 124.

50. Schutz, "Some Leading Concepts . . . ," *op. cit.,* p. 111.

51. G. K. Plochmann, "On the Organic Logic of Teaching and Learning," in Donald Vandenberg (ed.), *Theory of Knowledge and Problems of Education, op. cit.,* p. 244.

52. *Cf.* note 10.

53. Michael Novak, *The Experience of Nothingness* (New York: Harper & Row, 1970), p. 94.

54. Schutz, "Symbols, Reality, and Society," *Collected Papers* I, *op. cit.,* p. 315.

55. Merleau-Ponty, *Phenomenology of Perception, op. cit.,* p. xix.

56. *Ibid.,* pp. 455–56.

19. AN APPROACH TO THE STUDY OF CURRICULA AS SOCIALLY ORGANIZED KNOWLEDGE[1]

Michael F. D. Young

The almost total neglect by sociologists of how knowledge is selected, organized and assessed in educational institutions (or in any other institutions for that matter) hardly needs documenting. Some answers to the question why this happened, and an attempt to show that this neglect arises out of narrow definitions of the major schools of sociological thought (in particular, those stemming from Marx, Weber and Durkheim) rather than out of their inadequacies, may provide a useful perspective from which to suggest the directions in which such work might develop. This paper explicitly does not set out to offer a general theory of culture, or to be a direct contribution to the sociology of knowledge, except to the extent that it raises questions about what might be meant by the notion of knowledge being socially organized or constructed. It has the more limited aim of trying to suggest ways in which questions may be framed about how knowledge is organized and made available in curricula. However, it would be my contention that if such questions became the foci of research in the sociology of education, then we might well see significant advances in the sociology of knowledge in particular, and sociological theory in general. The paper then has four parts:

SOURCE. In Michael F. D. Young (ed.), *Knowledge and Control: New Directions for the Sociology of Education* (London: Collier-Macmillan, 1971), pp. 19–46.

1. The changing focus of the public debates about education in the last twenty years.

2. A brief examination of the limitations and possibilities of existing approaches to the sociology of education and the sociology of knowledge in generating either fruitful theories or research in the field of curricula.

3. An outline of some of the possibilities of the Marxist, Weberian and Durkheimian traditions.

4. An elaboration of the implications of the previous sections to suggest a framework and some possible directions for future research.[2]

1

One can only speculate on the explanations, but it is clearly possible to trace three stages in the public debates on education in England in the last fifteen to twenty years; the foci have been *equality of opportunity* and the *wastage of talent, organization and selection of pupils,* and the *curriculum.* In each case one can distinguish the political, sociological and educational components, and though both of the sets of distinctions are oversimplified and schematic, they do provide a useful context for considering the problems posed in this paper. The latter three distinctions do not refer to the content of issues, but to the groups involved and the way they defined the problems.[3] In the first stage, the facts of educational "wastage" were documented by the Early Leaving and Crowther Reports (and later by Robbins) and the "class" nature of the lack of opportunity was demonstrated by Floud and Halsey. Though the sociological research largely complemented the public reports and was tacitly accepted as a basis for an expansionist policy by successive ministers, it also threw up a new set of questions concerning the social nature of selection, and the organization of secondary education in particular. Thus, the second phase of public debate from the midsixties focused on the issues of *selection* and *comprehensive reorganization.* That the debate now became an issue of political conflict is an indication that the policies involved, such as the abolition of selective schools, threatened certain significant and powerful interests in society—particularly the career-grammar, direct-grant and public school staff and the parents of the children who expected to go to such schools. The manifest inefficiency and less well-documented injustice of the $11+$[4] made its abolition a convenient political commitment for reformist politicians. This debate was paralleled by an increasing interest by sociologists in all kinds of organizations and the possibility of applying the more general models of "organization theory" to schools and colleges.[5]

It is only in the last two or three years that the focus of the debate has moved again from *organization* to *curriculum,* and again one can only speculate on the reasons. Four might be worth exploring; the first three particularly, in relation to the kind of projects on curriculum reform sponsored by the Schools Council:

1.) *Government pressure for more and better technologists and scientists.* The origins and implications of this are highly complex and can only be briefly referred to here. Mcpherson (1969), Blaug and Gannicott (1969) and Gorbutt (1970) have all cast doubts on the widely held notions that pupils in secondary schools are "swinging from science." This swing has been an "official" problem, with various "official" sets of remedies since the publication of the Dainton Report (1968). Gorbutt (1970) draws on the earlier studies and suggests that what has been called the "swing from" science may be less the product of an identifiable change in the pattern of "subject" choice by school pupils, and more an indication of how particular interest groups "use" official statistics.

The failure of sociologists to make explicit the theoretical assumptions underlying contemporary definitions of this problem and the research it has generated is worth considering here. The whole "subject-choice" and "swing from science" debate presupposes taking as "given" the social definitions implicit in our commonsense distinction between "arts" and "sciences." What "does" and "does not" count as "science" depends on the social meaning given to science, which will vary not only historically and cross-culturally but within societies and situationally. The dominant English cultural definitions of science might be characterized as what Habermas (1970) calls "objectivistic," by which he means that we accept the scientists' claim that they "apply their method without thought for their guiding interests." In other words an idea of science has developed in which what is thought of as scientific knowledge is abstracted from the institutional contexts in which it is generated and used. Goodman (1969*b*) is making a similar point in discussing the implications of alternative social definitions of technology. Once the meanings associated with "science" and "technology," and "pure" and "applied," are seen as socially determined, not only does it become possible to explore how these social meanings become part of the school context of pupil preference, but a sociological enquiry into the intellectual content of what counts as science becomes possible (King, 1971).

2.) *The commitment to raising the school leaving age.* The implications of this change stem from the obvious if neglected fact that length of educational career is probably the single most important determinant of pupils' curricular experience. Thus for the 50 percent of pupils who at present leave when school is no longer legally compulsory, by 1973 teachers will be forced to conceive of curricula for a further "terminal year."

One development, which can be seen as a possible "solution" to the "extra year," has been the extension, to at least one half of all school leavers, of publicly recognized school exams. The extension of "mode 3" or "teacher based" exams has introduced a potentially greater flexibility in approach and the possibility of a more critical questioning of existing syllabi. The "guiding interests" of the examination boards have so far remained outside the field of sociological enquiry. It is possible that such "interests" may become more "public" if the various pressures to abolish G.C.E. '0' level grow.

3.) *Comprehensive amalgamations.* Many of these involve grammar schools which are obliged to receive an unselective pupil intake. Thus teachers who for years have successfully produced good "A" level results from highly selected groups of pupils are now faced with many pupils who appear to neither know how to "learn" the "academic knowledge," nor appear to want to. This inevitably poses for teachers quite new problems of finding alternatives.

4) *Student participation.* It is undeniable that as the demands of students in colleges and universities have moved from the arena of union and leisure activities to discipline and administrative authority and finally to a concern to participate in the planning of the structure and content of courses and their assessment, staff have themselves begun to re-examine the principles that underlay their curricula and which have for so long been taken for granted. It is more rather than less likely that this pressure from the students will increase and extend to the senior forms of the schools. Perhaps the most dramatic demonstration of this trend is the Negro students in the U.S.A. who are demanding courses in black studies.

Again the public debate has taken place on two levels, the "political" and the "educational"—though such a distinction is necessarily an over-simplification, and it is not intended to suggest that educational ideas do not have a political content. At the political level the main protagonists have been the Marxist "left" (Anderson, 1969) and the conservative or Black Paper (Cox and Dyson, 1969*a*, 1969*b*) "right." The "left" criticizes contemporary curricula for "mystifying the students" and "fragmenting knowledge into compartments." They also claim that such curricula, by denying students the opportunity to understand society as a "totality," act as effective agents of social control.* The conservative "right" criticize progressive teaching methods, unstreaming and the various curricular innovations in English, history, and maths, as well as the expansion of the "soft" social sciences. In the name of preserving "our cultural heritage" and providing opportunities for the most able to excel, they seek to conserve the institutional support for the educational tradition they believe in—particularly the public and direct-grant grammar schools. What is significant for the sociology of education is that in spite of attempts, the politics of the curriculum has remained outside of Westminster. Apart from compulsory religious instruction, the headmaster or

---

*Considerably more sophisticated versions of this thesis, which are not considered here, have been put forward by French and German social scientists (for instance, H. Lefebvre [1969]).

principal's formal autonomy over the curriculum is not questioned. That this autonomy is in practice extremely limited by the control of VIth-form (and therefore lower form) curricula by the universities, *both through their entrance requirements and their domination of all but one of the school examination boards, hardly needs emphasizing. Furthermore any likelihood of the new "polytechnics" developing alternative sets of criteria is limited by the powerful indirect control (of all degree-based courses) held by universities through their membership of the C.N.A.A. Boards. It becomes apparent that it is the legitimacy of university control, rather than teacher autonomy, that is being upheld.

It is as if by what has been called in another context the "politics of non-decision making" (Bachrach and Baratz, 1963) through which the range of issues for party political debate are limited, that consideration of the curriculum is avoided[6] except for broad discussions about the need for more scientists. There are sufficient parallels in other contexts to suggest that the avoidance of such discussion is an indication of the interrelationship between the existing organization of knowledge and the distribution of power, the consideration of which might not be comfortable in an era of consensus politics.[7]

The context of the "educationalists' " debate about the curriculum has been different and inevitably less contentious. This lack of contentiousness is in stark contrast with the kind of direct confrontation that exists in America between the American academic establishment and its critics (Goodman, Friedenberg, Chomsky, Holt, *et al.*). It is possible that this contrast may in part be accounted for by the different contexts and historical antecedents of the prevailing "liberal" orthodoxies in each country. The difference is also apparent when we consider some of the issues of the "educationalists' " debate in this country; early tracking into the sciences or arts, overspecialization and neglect of applied science in the VIth form, as well as the possibility of introducing new knowledge areas such as the social sciences. On another level, what has been labelled the "tyranny of subjects" typical of much secondary education has been opposed by suggestions for integrated curricula based on "themes" and "topics."

Three features that have characterized the educationalists' part in this debate should also be mentioned: 1) *The emphasis on secondary curricula.* Virtually all the issues have focused on aspects of secondary school curricula, which have in practice undergone least change; the absence of debate over changes at the primary level would seem to point, paradoxically, to the much greater autonomy of that part of the educational system with the lowest status. 2) *The stream of working papers and proposals of the Schools Council.* (This point will be taken up later in the paper.) 3)*The critiques of the philosophers of education.* Start-

---

*No direct control is implied here, but rather a process by which teachers legitimate their curricula through their shared assumptions about "what we all know the universities want."

ing from certain *a priori* assumptions about the organization (or forms) of knowledge (Hirst, 1969), their criticisms focus either on new topic-based syllabi which neglect these "forms of understanding," or on new curricula for the so-called "less able" or "Newsom child" which they argue are consciously restricting them from access to those forms of understanding which in the philosopher's sense are "education." The problem with this kind of critique is that it appears to be based on an absolutist conception of a set of distinct forms of knowledge which correspond closely to the traditional areas of the academic curriculum and thus justify, rather than examine, what are no more than the socio-historical constructs of a particular time. It is important to stress that it is not "subjects," which Hirst recognizes as the socially constructed ways that teachers organize knowledge, but forms of understanding, that it is claimed are "necessarily" distinct. The point I wish to make here is that unless such *necessary* distinctions or intrinsic logics are treated as problematic, philosophical criticism cannot examine the assumptions of academic curricula.

Unlike in the debates on *equality* and *organization,* sociologists, except as political protagonists, have remained silent. We have had virtually no theoretical perspectives or research to suggest explanations of how curricula, which are no less social inventions than political parties or new towns, arise, persist and change, and what the social interests and values involved might be.

2

Sociology of Education and the Curriculum

Having mapped out the context of the debates on the curriculum, let us turn to the sociology of education and consider why its contribution has been so negligible.[8] Sociologists seem to have forgotten, to paraphrase Raymond Williams, that education is not a product like cars and bread, but a selection and organization from the available knowledge at a particular time which involves conscious or unconscious choices. It would seem that it is or should be the central task of the sociology of education to relate these principles of selection and organization that underly curricula to their institutional and interactional setting in schools and classrooms and to the wider social structure. I want to suggest that we can account for the failure of sociologists to do this by examining on the one hand the ideological and methodological assumptions of the sociologists, and on the other hand the institutional context within which the sociological study of education has developed. However, perhaps as significant a fact as any in accounting for the limited conception of the sociology of education in Britain has been that in spite of the interest in the field reported by respondents to Carter's recent survey (Carter, 1967), *very few* sociologists have been involved in research in education.

Much British sociology in the late fifties and the sociology of education in particular drew its ideological perspective from Fabian socialism and its methodology from the demographic tradition of Booth and Rowntree. They broadened the notion of poverty from lack of income to lack of education, which was seen as a significant part of working-class life chances. The stark facts of the persistence of inequalities over decades and in spite of an overall expansion do not need repeating, but what is important is that these studies and those such as Douglas and Plowden which followed, in their concern for increasing equality of opportunity, focused primarily on the characteristics of the failures, the early leavers and the dropouts. By using a model of explanation of working-class school failure which justified reformist social policies, they were unable to examine the socially constructed character of the education that the working-class children failed at—for instance, the peculiar content of the grammar school curriculum for the sixteen-year-old in which pupils are obliged to do up to ten different subjects which bear little relation either to each other or to anything else. It would not be doing these studies an injustice to say that they developed primarily from a sociological interest in stratification in the narrow sense rather than education. They were concerned to show how the distribution of life chances through education can be seen as an aspect of the class structure. Inevitably this led to an overmechanistic conception of "class" which isolated the "class" characteristics of individuals from the "class" content of their educational experience. It may clarify this point by looking at the implicit model more normally as follows:

Assumptions	*Independent variable*	*Dependent variable*
Criteria of educational success—curricula, methods and evaluation. What counts as "knowledge and knowing" in school	Social characteristics of the success and failure groups	Distribution of success and failure at various stages—stream, 11+, 'O' level, etc.

Though the table illustrates the point in a crude and oversimplified form, it does show that within that framework the content of education is taken as a "given" and is not subject to sociological enquiry—the "educational failures" become a sort of "deviant."[9] We can usefully reformulate the problem in a similar way to that suggested by Cicourel and Kitsuse (1963a) in their discussion of how "official statistics" on crime are produced, and ask what are the processes by which rates of educational success and failure come to be produced. We are then led to ask questions about the context and definition of success and how they are legitimized. In other words, the methods of assessment, selection and organization of knowledge and the principles underlying them become our focus of study. The point is important because what is implied is that questions have to be raised about matters that have either not been considered important or have been tacitly accepted as "given." How does the education that poor working-class children fail at come to be provided? What are the social assumptions that are implicit in the criteria used in the Crowther Report to delineate a "second group" who "should be taught a sensible practicality—moral standards and a wise use of leisure time"? One could raise similar questions about the Newsom Report's "below average child," and in fact about much educational research. One can see that this kind of reformulation would not have been consistent either with the methods or with the ideology of most British sociological research, particularly that concerned with social class and educational opportunity. A similar point can be made about studies of schools and colleges as "organizations." They have either begun with "models" from "organizational theory" or have compared schools with mental hospitals and prisons as "people processing organizations."[10] In neither case is it recognized that it is not only people but knowledge in the educational institutions that is "processed," and that unless what is "knowledge" is to be taken as "given," it is the interrelation of the two processes of organization that must form the beginning of such studies.[11] An examination of the knowledge teachers have of children and how this influences the knowledge they make available to them would provide one way of tackling this empirically (Keddie, 1970).

Turning to the institutional context, it does seem clear that most of the teaching and published work in the sociology of education has taken place in colleges, institutes and departments of education. It is only very recently that university departments of sociology have offered main options at either B.Sc. or M.Sc. level in this field. Thus sociology of education has developed in institutions devoted to the "academic" study of education where ten to fifteen years ago it hardly existed. We can pose the question as to how did the new specialists legitimate their contribution to educational studies and justify their particular field of expertise—particularly when the ex-school subject specialists and the philosophers had defined their area of competence as covering the curriculum and pedagogy. Not surprisingly, the sociologists mapped out new unexplored areas. They started from the social context of education, with an emphasis on social class, relationships to the economy, the occupational structure and the family, and moved to the consideration of schools as organizations and pupil subcultures. Through an arbitrary division of labor which had no theoretical basis, this allowed the expansion of sociology of education with the minimum of "boundary disputes." Inevitably this is speculation, but it does suggest an explanation of what appears to have been a consensus among sociologists and nonsociologists alike that the curriculum was not a field for sociological research.

Although this discussion has focused on British sociology, the points are equally applicable to the American situation. Functionalist theory, which has been the perspective of the majority of sociologists in the U.S.A., presupposes at a very general level an agreed set of societal values or goals which define both the selection and organization of knowledge in curricula. With one or two notable exceptions,[12] even the best American work in the sociology of education has been concerned with the "organization" or "processing" of people (whether pupils or students), and takes the organization of knowledge for granted.[13] It is important to stress that this limitation has also been characteristic of the work of those who have criticized the structural-functionalists.[14] This is of importance as it points to the limitations of the symbolic interactionist perspective. This perspective, derived largely from the ideas of G. H. Mead, has given rise to valuable studies of lawyers, medical students, nurses and others. These studies have raised questions that are not considered by functionalists about the processes of interaction and the situational significance of beliefs and values. However, they have not been able to consider as problematic the knowledge that is made available in such interactions. This would have led to considering the structural contingencies influencing what is defined as legal, medical, nursing or other knowledge, and would inevitably take the research out of the "situated action" and therefore out of the symbolic interactionist framework.

Sociology of Knowledge and the Curriculum

It would have seemed that a field which was concerned with the social conditions influencing the development of knowledge, and with attempts to place ideas in their socio-historical setting, would have seen educational institutions and how knowledge is selected and organized in them as an obvious area for research. However, the main tradition which stems from Marx has been largely restricted to philosophies, political theories and theologies. These comments do not refer to the sociology of knowledge that stems from the phenomenology of Alfred Schutz, until recently totally neglected by sociologists. Schutz treats the institutional definitions or typifications (whether of education, or families or politics) as the intersubjective reality which men have constructed to give meaning to their world; therefore though they are part of the accepted world of everyday life for teachers, mothers and politicians, they can become the objects of sociological enquiry. In other words, if "knowledge" or "what is taken for knowledge" is ideal-typical in construction, Schutz is pointing to a study of the "construction" of subjects, disciplines and syllabi as sets or provinces of meaning which form the basis of the intersubjective understandings of educators. The school curriculum becomes just one of the mechanisms through which knowledge is "socially distributed." As Schaffer (1970) suggests, the question "how do children learn mathematics" presupposes answers to the prior question as to what is the social basis of the "set of meanings that come to be typified under the term mathematics?"

Three strands, which characterize the more familiar traditions in the sociology of knowledge, indicate not its lack of potential but why the direction it has taken has made its contribution to the sociology of education so insignificant. Firstly, except in the American work on mass media, most writings have either, like Child[15] and Mannheim, been on the border of sociology and epistemology and have been concerned primarily with the existential nature of knowledge, or more recently have been little more than overviews. In both cases, with the exception of Mannheim's essay on "Conservative Thought" (Mannheim, 1936), substantive empirical research has been eschewed. Secondly, there has been, since Marx, a persistent neglect of the cognitive dimension of the categories of thought and how they are socially constrained—studies have been restricted to the values, standards and "views of the world" of different groups.[16] Thirdly, and most importantly for the issues raised in this paper, the process of transmission, as *itself* a social condition, has not been studied. If it had, as we shall demonstrate in referring to Bourdieu's comments on Durkheim, the sociology of knowledge would have been inevitably concerned with the curricula through which knowledge is transmitted.

3

The Marxist Tradition

Marx himself wrote very little about education, though a notion of "polytechnical education" which underlies the educational policy of the "communist" countries can be found in one of his early speeches.[17] Though Marx does have a theory which at a very general level can account for the changes in men's consciousness or categories of thought in terms of the changing means of production and the social relations they generate, he does not extend this to a systematic analysis of the educational system of his time comparable with his analysis of the economy. The limitations of Marxist theory also relate to its focus on how the knowledge is controlled and legitimized and its neglect of the equally important process of its acquisition. However, Marx's claim that education in a "capitalist society" is a "tool of ruling class interest," does direct one to examine the relation between the interests of economically dominant groups and the prevailing ideas of education as "good" or "worthwhile" in itself. It follows that the dominant emphasis of the education systems of capitalist societies, which might be described as the competitive concern with exams, grades and degrees, can be seen as one expression of the principles of a market economy (Hellerich, 1970). It is difficult to avoid the view that while these ideas may be true up to a point, they are on such a general level as to make them of limited value as starting points for the analysis of elite curricula. They do not point to explanations of the dynamics and particular configurations of different curricula.

However, the Italian Marxist Antonio Gramsci was more specifically concerned with education, and although only fragments of his work (Gramsci, 1957, 1967) are available in English, his primary concern with both the role of intellectuals (and by implication "their kind of knowledge") and what he called the cultural hegemony which he saw as imposed on the working classes who are thus prevented from thinking for themselves, is important for any consideration of the content of education. Two aspects of Gramsci's thought that I refer to below are no more than illustrative and do not claim to be necessarily his most important ideas. His deep interest in the role of intellectuals in different kinds of society led him to consider many of the educational distinctions which we take for granted as historical products. They therefore become not "given" but open to explanation and change. Examples such as "theory" and "practice," creation and propagation of knowledge (or in contemporary terms "teaching" and "research"), and what he calls the "laws of scholarship" and the "limits of scientific research" are all unexamined parts of the framework within which most formal education takes place. The second aspect relates to his distinction between "common sense" and "philosophy" in which he sees that some people's common sense becomes formally recognized as philosophy, and other people's does not, depending on their access to certain institutional contexts. This suggests that sociologists should raise the wider question of the relation between school knowledge and commonsense knowledge, of how, as Gramsci suggests, knowledge available to certain groups becomes "school knowledge" or "educational" and that available to others does not.

The most interesting recent attempt within a Marxist framework is that of Anderson (1969) in which he attempts to relate the content of the humanities in English academic curricula to the historical development of the class struggle. It is relatively easy and not very helpful to show that the examples of English culture that he takes are not representative and are selected to suit his thesis. However, a more important theoretical weakness is in his claim to a *structural analysis*, which seems unwittingly to exhibit the same flaws as most functional analyses of institutions. It emphasizes the interrelations of existing patterns of culture rather than seeing them as developing through the interaction of competing beliefs and ideas in the context of developing knowledge and a changing institutional setting. This "structural" analysis allows Anderson to treat cases that do not fit as "deviant" and not in need of explanation, another parallel with functional theories.

With a neo-Marxist framework, Williams (1961) provides perhaps the most promising and (by sociologists) most neglected approach to the study of the content of education. He distinguishes four distinct sets of educational philosophies or ideologies which rationalize different emphases in the selection of the content of curricula, and relates these to the social position of those who hold them. He then suggests that curricula changes have reflected the relative power of the different groups over the last hundred years. These can conveniently be summarized in the table below. He makes the significant point that the last of the foci was only recognized as legitimate outside the formal educational system. It is paradoxical when one considers the persisting subordinate position of the manual worker, that aspects of the populist educational ideology are now being ''resurrected'' not by manual workers but in student demands for participation in the planning of curricula of universities,[18] institutions to which only about 3 percent of the sons of manual workers ever attain.

Ideology	Social position	Educational policies
1. Liberal/ conservative	Aristocracy/gentry	Non-vocational—the "educated" man, an emphasis on character
2. Bourgeois	Merchant and pro-fessional classes	Higher vocational and professional courses. Education as access to desired positions
3. Democratic	Radical reformers	Expansionist—"education for all"
4. Populist/ proletarian	Working classes/ subordinate groups	Student relevance, choice, participation

In placing curricular developments in their historical context, Williams's chapter is original and insightful though inevitably lacking in substantive evidence. It is only regrettable that in the nine intervening years no sociologist has followed it up. Perhaps the greatest weaknesses of the approach are that little attention is given to the changing power relations between the groups which might account for curricular changes, and one is left in doubt as to how the ''democratic'' and ''bourgeois'' ideologies arise from what would appear to be the same social group. Other attempts have been made to develop more systematically the Marxist concept of ideology for empirical research, though not primarily in the field of education. However, one study which warrants note in the context of this paper is Mills's (1943) early account of the professional ideology of social problem-orientated sociologists in the twenties and thirties. He characterized their ''common thought style'' from a content analysis of a wide range of popular texts, and showed the relation of this to their common social origins and professional experience. It is a model study of how to relate complex empirical data to a theoretical perspective in order to show how, in this case, university sociology syllabuses developed at a particular time. It would seem to have relevance as an approach, given the dominating influence of textbooks on secondary education, to a wide range of knowledge areas, particularly in the humanities.

The Weberian Contribution

Max Weber's ideas (and not only his writings on bureaucracy) have not been neglected by sociologists of education, for the well-known analyses of the changing function of universities have been based on his ideal-types of the "expert" and the "cultivated man."[19] However, with the exception of Musgrove,[20] the possibilities of his work for posing questions about the selection and organization of knowledge have not been examined. I shall not try here to redress the balance, but refer by way of illustration to his study of Confucian education.[21] Weber identified three characteristics of the education of the Chinese literati (or administrators):

1. An emphasis on propriety and "bookishness," with a curriculum largely restricted to the learning and memorizing of classical texts.
2. This curriculum was a very narrow selection from the available knowledge in a society where mathematicians, astronomers, scientists, and geographers were not uncommon. However, all these fields of knowledge were classified by the literati as "vulgar," or perhaps in more contemporary terms "non-academic."
3. Entry into the administrative elite was controlled by examinations on this narrow curriculum, so that the "non-bookish" were for the purpose of the Chinese society of the time "not educated."

Weber explains this curriculum selection by relating it to the characteristics of what he called the patrimonial bureaucracy, in which administration was carried out by referring to the classical texts. Any change in curriculum would have undermined the legitimacy of the power of the administration whose skills therefore had to be defined as "absolute." As the whole question is secondary to Weber's main interest in comparative religion, we do not get suggestions as to the relationships of those with access to "non-bookish" knowledge, and the possibility of their forming a competing power group with a radically different definition of education. Drawing on Weber, Wilkinson (1964) has a similar thesis about the classical curriculum of the nineteenth-century English public schools. Both writers are suggesting that curricula are defined in terms of the dominant group's idea of the "educated man," which directs us back to the question raised implicitly earlier as to what model of the educated man is implicit in the "worthwhile activities" or "forms of understanding" of contemporary philosophies of education. Each of these studies, like Ben-David's (1963) interesting comparison of the relative influence of local pressure groups and elite values on American and English university curricula, are limited by the lack of an overall framework for linking the principles of selection of content to the social structure. However, both Weber and Ben-David, as well as a recent symposium on elite education (Wilkinson, 1969), point to the value of comparative studies in suggesting how different definitions of legitimate academic study arise and persist.

Durkheim

His specific works on education, apart from the emphasis on the social nature of curricula and pedagogy, are not very helpful, though it is important to remember that these books are collections of his lectures to student teachers and not systematic studies in sociology. The familiar criticisms, which do not need elaborating, are however applicable—firstly, his undifferentiated view of society which blurs the culture/social structure distinction and assumes them to be either synonymous or congruent or functionally related; and secondly, an over-emphasis on the value-component of education which he envisages as having a primarily integrative rather than stratifying and differentiating function. However, recent writers such as Bourdieu (1967) and Bernstein (1967) have focused on Durkheim's work as a whole and suggested that it is his work on religion and primitive classification (Durkheim and Mauss, 1963) leading indirectly to a sociology of knowledge that are of most significance for the sociological study of education. Bourdieu suggests that there is an analogy between Durkheim's account of the social origins of the categories of thought in small-scale societies with the development of thought categories through the process of transmission of culture in the school. Implicit in this process of transmission are criteria of what is topical, and the legitimacy of a hierarchy of ''study objects'' becomes built into categories of thought themselves. Bernstein's work will be referred to in more detail later in the paper, but it is worth pointing out that he has extended Durkheim's work in two ways that are important here. He has elaborated the link between social change (mechanical to organic solidarity) and cultural change (the move from collection to integrated-type curricula) and secondly, by emphasizing language and the curriculum he has moved the Durkheimian approach to education to the cognitive as well as the evaluative level.

To summarize this section, an attempt has been made to show that sociological research drawing on the Marxist, Weberian and Durkheimian traditions can contribute to a reorientation of the sociology of education that would no longer neglect curricula nor, as Talcott Parsons treats ''power,'' consider it as an epiphenomenon.

4

The previous section has, from different points of view, suggested that consideration of the assumptions underlying the selection and organization of knowledge by those in positions of power may be a fruitful perspective for raising sociological question about curricula. We can make this more explicit by starting with the assumptions that those in positions of power will attempt to define what is to be taken as knowledge, how accessible to different groups any knowledge is, and what are the accepted relationships between different knowledge areas and between those who have access to them and make them available. It is thus the exploration of how these processes happen, since they tend in other than pre-literate societies to take place in and through educational institutions, that should form the focus of a sociology of education. Our understanding of the processes is so rudimentary at present, that it is doubtful if we can postulate any clear links between the organization of knowledge at the level of social structure and the process as it involves teachers in classrooms. However, from these assumptions we can, drawing on Bernstein (1969), pose three interrelated questions about how knowledge is organized in curricula.

1.) The power of some to define what is "valued" knowledge leads to problems of accounting for how "stratified" knowledge is and by what criteria. Implicit in this idea of "stratification of knowledge" is the distinction between the "prestige" and the "property" components of stratification. To the former are linked the different social evaluations placed on different knowledge areas,[22] and to the latter are the notions of "ownership" and freedom (or restriction of access).[23] Thus the "property" aspect of stratification points to "knowledge" in use, and the reward structure associated with it. It suggests that in different societies the dominant conception of knowledge may be akin to "private property," property shared by particular groups, or communally available on the analogy of "common land." The analysis which follows implicitly places greater emphasis on the prestige component of the stratification of knowledge. This is in part because the focus of the analysis is on curricula in one society rather than across societies, when it would become easier to conceptualize different definitions of "knowledge as property."

2.) The restriction of the accessibility of knowledge areas to different groups, poses the question in relation to curricula as to what is the *scope* of curricula available to different age groups, and more specifically to the social factors influencing the degree and kind of specialization at any age level.

3.) Earlier in the paper I raised the question as to what fields of enquiry were, at different times and in different cultures, embraced by a term like "science." More broadly this raises the question of the relation between knowledge areas and between those with access to them.

It may be useful to conceive of these three questions dichotomously and to represent the possible curricular alternative diagrammatically (see Table 1).

Bernstein's two ideal-type curricula, the "integrated" and "collection" types (1969) are shown to include different sub-types in which the stratification and specialization of knowledge is high or low. The conceptual structure implicit in the diagram was suggested by Bernstein (1969, 1970), though he concentrates

TABLE 1
Dimensions of the Social Organization of Knowledge in Curricula

		Open		Closed	
What is the scope of knowledge areas? (degree of specialization)		Narrow (specialized)	Broad	Narrow	Broad (unspecialized)
How stratified are the knowledge areas? (degree of stratification)	High	1	2	5	6
	Low	3	4	7	8

[alternatives 1-4 represent "integrated" types and 5-8 represent "collection" types in Bernstein's terminology]

his anaysis primarily on types 4 and 5 and some of their "variants" on account of their obvious historical significance. While it is not suggested, as some typologists do, that we should expect to find all of the types, it might be valuable to speculate on the conditions that we would expect to give rise to the various types.[24]

The expansion of knowledge, and the access to it, is paralleled by its increasing differentiation. *Empirically* we could no doubt also demonstrate that increasing differentiation is a necessary condition for some groups to be in a position to legitimize "their knowledge" as superior or of high value. This high value is institutionalized by the creation of formal educational establishments to "transmit" it to specially selected members of the society. Thus highly-valued knowledge becomes enshrined in the academy or school and provides a standard against which all else that is known is compared. That this description is analogous to the process described by Davis and Moore (1945) when discussing social stratification is not unintended; the limitations of the latter point also to those of the analysis presented above. The important point, made originally by Buckley (1958), is that, though empirically differential social evaluation often follows from increasing differentiation, there is no necessary relationship between the two processes. In other words the pattern of social evaluation must be explained, independently of the process of differentiation, in terms of the restricted access to certain kinds of knowledge and the opportunity for those who have access to them to legitimize their higher status and control their availability.

The framework presented focuses on the principles of organization and selection of knowledge and only implicitly suggests how these are related to the social structure. The sociological assumption is that the most explicit relation between the dominant institutional order and the organization of knowledge will be on the dimension of stratification; moves therefore to "destratify" or give equal value to different kinds of knowledge, or "restratify" (moves to legitimize other criteria of evaluation), by posing a theat to the power structure of that "order," will be resisted. This proposition is made on a very general level to which two qualifications should be made. Firstly, the notion of a dominant institutional order implies that among various economic, political, bureaucratic, cultural and educational interest groups which make up such an order, there is a consensus on the definitions of knowledge which is only likely under certain specific conditions. One would imagine, for example, that business and academic elites would not, except if faced with a common threat, share assumptions in their definitions of knowledge (see, for example, Thompson, 1970). Secondly, although one can trace historically (Williams, 1961; Birnbaum, 1970) some of the mechanisms of resistance and change, and also explore them in case studies at the organizational and interactional level, we still lack, as was indicated earlier, a way of conceptualizing the relationship between these levels.

Similarly, movements to make the scope of knowledge in a curriculum less restricted (a decrease in specialization), and the relations between knowledge areas more "open," will also pose threats to the patterns of social relations implicit in the more restricted and less open forms, and likewise will be resisted.[25] It should therefore be possible to account for the persistence of some characteristics, particularly of academic curricula, and the changes of others in terms of whether they involve changes in either the criteria of evaluation of knowledge, or its scope or relations.[26] I want to suggest, therefore, that it may be through this idea of the stratification of knowledge that we can suggest relations between the patterns of dominant values and the distribution of rewards and power, and the organization of knowledge. Such analysis would be necessary both historically and cross-culturally on the societal level[27] and also at different age levels and in different knowledge areas.[28]

Academic curricula in this country involve assumptions that some kinds and areas of knowledge are much more "worthwhile" than others: that as soon as possible all knowledge should become specialized and with minimum explicit emphasis on the relations between the subjects specialized in and between the specialist teachers involved. It may be useful, therefore, to view curricular changes as involving changing definitions of knowledge along one or more of the dimensions towards a less or more stratified, specialized and open organization of knowledge. Further, that as we assume some patterns of social relations associated with any curriculum, these changes will be resisted in so far as they are perceived to undermine the values, relative power and privileges of the dominant groups involved.

Before looking in more detail at the stratification of knowledge, I should like to indicate by examples the kind of questions that the ideas of scope and openness suggest.[29] First, *scope*: by referring to the degree of specialization, we are by implication concerned with the distribution of resources (pupil and teacher time, resources and materials).[30] This suggests why, in spite of much publicity to the contrary, specialization is so firmly entrenched. Its institutional basis in the schools would seem an important area of sociological enquiry.[31] Let us take as an illustration recent changes in medical and engineering curricula, which bring out the ways in which the characteristics and content of curricula are influenced by the changing values and interests of the controlling groups involved.

One feature that medical and engineering curricula have in common is that those controlling them have recently appeared concerned to introduce a social science component into the courses. In the absence of research, one can only speculate about the changing definitions of socially relevant knowledge involved in this broadening of the curriculum. Conceivably, these changes reflect a change in the position of the engineer and doctor, who both find themselves working increasingly in large organizations isolated from the direct consequences of their work, but still subject to public criticisms of what they do. The significance of this example is to point out the way changes in the social or occupational structure may influence definitions of relevant knowledge and thus curricula.

Turning to the question of *openness;* there are critical research problems here, for the idea of curricula consisting of knowledge areas in "open" or closed relation to each other presupposes that definitions of knowledge areas or "subjects" are not problematic. It is important to recognize that "subjects" or, even as was suggested earlier in this paper, broad fields like "arts" and "sciences," though they may be part of educators' taken for granted world, cannot be seen as such by sociologists. However, in order to conceptualize the changing relationships between teachers, some assumptions have to be made, and it may be valuable as an illustration of the utility of the framework to point to some of the differences that are likely to arise from "integration" in the "arts" and in the "sciences." The characteristic of all teaching of sciences at any level is that however strong subject loyalties and identification may be (and this is likely to be closely associated with the level of teaching), those teaching do tend to share implicitly or explicitly norms and values which define what science is about, and thus chemistry, physics and biology are at one level "integrated." It is not surprising, therefore, that in an area of the academic curriculum not striking for its innovations, the VIth form, both biological and physical sciences are increasingly taught as fully-integrated courses. An indication of the significance of the stratification dimension of knowledge is that the core base of the former is biochemistry and of the latter is mathematics: both high-status knowledge fields among scientists. Evidence of the different situation that arises when attempts to integrate appear to reduce the status of the knowledge is the failure of the general science movement after World War II. Whereas the physicist and biologist share a fairly explicit set of values through being scientists, it is doubtful if being in the "humanities" has any common meaning for historians, geographers and those in English and foreign languages (except in the situation where they all see themselves competing for resources with the scientists). In this case, any movement to "integration" involves the construction of new values to replace subject identities. It is not surprising that this side of the academic VIth-form curriculum has undergone very little change.

The third question that was raised about the organization of knowledge concerned how far and by what criteria were different knowledge areas *stratified*. I would argue that it is the most important, for it is through this idea that we are led to consider the social basis of different kinds of knowledge and we can begin to raise questions about relations between the power structure and curricula, the access to knowledge and the opportunities to legitimize it as "superior," and the relation between knowledge and its functions in different kinds of society.

If knowledge is highly stratified there will be a clear distinction between what is taken to count as knowledge, and what is not, on the basis of which processes of selection and exclusion for curricula will take place. It would follow that this type of curricular organization presupposes and serves to legitimate a rigid hierarchy between teacher and taught, for if not, some access to control by the pupils would be implied, and thus the processes of exclusion and selection would become open for modification and change. The degree to which this model characterizes the contemporary university and its implications for student movements would seem worth exploring. A further point is that access to control by pupils or student implies that alternative definitions of knowledge are available to them. It would be useful to examine the conditions under which such alternative definitions were available, and to compare different age groups, and different areas of study.

So taken for granted by most educators is the model referred to in the previous paragraph, that it is difficult to conceive of the possibility of a curriculum based on knowledge which is differentiated but not stratified. That it poses a revolutionary alternative is apparent, when one considers whether the terms teacher, pupil and examination in the sense normally used would have any meaning at all. It suggests that assumptions about the stratification of knowledge are implicit in our ideas of what education "is" and what teachers "are."

As previously suggested, the contemporary British educational system is dominated by academic curricula with a rigid stratification knowledge. It follows that if teachers and children are socialized within an institutionalized structure which legitimates such assumptions, then for teachers, high status (and rewards) will be associated with areas of the curriculum that are 1) formally assessed, 2) taught to the "ablest" children, 3) taught in homogeneous ability groups of children who show themselves most successful within such curricula.

Two other implications follow which would seem to warrant exploration.

1.) If pupils do identify high-status knowledge as suggested, and assume that the characteristics of "worthwhile knowledge" to be that it is taught in "sets," formally examined, and not studied by the "less able," they could well come to reject curricular and pedagogic innovations which necessarily involve changing definitions of relevant knowledge and teaching methods.

2.) If the criteria of high-status knowledge are associated with the value of the dominant interest groups, particularly the universities, one would expect maximum resistance to any change of the high status of knowledge associated with academic curricula. This, as I shall elaborate on later, is supported by evidence of the Schools Council proposals for curriculum reform. The Council has accepted the existing stratification of knowledge and produces most of its recommendations for reform in the low-status knowledge areas. These are associated with curricula which are for the young and less able and do not undermine the interests of those in positions of power in the social structure.

Let us explore a bit further the idea of knowledge being stratified. It does suggests two kinds of questions to be asked:

1.) In any society, by what criteria are different areas of, kinds of and approaches to knowledge given different social value? Those criteria will inevitably have developed in a particular social and historical context, but, if isolated, may be useful if related to social, political and economic factors in accounting for changes and resistances to changes in curricula.

2.) How can we relate the extent to which knowledge is stratified in different societies, and the kinds of criteria on which such stratification may be based,[32] to characteristics of the social structures?

The first question requires an attempt to postulate some of the common characteristics of academic curricula, and to show how, over a particular historical period, they have become legitimated as of high status by those in positions of power. As suggested earlier, these characteristics are not absolute, but sociohistorical constructs, so it is not inappropriate to draw on three strands of thinking which emphasize this. These are, first, the comparative perspective on pre- and post-literate societies (Mead, 1938); secondly, consideration of the consequences of literacy for contemporary culture (Goody and Watt, 1962); and thirdly the way a gradual "bureaucratization" of the education systems of industrializing societies has led to an increasing emphasis on "examinations" as the most "objective" means of assessing (and therefore identifying) "expert" knowledge (Weber, 1952). Weber discusses the process of what he calls the "bureaucratic domination of the nature of education." He implicitly suggests that the major constraint on what counts as knowledge in society will be whether it can be "objectively assessed."[33] There is an interesting and not entirely fortuitous parallel with Kelvin's sentiment that "when you cannot express it in numbers, your knowledge is of a meagre and unsatisfactory kind"[34] in the idea implicit in contemporary education that "if you cannot examine it, it's not worth knowing."[35] The way formal examinations place an increasing emphasis on literacy rather than oral expression is raised by Davie (1961), and the implications of the "literate" character of modern culture brought out by Goody and Watt (1962). They argue that so great is the discontinuity or even the contradictions between the private oral traditions of family and home and the public literate tradition of the school that "literate skills form one of the major axes of differentiation in industrial societies." They go on to suggest that reading and writing (which are the activities which occupy most of the timetable of most of those being educated) are inevitably solitary activities, and so a literate culture brings with it an increasing individualization. This individualization is symbolized in its most dramatic form in the various ways in which those being educated are assessed or examined.

In comparing literate and non-literate cultures Goody and Watt suggest that the peculiar characteristics of the former are "an abstraction which disregards an individual's social experience . . . and a compartmentalization of knowledge which restricts the kind of connections which the individual can establish and ratify with the natural and social world."[36] The final point they make is how most knowledge in a literate culture is fundamentally at odds with that of daily life and common experience. In discussing the way educational emphases have moved from "learning" to "teaching," Mead (1938) brings out a related point, when she links the idea of groups holding some kinds of knowledge as superior and the notion of "a hierarchical arrangement of cultural views of experience," to the increasing emphasis on changing the beliefs, habits, knowledge, ideas and allegiances that children bring with them to school.

Oversimplifying, we can draw together the main ideas of the previous paragraphs to suggest the dominant characteristics of high-status knowledge, which we will hypothesize as the organizing principles underlying academic curricula. These are literacy, or an emphasis on written as opposed to oral presentation; individualism (or avoidance of group work or co-operativeness),[37] which focuses on how academic work is assessed and is a characteristic of both the "process" of knowing and the way the "product" is presented; abstractness of the knowledge and its structuring and compartmentalizing independently of the knowledge of the learner;[38] finally and linked to the former is what I have called the unrelatedness of academic curricula, which refers to the extent to which they are "at odds" with daily life and common experience.[39]

If status of knowledge is accorded in terms of these criteria, academic curricula would be organized on such principles; in other words they will tend to be abstract, highly literate, individualistic and unrelated to non-school knowledge. It may also be useful as a preliminary way of posing questions to see curricula ranked on these characteristics which then become four dimensions in terms of which knowledge is stratified. Thus one can suggest conditions under which (non-academic) curricula will be organized in terms of oral presentation, group activity and assessment, concreteness of the knowledge involved and its relatedness to non-school knowledge.

One way is to view these characteristics as the specific historical consequences of an education system based on a model of bookish learning for medieval priests which was extended first to lawyers and doctors, and increasingly has come to dominate all education of older age groups in industrial societies (Goodman, 1969a). However, their use to sociologists may be to highlight the unquestioned dimensions of academic curricula—to elaborate—these characteristics can be seen as social definitions of educational value, and thus become problematic in the sense that if they persist it is not because knowledge is in any meaningful way best made available according to the criteria they represent, but because they are conscious or unconscious cultural choices which accord with the values and beliefs of dominant groups at a particular time.[40] It is thus in terms of these choices that educational success and failure are defined. One might speculate that it is not that particular skills and competences are associated with highly-valued occupations because some occupations ''need'' recruits with knowledge defined and assessed in this way. Rather it is suggested that any very different cultural choices, or the granting of equal status to sets of cultural choices that reflect variations in terms of the suggested characteristics, would involve a massive redistribution of the labels ''educational'' ''success'' and ''failure,'' and thus also a parallel redistribution of rewards in terms of wealth, prestige and power.

Two important limitations of this approach must be mentioned; firstly, not only are the categories highly tentative but they are formal, and no operational rules are suggested with direct relevance to analyzing questions of substantive content.[41] Their use in the analysis of texts, syllabi, reports, exam questions ''marking'' criteria and the day-to-day activities of the classroom would lead either to narrower but more substantive categories, or their modification, depending on the nature of the research problem posed. Secondly, by its primary emphasis on the social organization and not the social functions of knowledge, this approach does not make explicit that access to certain kinds of knowledge is also potential access to the means of changing the criteria of social evaluation of knowledge itself and therefore to the possibility of creating new knowledge, as well as the means of preserving these criteria. However, changing criteria involve social actions which inevitably are concrete, corporate and related as well as involving oral as well as written communication. Perhaps it is through the disvaluing of social action and the elevation of the value placed on ''knowledge for its own sake" through the separation of knowledge from action, well symbolized by the values implicit in such distinctions as "pure and applied" and "theory and practice," that knowledge of social alternatives in our educational system is both restricted and, when available, is perceived as "alternatives in theory."[42] However, we can illustrate some more specific ways in which this approach might be useful for a sociology of educational knowledge.

1.) If the relations between the patterns of domination and the organization of knowledge are as have been suggested, one would only expect a reduction in specialization for any particular age group, an increase in inter-subject integration, or a widening of the criteria of social evaluation of knowledge, if they were to follow or be closely dependent on changes in these patterns of domination.[43]

If we assume the absence of such changes we would expect most so-called "curricular innovations" to be of two kinds:

a.) Those in which existing academic curricula are modified but there is no change in the existing social evaluation of knowledge.[44] Two examples are the new Nuffield 'O' level science syllabuses and the integrated science projects referred to earlier. A significant research problem would be to examine the influence of the Nuffield sponsors, the Science Masters' Association (now the Association for Science Education, and an organization which has close links with the universities and traditionally an active membership drawn largely from public, direct-grant and grammar schools with large science VIths) and the university advisors, which led to the Nuffield Project being directed, in the first place, to 'O' level, which is taken by a maximum of 30 percent of pupils, rather than to reforming secondary school science as a whole.

b.) "Innovations" which disregard the social evaluations implicit in British academic curricula, but are restricted in their availability to less able pupils. In becoming the major sponsor for such innovations, the Schools Council can be seen as legitimizing the existing organization of knowledge in two ways. Firstly, by taking the assumptions of the academic curricula for granted, the social evaluations of knowledge implicit in such curricula are by implication being assumed to be in some sense "absolute" and therefore not open to enquiry. Secondly, by creating new courses in "low status" knowledge areas, and restricting their availability to those who have already "failed" in terms of academic definitions of knowledge, these failures are seen as individual failures, either of motivation, ability or circumstances, and not failures of the academic system itself. These courses, which explicitly deny pupils access to the kinds of knowledge which are associated with rewards, prestige and power in our society are thus given a kind of legitimacy, which masks the fact that educational success in terms of them would still be defined as "failure." The link with teachers' definitions of the raising of the school leaving age as being a problem of social control rather than of intellectual development is not difficult to see.

2.) It should be fruitful to explore the syllabus construction of knowledge practitioners in terms of their efforts to enhance or maintain their academic legitimacy. Some examples worth investigation would be the various professional examining bodies, the attempts to obtain university entrance recognition for new knowledge areas, and the presentation of previously non-degree knowledge areas (particularly technical and administrative fields, art, dance and physical education) as suitable for degree status.[45]

Returning to the second question of this section, which was concerned with how we account for the criteria implicit in the different ways knowledge is stratified, we do not know how relations between the economy and the educational system produce different degrees and kinds of stratification of knowledge. It is possible to trace schematically a set of stages from non-literate societies where educational institutions are not differentiated from other institutions, to feudal type societies where formal education in separate schools is almost entirely restricted to a priestly caste, and, through the church ownership of land, such schools remained largely independent (at least in regard to the curricula) of the economic and political processes of the time. Gradually schools and colleges became increasingly differentiated and dependent on the economies of the societies they were in, when clearly the dominant economic and political orders became the major determinants of the stratification of knowledge. Comparative studies of educational arrangements in developing countries might shed light on these relationships in more detail. One way would be to compare the kinds of knowledge stratification in countries like North Korea where the schools are less separate from the economy and many activities of learning are also activities of production, with systems like our own where in school nothing is "for real," even in the workshops.

To sum up, then, an attempt has been made to offer a sociological approach to the organization of knowledge in curricula. The inevitably limited and schematic nature of the outline presented together with the total lack of research by sociologists in the field turns us back to the question posed at the beginning of this paper. Why no sociology of the curriculum? Perhaps the organization of knowledge implicit in our own curricula is so much part of our taken for granted world that we are unable to conceive of alternatives. Are we then reluctant to accept that academic curricula and the forms of assessment associated with them are sociological inventions to be explained like men's other inventions, mechanical and sociological?

ACKNOWLEDGEMENTS

I should like to thank my colleagues, Basil Bernstein and Brian Davies for their comments of earlier drafts, and to express my appreciation to them and the other members of the departmental seminar for the valuable discussion that arose out of some of the preliminary ideas in this paper. A similar debt is owed to those graduate students of the department with whom I have benefited from many discussions around the themes of this paper. This extended and revised version owes much to the many hours of discussion I had with Basil Bernstein, whose constructive criticisms I only came to appreciate fully when it came to re-writing. Also I have continued to learn much from my graduate students, in particular, Nell Keddie and Geoff Esland.

NOTES AND REFERENCES

1. First published in this volume. An earlier and shorter version of this paper was presented at the Annual Conference of the British Sociological Association, April 1970, and will be published under the title "Curricula and the Social Organization of Knowledge" in the collection of the Conference papers—*Sociology of Education,* edited by Richard Brown (Tavistock).

The title would imply that we can make statements about curricula in general which when one considers the diversities within even one education system, would seem unwarranted. In effect, the paper focuses largely on what is commonly called the "academic curriculum" of secondary and higher education in England. The relevance of any of the general ideas presented for infant and junior curricula or the various technical courses available must remain doubtful.

2. These ideas represent a development from a preliminary attempt by the author (Young, 1967) to begin a "sociology of the curriculum." Here the analogy between explanations of "educational failure" and "deviance" in contemporary sociology is explored in more detail.

3. A detailed historical study of the social composition of the groups involved and the social and political circumstances in which their educational ideas developed and influenced "educational practice" would make an important contribution to our understanding of the origins, persistence and change of educational ideologies. Banks (1955) and Taylor (1963) are perhaps the only significant attempts to carry out such a study in this country. Each, however, is limited by an implicit conceptual framework which takes "academic knowledge" as "given" rather than "to be explained."

The unsatisfactory use of the concept "educational ideology" in the literature stems in large part from a lack of substantive studies, but in part also from the failure to relate the sets of beliefs, their social contexts and their implications for practical action. Those using the concept have either, like Hoare (1967), Burnett and Palmer (1967) and D. I. Davies (1969), relied on broad "political" categories without demonstrating that they have any necessary "educational" implications, or like Brameld (1967) have developed typologies of educational ideas without linking them to either a theory of social change or to the social origins of those who are assumed to have held them. It seems likely that the more limited approach of exploring how "beliefs" about children implicit in psychological theories become institutionalized and situationally significant in providing "explanations" for various curricular and pedagogic practices, may be more fruitful (Friedman, 1967; Eastman, 1967; Esland, 1970).

4. This "inefficiency" refers to the evidence collected or summarized by writers such as Vernon (1957) and Westergaard and Little (1964) concerning the arbitrariness of the

11+ (in terms of predicting future attainment) and the discrepancy between the distribution of opportunity for selective education and the distribution of *measured* intelligence that has been produced by the 11+; in neither case does one find serious counterclaims in the literature. The "injustice" presupposes that some other administrative technique which would replace the 11+ (e.g., parental "choice," teacher recommendation, "flexible grouping in non-selective secondary schools"), would be both "less arbitrary" and in some sense "fairer." The evidence, such as it is, points to the opposite being as likely an outcome of the change (Floud, 1957; Douglas, 1969; Ford, 1969).

5. The possible explanations of why such studies have focused on "pupil subcultures" is discussed fully elsewhere (W. B. Davies, 1970; Seaman, 1970). In this context it is perhaps worth pointing out that as in the earlier phase of the educational debate which focused on "equality" and "wastage," the sociological definition of the problem complements those of teachers and research sponsors. In this case the problem is one of "control" of pupils, which leads to a concern to isolate their common characteristics. These are conceptualized as the "subculture," particularly of the least "controllable" pupils. Though there is much more in each study, this is the primary emphasis of both Hargreaves (1968) and Lacey (1970).

6. The financing of a new statutory body, the Schools Council, with responsibility for sponsoring curriculum development "projects," and having specific powers over how secondary school children are examined, is itself an indication of an increasing political concern over the control of educational knowledge. The Schools Council's much-publicized "autonomy" from the D.E.S., together with the recruitment of "practising teachers" on to its staff and committees, suggests an attempt to deny that the Schools Council marks anything other than an extension by teachers of their "traditional" control over the curriculum.

7. This point needs exploring in specific circumstances, but might be illustrated by referring to examples from other kinds of institutions. With regard to the Church, we might consider the Vatican's resistance to allowing celibacy and "natural law" to be on the agenda of the Bishops' Conference. A similar example was the persistent refusal of those controlling the Anglican Lambeth Conference to allow "freemasonry" to be discussed. Other examples from political parties would also point to the way legitimate areas of discussion are defined by existing hierarchies.

8. It is ironical that the one outstanding study, which looks at the various social, cultural and institutional factors influencing the organization of knowledge, is by a philosopher, G. E. Davie. His study of curricular change in the nineteenth-century Scottish universities raises many of the issues about selection of content and relation between areas of knowledge that are considered later in the paper (Davie, 1961).

9. The analogy between explanations of "deviancy" and "educability" which take social class as their independent variable is explored in more detail (Young, 1967). The analogy points to how both explanations rely on similar functionalist presuppositions which, in each case, demonstrate the significance of *social class,* but are unable to account for the process through which this significance is active.

10. For example, Swift (1969) and Shipman (1968).

11. One of the few empirical studies to attempt this is Burton Clark's *Open Door College* (1961).

12. See Burton Clark (1960).

13. See Gross, *et al.* (1957).

14. Cicourel and Kitsuse (1963*b*), Becker, *et al.* (1961, 1969).

15. Child (1943).

16. A useful outline of trends in the sociology of knowledge which implicitly makes this point is given by Bottomore (1956).

17. Blake (1968).

18. The most dramatic example has been the development of demands for black studies courses in the U.S.A.

19. Halsey (1960).

20. Musgrove (1968).

21. Weber (1952).

22. By the use of such terms as "academic," "pure," "theoretical," etc.

23. I am referring here to the secret knowledge that "professionals" protect as if it was their own.

24. A much more detailed analysis than those yet available, of the genesis of examples of any particular curricular-types, would be a necessary preliminary to such an exercise.

25. It may be possible to examine the whole history of the arguments about secondary school specialization from Crowther (1959) and Petersen (1960) to today in this perspective.

26. An illustration of this is to compare the resistance to the introduction of new knowledge areas for the curriculum for the same age group in different institutions (e.g., the grammar school VIth form and the College of Further Education).

27. The works of Ben-David (1963), Davie (1961) and Rothblatt (1969) are a valuable beginning in this direction.

28. Perhaps the only significant study here is that of Reisman, Gusfield and Gamson (1970 in press).

29. The possible implications of this specialization and the degree of insulation between what is studied as well as of changes are explored in detail by Bernstein (1971).

30. It is a paradox of the English educational system worth exploring, that while those most in need of education get least of it, those with the longest educational careers have curricula of the most limited scope.

31. Studies relating the career structure of teachers in different knowledge areas and the strategies of the various subject-based associations would be one possible way of exploring this question empirically.

32. Ben-David (1963) in comparing university curricula in the U.S.A., U.S.S.R. and U.K., among other countries, shows wide variations in the criteria on which the stratification of knowledge is based in different countries.

33. There are two ways in which Weber's discussion is unsatisfactory, both of which raise important questions for any sociological research on examinations. First he took for granted that process by which some activities are selected as "worth objective assessment," a prior question to his consideration of the "effects" of examinations. Secondly the notion of what is meant by the "objectivity" of examinations is left unexplored. The point touched on briefly elsewhere about the priority given to "knowledge as product" as opposed to "knowing as process" is only one aspect of this.

34. Curiously but significantly the façade of the University of Chicago Social Science Research Building!

35. The fact that non-examined curricula are relegated to "leisure" courses, liberal and general studies, and courses for the "less able" is indicative of the implicit validity of this thesis.

36. Goody and Watt, *op. cit.*

37. The term *individualism* is far from satisfactory, as it is ambiguous and has a much wider meaning than is intended here.

38. There are problems in the use of the term "abstract" because it presupposes some kind of absolute notion of what is "abstract," and neglects the way in which one can have different "kinds of abstraction," some of which may be "labelled" concrete by others using different "abstraction" criteria. Horton (1967, 1968) explores this question indirectly, but it is an area that sociologists have too readily taken as not requiring research. While "abstractness" seems to be a satisfactory category for describing academic curricula, the problems raised by Horton mean that as an analytic category it presupposes just those assumptions that one would want to treat as problematic. It may be possible to reconceptualize the problem by treating "abstractness" as an "educators' category" to be explained.

39. See the section earlier on Gramsci for a more detailed consideration of this. The concept *"unrelatedness"* refers to a similar characteristic of formal educational systems that Henry (1960) calls "disjunctiveness." Again we are faced with conceptual problems, not surprisingly since the question of school and non-school knowledge has hardly been considered by sociologists. Similarly (and I am very grateful to Mr. Derek Frampton of Garnett College for pointing this out to me), these categories are unable to deal with professional curricula where the knowledge is undoubtedly of high status, but not on the criteria that have been suggested in this paper.

40. See note 31.

41. For instance, the gradual disappearance of classics (particularly Greek) from most secondary school curricula is not accountable in these terms. Nor specifically is the changing content of school history, geography or English literature.

42. An interesting example of the "philosophical sleight of hand" required to reach this position appears in an otherwise excellent paper by Rytina and Loomis (1970). After criticizing Marx and Dewey for using *metaphysical* justifications of the truth of what men "know" in terms of what men "do," they do likewise in drawing on a *metaphysical* "out there" in terms of which, they claim, we must check out our theories against our practice.

43. Specific reservations were made earlier about such an all-embracing phrase. Clearly the crucial "dominating" factor is the limited access to higher education, which enables universities to control secondary school curricula. Limited changes, such as the breakdown of the near monopoly, by university boards, of school examinations, would be important but secondary to this.

44. Most of the discussion of curriculum reform is of this kind. In general the question is asked, given that we know our objectives, how can we more efficiently achieve them? There is an enormous literature in this field which demonstrates the concern of those who have been aptly labelled "the curriculum mongers" (a term first suggested by John White (Department of Philosophy, University of London Institute of

Education), in an article with that title in *New Society* (March 1969)) to create and institutionalize an autonomous discipline "curriculum studies" with its own so-called "theory," house journals and professors. Most of the writing, with the exception of parts of Miles (1964), is more informative about the writer's perspectives and beliefs than about school curricula.

45. The activities of the Council for National Academic Awards Board of Studies would be particularly important to study in terms of the assumptions polytechnic staff have of what these boards will recognize as "honors degree standard."

BIBLIOGRAPHY

Anderson, P. "Patterns of National Culture" in Cockburn, A., and Anderson, P. (eds.), *Student Power* (Harmondsworth: Penguin, 1969).

Bachrach, P., and Baratz, M. S. "Decisions and Non-Decisions: An Analytical Framework." *American Political Science Review* 57 (No. 3, 1963).

Banks, O. *Parity and Prestige in British Education* (London: Routledge & Kegan Paul, 1955).

Becker, H. S., Geer, B., Hughes, E., and Strauss, A. *Making the Grade* (New York: John Wiley & Sons, 1969).

Ben-David, J. "The Professions and the Class Structure." *Current Sociology* 5 (No. 12, 1963–64).

Bernstein, B. B. "Open Schools, Open Society," *New Society* (September 14, 1967).

———. "On the Curriculum." (Unpublished.)

———. "On the Classification and Framing of Educational Knowledge" in Young, M. F. D. (ed.), *Knowledge and Control* (London: Collier-Macmillan, 1971).

Birnbaum, N. *The Crisis of Industrial Society* (London: Oxford University Press, 1970).

Blake, R. "Karl Marx and Education." *Annual Proceedings of the Philosophy of Education Society,* 1968.

Blaug, M., and Gannicott, K. "Manpower Forecasting since Robbins; a Science Lobby in Action." *Higher Education Review* (Autumn, 1969).

Bottomore, T. B. "Some Reflections on *The Sociology of Knowledge.*" *British Journal of Sociology* 7 (No. 1, 1956).

Bourdieu, P. "Systems of Education and Systems of Thought." *International Social Science Journal* 19 (No. 3, 1967), and in Young, M. F. D. (ed.), *Knowledge and Control* (London: Collier-Macmillan, 1971).

Brameld, T. *Education as Power* (New York: Holt, Rinehart & Winston, 1967).

Buckley, W. "Social Stratification and the Functional Theory of Stratification." *American Sociological Review* 23 (1958).

Carter, M. P. *A Report of a Survey of Sociological Research in Britain.* British Sociological Association, 1967.

Child, A. "On the Theoretical Possibility of the Sociology of Knowledge." *Ethics* 51 (1943).

Cicourel, A., and Kitsuse, J. I. "A Note on the Use of Official Statistics." *Social Problems* 2 (1963). (*a*)

————. *The Educational Decision Makers* (Indianapolis: Bobbs-Merrill, 1963). (*b*)

Clark, B. R. *The Open Door College* (New York: McGraw-Hill, 1960).

Cox, C. B., and Dyson, A. E. "The Fight for Education." *Black Paper* 1 *Critical Quarterly* (1969). (*a*)

————. "The Crisis in Education." *Black Paper* 2 *Critical Quarterly* (1969). (*b*)

Cremin, L. *The Transformation of the School* (New York: Alfred A. Knopf, 1964).

Crowther, G. *15-18th Report of the Central Advisory Council for Education* (London: H.M.S.O, 1959).

Dainton, F. S. *Enquiry into the Flow of Candidates in Science and Technology into Higher Education* (London: H.M.S.O., 1968).

Davie, G. E. *The Democratic Intellect* (Edinburgh: Edinburgh University Press, 1961).

Davies, D. I. "Education and Social Science." *New Society* (May 8, 1969).

Davies, W. B. "On the Contribution of Organizational Analysis to the Study of Educational Institutions." To be published in the papers of the British Sociological Association Annual Conference, 1970.

Davis, K., and Moore, W. E. "Some Principles of Stratification." *American Sociological Review* 10 (No. 2, 1945).

Douglas, J. W. B. *All Our Future* (London: Weidenfeld & Nicolson, 1969).

Durkheim, E., and Mauss, M. *Primitive Classification* (R. Needham, trans.) (London: Cohen & West, 1963).

Eastman, G. "The Ideologizing of Theories; John Dewey, a Case in Point." *Educational Theory* 1 (No. 1, 1967).

Esland, G. *Subject and Pedagogical Perspectives in Teaching.* M.A. (Ed.) Thesis, University of London. (See Young, M. F. D., *Knowledge and Control* (London: Collier-Macmillan, 1971).)

Floud, J., Halsey, A. H., and Martin, F. M. *Social Class and Educational Opportunity* (London: Heinemann, 1957).

Ford, J. *Social Class and the Comprehensive School* (London: Routledge & Kegan Paul, 1969).

Friedman, N. L. "Cultural Deprivation—A Commentary on the Sociology of Knowledge." *Journal of Educational Thought* 1 (August 1967).

Goodman, P. "The Present Moment in Education." *New York Review of Books* (April 1969). (*a*)

————. "Can Technology be Human?" *New York Review of Books* (November 1969). (*b*)

Goody, J., and Watt, I. "The Consequences of Literacy." *Comparative Studies in History and Society* 5 (No. 3, 1962).

Gorbutt, D. A. *Subject Choice and the "Swing from Science," a Sociological Critique.* M.A. Thesis, University of London, 1970.

Gramsci, A. *The Modern Prince and Other Writings* (translation) (New York: Monthly Review Press, 1957).

————. "In Search of the Educational Principle" (translation) *New Left Review* (1967).

Gross, N., Mason, W. S., and McEachern, A. *Explorations in Role Analysis* (New York: John Wiley & Sons, 1957).

Habermas, J. "Knowledge and Interest" in Emmett, D., and McIntyre, A., *Philosophical Analysis and Sociological Theory* (London: Macmillan, 1970).

Halsey, A. H. "The Changing Functions of Universities" in Halsey, A. H., Floud, J., and Anderson, C. A. (eds.), *Education, Economy and Society* (New York: The Free Press, 1960).

Hargreaves, D. *Social Relations in the Secondary School* (London: Routledge & Kegan Paul, 1968).

Hellerich, G. "Some Educational Implications of Karl Marx's Communism." *Educational Forum* (May 1970).

Henry, J. "Education, a Cross Cultural Outline." *Current Anthropology* 1 (No. 4, 1960).

Hirst, P. H. "The Logic of the Curriculum." *Journal of Curriculum Studies* 1 (No. 2, May 1969).

Hoare, Q. "Education; Programmes and Men." *New Left Review* (1967).

Horton, R. "African Traditional Thought and Western Science." *Africa* 67 (1967), and in Young, M. F. D., *Knowledge and Control* (London: Collier-Macmillan, 1971).

————. "Neo-Tylorianism, Sound Sense or Sinister Prejudice." *Man* 3 (1968).

Keddie, N. *The Social Basis of Classroom Knowledge—A Case Study.* M.A. Thesis, University of London, 1970. (See also Keddie, N., "Classroom Knowledge" in Young, M. F. D., *Knowledge and Conrol* (London: Collier-Macmillan, 1971).)

King, M. "Reason, Tradition and Progressiveness of Science." (to be published in *History and Theory,* 1971).

Lacey, C. *Hightown Grammar* (Manchester: Manchester University Press, 1970).

Lefebvre, H. *Explosion; Marxism and the French Upheaval* (New York: Monthly Review Press, 1969).

McPherson, A. " 'Swing from Science,' Retreat from Reason?" *Universities Quarterly* (Winter 1969).

Mannheim, K. *Ideology and Utopia* (translated by Wirth and Shib) (New York: Harcourt Brace, 1936).

Mead, M. "Our Educational Emphases in Primitive Perspective." *American Journal of Sociology* 43 (1938).

Miles, M. *Innovation in Education* (New York: Teachers College Press, 1964).

Mills, C. W. "The Professional Ideology of Social Pathologists." *American Journal of Sociology* 49 (1943).

Musgrove, F. "The Contribution of Sociology to the Study of Curriculum" in Kerr, J. (ed.), *Changing the Curriculum* (London: University of London Press, 1968).

Petersen, A. D. C. "The Myth of Subject-Mindedness." *Universities Quarterly* 14 (No. 3, 1960).

Reisman, D., Gusfield, J., and Gamson, Z. *Academic Values and Mass Education* (New York: Doubleday, 1970).

Rothblatt, S. *The Revolution of the Dons* (London: Faber & Faber, 1969).

Rytina, J. H., and Loomis, C. P. "Marxist Dialectic and Pragmatism: Power as Knowledge." *American Sociological Review* 35 (No. 2, 1970).

Schaffer, H. "Alienation and the Sociology of Education." *Educational Theory* (1970).

Seaman, P. *On Planned Organizational Change.* M.A. Thesis, University of London, 1970.

Shipman, M. *Sociology of the School* (London: Longmans, 1968).

Swift, D. *The Sociology of Education* (London: Routledge & Kegan Paul, 1969).

Taylor, W. *The Secondary Modern School* (London: Faber & Faber, 1963).

Thompson, E. P. *Warwick University Ltd.* (Harmondsworth: Penguin, 1970).

Vernon, P. *Secondary School Selection* (London: Methuen, 1957).

Weber, M. *Essays in Sociology.* Translated and edited by H. Gerth and C. W. Mills (London: Routledge & Kegan Paul, 1952).

Westergaard, J., and Little, A. "The Trend of Social Class Differentials in Educational Opportunity." *British Journal of Sociology* 15 (1964).

Wilkinson, R. *The Prefects* (London: Oxford University Press, 1964).

―――. *Governing Elites* (London: Oxford University Press, 1969).

Williams, R. *The Long Revolution* (London: Chatto & Windus, 1961).

Young, M. F. D. *Towards a Sociological Approach to the Curriculum.* M.A. Thesis, University of Essex, 1967.

20. CLASSROOM KNOWLEDGE

Nell Keddie

One consequence of the particular normative orientation of much sociology of education has been its definition of educational failure: explanations of educational failure are most often given in terms of pupils' ethnic and social class antecedents[1] and rely on a concept of social pathology rather than one of cultural diversity.[2] It is only recently that attention has been given to the defining processes occurring within the school itself[3] and to the social organization of curriculum knowledge.[4] The studies suggest that the processes by which pupils are categorized are not self-evident and point to an overlooked consequence of a differentiated curriculum: that it is part of the process by which educational deviants are created and their deviant identities maintained.[5] Here I hope to raise questions about these processes by considering two aspects of classroom knowledge: what knowledge teachers have of pupils, and what counts as knowledge to be made available and evaluated in the classroom. This involves casting as problematic what are held to be knowledge and ability in schools rather than taking either as given.

The empirical data on which this account is based[6] were collected by observation, tape recording and questionnaire in a large mixed comprehensive school with a fairly heterogeneous social class intake, although in the school, as in its catchment area, social class III is over-represented. Pupils from social

SOURCE. First published in Michael F. D. Young (ed.), *Knowledge and Control: New Directions for the Sociology of Education* (London: Collier-Macmillan, 1971), pp. 133–60.

classes I and II tend to be placed in A streams and those from social classes IV and V in C streams.[7] The study is focused on the humanities department which in 1969/70 introduced an examination course based on history, geography and social science to fourth-year pupils. The course was constructed to be taught as an undifferentiated program across the ability range, and to be examined by mode 3 at ordinary level and C.S.E. at the end of the fifth year.[8] The course is described as "enquiry based" and is taught by "key lessons" to introduce a topic, and a workcard system to allow children to work individually and at their own speed. In the fifth year the work is often organized around topics; in the fourth year it is generally organized in "blocks" of different subjects. This study is concerned with the first social science block which has socialization as its theme and follows directly after a geographical study of regions of Britain. Both were taught from material prepared by the department's teachers (in this case sociologists, a psychologist, an economist and geographers), so that each class keeps the same teacher for both geographical and social science studies.

The school is probably atypical of secondary schools in this country in its high degree of institutionalized innovation (every subject is now examined by mode 3 at C.S.E.) and therefore if the data has any claim to generality it must be because the school stands as a critical case and illustrates the fate of innovatory ideals in practice. Throughout this account references to teachers and pupils are specifically references to teachers and pupils of this one school.

A central issue for teachers in the school is whether or not the school should unstream. Bourdieu[9] points out that conflict indicates consensus about which issues are deemed worthy of conflict. In this debate consensus that is not articulated is the most interesting because it is not questioned and includes, as I shall show, evaluations of what constitutes knowledge and ability and thus evaluations of what pupils are and ought to be like in critical respects. In the fourth year pupils are divided into three broad ability bands, A, B and C, and some departments stream rigidly within these bands. The humanities department divides pupils into parallel groups within each band and looks forward to teaching completely mixed ability groups.

In casting as problematic what counts as knowledge and ability, I begin with what teachers themselves find problematic: the teaching of C stream pupils. C stream pupils present teachers with problems both of social control and in the preparation and presentation of teaching material. By their characterization of C stream pupils as "that type of child" and "these children," teachers tell that they feel that C stream pupils are unlike themselves. By inference, teachers feel that A stream pupils are more like themselves, at least in ways that count in school. Teaching A stream pupils seems to be relatively unproblematic for teachers: they take the activities in these classrooms for granted, they rarely make explicit the criteria which guide the preparation and presentation of teaching material for these pupils, and what counts as knowledge is left implicit, and, apparently, consensual. The "question" to which C. Wright Mills[10] refers rarely arises: the empirical problem is the phenomen on which Garfinkel calls the "unavailability" of the "formal structures of practical actions."[11] The assumption underlying my interpretation of data is that C stream pupils disrupt teachers' expectations and violate their norms of appropriate social, moral and intellectual pupil behavior. In so far as C stream pupils' behavior is explicitly seen by teachers as inappropriate or inadequate, it makes more visible or available what is held to be appropriate pupil behavior because it provokes questions about the norms which govern teachers' expectations about appropriate pupil behavior.

THE IDEAL PUPIL

Becker[12] developed the concept of the *ideal pupil* to refer to that set of teacher expectations which constitute a taken for granted notion of appropriate pupil behavior. In examining discrepancies between what I shall call *educationist* and *teacher* contexts I shall argue that it is in the likeness of the images of the ideal pupil from one context to the other that the relation and the disjunction between the views expressed by teachers in these contexts is explained.

The fundamental discrepancy between the views of teachers as they emerge in these contexts can be expressed as that between theory and practice, or what Selznick calls doctrine and commitment:

Doctrine, being abstract, is judiciously selective and may be qualified at will in discourse, subject only to restrictions of sense and logic. But action is concrete, generating consequences which define a sphere of interest and responsibility together with a corresponding chain of commitments. Fundamentally, the discrepancy between doctrine and commitment arises from the essential distinction between the interrelation of ideas and the interrelation of phenomena.[13]

This is a distinction between "words" and "deeds"[14] and it is necessary to remember that words like deeds are situated in the ongoing interaction in which they arise. "Doctrine" as the ideology and theory of the humanities department is enunciated in the educationist context, which may also be called the context of *discussion* of school politics, in particular discussion which evokes interdepartmental conflicts, especially those about streaming. (The actual context of school politics, for example, heads of departments' meetings, may provoke something else again.) The other aspect of the educationist context is the discussion of educational theory, and here talk of the department's policy often evokes statements about its alignment with or opposition to other humanities programs[15] constructed by other course makers. The educationist context may be called into being by the presence of an outsider to whom explanations of the department's activities must be given or by a forthcoming school meeting which necessitates discussion of policy of how things *ought* to be in school.

By contrast, the teacher context is that in which teachers move most of the time. It is the world of *is* in which teachers anticipate interaction with pupils in planning lessons, in which they act in the classroom and in which when the lesson is over they usually recount or explain what has happened. I shall elaborate on the characteristics of both contexts to suggest their relation to each other and the implications for the possible fate of educational innovation in schools.

THE EDUCATIONIST CONTEXT

The educational policy of the course and of the department draws selectively and consciously on educational theory and research, and is seen by at least some of the department as an informed and expert view of education, as opposed to the lay and commonsense views advanced by other departments. The "pure" educational policy of the department seems to contain the following as its components:

1. Intelligence is not primarily determined by heredity. Differential educational performance may be accounted for by differential motivation rather than differential intelligence. Ability is to be accounted for as much by motivation as by intelligence and is largely determined by the child's social class antecedents.
2. Streaming by ability weights the school environment against those whose family background has already lessened their chances of educational achievement because it "fixes" the expectations that both teachers and pupil have of a pupil's performance and is thereby likely to lower the motivation of pupils with low achievement-orientation who have been assigned to low streams.
3. The criteria by which pupils are allocated to streams or sets when they enter the school (the mathematics department, for example, are said to use verbal I.Q. scores) have been discredited by both psychologists and sociologists; but their lack of reliability is not understood by those who use them.
4. Streaming perpetuates the distinction between grammar and secondary modern school under one roof, and creates or maintains social divisiveness, since like the grammar school it favors middle-class children.
5. A differentiated curriculum divides pupils. The school should try to unite them.

Those in the school who favor streaming oppose the views given above on the grounds that the individual child is best helped by being placed in a stream with those like himself so that he can receive teaching appropriate to his pace and level.

I have insufficient data about the extent to which teachers in the humanities department hold this educational policy in its "pure" form. Probably most select out of it aspects of it that are most relevant to them. Outwardly at least, all members of the department are in favor of the mixed ability teaching which the department has introduced into the first and second years. The department is committed eventually to teaching mixed ability groups in the higher forms, but sees the matter as sufficiently problematic to delay until a new teaching block is ready in a couple of years' time. The main point, however, is that those teachers who will advance the educationist view in the discussion of school and educational policy will speak and act in ways that are discrepant with this view when the context is that of the *teacher*. While, therefore, some educational aims may be formulated by teachers as *educationists,* it will not be surprising if "doctrine" is contradicted by "commitments" which arise in the situation in which they must act as *teachers*.

The way in which the course is set up reveals how teachers can hold discrepant views without normally having to take cognizance of the contradictions which may arise. For example, a resolution is partially effected by shifting the meaning of motivation from an assertion of the desirable in the educationist context to an explanation of the desirable in the teacher context. Thus the educationist assumes that in the ideal environment of the unstreamed school with an undifferentiated curriculum, the differential motivation which now leads to underachievement will be greatly reduced. In the teacher context, in which teachers move in their everyday activities as teachers, motivation becomes an explanation of pupils' behavior. In this exchange, two teachers who also hold the educationist's view in part are talking about the A stream class of the teacher who speaks first:

TEACHER J: [Some of the class] have written to Oldham Town Council for material for the New Town project.
TEACHER C: They're really bright, are they?
TEACHER J: Mostly from middle-class families, well motivated.

Here the relationship between initiative, intelligence, social class and motivation is the assumption taken for granted that makes the exchange of comments possible, and also illustrates well the portrayal of social skills as cognitive ones.

In the educationist's view, motivation is subsumed in a notion of rationality as leading to autonomy for the individual. The ideal pupil in the educationist context is the one who can perceive and rationally evaluate alternatives. He will become the ideal man of a society which embraces consensus politics and a convergence thesis of social class. In an interview[16] the head of department spoke of the "qualities of mind" that the course will attempt to develop:

I think mainly rationality—this is the essence of what we're trying to teach. Not, I hope, a belief that rationality will always . . . produce good moral answers because it won't, clearly; but a person who is prepared to weigh evidence. . . . This is the last opportunity many of them get for a structured view of society. This is political education . . . a participating society does not mean to my mind a population that is attending lots of planning meetings. It's a population that's aware of what's involved in planning. . . . It's educating people to be aware of what's involved in making political decisions. . . .

Whether or not all the department's teachers share these educational aims and subscribe to this image of society, the course is set up with intentions of developing in pupils modes of work and thought which will help them to become more autonomous and rational beings. That is, it is set up in the hope that the conception of enquiry-based work will help to create the ideal pupil. I select three main aspects of the course to show how it also in fact caters for a pupil who already exists: the A stream academic and usually middle-class pupil. Thus the course embodies not only an image of what the ideal pupil ought to be, but also what he already is. These three aspects are:

1.) "Working at your own speed"—this notion is very firmly embedded in the ideology of the course and it is significant that a teacher I heard "selling" the course to pupils described it as "self-regulating work which allows you to get ahead." The corollary of this is that others fall behind, at least in relation to the pace of the course. Teachers were constantly urging pupils: "You must finish that this week because next week we're going on to a new topic." Teachers frequently remarked how much more quickly A pupils work than C pupils, and A pupils generally expressed approval of the notion of "working at your own speed"—it is *their* speed. It would seem inevitable that the principle of individual speeds should be incompatible with a course that moves in a structured way from topic to topic. The only leeway is for some pupils to work through more workcards than others.

2.) All the studies on achievement orientation stress the middle-class child's tendency to thrive on an individualistic and competitive approach to learning. It follows that a workcard system which puts a premium on the individual working by himself rather than in a group, is probably set up in advance for the success of some pupils rather than others because they already value that kind of autonomy. Observation suggested that the result of this was that while pupils worked or rested from working, they talked in the peer group about matters like football and boy friends. Talk about work tended to be of the order: "Do you know the answer to question 2?" Thus the content of the work rarely becomes the content of peer-group interaction but becomes separate from it. An analogy might be drawn with the doing of repetitive industrial tasks, where satisfaction derives from group interaction rather than from the work which brings in the money (or grades). The possibility for pupils of continuous interaction with friends may, however, be an important element in reducing social control problems for teachers.

3.) Teachers express regret that a problem in motivating C stream pupils is their tendency to see education in vocational terms. It was never made explicit (if realized at all by some teachers) that the educational aims of a course like this one also fulfill the vocational purposes of the more successful pupils. A stream pupils have been told, and they told me, that learning to work independently (of teacher and textbook) will help them "in the sixth form and at university." I also heard a teacher telling a B group that "any worker who can think for himself is worth his weight in gold to his employer." It is likely that lower stream pupils know this to be a highly questionable statement and do not look forward to this kind of satisfaction from their work. Thus while teachers do not, on the whole, perceive higher education as vocational, C stream pupils do not find the vocational rationale of the course commensurate with their expectations of what work will be like.

Both 1.) and 2.) suggest that the short-term aims of the course, where it impinges immediately on the pupils' work situation, are weighted in favor of A stream pupils, giving priority to skills and attitudes they are most likely to possess. In its long-term aims the same pattern emerges. It seems likely that an undifferentiated course will be set up with an image of the pupil in mind. Because in the educationist context the perspective is one of how things *ought* to be, it is not so obvious to teachers that they are drawing, albeit selectively, on what already *is*. As I shall show, in the teacher context teachers organize their activities around values which as educationists they may deny. These values arise from the conjunction of social class and ability in the judgments teachers make on pupils. It is by exploring what is judged to be appropriate behavior that it becomes clear how ability and social class which are held separate in the educationist context are confounded in the teacher context.

THE TEACHER CONTEXT

Normal Pupils

In this context what a teacher "knows" about pupils derives from the organizational device of banding or streaming, which in turn derives from the dominant organizing category of what counts as ability. The "normal" characteristics (the term is taken from Sudnow[17]) of a pupil are those which are imputed to his band or stream as a whole. A pupil who is perceived as atypical is perceived in relation to the norm for the stream: "She's bright for a B" (teacher H); or in relation to the norm for another group: "They're as good as Bs" (teacher J of three hardworking pupils in his C stream group). This knowledge of what pupils are like is often at odds with the image of pupils the same teachers may hold as educationists, since it derives from streaming whose validity the educationist denies.

Although teachers in the humanities department might express disagreement with other teachers over teaching methods, evaluations of pupils and so on, there seems, in the teacher context, to be almost complete consensus about what normal pupils are like. It is probable, given the basis of categorization, that members of the department are, in terms of "what everyone knows" about pupils, much closer to other teachers in the school than they themselves commonly imply. As house tutors, most of their negotiations with teachers outside the department must be carried on in terms of shared meanings. Because these meanings are taken for granted both within and outside the department they are not made explicit as a set of assumptions because they continue to refer to an unquestionable reality "out there." It is possible to disagree about an individual pupil and to couch the disagreement in terms of his typical or atypical "B-ness," but in the teacher context it would be disruptive of interaction and of action-to-be-taken to question that "B-ness" exists. Like the concept of ability from which it derives it is unexamined in the teacher context since it belongs to the shared understandings that make interaction possible. In the educationist context, where other interests are at stake, "ability" and "streaming" shift into new categories of meaning. Although the teacher may be the same person in both contexts, what he "knows" as educationist about pupils may not be that which he as teacher "knows" about them. The frame of reference shifts from a concern with "things as they *are*" to "things as they *ought* to be,"[18] and in this context both ability and streaming may become problematic as they cannot be for the practical on-going purpose of the teacher.

The imputation of normal attributes to pupils by teachers does not tell us objectively about pupils. Rather it is the case that in certain areas of school life teachers and different groups of pupils maintain conflicting definitions of the situation. For the teacher, social control may depend on his being able in the classroom to maintain publicly his definition of the situation. He may do this by attempting to render pupil definitions invalid. Thus he may treat pupils' complaints about the course with scepticism and subsume them under normal categories like: "he's trying to get out of work," "it's just a bit of 'agro,' " "they'll try anything on." These explanations may or may not coincide with pupils' explanations of their motives. The general effect of teachers' explanations is to recognize the situation as conflictual, but to render invalid the particular point the pupil is making and thus to delineate the extent of pupils' rights. Equal rights are not granted to all pupils since the "same" behavior may have different meanings attributed to it, depending on the normal status of the pupil. In one C stream lesson a pupil asked the teacher:

PUPIL: This is geography, isn't it? Why don't we learn about where countries are and that?

TEACHER: This is socialization.

PUPIL: What's that? I'd rather do geography. . . . Netsilik Eskimo—I don't know where that is.

TEACHER [ironically]: After the lesson we'll go and get the atlas and I'll show you. (Teacher D)

A few days earlier I had asked this teacher whether any pupil had asked in class (as they had in some other classes): "Why should we do social science?" and had had the reply:

TEACHER: No, but if I were asked by Cs I would try to sidestep it because it would be the same question as "Why do anything? Why work?"

OBSERVER: What if you were asked by an A group?

TEACHER: Then I'd probably try to answer.

For me, as observer, learning how to recognize normal pupils was an important aspect of my socialization as observer from the teachers' point of view. Teachers took some care that I should understand what pupils were like, especially C pupils. In my first days in the school they frequently prepared me for what I should expect when I attended their lesson, and they afterwards explained to me why the lesson had gone as it had. These explanations tended to take the form: "C stream pupils are . . ." or "low ability pupils . . . ." This aspect of "learning the ropes"[19] is presumably an important element in the socialization of student and probationary teachers.

The "normalization" of pupils tends to produce a polarity between A and C pupils in which they reflect reversed images of each other. The B stream pupil is left in the middle and tends to shift around in the typology. Generally when special workcards are prepared it is for C groups and it is assumed that Bs will follow the same work as A pupils. On the other hand, teachers often see B pupils as posing the same social control problems as C streams. One teacher saw this as the *result* of their undefined status and characterized B stream pupils as suffering from identity problems. His characterization could as well refer to teachers' problems in being unable to define clearly the normal B pupil, as to the perspective of the pupils themselves, who may have quite clear notions of their own positions and status, though they are liable to be defined out by the teachers. Similarly A pupils who present discipline problems to teachers are likely to be described as pupils who "are really Bs." This characterization is not necessarily applied to those A pupils who will probably be entered for C.S.E. and not "O" level in the humanities examinations and might therefore be seen as right for a B stream. This is in keeping with the tendency not only for normative judgments to predominate—teachers speak more about the "moral" and "social" qualities of pupils than of their cognitive skills—but for the former qualities to be presented as though they were cognitive skills:

TEACHER K. If you want, you can go on to the Depression later in the term. There's also material on America in the twenties.

TEACHER B: Isn't it true to say that although it's C material in a sense, the level of response depends on the level of intelligence. For example, some of the moral problems you pose—it would take an A child really to see the implications. Some of the girls would find it interesting.

TEACHER K: Yes, it could be used at all levels.   (At a staff meeting)

Ability and Social Class

Most children enter secondary schools with their educational identities partially established in the records, and by the fourth year the question is rather how these identities are maintained than how they were established. Teachers appear to have two principal organizing categories: ability and social class. Social class, however, tends to be a latent and implicit category for sorting pupil behavior. On occasion though, some teachers appear to use social class as an explanation of educational performance:

Teacher B of a group of boys he described as "working class who belong to a B group": "they don't work but they came up high in a test which tested their grasp of concepts." On another occasion he spoke of the same boys as "really from a higher stream—able but they don't work." Teacher H distinguished between the performance of two "bright" girls in his A stream class: "one is the daughter of a primary school headmaster; a home with books and lots of encouragement . . . [the other one] comes from quite a different kind of home which doesn't encourage homework. . . ." He felt that the latter had potential ability she was not using to the full.

Another teacher (L) characterized a girl whom he thought "works only for grades" as a "trade unionist."

Teacher J had a threefold typology of his C stream class (which he told me before I observed his class for the first time) in which he linked certain kinds of psychological disturbance with a working-class culture. It is possible to identify two types of pupil in what follows: the remedial child and the pathologically disturbed child:

TEACHER: The difficulties with the least able child are those of remedial children: children who don't work in normally accepted ways in school—with these children I'm not succeeding, humanities aren't succeeding. The Cs who fail can't meet [the head of department's] criteria [of autonomous work]. They need to be in a group with only a few teachers. . . . Many have working-class parents—Jane's got problems. Her father's a not-very-bright milkman and her mother ran away. Lots of difficult children have disturbed backgrounds and this is often more important than innate abilities.

OBSERVER: What do you mean by disturbed?

TEACHER: Fathers who beat mothers, nervous breakdowns in the family, that sort of thing.

He speaks of "that kind of child" and says they "fluctuate in behavior" . . . "Jane has little idea of how to behave generally . . . [but Susan] is a big mouthing fishwife who can, on occasion, work solidly and be pleasant."

The third type of child was identified only after the lesson: the quiet child who works fairly hard through most lessons. In terms of social control this pupil is not a problem and this is why the casual listener-in to teachers' talk might get the impression that all C stream pupils are constant problems for teachers.

After the lesson this teacher, like others, wondered if he were too lenient with the problem pupils; he said of Jane, "Perhaps she gets away with too much . . . [but] she can't concentrate and needs the teacher all the time." The key phrase in his general description is probably the reference to "children who don't work in normally accepted ways in school." These pupils' behavior can be seen as generally inappropriate. Like the concept of the disadvantaged child the reference contains a notion of "under-socialization" and instability originating in the social disorganization[20] of the "background" of the pupil. The dominant notion here seems akin to some social psychological accounts of delinquency[21] which specify a multiplicity of factors like a "bad" home as a cause of deviance without making it clear what a bad home is, how it causes deviance or why other homes, which should on the same criteria be "bad," do not produce delinquents. Because the social pathology approach allows explanations of pupil behavior to be made in terms of discrete factors, teachers tend not to perceive the collective social class basis of pupils' experience but to fragment that experience into the problems of individual (and "disadvantaged") pupils. This makes it likely that the pupils' collective definition of the educational situation will be rendered invisible to teachers,[22] and failure individualized.

This teacher's (J) normal C pupil is probably cast in a more explicit model of psychological disturbance than many, but this does not affect the essential outline of the image, in which instability plays a large part and is frequently linked with aggression. In terms of social control instability means unpredictability and the social control problems as perceived by the teacher are demonstrated in the remark of this teacher who said that many C stream pupils are "awkward customers" and are allowed to get away with too much: "it's important if you're to get anywhere not to antagonize these children." This teacher, like most of the teachers in the department, expects his C pupils to behave differently in class from his A pupils: for example, he expects and allows them to make more noise and to achieve a great deal less work than A pupils. It is not possible to estimate the degree to which his expectations are instrumental in creating the situation as he defines it.

Frequently C, and occasionally, B pupils become "characters"; for example: "Clare will envelop Dick one of these days. The girls think Dick is very sexy." A stream pupils are not spoken of in this way. This is linked with another normal characteristic of C pupils—their immaturity.[23] Thus after showing a film called *The First Fifteen Minutes of Life* to groups of pupils, the noise made by B and C groups was described as "covering up embarrassment" and as "the back row of the cinema," indicating the pupils' response had been characterized as contextually inappropriate. A pupils who were much more silent (but were also, . hushed quite systematically) were characterized as more "mature" in their response, although the comments of a girl to her friends: "they shouldn't show films like that to fifteen year olds," suggested that some of these pupils, at least, found the film difficult to accept. It may have been relevant to the C pupils' response that they were quite unable to see a rationale for the showing of the film since the label "socialization" had no explanatory significance for them. Many defined the film as "biology" and said "we've done it before."

Clearly, A stream pupils' definition of appropriate behavior in the situation was taken over from or coincided with that of the teachers. It is already clear that teachers are most concerned with what they perceive as the negative characterastics of C pupils' behavior and that this is to some extent linked with expectations of appropriate behavior that have a social class basis and differentiation. C stream pupils are often seen to lack those qualities which are deemed by teachers desirable in themselves and appropriate to school,[24] whereas A stream pupils appear to possess these qualities. The negative aspects of the normal C pupil emerge whenever a teacher compares C and A pupils:

It's amazing how much quicker As are than Cs. The As have almost caught Cs now. (Teacher D)

I did it slightly differently with the As because they're rushed for time. With the As I used the pink card more, but I still put diagrams on the board. But it was still quicker. (Teacher J)

I meant to find out [what "ulu" an Eskimo word, meant] but I knew the Cs wouldn't ask. It's remarkable how they can read through and not notice words they don't understand. (Teacher D)

I didn't know any more than was on the workcard—this was all right with Cs, but it wouldn't be with As. (Teacher G)

These comments indicate that teachers have notions about the organization of time and material (and the degree of preparation necessary) in the classroom which depend on the normal characteristics of the ability group they are teaching. Thus what teachers "know" about pupils as social, moral, and psychological persons is extended to what they know about them as intellectual persons, which as I shall show leads to the differentiation of an undifferentiated curriculum.

Ability and Knowledge

One of the remarkable features of the tendency to attribute to pupils the normal characteristics of their ability band is that what is held to constitute ability is rarely made explicit. When teachers discuss whether material is suitable for teaching to A, B or C streams, the criteria on which they make judgments remain largely implicit and consensual. Throughout it is difficult to separate out references to cognitive skills from imputed social and moral characteristics on the one hand and from characterization of teaching material on the other. This comment on teaching material about the Depression is typical:

Some of the economic implications are difficult—it's O level type of material . . . but some of the human elements may be C material.   (Teacher at staff meeting)

Material is categorized in terms of its suitability for a given ability band and, by implication, ability is categorized in terms of whether or not these pupils can manage that material. Like the pupils who are categorized in terms of levels of ability, knowledge in school is categorized in terms of its supposed hierarchical nature with reference to criteria of age and ability. I shall be concerned with how teachers organize knowledge in relation to the normal attributes of the pupils they are teaching, according to criteria used to establish the hierarchies of ability and knowledge. This approach involves starting from the assumption that not only is ability not a given factor but also that we do not know what the knowledge to be got or the subject to be mastered properly is. We can only learn what they are by learning what teachers and pupils who are involved in defining that knowledge claim to be doing: subjects are what practitioners do with them.

Within the course itself, the enquiry-based mode is intended to change the emphasis from mastery of given contents of a subject to mastery of the method of enquiry itself. The workcards are to some extent structured around the "concepts" it is desirable for pupils to acquire through working through the material. Thus the teacher who speaks of the "working-class" boys in his B group who are "able but don't work, but come up high in a test which tested their grasp of concepts," is using the term concept partly in the in-language of the course. The term derives from Bloom,[25] who uses it in his taxonomy of the hierarchical organization of knowledge where each level subsumes, under more general categories, the categories of the level below. The head of the humanities department here shows how the notion of concept, which appears to be glossed as "idea" or "structure," is embedded in the organization of the teaching material:

When you begin to think in terms of drawing things together, although, as I say, there are certain contents more important than other contents, and that's why we do the British economy rather than endless regional studies of Britain or endless historical studies of the treaties of the nineteenth century, the most important element in the work is teaching the children how to work. Teaching them a mode of enquiry is, I think, fundamental to the whole thing. Because this is the common ingredient of the historian's work, the geographer's work, the social scientist's work and this is the lasting influence on the child, not the memory of a particular date, and I regard as part of the teaching of that mode of enquiry the development of concepts and ideas which obviously increases the degree of sophistication in their mode of enquiry. The more ideas they've got, the more ideas of structures they've got, the better equipped they are to think in an orderly mode of enquiry. [See note 16.]

It appears from this that what he is describing is not so much a change from an emphasis on contents to an emphasis on method, but a change in content in terms of how that content is organized. It may not be intrinsic to the way the course is set up that teachers treat the teaching material as a body of knowledge or "facts" to be got across to pupils, rather than as ways of organizing facts or contents in relation to each other. In the classroom it often seems that pupils are more enquiry-minded than teachers, whose presentation of material does not allow concepts to be distinguished from content because the concept is presented in terms of its content. This relationship is also clearly illustrated in the end-of-topic test where many questions ask the pupil to match a content to a term or "concept," for example:

In some experiments hungry animals are given a food pellet each time they produce a particular response, such as pressing a bar or pecking at a disc. This is called: *stimulus, extinction, motivation, reinforcement.*

Thus although the course was deliberately set up by teachers as educationists to counteract what they saw as an inappropriate exercise of authority by the teacher in the traditional talk-and-chalk presentation of material, in the teacher context enquiry for the pupil is still heavily teacher directed.

In the following extract from a C stream lesson, the teacher (E)—who is not a sociologist and has to rely on prepared material on a pink card[26] which includes a description of the joint family, but not of the extended family as it is defined in Britain today—rejects alternative definitions to the nuclear family suggested by pupils because his reading of the material leads him to see common residence as a critical criterion:

TEACHER: Now who'd like to tell me what we mean by the family? [Pause] It's not as obvious as you might think. What is a family? Derek?

DEREK: A mother, a daddy.

TEACHER: Yeah.

DEREK: A couple of kids if they got them.

TEACHER: Yes.

DEREK: A granddaddy, a grandmummy.

TEACHER: Yes.

DEREK: An aunt, an uncle.

TEACHER: You'd include that in the family.

BOY: Yes, you would.

GIRL: [untranscribable]

TEACHER: Anybody disagree with that—that in a family you'd include grandparents?

DEREK: Well they are 'cos they're your mother's and father's mothers and fathers.

TEACHER: And it's all part of one family?

BOY: Yeah.

TEACHER: Anybody disagree or like to add to it at all? What we mean by the family?

GIRL [she has probably been reading the pink card]: It's also a group of people living under one roof.

GIRL: No, it's not. [Other pupils agree and disagree].

TEACHER: Ah, a group of people living under one roof—aah—that differs from what Derek said, isn't it? Because the group—ssh, Derek . . .

DEREK [his voice emerges above the teacher's voice]: . . . would still be the same as your mum, wouldn't it? It'd still be your family.

TEACHER: Yeah, the group that Derek mentioned doesn't live under one roof. Now we can limit the family to say its a group of people related by blood, er, who live under one roof; or we can extend its meaning to include what Derek said: grandparents, aunts and uncles and so on, who may in individual cases live under the same roof, but it's not normal. The British family, I say the British family because the idea of families differs, as we shall see, over the world. Peter and Derek, you're not listening.

PETER: I am.

TEACHER: . . . British family is parents and children, that is what you might call the, er, nuclear family; in other words, the core of the family. They tend to live together until the children have developed, matured, if you like, into adults. . . .

The way the exchange goes is not entirely a matter of "how much" sociology this teacher knows; it is also a question of the relation between the categories he is using to structure this knowledge in the classroom and those used by the boy which derive from his everyday knowledge of "what everyone knows" about families. The teacher moves outside this everyday knowledge since there must be occasions when he refers to his own relations as "family" even if his ties with them are less close than those of Derek with his extended kin. The teacher cues the class that he wants them to move into another reality[27] with the words: "It's not as obvious as you might think." The C girls who said to me "why should we learn about families? I mean we know about families, we live in them," have not made this shift to seeing that the family might be viewed as problematic. It appears at this point, and I discuss the matter further below, that the ability to "grasp a concept" in the context of the course and probably in its wider sense, refers to a pupil's willingness or ability to take over or accept the teacher's categories. This may mean, as it would have done for Derek, having to make a choice between apparently contradictory sets of statements unless he can see a reason for shifting his perspective to another set of categories. I shall suggest that Derek's stance is common among C pupils and differs from that of A stream pupils, who assume that the knowledge the teacher will purvey to them has a structure in which what they are asked to do has some place. This does not mean that the A pupil expects that knowledge to be relevant to his everyday experience. The argument is that A and C pupils tend to approach classroom knowledge from different positions and with different expectations. This argument makes no assumptions about the hierarchical status of the knowledge they are being asked to "grasp" or about the degree of generalization of "abstraction" involved. The concept of intelligence as a differential ability to deal with abstractions is implicit in the teachers' frequent reference to the "levels" of difficulty in the material and the "levels" of pupils' response.

I turn now to teachers' discussion of teaching material before and after use in the classroom, and follow this with a consideration of the data provided by pupils' responses to a questionnaire and to the teaching material in the classroom.

The Teaching Material: "Subjects" and Pupils

When teachers talk about how they have or will teach material they speak nearly always about the problems of teaching C stream pupils. Teaching the material to the A stream pupils for whom it is primarily prepared and who stand in some sense as ideal pupils appears relatively unproblematic; although, as I shall argue, there are reasons why it might be regarded as highly problematic. I have already quoted comments from staff meetings which showed the difficulty of "economic implications" as opposed to "human elements." Similarly the comments showed a link between the level of response to "moral problems" and the "level of intelligence." The following extracts from teachers' comments bring out these points more clearly:

Yes, worth bringing out with the more able group. (Teacher B)

I envisage problems with 4Cs in understanding unusual relationships. The meaning of relationships, it's going to be very difficult to get this over to them. (Teacher J)

Yes, um, when we did it with the 4Cs before they, er, didn't seem particularly interested that, er, other people had family groups of their own. Because it wasn't real to them, it was so far removed, it didn't seem of complete . . .of any relevance to them. (Teacher L)

I think if you're dealing with it purely in terms of kinship diagrams and white sheets [see note 26], again you're actually reducing the interest again, if you make it too intellectual. What illustrative material is there on this? . . . I think I've said this before . . . that sociology has its validity in its abstractions and in its intellectual [untranscribable] . . . to what extent the 4Cs will take that or to what extent it will remain a series of stories about families. . . . (Teacher J—not himself a sociologist)

The picture that emerges from these comments which are highly representative, is one of oppositions that describe material and pupils: "intellectual" is opposed to "real," and "abstractions" to "stories." One teacher implies that so long as the material is accessible only in terms of kinship diagrams and buff cards it will be too "intellectual." To make it "real," illustrative material is needed. The points they make are not ones simply of method, but are about methods relating to C stream pupils, and so questions arise not only about why C pupils are believed to need non-intellectual material, but also why A pupils are believed not to need illustrative material and not to have problems in understanding "the meaning of relationships." The suggestion in these comments is that there is something in the material which "it might be possible to bring out with the As." The phrases "bring it out," "make explicit," the "implications of moral problems," "economic implications," seem to point to a range of understanding that is not available to C pupils who can engage only marginally with the material. Teacher J provides a further gloss[28] on this when he says after a lesson with a C group:

"This stuff [on language] is much too difficult for them. . . . On the other hand they could cope with the family stuff. They could say something in their own words about different kinds of family, because they already knew something about them even if they did not know the correct term.

"The correct term" implies something about how status may be attributed to knowledge. The pupils' ignorance of the "correct term" suggests their deficiency. In the following discussion it is further suggested that the range of understanding that is available to C stream pupils must be rooted in their "experience," and that this is linked with another phrase teachers often use about adapting teaching material for C pupils: "putting it in language they can understand":

TEACHER J: How about the family for the Cs? It may have more in it for them because it's nearer home.
TEACHER B: There'll be a lot of visual stimulus for discussion. . . . The Cs should be able to get somewhere with discussion . . . we won't do the history of the family with them, it's too difficult, probably too difficult for anyone.

What seems to emerge overall from the way teachers discuss teaching material in relation to pupils' abilities is an assumption that C pupils cannot master subjects: both the "abstractions of sociology" and the "economic implications" are inaccessible to them. The problem then in teaching C pupils is that you cannot teach them subjects. When A pupils do subjects it can be assumed by teachers that they do what, in terms of the *subject*, is held to be appropriate, and material is prepared with regard to what is seen as the demands of the *subject*. In teaching C pupils modifications must be made with regard to the *pupil*, and it is as though the subject is scanned for or reduced to residual "human elements" or a "series of stories."

The clearest statement of the differential emphasis on subject and pupils is that made by Teacher K. He is describing how he is able to "gear" his study of the British economy for a C pupil at "quite a different level" from the level at which he teaches it to his A group. He says:

I can streamline it so it's got various grades of content and I can, I hope, do things which are very useful and valuable to the C child which I don't feel are as necessary for the A child. But they're all doing economics, they're all doing certain vital basic studies in how the economy works. . . .

He describes how the study is dealing with "land, labor and capital . . . in answer to what we call the 'for whom' question in economics":

Well, that leads on to a special study of labor for the Cs. Rewards for labor—wages. Wages can then be considered for girls in terms of why they're paid often lower than men's pay and what sorts of factors determine the different wages rates for different sorts of employment—something that's very immediate for these children.

Later he says:

Looking at a mixed economy he can angle that study much more towards taxation and the practical elements of how to fill in tax forms and what you get relief for, whereas . . . I'd be much more concerned with how the different types of taxation work, with the higher ability child: the difference between direct and indirect taxation and S.E.T. and so on. And also the effects that different forms of taxation have on the rates of economic growth—the more sophisticated elements which the lower ability child, it may not be possible for him to grasp the ideas that are part of that type of study but he's still able to study taxation and at a simpler level; but he's not being discriminated against.

Here it is clear that one consequence of a differential treatment of the economy is the way in which categories of analysis are made available to or withheld from pupils. This teacher held the educationist view in almost its pure form, and the political implications of his teaching of economics should probably be seen as an unintentional and unrecognized manifestation of consensus politics arising from an image of society as consensus. The teaching cannot be said to be intentionally prescriptive: it is presented as an objective account of the economic system rather than one of a number of possible accounts. He is not deliberately restricting the categories that are available to A pupils, since his teaching reflects his own thinking. When he further restricts C stream pupils to a study of labor and that in terms of differential wages, he sees this as "valuable" for the C pupils in terms of their ascribed status as workers. He does not intentionally withhold the framework which would allow the pupil to raise questions about the taxation policy as a whole, but he does effectively prevent, by a process of fragmentation, the question of how such knowledge becomes available.[29]

The Pupils' Response

I shall now attempt some account of the relation between teachers' and pupils' definitions of the classroom situation. The main contention is that the differences attributed to A and C pupils by teachers are substantive, but they may be open to interpretations other than those habitually made by teachers. In presenting the data I look at the ways in which teachers and pupils scan each others' activities in the classroom and attribute meaning to them.

The first indication of a differentiated response of A and C pupils comes from the responses to a questionnaire administered to the whole fourth year which sought information on the degree to which pupils have access to or have taken over the teachers' definitions of the humanities course.

A pupils all knew the terminology of the course and did not have to ask what "key lesson" or pink card meant. Question 2 is quite open-ended: "Do you think key lessons are a good idea or not, and why?" The majority of A pupils chose to answer it in terms of the structure of the course as teachers defined it, with answers that indicate that they saw the key lesson as an introduction to a new topic suggesting the nature of the work to follow:

It introduces you to the topic.
It helps you to understand the topic better.
You see what a subject is about.
You're not dropped into a mass of facts.

Table 1 shows the pattern of responses to questions 2 and 3 of the questionnaire. Question 3 asked pupils to explain what a pink card, a buff card and a yellow workcard are respectively. A pupils show a much higher tendency to distinguish the "blue sheet" from the "white sheet" as a "summary," "an introduction to a topic" or "a key lesson on paper," and not to describe both simply as "information sheets." A pupils were also more likely to pick up and use the terms "social science" or "sociology" as an overall label for their studies and were more likely to characterize the film, *The First Fifteen Minutes of Life,* which introduced the study of socialization, as about "learning" rather than as "biology" or as well as "biology"; although they were generally unable, when asked, to gloss [see note 28] the term "learning" despite the fact that they had written up notes on it.

A pupils are generally more sensitive to what they have been told *about* the course. Thus when I asked them what they thought of the course, typical responses were:

It's very good; you can disagree with the teacher.
You can link up subjects.
You can think out things for yourself.
It's good for learning how to work at university.

TABLE 1

Percentages of those accepting the teachers' definition of:

Stream	(a) The course	(b) Pink cards	(c) Yellow workcards
A	68	68	40^3
B	50^1	44	23
C	8^2	19	3

Total number of respondents: A—111; B—102; C—112.

[1] Nearly half of these responses, 23 from a class of 29, came from one class, which suggests that the teacher is in some way acting differently with this B group.

[2] C pupils' answers are very diverse and no distinct trend emerges, although they tend to be more concerned with how the lesson is organized for learning, and the showing of films is contrasted favorably with "just talking" and workcards as teaching methods.

[3] It is likely that A pupils are more often encouraged to think of the yellow workcards as a "guide" to using other workcards rather than as just "questions on the white sheet."

It seems likely they had accepted definitions received from teachers, because when I asked these pupils to tell me about a time they had disagreed with the teacher or about a time when they had been able to link up between subjects, they could recall no instances of either. There appears to be a discrepancy between their definition and their experience of the course of which they were not aware.

It seems probable that the pupils who come to be perceived by teachers as the most able, and who in a streamed school reach the top streams, are those who have access to or are willing to take over the teachers' definition of the situation. As A pupils' behavior is generally seen by the teachers as appropriate, so also is their handling of what is presented as knowledge. Appropriate pupil behavior here seems to be defined by the pupil's ability to do a subject. This is not necessarily a question of the ability to move to higher levels of generalization and abstraction so much as an ability to move into an alternative system of thought from that of his everyday knowledge. In practical terms this means being able to work within the framework which the teacher constructs and by which the teacher is then himself constrained, as the position of the teacher (E) teaching the family (quoted earlier) suggests. In teacher E's lesson pupils' definitions of the family which stemmed from their everyday knowledge of families conflicted with the teacher's "expert" definition. The following extracts are from a lesson on the same material with A pupils and teacher D:

TEACHER: Ninety percent of British families are nuclear families.
BOY: What are the other ten percent?
TEACHER: We're going on to those. . . .

BOY: What are joint families?

TEACHER: Where you have two or more related families living in the same house. There may be three generations.
GIRL: If you have your granny and grandad living with you is that a joint family?
TEACHER: Yes. . . .

PUPIL: What about single people?
TEACHER: They're not really a family unless they have children. . . .

TEACHER: Another group that's rare throughout the world but is found among the Netsilik Eskimo is the polyandrous group. . . .
PUPIL: What country is that found in? . .

Here the questions from the pupils take the framework the teacher presents for granted, and the pupils show a willingness to accept the terminology (the "correct term") as part of that framework. The scepticism of many C pupils, which leads them to question the teachers' mode of organizing their material, means that they do not learn what may be taken for granted within a subject, which is part of the process of learning what questions may be asked within a particular subject perspective.[30]

It would appear that the willingness to take over the teacher's definition of what is to constitute the problem and what is to count as knowledge may require pupils to regard as irrelevant or inappropriate what they might see as problems in a context of everyday meaning. (In this they resemble the teacher who made irrelevant the everyday use of the term "family.") This means that those pupils who are willing to take over the teachers' definitions must often be less rather than more autonomous (autonomy being a quality or characteristic the enquiry mode is intended to foster) and accept the teacher's presentation on trust. One unit of the socialization theme was work on isolated children, intended to show the necessity of socialization by presenting a negative case. In one account of an isolated child, Patrick, the description did not make clear that he was isolated in a henhouse because he was illegitimate and that the woman who put him there was his mother. In doing this workcard, A pupils generally did not raise problems about why the boy's mother treated him as she did, but got on with the workcard, although it emerged when they were questioned that they had not realized that the child was illegitimate. Some C pupils who wanted first to know why the woman had treated the child like this were told by their teacher: "Well, we're not too interested in that but in the actual influence on the development of the child." Here not only is there a clear resemblance between the way that A pupils and the teacher had each shifted categories of meaning so that enquiry into the question "Why would anyone treat a child like that?" becomes inappropriate, but also that the material is already in some sense "real" and "immediate" to C pupils, but that the teacher took no cognizance of this. It is often assumed by teachers that the comprehension of everyday meaning of material will be obvious to A pupils. Here it is suggested that this cannot be taken for granted. It may be clear to C pupils, whose first concern is likely to be with this kind of meaning.

It may be that the important thing for A pupils is the belief that the knowledge is structured and that the material they are asked to work with has sufficient closure to make "finding the answer" possible. They are usually willing to work within the framework outlined by the teacher and within his terms. Thus a new term like "social science" is at first a label with little meaning but is self-legitimating, and A pupils seem content to wait and let the content emerge so long as they can undertake the immediate task of completing a workcard. This means they frequently do not understand the generalizations teachers make to explain the theme which links several units of work, but this is not apparent to teachers or pupils so long as the work is structured in more or less self-contained units.

Because A pupils are prepared to take over teachers' definitions on trust, they were much quicker to accept social science as a new "subject" within the course, while C pupils continued to refer to the material on socialization in terms of subjects they already knew, like geography or biology, and to question the validity of what they saw as an unjustifiable change of content. A pupils were not generally able to explain the rationale of the socialization theme as teachers had explained it to them[31] but they accepted that the study could be legitimated and were prepared to operate within the "finite reality" of the subject as the teacher established it. This enabled them to move more quickly into what Blum[32] calls the "common culture" of the subject and to use its terminology. A striking example of this mastery of the language of the subject comes from an A class taught by a psychologist where pupils have acquired a set of terms they can use without gloss [see note 28]. This is from a discussion of Patrick, the child shut in the henhouse:

TEACHER: So we should, when he was found at the age of eight and a half, have been able to teach him to speak?

GIRL: Yes.

BOY: Yes, it was like he'd, um, he'd, um, been sort of lost for ages and had difficulties in speaking.

TEACHER: It's not quite the same. Yes, er . . .

BOY: He's just regressed in er er er in understanding things like.

TEACHER: Mm, but he has been using his vocal chords in some way, as Graham pointed out. He's been imitating chickens. Do you think this could retard his development at all?

BOY: Yes, associating—if you asso—if we associate foreign language words with one of those, it does mean the same thing in his language—

TEACHER: Do you th—

BOY: —he'd be able to speak but he wouldn't think in that language.

The following extract from a C lesson makes an interesting contrast since it may be that the mastery of terms like "regression" represents closure in the questions likely to be asked. In the following, the boy is able to pose the "common sense" question about "unlearning" because the material has suddenly enabled him to see something taken for granted as problematic:

BOY: Who knew he was in there, then?

TEACHER: Only his mother.

BOY: Where was his father, then?

TEACHER: His mother had separated from his father—she pretended to be a respectable widow. . . . The interesting thing is that the boy was fostered out. He was illegitimate, you see. If you think about it he must have learnt to walk and probably had the beginnings of speech—so what do you think happened?

BOY: The woman who put him in the chicken coop had made him go backwards.

TEACHER: Very good . . .

BOY 2: Well done . . .

BOY: How do you unlearn?

TEACHER: Well you simply forget—in school—tests show that.

BOY: [makes some objection—untranscribable].

TEACHER: You need to keep practising skills.

A noticeable feature of this sequence is that the teacher's response renders the question unproblematic: "Well you simply forget." Here is another extract where the same process can be seen. The group is a C group, the teacher has been through the pink cards with the class as a whole and the pupils are now working with workcards. Most pupils are having difficulty with a question which runs: "Is it biologically absolutely necessary that this division of labor (between the sexes) should be as rigid as it is?"

TEACHER: Yeah, in other words is it bio-um-physically impossible for the women to do the men's tasks. . . . Well, supposing you said is it biologically necessary for that division. . . . It is *not* biologically necessary. It's um er social reasons.

BOY: Will you come and tell us that, sir, please.

TEACHER: Well it's obviously not biologically necessary. I mean there's no physical reason why the women can't do the men's jobs; they wouldn't be able to do it as well because they're not as strong.

BOY: Aren't women the stronger sex?

TEACHER: Not in the [. . .] sense. The [. . .] says that they have more resistance to pain usually, and so on, and tend to live longer—they're stronger in that sense.

BOY: [untranscribable] . . . feel it.

TEACHER: No, they feel the same pain but they have a greater resistance to it.

BOY: What they always crying for?

TEACHER: Well, that's temperament, isn't it? Anyway we're getting away from the point about the Eskimos, aren't we?

In each of the last two sequences the material had led the pupil to pose as problematic an event he had probably previously taken for granted, and in each case the teacher closes the question in such a way as to render it (for himself if not for the pupil) unproblematic again, apparently because he is not able to accommodate it within the structure he is using. In the first instance the pupil's question could have opened up major issues about learning, in the second about the relative strength of heredity and environment. In neither instance was the pupil's enquiry integrated into the unfolding of the lesson although very germane to its theme.

The matter is complicated here by the teacher's unfamiliarity with the material, but it seems that what counts is whether the pupil's comment or question may be seen as having meaning within the relevance structure[33] the teacher is using, which derives from his notion of what counts as knowledge within a given subject. This relevance structure may, however, shift with respect to the knowledge the teacher has about the pupil, so that the pupil's questions and comments are seen by the teacher as deriving from different relevance structures depending on the statuses of the pupil with respect to his imputed ability. Thus both the "knowledge" the teacher has of his subject and the "knowledge" he has of the pupil must be seen as variables in the organization and evaluation of what counts as knowledge in the classroom. This may mean that when similar questions are asked by A and C pupils they are categorized differently by the teacher. This is a consequence of the implied notion that A pupils can master subjects while C pupils cannot. The A pupils' questions will be seen as relevant if they can be seen as helping to make explicit the implications of the subject. C pupils' questions are seen as ends in themselves: they arise out of "experience" or everyday reality, beyond which these pupils supposedly cannot go, and are therefore scanned for different kinds of meaning. It seems likely that it is here that teachers' expectations of pupils most effectively operate to set levels of pupil achievement: C pupils are not expected to progress in terms of mastering the nature of a subject, and so their questions are less likely to be seen as making a leap into the reality of the subject. These expectations seem to be implied in the remarks of teachers who said they could get away with not preparing work for C pupils but would not risk that with A pupils. The questions of the latter will require the knowledge of the teacher as "expert."

It seems that in considering what might be involved in the pupil's educational career it would be necessary to specify possible interactional sequences between teacher and pupil in which the pupil's educational identity is established in terms of the expectations the teacher has of him. It is likely that one of the crucial differences in the "latent cultures"[34] from which pupils come is in providing children with modes of acquiring knowledge that leads to differential access to the ways in which teachers structure knowledge: not so much to the particular structures as to the notion that it will be structured in ways that may make it remote from everyday experience. It may be that it is this remoteness from everyday life that is an important element in legitimating academic knowledge in schools. Pupils who have easy access to this knowledge need an ability to sustain uncertainty about the nature of the learning activity in the belief that some pattern will emerge. This requires a willingness to rely on the teacher's authority in delineating what the salient areas of a problem are to be. This will often mean a pupil putting aside what he "knows" to be the case in an everyday context. Children who demonstrate this facility are likely to be regarded as more educable, and to find their way into high-ability groups or to be defined as of high ability, since these are pupils with whom teachers can feel they are making progress. It is likely, as C pupils' questions demonstrate, that all pupils can move between "common sense" and "finite provinces of meaning," but that the particular shifts that the school requires and legitimates are based on a social organization of knowledge that is most likely to be achieved by the predominantly middle-class pupils in A streams.

Once pupils are placed in high-ability groups the wish to achieve at school in the school's terms is confirmed and situated in school activities, and is reinforced by their long-term vocational expectations. These are the pupils in the study who when asked about the humanities course in general terms show they tend to see it in the terms in which teachers define it. These pupils are more likely to move towards using the language of the subject as the teacher presents it and, equally important, their behavioral style is more likely to seem to the teacher appropriate to the occasion, than the style of C pupils.[35] Once pupils are accredited by streaming or some other device as of high ability, their questions are likely to be scanned by teachers for a different kind of meaning and to be used to a different end from those of C pupils. Teachers will also tend to assume for A pupils that the ability to move into the structure of a subject presupposes that understanding at a "lower," "concrete," "experiential" level which they attribute to C pupils as the limits of their ability. However, it can be argued that A pupils do not necessarily have this understanding, which may involve a different mode of thought and not a simple hierarchical progression from low- to high-order generalizations as teachers seem often to suppose, at least implicitly. It was assumed, for example, that A pupils had a commonsense understanding of why Patrick had been isolated, which in many cases they did not. They had, like the teacher of the C stream group who asked why he had been isolated, apparently defined it out of what it was relevant to enquire into, because neither teacher nor workcard referred to it.

Teachers also tend to assume that A pupils grasp the rationale of the subject in terms of the way teachers indicate progression of linkage from one piece of work to the next. In view of the fact that A pupils generally did not seem to have grasped what the linkage was except in the most general terms, it appears that teachers make assumptions about A pupils' ability to master subjects that are not justified; but because they present and evaluate material in discrete units, this assumption is not often tested.

CONCLUSIONS

In the presentation and discussion of data an attempt has been made to examine what teachers "know" about their pupils and how that knowledge is related to the organization of curriculum knowledge in the classroom. Ability is an organizing and unexamined concept for teachers whose categorization of pupils on the grounds of ability derives largely from social class judgments of pupils' social, moral and intellectual behavior. These judgments are frequently confounded with what are held to be rational values of a general nature. There is between teachers and A pupils a reciprocity of perspective which allows teachers to define, unchallenged by A pupils, as they may be challenged by C pupils, the nature and boundaries of what is to count as knowledge. It would seem to be the failure of high-ability pupils to question what they are taught in schools that contributes in large measure to their educational achievement.

It seems that one use to which the school puts knowledge is to establish that subjects represent the way about which the world is normally known in an "expert" as opposed to a "commonsense" mode of knowing. This establishes and maintains normative order [see note 32] in and within subjects, and accredits as successful to the world outside school those who can master subjects. The school may be seen as maintaining the social order through the taken for granted categories of its superordinates who process pupils and knowledge in mutually confirming ways. The ability to maintain these categories as consensual, when there are among the clients in school conflicting definitions of the situation, resides in the unequal distribution of power. There is a need to see how this enters into and shapes the interactional situation in the classroom. Clearly there is also a need to examine the linkages between schools and other institutions, and attempt to understand the nature of the relationship between what counts as knowledge in schools and what counts as knowledge in other relevant societal areas. In particular, there is a need to understand the relationship between the social distribution of power and the distribution of knowledge, in order to understand the generation of categorizations of pupil, and categories of organization of curriculum knowledge in the school situation. (Because these linkages are unspecified here, the comments I have made about teachers may at times appear to be critical of the "failures" of individuals.)

In the wider context of educational discussion, two panaceas currently put forward to reform the educational system are unstreaming and an undifferentiated curriculum. It seems likely that these prescriptions overlook the fact that streaming is itself a response to an organizing notion of differential ability. It seems likely that the hierarchical categories of ability and knowledge may well persist[36] in unstreamed classrooms and lead to the differentiation of undifferentiated curricula, because teachers differentiate in selection of content and in pedagogy between pupils perceived as of high and low ability. The origins of these categories are likely to lie outside the school and within the structure of the society itself in its wider distribution of power. It seems likely, therefore, that innovation in schools will not be of a very radical kind unless the categories teachers use to organize what they know about pupils and to determine what counts as knowledge undergo a fundamental change.

ACKNOWLEDGEMENTS

My thanks are first and foremost to the teachers and pupils of the school of the study. The teachers in the humanities department were, throughout the time I was at the school, unfailingly helpful in giving me their time and allowing me into their lessons with a tape recorder. I am indebted to Gillian Frost, who was also carrying out research at the school, both for the discussions we had, and for the data she made available to me.

The London Borough of Bromley made it possible for me to study for the Master's Degree of the University of London, by seconding me for a year, giving me the time to carry out the study on which this paper is based. I should like to thank Professor Basil Bernstein for his encouragement and for his assistance in getting the tape recordings transcribed. My thanks are also due to John Hayes and Michael Young with whom I discussed the material at various stages and to whom I owe very many insights that helped me to organize the data. I owe similar thanks to my fellow graduate students, in particular to John Bartholomew, and also to John Beck. My thanks are also to Michael Young for reading this paper in an earlier draft and making many detailed and constructive comments which helped me to clarify confusions and inconsistencies. .

NOTES AND REFERENCES

1. The direction of mainstream sociology of education in this respect can be seen in the very comprehensive account of available studies in Chapters 3, 4 and 5 of Olive Banks's *The Sociology of Education,* 1968.

2. Baratz and Baratz (1970).

3. Cicourel and Kitsuse (1963); Dumont and Wax (1969); Wax and Wax (1964).

4. Bernstein (1971); Young (1971).

5. Cicourel and Kitsuse (1963) show the importance in this context of the processes by which students are allocated to college or non-college courses. The Schools Council's acceptance of a differentiated curriculum, like the Newsom Report, maintains a distinction between the "academic" and the "non-academic" child.

6. Keddie (1970).

7. I have to thank Gillian Frost for making this information available to me.

8. This mode of examination allows teachers to construct and examine their own courses with moderation from an external examiner.

9. Bourdieu (1967).

10. C. Wright Mills (1940).

11. Garfinkel and Sacks (1970).

12. Becker (1952).

13. Selznick (1949), p. 70, I have to thank John Bartholomew for bringing this to my notice.

14. Deutscher (1966).

15. For example, the Humanities Curriculum Project of the Schools Council directed by Lawrence Stenhouse.

16. An interview with Gillian Frost, whom I thank for making it available to me.

17. Sudnow (1968).

18. "Is" and "ought" are not necessarily discrepant. There is no reason why there should not be a fit between them.

19. Greer, *et al.* (1968).

20. Cohen, A. K. (1959).

21. Deutsch (1963).

22. Dumont and Wax (1969) make a similar point about the culture of the Cherokee Indian. There is clearly a relationship between individualization of failure and the psychologistic notion of a curriculum based on pupils' "needs." See also Friedman (1967).

23. This relationship is also apparent in the data of Hargreaves (1967), p. 95: "On one occasion a teacher left the room to investigate some noise in the corridor. 'Who are you lot?' he cried. '3B, sir,' came the reply. 'You sound more like 1E than 3B,' was the master's crushing retort."

24. Wax and Wax (1964) find the same situation in what they call a "vacuum ideology" which is attributed to the Cherokee Indian by white teachers.

25. Bloom (1956).

26. Workcards for pupils are of three kinds: pink cards written by a member of staff which give an overview of the topic to be studied ("concepts" are generally printed in capital letters to point the organization of material to the pupils); buff cards which are also referred to as "documents" because they often reproduce original sources and deal with areas of the topic in more detail; yellow workcards which have questions intended to guide pupils in the use of the other workcards. Many pupils treated these straightforwardly as question sheets.

27. The concept here is that of "multiple realities" developed by Schutz (1967). In organizing the data I have also been greatly influenced by the distinction between "commonsense" and "expert" knowledge made by Horton (1967). I have also used this article in attempting to conceptualize A and C pupils' approaches to knowledge as the outcome of alternative thought systems, as opposed to seeing the differences in terms of a hierarchical relationship.

28. Garfinkel and Sacks (1970), pp. 342–45 and 362–66.

29. There is a need for studies of the models of society inherent in subjects as they are taught in schools and in textbooks. T. S. Kuhn (1970) suggests how an authoritarian model of science is built into science subjects as they are taught and the textbooks as they are used. Other studies might cast light on how a normative order is transmitted through the contents of subjects in schools and, in relation to this, what counts as "objectivity" in that subject and how it operates to maintain that normative order.

30. One exposition of a subject from this point of view is made by Merton (1959).

31. For example, most teachers explained to pupils that the film showed how early the human child begins to learn, and that the study of isolated children showed how necessary it is for a child to be brought up among human beings if his learning is to proceed and he is to become human. Nevertheless most pupils were unable to point to any link between the two units of study. At the most they were able to say both were "about learning."

32. Blum (1970).

33. Schutz (1967), p. 5 following.

34. The concept here is that the school represents the *manifest* culture. See Becker (1960).

35. It seems likely that teachers frequently pay more attention to the style than to the content of pupils' comments. Clearly this is linked to problems of social control. C pupils in particular tend to call out in class. There is probably also a problem for teachers in how C pupils actually phrase their comments or questions. When I reported to the humanities department on the research, I gave as examples of pupils asking questions from the point of view of their own commonsense views of the world, one question already quoted: "what are they [women] always crying for then?" and another from the key lesson in which pupils were shown slides of the foetus in the womb, when a C boy asked about the foetus: "How does it go to the toilet then?" This latter question, which seems to be an intelligent one, probably could not be asked more precisely without a concept of the body's "functions." When I gave these two questions as examples one teacher said the boys "must have been joking." At the least he implies that these questions are not appropriate to the business of learning and it is likely that his reponse is to the pupil's language and has a social class basis. Probably this teacher made explicit what many teachers feel: that the C pupil's attitudes and manners are inappropriate to the classroom; similar attitudes of teachers are to be found in: Hargreaves, *op. cit.*, and Werthman.

36. Barker Lunn (1970) suggests that teachers often carry attitudes appropriate to streaming into unstreamed classes and that this is particularly damaging for the "low-ability" working-class child.

BIBLIOGRAPHY

Banks, O. *The Sociology of Education* (London: Batsford, 1968).

Baratz, S., and Baratz, J. "Early Childhood Intervention: the Social Science Basis of Institutionalized Racism." *Harvard Educational Review* 40 (February 1970).

Barker Lunn, J. C. *Streaming in the Primary School* (Slough: National Foundation for Educational Research, 1970).

Becker, H. S. "Social Class Variations in the Teacher–Pupil Relationship." *Journal of Educational Sociology* 25 (April 1952). Also in Bell, R., and Stubb, H. (eds.), *The Sociology of Education: A Sourcebook* (Homewood, Ill.: The Dorsey Press, 1968).

Becker, H. S., and Geer, B. "Latent Culture: a Note on the Theory of Latent Social Roles." *Administrative Science Quarterly* 5 (No. 2, 1960).

Bernstein, B. B. "On the Framing and Classification of Educational Knowledge" in

Young, M. F. D. (ed.), *Knowledge and Control* (London: Collier-Macmillan, 1971).

Bloom, B. S. *Taxonomy of Educational Objectives* (New York: David McKay, 1956).

Blum, A. "The Corpus of Knowledge as a Normative Order." Reprinted in Young, M. F. D. (ed.), *Knowledge and Control* (London: Collier-Macmillan, 1971).

Bourdieu, P. "Systems of Education and System of Thought." *International Social Science Journal* 19 (No. 3, 1967) and reprinted in Young, M. F. D. (ed.), *Knowledge and Control* (London: Collier-Macmillan, 1971).

Cicourel, A. V., and Kitsuse, J. I. *The Educational Decision Makers* (Indianapolis: Bobbs-Merrill, 1963).

Cohen, A. K. "The Study of Social Disorganization and Deviant Behaviour" in Merton, R. K., Broom, L., and Cottrell, L. S. (eds.), *Sociology Today: Problems and Prospects* (New York: Basic Books, 1959).

Deutsch, M. "The Disadvantaged Child and the Learning Process" in Passow, H. (ed.), *Education in Depressed Areas* (New York: Teachers College Press, 1963).

Deutscher, I. "Words and Deeds: Social Science and Social Policy." *Social Problems* 13 (Winter 1966).

Dumont, R. V., and Wax, M. L. "Cherokee School Society and the Intercultural Classroom." *Human Organization* 28 (No. 3, Fall 1969).

Friedman, N. L. "Cultural Deprivation: A Commentary in the Sociology of Knowledge." *Journal of Educational Thought* 1 (August 1967).

Garfinkel, H., and Sacks, H. "On Formal Structures of Practical Actions" in McKinney, J., and Tiryakian, E., *Theoretical Sociology: Perspectives and Development* (New York: Appleton-Century-Crofts, 1970).

Geer, B., Haas, J., Vivona, C., Miller, S. J., Miller, C., and Becker, H. S. "Learning the Ropes: Situational Learning in Four Occupational Training Programmes" in Deutscher, I., and Thompson, E. J., *Among the People: Encounters with the Poor* (New York: Basic Books, 1968).

Hargreaves, D. *Social Relations in a Secondary School* (London: Routledge & Kegan Paul, 1967).

Horton, R. "African Traditional Thought and Western Science." *Africa* 67 (1967). Reprinted in Young, M. F. D. (ed.), *Knowledge and Control* (London: Collier-Macmillan, 1971).

Keddie, N. G. *The Social Basis of Classroom Knowledge: A Case Study.* M.A. Thesis, University of London, 1970.

Kuhn, T. S. *The Structure of Scientific Revolutions.* 2nd ed. (Chicago: University of Chicago Press, 1970).

Merton, R. K. "Notes on Problem-Finding" in Merton, R. K., Broom, L., and Cottrell, L. S. (eds.), *Sociology Today: Problems and Prospects* (New York: Basic Books, 1959).

Mills, C. W. "Situated Action and Vocabularies of Motive." *American Sociological Review* 4 (No. 5, 1940).

Schutz, A. *Collected Papers.* Volume 1: *The Problem of Social Reality* (The Hague: Martinus Nijhoff, 1967).

Selznick, P. *T.V.A. and the Grass Roots: a Study in the Sociology of Formal Organizations* (Berkeley and Los Angeles: University of California Press, 1949).

Sudnow, D. "Normal Crimes: Sociological Features of the Penal Code in a Public Defender Office." *Social Problems* 15 (Winter 1968).

Wax, M. L., and Wax, R. H. "Formal Education in an American Indian Community." *Social Problems Monograph* 2 (Spring 1964).

Werthman, C. "Delinquency in Schools. A Test for the Legitimacy of Authority." *Berkeley Journal of Sociology* 8 (1963).

Young, M. F. D. "An Approach to the Study of Curricula as Socially Organized Knowledge." In Young, M. F. D. (ed.), *Knowedge and Control* (London: Collier-Macmillan, 1971).

CHAPTER **4**

How Should the Curriculum Be Evaluated?

. . . we must . . . rise above that rude, empirical style of judging displayed by those more intelligent people who do bestow some care in overseeing the cultivation of their children's minds. It must not suffice simply to *think* that such or such information will be useful in after life, or that this kind of knowledge is of more practical value than that; but we must seek out some process of estimating their respective values, so that as far as possible we may positively *know* which are most deserving of attention.

Herbert Spencer
"What Knowledge is of Most Worth?"

In curriculum development as in all activities serving human purposes, notions about what constitutes success in the enterprise take on special significance. Given the pluralistic nature of contemporary society, it is not unexpected that sharp differences of opinion are expressed by educators and laymen not only about what constitutes a "good" curriculum, but even about how evaluations should be carried out. These divergent viewpoints are reflected in a wide range of criteria and procedures used by evaluators in assessing curricula.

Rather than presenting a compilation of technical writing in the field of curriculum evaluation, therefore, this chapter concentrates on broad conceptual and ideological issues that confront the curriculum field when it seeks to address questions of "good" and "bad." Too often, such a complex issue is reduced to a question of whether the experimental group or the control group scores higher on an achievement test.

317

In a well-known essay (reading #21), "Course Improvement Through Evaluation," Lee J. Cronbach attempts to broaden the concept of educational evaluation beyond the administration of tests. Course evaluation, according to Cronbach, should emphasize the widest possible description of outcomes rather than mere comparison of achievement scores. In reading #22, building on Cronbach's work, Michael Scriven launches into an extensive review of issues involved in curriculum evaluation. A major portion of the article contrasts the implications of formative and summative evaluation. Robert E. Stake, considering issues raised by Cronbach and Scriven, maps out a plan for evaluating educational programs in reading #23.

Urban Dahllöf, a Swedish researcher, next considers the ways in which process data may contribute toward a conceptual understanding of educational evaluation. In a reanalysis of a series of studies on the influence of curriculum factors on student achievement, Dahllöf in reading #24 emphasizes the importance of explantory power as opposed to "massive correlational fishing trips." In the article that follows (reading #25), Decker F. Walker and Jon Schaffarzick undertake a major review of the attempts to evaluate post-Sputnik curriculum development. Their conclusions emphasize the weaknesses of comparing curricula to see which is "better" as opposed to evaluations that point up the different consequences and outcomes associated with different programs of study.

The final two articles in this chapter deal with the politics and ideology of evaluation practices. In reading #26 David K. Cohen sees evaluation largely as a political activity in that the information it provides becomes a basis for changing power relationships. His recommendations have particular relevance for evaluation of social action programs such as those supported by Title I. Michael W. Apple emphasizes in reading #27 the social nature of the evaluation process as opposed to treating evaluation as a technical problem. What we choose to evaluate, he points out, is a complex ideological and ethical issue.

21. COURSE IMPROVEMENT THROUGH EVALUATION

Lee J. Cronbach

The national interest in improving education has generated several highly important projects to improve curricula, particularly at the secondary-school level. In conferences of directors of "course content improvement" programs sponsored by the National Science Foundation, questions about evaluation are frequently raised.[1] Those who inquire about evaluation have various motives, ranging from sheer scientific curiosity about classroom events to a desire to assure a sponsor that money has been well spent. While the curriculum developers sincerely wish to use the skills of evaluation specialists, I am not certain that they have a clear picture of what evaluation can do and should try to do. And, on the other hand, I am becoming convinced that some techniques and habits of thought of the evaluation specialist are ill suited to current curriculum studies. To serve these studies, what philosophy and methods of evaluation are required? And particularly, how must we depart from the familiar doctrines and rituals of the testing game?

PROGRAMMATIC DECISIONS

To draw attention to its full range of functions, we may define "evaluation" broadly as the *collection and use of information to make decisions about an educational program.* The program may be a set of instructional materials distributed nationally, the instructional activities of a single school, or the educa-

---

SOURCE. *Teachers College Record* 64 (No. 8, May 1963), pp. 672–83.

tional experiences of a single pupil. Many types of decisions are to be made, and many varieties of information are useful. It becomes immediately apparent that evaluation is a diversified activity and that no one set of principles will suffice for all situations. But measurement specialists have so concentrated upon one process—the preparation of pencil-and-paper achievement tests for assigning scores to individual pupils—that the principles pertinent to that process have somehow become enshrined as *the* principles of evaluation. "Tests," we are told, "should fit the content of the curriculum." Also, "only those evaluation procedures should be used that yield reliable scores." These and other hallowed principles are not entirely appropriate to evaluation for course improvement. Before proceeding to support this contention, I wish to distinguish among purposes of evaluation and to relate them to historical developments in testing and curriculum making.

We may separate three types of decisions for which evaluation is used:

1. Course improvement: deciding what instructional materials and methods are satisfactory and where change is needed.
2. Decisions about individuals: identifying the needs of the pupil for the sake of planning his instruction, judging pupil merit for purposes of selection and grouping, acquainting the pupil with his own progress and deficiencies.
3. Administrative regulation: judging how good the school system is, how good individual teachers are, etc.

Course improvement is set apart by its broad temporal and geographical reference; it involves the modification of recurrently used materials and methods. Developing a standard exercise to overcome a misunderstanding would be course improvement, but deciding whether a certain pupil should work through that exercise would be an individual decision. Administrative regulation likewise is local in effect, whereas an improvement in a course is likely to be pertinent wherever the course is offered.

It was for the sake of course improvement that systematic evaluation was first introduced. When that famous muckraker Joseph Rice gave the same spelling test in a number of American schools, and so gave the first impetus to the educational testing movement, he was interested in evaluating a curriculum. Crusading against the extended spelling drills that then loomed large in the school schedule—"the spelling grind"—Rice collected evidence of their worthlessness so as to provoke curriculum revision. As the testing movement developed, however, it took on a different function.

THE TURNING TIDES

The greatest expansion of systematic achievement testing occurred in the 1920s. At that time, the content of any course was taken pretty much as established and beyond criticism save for small shifts of topical emphasis. At the administrator's direction, standard tests covering the curriculum were given to assess the efficiency of the teacher or the school system. Such administrative testing fell into disfavor when used injudiciously and heavyhandedly in the 1920s and 1930s. Administrators and accrediting agencies fell back upon descriptive features of the school program in judging adequacy. Instead of collecting direct evidence of educational impact, they judged schools in terms of size of budget, student-staff ratio, square feet of laboratory space, and the number of advanced credits accumulated by the teacher. This tide, it appears, is about to turn. On many university campuses, administrators wanting to know more about their product are installing "operations research offices." Testing directed toward quality control seems likely to increase in the lower schools as well, as is most forcefully indicated by the statewide testing recently ordered by the California legislature.

After 1930 or thereabouts, tests were given almost exclusively for judgments about individuals—to select students for advanced training, to assign marks within a class, and to diagnose individual competences and deficiencies. For any such decisions, one wants precise and valid comparisons of one individual with other individuals or with a standard. Much of test theory and test technology has been concerned with making measurements precise. Important though precision is for most decisions about individuals, I shall argue that in evaluating courses we need not struggle to obtain precise scores for individuals.

While measurers have been well content with the devices used to make scores precise, they have been less complacent about validity. Prior to 1935, the pupil was examined mostly on factual knowledge and mastery of fundamental skills. Tyler's research and writings of that period developed awareness that higher mental processes are not evoked by simple factual tests, and that instruction that promotes factual knowledge may not promote—indeed, may interfere with—other more important educational outcomes. Tyler, Lindquist, and their students demonstrated that tests can be designed to measure such general educational outcomes as ability to comprehend scientific method. Whereas a student can prepare for a factual test only through a course of study that includes the facts tested, many different courses of study may promote the same *general* understandings and attitudes. In evaluating today's new curricula, it will clearly be important to appraise the student's general educational growth, which curriculum developers say is more important than mastery of the specific lessons presented. Note, for example, that the Biological Sciences Curriculum Study offers three courses with substantially different "subject matter" as alternative routes to much the same educational ends.

Although some instruments capable of measuring general outcomes were prepared during the 1930s, they were never very widely employed. The prevailing philosophy of the curriculum, particularly among "progressives," called for developing a program to fit local requirements, capitalizing on the capacities and experiences of local pupils. The faith of the 1920s in a "standard" curriculum was replaced by a faith that the best learning experience would result from teacher-pupil planning in each classroom. Since each teacher or each class could choose different content and even different objectives, this philosophy left little place for standard testing.

TESTS AS TRAINING

Many evaluation specialists came to see test development as a strategy for training the teacher in service, so that the process of test making came to be valued more than the test—or the test data—that resulted. The following remarks by Bloom (1962) are representative of a whole school of thought:

The criterion for determining the quality of a school and its educational functions would be the extent to which it achieves the objectives it has set for itself. . . . Our experiences suggest that unless the school has translated the objectives into specific and operational definitions, little is likely to be done about the objectives. They remain pious hopes and platitudes. . . . Participation of the teaching staff in selecting as well as constructing evaluation instruments has resulted in improved instruments on one hand and, on the other hand, it has resulted in clarifying the objectives of instruction and in making them real and meaningful to teachers. . . . When teachers have actively participated in defining objectives and in selecting or constructing evaluation instruments, they return to the learning problems with great vigor and remarkable creativity. . . . Teachers who have become committed to a set of educational objectives which they thoroughly understand respond by developing a variety of learning experiences which are as diverse and as complex as the situation requires.[2]

Thus, "evaluation" becomes a local and beneficial teacher-training activity. The benefit is attributed to thinking about what data to collect. Little is said about the actual use of test results; one has the impression that when test-making ends, the test itself is forgotten. Certainly, there is little enthusiasm for refining tests so that they can be used in other schools, for to do so would be to rob those teachers of the benefits of working out their own objectives and instruments.

Bloom and Tyler describe both curriculum making and evaluation as integral parts of classroom instruction, which is necessarily decentralized. This outlook is far from that of "course improvement." The current national curriculum studies assume that curriculum making can be centralized. They prepare materials to be used in much the same way by teachers everywhere. It is assumed that having experts draft materials, and revising these after tryout, produces better instructional activities than the local teacher would be likely to devise. In this context, it seems wholly appropriate to have most tests prepared by a central staff and to have results returned to that staff to guide further course improvement.

When evaluation is carried out in the service of course improvement, the chief aim is to ascertain what effects the course has—that is, what changes it produces in pupils. This is not to inquire merely whether the course is effective or ineffective. Outcomes of instruction are multidimensional, and a satisfactory investigation will map out the effects of the course along these dimensions separately. To agglomerate many types of post-course performance into a single score is a mistake, because failure to achieve one objective is masked by success in another direction. Moreover, since a composite score embodies (and usually conceals) judgments about the importance of the various outcomes, only a report that treats the outcomes separately can be useful to educators who have different value hierarchies.

The greatest service evaluation can perform is to identify aspects of the course where revision is desirable. Those responsible for developing a course would like to present evidence that their course is effective. They are intrigued by the idea of having an "independent testing agency" render a judgment on their product. But to call in the evaluator only upon the completion of course development, to confirm what has been done, is to offer him a menial role and to make meager use of his services. To be influential in course improvement, evidence must become available midway in curriculum development, not in the home stretch, when the developer is naturally reluctant to tear open a supposedly finished body of materials and techniques. Evaluation, used to improve the course while it is still fluid, contributes more to improvement of education than evaluation used to appraise a product already placed on the market.

EFFECTS AND EFFECTIVENESS

Insofar as possible, evaluation should be used to understand how the course produces its effects and what parameters influence its effectiveness. It is important to learn, for example, that the outcome of programmed instruction depends very much upon the attitude of the teacher; indeed, this may be more important than to learn that on the average such instruction produces slightly better or worse results than conventional instruction.

Hopefully, evaluation studies will go beyond reporting on this or that course and help us to understand educational learning. Such insight will, in the end, contribute to the development of all courses rather than just the course under test. In certain of the new curricula, there are data to suggest that aptitude measures correlate much less with end-of-course achievement than they do with achievement on early units (Ferris, 1962). This finding is not well confirmed, but it is highly significant if true. If it is true for the new curricula and only for them, it has one implication; if the same effect appears in traditional courses, it means something else. Either way, it provides food for thought for teachers, counselors, and theorists. Evaluation studies should generate knowledge about the nature of the abilities that constitute educational goals. Twenty years after the Eight-Year

Study of the Progressive Education Association, its testing techniques are in good repute, but we still know very little about what these instruments measure. Consider "Application of Principles in Science." Is this in any sense a unitary ability? Or has the able student only mastered certain principles one by one? Is the ability demonstrated on a test of this sort more prognostic of any later achievement than is factual knowledge? Such questions ought to receive substantial attention, although to the makers of any one course they are of only peripheral interest.

The aim to compare one course with another should not dominate plans for evaluation. To be sure, decisionmakers have to choose between courses, and any evaluation report will be interpreted in part comparatively. But formally designed experiments, pitting one course against another, are rarely definitive enough to justify their cost. Differences between average test scores resulting from different courses are usually small relative to the wide differences among and within classes taking the same course. At best, an experiment never does more than compare the present version of one course with the present version of another. A major effort to bring the losing contender nearer to perfection would be very likely to reverse the verdict of the experiment.

Any failure to equate the classes taking the competing courses will jeopardize the interpretation of an experiment—and such failures are almost inevitable. In testing a drug, we know that valid results cannot be obtained without a double-blind control in which the doses for half the subjects are inert placebos; the placebo and the drug look alike, so that neither doctor nor patient knows who is receiving medication. Without this control, the results are useless even when the state of the patient is checked by completely objective indices. In an educational experiment, it is difficult to keep pupils unaware that they are an experimental group. And it is quite impossible to neutralize the biases of the teacher as those of the doctor are neutralized in the double-blind design. It is thus never certain whether any observed advantage is attributable to the educational innovation as such, or to the greater energy that teachers and students put forth when a method is fresh and "experimental." Some have contended that any course, even the most excellent, loses much of its potency as soon as success enthrones it as "the traditional method."

WEAKNESS OF COMPARISONS

Since group comparisons give equivocal results, I believe that a formal study should be designed primarily to determine the post-course performance of a well described group with respect to many important objectives and side effects. Ours is a problem like that of the engineer examining a new automobile. He can set himself the task of defining its performance characteristics and its dependability. It would be merely distracting to put his question in the form, "Is this car better or worse than the competing brand?'' Moreover, in an experiment where the treatments compared differ in a dozen respects, no understanding is gained from the fact that the experiment shows a numerical advantage in favor of the new course. No one knows which of the ingredients is responsible for the advantage. More analytic experiments are much more useful than field trials applying markedly dissimilar treatments to different groups. Small-scale, well controlled studies can profitably be used to compare alternative versions of the same course; in such a study, the differences between treatments are few enough and well enough defined that the results have explanatory value.

The three purposes—course improvement, decisions about individuals, and administrative regulation—call for measurement procedures having somewhat different qualities. When a test will be used to make an administrative judgment on the individual teacher, it is necessary to measure thoroughly and with conspicuous fairness; such testing, if it is to cover more than one outcome, becomes extremely time consuming. In judging a course, however, one can make satisfactory interpretations from data collected on a sampling basis, with no pretense of measuring thoroughly the accomplishments of any one class. A similar point is to be made about testing for decisions about individuals. A test of individuals must be conspicuously fair and extensive enough to provide a dependable score for each person. But if the performance will not influence the fate of the individual, we can ask him to perform tasks for which the course has not directly prepared him, and we can use techniques that would be prohibitively expensive if applied in a manner thorough enough to measure each person reliably.

Evaluation is too often visualized as the administration of a formal test, an hour or so in duration, at the close of a course. But there are many other methods for examining pupil performance, and pupil attainment is not the only basis for appraising a course.

It is quite appropriate to ask scholars whether the statements made in the course are consistent with the best contemporary knowledge. This is a sound and even a necessary procedure. One may go on to evelute the pedagogy of the new course by soliciting opinions, but here there is considerable hazard. If the opinions are based on some preconception about teaching method, the findings will be controversial and very probably misleading. There are no theories of pedagogy so well established that one can say, without tryout, what will prove educative.

SYSTEMATIC OBSERVATION

One can accept the need for a pragmatic test of the curriculum and still employ opinions as a source of evidence. During the tryout stages of curriculum making, one relies heavily on the teachers' reports of pupil accomplishment—

"Here they had trouble"; "This they found dull"; "Here they needed only half as many exercises as were provided," etc. This is behavior observation even though unsystematic, and it is of great value. The reason for shifting to systematic observation is that this is more impartial, more public, and sometimes more penetrating. While I bow to the historian or mathematician as a judge of the technical soundness of course content, I do not agree that the experienced history or mathematics teacher who tries out a course gives the best possible judgment on its effectiveness. Scholars have too often deluded themselves about their effectiveness as teachers—particularly, have they too often accepted parroting of words as evidence of insight—for their unaided judgment to be trusted. Systematic observation is costly, and introduces some delay between the moment of teaching and the feedback of results. Hence, systematic observation will never be the curriculum developer's sole source of evidence. Systematic data collection becomes profitable in the intermediate stages of curriculum development, after the more obvious bugs in early drafts have been dealt with.

The approaches to evaluation include process studies, proficiency measures, attitude measures, and follow-up studies. A process study is concerned with events taking place in the classroom, proficiency and attitude measures with changes observed in pupils, and follow-up studies with the later careers of those who participated in the course.

The follow-up study comes closest to observing ultimate educational contributions, but the completion of such a study is so far removed in time from the initial instruction that it is of minor value in improving the course or explaining its effects. The follow-up study differs strikingly from the other types of evaluation study in one respect. I have already expressed the view that evaluation should be primarily concerned with the effects of the course under study rather than with comparisons of courses. That is to say, I would emphasize departures of attained results from the ideal, differences in apparent effectiveness of different parts of the course, and differences from item to item; all these suggest places where the course could be strengthened. But this view cannot be applied to the follow-up study, which appraises effects of the course as a whole and which has very little meaning unless outcomes can be compared with some sort of base rate. Suppose we find that 65 percent of the boys graduating from an experimental curriculum enroll as scientific and technical majors in college. We cannot judge whether this is a high or low figure save by comparing it with the rate among boys who have not had the course. In a follow-up study, it is necessary to obtain data on a control group equated at least crudely to the experimental cases on the obvious demographic variables.

Despite the fact that such groups are hard to equate and that follow-up data do not tell much about how to improve the course, such studies should have a place in research on the new curricula, whose national samples provide unusual opportunity for follow-up that can shed light on important questions. One obvious type of follow-up study traces the student's success in a college course founded upon the high-school course. One may examine the student's grades or ask him what topics in the college course he found himself poorly prepared for. It is hoped that some of the new science and mathematics courses will arouse greater interest than usual among girls; whether this hope is well founded can be checked by finding out what majors and what electives these ex-students pursue in college. Career choices likewise merit attention. Some proponents of the new curricula would like to see a greater flow of talent into basic science as distinct from technology, whereas others would regard this as potentially disastrous; but no one would regard facts about this flow as lacking significance.

MEASURING MEANINGS

Attitudes are prominent among the outcomes with which course developers are concerned. Attitudes are meanings or beliefs, not mere expressions of approval or disapproval. One's attitude toward science includes ideas about the matters on which a scientist can be an authority, about the benefits to be obtained from moon shots and studies of monkey mothers, and about depletion of natural resources. Equally important is the match between self-concept and concept of the field: What roles does science offer a person like me? Would I want to marry a scientist? And so on. Each learning activity also contributes to attitudes that reach far beyond any one subject, such as the pupil's sense of his own competence and desire to learn.

Attitudes can be measured in many ways; the choices revealed in follow-up studies, for example, are pertinent evidence. But measurement usually takes the form of direct or indirect questioning. Interviews, questionnaires, and the like are quite valuable when not trusted blindly. Certainly, we should take seriously any *un*desirable opinion expressed by a substantial proportion of the graduates of a course (*e.g.*, the belief that the scientist speaks with peculiar authority on political and ethical questions, or the belief that mathematics is a finished subject rather than a field for current investigation).

Attitude questionnaires have been much criticized because they are subject to distortion, especially where the student hopes to gain by being less than frank. Particularly if the questions are asked in a context far removed from the experimental course, the returns are likely to be trustworthy. Thus, a general questionnaire administered through homerooms (or required English courses) may include questions about liking for various subjects and activities; these same questions administered by the mathematics teacher would give much less trustworthy data on attitude toward mathematics. While students may give reports more favorable than their true beliefs, this distortion is not likely to be greater one year than another, or greater among students who take an experimental course than among those who do not. In group averages, many distortions balance out. But questionnaires insufficiently valid for individual testing can be used in evaluating curricula, both because the student has little motive to distort and because the evaluator is comparing averages rather than individuals.

PROCESS AND PROFICIENCY

For measuring proficiency, techniques are likewise varied. Standardized tests are useful. But for course evaluation it makes sense to assign *different* questions to different students. Giving each student in a population of 500 the same test of 50 questions will provide far less information to the course developer than drawing for each student 50 questions from a pool of, say, 700. The latter plan determines the mean success of about 75 representative students on every one of the 700 items; the former reports on only 50 items (Lord, 1962). Essay tests and open-ended questions, generally too expensive to use for routine evaluation, can profitably be employed to appraise certain abilities. One can go further and observe individuals or groups as they attack a research problem in the laboratory or work through some other complex problem. Since it is necessary to test only a representative sample of pupils, costs are not as serious a consideration as in routine testing. Additional aspects of proficiency testing will be considered below.

Process measures have especial value in showing how a course can be improved because they examine what happens during instruction. In the development of programmed instructional materials, for example, records are collected showing how many pupils miss each item presented; any piling up of errors implies a need for better explanation or a more gradual approach to a difficult topic. Immediately after showing a teaching film, one can interview students, perhaps asking them to describe a still photograph taken from the film. Misleading presentations, ideas given insufficient emphasis, and matters left unclear will be identified by such methods. Similar interviews can disclose what pupils take away from a laboratory activity or a discussion. A process study may turn attention to what the teacher does in the classroom. In those curricula that allow choice of topics, for example, it is worthwhile to find out which topics are chosen and how much time is allotted to each. A log of class activities (preferably recorded by a pupil rather than the teacher) will show which of the techniques suggested in a summer institute are actually adopted and which form "part of the new course" only in the developer's fantasies.

I have indicated that I consider item data to be more important than test scores. The total score may give confidence in a curriculum or give rise to discouragement, but it tells very little about how to produce further improvement. And, as Ferris (1962) has noted, such scores are quite likely to be mis- or overinterpreted. The score on a single item, or on a problem that demands several responses in succession, is more likely than the test score to suggest how to alter the presentation. When we accept item scores as useful, we need no longer think of evaluation as a one-shot, end-of-year operation. Proficiency can be measured at any moment, with particular interest attaching to those items most related to the recent lessons. Other items calling for general abilities can profitably be administered repeatedly during the course (perhaps to different random samples of pupils) so that we can begin to learn when and from what experiences change in these abilities comes.

In course evaluation, we need not be much concerned about making measuring instruments fit the curriculum. However startling this declaration may seem, and however contrary to the principles of evaluation for other purposes, this must be our position if we want to know what changes a course produces in the pupil. An ideal evaluation would include measures of all the types of proficiency that might reasonably be desired in the area in question, not just the selected outcomes to which this curriculum directs substantial attention. If you wish only to know how well a curriculum is achieving *its* objectives, you fit the test to the curriculum; but if you wish to know how well the curriculum is serving the national interest, you measure all outcomes that might be worth striving for. One of the new mathematics courses may disavow any attempt to teach numerical trigonometry, and indeed, might discard nearly all computational work. It is still perfectly reasonable to ask how well graduates of the course can compute and can solve right triangles. Even if the course developers went so far as to contend that computational skill is no proper objective of secondary instruction, they will encounter educators and laymen who do not share their view. If it can be shown that students who come through the new course are fairly proficient in computation despite the lack of direct teaching, the doubters will be reassured. If not, the evidence makes clear how much is being sacrificed. Similarly, when the biologists offer alternative courses emphasizing microbiology and ecology, it is fair to ask how well the graduate of one course can understand issues treated in the other. Ideal evaluation in mathematics will collect evidence on all the abilities toward which a mathematics course might reasonably aim; likewise in biology, English, or any other subject.

Ferris states that the ACS Chemistry Test, however well constructed, is inadequate for evaluating the new CBA and CHEM programs because it does not cover their objectives. One can agree with this without regarding the ACS test as inappropriate to use with these courses. It is important that this test not stand *alone,* as the sole evaluation device. It will tell us something worth knowing, namely, just how much "conventional" knowledge the new curriculum does or does not provide. The curriculum developers deliberately planned to sacrifice some of the conventional attainments and have nothing to fear from this measurement, competently interpreted (particularly if data are examined item by item).

SECURITY, CONTENT, TERMS

The demand that tests be closely matched to the aims of a course reflects awareness that examinations of the usual sort "determine what is taught." If questions are known in advance, students give more attention to learning their answers than to learning other aspects of the course. This is not necessarily detrimental. Wherever it is critically important to master certain content, the knowledge that it will be tested produces a desirable concentration of effort. On the other hand, learning the answer to a set question is by no means the same as acquiring understanding of whatever topic that question represents. There is, therefore, a possible advantage in using "secure" tests for course evaluation. Security is achieved only at a price: One must prepare new tests each year and consequently cannot make before-and-after comparisons with the same items. One would hope that the use of different items with different students, and the fact that there is less incentive to coach when no judgment is to be passed on the pupils and the teachers, would make security a less critical problem.

The distinction between factual tests and tests of higher mental processes, as elaborated for example in the *Taxonomy of Educational Objectives,* is of some value in planning tests, although classifying items as measures of knowledge, application, original problem solving, etc., is difficult and often impossible. Whether a given response represents rote recall or reasoning depends upon how the pupil has been taught, not solely upon the question asked. One may, for example, describe a biological environment and ask for predictions regarding the effect of a certain intervention. Students who have never dealt with ecological data will succeed or fail according to their general ability to reason about complex events; those who have studied ecological biology will be more likely to succeed, reasoning from specific principles; and those who have lived in such an ecology or read about it may answer successfully on the basis of memory. We rarely, therefore, will want to test whether a student "knows" or "does not know" certain material. Knowledge is a matter of degree. Two persons may be acquainted with the same facts or principles, but one will be more expert in his understanding, better able to cope with inconsistent data, irrelevant sources of confusion, and apparent exceptions to the principle. To measure intellectual competence is to measure depth, connectedness, and applicability of knowledge.

Too often, test questions are course-specific, stated in such a way that only the person who has been specifically taught to understand what is being asked for can answer the question. Such questions can usually be identified by their use of conventions. Some conventions are commonplace, and we can assume that all the pupils we test will know them. But a biology test that describes a metabolic process with the aid of the $\rightleftharpoons$ symbol presents difficulties for students who can think through the scientific question about equilibrium but are unfamiliar with the symbol. A trigonometry problem that requires use of a trigonometric table is unreasonable, unless we want to test familiarity with the conventional names of functions. The same problem in numerical trigonometry can be cast in a form clear to the average pupil *entering* high school; if necessary, the tables of functions can be presented along with a comprehensible explanation. So stated, the problem becomes course-independent. It is fair to ask whether graduates of the experimental course can solve such problems, not previously encountered, whereas it is pointless to ask whether they can answer questions whose language is strange to them. To be sure, knowledge of certain terminology is a significant objective of instruction, but for course evaluation, testing of terminology should very likely be separated from testing of other understandings. To appraise understanding of processes and relations, the fair question is one comprehensible to a pupil who has not taken the course. This is not to say that he should know the answer or the procedure to follow in attaining the answer, but he should understand what he is being asked. Such course-independent questions can be used as standard instruments to investigate any instructional program.

Pupils who have not studied a topic will usually be less facile than those who have studied it. Graduates of my hypothetical mathematics course will take longer to solve trigonometry problems than will those who have studied trig. But speed and power should not be confused; in intellectual studies, power is almost always of greater importance. If the course equips the pupil to deal correctly, even though haltingly, with a topic not studied, we can expect him to develop facility later when that topic comes before him frequently.

TWO TYPES OF TRANSFER

The chief objective in many of the new curricula seems to be to develop aptitude for mastering new materials in the field. A biology course cannot cover all valuable biological content, but it may reasonably aspire to equip the pupil to understand descriptions of unfamiliar organisms, to comprehend a new theory and the reasoning behind it, and to plan an experiment to test a new hypothesis. This is transfer of learning. It has been insufficiently recognized that there are two types of transfer. The two types shade into one another, being arranged on a continuum of immediacy of effect; we can label the more immediate pole *applicational transfer,* and speak of slower-acting effects as *gains in aptitude* (Ferguson, 1954).

Nearly all educational research on transfer has tested immediate performance on a partly new task. We teach pupils to solve equations in x, and include in the test equations stated in a or z. We teach the principles of ecological balance by referring to forests, and as a transfer test, ask what effect pollution will have on the population of a lake. We describe an experiment not presented in the text, and ask the student to discuss possible interpretations and needed controls. Any of these tests can be administered in a short time. But the more significant type of transfer may be the increased ability to learn in a particular field. There is very likely a considerable difference between the ability to draw conclusions from a neatly finished experiment, and the ability to tease insight out of the disorderly and inconsistent observations that come with continuous laboratory work on a problem. The student who masters a good biology course may become better able to comprehend certain types of theory and data, so that he gains more from a subsequent year of study in ethnology; we do not measure this gain by testing his understanding of short passages in ethnology. There has rarely been an appraisal of ability to work through a problem situation or a complex body of knowledge over a period of days or months. Despite the practical difficulties that attend an attempt to measure the effect of a course on a person's subsequent learning, such "learning to learn" is so important that a serious effort should be made to detect such effects and to understand how they may be fostered.

The techniques of programmed instruction may be adapted to appraise learning ability. One may, for example, test the student's rate of mastery of a self-contained, programmed unit on the physics of heat or some other topic not studied. If the program is truly self-contained, every student can master it, but the one with greater scientific comprehension will hopefully make fewer errors and progress faster. The program can be prepared in several logically complete versions, ranging from one with very small "steps" to one with minimal internal redundancy, on the hypothesis that the better educated student could cope with the less redundant program. Moreover, he might prefer its greater elegance.

TOWARD DEEPER UNDERSTANDING

Old habits of thought and long established techniques are poor guides to the evaluation required for course improvement. Traditionally, educational measurement has been chiefly concerned with producing fair and precise scores for comparing individuals. Educational experimentation has been concerned with comparing score averages of competing courses. But course evaluation calls for description of outcomes. This description should be made on the broadest possible scale, even at the sacrifice of superficial fairness and precision.

Course evaluation should ascertain what changes a course produces and should identify aspects of the course that need revision. The outcomes observed should include general outcomes ranging far beyond the content of the curriculum itself—attitudes, career choices, general understandings and intellectual powers, and aptitude for further learning in the field. Analysis of performance or single items or types of problems is more informative than analysis of composite scores. It is not necessary or desirable to give the same test to all pupils; rather, as many questions as possible should be given, each to a different, moderate sized sample of pupils. Costly techniques, such as interviews and essay tests, can profitably be applied to samples of pupils, whereas testing everyone would be out of the question.

Asking the right questions about educational outcomes can do much to improve educational effectiveness. Even if the right data are collected, however, evaluation will have contributed too little if it only places a seal of approval on certain courses and casts others into disfavor. Evaluation is a fundamental part of curriculum development, not an appendage. Its job is to collect facts the course developer can and will use to do a better job, and facts from which a deeper understanding of the educational process will emerge.

NOTES

1. My comments on these questions, and on certain more significant questions that *should* have been raised, have been greatly clarified by the reactions of several of these directors and of my colleagues in evaluation to a draft of this paper. J. Thomas Hastings and Robert Heath have been especially helpful. What I voice, however, are my personal views, deliberately more provocative than "authoritative."

2. Elsewhere, Bloom's paper discusses evaluation for the new curricula. Attention may also be drawn to Tyler's (1951) highly pertinent paper.

REFERENCES

Bloom, B. S. (ed.) *Taxonomy of Educational Objectives* (New York: Longmans, Green, 1956).

————. "Quality Control in Education" in *Tomorrow's Teaching* (Oklahoma City: Frontiers of Science Foundation, 1961), pp. 54–61.

Ferguson, G. A. "On Learning and Human Ability." *Canadian Journal of Psychology* 8 (1954): 95–112.

Ferris, F. L., Jr. "Testing in the New Curriculums: Numerology, Tyranny, or Common Sense?" *School Review* 70 (1962): 112–31.

Lord, F. M. "Estimating Norms by Item-Sampling." *Educational Psychology Measurement* 22 (1962): 259–68.

Tyler, R. W. "The Functions of Measurement in Improving Instruction." In E. F. Lindquist (ed.) *Educational Measurement* (Washington, D.C.: American Council of Education, 1951), pp. 46–67.

22. THE METHODOLOGY OF EVALUATION

Michael Scriven[1]

INTRODUCTION

Current conceptions of the evaluation of educational instruments (e.g., new curricula, programmed texts, inductive methods, individual teachers) are still inadequate both philosophically and practically. This paper attempts to exhibit and reduce some of the deficiencies. Intellectual progress is possible only because newcomers can stand on the shoulder of giants. This feat is often confused with treading on their toes, particularly but not only by the newcomer. I confess a special obligation to Professor Cronbach's (1963) work,[2] and to valuable discussions with the personnel of CIRCE at the University of Illinois, as well as thoughtful correspondence from several others, especially James Shaver.

1. OUTLINE

The main focus of this paper is on curricular evaluation but almost all the points made transfer immediately to other kinds of evaluation. Section headings are reasonably self-explanatory and occur in the following order:

1. Outline.
2. Goals of Evaluation versus Roles of Evaluation: Formative and Summative Evaluation.

SOURCE. In Ralph W. Tyler, Robert M. Gagné, and Michael Scriven (eds.), *Perspectives of Curriculum Evaluation*. AERA Monograph Series on Curriculum Evaluation. No. 1 (Chicago: Rand McNally, 1967), pp. 39–83.

3. Professional versus Amateur Evaluation.
4. Evaluation Studies versus Process Studies.
5. Evaluation versus Estimation of Goal Achievement.
6. "Intrinsic" Evaluation versus "Pay-off" Evaluation.
7. Practical Procedures for Mediated Evaluation.
8. The Possibility of Pure "Pay-off" Evaluation.
9. Comparative versus Noncomparative Evaluation.
10. Practical Procedures for Control-Group Evaluation.
11. Criteria of Educational Achievement for Evaluation Studies.
12. Values and Costs.
13. A Marginal Kind of "Evaluation"—"Explanatory Evaluation."
14. Conclusions.

The discussion in the earlier sections is relatively elementary and etiological, progressing to an occasionally more difficult and generally more practical level in later sections.

2. GOALS OF EVALUATION VERSUS ROLES OF EVALUATION: FORMATIVE AND SUMMATIVE EVALUATION

The function of evaluation may be thought of in two ways. At the methodological level, we may talk of the *goals* of evaluation; in a particular sociological or pedagogical context we may further distinguish several possible *roles* of evaluation.

In the abstract, we may say that evaluation attempts to answer certain *types of question* about certain *entities*. The entities are the various educational "instruments" (processes, personnel, procedures, programs, etc.). The types of question include questions of the form: *How well* does this instrument perform (with respect to such-and-such criteria)?, Does it perform *better* than this other instrument?, *What* does this instrument do (i.e., what variables from the group in which we are interested are significantly affected by its application)?, Is the use of this instrument *worth* what it's costing? Evaluation is itself a methodological activity which is essentially similar whether we are trying to evaluate coffee machines or teaching machines, plans for a house or plans for a curriculum. The activity consists simply in the gathering and combining of performance data with a weighted set of goal scales to yield either comparative or numerical ratings, and in the justification of (a) the data-gathering instruments, (b) the weightings, and (c) the selection of goals.

But the *role* which evaluation has in a particular educational context may be enormously various; it may form part of a teacher training activity, of the process of curriculum development, of a field experiment connected with the improvement of learning theory, of an investigation preliminary to a decision about purchase or rejection of materials; it may be a data-gathering activity for supporting a request for tax increases or research support, or a preliminary to the reward or punishment of people as in an executive training program, a prison, or a classroom. Failure to make this rather obvious distinction between the roles and goals of evaluation, not necessarily in this terminology, is one of the factors that has led to the dilution of the process of evaluation to the point where it can no longer serve as a basis for answering the questions which are its goal. This dilution has sacrificed goals to roles. One can be against evaluation only if one can show that it is improper to seek an answer to questions about the merit of educational instruments, which would involve showing that there are *no* legitimate activities (roles) in which these questions can be raised, an extraordinary claim. Obviously the fact that evaluation is sometimes given an inappropriate role hardly justifies the conclusion that we *never* need to know the answers to the goal questions. Anxiety about "evaluation," especially among teachers or students, is all too frequently an illicitly generalized response originating in legitimate objections to a situation in which an evaluation was given a role quite beyond its reliability or comprehensiveness.

One role that has often and sensibly been assigned to evaluation is as an important part of the process of curriculum *development* (another is teacher self-improvement). Obviously such a role does not preclude evaluation of the *final* product of this process. Evaluation can and usually should play several roles. But it is clear from the treatment of evaluation in some of the recent literature and in a number of recent research proposals involving several million dollars that the assumption is being made that one's obligations in the direction of evaluation are fully discharged by having it appear *somewhere* in a project. Not only can it have several roles with respect to one educational enterprise, but with respect to each of these it may have several specific goals. Thus, it may have a role in the on-going improvement of the curriculum, and with respect to this role several types of questions (goals) may be raised, such as: Is the curriculum at this point really getting across the distinction between prejudice and commitment?, Is it taking too large a proportion of the available time to make this point?, etc. In another role, the evaluation process may serve to enable administrators to decide whether the entire finished curriculum, refined by use of the evaluation process in its first role, represents a sufficiently significant advance on the available alternatives to justify the expense of adoption by a school system.

One of the reasons for the tolerance or indeed encouragement of the confusion between roles and goals is the well-meaning attempt to allay the anxiety on the part of teachers that the word "evaluation" precipitates. By stressing the constructive part evaluation may play in nonthreatening activities (roles) we slur over the fact that its goals always include the estimation of merit, worth, value, etc., which all too clearly contribute in another role to decisions about promotion and rejection of personnel and courses. But we cannot afford to tackle anxiety about evaluation by ignoring its importance and confusing its presentation; the loss in efficiency is too great. Business firms can't keep executives or factories when they know they are not doing good work and a society shouldn't have to retain textbooks, courses, teachers, and superintendents that do a poor job when a good performance is possible. The appropriate way to handle anxiety of this kind is by finding tasks for which a better prognosis is possible for the individuals whose positions or prestige are threatened. Failure to evaluate pupils' performance leads to the gross inefficiencies of the age-graded classroom or the "ungraded" reports on pupils, and failure to evaluate teachers' performances leads to the correlative inefficiency of incompetent instruction and the substitution of personality for performance. A little toughening of the moral fiber may be required if we are not to shirk the social responsibilities of the educational branch of our culture. Thus, it may even be true that "the greatest service evaluation can perform is to identify aspects of the course where revision is desirable" (Cronbach, p. 236—see note 2), though it is not clear how one would establish this, but it is certainly also true that there are other extremely important evaluation services which must be done for almost any given curriculum project or other educational innovation. And there are many contexts in which calling in an evaluator to perform a final evaluation of the project or person is an act of proper recognition of responsibility to the person, product, or taxpayers. It therefore seems a little excessive to refer to this as simply "a menial role," as Cronbach does. It is obviously a great service if this kind of terminal, overall, or "outcome" evaluation can demonstrate that a very expensive textbook (etc.) is not significantly better than the competition, or that it is enormously better than any competitor. In more general terms it may be possible to demonstrate that a certain type of approach to (for example) mathematics is not yielding significantly better pupil performance on any dimension that mathematicians or vocational users are prepared to regard as important. This would certainly save a great deal of expenditure of time and money and constitute a valuable contribution to educational development, as would the converse, favorable, result. Thus there seem to be a number of qualifications that would have to be made before one could accept a statement asserting the greater importance of formative evaluation by comparison with summative. ("Evaluation, used to improve the course while it is still fluid, contributes more to improvement of education than evaluation used to appraise a product already placed on the market."—Cronbach, p. 236—see note 2.) Fortunately we do not have to make this choice. Educational projects, particularly curricular ones, clearly must attempt to make best use of evaluation in both these roles. As a matter of terminology, I think that novel terms are worthwhile here, to avoid inappropriate connotations, and I propose to use the terms "formative" and "summative" to qualify evaluation in these roles.

Now any curriculum builder is almost automatically engaged in formative evaluation, except on a very strict interpretation of "evaluation." He is presumably doing what he is doing because he judges that the material being presented in the existing curriculum is unsatisfactory. So, as he proceeds to construct the new material, he is constantly evaluating his own material as better than that which is already current. Unless entirely ignorant of one's shortcomings as a judge of one's own work, he is also presumably engaged in field-testing the work while it is being developed, and in so doing he gets feedback on the basis of which he again produces revisions; this is of course formative evaluation. If the field-testing is elaborate, it may amount to summative evaluation of *the early forms* of the new curriculum. He is usually involved with colleagues, e.g., the classroom teacher or peers, who comment on the material as they see it—again, this is evaluation, and it produces changes which are allegedly for the better.

If a recommendation for formative evaluation has any content at all, it presumably amounts to the suggestion that a *professional* evaluator should be added to the curriculum construction project. There certainly can be advantages in this, though it is equally clear from practical experience that there can be disadvantages. But this question is clearly not the same as the question whether to have summative evaluation. We devote part of the next section to a discussion of these two questions.

3. PROFESSIONAL VERSUS AMATEUR EVALUATION

The basic fact is that the evaluator, while a professional in his own field, is usually not a professional in the field relevant to the curriculum being reformed or, if he is, he is not committed to the particular development being undertaken. This leads to clashes and counter-charges of a kind which are all too familiar to project directors today.

From these "failures of communication" between evaluators and teachers or curriculum makers there have sprung some unfortunate overreactions. The hard-nosed anti-evaluation line is all too frequently a rationalization of the anxiety provoked by the presence of an external judge who is not identified with or committed to (or perhaps does not even understand) the ideals of the project. The equally indefensible opposite extreme is represented by the self-perceived tough-minded operationalist evaluator, all too likely to say "If you can't tell me what variables you claim to be affecting, in operational terms, we can't construct a test for their variation, and as long as they haven't been tested you haven't any reason for thinking you are making a contribution."

In order to develop a fair treatment of these views let us consider the difference between a contemporary educational project involving the development of a new curriculum or teaching method, and the co-authoring of a new ninth-grade algebra text by two or three teachers in the late 1930's. In the first place, the present projects are often supported from government funds on a very large scale. The justification of this expenditure calls for some kind of objective evidence that the product is valuable. Moreover *future* support for work in this area or by these same workers requires some objective evidence as to their merit at this kind of job. Since there are not sufficient funds to support all applicants, judgments of comparative merit are necessary; and objective bases for this are obviously superior to mere person-endorsements by peers, etc. Finally, the enormous costs involved in the *adoption* of such products by school systems commit another great slice of taxpayers' money, and this kind of commitment should presumably be made only on the basis of rather substantial evidence for its justification. In this context, summative evaluation is an inescapable obligation on the project director, an obvious requirement by the sponsoring agency, and a desideratum as far as the schools are concerned. And since formative evaluation is a necessary part of any rational approach to producing good results on the summative evaluation, it can hardly be wholly eschewed; indeed, as we have shown, its occurrence is to some degree guaranteed by the nature of the case. But the separate question of whether and how professional evaluators should be employed depends very much upon the extent to which they do more harm than good—and there are a number of ways in which they can do harm.

Professional evaluators may simply exude a kind of skeptical spirit that dampens the creative fires of a productive group. They may be sympathetic but impose such crushing demands on operational formulation of goals as to divert too much time to an essentially secondary activity. ("Secondary" in the sense that there cannot be any evaluation without a curriculum.) The major compromise that must be effected is to have the evaluator recognize it as partly *his* responsibility to uncover and formulate a testable set of criteria for the course. He may be substantially helped by the fact that the project has explicitly espoused certain goals, or rejected others, and he will certainly be aided by the writing team's criticism of his formulations. However, the exchange has to be a two-way one; curriculum writers are by no means infallible, and often are extremely prejudiced or grandiose in describing their operations. Evaluators, on the other hand, are handicapped so long as they are less than fully familiar with the subject matter being restructured, and less than fully sympathetic with the aims of the creative group. Yet once they become identified with those aims, emotionally as well as economically, they lose something of great importance to an objective evaluation—their independence. For this reason the formative evaluators should, if at all possible, be sharply distinguished from the summative evaluators, with whom they may certainly work in developing an acceptable summative evaluation schema, but the formative evaluators should ideally exclude themselves from the role of judge in the summative evaluation. If this distinction between formative and summative evaluation personnel is made, it becomes possible to retain the advantages of eventual objective professional evaluation without the risks of disrupting the team spirit during development.

There are other problems about the intrusion of evaluation into education, and the intrusion of an evaluator into the curriculum-making process. Several of these have been admirably expressed by J. Myron Atkin (1963). Some of them are taken up elsewhere in this paper, but some mention of two of them should be made here. The first suggestion is that testing for the extent of learning of certain rather delicate and pervasive concepts may be itself destructive, in that it makes the student too self-conscious about the role of a concept at too early a stage, thereby preventing its natural and proper development. The problem is that with respect to some of these concepts, e.g., symmetry, equilibrium, and randomness, it might be the case that very little accretion occurs in the understanding of a child during any particular course or indeed any particular year of his education, but that tiny accretion may be of very great importance in the long-run development of good scientific understanding. It would not show up on tests, indeed it might be stultified by the intrusion of tests, in any given year, but it has to be in the curriculum in order to produce the finished product that we desire. In this case, evaluation seems to be both incompetent and possibly destructive.

Such a possibility should serve as an interesting challenge to the creative curriculum maker. While not dismissing it, he would normally respond by attempting to treat it more explicitly, perhaps at a somewhat later stage in the curriculum than it is normally first mentioned, and see whether some significant and satisfactory accretion of comprehension cannot be produced by this direct attack. Only if this failed would he turn to the evaluator and demand a considerably more sensitive instrument. Again, it would also be possible to deliberately avoid testing for this during all the early years of its peripheral introduction, and test only in the senior year in high school, for example. We can acknowledge the *possibility* that concerns Atkin and allow some extra material in the curriculum to handle it even without any justification in the early feedback from tests. Errors of excess are much less significant than errors of commission or omission in curriculum making.

It is well known that there are dangers from having a curriculum-making group discuss its work with teachers of the present curriculum—although there are obviously possible advantages from this—so there are dangers and advantages in bringing the evaluator in early. In such situations, some ingenuity on the part of the project director will often make the best of both worlds possible; for example, the evaluator may be simply introduced to the materials produced, but not to the people producing them, and his comments studied by the director with an eye to feeding back any fundamental and serious criticisms, but withholding the others until some later stage in the curriculum development activities where, for example, an extensive process of revision is about to begin. But these are practical considerations; there remain two more fundamental kinds of objection that should be mentioned briefly, of which the first is central to Atkin's misgivings.

No one who has been involved in the field-testing of a new curriculum has failed to notice the enormous variability in its appeal to students, often unpredictable from their previous academic performance. The child already interested in bird-watching may find one approach to biology far more attractive than another. Similarly, for some children the relevance of the material to problems with which they are familiar will make an enormous difference to their interest, whereas for others the properties of those curious entities the hexaflexagons and the Moebius strips are immediately fascinating. More fundamentally, the structuring of the classroom situation may wholly alter the motivation for different students in different ways; the nondirective style of treatment currently regarded as desirable, partly for its supposed connection with the inductive approach, is totally unstimulating for some children, although an aggressive, competitive, critical interaction will get them up and running. In the face of this kind of variation, we are often committed to the use of the very blunt evaluation instrument of the performance, on tests, of the class as a whole. Even if we break this down into improvements in individual performances, we still have not fully exploited the potentialities of the material, which would be manifested only if we were to select the right material *and* the right instructional technique for a child with a particular background, attitudes, interests, and abilities. Perhaps, the antievaluation skeptic suggests, it is more appropriate to place one's faith in the creative and academically impeccable curriculum maker, using the field tests simply to make sure that it is *possible* to excite and teach students with the material, under appropriate circumstances. That is, our criterion should be markedly improved performance by *some,* even by a *substantial* number, rather than by the class as a whole. To this the evaluator must reply by asking whether one is to disregard possibilities such as serious lack of comprehensibility to many students at this age-level, a marked relative deterioration of performance in some of the students more than offsetting the gains in others, the possibility that it is the pedagogical skill or enthusiasm of the teacher that is responsible for the success in the field tests and not the materials. The material is to go out to other teachers; it must be determined whether it will be of any use to them. To answer these questions—and indeed for the field tests themselves—a professional job in evaluation is necessary.

We can learn something important from this criticism, however. We must certainly weigh seriously the opinions of the subject matter expert as to the flavor and quality of the curriculum content. Sometimes it will be almost all we have to go on, and sometimes it will even be enough for some decisions. It should in any event be seriously considered and sometimes heavily weighted in the evaluation process, for the *absence* of supporting professional consensus of this kind is often adequate grounds for complete rejection of the material.

Finally, there is the objection that hovers in the background of many of these discussions, the uneasy feeling that evaluation necessitates making value judgments and that value judgments are essentially subjective and not scientific. This is about as intelligent a view as the view that statements about oneself are essentially subjective and hence incapable of rational substantiation. Some value judgments are essentially assertions about fundamental personal preferences ("matters of taste") and as such are factual claims which can be established or refuted by ordinary (though sometimes not easy) procedures of psychological investigation. The process of establishing this kind of claim does not show that it is right or wrong for everyone to hold these values; it only shows that it is true that somebody does or does not hold them. Another kind of value judgment is the assessment of the merit or comparative merit of some entity in a clearly defined context where this amounts to a claim that its performance is as good as or better than another's on clearly identifiable and clearly weighted criterion variables. With respect to value judgments of this kind, it is not only possible to find out whether or not they are believed by the individuals who assert them, but it is also possible to determine whether it is right or wrong for anyone to believe them. They are simply complex conflations of various performance ratings and the weightings of the various performances; it is in this sense that we can correctly assert that the Bulova Accutron is the best wrist chronometer currently available or that a particular desk dictionary is the best one for somebody with extensive scientific interests. Finally, there are value judgments in which the criteria themselves are debatable, a type of value judgment which is only philosophically the most important and whose debatability merely reflects the fact that important issues are not always easy ones. Examples of this would be the assertion that the most important role of evaluation is in the process of curriculum writing, or that the IQ test is an unfortunate archaism, or that the Copenhagen interpretation of quantum physics is superior to any known alternative. In each of these cases, the disputes turn out to be mainly disputes about what is to count as good, rather than to be arguments about the straightforward "facts of the situation," i.e., what is in fact good. It is immature to react to this kind of judgment as if it is contaminated with some disgusting disease; the only proper reaction is to examine the reasons that are put forward for them and see if and how the matter may be rationally discussed. The history of the greatest developments in science is the history of the rational triumph of such value judgments, of new conceptions of "good explanation," "good theory," "good model" ("paradigm"), not just of one theory over another in a contest where the rules are agreed.

It is sometimes thought that in dealing with people, as we must in the field of education, we are necessarily involved in the field of *moral* value judgments, and that at least *these* really are essentially subjective. But in the first place value judgments about people are by no means necessarily moral, since they may refer to their health, intelligence, and achievements; secondly, even if they are moral, we are all presumably committed to one moral principle (the principle of the equality of rights of men) and by far the greater part of public moral discourse depends only on the framework built on this assumption with complicated empirical judgments about the consequences of alternatives.[3] So, unless one is willing to challenge this axiom, and to provide rational support for an alternative, even moral value judgments are within the realm of rational debate. But whatever the outcome of such a discussion, the facts that some evaluation is moral evaluation and that some moral evaluation is controversial do not conjointly imply the least degree of support for the conclusion that curricular evaluation is less than a fully appropriate goal for applied science.

4. EVALUATION STUDIES VERSUS PROCESS STUDIES

In the course of clarifying the concept of evaluation it is important not to simplify it. Although the *typical* goals of evaluation require judgments of merit and worth, when somebody is asked to evaluate a situation or the impact of certain kinds of materials on the market, then what is being called for is an analytical description of the process, usually with respect to certain possible causal connections, indeed an *interpretation* (see Section 13 below). In this sense it is not inappropriate to regard some kinds of process investigation as evaluation. But the range of process research only overlaps with and is neither subsumed by nor equivalent to that of evaluation. We may conveniently distinguish three types of process research, as the term is used by Cronbach and others.

1. The noninferential study of what actually goes on in the classroom. Perhaps this has the most direct claim to being called a study of the process of teaching (learning, etc.). We might for example be interested in the proportion of the class period during which the teacher talks, the amount of time that the students spend in homework for a class, the proportion of the dialogue devoted to explaining, defining, opining, etc. (Milton Meux and B.O. Smith, 1961). The great problem about work like this is to show that it is worth doing, in *any* sense. *Some* pure research is idle research. The Smith and Meux work is specifically mentioned because *it* is clearly original and offers promise in a large number of directions. Skinner's attack on controlled studies and his emphasis on process research are more than offset by his social-welfare orientation which ensures that the process work is aimed at valuable improvements in control of learning. It is difficult to avoid the conclusion, however, that most process research of this kind in education, as in psychotherapy (though apparently not in medicine), is fruitful at neither the theoretical nor the applied level.

2. The second kind of process research involves the investigation of causal claims ("dynamic hypotheses") about the process. Here we are interested in such questions as whether an increase of time spent on class discussions of the goals of a curriculum at the expense of time spent on training drills leads to

improved comprehension in (a) algebra, (b) geography, etc. This kind of investigation is essentially a miniature limited-scope "new instrument" project. Another kind looks for the answer to such questions as: Is the formation of subgroup allegiance and identification with the teacher facilitated by strong emphasis on pupil-teacher dialogue? The feature of this subgroup of process hypotheses that distinguishes them from evaluation hypotheses is that the dependent variables either are ones which would not figure among the set of criteria we would use in a summative evaluation study (though we might think of them as important because of their relevance to improved teaching techniques) or they are only a subgroup of such summative criteria; and in either case no attempt is made to justify any correlative assignments of merit.

Process hypotheses of this second kind are in general about as difficult to substantiate as any "outcome" hypothesis, i.e., summative evaluation. Indeed they are sometimes harder to substantiate because they may require identifying the effects of only one of several independent variables that are present, and it is extremely hard—though usually not impossible—to apply ordinary matching techniques to take care of the others. The advantage of some summative evaluation investigation is that it is concerned with evaluating the effects of a whole teacher-curriculum package and has no need to identify the specific agent responsible for the overall improvement or deterioration. That advantage lapses when we are concerned to identify the variance due to the curriculum as opposed to the teacher.

3. Formative Evaluation. This kind of research is often called process research, but it is of course simply outcome evaluation of an intermediate stage in the development of the teaching instrument. The distinction between this and the first kind of dynamic hypothesis mentioned above is twofold. There is a distinction of role: the role of formative evaluation is to discover deficiencies and successes in the intermediate versions of a new curriculum; the role of dynamic hypothesis investigation is *sui generis:* it is to provide the answer to an important question about the mechanism of teaching. And there is a distinction in the extent to which it matters whether the criteria used are an adequate analysis of the proper goals of the curriculum. The dynamic hypothesis study has no obligation to this; the formative evaluation does. But the two types of study are not always sharply distinct. They both play an important role in good curriculum research.

Now of course it is true that anybody who does an experiment of any kind at all should at some stage evaluate *his results*. It is even true that the experiment itself will usually be designed in such a way as to incorporate procedures for evaluation of the results—e.g., by using an "objectively validated" test, which has a certain kind of built-in comparative evaluation in the scoring key. None of this shows that most research is evaluation research. In particular, even process research is not all evaluation research. That interpretation of data can be described as evaluation of results does not show that the interpretations (and the explanations) are about the *merit* of a teaching instrument. They may, for example, be about the temporal duration of various elements of the instrument, etc. Such points are obvious enough, but a good deal of the comment pro and con evaluation research betokens considerable lack of clarity about its boundaries.

5. EVALUATION VERSUS ESTIMATION OF GOAL ACHIEVEMENT

One of the reactions to the threat of evaluation, or perhaps to the use of over-crude evaluative procedures, was the extreme relativization of evaluation research. The slogan became: How well does the course achieve its goals? instead of How good is the course? but it is obvious that if the goals aren't worth achieving then it is uninteresting how well they are achieved. The success of this kind of relativism in the evaluation field rests entirely upon the premise that judgments of goals are subjective value judgments not open to rational argument. No doubt they often are; but this in no way indicates that the field is one in which objectivity is impossible. An American History curriculum, K-14, which consisted in the memorization of names and dates would be absurd—it could not possibly be said to be a good curriculum, no matter how well it attained its goals. Nor could one which led to absolutely no recall of names or chronology. A "Modern Math" curriculum for general use which produced high school graduates largely incapable of reliable addition and multiplication would be (and possibly is) simply a disgrace, no matter what else it conveyed. This kind of value judgment about goals is not beyond debate, but *good* arguments to the contrary have not been forthcoming so far. These are value judgments with excellent backing. Nor is their defensibility due to their lack of specificity. Much more precise ones can be given just as excellent backing; a physics curriculum which does not discuss the kinetic theory at any stage would be deficient, no matter how well it achieved whatever goals it had. And so on.

Thus evaluation proper must include, as an equal partner with the measuring of performance against goals, procedures for the evaluation of the goals. That is, if it is to have any reference to goals at all. In the next two sections we will discuss procedures of evaluation that involve reference to goals and procedures which attempt to short-circuit such reference. First it should be pointed out that it is one thing to maintain that judgment of goals is part of evaluation, i.e., that we cannot just accept anyone's goals, and quite another to maintain that these goals should be the same for every school, for every school district, for every teacher, for every level, etc. It is entirely appropriate that a school with primarily vocational responsibilities should have somewhat different goals from those of a school producing 95 percent college-bound graduates. It just does not follow from this that the people who give the course or run the school or design the curriculum can be regarded as in any way immune from criticism in setting up their goals. A great deal of the energy behind the current attempts to reform the school curriculum springs straight out of the belief that the goals have been fundamentally wrong, that life-adjustment has been grossly overweighted, etc. To swing in the opposite direction is all too easy, and in no way preferable.

The process of relativization, however, has not only led to overtolerance for over-restrictive goals, but has also led to incompetent evaluation of the extent to which these are achieved. Whatever one's views about evaluation, it is easy enough to demonstrate that there are very few professionally competent evaluators in the country today. The United States Office of Education's plans for Research and Development centers, relatively modest in terms of the need, will certainly be unfulfillable because of the staffing problem as far as their evaluation commitments are concerned. The heavily financed curriculum projects already in existence are themselves badly understaffed on the evaluation side, even on the most conservative view of its role. The staff are themselves often well aware of their limitations, and in-service training projects for them are badly needed. The very idea that every school system, or every teacher, can today be regarded as capable of meaningful evaluation of his own performance is as absurd as the view that every psychotherapist today is capable of evaluating his work with his own patients. Trivially, they can learn something very important from carefully studying their own work; indeed they can identify some good and bad features about it. But if they or someone else need to know the answers to the important questions, whether process or outcome, they need skills and resources which are conspicuous by their rarity even at the *national* level.

6. "INTRINSIC" EVALUATION VERSUS "PAY-OFF" EVALUATION

Two basically different approaches to the evaluation of a teaching instrument appear possible, and are often contrasted in the literature. If you want to evaluate a tool, say an axe, you might study the design of the bit, the weight distribution, the steel alloy used, the grade of hickory in the handle, etc., or you might just study the kind and speed of the cuts it makes in the hands of a good axeman. (In either case, the evaluation may be either summative or formative, for these are roles of evaluation, not procedures for doing evaluation.)

The first approach involves an appraisal of the instrument itself; in the analog this would involve evaluation of the content, goals, grading procedures, teacher attitude, etc. We shall call this kind of approach intrinsic evaluation. The criteria are usually not operationally formulated, and they refer to the instrument itself. The second approach proceeds via an examination of the effects of the teaching instrument on the pupil, and these alone, and it usually specifies these rather operationally. It involves an appraisal of the differences between pre- and post-tests, between experimental group tests and control group tests, etc., on a number of criterial parameters. We can call this pay-off evaluation. Defenders of the second procedure would support their approach by arguing that all that really counts are the effects of the course on the pupils, appeal to the evaluation of goals and content being defensible only insofar as evaluations of these really correlate with pay-off evaluations. Since these correlations are largely a priori in our present state of knowledge, they argue, the intrinsic approach is too much an arm-chair affair. The intrinsic evaluator is likely to counter by talking about important values that do not show up in the outcome study to which the pay-off man restricts himself, due to the deficiencies of present test instruments and scoring procedures: he is likely to exemplify this claim by reference to qualities of a curriculum such as elegance, modernity, structure, integrity, readiness considerations, etc., which can best be judged by looking at the materials directly.

The possibility obviously emerges that an evaluation involving some weighting of intrinsic criteria and some of pay-off criteria might be a worthwhile compromise. There are certain kinds of evaluation situation where this will be so, but before any assessment of the correct relative weighting is possible it is necessary to look a little further into the nature of the two pure alternatives.

It was maintained in the preceding section that evaluation in terms of goal achievement is typically a very poor substitute for good summative evaluation, since it merely relativizes the problem. If we are going to evaluate in a way that brings in goals at all, then we shall typically have some obligation to evaluate the goals. The trouble with "intrinsic" evaluation is that it brings in what might be called intermediate goals or criteria, and hence automatically raises the question of the value of these criteria, presumably by reference to the pay-off criteria. One of the charms of the pay-off type of evaluation is the lack of charm, indeed the messiness, of a thorough intrinsic evaluation.

A major difficulty with evaluation involving intermediate goals, which is the key feature of an "intrinsic" approach, lies in the *formulation* of the goals. In the first place the verbally espoused goals of a curriculum maker are often not the implicit goals of his curriculum. Moreover, it is not always the case that this kind of error should be corrected in favor of the espoused goals by revising the curriculum or in favor of the implicit goals by revising the espoused goals. How do we decide which should receive precedence? Even if we were able to decide this, there is the perennial headache of translating the description of the goals that we get from the curriculum maker or the curriculum analyst into testable terms. Many a slip occurs between that lip and the cup.

In addition to this, there is the problem already mentioned, that putting pressure on a writer to formulate his goals, to keep to them, and to express them in testable terms may enormously alter his product in ways that are certainly not always desirable. Perhaps the best way of handling this third problem is to give prospective curriculum builders an intensive short course in evaluation techniques and problems prior to their commencing work. Such a course would be topic-neutral, and would thereby avoid the problems of criticism of one's own "baby." Interaction with a professional evaluator can then be postponed substantially and should also be less anxiety-provoking. Short courses of the kind mentioned should surely be available for subsidized attendance every summer at one or two centers in the country. Ignoring any further consideration of the problem of in-group harmony, and this proposal for improving formative evaluation, we can turn to the practical problem of evaluation.

7. PRACTICAL SUGGESTIONS FOR MEDIATED EVALUATION

Any curriculum project has some kind of general objectives at the very beginning. Even if these are only put in terms of producing a more interesting or more up-to-date treatment, there must be some kind of grounds for dissatisfaction with the present curriculum if the project is to be a worthwhile activity. Usually something rather more specific emerges in the course of planning discussions. For example, the idea of a three-track approach, aimed at various kinds of teacher or student interest, may emerge out of a rather explicit discussion of the aims of a project, when it becomes clear that three equally defensible aims can be formulated which will lead to incompatible requirements for the curriculum. Or, which amounts to the same, the same aim—in a very general sense—can be served in three equally defensible ways. These "ways" then become intermediate goals to be served by the curriculum. The mere fact that these aims can be seen as incompatible makes clear that they must have fairly substantial content. Another typical content presupposition refers to coverage; it is recognized from the beginning that at least certain topics should be covered, or if they are not then there must be some compensatory coverage of other topics. Typically, a project involves at least some of these abstractly formulated goals, and we shall call such studies "mediated." This is not quite the same as a pure intrinsic evaluation, because it may involve *some* pay-off criteria.

At this early stage of discussing the curriculum a member or members of the project team should be appointed to the task of goal-formulation. Many of the objections to this kind of activity stem from reactions to over-rigid requirements for the way in which goals can be formulated at this stage. Any kind of goal on which the group agrees, however abstractly or specifically formulated, even goals which it agrees should be considered as a possibility in the developing stage, should be listed at this point. None of them should be regarded as absolute commitments in any way—simply as reminders. It is not possible to overlook the unfortunate examples of projects in which the creative urge has outdistanced reality restraints; it has to be faced from the beginning that too gross a divergence from a certain minimum coverage is going to make the problem of adoption insuperable. If adoption is a goal, it should be listed along with the motivational and cognitive ones. Having market-type goals such as substantial adoption on the list is in no way inappropriate: one can hardly reform education with curricula that never reach the classroom. But one may think it desirable at an early stage (if it is possible) to translate such goals into constraints on content, e.g., on coverage, vocabulary, and attitudes towards society's sacred cows, etc.

As the project develops, three types of activities centering around the formulation of goals should be distinguished and encouraged. In the first place the goals as so far formulated should be regularly reexamined and modified in the light of divergences from them that have arisen during the developmental activities, where it is felt that these changes have led to other, more valuable goals. Even if no modification seems appropriate, the reexamination serves the useful purpose of reminding the writers of overall goals.

Secondly, work should be begun on the construction of a test-question pool. Progress tests will be given, and the items in these can be thrown into this pool. The construction of this pool is the construction of the operational version of the goals. It should therefore be scrutinized at the same time as reexamination of the more abstractly formulated goals occurs. Even though the project is only at the stage of finishing the first unit of a projected ten-unit curriculum, it is entirely appropriate to be formulating questions of the kind that it is proposed to include in the final examination on the final unit or, for that matter, in a follow-up quiz a year later. It is a commonplace that in the light of formulating such questions, the conception of the goals of the course will be altered. It is undesirable to devote a large proportion of the time to this activity, but it is typically not "undue influence" to encourage thinking about course goals in terms of "What kind of question would tap this learning achievement or motivation change in the final examination or in a follow-up test?" At times the answer to this will rightly be "None at all!" because not all values in a course manifest themselves in the final or later examinations. But where they do *not* thereby manifest themselves, some indication should be given of the time and manner in which they might be expected to be detectable; as in career choices, adult attitudes, etc.

The third activity that should commence at an intermediate stage in curriculum development is that of getting some external judgments as to the cohesiveness of the alleged goals, the actual content, and the test question pool. Without this, the validity of the tests and/or the utility of the curriculum will suffer, possibly fatally. There is no need at all for the individual judge at this task to be a professional evaluator; indeed professional evaluators are frequently extremely bad at this. A good logician, a historian of science, a professional in the subject-matter field, an educational psychologist, or a curriculum expert are possible resource categories. The necessary skill, a very striking one when located, is not co-extensive with any standard professional requirement; we might call it "consistency analysis." This is an area where appointments should not be made without trial periods. It is worth considering whether the activities of this individual, at least in a trial period, may be best conducted without face-to-face confrontation with the project team. A brief written report may be adequate to indicate the extent of possible useful information from this source at this stage. But at some stage, and the earlier the better, this kind of activity is essential if gross divergences between (a) espoused, (b) implicit, and (c) tested-for goals are to be avoided. Not only can a good consistency analyst prevent sidetracking of the project by runaway creative fervor, misconceptions of its actual achievement, etc., but he can provide a valuable stimulus to new lines of development. He must be alert for deficiencies in the item-pool as well as super-fluities, for omissions in the general list of goals as well as irrelevancies. Ultimately, the justification of psychotherapy does not lie in the fact that the therapist *felt* he was doing the patient some good, but in the fact that he was; and the same applies to curricular research.

If the above procedure is followed throughout the development of a curriculum, we will end up with an oversize question pool of which one should be prepared to say that any significant desired outcome of the course will show up on the answers to these questions and that what does show up will (normally) only come from the course. Possession of this pool has various important advantages. In the first and second place, it is an operational encapsulation of the goals of the course (if the various cross-checks on its construction have been adequate) which can be used (i) to give the students an idea of what is expected of them as well as (ii) to provide a pool from which the final examinations can be constructed. In the third place it can be used by the curriculum-developer to get an extremely detailed picture of his own success (and the success of the cross-checks on pool construction) by administering a different random sample of questions from this pool to each student in a formative evaluation study, instead of administering a given random sample to every student as justice perhaps requires in a final examination.[4]

What has been described is the bare bones of an adequate mediated evaluation. We have made some reference to content characteristics as one of the types of goal, because curriculum groups frequently argue that one of the merits of their output is its superiority as a representation of contemporary advanced thinking about the subject. The natural way to test this is to have the course read through by some highly qualified experts in the field. It is obvious that special difficulties arise over this procedure. For the most that we can learn from it is that the course does not contain any gross distortions of the best contemporary views, or gross deficiencies with respect to them. There remains the question, as the pay-off evaluator would be the first to point out, of the extent to which the material is being communicated. Even a course with gross oversimplifications, professionally repugnant though it may be to the academic expert, may be getting across a better idea of the truth about its subject than a highbrow competitor. The real advantage of the preceding methodology is to provide a means for jumping the gap between intrinsic and pay-off evaluation, between mere measures of goal-achievement and complete evaluation.

A number of further refinements on the above outline are extremely desirable, and necessary in any serious study. They center around the role of the consistency analysis, and they are crucial for formative evaluation studies, rather than summative, since they help diagnose the cause of poor results. Essentially, we need to know about the success of three connected matching problems: first, the match between goals and course content; second, the match between goals and examination content; third, the match between course content and examination content. Technically we only need to determine two of these in order to be able to evaluate the third; but in fact there are great advantages in attempting to get an estimate of each independently, in order to reduce the error range. We have talked as if one person or group might make each of these matching estimates. It is clearly most desirable that they should all be done independently, and in fact duplicated by independent workers. Only in this way are we likely to be able to track down the real source of disappointing results. Even the P.S.S.C. study, which has been as thoroughly tested as most recent curriculum projects, has nowhere approached the desirable level of analysis indicated here.

In general, of course, the most difficult problem in tests and measurement theory is the problem of construct validity, and the present problem is essentially an exercise in construct validity. The problem can be ignored only by someone who is prepared to accept immediately the consequence that their supposed goals cannot be regarded as met by the course, or that their examinations do not test what the course teaches, or that the examinations do not test the values/materials that are supposed to be imparted by the course. There are, in practice, many ways in which one can implement the need for the comparisons here described; the use of Q-sorts and R-sorts, matching the projective tests for the analysis, etc. In one way or another the job has to be done, if we are going to do a mediated evaluation at all, i.e., if we are going to bring in goals described in any way except by simply giving the questions to be asked on the final examination.

8. THE POSSIBILITY OF PURE PAY-OFF EVALUATION

The operationalist in this area, the "pay-off" evaluator, watches the developing intricacies of the above kind of experimental design with scorn, for he believes that the whole idea of bringing in goal- or content-assessment is not only an irrelevant but also an extremely unreliable procedure for doing the job of course evaluation. In his view it isn't very important to examine what a teacher says he is doing, or what the students say he is doing (or they are learning), or even what the teacher says in class and the students read in the texts; the only important datum is what the student says (does, believes, etc.) at the end of the course that he wouldn't have said at the beginning (or, to be more precise, would not have said at the end if he had not taken this course). In short, says the hardheaded one, let's just see what the course does, and let's not bother with the question of whether it had good intentions.

But the operationalist has difficulties of his own. He cannot avoid the construct validity issue entirely, that is, he cannot avoid the enormous difficulties involved in correctly describing *at a useful level of generality* what the student has learned. It is easy enough to give the exact results of the testing in terms of the percentage of the students who gave certain answers to each specific question; but what we need to know is whether we can say, in the light of their answers, that they have a *better* understanding of the elements of astronomy, or the chemical-bond approach to chemistry, or the ecological approach to biology. And it is a long way from data about answers to specific questions, to that kind of conclusion. It is not necessary for the route to lie through a discussion of abstract, intermediate goals—the operationalist is quite right about this. But *if* it does not lie through a discussion of goals, then we shall not have available the data that we need (a) to distinguish between importantly different explanations of success of failure, (b) to give reasons for using the new text or curriculum to those whose explicit aim *is* the provision of better understanding of the chemical-bond approach. And the latter really *is* a responsibility of the evaluator. For an example of (a), if we attempt a pure pay-off approach to evaluating the curriculum, and discover that the material retained and/or regurgitated by the student is regarded as grossly inadequate by the subject-matter specialists, we have no idea whether this is due to an inadequacy in the intentions of the curriculum makers, or to imperfections in their curriculum with respect to these goals, or to deficiencies in their examinations with respect to either of the preceding. And thus we cannot institute a remedial program—our only recourse is to start all over. The pay-off approach can be very costly.

To illustrate (b): Suppose that we try a pure pay-off approach and have the students' performance at the end of the course, and only this, rated by an external judge. Who do we pick for a judge? The answer to that question appears to depend on our commitment on our own part to certain intermediate goals which we might as well have acknowledged explicitly. The evaluator will have to relate the students' performance to *some* abstract criterion, whether it is his conception of an adequate professional comprehension, or what he thinks it is reasonable to expect a tenth-grader to understand, or what somebody should understand who will not continue to college, etc. The operationalist is right in saying that we can dispense with any discussion of goals and still discover exactly what students have learned, and right to believe that the latter is the most important variable; but he is mistaken if he supposed that we can in general give the kind of description of what is learned that is valuable for our purposes, or give a justification for the curriculum without any reference to abstract goals. At some stage, someone is going to have to decide what performances count as adequate comprehension for students at a particular level, for a particular subject, and then apply this decision to the data about the students' subsequent behavior, in order to come up with the overall evaluation. So the operationalism of pay-off evaluation is somewhat superficial. At this stage of the debate between the supporter of pure pay-off and that of mediated evaluation, the latter would seem to be having the best of it.

But the issue is not so one-sided; the operationalist is performing an invaluable service in reminding us of the potential irresponsibility of producing "elegant," "up-to-date," "rigorous" curricula if these qualities are not coming through to the students. We can take them on faith insofar as they are recognized as being the frosting on the cake, but we can't take the food-value of the cake on faith. The only real alternative which the operationalist position leads to is the use of an academic evaluator who is asked to look, not at the curriculum materials nor the test-item pool, but at the exact performance of the class on each question, and from this directly assess the adequacy of the course to the subject as he sees it. Of course, we still suffer with respect to diagnosing the cause of deficiencies and hence this is poor formative methodology; but we can simplify summative evaluation by this device.

So we must add to our comprehensive design a thorough analysis of the *results* of the students' tests, and not only of the course and examination content. It is not adequate to go to great trouble setting up and cross-analyzing the goals, tests, and content of a curriculum and then attempt to use a percentage-of-possible-maximum-points figure as the indication of goal achievement (unless the figure happens to be pretty close to 100 percent or 0 percent). This kind of gross approach is no longer acceptable as evaluation. The performance of the students on the final tests, as upon the tests at intermediate stages, must be analyzed in order to determine the exact locations of shortcomings of comprehension, shortages of essential facts, lack of practice in basic skills, etc. Percentages are not very important. It is the *nature* of the mistakes that is important in evaluating the curriculum, and in rewriting it. The technique of the large question pool provides us with an extremely refined instrument for locating deficiencies in the curriculum. But this instrument can only be exploited fully if evaluation of the results is itself handled in a refined way, with the same use of independent judges, hypothesis formation and testing about the nature of the mistakes, longitudinal analysis of same-student variations, etc. It should be clear that the task of proper evaluation of curriculum materials is an enormous one. The use of essay type questions, the development and use of novel instruments, the use of reports by laboratory-work supervisors, the colligation of all this material into specially developed rating schemata, all of this is expensive and time-consuming. It is not more time-consuming that good R & D work in engineering, however. In a later section some comment will be made on the consequences of this conception of the scale of evaluation activities. At this point, however, it becomes necessary to look into a further and final divergence of approaches.

9. COMPARATIVE VERSUS NONCOMPARATIVE EVALUATION

The result of attempts to evaluate recent new curricula has been remarkably uniform; comparing students taking the old curriculum with students taking the new one, it usually appears that students using the new curriculum do rather better on the examinations designed for that curriculum and rather worse on those designed for the old curriculum, while students using the old curriculum perform in the opposite way. Certainly, there is a remarkable absence of striking improvements on the same criteria (with some exceptions, of which the most notable is the performance of students in studies of good programmed texts). Initially, one's tendency is to feel that the mountain has labored and brought forth a mouse—and that it is a positive mouse and not a negative one entirely depends upon the evaluation of the criteria, i.e., (mainly) tests used. A legitimate reaction is to look very seriously into the question of whether one should not weight the judged merit of content and goals by subject-matter experts a great deal more heavily than small differences in level of performance on unassessed criteria. If we do this, then relatively minor improvements in performance, on the right goals, become very valuable, and in these terms the new curriculum looks considerably better. Whether this alteration of weights can really be justified is a matter that needs very serious investigation; it requires a rather careful analysis of the real importance to the understanding and use of contemporary physics, as it is seen by, e.g., physicists, of the missing elements in the old curriculum. It is all too tempting to feel that the reweighting must be correct because one is so thoroughly convinced that the new course is better.

Another legitimate reaction is to wonder whether the examinations are really doing a good job testing the depth of understanding of the people trained on the new curriculum. Here the use of the oversize question pool becomes extremely important. Cronbach speaks of a 700-item pool (without flinching!) and this is surely the order of magnitude that makes sense in terms of a serious evaluation of a one- or two-year curriculum. Again, it is going to be tempting to put items into the pool that reflect mere differences of terminology in the new course, for example. Of course if the pool consists mainly of questions of that kind, the new-curriculum students will do much better. But their superiority will be almost entirely illusory. Cronbach warns us against this risk of course-dependent terminology, although he goes too far in segregating understanding from terminology (this point is taken up below). So here, too, we must be certain to use external evaluators in the construction or assessment of the question pool.

Illegitimate reactions run from the charming suggestion that such results simply demonstrate the weaknesses of evaluation techniques, to a more interesting suggestion implicit in Cronbach's paper. He says:

Since group comparisons give equivocal results, I believe that a formal study should be designed primarily to determine the post-course performance of a well-described group, with respect to many important objectives and side-effects. [5]

Cronbach is apparently about to suggest a way in which we can avoid comparison, not with goals or objectives, but with another group, supposedly matched on relevant variables. What is this noncomparative alternative procedure for evaluation? He continues:

> Ours is a problem like that of the engineer examining a new automobile. He can set himself the task of defining its performance characteristics and its dependability. It would be merely distracting to put his question in the form: 'Is this car better or worse than the competing brand?'

It is perfectly true that the automobile engineer *might* only just be interested in the question of the performance and dependability of the new automobile. But no automobile engineer ever has had this pure interest, and no automobile engineer ever will have it. Objectives do not become "important" except in a context of practical choice. Unrealistic objectives, for example, are not important. The very measures of the performance and dependability of an automobile and our interest in them spring *entirely* from knowledge of what has and has not so far proved possible, or possible within a certain price-class, or possible with certain interior space, or with a certain overall weight, etc. The use of calibrated instruments is not an alternative to, but only a mediated way of, doing comparative studies. The same applies in the field of curriculum development. We already have curricula aimed at almost every subject known to man, and there isn't any real interest in producing curricula for curricula's sake; to the extent that there is, there isn't any interest in evaluating them. We are interested in curricula because they may prove to be better than what we now have, in some important way. We may assign someone the task of rating a curriculum on certain variables, without asking them simultaneously to look up the performance of other curricula on these variables. But when we come to *evaluate* the curriculum, as opposed to merely describing its performance, then we inevitably confront the question of its superiority or inferiority to the competition. To say it's a "valuable contribution," a "desirable" or "useful" course, even to say—in the usual context—that it's very good, is to imply relative merit. Indeed the very scales we use to measure its performance are often percentile scales or others with a built-in comparison.

There are even important reasons for putting the question in its comparative form immediately. Comparative evaluations are often very much easier than noncomparative evaluations, because we can often use tests which yield differences instead of having to find an absolute scale and then eventually compare the absolute scores. If we are discussing chess-teaching courses, for example, we might match two groups for background variables, and then let them play each other off in a round-robin tournament. Attempting to devise a measure of skill of an absolute kind would be a nightmare, but we might easily get consistent and significant differences from this kind of comparative evaluation. Cronbach is not making the "pure pay-off" mistake of thinking that one can avoid all reference to general goals; but he is proposing an approach which underestimates the implicit comparative element in any field of social engineering including automobile assessment and curriculum evaluation, just as the payoff approach underestimates the implicit appeal to abstract intermediate qualities.

Cronbach continues in this paragraph with a line of thought about which there can be no disagreement at all; he points out that in any cases of comparisons between importantly different teaching instruments, no real understanding of the reason for a difference in performance is gained from the discovery that one of them *is* notably superior to the other: "No one knows which of the ingredients is responsible for the advantages." But understanding is not our *only* goal in evaluation. We are also interested in questions of support, encouragement, adoption, reward, refinement, etc. And these extremely important questions can be given a useful though in some cases not a complete answer by the mere discovery of superiority. It will be recalled that in an earlier section we argued that the pure pay-off position suffers by comparison with the supporter of mediated evaluation in that his results will not include the data we need in order to locate sources of difficulty, etc. Here Cronbach is arguing that his noncomparative approach will be more likely to give us the data we need for future improvement. But this is not in any way an advantage of the noncomparative method as such. It is simply an advantage of methods in which more variables are examined in more detail. If we want to pin down the exact reasons for differences between programs, it is quite true that "small-scale, well-controlled studies can profitably be used to compare alternative versions of the same course" whereas the large-scale overall comparison will not be so valuable. But that in no way eliminates the need for comparative studies at some point in our evaluation procedures. In short, his argument is simply that in order to get *explanations,* one needs more control groups, and possibly more short-run studies, than one needs for summative *evaluation.* This is incontestible; but it does not show that for the purposes of overall evaluation we can or should avoid overall comparison.

One might put the point in terms of the following analogy: in the history of automobile engine design there have been a number of occasions when a designer has turned out an engine that was quite inexplicably superior to the competition—the Kettering GM V8, the Coventry Climax and the Weslake Ford conversions are well-known examples. Perhaps thirty variables are significantly changed in the design of any new engine and for a long time after these had been in production nobody, including the designer, knew which of them had been mainly responsible for the improvement. But the decision to go into production, the decision to put the further research into the engine that led to finding out what made it great, indeed the beginning of a new era in engine design, required *only the comparative evaluation.* You set a great team to work and you hope they are going to strike gold; but then you assay the ore before you start the big capital expenditure involved in finding out the configuration of the lode and mining. This is the way we have to work in any field where there are too many variables and too little time.

10. PRACTICAL PROCEDURES FOR CONTROL-GROUP EVALUATION

It is a major theme of Cronbach's that control group comparisons in the curriculum game are not really very suitable. We have just seen how his attempt to provide a positive alternative does not develop into a realistic answer in the context of typical evaluation enquiries. It is therefore appropriate for us to attempt to meet some of the objections that he raises to the control group method since we are recommending that this be left in possession of the field.

The suggestion that gross comparisons yield only small differences must first be met, as indicated above (and as Cronbach recommends elsewhere), by increasing the power of the microscope—that is, by increasing the type and number of items that are being tested, increasing the size of the group in order to get more reliability into differences that do appear, and developing new and more appropriate tests where the present ones seem to be the weakness. And where we pin down a beneficial factor, we then attempt to rewrite with more emphasis on it, to magnify the gain. But once all this has been said, the fact remains that it is probably the case that we shall often have to proceed in terms of rather small differences; that producing large differences will usually require a multiple-push approach, one that attacks not only the curriculum but the student-grouping procedures, the teacher presentation, the classroom time allocation, seeking above all to develop positive feedback via the long-term effects that improvements in every subject in the school curriculum will eventually produce for us—a general increase in the level of interest and preparedness. This is not too depressing a prospect, and it is exactly paralleled in that other field in which we attempt to change human behavior by applying pressure on the subjects for a few hours a week over a period of one or several years—the field of psychotherapy. We are perhaps too used to the discovery of miracle drugs or technological breakthroughs in the aerospace field to recognize the atypicality of such (apparently) "instant progress." Even in the automobile engineering field, to stay with Cronbach's example, it is a well-known theorem that developing a good established design yields better results than introducing a promising but radically new design in about twice as many cases as engineers under forty are willing to believe. What one may reasonably expect as the reward for work is *not* great leaps and bounds, but slow and steady improvement. And of course we shall sometimes go down dead ends. Cronbach says that "formally designed experiments pitting one course against another are rarely definitive enough to justify their cost" but he does not allow sufficiently for the fact that the lack of definite results is often just the kind of knowledge that we need. If we have really satisfied ourselves that we are using good tests of the main criterion variable (and we surely can manage that, with care) then to discover parity of performance *is* to have discovered something extremely informative. "No difference" is not "no knowledge."

Of course, we cannot conclude from a null result that all the techniques involved in a new curriculum are worthless improvements. We must go on to make the micro-studies that will enable us to see whether any one of them is worthwhile. But we have discovered something very significant. Doing the gross comparative study is going to cost the same whatever kind of results we get, and we have to do it sooner or later. Of course it is absurd to stop after discovering an insignificant difference; we must continue in the direction of further analytical research, of the kind Cronbach enthusiastically recommends. The impact of his article is to suggest the unimportance of the control group study, whereas the case can only be made for its inadequacy as a *total* approach to *the whole of* curriculum research.[6] We shall here try to provide some practical suggestions for experimental designs that will yield more than a gross comparative evaluation.

A significant part of the reason for Cronbach's despair over comparative studies lies in his recognition that we are unable to arrange for double-blind conditions. "In an educational experiment it is difficult to keep people unaware that they are an experimental group. And it is quite impossible to neutralize the biases of the teacher as those of the doctor are neutralized in the double-blind design. It is thus never certain whether any observed advantage is attributable to the educational innovation as such, or to the greater energy that teachers and students put forth when a method is fresh and 'experimental.'" (p. 237). But Cronbach despairs too quickly. The analogy in the medical field is not with drug studies, where we are fortunate enough to be able to achieve double-blind conditions, but with psychotherapy studies where the therapist is obviously endowed with enthusiasm for his treatment, and the patient cannot be kept in ignorance of whether he is getting some kind of treatment. If Cronbach's reasoning is correct, it would not be possible to design an adequate psychotherapy outcome study. But it *is* possible to design such a study, and the way to do it—as far as this point goes[7]—is to use more than one comparison group. If we use only one control group, we cannot tell whether it's the enthusiasm or the experimental technique that explains a difference. But if we use several experimental groups, we can estimate the size of the enthusiasm effect. We make comparisons between a number of therapy groups, in each of which the therapist is enthusiastic, but in each of which the method of therapy is radically different. As far as possible, one should employ forms of therapy in which directly incompatible procedures are adopted, and as far as possible match the patients allocated to each type (close matching is not important). There are a number of therapies on the market which meet the first condition in several dimensions, and it is easy enough to develop pseudo-therapies which would be promising enough to be enthusiasm-generating for some practitioners (e.g., newly graduated internists inducted into the experimental program for a short period). The method of differences plus the method of concomitant variations (analysis of covariance) will then assist us in drawing conclusions about whether enthusiasm is the (or a) major factor in therapeutic success, even though double-blind conditions are unobtainable. Nor is this the only kind of design which can do this; other approaches are available (one more is discussed below), and ingenious experimenters will doubtless think of still more, to enable us to handle this kind of research problem. There is nothing indispensable about the double-blind study.

It is true that the curriculum field is slightly more difficult than the psychotherapy field, because it is harder to meet the condition of excluding common elements from the several comparison groups. Although the average intelligent patient will accept almost any nonsense as a form of therapy, thanks to the witchdoctor tradition, need to be healed, etc., it is not equally easy to convince students and teachers that they are receiving and giving instruction in geometry unless what is going on really is a kind of geometry that makes some sense. And if it is, then interpretation of one of the possible outcomes is ambiguous, i.e., if several groups do about as well, it may be *either* because enthusiasm does the trick, or because the common content is efficacious. However, comparative evaluation is still well worthwhile, because if we find a very marked *difference* between the groups, when enthusiasm on the part of the teachers and students occurs in both cases, we may be reasonably sure that the difference is due to the curriculum content. And it is surely possible to vary presentation sequence, methods, difficulty, example, etc., enough so that indistinguishable results are improbable.

Now it is not particularly difficult to arrange for the enthusiasm matching. Corresponding to the cut-rate "new therapy" comparison groups, where the therapy procedures are brainstormed up in a day or two of wild free-associating by the experimenters assisted by a lot of beer and some guilt-ridden eclectic therapists, we set up some cut-rate "new curricula" in the following way. First, we get two bright graduate students or instructors in (let us suppose) economics, give them a vocabulary list for the tenth grade and pay them $500 a chapter for a translation of Samuelson's text into tenth-grade language, encouraging them to use their originality in introducing the new ideas. They could probably handle the whole text in a summer and so for a few thousand dollars, including costs of reproducing pilot materials, we have something we could set up against one of the fancier economics curricula, based on a great deal of high-priced help and laborious field-testing. Then we find a couple of really bright college juniors, majoring in economics, from different colleges, and give *them* a summer to turn their recent experience at the receiving end of introductory economics courses, and their current direct acquaintance with the problems of concept grasping in the field, into a curriculum outline (filled in as much as possible) of a brief introduction to economics for the tenth grade, not centered around any particular text.

And for a third comparison group we locate some enthusiasts for one of the *current* secondary school texts in "economics" and have them work on a revision of it with the author(s) and in the light of some sampling of their colleagues' reactions to the text in class use.

Preferably using the curriculum makers as teachers (*pace* State Departments of Education) we then turn them loose on loosely matched comparison groups, in school systems geographically well removed from the ones where we are running the tests on the high-priced spread. We might toss in a little incentive payment in the way of a preannounced bonus for these groups if they don't get significantly outscored by the supercurriculum. Now then, if we *still* get a big difference in favor of the supercurriculum, we have good reason for thinking that we have taken care of the enthusiasm variable. Moreover we don't have to pull this stunt with every kind of subject matter, since enthusiasm is presumably reasonably (though definitely not entirely) constant in its effects across subject matter. At any rate, a modest sampling should suffice to check this.

One of the nice things about this kind of comparative study is that even if we get the slightly ambiguous negligible-difference result, which will leave us in doubt as to whether a common enthusiasm is responsible for the result, or whether a roughly comparable job in teaching economics is being done by all the curricula, we get a nice economic bonus. If we can whomp up new curricula on a shoestring which are going to produce pretty good results, so much the better; we can do it often and thereby keep up the supply of enthusiasm-stoked project directors, and increase the chances of hitting on some really new big-jackpot approach from a Newton of curriculum reform.

Moreover, still on a shoestring, we can settle the question of enthusiasm fairly quickly even in the event of a tie between the various curricula, by dumping them into the lap of some *antagonistic* and some *neutral* teachers to use during the next school year or two, while on the other hand arranging for the original curriculum makers to lovingly train a small group of highly selected and innovation-inclined teachers to do the same job. Comparisons between the performance of these three new groups and that of the old ones should enable us to pin down the role of enthusiasm rather precisely, and in addition the no-doubt variable immunity of the various curricula to lack of enthusiasm.

A few obvious elaborations of the above procedures, including an opportunity for the novice curriculum makers to spend a couple of afternoons on field-testing early sections of their new curriculum to give them some "feel" for the speed at which students at this level can grasp new concepts, the use of some care in selecting teachers for their conservatism, allergy, or lethargy, using self-ratings plus peer-ratings plus attitude inventories, would of course be incorporated in an actual study.

The enthusiasm "difficulty" here is simply an example of what we might call *measurement-interference effects* (or coupled-variable phenomena), of which the placebo effect in medicine and the Hawthorne effect in industrial and social psychology are well-known instances. In each case we are interested in finding out the effects of a certain factor, but we cannot introduce the factor into the experimental situation without producing a disturbance which may itself be responsible for the observed changes. In the drug field, the disturbance consists in the act of giving the patient something which he considers to be a drug, an event which does not ordinarily happen to him, and which consequently may produce effects of its own, quite apart from the "intrinsic" effects of the drug. In the Hawthorne effect, the disturbance is the alteration of, e.g., conditions of work, which may suggest to the worker that he is the subject of special study and interest, and *this* may lead to improved output, rather than the physical changes in the environment which are the intended control variables under study.

The cases so far mentioned are all ones where the beliefs of the subjects are the mediating factor between the disturbance and the ambiguous effects. This is characteristic in the field of psychology, but the situation is not essentially different from that occurring in technological research where we face problems such as the absorption of heat by a thermometer which thereby alters the temperature that it is supposedly measuring. That is, some of the effect observed (which is here the eventual length of the mercury column) is due to the fact that in order to get a measurement at all you have to alter what you are trying to measure. The measuring process introduces another physical object into proximity with the measured object, and the instrument itself has a certain heat capacity, a factor in whose influence you are not interested, though in order to find out what you do need to know you eventually have to make an estimate of the magnitude of the measurement-interference effect. The ingenious double-blind design is only appropriate in certain circumstances, and is only one of many ways in which we can compensate for these effects. It therefore seems unduly pessimistic of Cronbach to suppose that the impossibility of a double blind in curriculum work is fatal to comparative evaluation. Indeed, when he comes to discuss follow-up studies, he agrees that comparative work is essential (p. 240). The conclusion seems obligatory that comparative evaluation, mediated or not, is the method of choice for evaluation problems.

11. CRITERIA OF EDUCATIONAL ACHIEVEMENT FOR EVALUATION STUDIES

We may now turn to the problem of specifying in more detail the criteria which should be used in evaluating a teaching instrument. The checklist to follow serves as a useful mnemonic for the goal-formulator and consistency-analyst. We may retain Bloom's (Bloom *et al.*, 1956) convenient trichotomy of cognitive, affective, and motor variables, though we shall often refer to the last two as motivational and physical or nonmental variables, but under the first two of these we shall propose a rather different structure, especially under the knowledge and understanding subdivisions of the cognitive field.

Some preliminary notes follow:

(i) It should be stressed at the beginning that the word "knowledge" *can* be used to cover understanding (or comprehension) and even affective conditions ("knowing how it feels to be completely rejected by one's peer group"), but that it is here used in the sense in which it can be *contrasted* with comprehension and experience or valuation, i.e., in the sense in which we think of it as "mere knowledge." Comprehension or understanding, in terms of this contrast, refers to a psychological state involving knowledge, not of one item, nor of several separate items, but of a field. A field or structure is a set of items related in a systematic way, and knowledge of the field involves knowledge not only of the items but of their relations. Understanding particular items in a field requires knowledge of the relation of the item to other items in the field, i.e., some knowledge of the field. A field is often open-ended in the sense of having potential reference or applicability to an indefinite number of future examples. In this latter case, comprehension involves the capacity to apply to these novel cases the appropriate rule, rubric or concept. A field may be a field of abstract or practical knowledge, of thought or of skills: one may understand the field of patent law, or how to retime two-stroke engines.

(ii) With respect to any field of knowledge we can distinguish between a relatively abstract or *conceptual* description of the parameters (which are to occupy the role of dependent variables in our study) and a *manifestation* description, the latter being the next stage towards the specification of the particular tests to be used, which we may call the *operational* description. It is appropriate to describe the criteria at all three levels, although we finally apply only the third, just as it is appropriate to give the steps of a difficult proof in mathematics, because it shows us the conceptual foundations for adopting the particular final step proposed.

(iii) I have followed the usual practice here in listing positive goals (with the possible exception of the example in 5) but a word of caution is in order. Although most negatively desired effects are the absence of positively desired effects, this is not always true, and more generally we often wish to alter the weighting of a variable when it drops below a certain level. For example, we may not be worried if we get *no* change on socialization with a course that is working well in the cognitive domain, and we may give small credit for *large gains* in this dimension. But if it produces a marked rise in sociopathic behavior (i.e., large losses) we may regard this as a fatal defect in the course. The same applies to a by-product like forgetting or rejection of material in other subject areas. Another example is discussed below.

(iv) A word about originality or "creativity"; this may be manifested in a problem-solving skill, as an artistic skill (which combines motor and perceptual and perhaps verbal skills) and in many other ways. On the whole it seems as mistaken to make it a separate criterion as to make "cleverness" one.

(v) In general, I have tried to reduce the acknowledged overlap among the factors identified in Bloom's analysis, and am prepared to pay a price for this desideratum, if such a price must be paid. There are many reasons for avoiding overlap, of which one of the more important and perhaps less obvious ones is that when the comparative weighting of criteria is undertaken for a given subject, independence greatly simplifies the process, since a straight weighting by individual merit will overweight the hidden loading factors.

(vi) There is still a tendency in the literature to regard factual recall and knowledge of terminology with general disdain. But for many subjects, a very substantial score on that dimension is an absolutely necessary condition for adequate performance. This is not the same as saying that a sufficiently high score on that scale will compensate for lack of understanding, even where we use a single index compounded from the weighted scores: we must taper off the weighting in the upper ranges of the recall scales. There are other subjects, especially mathematics and physics, where knowing how to apply the terminology requires and hence guarantees a very deep understanding and terminology-free tests are just bad tests (cf. Cronbach, p. 245).

11.1 Conceptual Description of Educational Objectives

1. Knowledge, of
   a. Items of specific information including definitions of terms in the field.
   b. Sequences or patterns of items of information including sets of rules, procedures or classifications for handling or evaluating items of information (we are here talking about mere knowledge of the rule or classification and not the capacity to apply it).

2. Comprehension or Understanding, of
   a. Internal relationships in the field,[8] i.e., the way in which some of the knowledge claims are consequences of others and imply yet others, the way in which the terminology applies within the field; in short what might be called understanding of the intrafield syntax of the field or subfield.
   b. Interfield relations, i.e., relations between the knowledge claims in this field and those in other fields; what we might call the interfield syntax.
   c. Application of the field or the rules, procedures, and concepts of the field to appropriate examples, where the field is one that has such applications; this might be called the semantics of the field.

3. Motivation (Attitude/values/affect)
   a. Attitudes toward the course, e.g., acoustics.

b. Attitudes toward the subject, e.g., physics
c. Attitudes toward the field, e.g., science.
d. Attitudes toward material to which the field is relevant, e.g., increased skepticism about usual advertising claims about "high fidelity" from miniature radios (connection with 2c above).
e. Attitudes toward learning, reading, discussing, enquiring in general, etc.
f. Attitudes toward the school.
g. Attitudes toward teaching as a career, teacher status, etc.
h. Attitudes toward (feelings about, etc.) the teacher as a person.
i. Attitude toward classmates, attitude toward society (obvious further sub-headings).
j. Attitude toward self, e.g., increase of realistic self-appraisal (which also involves cognitive domain).

4. Nonmental Abilities
a. Perceptual
b. Psycho-motor.
c. Motor, including, e.g., some sculpting skills.
d. Social skills.

5. Noneducational Variables
There are a number of noneducational goals, usually implicit, which are served by many existing courses and even by new courses, and some of them are even justifiable in special circumstances as, e.g., in a prison. The crudest example is the "keeps 'em out of mischief" view of schooling. Others include the use of the schools to handle unemployment problems, to provide a market for textbook sales. It is realistic to remember that these criteria may be quite important to parents, teachers, publishers, and authors even if not to children.

11.2 Manifestation Dimensions of Criterial Variables

1. Knowledge
In the sense described above, this is evinced by
a. Recital skills.
b. Discrimination skills.
c. Completion skills.
d. Labeling skills.
Note: Where immediate performance changes are not discernible, there may still be some subliminal capacity, manifesting itself in a reduction in re-learning time, i.e., time for future learning to criterion.

2. Comprehension

This is manifested on some of the above types of performance and also on

a. Analyzing skills, including laboratory analysis skills, other than motor, as well as the verbal analytic skills exhibited in criticism, précis, etc.

b. Synthesizing skills.

c. Evaluation skills, including self-appraisal.

d. Problem-solving skills (speed-dependent and speed-independent).

3. Attitude

Manifestations usually involve simultaneous demonstration of some cognitive acquisition. The kinds of instrument involved are questionnaires, projective tests, Q-sorts, experimental choice situations, and normal lifetime choice situations (choice of college major, career, spouse, friends, etc.). Each of the attitudes mentioned is characteristically identifiable on a passive to active dimension (related to the distinctions expounded on in Bloom, but disregarding extent of systematization of value system which can be treated as a (meta-) cognitive skill).

4. The Nonmental Abilities

All are exhibited in performances of various kinds, which again can be either artificially elicited or extracted from life-history. Typical examples are the capacity to speak in an organized way in front of an audience, to criticize a point of view (not previously heard) in an effective way, etc. (This again connects with the ability conceptually described under 2c).

11.3 Follow-Up

The time dimension is a crucial element in the analysis of performance and one that deserves an extensive independent investigation. Retention, recall, depth of understanding, extent of imprinting, can all be tested by reapplications of the tests or observations used to determine the instantaneous peak performance, on the dimensions indicated above. However, some follow-up criteria are not repetitions of earlier tests or observations; eventual choice of career, longevity of marriage, extent of adult social service, career success, are relevant and important variables which require case history investigation. But changes of habits and character are often not separate variables, being simply long-term changes on cognitive and affective scales.

11.4 Secondary Effects

A serious deficiency of previous studies of new curricula has been a failure to sample the teacher population adequately. When perfecting a teaching instrument, we cannot justify generalizing from pilot studies unless not only the students but the teachers are fair samples of the intended population. This need to predict/select favorable classroom performance for the new materials also underlines the importance of studies of measurement-interference effects. Just as generalizing has been based upon inadequate analysis of the teacher sample, so criterion discussions have not paid sufficient attention to teacher benefits. It is quite wrong to evaluate a teaching instrument without any consideration of the effects on the operator as well as on the subjects. In an obvious sense, the operator *is* one of the subjects.

We may distinguish secondary effects (i.e., those on others than the students taking the course) from tertiary effects. Secondary effects are those arising from or because of direct exposure to the material, and it is mainly the teachers and teachers' helpers who are affected in this way. Tertiary effects are those effects on the school or other students brought about by someone who exhibits the primary or secondary effects.

11.41 Effects on the Teacher

A new curriculum may have very desirable effects on updating a teacher's knowledge or pedagogy, with subsequent pay-off in various ways including the better education of other classes at a later stage (a tertiary effect), whether he/she is there using the old curriculum or the new one. Similarly, it may have very bad effects on the teacher, perhaps through induction of fatigue, or through failing to leave her any feeling of status or significant role in the classroom (as did some programmed texts), etc.

It is easy to itemize a number of such considerations, and we really need a minor study of the taxonomy of these secondary effects under each of their several headings. Interestingly, what I have called the interference effects, e.g., those due to enthusiasm, may be of immediate value themselves. Very often the introduction of new curriculum material is tied to teacher in-service training institutes or special in-service training interviews. These of course have effects on the teacher herself with respect to status, self-concept, pay, interests, etc., and indirectly on later students. Many of these effects on the teacher show up in her other activities; at the college level there will normally be some serious reduction of research time resulting from association with an experimental curriculum, and this may have results for promotion expectations in either the positive or the negative direction, depending upon departmental policy. All of these results are effects of the new curriculum, at least for a long time, and in certain circumstances they may be sufficiently important to count rather heavily against other advantages. Involvement with curricula of a highly controversial kind may have such strongly damaging secondary effects for the teacher as to raise questions as to whether it is proper to refer to it as a good curriculum for schools in the social context in which these secondary effects are so bad.

11.42 Effects on Teacher's Colleagues

Tertiary effects are the effects on people other than those directly exposed to the curriculum: once again they may be highly significant. A simple example of a tertiary effect involves other members of the staff who may be called upon to teach less attractive courses, or more courses, or whose load may be reduced for reasons of parity, or who may be stimulated by discussions with the experimental group teachers, etc. In many cases, effects of this kind will vary widely from situation to situation, and such effects may then be less appropriately thought of as effects of the curriculum (although even the primary effects of this, i.e., the effects on the students, will vary widely geographically and temporally) but there will sometimes be constancies in these effects which will require recognition as characteristic effects of this particular teaching instrument. This will of course be noticeable in the case of controversial experimental courses, but it will also be significant where the course bears on problems of school administration, relation of the subject to other subjects, and so on. Good evaluation requires some attempt to identify effects of this kind.

11.43 Effects on Other Students

Another tertiary effect, already referred to in discussing the effect of the curriculum on the teacher, is the effect on other students. Just as a teacher may be improved by exposure to a new curriculum, and this improvement may show up in benefits for students that she has in other classes, or at a later period using the old curriculum, etc., so there may be an effect of the curriculum on students not in the experimental class through the intermediary of *students* who are. Probably more pronounced in a boarding school or small college, the communication between students is still a powerful enough instrument in ordinary circumstances for this to be a significant influence. The students may of course be influenced in other ways; there may be additions to the library as a result of the funds available for the new course that represent values for the other students, etc. All of these are educationally significant effects of the course adoption.

11.44 Effects on Administrators

The school administrators may be affected by new teaching instruments in various ways: their powers of appointment may be curtailed, if the teaching instrument's efficiency will reduce faculty; they may acquire increased prestige (or nuisance) through the use of the school as an experimental laboratory; they may find this leads to more (or less) trouble with the parents or alumni or legislators; the pay-off through more national scholarships may be a value to them, either intrinsically or incidentally to some other end, etc. Again, it is obvious that in certain special cases this variable will be a very important part of the total set that are affected by the new instrument, and evaluation must include some recognition of this possibility. It is not so much the factors common to the use of novel material, but the course-specific effects that particularly require estimation and almost every new science or social studies course has such effects.

11.45 Effects on Parents

Effects on the parents are of course well known, but they tend to be regarded as mainly nuisance-generating effects. On the contrary, many such effects should be regarded as part of the adult education program in which this country is still highly deficient. In some subjects, e.g., Russian, there is unlikely to be a very significant effect, but in the field of problems of democracy, elementary accounting, and literature this may be a most important effect.

11.46 Effects on the School or College

Many of these are covered above, particularly under the heading of effects on the administrator, but there are of course some effects that are more readily classified under this heading, such as improvement in facilities, support, spirit, applicants, integration, etc.

11.47 Effects on the Taxpayer

These are partly considered in the section on costs below, but certain points are worth mentioning. We are using the term taxpayer and not ratepayer here to indicate a reference to the total tax structure, and the most important kinds of effects here are the possibility of very large-scale emulation of a given curriculum reform project, which in toto, especially with evaluation on the scale envisioned here, is likely to add a substantial amount to the overall tax burden. For the unmarried or childless taxpayer, this will be an effect which may with some grounds be considered a social injustice. Insofar as evaluation of a national armament program must be directly tied to questions of fair and unfair tax loads, the same must be applied in any national considerations of very large-scale curriculum reforms.

12. VALUES AND COSTS

12.1 Range of Utility

No evaluation of a teaching instrument can be considered complete without reference to the range of its applicability and the importance of improvement of education in that range. If we are particularly concerned with the underprivileged groups, then it will be a value of considerable importance if our new teaching instrument is especially well adapted for that group. Its utility may not be very highly generalizable, but that may be offset by the special social utility of the effects actually obtained. Similarly, the fact that the instrument is demonstrably usable by teachers with no extra training sharply increases its short-term utility. Indeed it may be so important as to make it one of the goals of instrument development, for short-run high-yield improvements.

12.2 Moral Considerations

Considerations of the kind that are normally referred to as moral have a place in the evaluation of new curricula. If the procedures for grading, or treating students in class (the use of scapegoats, for example), although pedagogically effective, are unjust, then we may have grounds for judging the instrument undesirable which are independent of any directly testable consequences. If one conceives of morality as a system of principles aimed at maximizing long-run social utility, based on an egalitarian axiom, then moral evaluations will usually show up somewhere else on the criteria given above, as primary or secondary effects. But the time lag before they do so may be so long as to make it appropriate for us to introduce this as a separate category. There are a number of other features of teaching instruments to which we react morally; "the dehumanizing influence of teaching machines" is a description often used by critics who are partly affected by moral considerations; whether misguidedly or not is a question that must be faced. Curricula stressing the difference in performance on the standardized intelligence tests of Negro and white children have been attacked as morally undesirable, and the same has been said of textbooks in which the role of the United States in world history has been viewed somewhat critically. Considerations like this will of course show up on a content-mediated approach to evaluation but they deserve a separate entry because the reaction is not to the truth or insight provided by the program, but to some other consequences of providing what may well be truths or insights, namely the consequences involving the welfare of the society as a whole.

12.3 Costs

The costing of curriculum adoption is a rather poorly researched affair. Enthusiasts for new curricula tend to overlook a large number of secondary costs that arise, not only in the experimental situation, but in the event of large-scale adoption. Evaluation, particularly of items for purchase from public funds, should have a strong commitment to examination of the cost situation. Most of the appropriate analysis can be best obtained from an experienced industrial accountant, but it is perhaps worth mentioning here that even when the money has been provided for the salaries of curriculum-makers and field-testers and in-service training institutes there are a number of other costs that are not easily assessed, such as the costs of rearrangements of curriculum, differential loads on other faculty, diminished availability for supervisory chores of the experimental staff (and in the long run, where the instrument requires more of the teacher's time than the one it replaces, this becomes a permanent cost), the "costs" of extra demands on *student time* (presumably at the expense of other courses they might be taking), and of energy drain on the faculty as they acquire the necessary background and skills in the new curriculum, and so on through the list of other indirect effects, many of which have cost considerations attached, whether the cost is in dollars or some other valuable.

13. A MARGINAL KIND OF "EVALUATION"— "EXPLANATORY EVALUATION"

Data relevant to the variables outlined in the preceding section are the basic elements for almost all types of evaluation. But sometimes, as was indicated in the fourth section, evaluation refers to *interpretation* or *explanation*. While not considering this to be a primary or even a fully proper sense, it is clear from the literature that there is some tendency to extend the term in this direction. It seems preferable to distinguish between evaluation and the attempt to discover an explanation of certain kinds of result, even when both are using the same data. Explanation-hunting is sometimes part of process research and sometimes part of other areas in the field of educational research. When we turn to considerations of this kind, data of a quite different variety are called for. We shall, for example, need to have information about specific skills and attitudes of the students who perform in a particular way; we shall call upon the assistance of experts who—or tests which—may be able to demonstrate that the failure of a particular teaching instrument is due to its use of an inappropriately advanced vocabulary, rather than to any lack of comprehensible organization. Evaluation of this kind, however, is and should be secondary to evaluation of the kinds discussed previously, for the same reason and in the same sense that therapy is secondary to diagnosis.

14. CONCLUSIONS

The aim of this paper has been to move one step further in the direction of an adequate methodology of curriculum evaluation. It is clear that taking this step involves considerable complication of the model of an adequate evaluation study by comparison with what has passed under this heading all too frequently in the past. Further analysis of the problem may reveal even greater difficulties that must be sorted out with an attendant increase in complexity. Complex experiments on the scale we have been discussing are very expensive in both time and effort. But it has been an important part of the argument of this paper that no substitutes will do. If we want to know the answers to the questions that matter about new teaching instruments, we have got to do experiments which will yield those answers. The educational profession is suffering from a completely inappropriate conception of the cost scale for educational research. To develop a new automobile engine or a rocket engine is a very, very expensive business despite the extreme constancy in the properties of physical substances. When we are dealing with a teaching instrument such as a new curriculum or classroom procedure, with its extreme dependence upon highly variable operators and recipients, we must expect considerably more expense. The social pay-off is enormously more important, and this society can, in the long run, afford the expense. At the moment the main deficiency is trained evaluation manpower, so that short-term transition to the appropriate scale of investigation is possible only in rare cases. But the long-term transition must be made. We are dealing with something more important and more difficult to evaluate than an engine design, and we are attempting to get by with something like 1 percent of the cost of developing an engine design. The educational profession as a whole has a primary obligation to recognize the difficulty of good curriculum development with its essential concomitant, evaluation, and to begin a unified attack on the problem of financing the kind of improvement that may help us towards the goal of a few million enlightened citizens on the earth's surface, even at the expense of one on the surface of Mars.

NOTES

1. An earlier version of this paper was written and circulated during the author's tenure as director of the Evaluation Project of the Social Science Education Consortium, supported by a developmental grant from the U.S. Office of Education, and later by the Kettering Foundation.

2. In the form of personal comments and correspondence, as well as his well-known article, "Evaluation for Course Improvement," *Teachers' College Record* 64 (No. 8, May 1963) reprinted in R. Heath (ed.), *New Curricula* (New York: Harper & Row, 1964), pp. 231−248. References in this paper are to the latter version.

3. Discussed in more detail by the author in, e.g., "Morality" in *Primary Philosophy* (New York: McGraw-Hill, 1966).

4. See Cronbach, p. 242.

5. This and the succeeding quotation are from p. 238.

6. Yet he does agree with the necessity for making the practical decisions, e.g., between textbooks (p. 232), for which nothing less than a valid comparative study is adequate.

7. Other difficulties are discussed in more detail in "The Experimental Investigation of Psychoanalysis" in S. Hook (ed.) *Psychoanalysis, Scientific Method and Philosophy* (New York: NYU Press, 1959).

8. Typically, "the field" should be construed more widely than "the subject" since we are very interested in transfer from one subject to related ones and rate a course better to the extent it facilitates this. In rating transfer, we can range very far, e.g., from a course on psychology to reactions to commercials showing white-coated men.

23. THE COUNTENANCE OF EDUCATIONAL EVALUATION

Robert E. Stake

President Johnson, President Conant, Mrs. Hull (Sara's teacher) and Mr. Tykociner (the man next door) are quite alike in the faith they have in education. But they have quite different ideas of what education is. The value they put on education does not reveal their way of evaluating education.

Educators differ among themselves as to both the essence and worth of an educational program. The wide range of evaluation purposes and methods allows each to keep his own perspective. Few see their own programs "in the round," partly because of a parochial approach to evaluation. To understand better his own teaching and to contribute more to the science of teaching, each educator should examine the full countenance of evaluation.

Educational evaluation has its formal and informal sides. Informal evaluation is recognized by its dependence on casual observation, implicit goals, intuitive norms, and subjective judgment. Perhaps because these are also characteristic of day-to-day, personal styles of living, informal evaluation results in perspectives which are seldom questioned. Careful study reveals informal evaluation of education to be of variable quality—sometimes penetrating and insightful, sometimes superficial and distorted.

Formal evaluation of education is recognized by its dependence on checklists, structured visitation by peers, controlled comparisons, and standardized testing of students. Some of these techniques have long histories of successful use.

SOURCE. *Teachers College Record* 68 (No. 7, April 1967), pp. 523–40.

Unfortunately, when planning an evaluation, few educators consider even these four. The more common notion is to evaluate informally: to ask the opinion of the instructor, to ponder the logic of the program, or to consider the reputation of the advocates. Seldom do we find a search for relevant research reports or for behavioral data pertinent to the ultimate curricular decisions.

Dissatisfaction with the formal approach is not without cause. Few highly-relevant, readable research studies can be found. The professional journals are not disposed to publish evaluation studies. Behavioral data are costly, and often do not provide the answers. Too many accreditation-type visitation teams lack special training or even experience in evaluation. Many checklists are ambiguous; some focus too much attention on the physical attributes of a school. Psychometric tests have been developed primarily to differentiate among students at the same point in training rather than to assess the effect of instruction on acquisition of skill and understanding. Today's educator may rely on formal evaluation because its answers have seldom been answers to questions *he* is asking.

POTENTIAL CONTRIBUTIONS OF FORMAL EVALUATION

The educator's disdain of formal evaluation is due also to his sensitivity to criticism—and his *is* a critical clientele. It is not uncommon for him to draw before him such curtains as "national norm comparison," "innovation phase," and "academic freedom" to avoid exposure through evaluation. The "politics" of evaluation is an interesting issue in itself, but it is not the issue here. The issue here is the *potential* contribution to education of formal evaluation. Today, educators fail to perceive what formal evaluation could do for them. They should be imploring measurement specialists to develop a methodology that reflects the fullness, the complexity, and the importance of their programs. They are not.

What one finds when he examines formal evaluation activities in education today is too little effort to spell out antecedent conditions and classroom transactions (a few of which visitation teams do record) and too little effort to couple them with the various outcomes (a few of which are portrayed by conventional test scores). Little attempt has been made to measure the match between what an educator intends to do and what he does do. The traditional concern of educational-measurement specialists for reliability of individual-student scores and predictive validity (thoroughly and competently stated in the American Council on Education's 1950 edition of *Educational Measurement*) is a questionable resource. For evaluation of curricula, attention to individual differences among students should give way to attention to the contingencies among background conditions, classroom activities, and scholastic outcomes.

This paper is not about what should be measured or how to measure. It is background for developing an evaluation plan. What and how are decided later.

My orientation here is around educational programs rather than educational products. I presume that the value of a product depends on its program of use. The evaluation of a program includes the evaluation of its materials.

The countenance of educational evaluation appears to be changing. On the pages that follow, I will indicate what the countenance can, and perhaps, should be. My attempt here is to introduce a conceptualization of evaluation oriented to the complex and dynamic nature of education, one which gives proper attention to the diverse purposes and judgments of the practitioner.

Much recent concern about curriculum evaluation is attributable to contemporary large-scale curriculum-innovation activities, but the statements in this paper pertain to traditional and new curricula alike. They pertain, for example, to Title I and Title III projects funded under the Elementary and Secondary Act of 1966. Statements here are relevant to any curriculum, whether oriented to subject-matter content or to student process, and without regard to whether curriculum is general-purpose, remedial, accelerated, compensatory, or special in any other way.

The purposes and procedures of educational evaluation will vary from instance to instance. What is quite appropriate for one school may be less appropriate for another. Standardized achievement tests here but not there. A great concern for expense there but not over there. How do evaluation purposes and procedures vary? What are the basic characteristics of evaluation activities? They are identified in these pages as the evaluation acts, the data sources, the congruence and contingencies, the standards, and the uses of evaluation. The first distinction to be made will be between description and judgment in evaluation.

The countenance of evaluation beheld by the educator is not the same one beheld by the specialist in evaluation. The specialist sees himself as a "describer," one who describes aptitudes and environments and accomplishments. The teacher and school administrator, on the other hand, expect an evaluator to grade something or someone as to merit. Moreover, they expect that he will judge things against external standards, on criteria perhaps little related to the local school's resources and goals.

Neither sees evaluation broadly enough. *Both* description and judgment are essential—in fact, they are the two basic acts of evaluation. Any individual evaluator may attempt to refrain from judging or from collecting the judgments of others. Any individual evaluator may seek only to bring to light the worth of the program. But their evaluations are incomplete. To be fully understood, the educational program must be fully described and fully judged.

TOWARDS FULL DESCRIPTION

The specialist in evaluation seems to be increasing his emphasis on fullness of description. For many years he evaluated primarily by measuring student progress toward academic objectives. These objectives usually were identified with the traditional disciplines, e.g., mathematics, English, and social studies. Achievement tests—standardized or "teacher-made"—were found to be useful in describing the degree to which some curricular objectives are attained by individual students in a particular course. To the early evaluators, and to many others, the countenance of evaluation has been nothing more than the administration and normative interpretation of achievement tests.

In recent years a few evaluators have attempted, in addition, to assess progress of individuals toward certain "inter-disciplinary" and "extracurricular" objectives. In their objectives, emphasis has been given to the integration of behavior within an individual; or to the perception of interrelationships among scholastic disciplines; or to the development of habits, skills, and attitudes which permit the individual to be a craftsman or scholar, in or out of school. For the descriptive evaluation of such outcomes, the Eight-Year Study (Smith and Tyler, 1942) has served as one model. The proposed National Assessment Program may be another—this statement appeared in one interim report (ETS, 1963):

> . . . all committees worked within the following broad definition of 'national assessment.'
> 1. In order to reflect fairly the aims of education in the U.S., the assessment should consider both traditional and modern curricula, and take into account ALL THE ASPIRATIONS schools have for developing attitudes and motivations as well as knowledge and skills . . . [caps added].

In his paper, "Evaluation for Course Improvement," Lee Cronbach urged another step: a most generous inclusion of behavioral-science variables in order to examine the possible causes and effects of quality teaching. He proposed that the main objective for evaluation is to uncover durable relationships—those appropriate for guiding future educational programs. To the traditional description of pupil achievement, we add the description of instruction and the description of relationships between them. Like the instructional researcher, the evaluator—as so defined—seeks generalizations about educational practices. Many curriculum project evaluators are adopting this definition of evaluation.

THE ROLE OF JUDGMENT

Description is one thing, judgment is another. Most evaluation specialists have chosen not to judge. But in his recent *Methodology of Evaluation* Michael Scriven has charged evaluators with responsibility for passing upon the merit of an educational practice. (Note that he has urged the evaluator to do what the educator has expected the evaluator to be doing.) Scriven's position is that there is no evaluation until judgment has been passed, and by his reckoning the evaluator is best qualified to judge.

By being well experienced and by becoming well-informed in the case at hand in matters of research and educational practice the evaluator does become at least partially qualified to judge. But is it wise for him to accept this responsibility? Even now when few evaluators expect to judge, educators are reluctant to initiate a formal evaluation. If evaluators were *more* frequently identified with the passing of judgment, with the discrimination among poorer and better programs, and with the awarding of support and censure, their access to data would probably diminish. Evaluators collaborate with other social scientists and behavioral research workers. Those who do not want to judge deplore the acceptance of such responsibility by their associates. They believe that in the eyes of many practitioners, social science and behavioral research will become more suspect than it already is.

Many evaluators feel that they are not capable of perceiving, as they think a judge should, the unidimensional *value* of alternative programs. They anticipate a dilemma such as Curriculum I resulting in three skills and ten understandings and Curriculum II resulting in four skills and eight understandings. They are reluctant to judge that gaining one skill is worth losing two understandings. And, whether through timidity, disinterest, or as a rational choice, the evaluator usually supports "local option," a community's privilege to set its own standards and to be its own judge of the worth of its educational system. He expects that what is good for one community will not necessarily be good for another community, and he does not trust himself to discern what is best for a briefly-known community.

Scriven reminds them that there are precious few who can judge complex programs, and fewer still who will. Different decisions must be made—P.S.S.C. or Harvard Physics?—and they should not be made on trivial criteria, e.g., mere precedent, mention in the popular press, salesman personality, administrative convenience, or pedagogical myth. Who should judge? The answer comes easily to Scriven partly because he expects little interaction between treatment and learner, i.e., what works best for one learner will work best for others, at least within broad categories. He also expects that where the local good is at odds with the common good, the local good can be shown to be detrimental to the common good, to the end that the doctrine of local option is invalidated. According to Scriven the evaluator must judge.

Whether or not evaluation specialists will accept Scriven's challenge remains to be seen. In any case, it is likely that judgments will become an increasing part of the evaluation report. Evaluators will seek out and record the opinions of persons of special qualification. These opinions, though subjective, can be very useful and can be gathered objectively, independent of the solicitor's opinions. A responsibility for processing judgments is much more acceptable to the evaluation specialist than one for rendering judgments himself.

Taylor and Maguire (1966) have pointed to five groups having important opinions on education: spokesmen for society at large, subject-matter experts, teachers, parents, and the students themselves. Members of these and other groups are judges who should be heard. Superficial polls, letters to the editor, and other incidental judgments are insufficient. An evaluation of a school program should portray the merit and fault perceived by well-identified groups, systematically gathered and processed. Thus, judgment data and description data are both essential to the evaluation of educational programs.

DATA MATRICES

In order to evaluate, an educator will gather together certain data. The data are likely to be from several quite different sources, gathered in several quite different ways. Whether the immediate purpose is description or judgment, three bodies of information should be tapped. In the evaluation report it can be helpful to distinguish between *antecedent, transaction,* and *outcome* data.

An antecedent is any condition existing prior to teaching and learning which may relate to outcomes. The status of a student prior to his lesson, e.g., his aptitude, previous experience, interest, and willingness, is a complex antecedent. The programmed-instruction specialist calls some antecedents "entry behaviors." The state accrediting agency emphasizes the investment of community resources. All of these are examples of the antecedents which an evaluator will describe.

Transactions are the countless encounters of students with teacher, student with student, author with reader, parent with counselor—the succession of engagements which comprise the process of education. Examples are the presentation of a film, a class discussion, the working of a homework problem, an explanation on the margin of a term paper, and the administration of a test. Smith and Meux studied such transactions in detail and have provided an 18-category classification system. One very visible emphasis on a particular class of transactions was the National Defense Education Act support of audio-visual media.

Transactions are dynamic whereas antecedents and outcomes are relatively static. The boundaries between them are not clear, e.g., during a transaction we can identify certain outcomes which are feedback antecedents for subsequent learning. These boundaries do not need to be distinct. The categories should be used to stimulate rather than to subdivide our data collection.

Traditionally, most attention in formal evaluation has been given to outcomes—outcomes such as the abilities, achievements, attitudes, and aspirations of students resulting from an educational experience. Outcomes, as a body of information, would include measurements of the impact of instruction on teachers, administrators, counselors, and others. Here too would be data on wear and tear of equipment, effects of the learning environment, cost incurred. Outcomes to be considered in evaluation include not only those that are evident, or even existent, as learning sessions end, but include applications, transfer, and relearning effects which may not be available for measurement until long after. The description of the outcomes of driver training, for example, could well include reports of accident-avoidance over a lifetime. In short, outcomes are the consequences of educating—immediate and long-range, cognitive and conative, personal and community-wide.

Antecedents, transactions, and outcomes, the elements of evaluation statements, are shown in Figure 1 to have a place in both description and judgment. To fill in these matrices the evaluator will collect judgments (e.g., of community prejudice, of problem-solving styles, and of teacher personality) as well as descriptions. In Figure 1 it is also indicated that judgmental statements are classified either as general standards of quality or as judgments specific to the given program. Descriptive data are clasified as intents and observations. The evaluator can organize his data-gathering to conform to the format shown in Figure 1.

The evaluator can prepare a record of what educators intend, of what observers perceive, of what patrons generally expect, and of what judges value the immediate program to be. The record may treat antecedents, transactions, and outcomes separately within the four classes identified as *Intents, Observations, Standards,* and *Judgments,* as in Figure 1. The following is an illustration of 12 data, one of which could be recorded in each of the 12 cells, starting with an intended antecedent, and moving down each column until an outcome judgment has been indicated.

Knowing that (1) Chapter XI has been assigned and that he intends (2) to lecture on the topic Wednesday, a professor indicates (3) what the students should be able to do by Friday partly by writing a quiz on the topic. He observes that (4) some students were absent on Wednesday, that (5) he did not quite complete the lecture because of a lengthy discussion and that (6) on the quiz only about ⅔ of the class seemed to understand a certain major concept. In general, he expects (7) some absences but that the work will be made up by quiz-time; he expects (8) his lectures to be clear enough for perhaps 90 percent of a class to follow him without difficulty; and he knows that (9) his colleagues expect only about one student in ten to understand thoroughly each major concept in such lessons as these. By his own judgment (10) the reading assignment was not a sufficient background for his lecture; the students commented that (11) the lecture was provocative; and the graduate assistant who read the quiz papers said that (12) a discouragingly large number of students seemed to confuse one major concept for another.

Evaluators and educators do not expect data to be recorded in such detail, even in the distant future. My purpose here was to give twelve examples of data that could be handled by separate cells in the matrices. Next I would like to consider the description data matrix in detail.

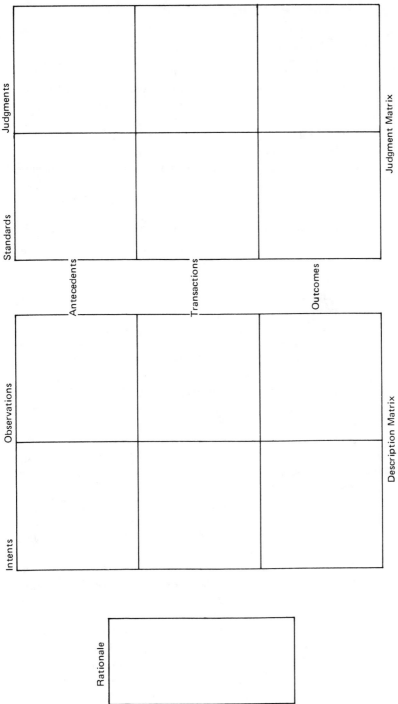

FIGURE 1

A Layout of Statements and Data To Be Collected by the Evaluator of an Educational Program

GOALS AND INTENTS

For many years instructional technologists, test specialists, and others have pleaded for more explicit statement of educational goals. I consider "goals," "objectives," and "intents" to be synonomous. I use the category title *Intents* because many educators now equate "goals" and "objectives" with "intended student outcomes." In this paper Intents includes the planned-for environmental conditions, the planned-for demonstrations, the planned-for coverage of certain subject matter, etc., as well as the planned-for student behavior. To be included in this three-cell column are effects which are desired, those which are hoped for, those which are anticipated, and even those which are feared. This class of data includes goals and plans that others have, especially the students. (It should be noted that it is not the educator's privilege to rule out the study of a variable by saying, "that is not one of our objectives." The evaluator should include both the variable and the negation.) The resulting collection of *Intents* is a priority listing of all that may happen.

The fact that many educators now equate "goals" with "intended student outcomes" is to the credit of the behaviorists, particularly the advocates of programmed instruction. They have brought about a small reform in teaching by emphasizing those specific classroom acts and work exercises which contribute to the refinement of student responses. The A.A.A.S. Science Project, for example, has been successful in developing its curriculum around behavioristic goals (see Gagné). Some curriculum-innovation projects, however, have found the emphasis on behavioral outcomes an obstacle to creative teaching (see Atkin, 1963). The educational evaluator should not list goals only in terms of anticipated student behavior. To *evaluate* an educational program, we must examine what teaching, as well as what learning, is intended. (Many antecedent conditions and teaching transactions can be worded behavioristically, if desired.) How intentions are worded is not a criterion for inclusion. Intents can be the global goals of the Educational Policies Commission or the detailed goals of the programmer (Mager, 1962). Taxonomic, mechanistic, humanistic, even scriptural—any mixture of goal statements are acceptable as part of the evaluation picture.

Many a contemporary evaluator expects trouble when he sets out to record the educator's objectives. Early in the work he urged the educator to declare his objectives so that outcome-testing devices could be built. He finds the educator either reluctant or unable to verbalize objectives. With diligence, if not with pleasure, the evaluator assists with what he presumed to be the educator's job: writing behavioral goals. His presumption is wrong. As Scriven has said, the responsibility for describing curricular objectives is the responsibility of the evaluator. He is the one who is experienced with the language of behaviors, traits, and habits. Just as it is his responsibility to transform the behaviors of a teacher and the responses of a student into data, it is his responsibility to transform the intentions and expectations of an educator into "data." It is necessary for him to continue to ask the educator for statements of intent. He should augment the replies by asking, "Is this another way of saying it?" or "Is this an instance?" It is not wrong for an evaluator to teach a willing educator about behavioral objectives—they may facilitate the work. It is wrong for him to insist that every educator should use them.

Obtaining authentic statements of intent is a new challenge for the evaluator. The methodology remains to be developed. Let us now shift attention to the second column of the data cells.

OBSERVATIONAL CHOICE

Most of the descriptive data cited early in the previous section are classified as *Observations*. In Figure 1 when he described surroundings and events and the subsequent consequences, the evaluator* is telling of his Observations. Sometimes the evaluator observes these characteristics in a direct and personal way. Sometimes he uses instruments. His instruments include inventory schedules, biographical data sheets, interview routines, checklists, opinionnaires, and all kinds of psychometric tests. The experienced evaluator gives special attention to the measurement of student outcomes, but he does not fail to observe the other outcomes, nor the antecedent conditions and instructional transactions.

Many educators fear that the outside evaluator will not be attentive to the characteristics that the school staff has deemed most important. This sometimes does happen, but evaluators often pay *too much* attention to what they have been urged to look at, and too little attention to other facets. In the matter of selection of variables for evaluation, the evaluator must make a subjective decision. Obviously, he must limit the elements to be studied. He cannot look at all of them. The ones he rules out will be those that he assumes would not contribute to an understanding of the educational activity. He should give primary attention to the variables specifically indicated by the educator's objectives, but he must designate additional variables to be observed. He must search for unwanted side effects and incidental gains. The selection of measuring techniques is an obvious responsibility, but the choice of characteristics to be observed is an equally important and unique contribution of the evaluator.

An evaluation is not complete without a statement of the rationale of the program. It needs to be considered separately, as indicated in Figure 1. Every program has its rationale, though often it is only implicit. The rationale indicates

---

*Here and elsewhere in this paper, for simplicity of presentation, the evaluator and the educator are referred to as two different persons. The educator will often be his own evaluator or a member of the evaluation team.

the philosophic background and basic purposes of the program. Its importance to evaluation has been indicated by Berlak (1966). The rationale should provide one basis for evaluating Intents. The evaluator asks himself or other judges whether the plan developed by the educator constitutes a logical step in the implementation of the basic purposes. The rationale also is of value in choosing the reference groups, e.g., merchants, mathematicians, and mathematics educators, which later are to pass judgment on various aspects of the program.

A statement of rationale may be difficult to obtain. Many an effective instructor is less than effective at presenting an educational rationale. If pressed, he may only succeed in saying something the listener wanted said. It is important that the rationale be in his language, a language he is the master of. Suggestions by the evaluator may be an obstacle, becoming accepted because they are attractive rather than because they designate the grounds for what the educator is trying to do.

The judgment matrix needs further explanation, but I am postponing that until after a consideration of the bases for processing descriptive data.

CONTINGENCY AND CONGRUENCE

For any one educational program there are two principal ways of processing descriptive evaluation data: finding the contingencies among antecedents, transactions, and outcomes and finding the congruence between Intents and Observations. The processing of judgments follows a different model. The first two main columns of the data matrix in Figure 1 contain the descriptive data. The format for processing these data is represented in Figure 2.

The data for a curriculum are *congruent* if what was intended actually happens. To be fully congruent the intended antecedents, transactions, and outcomes would have to come to pass. This seldom happens—and often should compare the cells containing Intents and Observations, to note the discrepancies, and to describe the amount of congruence for that row. (Congruence of outcomes has been emphasized in the evaluation model proposed by Taylor and Maguire.) Congruence does not indicate that outcomes are reliable or valid, but that what was intended did occur.

Just as the Gestaltist found more to the whole than the sum of its parts, the evaluator studying variables from any two of the three cells in a column of the data matrix finds more to describe than the variables themselves. The relationships or *contingencies* among the variables deserve additional attention. In the sense that evaluation is the search for relationships that permit the improvement of education, the evaluator's task is one of identifying outcomes that are contingent upon particular antecedent conditions and instructional transactions.

Lesson planning and curriculum revision through the years has been built upon faith in certain contingencies. Day to day, the master teacher arranges his

Descriptive data

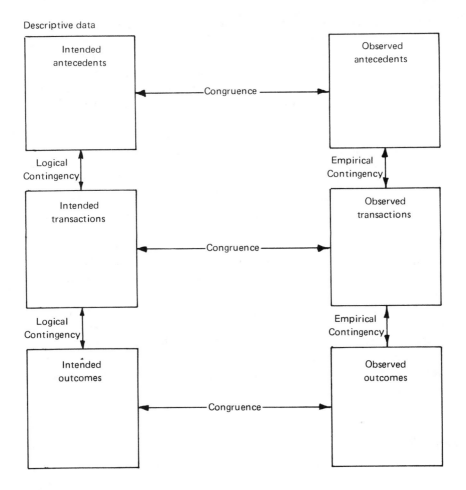

FIGURE 2

A Representation of the Processing of Descriptive Data

presentation and selects his input materials to fit his instructional goals. For him the contingencies, in the main, are logical, intuitive, and supported by a history of satisfactions and endorsements. Even the master teacher and certainly less-experienced teachers need to bring their intuited contingencies under the scrutiny of appropriate juries.

As a first step in evaluation it is important just to record them. A film on floodwaters may be scheduled (intended transaction) to expose students to a background to conservation legislation (intended outcome). Of those who know both subject matter and pedagogy, we ask, "Is there a logical connection between this event and this purpose?'' If so, a logical contingency exists between these two Intents. The record should show it.

Whenever Intents are evaluated the contingency criterion is one of logic. To test the logic of an educational contingency the evaluators rely on previous experience, perhaps on research experience, with similar observables. No immediate observation of these variables, however, is necessary to test the strength of the contingencies among Intents.

Evaluation of Observation contingencies depends on empirical evidence. To say, ''this arithmetic class progressed rapidly because the teacher was somewhat but not too sophisticated in mathematics'' demands empirical data, either from within the evaluation or from the research literature (see Bassham, 1962). The usual evaluation of a single program will not alone provide the data necessary for contingency statements. Here too, then, previous experience with similar observables is a basic qualification of the evaluator.

The contingencies and congruences identified by evaluators are subject to judgment by experts and participants just as more unitary descriptive data are. The importance of non-congruence will vary with different viewpoints. The school superintendent and the school counselor may disagree as to the importance of a cancellation of the scheduled lessons on sex hygiene in the health class. As an example of judging contingencies, the degree to which teacher morale is contingent on the length of the school day may be deemed cause enough to abandon an early morning class by one judge and not another. Perception of importance of congruence and contingency deserve the evaluator's careful attention.

STANDARDS AND JUDGMENTS

There is a general agreement that the goal of education is excellence—but how schools and students should excell, and at what sacrifice, will always be debated. Whether goals are local or national, the measurement of excellence requires explicit rather than implicit standards.

Today's educational programs are not subjected to ''standard-oriented'' evaluation. This is not to say that schools lack in aspiration or accomplishment. It is to say that standards—benchmarks of performance having widespread reference value—are not in common use. Schools across the nation may use the same evaluation checklist* but the interpretations of the checklisted data are couched

---

*One contemporary checklist is *Evaluative Criteria,* a document published by the National Study of Secondary School Evaluation (1960). It is a commendably thorough list of antecedents and possible transactions, organized mostly by subject-matter offerings. Surely it is valuable as a checklist, identifying neglected areas. Its great value may be a catalyst, hastening the maturity of a developing curriculum. However, it can be

in inexplicit, personal terms. Even in an informal way, no school can evaluate the impact of its program without knowledge of what other schools are doing in pursuit of similar objectives. Unfortunately, many educators are loathe to accumulate that knowledge systematically (Hand, 1965; Tyler, 1965).

There is little knowledge anywhere today of the quality of a student's education. School grades are based on the private criteria and standards of the individual teacher. Most "standardized" test scores tell where an examinee performing "psychometrically useful" tasks stands with regard to a reference group, rather than the level of competence at which he performs essential scholastic tasks. Although most teachers are competent to teach their subject matter and to spot learning difficulties, few have the ability to *describe* a student's command over his intellectual environment. Neither school grades nor standardized test scores nor the candid opinions of teachers are very informative as to the excellence of students.

Even when measurements are effectively interpreted, evaluation is complicated by a multiplicity of standards. Standards vary from student to student, from instructor to instructor, and from reference group to reference group. This is not wrong. In a healthy society, different parties have different standards. Part of the responsibility of evaluation is to make known which standards are held by whom.

It was implied much earlier that it is reasonable to expect change in an educator's *Intents* over a period of time. This is to say that he will change both his criteria and his standards during instruction. While a curriculum is being developed and disseminated, even the major classes of criteria vary. In their analysis of nationwide assimilation of new educational programs, Clark and Guba (1965) identified eight stages of change through which new programs go. For each stage they identified special criteria (each with its own standards) on which the program should be evaluated before it advances to another stage. Each of their criteria deserves elaboration, but here it is merely noted that there are quite different criteria at each successive curriculum-development stage.

Informal evaluation tends to leave criteria unspecified. Formal evaluation is more specific. But it seems the more careful the evaluation, the fewer the criteria; and the more carefully the criteria are specified, the less the concern given to standards of acceptability. It is a great misfortune that the best trained evaluators have been looking at education with a microscope rather than with a panoramic view finder.

There is no clear picture of what any school or any curriculum project is accomplishing today partly because the methodology of processing judgments is

---

of only limited value in *evaluating,* for it guides neither the measurement nor the interpretation of measurement. By intent, it deals with criteria (what variables to consider) and leaves the matter of standards (what ratings to consider as meritorious) to the conjecture of the individual observer.

inadequate. What little formal evaluation there is is attentive to too few criteria, overly tolerant of implicit standards, and ignores the advantage of relative comparisons. More needs to be said about relative and absolute standards.

COMPARING AND JUDGING

There are two bases of judging the characteristics of a program, (1) with respect to absolute standards as reflected by personal judgments and (2) with respect to relative standards as reflected by characteristics of alternate programs. One can evaluate SMSG mathematics with respect to opinions of what a mathematics curriculum should be or with regard to what other mathematics curricula are. The evaluator's comparisons and judgments are symbolized in Figure 3. The upper left matrix represents the data matrix from Figure 2. At the upper right are sets of standards by which a program can be judged in an absolute sense. There are multiple sets because there may be numerous reference groups or points of view. The several matrices at the lower left represent several alternate programs to which the one being evaluated can be compared.

Each set of absolute standards, if formalized, would indicate acceptable and meritorious levels for antecedents, transactions, and outcomes. So far I have been talking about setting standards, not about judging. Before making a judgment the evaluator determines whether or not each standard is met. Unavailable standards must be estimated. The judging act itself is deciding which set of standards to heed. More precisely, judging is assigning a weight, an importance, to each set of standards. Rational judgment in educational evaluation is a decision as to how much to pay attention to the standards of each reference group (point of view) in deciding whether or not to take some administrative action.*

Relative comparison is accomplished in similar fashion except that the standards are taken from descriptions of other programs. It is hardly a judgmental matter to determine whether one program betters another with regard to a single characteristic, but there are many characteristics and the characteristics are not equally important. The evaluator selects which characteristics to attend to and which reference programs to compare to.

From relative judgment of a program, as well as from absolute judgment we can obtain an overall or composite rating of merit (perhaps with certain qualifying statements), a rating to be used in making an educational decision. From this final act of judgment a recommendation can be composed.

---

*Deciding which variables to study and deciding which standards to employ are two essentially subjective commitments in evaluation. Other acts are capable of objective treatment; only these two are beyond the reach of social science methodology.

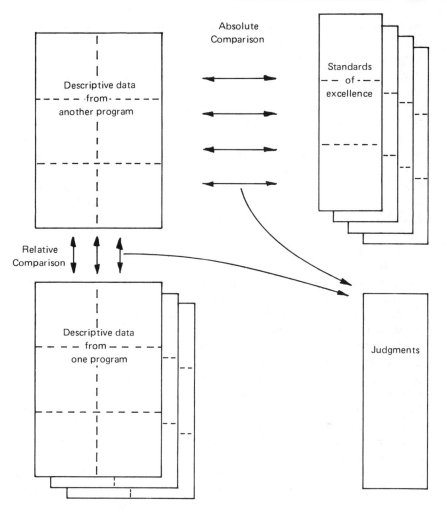

FIGURE 3

A Representation of the Process of Judging the Merit of an Educational
Program

ABSOLUTE AND RELATIVE EVALUATION

As to which kind of evaluation—absolute or relative—to encourage, Scriven
and Cronbach have disagreed. Cronbach (1963) suggests that generalizations to
the local-school situation from curriculum-comparing studies are sufficiently

hazardous (even when the studies are massive, well-designed, and properly controlled) to make them poor research investments. Moreover, the difference in purpose of the programs being compared is likely to be sufficiently great to render uninterpretable any outcome other than across-the-board superiority of one of them. Expecting that rarely, Cronbach urges fewer comparisons, more intensive process studies, and more curriculum "case studies" with extensive measurement and thorough description.

Scriven, on the other hand, indicates that what the educator wants to know is whether or not one program is better than another, and that the best way to answer his question is by direct comparison. He points to the difficulty of describing the outcomes of complex learning in explicit terms and with respect to absolute standards, and to the ease of observing relative outcomes from two programs. Whether or not Scriven's prescription is satisfying will probably depend on the client. An educator faced with an adoption decision is more likely to be satisfied, the curriculum innovator and instructional technologist less likely.

One of the major distinctions in evaluation is that which Scriven identifies as *formative* versus *summative* evaluation. His use of the terms relates primarily to the stage of development of curricular material. If material is not yet ready for distribution to classroom teachers, then its evaluation is formative; otherwise it is summative. It is probably more useful to distinguish between evaluation oriented to developer-author-publisher criteria and standards and evaluation oriented to consumer-administrator-teacher criteria and standards. The formative-summative distinction could be so defined, and I will use the terms in that way. The faculty committee facing an adoption choice asks, "Which is best? Which will do the job best?" The course developer, following Cronbach's advice, asks, "How can we teach it better?" (Note that neither are now concerned about the individual student differences.) The evaluator looks at different data and invokes different standards to answer these questions.

The evaluator who assumes responsibility for summative evaluation—rather than formative evaluation—accepts the responsibility of informing consumers as to the merit of the program. The judgments of Figure 3 are his target. It is likely that he will attempt to describe the school situations in which the procedures or materials may be used. He may see his task as one of indicating the goodness-of-fit of an available curriculum to an existing school program. He must learn whether or not the intended antecedents, transactions, and outcomes for the curriculum are consistent with the resources, standards, and goals of the school. This may require as much attention to the school as to the new curriculum.

The formative evaluator, on the other hand, is more interested in the contingencies indicated in Figure 2. He will look for covariations within the evaluation study, and across studies, as a basis for guiding the development of present or future programs.

For major evaluation activities it is obvious that an individual evaluator will not have the many competencies required. A team of social scientists is needed for many assignments. It is reasonable to suppose that such teams will include specialists in instructional technology, specialists in psychometric testing and scaling, specialists in research design and analysis, and specialists in dissemination of information. Curricular innovation is sure to have deep and widespread effect on our society, and we may include the social anthropologist on some evaluation teams. The economist and philosopher have something to offer. Experts will be needed for the study of values, population surveys, and content-oriented data-reduction techniques.

The educator who has looked disconsolate when scheduled for evaluation will look aghast at the prospect of a team of evaluators invading his school. How can these evaluators observe or describe the natural state of education when their very presence influences that state? His concern is justified. Measurement activity—just the presence of evaluators—does have a reactive effect on education, sometimes beneficial and sometimes not—but in either case contributing to the atypicality of the sessions. There are specialists, however, who anticipate that evaluation will one day be so skilled that it properly will be considered "unobtrusive measurement" (Webb et al., 1966).

In conclusion I would remind the reader that one of the largest investments being made in U.S. education today is in the development of new programs. School officials cannot yet revise a curriculum on rational grounds, and the needed evaluation is not under way. What is to be gained from the enormous effort of the innovators of the 1960's if in the 1970's there are no evaluation records? Both the new innovator and the new teacher need to know. Folklore is not a sufficient repository. In our data banks we should document the causes and effects, the congruence of intent and accomplishment, and the panorama of judgments of those concerned. Such records should be kept to promote educational action, not obstruct it. The countenance of evaluation should be one of data gathering that leads to decision-making, not to trouble-making.

Educators should be making their own evaluations more deliberate, more formal. Those who will—whether in their classrooms or on national panels—can hope to clarify their responsibility by answering each of the following questions: (1) Is this evaluation to be primarily descriptive, primarily judgmental, or both descriptive and judgmental? (2) Is this evaluation to emphasize the antecedent conditions, the transactions, or the outcomes alone, or a combination of these, or their functional contingencies? (3) Is this evaluation to indicate the congruence between what is intended and what occurs? (4) Is this evaluation to be undertaken within a single program or as a comparison between two or more curricular programs? (5) Is this evaluation intended more to further the development of curricula or to help choose among available curricula? With these questions answered, the restrictive effects of incomplete guidelines and inappropriate countenances are more easily avoided.

REFERENCES

American Council on Education. E. F. Lindquist (ed.), *Educational Measurement* (Washington, D.C.: The Council, 1951).

Atkin, J. M. "Some Evaluation Problems in a Course Content Improvement Project." *Journal of Research in Science Teaching* 1 (1963): 129–32.

Bassham, H. "Teacher Understanding and Pupil Efficiency in Mathematics: A Study of Relationship." *Arithmetic Teacher* 9 (1962):383–87.

Berlak, Harold. Comments recorded in Irving Morrissett (ed.), *Concepts and Structure in the New Social Science Curricula* (Lafayette, Indiana: Social Science Education Consortium, Purdue University, 1966), pp. 88–89.

Clark, David L., and Guba, Egon G. *An Examination of Potential Change Roles in Education* (Columbus: The Ohio State University, 1965). Multilith.

Cronbach, Lee. "Evaluation for Course Improvement." *Teachers College Record* 64 (1963):672–83.

Educational Testing Service. "A Long, Hot Summer of Committee Work on National Assessment of Education." *ETS Developments* 13 (November 1965).

Gagné, Robert M. "Elementary Science: A New Scheme of Instruction." *Science* 151 (No. 3706), pp. 49–53.

Hand, Harold C. "National Assessment Viewed as the Camel's Nose." *Phi Delta Kappa* 47 (September 1965):8–12.

Mager, R. F. *Preparing Objectives for Programmed Instruction* (San Francisco: Fearon Publishers, 1962).

Scriven, Michael. "The Methodology of Evaluation." In Ralph W. Tyler, Robert M. Gagné, and Michael Scriven (eds.), *Perspectives of Curriculum and Evaluation.* AERA Monograph Series on Curriculum Evaluation. No. 1 (Chicago: Rand McNally, 1967), pp. 39–83.

Smith, B. Othanel, and Meux, M. O. *A Study of the Logic of Teaching* (Urbana: Bureau of Educational Research, University of Illinois). No date.

Smith, E. R., and Tyler, Ralph W. *Appraising and Recording Student Progress* (New York: Harper and Row, 1942).

Taylor, Peter A., and Maguire, Thomas O. "A Theoretical Evaluation Model." *The Manitoba Journal of Educational Research* 1 (1966):12–17.

Tyler, Ralph W. "Assessing the Progress of Education." *Phi Delta Kappan* 47 (September 1965):13–16.

Webb, Eugene J., Campbell, Donald T., Schwartz, Richard D., and Sechrist, Lee. *Unobtrusive Measures: Nonreactive Research in the Social Sciences* (Chicago: Rand McNally, 1966).

24. TRENDS IN PROCESS-RELATED RESEARCH ON CURRICULUM AND TEACHING AT DIFFERENT PROBLEM LEVELS IN EDUCATIONAL SCIENCES*

Urban Dahllöf

INTRODUCTION

One of the most important questions that can be put to educational scientists today seems to be *under what conditions* do process-data make any difference to non-significant test differences. The question highlights the need for a more profound understanding of relationships in an area that has been dominated for too long by numerous empirical studies with only weak theoretical skeletons. In a survey of Swedish school research, Alkin and Johnson (1971, p. 20. Cf. also 1972, p. 56) recently had good reasons to warn against "massive correlational

SOURCE. *Scandinavian Journal of Educational Research* 19 (1974), pp. 55–77.

*This is a slightly revised version of an invitational address presented to Division B of the American Educational Research Association at the annual meeting in New Orleans, February 27, 1973. The address was given under the title "Data on curriculum and teaching process: Do they make any difference to non-significant test differences—and under what conditions?" I wish to thank Professor Arno A. Bellack, Teachers College, Columbia University, who has stimulated our thinking and promoted our research in a number of ways during the last few years and Dean David Turney, Indiana State University, Terre Haute, Ind., who as program director has given me most valuable assistance. Thanks are also due to Dr. Ulf P. Lundgren, Assistant Professor at the University of Göteborg, and associate project director, and to Mr. Daniel Kallós, fil. lic., Institute of Education, University of Lund (cf. Kallós, 1973).

fishing-trips''—a warning that no doubt is justified in the area of curriculum, teaching, and education process research on both sides of the Atlantic. There is hardly any scholar today who would dare to say that he is satisfied with the state of affairs of research in the area. On the contrary, most researchers seem to suffer from something like frustration.

But as long as there is frustration, there is hope: frustration leads to activity and there is, indeed, quite a lot of activity in the field. Something substantial will certainly come out of all this sooner or later. We are, however, searching for outlets in many directions, all of which may not be equally fruitful. The purpose of this paper is to discuss some of the main problems of strategy that arise out of this frustrating situation.

The question takes it for granted that there is agreement so far that there is an abundance of studies showing non-significant test differences. The question also takes the position that data on the educational process—somehow and under some conditions—may be of some help, but nothing is said about the kind of research we have in mind, nor is anything mentioned about the independent variables. Let us therefore first discuss some general statements about levels of educational research.

LEVELS OF EDUCATIONAL RESEARCH

- Educational phenomena can be studied at different levels, ranging from very detailed studies of classroom behavior to the systems analysis of comparative education.

- This range can be regarded as a micro-macro dimension. If so, it has, however, to be borne in mind that these terms are relative to the general definition of the field. From the standpoint of psychology—and especially the psychology of learning—the microstudies of classroom behavior would no doubt represent a macro-level. On the other hand, social economists working in the field of educational planning have good reasons to classify our approach to systems analysis in comparative education as micro-level studies from their point of view.

- Psychology of learning, like educational psychology in general, has been deliberately left outside this treatment. There seem to be no good reasons for any reductionism between psychology and education. As things stand, it appears to be wiser to assume that the problems of education cannot entirely be reduced to psychological principles, than the opposite, nor are there any good reasons to expect that problems of curriculum and teaching can be entirely reduced to the laws of learning.

- On the other hand: in order to be fruitful, educational research must clearly be *compatible* with established facts and principles of learning and also with the status of other neighbor sciences. Thus, compatibility with the psychology of learning is a necessary but probably not a sufficient condition for educational research.

- If the reasons in favor of reductionism over the boundaries between psychology and education are weak, there are for similar reasons no good arguments for any reductionism between the different levels of research within the field of education. Thus, it does not seem fruitful to expect that problems at the systems level of comparative education can be reduced to microteaching principles.

- The principle of compatibility and the distinction between necessary and sufficient conditions do not prevent researchers working at different levels from helping each other. Quite the contrary. There can probably be a fruitful exchange of ideas, concepts and approaches in both directions provided that the discussion is continuously adapted to the problems characteristic of each level.

- At present there seems to be a striking similarity between different levels of study within education, at least in so far as there are signs of frustration caused by the anemia of non-significant outcome differences both at the micro-, medium- and macro-levels.

CLASSROOM BEHAVIOR AND INTERACTION

One wide field is *classroom behavior and interaction*. It is, indeed, too vast and contains too many research traditions to be summarized in a few words. In this connection, however, we are primarily interested in those studies within these traditions that have investigated the direct relationships between different types of behavior or interaction patterns and educational outcomes. Here, Rosenshine (1970, 1971a, 1971b) has recently published a series of analytic surveys of the research field. In spite of the vivid activities in developing observation systems in the affective domain such as those of Flanders (1965, 1970) and others (Amidon and Hunter, 1967), in the cognitive area (Bellack *et al.*, 1966) or of a topic-centered kind (Gallagher, 1970a, b), the net result of established findings seems to be fairly meager when it comes to the relationships between specific behavior as well as patterns of behavior in the classroom on the one hand and student achievement on the other. This is partly due to the fact that there is a rapid decrease in the number of studies on this particular problem, but Rosenshine (1971a) does also note quite a lot of puzzling inconsistencies among those investigations that fulfill demands of comparability. Now and then Rosenshine is forced to conclude that findings are running counter to what seem to be quite trivial expectations, at least when they are based on psychology of learning. One of the main conclusions from the Rosenshine reviews is a warning against too far-reaching practical conclusions, e.g., for teacher training purposes, before we have arrived at a more coherent understanding of the relationships within the field of teaching. A warning of a corresponding kind is also issued by Nuthall (1971).

When it comes to recommendations for further research, Rosenshine (1971a) reminds us about the reviews of Ackerman (1954) and Morsh and Wilder (1954), who recommended a shift from high-inference rating scales to low-inference techniques for a more objective observation of teaching behavior. This shift has now taken place—but we are still confused.

The main point in the sympathetic message from Rosenshine is the following: "The next shift should be toward greater precision in recording, reporting and analyzing results" (Rosenshine, 1971a, p. 94). Let us in this connection only make the comment that improvements of this technical kind will of course be welcome as helpful, but let us also insert a question-mark in order to stimulate the discussion on this point: although a greater technical refinement would be a helpful tool or even a necessary condition, will such a greater precision really be a sufficient condition?

It is, by the way, a little easier to follow Rosenshine when he joins Norma Furst in another survey, which seems to put somewhat more stress on the theoretical considerations, e.g., when they propose more experimental research. Similar points of view are touched upon when Rosenshine and Furst (1971) discuss the selection of variables. One gets the feeling that this is fruitful ground, which, however, is still hiding if not treasures, at least some coins. Referring to, among others, Nuthall (1968) and B. O. Smith and co-workers (1962, 1966), they also point to the fact that bridges are occasionally built between classroom and laboratory research. Let us in this connection put another question this way: What about bridges between classroom research—as traditionally carried out— and research on a macro- or systems-level?

Before reaching the other end of the research continuum let us make two short stops not far from the classroom observation research level.

TEACHER EFFECTIVENESS

The first stop is, indeed, part of the classroom interaction field, although it may be looked upon as somewhat more concentrated upon the characteristic behavior patterns of the teacher. Another reason for a special discussion is the influence that in this area is exerted by Gage and his group at Stanford. In his recent book *Teacher Effectiveness and Teacher Education* (Gage, 1972), Gage seems to take a relatively optimistic position to the problems of concern here—or at least the publisher tries to convince us in the text on the dust jacket that Gage is optimistic.

The starting point for a shift towards optimism is, however, a pessimism that according to the publisher is no longer warranted. So far there has no doubt been much to support such a pessimistic attitude. Let me just quote one passage from Gage.

The early years of research on teaching have not paid off in solid, replicable, meaningful results of considerable theoretical or practical value. Positive and significant results have seldom been forthcoming, and they have survived replication even less often. The research has yielded many findings that do not make sense, that do not hang together in any meaningful way (1972, p. 114).

What about the support for a shift towards an attitude of optimism? One point is some trends towards significant positive relationships as regards such variables as warmth, indirectness, cognitive organization and enthusiasm—factors among which Rosenshine (1971a) found so many inconsistencies that he took a much less favorable position.

Another point is the neglected area of individualization that almost by definition can be expected to be a gateway to a more prosperous future, not the least in terms of what Cronbach has named "aptitude-treatment interaction studies," which will be considered at the next step, with little support for any optimism.

In these and other respects Gage provides arguments for expectations of a theoretically meaningful pattern of positive findings, provided that future researchers make certain changes in their designs and research strategies. So far there is little *evidence* of a more positive attitude today—but some *hope* for the future. This depends in turn on the fruitfulness of the recommendations stated.

There is, indeed, a great variety of considerations to be adopted. Among many other things Gage offers a perspicacious discussion of the relation of theories of teaching to theories of learning, he analyzes the importance of theories and paradigms in general, he reminds us of the somewhat distressing fact that none of the models reviewed "has come to grips with the complication that teachers typically deal with more than one pupil at a time. . . . Just how interactions between teachers and pupils should be combined to characterize significant processes and outcomes in the classroom has not been dealt with in the foregoing paradigms."

Having said this, Gage, however, continues: "At the present stage of paradigm development this gap does not seem to be an urgent one. When more experience has been gained in providing operational definitions for the paradigms, the problem of combining interacts into educationally significant units will become more realistic" (Gage, 1972, p. 109).

As far as I can see this statement is equivalent to taking the position that the most fruitful paradigms are those which take their starting point on a psychological level—perceptual and/or behavioral. This is also in line with the two main recommendations that seem to be the very core of the message. The one is the development of programmed learning and machine paradigms—mainly in accordance with recommendations by Stolurow (1965), when he put his famous question: To model the master teacher or master the teaching model? One main reason for Gage's recommendation of machine paradigms is that they help the understanding of the function of live teachers: "Systematic comparison of machine functions and those of human teachers, function by function, may reveal the proper and unique role of each. Paradigms for human teaching comparable for those for teaching machines will help in making such analyses" (Gage, 1972, p. 113).

The other main recommendation is micro-teaching analysis, "breaking down the complexities that have proven to be so unmanageable when dealt with as a whole" (Gage, 1972, p. 123).

There are, no doubt, good arguments in favor of multidimensional criteria of successful teaching—even on a micro-level. So far, micro-teaching is an interesting field of research *per se,* the development of which may be a necessary condition for understanding the relationship between teaching and student achievement. Once again, however, we may question if the recommendations discussed here at the same time represent a sufficient condition. There is much in Gage's own book to support such a doubt. Among other things, Gage (1972, p. 97) reminds us about Jackson's (1966) distinction between preactive and interactive phases of teaching. Referring to Cronbach (1967) he also reminds us about the spontaneous facets of the game, "the uncontrived character, speed and uncontrollability of teaching moves" (Gage, 1972, p. 97). And—in connection with the Stolurow-based recommendation of machine-paradigms as guides to human teaching—we are requested to analyze the programs that teachers carry around "in their heads."

But shall we really take it for granted that what goes on in the heads of the teachers and at the same time means something for their decisions and behavior, shall we really assume that all this is limited to the micro-level of the present situation? What about the interaction between the preactive and interactive phases of instruction, between the long term and middle term plans, intentions in relation to curriculum objectives on the one hand and on the other hand the various steps and decisions taken within a single lesson or a short series of lessons? Isn't there a risk that to rely only on a breakdown of the complexities will lead us to another blind alley? Do not Jackson's contribution and not least "the complexities of an urban classroom" as analyzed so cleverly by Smith and Geoffrey (1968) urge us to take even higher-order complexities into systematic account in our paradigms on teaching?

APTITUDE-TREATMENT INTERACTION

The next step will be much shorter, even though the field is also a complex one. We are now approaching the program level, where a certain method or style of teaching is applied for a shorter or longer period in order to suit the specific needs or abilities of the students. According to the summaries by Cronbach and Snow (1969) and Bracht (1970) there is no doubt that the whole field of aptitude-treatment interaction is suffering from the frustration of non-significant differences, and yet this is a field in which differences of a certain direction could in many cases be expected for very good theoretical reasons. Typical of research in this field seems among other things to be the short duration of the treatment and the little concern for what really goes on under the label of treatment. Thus one main conclusion by reviewers of this field is to concentrate more on the educational process that is actually taking place both in terms of teaching and learning, avoiding taking for granted that what is expected from the instruction is also taking place among all participants.

This area is by definition relatively close to the field of teacher effectiveness and micro-analysis of teaching behavior and classroom interaction. It has, however, to be noted that—in spite of the common characteristic of frustration—there seems to be a difference in the symptoms of the disease: at the micro-level, behaviors and behavior patterns of different kinds are in various combinations taking the place of independent variables and so far there is no lack of information about the details of the process, as seems to be the case at the research level of aptitude-treatment interaction.

Here, on the other hand, much attention is paid to individual differences and their role for the students' ability to profit from a certain type of instruction—while at the classroom interaction analysis level students are generally treated as equal, little attention being paid to individual differences or to subgroups of students.

It has also to be noted that in both cases factors like curriculum contents, type and level of objectives as well as the general environment are kept constant according to the established rules and massive tradition of experimental psychology. This may be quite in order for the single study and from a general point of view of design. But when it happens that in the long run the same factors or a certain set-up of factors are always kept constant, these factors are running the risk of total neglect even though they do in fact exert a certain influence.

RESEARCH ON THE ENVIRONMENT AND FRAME CONDITIONS

In order to survey research on environmental factors and their influence on scholastic achievement we have to take another step on the ladder up to field studies of a sociological kind and on a level of complex systems as in comparative education.

Environments can be classified in many ways. Let us start with factors relatively close to the teaching situation, such as size and characteristics of the school and the class that is subject to our teaching efforts. Typical of research in this field, among other things are:

—The assessment is generally made by means of standard group tests of a fairly general type, data being collected at the end of the school year or even longer after the environmental factors under study have been introduced to the students.

—When corrected for differences in initial ability, social background and the like, the tests generally show few significant differences, if any at all. Moreover, the pattern of significance is in many cases inconsistent and the differences are often too small to be of any practical importance for planning or other types of decisions.

—The investigations are generally held at a purely descriptive level. Although differences are often expected not only by teachers, school leaders and the general public but apparently also by the researchers themselves, there are few, if any, efforts to explain the outcomes by means of an alternative model or pattern of hypotheses.

—Almost nothing is known about the characteristics of the educational processes behind the test results (Dahllöf, 1971a).

It is at this point that our own empirical data from project Compass for the first time have a chance to make a contribution. Originally they were collected in a curriculum study (Dahllöf, 1960) that was carried out in the late fifties under Torsten Husén in connection with the Swedish comprehensive school reform (Husén and Dahllöf, 1960, 1965).

Before turning to research details some words should perhaps be mentioned about Sweden and Swedish school reforms. The school system is highly centralized. For each school form there is just one curriculum, issued by the National Board of Education, stating the same objectives for all students in a subject in a certain grade. The same organization covering optional courses and subjects is used in all school districts. There is, however, a considerable freedom for the local boards of education and for the single teacher to choose textbooks, sequence the contents and also to choose methodology of teaching and working forms for the pupils.

From 1950 the old European parallel school system has been integrated into a comprehensive school, starting at the age of 7 and lasting for 9 years. Then there is a three-year senior high school preceding the university level.

The comprehensive school was to a large extent introduced in order to promote social equality. Its curriculum philosophy is progressive with great stress on the development of the whole child, cooperation and group work as well as on the unselected heterogeneous class as the best environment for the fulfillment of these ends. The reform called for a radical change of teaching methods from traditional classroom instruction to a great deal of individualization within the comprehensive class (Husén and Henrysson, 1959; Paulston, 1968; Marklund and Söderberg, 1968; Beauchamp and Beauchamp, 1972).

The committees preparing the reform drew considerably on educational and sociological research in their planning. One of the most important fields of research and argumentation was the influence of social background factors on the enrollment to higher studies and success at school. Here, early studies by Boalt (1947) and Husén (1948) played an important role. This theme has been followed up in a number of later studies by Husén, who became one of the most prominent spokesmen for the reform. (See Husén and Boalt, 1968 for further references.) Among the research studies ought also to be mentioned a series of investigations by Härnqvist (1958, 1960, 1965; cf. also Härnqvist and Bengtsson, 1972) on the reserve of talent, inter- and intraindividual differences in relation to the problems of differentiation, enrollment in relation to social background, etc.

Between 1950 and 1962 a first version of the comprehensive school was tried out in a number of school-districts clustered in regional areas. The intent was to test different ways of organizing the upper section, i.e., grades 7-9, corresponding to junior high-school, but for various reasons very little came of this experiment that could serve as a guide for the decision-makers about the merits and demerits of different ways of organizing the school work. So when the final decision was to be taken in 1962 there was only one study in the area of ability grouping and scholastic achievement.

The only study about the effectiveness of different kinds of school organization that existed before the final decision on the Swedish comprehensive school, made a comparison between the old selective system and the experimental comprehensive system that were running parallel to each other in different parts of the city of Stockholm (Svensson, 1962). It was, from a technical point of view, a very good study, introducing analysis of co-variance on field data. When keeping initial ability and social background constant, as usual no differences were found between classes belonging to the selective and comprehensive system.

A re-analysis some years later, however, showed two things (Dahllöf 1967, 1971a). First, it was found that the tests used were very basic, and—incidentally—not equally fair to the systems under comparison. As a matter of fact, the functions studied were so basic that they had already been subject to teaching and learning before any differential treatment had taken place, the effects of which formed the main purpose of the Stockholm investigation.

Second, from the old curriculum studies (Dahllöf, 1960) we happened to have access to data on the educational process. These in turn were of two kinds (Dahllöf 1967, 1971a). (1) Data about the general pattern of teaching were collected. Here it was revealed—contrary to recommendations and expectations—that traditional classroom instruction was equally prominent in both types of school. Thus, when the great majority of teachers (95 percent) had to introduce a new curriculum unit or topic, they addressed the whole class at one and the same time. Some individualization did occur but only in the training phase within a certain topic and not over curriculum units. Thus, the more clever students had to wait for their slower classmates before they could proceed by taking up a new unit. This condition is very important for the theoretical model to be presented a little later on. (2) The curriculum was divided into a great number of units and main units, each unit being classified as to content and the corresponding taxonomical level. In this connection it may suffice to distinguish only between basic or elementary units and advanced units. For each unit we had assessments from a representative sample of teachers as to the number of lessons that were devoted to the different units during the school year. The first analysis was made in Mathematics for grade 7, distinguishing between students who had been transferred to the selective junior high-school classes from grade 5 and from grade 7, the latter having spent grades 5-6 in comprehensive classes. The total number of hours was about the same.

The main findings were as follows. With regard to basic teaching strategy, there was no difference, nor were there any differences in the total amount of time spent on the subject. Let us then turn to the amount of lessons spent on the elementary curriculum units, the attainment of which was studied in the tests. Here we have a difference that is not only significant but also relatively great. The number of lessons in the comprehensive classes were 42 out of a total of 96, whereas the positively selected classes did not spend more than 13 lessons on this kind of unit. The plus-selected classes spent more than 80 of the 95 lessons on the more advanced units, in contrast to 56 in the comprehensive classes, but here the attainments were not tested. This being the case—and provided that there is any correspondence between the general ability of the class and the number of lessons needed for teaching a unit by the method used—the level of achievement ought to be higher.

Thus there was a difference between the grouping systems, but it did not appear as a difference in the level of performance in the standardized tests of elementary Mathematics. Instead the difference came out in terms of time in a ratio as big as 1:3 for an equal level of attainment in basic curriculum units— and in terms of time as well as level of performance in advanced units.

From a practical and political point of view this outcome will of course involve some frustration for those who had drawn the too simple and far-reaching conclusion that ability grouping does not have any influence at all. But since most of the advocates of the reform had been criticizing the old secondary school and its medieval tradition for putting too much stress on memory and intellectual goals, the first results, as reported by Svensson (1962), may be said to be too good to be true: they simply meant that there was no price to be paid at all on the intellectual side for favors in other respects, socially and with regard to the personal development of the students. Now there appeared a price—so why not pay it, which most of the spokesmen no doubt had been prepared to do, or try to lower the cost by breaking up the basic pattern of teaching in favor of individualization within the comprehensive class.

From a theoretical point of view the inclusion of process data gives rise to a systematic model about the relationship between objectives, environmental conditions, teaching method, teaching time and level of attainment of the students. The details of the model have been presented elsewhere (Dahllöf, 1967, 1971a). Here we will underline only some main points that need to be considered in order to arrive at an explanation that at the same time is compatible with facts and models from situations where there is a great deal of individualization, at least with regard to pacing, as in programmed instruction.

(1) The level of objectives is important. In this particular case this can already be illustrated by the rough distinction between elementary and advanced curriculum units. The elementary units are basic and important to the extent that there is a demand for a high level of performance not only in both school systems but also by the great majority of students within each system. Skewed distributions and ceiling effects in the tests are also shown. So far, the findings may be regarded as a special case under limited conditions of the Carroll (1963, 1965, 1971) school learning model and the Bloom (1968, 1971a, 1971b, 1971c) mastery learning principles. Even though Cronbach (1971) has questioned parts of the Carroll and Bloom models as a general principle, I would like to point out that this particular case—elementary curriculum units of Mathematics—seems to correspond fairly well to the criteria held up by Bloom (1971c). Things like addition and multiplication, basic problem-solving tasks such as percent, discount and interest, etc. quite simply are so important both for further studies in the subject and for practical life, that something very close to mastery is demanded, even though it takes many more lessons to reach that level in randomly grouped, heterogeneous classes when traditional classroom instruction is used.

(2) It has to be observed that the time factor here does not directly reflect school learning—but school teaching of mastery learning. Thus the model does not say anything about the psychological details of the learning process except for the basic fact that students need different amounts of time irrespective of what kind of learning is involved. Whether it is a unidimensional training process or, as Cronbach (1971) suggests, a cognitive process of a multidimensional kind is of secondary interest in this connection.

(3) In this case we are interested in the influence that is exerted by a certain set-up of environmental factors. When systems are compared with regard to the effectiveness in their operation, it follows by definition that the outcome measures ought to be strongly related to objectives as well as to the processes that really have been going on when the factors have been operating. Thus, there is a demand for high *content validity*.

(4) Concerning the environment, let us make another rough distinction between, on the one hand, the general social, economic and cultural aspects of the environment and, on the other hand, such factors that constitute the immediate background and the environmental conditions for the teaching. The general background as here defined is a fixed feature of the school system that cannot within reasonable time be subject to change and in any case not by the school authorities.

(5) The immediate background for the teaching situations, on the other hand, consists of such conditions that at least in principle are under the control of the school system (if not of the single teacher).

Three main factors belong to this group: *first,* the physical characteristics of the school: size and structure of school buildings; distance between school and home; supply of teaching aids, etc. *Second,* administrative factors or rules of organization: principles for class-size and grouping of students; length of school-year and school-day; number of lessons a week in a given subject, and so on and so forth. We would also like to include, *third*, the characteristics of the teacher with regard to the repertoire of teaching patterns which he has been trained to use.

Although these factors may be changed now and then, they are, from the point of view of the single teacher, very often permanent for a considerable amount of time, e.g., a school-year. They represent the conditions under which the teacher has to do his job when trying to fulfill the objectives of the curriculum. In order to underline the role of these immediate environmental factors in the front line of the teaching situation for the dynamics of the teaching process we have used the term *direct frame factors* or simply *frame factors* (Dahllöf, 1967, 1971*a*, 1971*b*).

The main point is that these frame factors may be regarded as the primary expression of the very fundamental fact that schools are operating with limited resources. The frame factors thus restrict the time and space for the different types of teaching activities, which means that certain, psychological and/or physical barriers are being developed from the point of view of the teacher in his role as an administrator and coordinator of the learning activities of the students. This view of the frame factors has been developed in much more detail in more recent studies within our project by Lundgren (1972*a*). He also points out that even the objectives may act and be regarded as frames, e.g., when time is restricted and there are several objectives to be achieved, the time for teaching the first units restricts the degree of freedom to be used on the latter ones. Since the goals and objectives already have an established place in our paradigm and since they also may be said to exert an activating force, we prefer in this connection to treat them separately and to reserve the term frame factors for the immediate and strategic environment of the teaching situation.

Now, in the ability grouping case just mentioned a combination of three frame factors is of strategic interest:

(1) The total time at disposal during the school year for the Mathematics was about the same in the positively selected and in the comprehensive classes.

(2) Lack of appropriate teaching aids as well as lack of sufficient in-service training restricted the repertoire of the teacher to the traditional class-centered teaching pattern.

(3) The composition of the classes was different with regard to general ability, prior knowledge and social background. Even though the size of the classes was somewhat greater in positively selected settings, the main difference between the heterogeneous comprehensive school classes on the one hand and the positively selected, homogeneous classes on the other hand is the relative lack of so-called slow students in the latter. Thus the difference between the systems in general ability is greater at the 10th-25th percentile than at the median.

These frame conditions now—according to the model—interact in the following way. Since there is a demand for something not far from mastery in the elementary curriculum units, this means that the teacher is under pressure to see to it that the great majority of the students in the class reach the level of objectives. Thus the students somewhere in the region between the 10th and 25th percentile within the class become something like a *reference group* or—as we have called it—a *steering criterion group* for the teacher's appraisal of the progress of his students and for his decision to leave the old curriculum unit and to proceed to a new one.

When various other studies are combined—e.g., the Swedish reports and the Borg (1965) study from Utah—there are already supporting indications for the operation of such a steering group (Dahllöf, 1967, 1971). Since total time was not only restricted but also the same in the two systems under comparison and since it takes more time to teach the slow learners at the lower end of the distribution in the comprehensive classes to reach mastery, a greater part of the total available time is spent on elementary units in these classes than in the positively selected ones. This also means that the clever students in the comprehensive classes must wait a longer time for their slower classmates before they are allowed to take up a new topic. Meanwhile they are doing something else or are busy with so-called enrichment exercises, which in elementary units often imply no more than a greater number of numerically—but not necessarily logically— more difficult examples. The outcome of this is overlearning of low additional return.

We have here at some length presented notions that hold a key position in our curriculum-related model of classroom teaching, viz. the concepts of *frame factors* and *steering criterion group*. Of these the frame concept is of a more general kind, while the phenomenon of a steering group is subordinate so far as it may appear in the traditional class-centered instruction under certain frame conditions, such as when time is restricted but the objectives still call for a high level of performance. This also means that it is not bound to a certain part of the distribution. The indication of a steering group somewhere in the lowest quarter of the distribution is consequently a function of high demands and relatively plenty of time. When there is a change, e.g., in terms of an unexpected loss of a number of lessons at the end of the school year, then the steering group may move upwards, which simply means that the teacher is forced by the conditions to lower his ambition on part of a greater number of pupils, leaving more of them behind. On the other hand, when instructional aids and teaching competence are at hand and time is not restricted, no steering group phenomenon can be expected—and this is the frame condition for an individualized instruction for all students as a necessary (but probably still not sufficient) condition for mastery learning.

Before we go down to the classroom instruction level again, let us make two short comments, the one on mastery learning and the other on frame factors and comparative education.

As regards the mastery learning problem, I should like to draw attention to the very simple fact that time almost always seems to be restricted as far as schools and other similar institutions are concerned. This calls for a new concern for the priority problem and balance problem within curriculum theory. What part of the curriculum should be subject to our mastery teaching efforts and at the expense of what kinds of units and activities? (Cf. Dahllöf, 1973.)

As regards frame factors and mass investigations of a sociological and comparative kind, there seems to be a quite common methodological problem that is seldom discussed. When group tests and questionnaires are distributed, researchers often collect all the data at the same time on all kinds of variables, and this is so far quite in order. This is, however, often connected with the assumption that variables treated as independent also have been operating parallel to the teaching and learning of the functions studied as dependent variables in the tests. This assumption, however, can be questioned. If the tests, such as the ones discussed above, are of a basic character containing a great number of elementary items, this is very often not the case.

Let us take class-size or age of the teacher as an example—frame factors that are fairly constant for a school year but that may often be subject to change between school years. In general, the analysis is carried through *as if* the tests have a high content validity and *as if* the independent factor has constantly held the values for each class that is observed in the group test situation at the end of the period.

The problem case we have in mind can be characterized as a lack of consonance between the operation of the frame factors on the one hand and the teaching and learning of the functions assessed by the test items on the other, either because the test is measuring things that were subject to educational treatment at an earlier stage than anticipated, because there have been unconsidered changes in the frame factors or because both types of errors have been operating. The consequence of this type of error is underestimation of the real role of the frame factor. If factors like these are not under control in more complex analyses, e.g., in comparisons between school systems in comparative education (cf. Husén *et al.*, 1967; cf. also Dahllöf, 1971*b*, 1971*c*), it may lead to serious errors in the conclusions.

A RETURN TO THE MICRO LEVEL

It ought to be obvious from this outline of a model on the macro level, that it does contain a number of assumptions about the detailed interaction pattern of the classroom. Some of these assumptions and consequences have been investigated in a second phase of our project that has recently been reported in a dissertation by Lundgren (1972*a*). Here 46 classes at the senior secondary school level were followed during the school year in five subjects with special regard to the teachers' plans and intentions on the one hand and the actual process on the other hand. Changes of strategy were of prime interest. In one of the subjects, Mathematics, 8 of the 46 classes, in addition to this, were followed by means of interaction analysis, based on tape-recordings of every third lesson during the fall semester (cf. also Dahllöf and Lundgren, 1970; Dahllöf, Lundgren, and Siöö, 1971).

It would lead too far to report on the details of this study here. Let us only point out some main characteristics.

—The studies by B. O. Smith *et al.* (1962), Smith and Meux *et al.* (1966) as well as by Bellack *et al.* (1966) have both from a theoretical and a methodological point of view been of utmost importance for the studies.

—The interaction analysis has been carried out through a combination of the systems by Bellack *et al.* (1966), Flanders (1964) and Bales (1950). For our purposes it was—with special regard to the hypothesis connected with the steering-group phenomenon—of prime importance to identify every individual student taking part in the interaction. Also in other respects the systems were supplemented by new variables.

—The teacher's perception of the class as a whole and his distinction of different subgroups of students were tested by Lundgren (1972a) by means of a technique of free recall based on Miller's (1967) communication theory. This part of the study sheds new light on the dynamics of the teaching situation in general, and on the frame concept as well as on the steering-group phenomenon in particular.

—The analyses of the interaction patterns also revealed patterns of behavior that hang together in a meaningful way and also confirm the influence of the limiting frame factors as well as the existence of a steering-group under certain conditions. The analyses seem to give support to the general directions from the earlier phase of the Compass project about the possible role of process data in order to highlight the educational processes behind achievement test results (cf. also Lundgren, 1972b).

CONCLUSIONS

Our re-analysis of research on the influence of certain environmental factors on student achievement has indicated that educational process data seem to be helpful in building up an explanatory model not only on the macro or systems level but also on the classroom interaction level. Some of the more important and promising characteristics of the approach may be summarized as follows:

—Data are curriculum-related, reflecting the goals and intentions of the instructional program as well as the ambitions of the teacher.

—Data are related to basic patterns of teaching, in this particular case class-centered instruction of a fairly traditional type.

—Data reflect the cumulative character of the teaching process and its long-term effects.

—Data mirror the teaching process as a continuous change of perceptions and behaviors over time towards certain goals. They do this also if time for teaching a certain curriculum unit is analyzed as an important variable related systematically to level of achievement.

—The analysis takes into consideration that the teaching of a certain curriculum unit is generally running through a series of phases like presentation, training and control—each phase with its own characteristic pattern with regard to communication and interaction.

—Data are dynamic also in as much as they can be related in a meaningful way to the restrictions that are imposed upon most teaching situations by frame factors like limits of space and time.

—Data are also dynamic in so far as they try to describe and do justice to the role that in the teaching situation and its different phases—and because of the combined effects of goals and frames—is played by different groups of students.

The consequence of this is to broaden the paradigms and models of research on teaching. To broaden instead of breaking down—and to do it in a way that both keeps control of strategic factors and facilitates theoretically meaningful interpretations—is by no means an easy task. It is, however, a challenge that has to be met by varied and systematic attacks in the field instead of by avoidance behavior in the laboratory. And yet, experimental designs, refined procedures of measurement and analysis may still be helpful, even though they do not represent conditions that are sufficient for a real advancement of research in this area.

When related to already existing research data both on the systems and classroom interaction level, the Swedish findings and models that have been drawn upon here, both theoretically and empirically give strong support to claims for a reorientation of educational research as published by Westbury (1971), Gowin (1972) and Scriven (1972). It would lead too far to take up their recent contributions to discussion in this connection. These new trends in the thinking about educational research are interesting not only because they may promise significant differences—even though they are located at other places in the model than traditionally anticipated—but also, and more important, because they build bridges between different subfields of educational research, facilitating the development of educational theory. Methodologically and theoretically these new trends also support the development of new strategies of planning and evaluation. To take only one example, part of our own project group will now enter upon a project, aiming at an evaluation—curriculum-related and process-centered—of non-graded schools (Goodlad and Anderson, 1963) as a means of a deliberate policy of supporting and strengthening distant rural areas as a living local society (Andrae and Dahllöf, 1973).

REFERENCES

Ackerman, W. I. "Teacher Competence and Pupil Change." *Harvard Educational Review* 24 (1954): 273–89.

Alkin, M. C., and Johnson, M. "Comments on the Research and Development Program of Byra L4:1." *Newsletter School Research* 24 (1971). National Board of Education, Stockholm, Sweden. Mimeo.

Alkin, M. C., and Johnson, M. "Some Observations on Educational Research and Development in Sweden." *Scandinavian Journal of Educational Research* 16 (1972): 41-60.

Amidon, E., and Hunter, E. *Improving Teaching. The Analysis of Verbal Interaction* (New York: Holt, Rinehart & Winston Inc., 1967).

Andrae, A., and Dahllöf, U. "Process Analysis of Non-Graded Rural Schools in Sweden. Outline of an Evaluation Program." Project PANG 5. Reports from the Institute of Education No. 31. University of Göteborg, Göteborg. Mimeo.

Bales, R. F. *Interaction Process Analysis* (Reading, Mass.: Addison & Wesley, 1950).

Beauchamp, G. A., and Beauchamp, K. E. *Comparative Analysis of Curriculum Systems*. 2nd ed. (Wilmette, Ill.: The Kagg Press, 1972).

Bellack, A. A., et al. *The Language of the Classroom* (New York: Teachers College Press, 1966).

Block, J. H. (ed.) *Mastery Learning. Theory and Practice* (New York: Holt, Rinehart & Winston Inc., 1971).

Bloom, B. S. "Learning for Mastery." UCLA-CSEIP *Evaluation comment* 2 (No. 1, 1968).

———. "Mastery Learning." In Block, J. H. (ed.) *Mastery Learning. Theory and Practice* (New York: Holt, Rinehart & Winston Inc., 1971), pp. 47–63. (a)

———. "Individual Differences in School Achievement: A Vanishing Point?" *Education at Chicago* (Winter 1971): 4–14. (b)

———. "Mastery Learning and Its Implications for Curriculum Development." In Eisner, E. W. (ed.) *Confronting Curriculum Reform* (Boston: Little, Brown & Co., 1971), pp. 17–49. (c)

Boalt, G. *Skolutbildning och skolresultat för barn ur olika samhällsgrupper i Stockholm.* Akad. avh. Monografier utgivna av Stockholms kommunalförvaltning (Stockholm: P. A. Norstedt & Söner, 1947).

Borg, W. R. "Ability Grouping in the Public Schools." *Journal of Experimental Education* 34 (No. 2, 1965): 1–97.

Bracht, G. H. "Experimental Factors Related to Aptitude-Treatment Interactions." *Review of Educational Research* 40 (1970): 627–45.

Carroll, J. B. "A Model for School Learning." *Teachers College Record* 64 (1963): 723–33.

———. "School Learning Over the Long Haul." In Krumboltz, J. D. (ed.) *Learning and the Educational Process* (Chicago: Rand McNally, 1965), pp. 249–69.

———. "Problems of Measurement Related To the Concept of Learning for Mastery." In Block, J. H. (ed.) *Mastery Learning. Theory and Practice* (New York: Holt, Rinehart & Winston Inc., 1971), pp. 29–46.

Cronbach, L. J. "How Can Instruction Be Adapted to Individual Differences?" In Gagné, R. M. (ed.) *Learning and Individual Differences* (Columbus, Ohio: Charles E. Merrill Books, 1967), pp. 23–39.

————. "Comments on Mastery Learning and Its Implications for Curriculum Development." In Eisner, E. W. (ed.) *Confronting Curriculum Reform* (Boston: Little, Brown & Co., 1971), pp. 49–55.

Cronbach, L. J., and Snow, R. E. *Individual Differences in Learning Ability as a Function of Instructional Variables*. Final report (Stanford, Calif.: Stanford University Press, 1969).

Dahllöf, U. *Kursplaneundersökningar i matematik och modersmalet*. Diss. 1957 ars skolberedning III. SOU 1960:15. Ecklesiastikdepartementet, Stockholm.

————. *Skoldifferentiering och undervisningsförlopp*. Göteborg Studies in Educational Sciences 2 (Stockholm: Almqvist & Wiksell, 1967).

————. *Ability Grouping, Content Validity and Curriculum Process Analysis* (New York: Teachers College Press, 1971). (*a*)

————. "Relevance and Fitness Analysis in Comparative Education." *Scandinavian Journal of Educational Research* 15 (No. 3, 1971): 101–21. (*b*)

————. "Curriculum Process Analysis and Comparative Education of School Systems." *Paedagogica Europaea* (1970/71): 21–36. (*c*)

————. "Rahmenfaktoren und zielreichendes Lehren." In Edelstein, W., and Hopf, D. (eds.) *Bedingungen des Bildungsprozesses* (Stuttgart: Ernst Klett Verlag, 1973), pp. 271–84.

Dahllöf, U. S., and Lundgren, U. P. "Macro and Micro Approaches Combined for Curriculum Process Analysis: A Swedish Educational Field Project." Project Compass 23. Reports from the Institute of Education No. 10. University of Göteborg, Göteborg. Mimeo.

Dahllöf, U., Lundgren, U. P., and Siöö, M. "Reform Implementation Studies As a Basis for Curriculum Theory: Three Swedish Approaches." *Curriculum Theory Network* 7 (1971): 99–117.

Flanders, N. A. *Teacher Influence, Pupils Attitudes and Achievement* (Washington, D.C.: U.S. Government Printing Office, 1965).

————. *Analyzing Teaching Behavior* (Reading, Mass.: Addison & Wesley Publ. Co., 1970).

Gage, N. L. *Teacher Effectiveness and Teacher Education. The Search for a Scientific Basis* (Palo Alto, Calif.: Pacific Books, 1972).

Gagné, R. M. (ed.) *Learning and Individual Differences* (Columbus, Ohio: Charles E. Merrill Books, 1967).

Gallagher, J. J. "Three Studies of the Classroom." In Gallagher, J. J., Nuthall, G. A., and Rosenshine, B. *Classroom Observation*. AERA Monograph Series on Curriculum Evaluation 6 (Chicago: Rand McNally & Co., 1970), pp. 74–108.

————. "A 'Topic Classification System' for Classroom Observation." In Gallagher, J. J., Nuthall, G. A., and Rosenshine, B. *Classroom Observation*. AERA Monograph Series on Curriculum Evaluation 6 (Chicago: Rand McNally & Co., 1970), pp. 30–73.

Goodlad, J. I., and Anderson, R. H. *The Nongraded Elementary School*. Revised edition (New York: Harcourt, Brace & World, Inc., 1963).

Gowin, D. B. "Is Educational Research Distinctive?" In Thomas, L. G. (ed.) *Philo-

sophical Redirection of Educational Research. Seventy-First Yearbook of the National Society for the Study of Education. Part 1 (Chicago: The University of Chicago Press, 1972), pp. 9–25.

Härnqvist, K. "Beräkning av reserver för högre utbildning." Pp. 7–92 in SOU 1958:11. *Reserverna för högre utbildning. Beräkningar och metoddiskussion* (Stockholm: Ecklesiastikdepartementet, 1958).

———. *Individuella differenser och skoldifferentiering*. 1957 ars skolberedning II. SOU 1960:13 (Stockholm: Ecklesiastikdepartementet, 1960).

———. "Social Factors and Educational Choice." Reports from the Institute of Education No. 3. University of Göteborg, Göteborg. Mimeo.

Härnqvist, K., and Bengtsson, J. "Educational Reform and Educational Equality. Contribution to a Reader on Social Stratification." R. Scase (ed.) Reports from the Institute of Education No. 20. University of Göteborg, Göteborg. Mimeo.

How Teachers Make a Difference. U.S. Office of Education (Washington, D.C.: U.S. Government Printing Office, 1971).

Husén, T. *Begavning och miljö* (Stockholm: Gebers, 1948).

Husén, T., et al. *International Study of Achievement in Mathematics. A Comparison of Twelve Countries*. Vol. I-II (Stockholm: Almqvist & Wiksell; and New York: John Wiley & Sons, 1967).

Husén, T., and Boalt, G. *Educational Research and Educational Change. The Case of Sweden* (Stockholm: Almqvist & Wiksell; and New York: John Wiley & Sons, 1968).

Husén, T., and Dahllöf, U. *Mathematics and Communication Skills in School and Society* (Stockholm: The Industrial Council for Social and Economic Studies, 1960).

Husén, T., and Dahllöf, U. "An Empirical Approach to the Problem of Curriculum Content." *International Review of Education* 11 (1965): 51–76.

Husén, T., and Henrysson, S. (eds.) *Differentiation and Guidance in the Comprehensive School* (Stockholm: Almqvist & Wiksell, 1959).

Jackson, P. W. "The Way Teaching Is." In *The Way Teaching Is*, 7–27.

Kallós, D. "On Educational Scientific Research." Report from the Institute of Education No. 36. University of Lund, Lund. Mimeo.

Lundgren, U. P. *Frame Factors and the Teaching Process*. Project Compass. Göteborg Studies in Educational Sciences 8 (Stockholm: Almqvist & Wiksell, 1972). (a)

———. "Educational Process Analysis." Two articles. Reports from the Institute of Education No. 24. University of Göteborg, Göteborg, 1972. Mimeo. (b)

Marklund, S. "Comparative School Research and the Swedish School Reform." *International Review of Education* 17 (1971): 39–49.

Marklund, S., and Söderberg, P. *The Swedish Comprehensive School* (New York: Humanities Press, 1968).

Miller, G. A. *The Psychology of Communication* (New York: Basic Books, Inc., 1967).

Morsh, J. E., and Wilder, E. W. "Identifying the Effective Instructor: A Review of the Quantitative Studies, 1900-1952." USAF Pers. Train. Res. Cent. Res. Bull., No. AFPTCR–TR–54–44, 1954.

Nuthall, G. A. "An Experimental Comparison of Alternative Strategies for Teaching Concepts." *American Educational Research Journal* 5 (1968): 561–84.

———. "A Review of Some Selected Recent Studies of Classroom Interaction and Teaching Behavior." In Gallagher, J. J., Nuthall, G. A., and Rosenshine, B. *Classroom Observation.* AERA Monograph Series on Curriculum Evaluation 6 (Chicago: Rand McNally, 1971), pp. 6–29.

Paulston, R. G. *Educational Change in Sweden: Planning and Accepting the Comprehensive School Reforms* (New York: Teachers College Press, 1968).

Rosenshine, B. "The Stability of Teacher Effects Upon Student Achievement." *Review of Educational Research* 40 (1970): 647–62.

———. "Teaching Behaviors Related To Pupil Achievement: A Review of Research." In Westbury, I., and Bellack, A. A. (eds.) *Research into Classroom Processes* (New York: Teachers College Press, 1971), pp. 51–98. (*a*)

———. "New Directions for Research on Teaching." In *How Teachers Make a Difference.* U.S. Office of Education (Washington, D.C.: U.S. Government Printing Office, 1971), pp. 66–95. (*b*)

Rosenshine, B., and Furst, N. "Research on Teacher Performance Criteria." In Smith, B. O. (ed.) *Research in Teacher Education. A Symposium* (Englewood Cliffs, N.J.: Prentice Hall Inc., 1971), pp. 37–72.

Scriven, M. "Objectivity and Subjectivity in Educational Research." In Thomas, L. G. (ed.) *Philosophical Redirection of Educational Research.* Seventy-First Yearbook of the National Society for the Study of Education. Part 1 (Chicago: The University of Chicago Press, 1972), pp. 94–142.

Smith, B. O., et al. *A Study of the Logic of Teaching* (Urbana: University of Illinois, 1962).

Smith, B. O., and Meux, et al. *A Study of the Strategies of Teaching* (Urbana: Bureau of Educational Research, College of Education, University of Illinois, 1966).

Smith, B. O., and Geoffrey, L. *The Complexities of an Urban Classroom* (New York: Holt, Rinehart & Winston Inc., 1968).

Stolurow, L. M. "Model the Master Teacher or Master the Teaching Model?" In Krumboltz, J. D. (ed.) *Learning and the Educational Process* (Chicago: Rand McNally & Co., 1965), pp. 223–47.

Svensson, N.-E. *Ability Grouping and Scholastic Achievement.* Diss. Stockholm Studies in Educational Psychology 5 (Stockholm: Almqvist & Wiksell, 1962).

Thomas, L. G. (ed.) "Philosophical Redirection of Educational Research." Seventy-First Yearbook of the National Society for the Study of Education. Part 1 (Chicago: The University of Chicago Press, 1972).

The Way Teaching Is. Report of the Seminar on Teaching. 1966 (Washington, D.C.: NEA, ASCD and CSI, 1966).

Westbury, I. "Problems and Prospects." In Westbury, I., and Bellack, A. A. *Research into Classroom Processes* (New York: Teachers College Press, 1971), pp. 227–52.

25. COMPARING CURRICULA*

Decker F. Walker and Jon Schaffarzick

Since the launching of Sputnik in 1957, Americans have spent millions of dollars and occupied the time of hundreds of scholars and scientists on curriculum development projects. Most of this money and effort has gone to design new sets of course materials—textbooks, learning materials and apparatus of all kinds, teachers' guides, and tests—and to prepare teachers to use them. For the most part, the new course materials were intended to replace existing materials in standard school subjects, not to add new subjects to the school curriculum. After the urgency and excitement of the early years of this new curriculum movement had passed, many individuals and groups, including the Congress of the United States, demanded objective evidence of the value of the new courses. To provide this evidence, a number of studies were designed and carried out to compare the achievement of students who studied from traditional materials with that of students who studied from the new materials. Such experimental or quasi-experimental comparisons would, many hoped, definitively answer questions about the relative value of the new and old courses.

This paper began as a review of the experiments done since 1957 that were

SOURCE. *Review of Educational Research* 44 (Winter 1974), pp. 83–111.

*We thank Edward G. Begle, Leonard Berk, Robert Bridgham, Robert Calfee, Lee Cronbach and Elliot Eisner of Stanford University and Barak Rosenshine of the University of Illinois for criticism of earlier drafts of this paper. Errors that remain are the responsibility of the authors.

412

designed to compare the subject matter achievement of students using new or innovative curricula with that of students using traditional curricula. We reasoned that if the innovative curricula were substantial improvements over traditional ones then these experiments should show a consistent advantage for students using innovative curricula. The pattern of results we found in the reports we read seemed at first to show such a result. But a more thorough analysis showed that innovative curricula were superior only in their own terms. More precisely, these studies showed that students using different curricula in the same subject generally exhibited different patterns of test performance, and that these patterns generally reflected differences in content inclusion and emphasis in the curricula.

The first part of this paper is a review of research from which we draw some tentative conclusions about the influence of curricula on school achievement. The second part is an exploration of some implications of this review for educational theory, research, evaluation, and practice.

REVIEW OF STUDIES

Our search through educational reference works and journals led us to twenty-six studies which compared students exposed to different curricula in the same subject on some measure of school achievement. We did not look for and did not find any studies comparing different curricula solely on affective measures, such as measures of attitudes, personality structure, social or political beliefs or orientations. Also, out of practical necessity we excluded studies comparing reading programs. We realize that we have not located all studies comparing achievement under different curricula that have been carried out, since these studies are reported in a great many journals, newsletters, monographs, and books in various fields, but conclusions based upon these twenty-six studies are not likely to be reversed by the additional studies that an exhaustive search would disclose.

Of the studies we found, twenty-three were designed in such a uniform way as to permit direct comparison of their results. Each of these studies compared two or more groups of students, at least one group of which had studied a school subject in American public schools using a traditional curriculum and at least one other of which had studied the same subject under comparable conditions in the same school(s) using an innovative curriculum. The principal criterion measure in each of these studies was an "objective" pencil-and-paper test of subject matter achievement given immediately following completion of the curriculum.

Throughout this paper the term *curriculum* will be used synonymously with *curriculum materials*—textbooks, teachers' guides, workbooks, laboratory apparatus and other teaching and learning materials—in use by a teacher in a classroom. Disputes about the proper definition of the term *curriculum* form a literature in their own right to which we will not attempt to add. We are concerned in this paper with the curriculum as a policy variable, as a line of action which can be set in motion by an educational policymaker. The adoption, purchase, and use in classrooms of packages of curriculum materials certainly constitutes such a policy variable. Some other commonly used definitions like "the experience of students" imply that the curriculum is not directly controllable by a policymaker. Speaking of the curriculum as *curriculum materials in use* has the additional advantage of enabling us to specify the treatment variable in these experimental comparisons easily and, at least at one level of abstraction, completely. (Of course without a separate investigation we do not know exactly how teachers used the curriculum, so, the specification is not really complete. Nevertheless, separate investigations can, in theory, discover how curriculum materials are used in classrooms and thus complete the specification.)

The studies showed a great variety within this basic common pattern. Twelve of them were in the sciences, five were in mathematics, four were in social studies, and two were in English. Only five of the studies compared groups of elementary school students; the remainder compared high-school or junior-high-school students. About half of the studies included more than two groups. The additional groups permitted various other comparisons: e.g., of different innovative curricula with the traditional one; of groups taught by trained teachers with groups whose teachers had no special training; of different ability levels, amount of exposure to the innovative curriculum, and the like.

Several of these studies had more than a thousand students in both innovative and traditional groups. The smallest number of students in any group in any study was 28. The typical study compared from 4-8 *classes* of students. In most of the studies, the curricula were used for one school year before final achievement tests were administered. In a few studies, the course was completed and the achievement test administered after a shorter time, the shortest reported time being twenty-two school days (at one hour of study in class per day (Potterfield, 1968)). In the National Longitudinal Study of Mathematics Achievement, numerous groups composed of thousands of students were followed through five years of mathematics study. Welch and Walberg (1972) used the classes of a nationwide sample of fifty-three teachers.

In about half of the studies, some criterion measure in addition to subject matter achievement was administered including, in part, measures of critical thinking (4 studies), scientific reasoning (4 studies), political attitudes (1 study), attitudes toward the subject (3 studies), and preference among ways of using knowledge (1 study). All studies used a test of statistical significance, in this case either a t test or an F test, at the .05 level or below.

The use of an index of statistical significance as a criterion for judging that a difference is worth attending to presents all educational researchers with serious difficulties. A study with great statistical power can be designed merely by including large numbers of students and classes in each group. If any differences exist at all, no matter how small, a sufficiently powerful design will show statistically significant results. Yet these results may be of no theoretical or practical value whatever. When studies of greatly different power are lumped together simply on the basis of the statistical significance of the findings, a very rough and wandering criterion is being used. Short of calculating an index of power for each of these studies, an impossible task in many cases because of incomplete reporting, nothing can be done about this serious problem. Furthermore, even if it could be handled mathematically, the question of the educational significance of the criterion chosen would remain. Unhappily, we follow the established precedent of accepting the criterion of statistical significance and hope for a day when results are reported and compared in a different way.

In most of these studies, students and teachers were assigned to either the traditional or the innovative curriculum by unspecified procedures operating in each school district. Therefore, it is possible that the students and teachers studying from innovative curricula differed systematically from those studying from traditional curricula and that this initial difference, not the curriculum, was responsible for any achievement test differences that eventually showed up. In about half of the studies, the investigators used a regression procedure to correct achievement test scores for initial differences in measured academic ability. In some of the remaining studies, academic ability was dealt with explicitly in another way: by showing that different groups did not differ on pretests of academic ability, by forming subgroups of uniform ability, or by matching students on the basis of measured academic ability. None of these procedures insures that the groups are alike in all other ways. The surest guarantee against this threat is random assignment of teachers and students to curricula. Only two studies (Welch and Walberg, 1972 and Williams and Shuff, 1963) assigned subjects to curricula randomly. Thus we cannot be sure that effects assigned to curricula might not be due to unspecified initial differences among subjects.

It is impossible to say now just how likely it is that uncontrolled initial differences could be responsible for effects that would otherwise be assigned to studying from different curricula. Ultimately this is an empirical question, to be decided by checking the results of carefully controlled investigations against similar studies that are not so well controlled or by detailed study of the interactions of subject characteristics and outcome measures. Random assignment in school settings can disrupt normal routine and is expensive. It requires the cooperation of the individuals and institutions involved, which introduces the possibility of large numbers of potential subjects and schools declining to participate, thereby introducing still another threat to validity of the findings. Competent persons differ in their judgment of the value, in general, of quasi-experiments. Without taking a stand one way or the other on this general issue, we bow to the circumstance that virtually the only evidence available bearing on the question we are concerned with here is quasi-experimental. We shall try to make what we can of this evidence, keeping in mind its shortcomings.

Another design weakness of these studies as a group is the way in which students, teachers, schools, and communities were selected for study. In every case students and teachers selected were at least willing, if not anxious, to experiment with new curricula. Such schools, we suspect, are more often found in well-to-do localities than in poor ones, more often in suburbs than in rural areas or inner-cities. The teachers and students included in the studies are probably not typical even of those in such favored schools, since teacher and student volunteers were commonly used. Students with records of academic failure are almost certainly under-represented in these studies. Of course, many of these curricula were intended for students in academic tracks, and it is important to select samples that are representative of the clientele likely to adopt the curriculum. Even so, however, we must suppose that enthusiasm of student and teacher volunteers, at times augmented by special attention or even special teacher training provided by the investigators, would affect performance.

In summary, these studies were relatively long-term, large-scale efforts when judged by current standards in educational research. The criterion measures used were reasonably satisfactory and certainly up to the prevailing standard in most respects. Although the studies controlled for many common threats to validity, they were not as well-controlled as we would like or as we might reasonably expect given the state of the art of educational research in this period. In this respect, we are dealing in somewhat questionable data. The situations studied included a variety of ages, grades, school subjects, and geographical regions within the United States.

We plan to consider these studies as a single group, even though they are not fully comparable. Participants were selected differently. The curricula here labeled innovative (or traditional) differ among themselves in subject matter, form, and style. The achievement measures used are not directly comparable even within the same school subject, much less across subject matter and grade levels. Nevertheless, we expect a common pattern to appear across the studies. We hope to be able to say something not just about mathematics curricula or science curricula, but about curricula generally. To be sure, any conclusion about curricula in general will be indicated rather than demonstrated, since the curricula studied are not a representative sample of all curricula. With this reservation in mind, let us examine the studies, searching for a common pattern of results.

Results

Table 1 summarizes the studies and their findings. The first three columns show authors of the report and year of publication, the school subject to which the curricula were devoted, and the grade level of the students using the curricula.

The fourth column shows the number of separate comparisons made in each study of a group of students studying from a traditional curriculum with a group studying from an innovative curriculum. This column was necessary because many studies compared more than two treatment groups (adding additional treatment variables or further differentiating the simple innovative/traditional dichotomy) or more than one criterion measure. In these cases the results were usually mixed, one treatment group exceeding others on one measure but not on another, for example. In order to show the findings of such studies unambiguously, it was necessary to treat each comparison separately. (The careful reader may be bothered by the effect that this way of treating the studies has of weighting those with more separate parts more heavily in the conclusions. This reader may wish to verify that none of the conclusions we reach are changed if each study is reduced to a theoretical weight on one by dividing the figures in columns five, six, and seven of each row of Table 1 by the figure in column four of that row. The only effect of this correction is to reduce somewhat the proportionate factor by which the number of studies in one category exceeds the number in another. The direction and order of magnitude of the results are unchanged.)

Columns five, six, and seven in Table 1 show respectively the number of separate comparisons in each study that found the innovative group scoring significantly higher, and no statistically significant differences (i.e., $p \geq .05$).

The final column in Table 1 labeled "test content bias" needs some explanation. Sometimes groups studying from different curricula were compared on tests specifically designed to measure the learning of content in one of the two curricula. For example, several studies used the final examinations constructed for use with the innovative curriculum. In every case in which the report stated explicitly that the test was specifically designed for use with the innovative curriculum or in which the text was named and our examination of it left no doubt in our minds that the test content favored the innovative curriculum, we placed an "I" in the last column. Similarly, when the report stated that a test was designed specifically for use with the traditional curriculum or when a named test upon examination showed a substantial number of items covering content distinctive in the traditional curriculum, we placed a "T" in the last column opposite that study. When we were unable to determine without doubt whether a test favored one group or the other, we placed a "?" in the last column.

From the summary figures at the bottom of Table 1, it is clear that the innovative groups were superior about four times as often as the traditional groups in these comparisons. The proportion for the five studies using students in elementary grades (twenty-two separate comparisons) was three to one.

Table 2 shows the results analyzed by school subject. Of the twenty-nine separate comparisons of SMSG-taught students with students taught with more traditional texts, the SMSG groups were superior thirteen times, more than twice as many times as the traditional groups. The ratio was four to one for CHEM Study chemistry. For the five different innovative social studies courses for

TABLE 1

Summary of Studies and Findings

Study (1)	Subject (2)	Grade (3)	Total Number of Separate Comparisons (4)	Number of Comparisons Favoring The Innovative Group (5)	Number of Comparisons Favoring The Traditional Group (6)	Number of Comparisons Showing No Sig. Diff. (7)	Direction of Test Content Bias (8)
Stronk (1971)	science	7	4	0	2	2	?
Lance (1964)	biology	9,10	1	0	0	1	T
Wallace (1963)	biology	10	1	0	1	0	T
Wallace (1963)	biology	10	1	1	0	0	I
Wallace (1963)	biology	10	1	0	1	0	?
Lisonbee & Fullerton (1964)	biology	10	1	0	0	1	T
Lisonbee & Fullerton (1964)	biology	10	1	0	0	1	I
George (1965)	biology	10	3	1	0	2	?
Hardy (1970)	chemistry	secondary	1	1	0	0	T
Heath & Stickell (1963)	chemistry	secondary	2	0	2	0	T
Heath & Stickell (1963)	chemistry	secondary	2	2	0	0	I
Herron (1966)	chemistry	secondary	5	1	0	4	?
Rainey (1964)	chemistry	12	1	0	0	1	T
Rainey (1964)	chemistry	12	1	0	0	1	I
Wasik (1971)	physics	secondary	1	1	0	0	?
Heath (1964)	physics	11,12	1	0	0	1	T

TABLE 1 (Continued)

Study	Subject	Grade					
Heath (1964)	physics	11,12	1	1	0	0	I
Welch & Walberg (1972)	physics	11,12	1	0	0	1	?
Minn. Nat'l Labs. (1963)	mathematics	4	1	0	0	1	T
Hungerman (1967)	mathematics	6	1	0	1	0	T
Hungerman (1967)	mathematics	6	1	1	0	0	T
Rosenbloom (1961)	mathematics	7	2	1	0	1	T
Williams & Shuff (1963)	mathematics	7-10	4	0	1	3	T
Payette (1961)	mathematics	7-12	10	1	4	5	T
Payette (1961)	mathematics	7-12	10	10	0	0	—
Buxton (1958)	English	college	2	2	0	0	—
Burton (1971)	English	9	1	1	0	0	—
Taba (1966)	social studies	4-6	3	2	1	0	T
Taba (1966)	social studies	4-6	12	11	1	0	I
Patrick (1971)	social studies	secondary	18	13	0	5	I
Potterfield (1968)	anthropology	4-6	2	0	0	2	T
Derosier & Schuck (1970)	economics	1	1	1	0	0	?
TOTALS			98	53	13	32	

TABLE 2

Results Analyzed by School Subject

SMSG: (Hungerman, 1967; Minnesota National Laboratory, 1963; Payette, 1961; Rosenbloom, 1961; Williams & Shuff, 1963. Five studies, 29 separate comparisons)

number favoring innovative group:	13
number favoring traditional group:	6
number favoring neither:	10

CHEMS: (Hardy, 1970; Heath & Stickell, 1963; Herron, 1966; Rainey, 1964. Four studies, 11 separate comparisons.)

number favoring innovative group:	4
number favoring traditional group:	1
number favoring neither:	6

BSCS: (George, 1965; Lance, 1964; Lisonbee & Fullerton, 1964; Wallace, 1963. Four studies, 9 separate comparisons.)

number favoring innovative group:	2
number favoring traditional group:	2
number favoring neither:	5

Social Studies: (Derosier & Schuck, 1970; Patrick, 1971; Potterfield, 1968; Taba, 1966. Four studies, 38 separate comparisons.)

number favoring innovative group:	29
number favoring traditional group:	2
number favoring neither:	7

which we found experimental comparisons, the ratio was fifteen to one in favor of the innovative courses. Of all identifiable subject groups, only in BSCS biology did the traditional groups hold their own, winning just as often as the innovative groups.

The conclusion that seems to fit these results best is that those who studied from innovative curricula nearly always did as well as or better than those who studied from traditional curricula. In short, the new curricula seem from this analysis to have been a success, to have been genuine improvements over the courses they were designed to replace. But this conclusion is too hasty. Let us see what happens when we take into account the test content bias.

Table 3 shows the numbers of experimental comparisons in which each of the three possible outcomes was found. The column labeled "I > T" represents those independent comparisons in which the innovative group's achievement test scores were significantly higher than the traditional group's scores. The column labeled "T > I" represents those comparisons in which the opposite result was found. The column labeled "I = T" represents comparisons in which the two groups did not differ significantly.

TABLE 3

Results Analyzed by Test Content Bias

Number of separate comparisons with various outcomes:	1 > T	T > 1	1 = T	Total
from among those in which the test favored the *INNOVATIVE* curriculum:	44	1	7	52
from among those in which the test favored the *TRADITIONAL* curriculum.	5	9	16	30
from among those in which the test content bias could not be determined:	4	3	9	16
Total number	53	13	32	98

As the table shows, groups studying from the innovative curriculum scored higher on virtually every test which favored the innovative curriculum, *but* groups studying from the *traditional* curriculum scored higher on a substantial number of comparisons in which the test content more nearly resembled what *they* had studied. Clearly the overall superiority of the innovative groups comes almost entirely from the fifty-two comparisons in which the test content favored the innovative groups. In the remaining forty-six comparisons, the traditional groups were superior in twelve, whereas the innovative groups were superior in only nine. It might still seem as though the overwhelming superiority of the innovative groups on *their* tests more than offsets the slight advantage of the traditional groups on *theirs,* but such a judgment would be no more than guesswork since we cannot be certain that the *degree* of bias was the same in the tests favoring each of the two groups.

All that these results permit us to say is that innovative curricula almost always led to higher achievement scores on tests whose content more closely resembled that of the innovative curriculum, while traditional curricula occasionally led to higher scores on tests whose content more closely resembled that of the traditional curriculum. We cannot say with any confidence what accounts for the "margin of victory" in the two cases.

Some investigators seemed to be aware of the problem of test content bias and attempted to overcome it by using two achievement tests, one biased in favor of each curriculum. The studies using this procedure stand out in Table 1 as those represented by more than one row. We found nine such studies (Wallace, 1963;

Lisonbee and Fullerton, 1964; Heath and Stickell, 1963; Rainey, 1964; Heath, 1964; Hungerman, 1967; Payette, 1961; Taba, 1966; Potterfield, 1968) accounting for fifty-two separate comparisons, five in science, two each in mathematics and social studies. In twenty-one of these comparisons, the test content bias favored the traditional curriculum; in thirty-one, the bias favored the innovative curriculum. (The difference is due to three studies having either more innovative groups than traditional groups or more tests biased in favor of the innovative curriculum than the traditional curriculum.) Table 4 shows the results, and they mirror almost exactly the results for the entire group of twenty-two studies: innovative groups are overwhelmingly superior on tests biased in their direction, and traditional groups do noticeably, but not overwhelmingly, better on tests biased their way.

Other studies dealt with the problem of test bias by looking *within* each test for subscores reflecting patterns of emphasis within the curricula. Five studies proceeded in this way. Wasik (1971) classified physics achievement test items into three categories (derived from the Bloom, *et al. Taxonomy of Educational Objectives: Cognitive Domain*, 1956), comprehension, application, and analysis. He suspected that the innovative and traditional groups might differ in their emphasis on these different levels of cognitive functioning. He found the innovative group to be superior on all three subgroups of items. Unfortunately, the tests used had been revised recently to be more appropriate to the "new" physics, so it is difficult to determine the content bias of the items.

Herron (1966) constructed an achievement test in chemistry called the Taxonomy Test which yielded separate scores for each of the six categories in the Bloom, *et al. Taxonomy*—knowledge, comprehension, application, analysis,

TABLE 4

Results of Studies Using Tests Biased in Both Directions

Number of independent comparisons with various outcomes:[a]	I > T	T > I	I = T	Total
from among those in which the test favored the *INNOVATIVE* curriculum:	28	1	2	31
from among those in which the test favored the *TRADITIONAL* curriculum	3	8	10	21
Total number	31	9	12	52

[a]Including only the nine studies using tests biased in both directions.

synthesis, and evaluation. He found significant differences between innovative and traditional groups on only the application subtest, where the innovative groups scored higher. He noted that this finding was "consistent with the expressed intention of the CHEM Study writers who claim that [the student] is asked to learn facts by using them [p. 167]."

Hungerman (1967) used both a traditional test and an innovative test yielding subscores for various mathematical topics or skills. She found the traditional group scoring significantly higher on three of seven subtests in the traditional test and numerically but not significantly higher on the others. Similarly, the innovative group scored higher on each of the ten subtests in the innovative measure, though this difference was significant in only seven of the ten cases. She summarized the pattern of results in this way: "Examination of the textbooks studied indicated that these performances were closely related to the scope and emphases of the program that each treatment group had followed [p. 34]."

Burton (1971) compared three carefully designed curricular sequences chosen to represent three very different but widely-used patterns of course work in English. One curriculum, called tricomponent, used three more or less distinct units, one in literature, one in composition, and one in language. A second curriculum was literature-centered, featuring reading and writing on six literary themes. Language study was incidental. The third curriculum was organized around certain cognitive processes, rather than conventional subject matter categories. The author summarized the results found when the three groups were given a number of achievement tests as follows:

Student response to literature, when asked for formally in controlled situations, tends to parallel quite closely the kind of teaching the students have been exposed to. Students in the tri-component program, in which there were formal units on the genres and modes of literature, did somewhat better than the others on the short story and poetry tests and made more purely literary judgments on the free responses to the short story and poem . . . .
Students in the tri-component curriculum, which featured more formal and elaborate study of syntax than the other program, did better than the others on the Sentence Relationship Test and the Sentence Combining Test, but not on the writing samples. The implication here is not new: grammar teaches grammar, not writing [p. 27].

Overall, then, the examination of particular studies in which an attempt was made to discriminate finer and more subtle differences between innovative and traditional curricula than a single score on an achievement test confirms the result found earlier: innovative students do better when the criterion is well-matched to the innovative curriculum, and traditional students do better when the criterion is matched to the traditional curriculum.

Two other major recent studies—the International Study of Achievement in Mathematics and the National Longitudinal Study of Mathematical Abilities—

offer evidence on the comparative results of alternative curricula. The International Study of Achievement in Mathematics, a massive study of mathematics achievement in twelve countries including the U.S.A., did not compare curricula directly, but it did include some related investigations. As one part of the study, teachers were asked to indicate whether "the topic any particular question deals with has been covered by the students" taking the test in that school. This variable, which the authors of the study christened "opportunity to learn," yielded correlations of .96, .98, .80, .40 with total math achievement for the four populations studied. The authors concluded that "students have scored higher marks in countries where the tests have been considered by the teachers to be more appropriate to the experience of their students [Husén, 1967, Vol. II, p. 168]."

Teachers were also asked to report the "relative emphasis on certain topics" in their classrooms. These reports were transformed into an "index of emphasis" on the separate topics tested in the achievement test. Correlations with achievement were not computed. Instead the data were presented graphically, and the similarity thus exhibited between the indices of emphasis and achievement scores was striking. The authors conclude as follows:

> In Population 1b (students enrolled in the grade containing most 13-year-olds) there is a striking relation between the teachers' ratings and the students' achievement, and this holds true for all countries. . . . For Population 3b (Preuniversity students) the hypothesis is not supported as conclusively as for Population 1b. In some countries the relation between the emphasis in the teaching and the outcome is fairly strong . . .; in other instances the hypothesis seems to be disproved. . . . In general, the conclusion seems warranted that the profile of achievement of characteristic classifications of subject matter does follow the national emphasis as judged by the teachers [Husén, 1967, Vol. II, p. 174].

Many other curricular variables were tested for their correlation with total mathematics achievement, including time spent on school work, amount and type of teacher preservice preparation, and student participation in special opportunities such as "new mathematics." Most produced essentially zero correlation, and none were correlated with total mathematics achievement as highly as "opportunity to learn."

In their final summary of results, the authors offer the following cautiously stated conclusion on the relationship of the curriculum to achievement in mathematics in the twelve countries studied:

> The emphasis on a given topic in the respective national curricula rated by the teacher was related to students' achievement . . .
> Except for demonstrative geometry, emphasis and achievement followed each other closely. Thus, national differences (but not necessarily individual differences) can in part be explained by differences in emphasis in curriculum [Husen, 1967, Vol. II, p. 300].

The National Longitudinal Study of Mathematical Abilities (NLSMA) (Wilson, Cahen, and Begle, 1968-72) compared the achievement of 112,000 students in 1,500 schools in forty states across grades four through twelve over a five-year period. The textbook used by each class of students in the study was recorded, and the achievement test results were analyzed separately for all students using each textbook group during the years of the study. The unit of analysis in the study was the mean score of all eligible students (e.g., all students studying from the same set of textbooks) in each school rather than the scores of individual students. These means were adjusted for initial differences on verbal and nonverbal ability tests and pretests of mathematics achievement. The groups that had studied with each textbook series were then compared with respect to their adjusted score on a number of mathematics achievement scales. These scales were grouped into four clusters—computation, comprehension, application, and analysis—based on a model of mathematics achievement constructed by the School Mathematics Study Group and inspired by the *Taxonomy of Educational Objectives: Cognitive Domain* (Bloom, Engelhart, Furst, Hill, and Krathwohl, 1956).

The NLSMA results are presented in a multivolume report, the higher numbered volumes of which are still being issued. The results of primary interest here—the achievement of different textbook groups—have been reported in Reports 10 through 18. The results are quite complex, as might be expected in view of the number of measures employed. In essence, the NLSMA staff computed a profile of achievement for each group in their study. For example, the population of students who had studied from SMSG materials through grades 4, 5, and 6 was compared with other groups who had studied from other textbooks on 37 achievement test scales. (A scale consisted of several items thought to measure the same competence, for example, division of whole numbers.) These 37 scales, in turn, were grouped into four broad categories—those measuring computation, those measuring comprehension, those measuring applications, and those measuring analysis. The groups who had studied from different textbooks showed different profiles of achievement. Generally, students who studied from the SMSG text did slightly less well than students in the other five textbook groups on computation scales but noticeably better on the other three clusters of scales. The authors conclude:

In summary, two textbook groups appeared to stand apart from the remaining four as having been associated with generally high achievement. These two, T_1 and T_6, were very different in the character of their profiles. T_1 exhibited relatively low achievement for some measures of computation, whereas T_6 achievement was relatively high on these scales. On the other hand, T_6 exhibited relatively low achievement on certain comprehension measures, while T_1 was relatively high for most of these scales [Wilson, Cahen, and Begle, 1970, NLSMA Report No. 10, p. 182]. [T_6 was a traditional mathematics series; T_1 was the SMSG series.]

Later NLSMA Reports reveal similar findings. Perhaps Report Number 12 expresses it most simply.

One of the clearest conclusions to be drawn from the results is that student achievement, to a substantial extent, mirrors the content treated in the textbook: students are more likely to learn what they have been taught than something else [p. 82].

Conclusions Drawn From the Review

Four distinct lines of evidence tend to controvert our initial impression of the overall superiority of the innovative curricula. First, the studies on which the impression was based, when reanalyzed with test content bias taken into account, show that the advantage of groups studying from innovative curricula comes entirely from those studies in which the test content bias favors the innovative curriculum. Second, that subset of studies in which two agglomerate achievement tests were used—one biased in either direction—shows that traditional curricula more than hold their own in tests biased their way. Third, that subset of studies in which the agglomerate achievement test was analyzed into presumably more coherent and unified subscores show different patterns of achievement on the different components of the achievement measure. The NLSMA study offers particularly convincing evidence of differential patterns of achievement. Finally, the International Study of Achievement in Mathematics shows differences in overall achievement among the different countries, but it also shows that teachers' rankings of their students' opportunity to learn particular topics correlates highly with the students' achievement on items covering that topic. This finding adds further plausibility to the conclusion that different curricula produce different patterns of achievement, not necessarily greater overall achievement.

What these studies show, apparently, is *not* that the new curricula are uniformly superior to the old ones, though this may be true, but rather that *different curricula are associated with different patterns of achievement*. Furthermore, these different patterns of achievement seem generally to follow patterns apparent in the curricula. Students using each curriculum do better than their fellow students on tests which include items not covered at all in the other curriculum or given less emphasis there.

Although this conclusion may seem obvious, a great many seemingly obvious generalizations about education have proven embarrassingly difficult to confirm by research. For example, a substantial amount of research has been done on the effects on academic achievement of such variables as mode or medium of presentation of subject matter or method of teaching. Yet these variables have generally not been found to have an effect on achievement tests of the sort used in the studies reviewed here. Wallen and Travers (1963) reviewed research on teaching methods and concluded that "teaching methods do not seem to make a difference." Getzels and Jackson (1963) reviewed the research on the relationship of teacher personality to academic achievement of pupils and concluded that "very little is known for certain . . . about the relation between teacher personality and teacher effectiveness [p. 574]." Dubin and Taveggia (1968) found in their review of achievement in college courses that college students' final examination scores in their courses were unaffected by differences in teaching method.

Perhaps the most comprehensive recent review of research on variables generally thought likely to affect achievement is Stephens (1967). Stephens studied research reports and summaries concerning a large variety of educational variables: school attendance, instructional television, educational independent study and correspondence courses, size of classes, individual consulting and tutoring, counseling concentration on specific students, the student's involvement, the amount of time spent in study, distraction by jobs and extracurricular activities, size of school, the qualities of teachers that can be rated by principals and supervisors, nongraded schools, team teaching, ability grouping, progressivism vs. traditionalism, discussion vs. lecture, group-centered vs. teacher-centered approaches, the use of frequent quizzes and programmed instruction. Stephens failed to find consistent and significant differences in student achievement associated with any of these variables. So perhaps in considering the seemingly obvious conclusion that outcomes reflect content, we should take the attitude that it is comforting to have at least one of our commonsense notions about education confirmed by research.

A more important reason why we are inclined to regard this "obvious" conclusion as worthy of serious attention is the regularity with which it seems to be overlooked.

If the designers of the studies we have reviewed realized that the curricula they were comparing would have different patterns of outcomes, why did they try to compare these outcome patterns with an agglomerate achievement test yielding only one composite score? And why, if this conclusion is so obvious, is there no systematic apparatus at local, state, regional, or federal levels of school policy-making for considering the merits of various items of content that might be included in the school curriculum or in tests used to judge the success of students, teachers, or curricula? Why is it virtually impossible to find research which attempts to discover the consequences of studying different items of content, when there is so much research on the consequences of different media, methods, or strategies of teaching? And why do schools and funding agencies spend so much on organizational and technological innovations that have not been shown to produce different patterns of achievement and relatively little on innovations in curriculum materials?

Limitations of This Conclusion. Since these studies did not randomly assign students and teachers to curricula, the possibility exists that differential patterns of performance are not due to curricular differences but to initial differences in ability, interests, family background, or some other characteristic of the people involved. It is possible, for example, that students and teachers assigned to new curricula were more able than their counterparts assigned to traditional curricula. If so, then a representative group of students and teachers assigned to an innovative curriculum might conceivably fail to master either the new content or the old. Our conclusion that achievement patterns generally follow patterns of content inclusion and emphasis would then be shown to be limited to able students and teachers. Ability differences are not the only ones that might be responsible for such artifacts and therefore other limitations, presently unknown, may be in order. These possibilities can only be ruled out by further research which controls for them in some way, preferably by random assignment.

Quite likely the terms *coverage* and *emphasis* are merely rough and ready names for very complicated behavioral and social phenomena. Printing a few pages in a book will not magically produce students who can understand and use what is printed there. Including items on tests will not do so either. These actions can focus, direct, or orchestrate a variety of processes whose details may be entirely hidden from us. But there are surely limits to what the underlying phenomena will permit as well as to the directive capacity of variables we control. We would be foolish to expect, for example, that simply including more content in texts and tests would ensure ever greater knowledge and skill. Nor can we conclude that everything included in texts and emphasized by test and teacher will be learned. Strictly speaking, our conclusion is limited to patterns of relative achievement in large groups of students studying roughly similar kinds and amounts of content under similar institutional circumstances. It could no doubt easily be extended to greater differences in content: if one group studies algebra and another studies French, we would certainly expect different patterns of outcomes. On the other hand, it seems doubtful that a group asked to learn ten times as much algebra (as measured, say, by pages of text) in the same time would be able to do so. The line of reasoning used to justify the conclusion can be adapted readily to the case of the individual learner, and future studies could explore the limits of the conclusion as it is applied to individuals.

We will need a more direct test of this conclusion before we can rest content with it. Ideally such a test would consist of experiments in which the differences in content inclusion and emphasis found within two curricula were identified before the test results were known. Then a search would need to be made for differences in achievement corresponding to each major difference in content and emphasis found in the curricula. Each difference identified would offer an hypothesis to be tested. The fate of the general conclusion would depend on the oucome of the tests of the individual hypotheses. Until such evidence is available, the wiser course would seem to be to follow the preponderance of existing circumstantial evidence reviewed here which indicates that patterns of content inclusion and emphasis are in part responsible for achievement differences.

SOME IMPLICATIONS FOR EDUCATION

Educational Theory

That different curricular content and emphasis produce correspondingly different patterns of achievement needs no elaborate theoretical interpretation. Presenting students with the opportunity and encouragement to learn different things should certainly lead to different patterns of achievement. What does seem to need theoretical explanation is that different curricula produce different patterns of achievement when other sorts of variables that seem intuitively likely to affect achievement do not. Why do more experienced or better trained teachers not produce different patterns of achievement? Why does it make no difference whether content is presented by a live teacher or by a television? Or in programmed form? In a large or a small class? What is wrong with the intuitions that lead us to expect differences we fail to find?

Of course, it is possible that differences in mode and medium of presentation *do* make a difference in achievement, but that we have just not learned how to find this difference. Perhaps our tests are not sensitive enough. (But they are sensitive enough to detect the changes associated with curricular differences.) Perhaps we are not measuring a wide enough range of outcomes. (But a wider range of outcome measures *might* show even greater differences due to content inclusion and emphasis.) Perhaps we have not interpreted our data with sufficient wit. Perhaps the lumping together of groups of students who are affected in different ways has obscured the effects. Maybe we have not tried the most powerful modes or media of presentation. Maybe we have not designed our curricula carefully enough and therefore have not taken full advantage of the potential effects of these other variables.

These alternative explanations of our failure to find achievement differences in connection with differences in mode or medium of presentation cannot be dismissed. But neither can we afford to accept them too readily. For if we accepted such explanations routinely, no line of research would ever be abandoned; each new negative finding would only confirm the inadequacy of our research methods and techniques.

A plausible explanation of the alternative hypothesis is that differences in mode or medium of presentation do not as a rule have as great an effect on subject matter achievement as content inclusion and emphasis. Curricula-in-use are multifaceted and redundant. Students, by the time they reach school, exhibit a considerable variety of active learning capacities which enable them to interpret and comprehend their world. Once an item of content has been included in the textbooks and identified as something children should learn, the multiple resources of the curriculum-in-use and the variety of active student learning processes combine to produce a level of achievement that is usually greater than any additional increment that might be produced by any further refinement of the curriculum or any improvement in teaching style or method, medium of instruction, or organizational change in the school or classroom. (This explanation owes a great deal to Stephens' (1967) theory of spontaneous schooling, though we place less emphasis on natural causes and more on policy variables. Carroll (1963) has also advanced a similar line of reasoning.) Students presented with two different curricula should be able to employ any of a number of their developed learning capacities—the vocabulary they understand, their capacity to ask questions that yield information they want or need, their ability to comprehend charts, graphs, tables, and other visual materials, and their ability to relate words to things, to name only a few—to extract meaning from the presentation of the curriculum. In addition, teachers may supplement or correct for defects in the curricular presentation. Students may ask their peers, parents, or older children for help. An exercise may clarify a point that remained obscure in the text. An end-of-unit test may reveal mistakes or deficiencies that the teacher then corrects. In the face of these multiple opportunities and multiple resources, any differences due to the manner or mode of presentation—provided it is a full presentation and not a stripped-down version for the purposes of research—are unlikely to produce differences comparable in size to the effect of not including an item of content at all. But, as this entire review shows, simple quantitative comparisons of outcomes are likely to be misleading. If two sets of curricular outcomes belong to somewhat different "domains," it is impossible to find a single index which will fully express their differences. Given two profiles of achievement, which is "better?"

Obviously, this explanation is highly intuitive. We would like to have some more explicit idea of the sorts of actions on our part that are likely to influence achievement to a larger or smaller degree and an explanation of why each sort of action has the influence that it does. We are not able to provide such an analysis at this time. But we can indicate approximately the direction we think such an analysis will take when it is available. We shall begin with the two variables— content inclusion and emphasis—that we have identified in this paper as likely to influence achievement in major ways, and then we will proceed along lines roughly parallel to those laid down by Carroll (1963) in his model of schooling. We emphasize that this is a preliminary foray for the purpose of illustrating a line of thought we think is likely to prove fruitful, and not a full-fledged explication of this line of thought.

Suppose we begin with what would appear to be the minimum essential for a curricular element to influence student achievement: the element must be presented to the student. (The "element" may be as large as a school curriculum or as small as a sentence or a paragraph. The elements most frequently mentioned, however, are the school *subject* or the *topic* within a school subject.) Examples of this minimal sort of influence might include posting material on the classroom walls, setting up exhibits of various kinds within the school, and making books available, for example, through the library.

In each of these cases, the school makes some things available and not others, thus implicitly giving its stamp of approval to the things it chooses to make available. So even in this minimal case, the school is influencing students by publicly, if implicitly, declaring the elements presented to be suitable and desirable for students to learn. In addition, teachers commonly try to persuade children to engage in certain activities, such as reading and mathematics. These influences are a second way the school curriculum can influence achievement.

Perhaps the most powerful tools for directly affecting children's activities in school are the rewards and punishments the school may dispense in the enforcement of direct orders or of generalized norms of behavior. Probably the simplest case of this is the teacher's power to reward students who carry out her directions and to punish those who do not. The teacher who was completely successful in using this tool could secure whatever pattern of activity he or she wished from children, and thus could have complete control over their apparent engagement with various curricular presentations. Other forms of this mode of curricular influence include the establishment of time schedules for engagement with various curricular elements (an activity of state officials and college entrance boards as well as of teachers and local school officials), making assignments, achievement testing, grading, and the myriad incentives used in connection with these, such as honor rolls and school awards. These processes—giving students access to a presentation of those items, influence stemming from the schools' implicit or explicit endorsement of the item presented, and the establishment of norms relating to the item and their enforcement with rewards and punishments—are called into play almost automatically in a traditional school or classroom, whether or not the teacher's role as "instructor" is exercised in a strong and active way. These processes are built into textbooks and learning materials of all kinds, especially tests. Improvements in the mode or medium of presentation of an item of content may make it easier for the students to whom the items are presented to learn it, or they may make it possible for more students to learn it under fixed constraints of time and resources. These results, however, are unlikely to seem as great as the achievement produced by the "natural" operation of factors which secure the engagement of the students' learning capacities with the item in its unimproved form.

Accepting this line of argument does not imply abandonment of the search for more effective methods of teaching or instruction. On the contrary, it suggests that, insofar as academic achievement is concerned, the selection and presentation of content be considered a vital part of the instructional process and that this entire process be investigated as a whole. At the present time instructional researchers arbitrarily select a body of content to be taught and then search for instructional variables that affect how well or how quickly students learn this fixed body of content. The line of argument developed in this section suggests that this procedure overlooks a cluster of variables—content inclusion and emphasis—known to influence academic achievement and that it may therefore not appreciate the role that the teacher's actions and the characteristics of the instructional materials play in modifying these variables.

The real point of this argument, then, is to suggest giving more attention to content inclusion and emphasis as variables in their own right and as one of the ways teachers and instructional devices affect achievement. (Barak Rosenshine (1971) has called for a similar sort of research integrating the study of teaching with the study of particular curriculum packages. He reached the same conclusion from the other side, as it were, from a consideration of the problem of research on teaching rather than the findings of research on curricula.) As we learn more about the consequences of including and emphasizing various sorts of content, we will be able to make better use of whatever techniques we have for improving their presentation. As our techniques for presentation become more effective, the decision to use them or not in presenting a given item will become even more important.

Educational Research

If the situation is as we have portrayed it, there is a great need for research that would reveal the consequences of studying *different* curricula. Most of the studies we have reviewed here have not addressed this problem. They have proceeded as though different curricula embodied the same intentions, and they have assumed the problem for research to be that of discovering which curriculum performed the common function best. Yet the new curricula of the 1960's were not intended to accomplish the same things as the traditional curricula they were designed to replace. The new curricula emphasized modern topics, giving students a clear idea of the structure of the subject and teaching them to use their knowledge to inquire, to find out more. To compare groups taught different things on a single common criterion measure is to claim, implicitly at least, that the single measure is equally appropriate to the two programs. This is a dubious assumption in any case, and is certainly false for the studies reviewed here.

Research which permits us to compare curricula is not a scientific impossibility. One way to do it is simply to check on the validity of the claims made for (and against) the alternative curricula. If someone claims that studying economics in school will help people to understand the economic aspects of public policy issues, then let us look carefully and determine whether adults who have studied economics in school do this better than those who have not. If someone claims an advantage for one economics curriculum, let us compare students who have studied from various curricula. Let us check claims that studying economics helps students to manage their personal financial affairs more effectively, that the study of economics facilitates the study of history or the social sciences, that it helps people to get and keep better jobs, and that it affects political preferences. We cannot check every claim, of course, and so a selection must be made. But we cannot avoid making selections of this sort no matter how we compare curricula. The person who wants to know which curriculum is better will have to determine the relative importance of the various benefits of concern to him or her from among the various benefits claimed for each curriculum and tested by research.

This strategy and the reasons for its use are in essence those recommended by Cronbach (1963) a decade ago.

Since group comparisons give equivocal results, I believe that a formal study should be designed primarily to determine the post-course performance of a well described group with respect to many important objectives and side effects. . . . Moreover, in an experiment where the treatments compared differ in a dozen respects, no understanding is gained from the fact that the experiment shows a numerical advantage in favor of the new course [p. 676].

In examining the patterns of outcomes produced by alternative curricula in the same subject, we should also test hypotheses about what elements in the curricula are responsible for the differences found. We have suggested that patterns of content inclusion and emphasis are likely to be associated with patterns in achievement. In some instances different sorts of presentations of an item of content will no doubt produce differences in achievement. One way of explaining something will prove less confusing than another, a visual presentation may prove to give better results than a verbal explanation, or whatever. By detailing differences between curricula and by looking for outcomes that are associated with curricular differences, we may begin to understand why certain ingredients contribute to a successful curricular presentation. (Also, in searching for what makes curricula effective, we must be alert for the possibility that the effectiveness of a curriculum is not a simple function of its obvious properties, but a result of an overall constellation or configuration to which many elements, great and small, contribute.)

Whatever strategy is adopted for comparing different curricula, the achievement measure should permit the derivation of a pattern of scores rather than simply one conglomerate score. Conventional achievement tests are attractive as outcome measures for many reasons: they are convenient, reliable, known to correlate highly with school grades and other reasonable criteria of subject matter achievement and to cover many of the topics normally included in school curricula. Since they have generally been used in many other studies, including validation studies, the investigator has some assurance that the scores they yield are stable and well-behaved, an assurance that could not be obtained in the case of a test designed specifically for a single study. But, as this review has shown, agglomerate tests have severe limitations for comparing curricula. The single score they yield is not easily relatable to any particular curriculum or to any other way of considering achievement in the subject because the items on the test are drawn in an unspecified way from an unspecified universe of content and skill, and because scores on the individual items are combined in an arbitrary way that obscures the meaning of the separate performances.

We can cope with this problem of determining the meaning of achievement test scores in a number of ways, none of which is completely satisfactory. The NLSMA test batteries are models of what can be done to relate performance on test items to a model of achievement in the subject. The NLSMA staff devised a model of mathematics achievement consisting of four main elements that can be measured with respect to any mathematics content: computation, comprehension, application, and analysis. These were defined theoretically in the following way:

Computations — Items designed to require straightforward manipulation of problem elements according to rules the subjects presumably have learned. Emphasis is upon performing operations and not upon deciding which operations are appropriate.
Comprehension —Items designed to require either recall of concepts and generalizations or transformation of problem elements from one mode to another. Emphasis is upon demonstrating understanding of concepts and their relationships and not upon using concepts to produce a solution.
Application — Items designed to require (1) recall of relevant knowledge, (2) selection of appropriate operations, and (3) performance of the operations. Items are of a routine nature. They require the subject to use concepts in a specific context and in a way he has presumably practiced.
Analysis — Items designed to require a nonroutine application of concepts [Wilson, Cahen, and Begle, *NLSMA Reports,* 10, pp. 3–4].

The staff then wrote a number of items designed to test each type of achievement in each content category. Intercorrelations between items were determined, and a small number of related items were selected for each of a large number of scales. The items from a number of scales were mixed together in a single achievement test that looked very much like a conventional agglomerate achievement test, but no overall score for the entire "test" was computed. Instead, scores on each scale of related items were computed. In this way, each cell on the content-process grid could be assessed by a number of items (indeed, usually by a number of different scales), and scores on these items could be combined into a more reliable scale score which was still readily interpretable.

Welch and Walberg (1972) used expert judges to help select the most important measures from a list of nearly forty instruments being considered for use in comparing different physics curricula. Their procedure of asking judges to make global ratings of the relative importance of various instruments could probably be improved, however, by identifying particular questions, issues, or concerns of major interest in the evaluation and then asking judges to identify the instruments that seem likely to give the most useful and highest quality information for resolving the issues, answering the questions, or addressing the concerns. Stake's (1970) review of techniques for measuring objectives and priorities should provide interested readers with ideas for other practical ways to cope with this problem.

The most important shortcoming of conventional achievement tests and the most serious single limitation of the comparative curricular studies done so far is the restricted range of outcomes measured. The studies we reviewed made few attempts to assess outcomes other than paper-and-pencil achievement at the end of the course, and those few attempts showed little of interest. Four studies administered tests of critical thinking. Two of these showed no significant differences between experimental and traditional curricula, one showed a significant difference in favor of the experimental curriculum in only one of three comparisons, and the other found a significant difference in favor of the traditional curriculum. None of the measures of attitudes or scientific reasoning showed statistically significant differences. Considering the range and scope of claims made for the new curricula, it is difficult to understand how studies based on such a meager selection of outcomes would help people who are genuinely perplexed about the relative merits of the two types of courses to make up their minds.

The only hopeful sign of an expanded range of outcomes that we found in these studies were the Welch and Walberg study and Heath's (1964) attempt to measure an aspect of cognitive style as an outcome of a physics course. Each item of Heath's Cognitive Preference Test presented a true statement drawn from the lore of physics and asked the student to express a preference for one of a given set of related statements. These related statements were designed to express one of four different modes of dealing with the knowledge presented in the stem of the item: remembering the knowledge, applying the knowledge, relating the knowledge to a general principle, and identifying the evidential grounds or basis for the knowledge. Heath found that the thirty classes enrolled in the experimental PSSC physics course demonstrated a stronger preference for relating knowledge to principles and for questioning it than did students studying from the traditional curriculum.

Welch and Wallberg (1972) used eleven measures: an achievement test in physics, a test of students' understanding of the scientific enterprise, a test of knowledge of the activities, assumptions, products and ethics of science, final grade in the physics course, a measure of interest in physical science, an inventory of science-related activities, a questionnaire assessing satisfaction with the course, a learning environment inventory characterizing classroom climate, a questionnaire assessing reactions to the course, a semantic differential test of attitudes toward physics, and a semantic differential test of perceptions of physics. This study is particularly interesting in that the innovative course was designed to improve performance on noncognitive outcomes (presumably without sacrificing on cognitive outcomes). The evaluation, therefore, appropriately emphasized these noncognitive outcomes.

Ways of relating end-of-course measures to more long-term and far-reaching outcomes are also needed. The most important outcomes are those that remain when, in Whitehead's (1929) phrase, "you have lost your textbooks, burnt your lecture notes, and forgotten the minutiae which you learnt by heart for the examination [p. 42]." This means, in particular, that an attempt should be made to measure two sorts of extended outcomes: lasting changes in ability and inclination to study and learn additional school subject matter or skills, and long-term life consequences of school learnings. It may be impractical to assess these extended outcomes in evaluation studies of this sort, but we can attempt in other studies to establish the relationship between end-of-course measures and long-term outcomes. Some such research seems absolutely necessary if educational research is to have a sound and comprehensive basis. Unless the many problems with this sort of research can be mitigated in some way, if not altogether overcome, studies comparing the effects of different curricula will be of little use to scholars or policy-makers. But even if we solve all these problems, experimental comparisons of different curricula may still be of little value.

The scholar interested in understanding relationships between various school practices or policies and school outcomes needs a much more detailed and intensive analysis of both than would be feasible in a study comparing two year-long curriculum programs. Furthermore, the scholar may very well want more control over the conditions of the research than would be possible in a study of real curricular alternatives in real schools. The scholar interested in long-term, large-scale life consequences of school practices and policies will probably want to examine more pervasive and radical curricular alternatives than two curricula in the same subject. If so, the scholar is not helped, and is probably hampered, by the element of comparison between programs. A comparison group may help the scholar to rule out alternative interpretations of his or her findings, but it is not at all obvious that the most useful comparison group is one studying the same subject from a different curriculum. It would seem that the best comparison group in any case would be one which differed from the group being studied in ways that highlight most vividly the differences of interest to the scholar.

The school policy-maker, on the other hand, may need to decide among fixed and competing curricular alternatives. For the policy-maker faced with such a decision the element of comparison is essential. But the policy-maker must compare the alternatives in a way that takes into account as many of the benefits and costs of each as is possible. A comparison of only a few kinds of outcomes will almost surely be open to the criticism that it favors those alternatives which emphasize those outcomes and penalizes those that emphasize unmeasured outcomes. The policy-maker's purposes would probably be better served by an investigation aimed at determining whether each curriculum lives up to the claims made for it by its proponents and whether the charges or doubts put forward by skeptics or critics of each alternative have any basis in fact. Attention to charges and doubts is also necessary because the proponents of each alternative will usually emphasize in their claims the distinctive positive features of their favorite. When this is so, information that each alternative shows up better than the others on the measures it emphasizes only confirms the issue; it does not begin to resolve it. This is exactly what has happened in most of the studies reviewed here. The new programs do a better job of teaching the content regarded as more important by their proponents, and the old programs do better at the things presumably considered most important by theirs.

Considering the advantages of checking up on claims as a strategy for helping the policy-maker choose between alternative curricula, and the advantages for the scholar of a more intensive, controlled, and carefully designed and conducted study that is not necessarily comparative, it is doubtful whether the direct experimental comparison of alternative curricula on a set of common measures is ever an optimum procedure.

Policy-making

A hypothetical Martian observer of our schooling system would no doubt wonder greatly how it happened that we so rarely, so sporadically, and so feebly consider what matters to address and what to emphasize in schools. Since our present knowledge indicates that this decision has as much influence on what students learn as any subsequent decision the school can make, this omission is indeed mysterious. Perhaps if as many people in schools, in government, and in foundations asked as insistently for evidence that schools were attempting to teach worthwhile and defensible things as ask whether the schools have taught what they set out to teach, we would have more and better research and maybe even better schools.

SUMMARY

We begin as people always begin, naively, to look for signs of superiority of innovative curricula over traditional curricula. What we found was not superiority, but parity: each curriculum did better on the distinctive parts of its own program, and each did about equally well on the parts they held in common.

Although this result is disappointing to those of us who hoped to find a royal road to learning superior to the footpaths we have heretofore been forced to use, it contains a ray of hope. It assures us that the application of funded wisdom to the creation and use of curriculum materials is generally producing a pattern of academic achievement consistent with the intentions of curriculum developers. It also alerts us to a powerful tool for securing the learning of the content we want pupils to learn: inclusion of the material to be learned in the school curriculum.

We suggested an interpretation of the conclusion that, if true, has many far-reaching implications for educational theory, practice, and research. We suggested that inclusion of an item of content in a curriculum brings many powerful forces into play to secure the engagement of the student's active learning capacities with the presentation. Our analysis also suggested that the additional benefits to be gained from improving the presentation beyond the standard in current use are not in general likely to yield results commensurate with the benefits of including the item in the unimproved version.

The difficulties we experienced in trying to interpret the results of these studies led us to question the wisdom of designing and conducting comparative experimental studies of different curricula. Studies which locate the distinctive outcomes of different curricula and studies which determine the long-term school-related and life consequences of these different outcomes would seem to be more useful to both policy-makers and scholars. Such studies require that a great deal more research be directed toward creating measures of a variety of outcomes other than achievement that commonly appear in claims made for and about curricula.

Finally, we suggested that policy-makers begin to take more seriously decisions about including various subjects and topics in the curriculum. Decisions that can be made now by every district in the nation, namely, decisions about content inclusion and emphasis, appear to influence substantially what students learn. If we are to take advantage of this tool, we will need to devise a better system for curriculum policy-making.

If there is a single moral to be drawn from this paper it is this: stop thinking of the curriculum as a fixed race course and begin to think of it as a tool, apparently a powerful one, for stimulating and directing the active learning capacities which are ultimately responsible for the achievement we want from schools.

REFERENCES

Begle, E. G. "SMSG: Where we are today." In Elliot W. Eisner (ed.), *Confronting Curriculum Reform* (Boston: Little, Brown, 1971), pp. 68–81.

Bloom, B. S., Engelhart, D., Furst, E. J., Hill, H., and Krathwohl, D. R. *Taxonomy of Educational Objectives: The Classification of Educational Goals. Handbook I: Cognitive domain* (New York: Longmans, Green and Co., 1956).

Burton, L. "English in No Man's Land: Some Suggestions for the Middle Years." *English Journal* 60 (1971): 23–30.

Buxton, E. W. "An Experiment to Test the Effects of Writing Frequency and Guided Practice upon Students' Skill in Written Expression." Unpublished doctoral dissertation, Stanford University, 1958. Ann Arbor, Mich.: University Microfilms, 1958. No. 58-3596.

Campbell, D. T., and Stanley, J. C. *Experimental and Quasi-Experimental Designs for Research* (Chicago: Rand McNally, 1963).

Carroll, J. B. "A Model of School Learning." *Teachers College Record* 64 (1963): 723–33.

Cronbach, L. J. "Course Improvement Through Evaluation." *Teachers College Record* 64 (1963): 672–83.

Derosier, R. F., and Schuck, R. F. "A Comparison of the Effectiveness of Two Social Studies Instructional Programs upon First-Grade Level Pupil Achievement in Economics." *Educational Leadership* (1970): 815–24.

Dubin, R., and Taveggia, T. C. *The Teaching-Learning Paradox: A Comparative Analysis of College Teaching Methods* (Eugene, Ore.: Center for the Advanced Study of Educational Administration, University of Oregon, 1968).

Education Commission of the States. *National Assessment of Educational Progress* (Washington, D.C.: Superintendent of Documents, U.S. Printing Office, 1970).

Finger, J. A., Jr., Dillon, J. A., and Corbin, F. "Performance in Introductory College Physics and Previous Instruction in Physics." *Journal of Research in Science Teaching* 3 (1965): 61–65.

Gallup, G. *How the Nation Views the Public Schools* (Princeton, N.J.: Gallup International, 1969). Also reported in *Life*, May 16, 1969.

George, K. D. "The Effect of BSCS and Conventional Biology on Critical Thinking." *Journal of Research in Science Teaching* 3 (1965): 293–99.

Getzels, J. W., and Jackson, P. W. "The Teacher's Personality and Characteristics." In N. L. Gage (ed.), *Handbook of Research on Teaching* (Chicago: Rand McNally, 1963), pp. 506–82.

Hardy, C. A. "CHEM Study and Traditional Chemistry: An Experimental Analysis." *Science Education* 54 (1970): 273–76.

Heath, R. W. "Curriculum, Cognition, and Educational Measurement." *Educational and Psychological Measurement* 24 (1964): 239–53.

Heath, R. W., and Stickell, D. W. "CHEM and CBA Effects on Achievement in Chemistry." *Science Teacher* 30 (1963): 45–46.

Herron, J. "Evaluation and the New Curricula." *Journal of Research in Science Teaching* 4 (1966): 159–70.

Hungerman, A. D. "Achievement and Attitude of Sixth-Grade Pupils in Conventional and Contemporary Mathematics Programs." *The Arithmetic Teacher* 14 (1967): 30–39

Husén, T. *International Study of Achievement in Mathematics: A Comparison of Twelve Countries*. Vols. I and II (New York: John Wiley, 1967).

Lance, M. "A Comparison of Gains in Achievement Made by Students of BSCS High School Biology and Students of a Conventional Course in Biology." Unpublished doctoral dissertation, University of Georgia, 1964.

Lisonbee, L., and Fullerton, B. J. "The Comparative Effects of BSCS and Traditional Biology on Student Achievement." *School Science and Mathematics* 64 (1964): 594–98.

Minnesota National Laboratory. "Evaluation of SMSG Text, Grade 4." *School Mathematics Study Group Newsletter* 15 (1963): 8–10.

Patrick, J. J. "The Impact of an Experimental Course, American Political Behavior, on the Knowledge, Skills, and Attitudes of Secondary School Students (Bloomington, Indiana: Indiana University, 1971). Mimeo.

Payette, R. F. "Educational Testing Service—Summary Report of the School Mathematics Study Group Curriculum Evaluation." *School Mathematics Study Group Newsletter* 10 (1961): 5–11.

Potterfield, J. E. "An Analysis of Elementary Children's Ability To Learn Anthropological Content of Grades Four, Five, and Six." *The Journal of Educational Research* 61 (1968): 297–99.

Rainey, R. G. "A Comparison of the CHEM Study Curriculum and a Conventional Approach in Teaching High School Chemistry." *School Science and Mathematics* 64 (1964): 539–44.

Rosenbloom, P. "Minnesota National Laboratory Evaluation of SMSG, Grades 7-12." *School Mathematics Study Group Newsletter* 11 (1961): 12–26.

Rosenshine, B. "New Directions for Research on Teaching." In *How Teachers Make a Difference* (Washington, D.C.: U.S. Government Printing Office, 1971), pp. 66–95.

Stake, R. E. "Objectives, Priorities and Other Judgment Data." *Review of Educational Research* 40 (1970): 181–212.

Stephens, J. M. *The Process of Schooling* (New York: Rinehart and Winston, 1967).

Stronck, D. R. "Comparative Effects of Three Seventh-Grade Science Programs with Different Laboratory Materials." *Science Education* 55 (1971): 125–30.

Taba, H. *Teaching Strategies and Cognitive Functioning in Elementary School Children.* U.S. Dept. of Health, Education, and Welfare, Office of Education, Cooperative Research Project No. 2404 (San Francisco: San Francisco State College, 1966).

Wallace, W. "The BSCS 1961-62 Evaluation Program—A Statistical Report." *BSCS Newsletter* 19 (1963): 22–24.

Wallen, N. E., and Travers, R. M. W. "Analysis and Investigation of Teaching Methods." In N. L. Gage (ed.), *Handbook of Research on Teaching* (Chicago: Rand McNally, 1963), pp. 448–505.

Wasik, J. L. "A Comparison of Cognitive Performance of PSSC and non-PSSC Physics Students." *Journal of Research in Science Teaching* 8 (1971): 85–90.

Welch, W. W., and Walberg, H. J. "A National Experiment in Curriculum Evaluation." *American Educational Research Journal* 9 (1972): 373–83.

Whitehead, A. N. *The Aims of Education and Other Essays* (New York: Macmillan, 1929).

Williams, E. D., and Shuff, R. V. "Comparative Study of SMSG and Traditional Mathematics Text Material." *The Mathematics Teacher* 56 (1963): 495–504.

Wilson, J. W., Cahen, L. S., and Begle, E. G. *NLSMA Reports*. Vols. 1-25 (Stanford University: The Board of Trustees of Leland Stanford Junior University, 1968-72).

26. POLITICS AND RESEARCH: EVALUATION OF SOCIAL ACTION PROGRAMS IN EDUCATION

David K. Cohen[1]

Although program evaluation is no novelty in education, its objects have changed radically. The national thrust against poverty and discrimination introduced a new phenomenon with which evaluators must deal: large-scale programs of social action in education. In addition to generating much activity in city schools, these programs produced considerable confusion whenever efforts were made to find out whether they were "working." The sources of the confusion are not hard to identify. Prior to 1964, the objects of evaluation in education consisted almost exclusively of small programs concerned with such things as curriculum development or teacher training: they generally occurred in a single school or school district, they sought to produce educational change on a limited scale, and they typically involved modest budgets and small research staffs.

This all began to change in the mid-1960's when the federal government and some states established broad educational improvement programs. The programs—such as Project Headstart, Title I of the 1965 ESEA, and Project Follow-Through—differ from the traditional objects of educational evaluation in several important respects: (1) they are social action programs, and as such are not focused narrowly on teachers' in-service training or on a science curriculum, but aim broadly at improving education for the disadvantaged; (2) the new programs are directed not at a school or a school district, but at millions of children, in thousands of schools in hundreds of school jurisdictions in all the

SOURCE. *Review of Educational Research* 40 (No. 2, April 1970), pp. 213–37.

states; (3) they are not conceived and executed by a teacher, principal, a superintendent, or a researcher—they were created by the Congress and are administered by federal agencies far from the school districts which actually design and conduct the individual projects.

Simply to recite these differences is to suggest major new evaluation problems. How does one know when a program which reaches more than eight million children "works"? How does one even decide what "working" means in the context of such large-scale social action ventures? Difficulties also arise from efforts to apply the inherited stock-in trade evaluation techniques to the new phenomena. If the programs seek broad social change, is it sensible to evaluate them mainly in terms of achievement? If they are national action programs, should evaluation be decentralized?

This chapter is an effort to explore these and other questions about evaluating large-scale social action programs. It has three major parts. First, I delineate the political character of the new programs, in order to distinguish them from the traditional objects of educational evaluation. Second, to illustrate this point and define the major obstacles to evaluation, I review some evaluations of the new programs. Finally, I suggest some elements of a strategy which might improve the evaluation of social action programs.

POLITICS AND EVALUATION

There is one sense in which any educational evaluation ought to be regarded as political. Evaluation is a mechanism with which the character of an educational enterprise can be explored and expressed. These enterprises are managed by people, and they take place in institutions; therefore, any judgment on their nature or results has at least a potential political impact—it can contribute to changing power relationships. This is true whether the evaluation concerns a small curriculum reform program in a rural school (if the program is judged ineffective the director might lose influence or be demoted), or a teacher training program in a university (if it is judged a success its sponsors might get greater authority). Evaluation, as some recent commentators have pointed out, produces information which is at least potentially relevant to decision-making (Stufflebeam, 1967; Guba, 1968). Decision-making, of course, is a euphemism for the allocation of resources—money, position, authority, etc. Thus, to the extent that information is an instrument, basis, or excuse for changing power relationships within or among institutions, evaluation is a political activity.

These political aspects of evaluation are not peculiar to social action programs. They do, however, assume more obvious importance as an educational program grows in size and number of jurisdictions covered: the bigger it is, the greater the likelihood for the overt appearance of political competition.

There is another sense in which evaluation is political, for some programs explicitly aim to redistribute resources or power; although this includes such things as school consolidation, social action programs are the best recent example. They were established by a political institution (the Congress) as part of an effort to change the operating priorities of state and local governments and thus to change not only the balance of power within American education but also the relative status of economic and racial groups within the society. One important feature of the new social action programs, then, is their political origin; another is their embodiment of social and political priorities which reach beyond the schools; a third is that their success would have many far-reaching political consequences.

One political dimension of evaluation is universal, for it involves the uses of information in changing power relationships; the other is peculiar only to those programs in which education is used to rearrange the body politic. Although one can never ignore the former dimension, *its salience in any given situation is directly proportional to the overt political stakes involved;* they are small in curriculum reform in a suburban high school, somewhat larger in a state-wide effort to consolidate schools, and very great in the case of national efforts to eliminate poverty. The power at stake in the first effort is small, and its importance slight. In the social action programs, however, the political importance of information is raised to a high level by the broader political character of the programs themselves.

This should be no surprise. Information assumes political importance within local school jurisdictions, but political competition *among* school jurisdictions usually involves higher stakes—and the social action programs promote competition among levels of government. These programs are almost always sponsored by state or federal government, with at least the implicit or partial intent of setting new priorities for state and local governments. In this situation evaluation becomes a political instrument, a means to determine whether the new priorities are being met and to assess the differential effectiveness of jurisdictions or schools in meeting them. As a result, evaluation is affected by the prior character of intergovernmental relations. State resistance to federal involvement, for example, pre-dates recent efforts to evaluate and assess federal social action programs. The history colors the evaluation issue and the state response reflects the prior pattern of relations, for evaluation is correctly seen as an effort to assert federal priorities. Evaluation also can affect patterns of intergovernmental relations for it can help consolidate new authority for the superordinate government. In general, however, evaluation seems to reflect the established pattern of intergovernmental relations.

Of course, not all the novelties in evaluating large-scale social action programs are political. There are serious logistical difficulties—the programs are bigger than anything ever evaluated in education, which poses unique problems—and there is no dearth of methodological issues. These mostly center around making satisfactory comparisons between "treated" subjects and some criterion presumed to measure an otherwise comparable condition of non-treatment. These are difficult in any program with multiple criterion variables, and when the program is spread over the entire country the problems multiply enormously. But difficult though these issues may be, they are in all formal respects the same, irrespective of the size, age, aim, or outcome of the program in question. The large-scale programs do not differ in some formal property of the control-comparison problem, but only in its size. The bigger and more complicated the programs, the bigger the associated methodological headaches. What distinguishes the new programs are not the formal problems of knowing their effects, but the character of their aims and their organization. These are essentially political.

The politics of social action programs produce two sorts of evaluation problem. Some are conceptual—the programs' nature and aims have not been well understood or adequately expressed in evaluation design. Others are practical—the interested parties do not agree on the ordering of priorities which the programs embody. As a result of the first, evaluation is misconceived; as a result of the second, evaluation becomes a focus for expressing conflicting political interests.

CONCEPTUAL PROBLEMS

The central conceptual difficulty can be simply summarized: while the new programs seek to bring about political and social change, evaluators generally approach them as though they were standard efforts to produce educational change. This results in no small part from ambiguity of the programs—since they are political endeavors in education, the program content and much of the surrounding rhetoric is educational. It also occurs because evaluation researchers identify professionally and intellectually with their disciplines of origin (mostly education and psychology), and thus would rather not study politics. They prefer education and psychology; since that is what they know, what their colleagues understand, and—if done well—what will bring them distinction and prestige (Dentler, 1969).

But whatever the sources of the incongruence, it produces inappropriate evaluation. The aims and character of the programs are misconceived, and as a result evaluation design and execution are of limited value. Title I of ESEA (U.S. Congress, 1965a) is a good example with which to begin.

In the four years ESEA has been in existence, the federal government completed several special evaluation studies, undertaken either by the Office of the Secretary of HEW or the Office of Education.[2] They concentrated mainly on one question—has the program improved achievement over what otherwise might have been expected? The answer in each case was almost entirely negative, and not surprisingly, this led many to conclude that the Title I program was not "working." This, in turn, raised or supported doubts about the efficacy of the legislation or the utility of compensatory education. Yet such inferences are sensible only if two crucial assumptions are accepted:

(a) children's achievement test scores are a sufficient criterion of the program's aims—the consequences intended by the government—to stand as an adequate summary measure of its success; and
(b) the Title I program is sufficiently coherent and unified to warrant the application of *any* summary criterion of success, be it achievement or something else.

Both assumptions merit inspection.

It does not seem unreasonable to assume that improving the achievement of disadvantaged children is a crucial aim of the Title I program. Much of the program's rhetoric suggests that it seeks to reduce the high probability of school failure associated with poverty. Many educators and laymen regard achievement test scores as a suitable measure of school success, on the theory that children with higher achievement will have higher grades, happier teachers, more positive attitudes toward school, and therefore a better chance of remaining and succeeding.

There are, however, two difficulties with this view. One is that achievement scores are not an adequate summary of the legislation's diverse aims. The other is that hardly anyone cares about the test scores themselves—they are regarded as a suitable measure of program success only because they are believed to stand for other things.

The second point can easily be illustrated. Aside from a few intellectuals who think that schooling is a good thing in itself, people think test scores are important because they are thought to signify more knowledge, which will lead to more years in school, better job opportunities, more money, and more of the ensuing social and economic status Americans seem to enjoy. Poor people, they reason, have little money, undesirable jobs (if any) and, by definition, the lowest social and economic status presently available. The poor also have less education than most of their countrymen. On the popular assumptions just described, it is easy to argue that "poverty can be eliminated" by increasing the efficiency of education for the poor.

Although much abbreviated, this chain of reasoning is not a bad statement of the reasons why improved achievement is an aim of Title I. Improved schooling was a major anti-poverty strategy, and higher school achievement simply a proxy for one of the program's main aims—improving adults' social and economic status. The principal problem this raises for evaluation is that the criterion of program effectiveness is actually only a surrogate for the true criterion. This would pose no difficulty if reliable estimates of the causal relationship between schoolchildren's achievement and their later social and economic status existed. Unfortunately, no information of this sort seems to be available. There is one major study relating years of school completed and occupational status; it shows that once inherited status is controlled, years of school completed are moderately related to adult occupational status (Blau and Duncan, 1968). Other studies reveal no direct relationship between intelligence and occupational status, but they do show that the education-occupation relationship is much weaker for Negroes than whites (Duncan, 1968). The first of these findings should not encourage advocates of improved achievement, and the second is hardly encouraging to those who perceive blacks as a major target group for antipoverty programs.

There are studies which show that more intelligent people stay in school longer (Duncan, 1968), but it is hardly clear a priori that raising achievement for disadvantaged children will keep them in school, nor is it self-evident that keeping poor children in school longer will get them better jobs.[3] It is, for example, not difficult to imagine that the more intelligent children who stay in school longer do so because they also have learned different behavior patterns, which include greater tolerance for delayed gratification, more docility, less overt aggression, and greater persistence. Several compensatory programs are premised on these notions, rather than the achievement-production idea. Without any direct evidence on the consequence of either approach, however, it is difficult to find a rational basis for choice.

This does not mean that compensatory education programs founded on either view are a mistake—absent any data, one could hardly take that position. It does suggest, however, that using achievement—or any other form of school behavior—as a proxy for the actual long-range purpose of compensatory education is probably ill-founded. The chief difficulty with this variety of agnosticism, of course, is that the only alternative is evaluation studies whose duration would make them of interest only to the next generation. What is more, they would be extremely expensive. The current proportion of program budgets devoted to evaluation indicates that the probability of undertaking such studies is nil.

Even if this scientific embarrassment were put aside, there is the other major difficulty with using achievement as an evaluation criterion. Schoolmen must be expected to assume that the greater application of their efforts will improve students' later lives, but there is no evidence that the Congress subscribed to that view by passing Title I of the 1965 ESEA. Although the title did contain an unprecedented mandate for program evaluation—and even specified success in school as a criterion—this is scant evidence that the sole program aim was school achievement. The mandate for evaluation—like many Congressional authorizations—lacked any enabling mechanism: responsibility for carrying out the evaluation was specifically delegated to the state and local education authorities who operated the programs. It was not hard to see, in 1965, that this was equivalent to abandoning much hope of useful program evaluation.

The main point, however, is that the purposes of the legislation were much more complex: most of them could be satisfied without any evidence about children's achievement. Certainly this was true for aid to parochial school students, and it most likely was also true for many of the poorer school districts: for them (as for many of the congressmen who voted for the act) more money was good in itself. Moreover, the Congress is typically of two minds on the matter of program evaluation in education—it subscribes to efficiency, but it does not believe in Federal control of the schools. National evaluations are regarded as a major step toward Federal control by many people, including some members of Congress.

Although the purposes of the Congress may be too complicated to be summarized in studies of test scores, they are not by that token mysterious. The relevant Committee hearings and debates suggest that the legislative intent included several elements other than those already mentioned.[4] One involved the rising political conflict over city schools in the early 1960's; many legislators felt that spreading money on troubled waters might bring peace. Another concerned an older effort to provide federal financial assistance for public education: the motives for this were mainly political and ideological, and were not intimately tied to achievement. A third involved the larger cities; although not poor when compared to the national average expenditure, they were increasingly hard-pressed to maintain educational services which were competitive with other districts in their areas as property values declined, population changed, and costs and taxes rose. Educators and other municipal officials were among the warmest friends of the new aid scheme, because it promised to relieve some of the pressure on their revenues.

Indeed, many purposes of the legislation—and the Congress's implicit attitude toward evaluation—can be summarized in the form which it gave to fund apportionment. Title I is a formula grant, in which the amount of money flowing to any educational agency is a function of how many poor children it has, not of how well it educates them. In a sense, Title I is the educational equivalent of a rivers and harbors bill. There is no provision for withdrawing funds for non-performance, nor is there much suggestion of such intent in the original committee hearings or floor debates. Given the formula grant system, neither the Federal funding agency or the states have much political room to maneuver, even if they have the results of superb evaluation in hand. Without the authority to manipulate funds, achievement evaluation results could only be used to coax and cajole localities: the one major implicit purpose of program evaluation—more rational resource allocation—is seriously weakened by the Title I formula grant system.

It is, therefore, difficult to conclude that improving schools' production of poor children's achievement was the legislation's major purpose. The legislative intent embraced many other elements: improving educational services in school districts with many poor children, providing fiscal relief for the central cities and parochial schools, reducing discontent and conflict about race and poverty, and establishing the principle of federal responsibility for local school problems. The fact that these were embodied in a single piece of legislation contributed heavily to its passage, but it also meant that the resulting program was not single-purpose or homogeneous. If any supposition is in order, it is precisely the opposite. Title I is typical of reform legislation in a large and diverse society with a federal political system: it reflected various interests, decentralized power, and for these reasons a variety of programmatic and political priorities.

Additional References: Bateman, 1969; Campbell, 1969; Campbell and Stanley, 1966; Dyer, 1972; Evans, 1969; Hyman and Wright, 1966; Marris and Rein, 1967; McDill, McDill and Spreche, 1969; Rivlin, 1969; Rivlin and Wholey, 1967; Rothenberg, 1969; Swartz, 1961; Weiss and Rein, 1969; Wholey, 1969 *a* and *b*; Williams and Evans, 1969.

CONSEQUENCES FOR EVALUATION

Misconceptions about program aims result in omissions in evaluations and in distortions of the relationship among various aspects of evaluation. The first problem is mainly confined to program delivery. For Title I, for example, there are several criteria of program success which appear never to have been scrutinized. One involves impact of Title I on the fiscal position of the parochial schools: as nearly as I can tell, this purpose of the Act has never been explored.[5] Another involves the impact of Title I upon the fiscal situation of the central cities and their position vis-a-vis adjacent districts. Although the redistributive intent of the title was clear, there is little evidence of much effort to find out whether it has had this effect. With the exception of one internal Office of Education paper—which showed that Title I had reduced the per pupil expenditure disparity between eleven central cities and their suburbs by about half—this subject appears to have received no attention.[6] A third involves the quality of education in target as compared with non-target schools. Thus far no data have been collected which would permit an assessment of Title I's effectiveness in reducing intra-district school resource disparities, although this was one of the most patent purposes of the Act. There has been an extended effort, covering 465 school districts (Project 465), to gather information on resource delivery to Title I target schools. This might turn up interesting data on differences in Title I services among schools, districts, or regions, but comparison with schools which do not receive Title I aid is not provided. Since Title I seeks to provide better-than-equal education for the disadvantaged, measuring its impact upon resource disparities between Title I and non-Title I schools within districts would be crucial. This is recognized in the Office of Education regulations governing the Title, which provide that Title I funds must add to existing fiscal and resource equality between Title I and non-Title I schools. [7] Important as this purpose of the legislation is, only a few federal audits have been conducted; for the most part, states satisfy the federal requirements simply by passing on data provided by the local education agencies, most of which are so general they are useless.

Such things do not result simply from administrative lapses. Evidence on whether Title I provides better-than-equal schooling would permit a clear judgment on the extent to which Federal priorities were being met. But the legislation allocates money to jurisdictions on a strict formula, and it delegates the responsibility for monitoring performance to those same jurisdictions: this reflects both the decentralization of power in the national school system and the sense of the Congress that it should remain just so. An important source of inadequate program delivery studies is inadequate Federal power or will to impose its priorities on states and localities; the priorities are enunciated in the statute, but the responsibility for determining whether they are being met is left with the states and localities.

The distribution of power is not the sole source of such problems in evaluating program delivery; the sheer size and heterogeneity of the society, and the unfamiliarity of the problems are also important. Project Headstart is illustrative. This program was not initially established within the existing framework of education. It existed mostly outside the system of public schools; its clients were below the age of compulsory education, and its local operating agencies often were independent of the official school agencies. Since the program came into existence, several million dollars have been spent on evaluation, and not a little of it on studies of program delivery. Yet it is still impossible to obtain systematic information on this subject. Several annual national evaluations and U. S. Census studies of program delivery are unpublished. But even if these studies had all been long since committed to print, they would only allow comparisons within the Headstart program. They would provide no basis for comparing how the services delivered to children under this program compare with those available to more advantaged children. That is no easy question to answer, but it is hardly trivial: without an estimate of this program's efficacy in delivering services to children, its efficacy as an anti-poverty program could hardly be evaluated.

There have been some recent efforts to remedy the relative absence of information on Title I program delivery, through an extensive management information program under development in 21 states. Data are to be collected from a sample of schools which receive Federal aid under several programs; it is estimated that the universe of schools and districts from which the sample will be drawn includes roughly 90 percent of all public school students in those states.

Extensive information on teachers, on district and school attributes, and funding will be collected from self-administered questionnaires. Principals and teachers will provide information on school and classroom characteristics and programs, including compensatory efforts. In elementary schools the teachers will provide information on student background, but in secondary schools these data may be taken from the students themselves. Some effort also will be made to measure the extent of individual student's exposure to programs. In addition, common testing (using the same instruments in all schools) is planned, beginning with grades four and eleven. If this ambitious effort becomes operational in anything approaching the time planned, in a few years extensive data will be available with which to assess program delivery for Title I.

In summary, then, an underlying purpose of social action programs is to deliver more resources to the poor, whether they are districts, schools, children, or states. It is therefore essential to know how much more and for whom. It is important both because citizens should know the extent to which official intentions have been realized, and because without much knowledge on that score, it is hard to decide what more should be done. Satisfying these evaluative needs implies measurement that is both historical (keyed to the target population before the program began) and comparative (keyed to the non-target population).[8]

Studies of program delivery also serve a building-block function with respect to evaluating program outcomes. Whatever criterion of program effect one might imagine, it could not intelligibly be evaluated in the absence of data which describe the character of the program. Improved health, for example, is a possible outcome of the health care components of Title I and Headstart: one could not usefully collect evidence on changes in students' health without evidence on the character and intensity of the care they received from the program. And if one were interested in the impact of health care on school performance, it would be necessary to add some measure of students' achievement, classroom behavior, or attitudes. In the case of achievement outcomes, of course, evaluators commonly try to associate information about the type and intensity of academic programs with students' scores on some later test.

Despite the logical simplicity of these relationships, it is not easy to find large-scale social action programs in which outcome evaluation is linked to appropriate program delivery data. Without any direct evidence on program delivery, the only "input" which can be evaluated is inclusion in a program. But an acquaintance with national social action ventures leads quickly to the conclusion that an important aspect of such endeavors is the "non-treatment project." There is no reason to believe that mere inclusion necessarily leads to change either in the substance of education or in the level of resources. This phenomenon takes many forms: it may consist of teachers or specialists who never see the target children; it may involve supplies and materials never unpacked, or educational goods and services which reach students other than those for whom they were intended; in still other cases it may consist of using program monies to pay for goods and services already in use. Whatever the specific form the non-treatment project takes, however, recognizing it requires extensive program delivery data. In a decentralized educational system the probability of such occurrences must be fairly high, and the obstacles to discovering them are considerable.

Even if the non-treatment project problem could be ignored, inadequate evidence on program delivery has other consequences for the evaluation of program outcomes. One of them is illustrated by the following excerpt from one Office of Education study of pre- and post-test scores in 33 big-city Title I programs (Piccariello, undated, p. 4):

For the total 189 observations [each observation was one classroom in a Title I program], there were 108 significant changes (exceed 2 s.e.). Of these 58 were gains and 50 were losses. In 81 cases the change did not appear to be significant.

As the data in Appendix D show, success and failure seem to be random outcomes, determined neither clearly nor consistently by the factors of program design, city or state, area or grade level.

When one reads Appendix D, however, he finds that the categorization by program design rests exclusively on one-paragraph program descriptions of the sort often furnished by the local project directors in grant applications. This makes it difficult to grasp the meaning of the study's conclusions. Perhaps success and failure were random with respect to program content, but given the evidence at hand it is just as sensible to argue that program content is unrelated to project descriptions, and that some underlying pattern of causation exists.[9] Without evidence on program delivery, it is not easy to see what can be learned from evaluations of this sort.

There is, however, an important counterargument on this point. The recent Westinghouse evaluation of Project Headstart, for example, took as its chief independent variable *inclusion in Headstart projects*. The premise for this was that the government has a legitimate interest in determining whether a program produces the expected results. On this view, arguments about program delivery are irrelevant, since from the sponsoring agency's perspective, inclusion in the program is of overriding interest. (See Evans, 1969.)

There certainly is no question that in principle over-all program evaluation is justified. But the principle need not lead to a single summary evaluation in practice. Judgments about a program's over-all impact can just as well be derived from an evaluation which distinguishes program types or differentiates program delivery as from one which ignores them. From this perspective, rather than reporting whether the "average" Headstart project raised achievement, it would be more meaningful to identify the several program types and determine whether each improved achievement.

This may seem sensible, but it is not easy to put into practice. How does one collect data on program types or distinguish program characteristics? Assume a hypothetical program in which the outcome variable is school achievement. The first step would be to drop all projects whose purpose is not to improve achievement. But if one reads any compilation of project aims in Title I, he finds that only a minority aim only to improve achievement. Another minority aims to improve something else, and a majority aim to do both, or more. Given this heterogeneity of aims and the non-treatment project problem, one could not proceed on the basis of project descriptions—the stated purpose of improving achievement would have to be validated by looking at programs. The second step would be to distinguish the main approaches (the program types), from all those which actually sought to raise achievement. The main purpose of the evaluation is to distinguish the relative effectiveness of several approaches to this goal.

But if the logic seems clear, the procedure does not. To empirically distinguish the class of projects aimed at raising achievement one must first know what it is about schooling that affects achievement. Only on the basis of such information would it be possible to sort out those projects whose execution was consistent with their aims from those which were not. But when the new programs were established very little was known on this point: prior compensatory education efforts were few, far between, and mostly failures. The legislation was not the fruit of systematic experimentation and program development, but the expression of a paroxysm of concern. Although a good deal has been learned in the last four or five years, researchers are still a good way from an inventory of techniques known to improve school achievement. The only way one can tell if a project is of the sort which improves achievement, then, is not to inspect the treatment, but to inspect the results.

This creates an awkward situation. If there is no empirical typology of compensatory or remedial programs, what basis is there for distinguishing among programs? What basis is there for deciding which program characteristics to measure—if one does not know what improves achievement, how does one select the program attributes to measure? Some choice is essential, for evaluations cannot measure everything.

These questions focus attention on one important attribute of the new programs. To the extent that they seek to affect some outcome of schooling, such as attitudes or achievement, they represent a sort of muddling-through—an attempt at research and development on a national scale. This is not a comment on the legislative intent, but simply a description of existing knowledge. If program managers and evaluators do not know what strategies will affect school outcomes, it is not sensible to carry out over-all, one-shot evaluations of entire national programs: the results of strategies which improved achievement might be canceled out by the effects of those which did not. If the point is to find what "works," the emphasis should be on defining distinct strategies, trying them out, and evaluating the results. The highest priority should be maximum definition and differentiation among particular approaches. Program managers and evaluators must therefore devise educational treatments based on relatively little prior research and experience, carry them out under natural conditions, evaluate the results, and compare them with those from other similarly developed programs. Insofar as school outcomes are the object of evaluation, the work must take place in the context of program development and comparative evaluation. This requirement raises a host of new problems related to the intentional manipulation of school programs and organization within the American polity.

EXPERIMENTAL APPROACHES

The problem, then, is not only to identify what the programs deliver, but also to systematically experiment with strategies for affecting school outcomes. This idea has been growing in the Federal bureaucracy as experience with the social action programs reveals that the system of natural experiments (every local project does what it likes on the theory that good results would arise, be identified, and disseminated) has not worked. The movement toward experimentation presumes that the most efficient way to proceed is systematic trial and discard, discovering and replicating effective strategies.

Under what conditions might social action programs assume a partly experimental character? For Title I this would not be easy, because the legislation did not envisage it. It is a major operating program, and several of its purposes have nothing to do with achievement. Activities in Washington designed to carry out systematic research and development would generate considerable opposition among recipient state and local educational agencies, and in the Congress. Experimentation requires a good deal of bureaucratic and political control, and there is little evidence of that. The Office of Education, for example, does not require that the same tests be used in all Title I projects— indeed, it does not require that *any* tests be used. The Title I program's managers have neither the power nor the inclination to assign educational strategies to local educational agencies. Even if they did, the legislation would be at cross-purposes with such efforts. It aims to improve resource delivery—to ease the fiscal hardships of city and parochial schools, and to equalize educational resource disparities. Although the formula grant system is quite consistent with these aims, it is not consistent with experimentation. The two aims imply different administrative arrangements, reporting systems, and patterns of Federal-state-local relations. The experimental approach requires a degree of control over school program which seems incompatible with the other purposes of Title I.

The question is whether other programs offer a better prospect for experimentation in compensatory education. In mid-1968, the White House Task Force on Child Development recommended that Federal education programs adopt a policy of "planned variation"; the Task Force report argued that no learning from efforts to improve education was occurring with existing programs, and that it would result only from systematic efforts to try out different strategies under a variety of school and community conditions (White House Task Force, 1968).

The Task Force report focused its attention on Project Follow-Through. Follow-Through was originally intended to extend Headstart services from preschool to the primary grades, but severe first year budgetary constraints had greatly reduced its scope. Largely for this reason, the program seemed a natural candidate for experimentation. The Task Force (1968) recommended that Federal officials select a variety of educational strategies and develop evaluation plans using common measures of school outcomes in all cases.

The administration should explicitly provide budget and personnel allowances for a Follow-Through staff to stimulate and develop projects consistent with these plans ....

The Office of Education should select all new Follow-Through projects in accordance with these plans for major variation and evaluation.

After three years, can the effort be termed a success? Since the program is still under development it would be unwise to deal with the strategies or their impact upon achievement. My concern is only with the quality of the evaluation scheme and the discussion is meant to be illustrative; the evaluation design may change, but the underlying problems are not likely to evaporate.

The Follow-Through program of experimentation is designed to determine which educational strategies improve achievement over what might otherwise be expected, and what the relative efficiency of the strategies is. The program began with little knowledge about the determinants of academic achievement, and as a consequence, equating schools and programs becomes much more difficult. Assume, for example, that all the Follow-Through projects sought to change student achievement by changing teachers' classroom behavior, but no two projects used the same treatment or attacked the same dimension of behavior. Suppose further that in half the projects achievement gains for students resulted. How could one be sure that the gains derived from the Follow-Through strategies, and not from selection or other teacher attributes than those manipulated by the program? The obvious answer is to measure teacher attributes and use the data to "control" the differences. But, since the program begins with little knowledge of what it is about teachers and teaching that affects achievement, evaluators must either measure *all* the teacher attributes which might affect achievement or closely approximate an experimental design. The first alternative is logically impossible, for the phenomena are literally unknown. The second alternative poses no logical problems; it requires only that the Federal experimenter have extensive control over the assignment of subjects (school systems, and teachers) to treatment. The problems it raises are administrative and political.

The Follow-Through program has not been able to surmount them. Neither the districts nor the schools appear to have been selected in a manner consistent with experimental design. The districts were nominated by state officials; those nominated could accept or decline, and those who accepted could pretty much choose the strategy they desired from several alternatives. There was, then, room for self-selection. In addition, the purveyors of the strategies—the consultants who conceived, designed, and implemented or trained others to implement the strategies—seem also to have been recruited exclusively by self-selection. The usual ways of dealing with selection problems (never entirely satisfactory) seem even less helpful here. Although experimental and non-experimental schools could be compared to see if they differed in any important respects, the relevance of this procedure is unclear when little is known about what those "important respects" (vis-a-vis improving education for disadvantaged children) happen to be.

The weight of the evaluation strategy seems to fall on comparison or control groups. The present plan calls for selecting a sample of treatment and control classrooms, carrying out classroom observation, measuring teachers' background and attitudes, and using variables derived from these measurements in multivariate analyses of student achievement. Most of the instruments are still under development. But since there is neither a compulsion nor an incentive for principals in non-Follow-Through schools to participate as controls, how representative will the control classrooms be? What is more, these control or comparison groups cannot serve as much of a check on selectivity among the participants. Many of the comparison schools are in the same districts which selected themselves into the program and chose particular treatments; even those that are not are bound to be somewhat selected, because of the voluntary character of participation. Even if no "significant differences" are found between experimental and control schools, this would only prove that selected experimental schools are not very different from selected control schools.

There also may be some confounding of Follow-Through with related programs. Follow-Through operates in schools which are likely to receive other federal (and perhaps state and local) aid to improve education for disadvantaged children. Students will have the benefit of more than one compensatory program, either directly or through generally improved services and program in their school. There is little evidence at the moment of any effort to deal with this potential source of confounding.

In addition to selection, there are problems related to sample size. The design assumes that classrooms are the unit of analysis; this is appropriate, since they are the unit of treatment. Almost all measurements of program impact are classroom aggregates—i.e., they measure a classroom's teacher, its climate, its teaching strategy, etc. But it seems that relatively few classrooms will be selected from each project for evaluation (the 1969-70 plans call for an average of almost five per project, distributed over grades K-2). Since there are only a few classrooms per grade per project, it appears that in the larger projects there might be a dozen experimental units (classrooms) per grade. That is a very small number, especially when it is reasonable to expect some variation among classrooms on such things as teacher and student attributes, classroom styles, etc. In fact, since only six or eight of the strategies that are being tried involve large numbers of projects, the remaining strategies (more than half the total) probably will not have sufficient cases for much of an evaluation.

There has been some effort to deal with this problem by expanding the student achievement testing to cover almost all classrooms in Follow-Through. This has not, however, been paralleled by expanded measurement of what actually is done in classrooms, a procedure which is helpful only on the assumption that there is no significant variation among classrooms within projects or strategies on variables related to the treatment or the effect. If this is true, of course, then measuring *anything* about the content, staff, or style of the classroom is superfluous—one need only designate whether or not it is an experimental or control unit. Despite the evaluators' view that this approach is warranted, the inclusion of some classrooms for which the only independent variable is a dummy (treatment-nontreatment) variable seems dubious. This will inflate the case base and therefore produce more statistical "confidence" in the results, but it may so sharply reduce the non-statistical confidence that the exercise will be useless. The evaluators argue that given the fixed sum for evaluation, they cannot extend measurement of classroom content.

Sample size problems are compounded because the evaluation is longitudinal. Since there is inter-classroom mobility in promotion (all classes are not passed on from teacher to teacher *en bloc*), following children for more than one year will sharply reduce the number of subjects for which two- or three-year treatment and effect measures can be computed. Add to this the rather high inter-school pupil mobility which seems to be characteristic of slum schools, and nightmarish anxieties about sample attrition result. Although nothing is certain at this point, there will be considerable obstacles to tracing program effects over time.

A fourth problem relates to student background measures. Apparently these data are being collected only for a relatively small sample of families. The evaluators are not sure that it will be large enough to allow consideration of both project impact and family background variables at once, but budget constraints preclude expanding the sample.

There are a few additional difficulties that merit mention, though they do not arise from the evaluation strategy, but from the nature of social action programs.

There are reports of "leakage" of treatments from Follow-Through to comparison schools in some communities; there also seem to have been shifts in program goals in some projects, and apparently there has been conflict in definition of aims between the Follow-Through administration and some projects. In fact, there appears to be an element of non-comparability emerging among the strategies. Some involve very broad approaches, whose aims center around such things as parent involvement in or control of schools; others are more narrowly-defined and research-based strategies for improving cognitive growth. As long as traditional evaluation questions are asked (did treatment produce different results than an otherwise comparable non-treatment?), this poses no problem, but comparing treatments is close to the heart of Follow-Through. It is difficult to see how such comparative questions can be answered when the programs are so diverse. The general change programs, for example, appear to be hostile to the idea of evaluations based on achievement. They seem to be moving toward establishing other outcomes—"structural change" in schools, for example—as the program aim of primary concern. This heterogeneity of aims may well restrict the scope of comparative analysis for Follow-Through.

The common element in all these difficulties is that the Office of Education is largely powerless to remedy them. Random assignment of schools to treatments and securing proper control groups are the most obvious cases; lack of funds to generate adequate samples of experimental classrooms or parents are other manifestations of the same phenomenon. Although there is no doubt that some problems could have been eased by improved management, no amount of forethought or efficiency can produce money or power where there is none. Nor is it easy to see how the Office of Education could effectively compel project sponsors not to change some aspects of their strategies or not to alter their motion of program aims.

The experience thus far with Follow-Through suggests, then, that the serious obstacles to experimentation are political: first, power in the educational system is almost completely decentralized (at least from a national perspective), and federal experimentation must conform to this pattern; second, the resources allocated to eliminating educational disadvantage are small when compared to other federal priorities, which indicates the government's relatively low political investment in such efforts. Consequently, federal efforts to experiment begin with a grave deficit in the political and fiscal resources required to mount them, and there is little likelihood of much new money or more power with which to redress this imbalance. These difficulties are not peculiar to evaluation: they result from the same conditions which make it difficult to mount and operate effective reform programs. The barriers to evaluation are simply another manifestation of the obstacles to federally-initiated reform when most power is local and when reform is a relatively low national priority.

Several dimensions of social action program evaluation emerge from this analysis. My purpose here is not to provide a final typology of evaluation activities, but simply to suggest the salient elements. First among these is the identification of program aims; this ordinarily will involve the recognition of diversity, obscurity, and conflict within programs, and greater attention to program delivery. Evaluators of social action programs often complain that the programs lack any clear and concise statement of aims, a condition which they deplore because it muddies up evaluations. Their response generally has been to bemoan the imprecision and fuzzy-mindedness of the politicians and administrators who establish the programs, and then to choose a summary measure of program accomplishment which satisfies their more precise approach. I propose to stand this on its head and question the intellectually fuzzy single-mindedness of much educational evaluation. It generally has not grasped the diverse and conflicting nature of social action programs, and therefore produces unrealistically constrained views of program aims.

The second element is clarity about the social and political framework of measurement. In traditional evaluation the ideal standard of comparison (the control group or pre-measure) is one that is just like the treatment group in all respects except the treatment. But in social action programs the really important standard of comparison is the non-treatment group—what one is really interested in is how much improvement the program produces *relative to those who do not need it*. As a result the evaluation of social action programs is essentially comparative and historical, despite its often quantitative character: it seeks to determine whether a target population has changed, relative both to the same population before the program began and to the non-target population.

Finally, the evaluation of social action programs in education is political. Evaluation is a technique for measuring the satisfaction of public priorities; to evaluate a social action program is to establish an information system in which the main questions involve the allocation of power, status, and other public goods. There is conflict within the educational system concerning which priorities should be satisfied, and it is transmitted, willy-nilly, to evaluation. This puzzles and irritates many researchers; they regard it as extrinsic and an unnecessary bother. While this attitude is understandable; it is mistaken. The evaluation of social action programs is nothing if not an effort to measure social and political change. That is a difficult task under any circumstances, but it is impossible when the activity is not seen for what it is.

SUGGESTIONS FOR AN EVALUATION STRATEGY

What might be the elements of a more suitable evaluation strategy? The answer depends not only on what one thinks should be done, but on certain external political constraints. There is, for example, good reason to believe that federal education aid will be shifted into the framework of revenue sharing or block grants in the near future, and this is unlikely to strengthen the government's position as a social or educational experimenter. The only apparent alternative is continuing with roughly the present balance of power in education as categorical aid slowly increases the federal share of local expenditures. This seems unlikely to improve the government's position in the evaluation of large-scale social action programs. In addition, there seems to be a growing division over the criteria of program success. Researchers are increasingly aware that little evidence connects the typical criteria of program success (high achievement and good deportment), with their presumed adult consequences (better job, higher income, etc.). More important, in the cities—particularly in the Negro community—there is rising opposition to the view that achievement and good behavior are legitimate criteria of success. Instead, political legitimacy—in the form of parent involvement or community control—is advanced as a proper aim for school change programs. It is ironic that the recent interest in assessing schools' efficiency—which gained much of its impetus from black discontent with white-dominated ghetto schools—now meets with rising opposition in the Negro community as blacks seek control over ghetto education. Nonetheless, this opposition is likely to increase, and the evaluation of social action programs in city schools is sure to be affected.

There is, then, little reason to expect much relaxation of the political constraints on social action program evaluation. This suggest two principles which might guide future evaluation: experiment only when the substantive issues of policy are considerable and reasonably well-defined; reorient evaluation of the non-experimental operating programs to a broad system of measuring status and change in schools and schooling.

The first principle requires distinctions among potential experiments in terms of the political constraints they imply. One would like to know, for example, which pre-school and primary programs increase cognitive growth for disadvantaged children; whether giving parents money to educate their children (as opposed to giving it to schools) would improve the children's education; whether students' college entrance would suffer if high school curriculum and attendance requirements were sharply reduced or eliminated; whether school decentralization would improve achievement; or whether it would raise it as much as doubling expenditures.

These are among the most important issues in American education, but they are not equally difficult when it comes to arranging experiments to determine the answers. In most cases, large scale experimentation would be impossible. Experiments with decentralization, tuition vouchers, doubling per-pupil expenditures, and radical changes in secondary education have two salient attributes in common: to have meaning they would have to be carried out in the existing schools, and few schools would be likely to oblige. If experimentation occurs on such issues it would be limited—a tentative exploration of new ideas involving small numbers of students and schools. While this is highly desirable, it is not the same thing as mounting an experimental social action program in education.

This may not be the case with one issue, however—increasing cognitive growth for disadvantaged children. It already is the object of several social action programs and would not be a radical political departure. As a result of prior efforts, enough may be known to permit comparative experimental studies of different strategies for changing early intelligence. Several alternative approaches can be identified: rigid classroom drill, parent training, individual tutoring at early ages, and language training. Relatively little is known about the processes underlying these approaches, but there may be enough practical experience to support systematic comparative study. Since all the strategies have a common object, researchers probably could agree on common criterion measures. Since cognitive growth is widely believed to be crucial, investment in comparative studies seems worthwhile. But if such studies were undertaken, they should determine whether the treatment effect itself (higher IQ) is only a proxy for other things learned during the experiment, such as academic persistence, good behavior, and whether cognitive change produces any change on other measures of educational success, such as grades or years of school completed.

In effect, the chances for success of experimental approaches to social action will be directly related to a program's political independence, its specificity of aim, and its fiscal strength. The less it resembles the sort of broad-aim social action programs discussed in this paper, the more appropriate is an experimental approach and the more the "evaluation" looks like pure research. Of course, the further one moves down this continuum the less the program's impact is, and the less relevant the appellation "social action." Early childhood programs may be the only contemporary case in which the possibility of large-scale experimentation does not imply political triviality.

The second principle suggested above implies that the central purpose of evaluating most social action programs is the broad measurement of change. Evaluation is a comparative and historical enterprise, which can best be carried out as part of a general effort to measure educational status and change. The aims of social action programs are diverse, and their purpose is to shift the position of specified target populations relative to the rest of the society; their evaluation cannot be accomplished by isolated studies of particular aims with inappropriate standards of comparison. Evaluating broad social action programs requires comparably broad systems of social measurement.

A measurement system of this sort would be a census or system of social indicators of schools and schooling (not education). It would cover three realms: student, personnel, program, and fiscal inputs to schools; several outcomes of schooling, including achievement; temporal, geographic, political and demographic variation in both categories. If data of this sort were collected on a regular and recurring basis, they would serve the main evaluation needs for such operating programs as Title I. They would, for example, allow measurement of fiscal and resource delivery and of their variations over time, region, community, and school type. They would permit measurement of differences in school outcomes, as well as their changes over time. If the measurement of school outcomes were common over all schools, their variations could be associated with variations in other school attributes, including those of students, school resources, and the content and character of federal programs. Finally, if the measurement of outcomes and resources were particular to individual students, many of these comparisons could be extended from schools to individuals.

One advantage of such a measurement system would be its greater congruence with the structure and aims of large-scale multi-purpose programs. Another is that it would be more likely to provide data which could be useful in governmental decision-making—which, after all, is what evaluation is for. Most evaluation research in programs such as Title I is decentralized, non-recurring, and unrelated to either program planning or budgeting; as a result of the first attribute it is not comparable from community to community; as a result of the second it is not comparable from year to year; and as a result of the third it is politically and administratively irrelevant. Since the main governmental decisions about education involve allocating money and setting standards for goods, services, and performance, evaluation should provide comparable, continuing, and cumulative information in these areas. That would only be possible under a regular census of schools and schooling.

This is not to say there would be no deficiencies; there would be several, all of which are pretty well given in the nature of a census. By definition a census measures stasis, it quantifies how things stand. If done well, it can reveal a good deal about the interconnection of social structure; if it recurs, it can throw much light on how things change. But no census can reveal much about change other than its patterns—probing its causes and dynamics requires rather a different research orientation. And no census can produce qualitative data, especially on such complicated organizations as schools. There is, however, no reason why qualitative evaluation could not be systematically related to a census. Such evidence is much more useful when it recurs, and is connected with the results of quantitative studies. The same is true of research on the political dynamics and consequences of social action programs. Although valuable in itself, its worth would be substantially increased by relating it to other evidence on the same program.

The central problem, however, is experimentation. Using a census as the central evaluation device for large-scale multi-purpose programs assumes that systematic experimentation is very nearly impossible within the large operating programs and can best be carried on by clearly distinguishing census from experimental functions. It would be foolish to ignore experimentation—it should be increased—but it would be illusory to try to carry it out within programs which have other purposes. A clear view of the importance of both activities is unlikely to emerge until they have been distinguished conceptually and pulled apart administratively.

These suggestions are sketchy, and they leave some important issues open. Chief among them are the institutional and political arrangements required to mount both an effective census of schools and schooling and a long-term effort in experimentation.[10] Nonetheless, my suggestions do express a *strategy* of evaluation, something absent in most large-scale educational evaluation efforts. The strategy assumes that government has two distinct needs, which thus far have been confounded in the evaluation of large-scale action programs. One is to measure status and change in the distribution of educational resources and outcomes; the other is to explore the impact and effectiveness of novel approaches to schooling. If the first were undertaken on a regular basis the resulting time-series data would provide much greater insight into the actual distribution of education in America. It would thus build an information base for more informed decisions about allocation of resources, at both the state and Federal level. If the second effort were undertaken on a serious basis, it should be possible to learn more systematically from research and development. Perhaps the best way to distinguish this strategy from existing efforts is this: were the present approach to evaluating social action programs brought to perfection, it would not be adequate—it would not tell us what we need to know about the programs.

Second, my suggestions assume that the evaluation of social action programs is a political enterprise. This underlies the idea of separating experimentation from large-scale operating programs. It also underlies the notion of a census of schools and schooling, which would almost compel attention to the proper standards of comparison and would emphasize the importance of change. In addition, only a broad system of measurement can capture the political variety which social action programs embody. Perhaps most important, measuring the impact of social change programs in this way is not tied to a particular program or pattern of Federal aid.

Finally, such a strategy could be implemented within the existing political constraints. That is not a scientific argument, but that is the real point: evaluating social action programs is only secondarily a scientific enterprise. First and foremost it is an effort to gain politically significant information on the consequences of political acts. To confuse the technology of measurement with the real nature and broad purposes of evaluation will be fatal. It can only produce increasing quantities of information in answer to unimportant questions.

NOTES

1. Research for this paper was supported by a grant from the Carnegie Corporation of New York to the Center for Educational Policy Research, Harvard University. Henry

Dyer, Frederick Mosteller, and Martin Rein served as consultants to Dr. Cohen on the preparation of this chapter.

2. The national evaluations of Title I are little more than annual reports based on the state evaluation reports, which are little more than compilations of LEA reports. This is not to say that the reports are useless—but simply that they are not evaluations. The Office of the HEW Secretary was responsible for a study by Tempo (1968). Also, see Piccariello, undated.

3. By "achievement," I mean measures of reading or general verbal ability; I do not include therein more specialized measures of achievement such as math, social studies, science, or driver education.

4. A good general treatment is Bailey and Mosher, 1968. See also: U.S. Congress, 1965*b*; U.S. House Education and Labor Committee, 1965*a* and *b*; U.S. Senate Appropriations Committee, 1965; and U.S. Senate Labor and Public Welfare Committee, 1965.

5. The most recent report of the National Advisory Council on the Education of Disadvantaged Children (1969) contains a brief section on this issue. It does not deal with program impact, but with private-parochial school relations.

6. Jackson, P. B. (1969). Hartman (undated) concluded that the aims of Title I are so vague as to make the act little more than a general (i.e., non-categorical) vehicle for redistributing educational revenues.

7. The requirement is found in U.S. Dept. of Health, Education, and Welfare (1968). There also is a special memorandum (Howe, 1968) covering this issue.

8. Not all the purposes of social action programs are so neat or abstract, nor can they all be evaluated by counting dollars, teachers, or special programs. One of the aims of large-scale social action programs is to produce peace, or at least to reduce conflict. Whether or not they serve these ends is well worth investigating.

Similarly, little is known about the ways in which educational institutions change. This has been highlighted by the ability of many big-city school systems to absorb large amounts of activity and money designed to change them, and emerge apparently unchanged. If any question about the efficacy of social action programs is crucial, it is how such efforts at change succeed or fail. The requirement here may not be quantitative research, but political and social analysis, which follows the political and administrative history of social change programs. It may be possible to learn as much about the sources of programs' success from studying the politics of their intent and execution as from analyzing the quantitative relationships between program components and some summary measure of target group performance. Although such studies would be inapplicable in traditional educational evaluation, they are crucial in the evaluation of social action programs. These programs represent an effort to rearrange political relationships, and the sources of variation in their success are therefore bound to have as much to do with political and administrative matters as with how efficiently program inputs are translated into outcomes.

9. Actually, the evaluation found that gains were more common among classrooms which had low scores on the pre-tests and that losses were more common among those classrooms which had higher pre-tests. The most economical hypothesis, then, is a regression effect (Piccariello, undated).

10. Creating the capacity for experimentation would involve a few major decisions. One probably would be to separate the activity from the Office of Education, retaining its

connection with HEW at the Assistant Secretary level. Another would be to create greater institutional capacity for support and evaluation in the private (or quasipublic) sector; at the moment, this important resource is not well enough developed to bear the load. A third would be to so arrange its management that the decisions about what experiments to fund resulted from systematic and sustained interaction between the political governors of such an institution, its scientific staffers and constituents, and the educational practitioners. Without this, it would probably do interesting but politically unimportant work.

Creating the capacity for a census or system of schooling indicators involves different issues. Here there is good reason for it to be part of USOE. The question is where, and what capacity would be required; though these require more detailed work than is possible here, a bit of speculation is possible. There is some reason to think, for example, that the new 21 state management information system might be a good base from which to begin. There already is an ongoing program, it seems to have promise conceptually, and there seems to be a good state-Federal relationship.

BIBLIOGRAPHY

Bailey, S., and Mosher, E. ESEA: *The Office of Education Administers a Law* (Syracuse, N.Y.: Syracuse Univ. Press, 1968).

Blau, P., and Duncan, O. *The American Occupational Structure* (New York: Wiley, 1968).

Dentler, R. "The Phenomenology of the Evaluation Researcher." Paper presented to the Conference on Evaluating Social Action Programs, American Academy of Arts and Sciences, May 1969 (New York: Center for Urban Education, 105 Madison Avenue). Typewritten.

Duncan, O. *Socioeconomic Background and Occupational Achievement* (Ann Arbor: Univ. of Mich. Press, 1968).

Guba, E. "Development, Diffusion, and Evaluation." In Terry Eidell and Joanne Kitchel (eds.), *Knowledge Production and Utilization in Educational Administration* (Eugene, Ore.: Univ. Council for Educational Administration and Center for the Study of Educational Administration, 1968), chapter 3, pp. 37–63.

Hartman, R. "Evaluation in Multi-Purpose Grant-in-Aid Programs" (Washington, D.C.: The Brookings Institution, undated). Typewritten.

Howe, Harold (Commissioner). *Special memorandum* (Washington, D.C.: U.S. Dept. of Health, Education, and Welfare, Office of Education, June 14, 1968).

Jackson, P. B. "Trends in Elementary and Secondary Education Expenditures: Central City and Suburban Comparisons, 1965–1968" (Washington, D.C.: U.S. Dept. of Health, Education, and Welfare, Office of Education, Office of Program Planning and Evaluation, 1969). Mimeo.

National Advisory Council on the Education of Disadvantaged Children. *Title I ESEA: A Review and a Forward Look* (Washington, D.C.: The Council, 1969).

Piccariello, H. "Evaluation of Title I." Paper presented to the Dept. of Health, Education, and Welfare, Office of Education, Washington, D.C., undated. Typewritten.

Stufflebeam, D. "The Use and Abuse of Evaluation in Title III." *Theory into Practice* 6 (1967): 126–33.

Tempo, G. *Survey and Analysis of Title I Funding for Compensatory Education* (Washington, D.C.: U.S. Dept. of Health, Education, and Welfare, Office of the Secretary, 1968).

U.S. Congress, Eighty-nine, First Session. Title I. *Elementary and Secondary Education Act of 1965.* Public Law 89–10. U.S. Statutes at Large, 89th Congress, First Session. 1965. (*a*)

U.S. Congress, Eighty-nine, First Session. House Report No. 143. *Report of the Committee on Education and Labor, on the Elementary and Secondary Education Act of 1965.* 1965. (*b*)

U.S. Department of Health, Education, and Welfare. *Criteria for Applications Grants to Local Educational Agencies Under Title I, ESEA* (Washington, D.C.: The Department, 1968).

U.S. Department of Health, Education, and Welfare. *Summary Report of 1968 White House Task Force on Child Development* (Washington, D.C.: USGPO, 1968).

U.S. House Education and Labor Committee. *Hearings before General Subcommittee on Education, Eighty-Ninth Congress, First Session, on Aid to Elementary and Secondary Education.* 1965. (*a*)

U.S. House Education and Labor Committee. *Hearings before General Subcommittee on Education, Eighty-Ninth Congress, First Session, on the Elementary and Secondary School Act Formulas.* 1965. (*b*)

U.S. Senate Appropriations Committee. *Hearings before Subcommittee on Departments of Labor and HEW Appropriations for 1966, Departments of Labor and HEW Supplemental Appropriations for 1966, Eighty-Ninth Congress, First Session.* 1965.

U.S. Senate Labor and Public Welfare Committee. *Hearings before Subcommittee on Education, Eighty-Ninth Congress, First Session, on the Elementary and Secondary Education Act of 1965.* 1965.

ADDITIONAL REFERENCES

Aldrich, Nelson (Issues Editor). *The Urban Review* 2 (No. 6 and No. 7, 1968).

Bateman, W. *An Experimental Approach to Program Analysis: Stepchild in the Social Sciences.* Paper presented to the Operations Research Society of America, Denver, Colo., June 1969 (Washington, D.C.: The Urban Institute, 1969).

Campbell, D. "Reforms as Experiments." *American Psychologist* 24 (1969): 409–29.

Campbell, D., and Stanley, J. *Experimental and Quasi-Experimental Designs for Research* (Chicago: Rand McNally, 1966).

Dyer, H. "Some Thoughts About Future Studies." In D. Moynihan and F. Mosteller (eds.) *On Equality of Educational Opportunity* (New York: Random House, 1972).

Evans, J. "Evaluating Social Action Programs" (Washington, D.C.: Office of Economic Opportunity, 1969). Typewritten.

Hyman, H., and Wright, C. "Evaluating Social Action Programs." In Paul Lazarsfeld, William Sewall, and Harold Wilensky (eds.), *The Uses of Sociology* (New York: Basic Books, 1966), chapter 27, pp. 741−82.

Marris, P., and Rein, M. *Dilemmas of Social Reform* (Atherton, N.Y.: Atherton Press, 1967).

McDill, E., McDill, M., and Sprehe, T. "An Analysis of Evaluation of Selected Compensatory Education Programs." Presented to the American Academy of Arts and Sciences Conference, May 1969 (Baltimore, Md., Johns Hopkins Univ., 1969). Typewritten.

Rivlin, A. "PPBS in HEW: Some Lessons from Experience." Paper prepared for the Joint Economic Committee, Mar. 1969 (Washington, D.C.: The Brookings Institution, 1969). Typewritten.

Rivlin, A., and Wholey, J. "Education of Disadvantaged Children." Paper presented to the Symposium on Operations Analysis of Education, Nov. 1967 (Washington, D.C.: The Brookings Institution, 1967). Typewritten.

Rothenberg, J. "Cost Benefit Analysis: A Methodological Exposition." Paper presented to the American Academy of Arts and Sciences Conference, May 1969 (Cambridge: Mass. Institute of Technology, 1969). Typewritten.

Swartz, R. "Experimentation in Social Research." *Journal of Legal Education* 13 (1961): 401−10.

Weiss, R., and Rein, M. "Evaluation of Broad-Aim Social Programs." Paper presented to the American Academy of Arts and Sciences Conference, May 1969 (Roxbury, Mass.: Harvard Medical School, 1969). Typewritten.

Wholey, J. "Federal Evaluation Practices" (Washington, D.C.: The Urban Institute, 1969). Typewritten. (*a*)

————. "Program Evaluation in the Department of Health, Education, and Welfare." *Federal Program Evaluation Practices.* Appendix I (Washington, D.C.: The Urban Institute, 1969). (*b*)

Williams, W., and Evans, J. "The Politics of Evaluation: The Case of Headstart." *Annals* 385 (1969): 118−32.

27. THE PROCESS AND IDEOLOGY OF VALUING IN EDUCATIONAL SETTINGS

Michael W. Apple

The language and slogans of school people provide symbols for key educational ideas and movements. They serve as standards or beacons that attract adherents and often generate vast amounts of literature.[1] Sometimes, though less often than we suppose, they have a significant effect in reorienting educational practice. The language of accountability and evaluation provides an excellent instance of this phenomenon today. While evaluation is not a new concern to be sure, its recent emphasis—some might argue overemphasis—is striking to anyone familiar with the professional journals that indicate the state of the field.

There is reason to believe that the patterns of interaction among people concerned with evaluation affect the types of discourse that dominate the topic. There has been and, unless patterns change drastically, there will continue to be little debate among educators who hold distinctly different positions about many of the valuative and fundamental questions concerning evaluation because of what has been commonly called "invisible colleges." That is, individuals discuss and engage in debate only with others who already share much of their basic orientation. They never have to take seriously alternative conceptions of their activity because this professional activity is not open to challenge by others of a different persuasion. In this way there is little genuine synoptic progress in education as a whole and in evaluation in particular.

Therefore, a number of the arguments in this chapter will be guided by a

SOURCE: Michael W. Apple, Michael J. Subkoviak, and Henry S. Lufler, Jr. (eds.), *Educational Evaluation: Analysis and Responsibility* (Berkeley, Calif.: McCutchan Publishing Corp., 1974), pp. 3–34. Reprinted by permission of the publisher.

perspective that might best be called "critical" in that it seeks to illuminate the problematic character of the commonsense reality most educators take for granted. The critical spirit of the chapter should be interpreted as a step toward engaging other members of the field in the essential argumentation over the role evaluation has played and will play in education. Such intellectual conflict and debate are of fundamental importance if we are serious about confronting educational problems in a manner that does justice to their complexity and subtlety. We need to reflect on Toulmin's dictum that any field that seeks to make programmatic and conceptual headway must stand open to even quite basic criticism and change if it is to be more than a pretender to rationality.[2] Unfortunately, curriculum discourse and a good deal of educational thought in general have been more concerned with both conceptual and social stability than with change, more interested in a search for prior consensus than in the critical give-and-take that supports genuine advances. The original papers and debates that this book presents are part of a response to the need for such informed discussion.

A basic aim of this chapter is to suggest the complexity of the problems that so much recent educational thought has tended to ignore. A good deal of what I shall say stresses the conservative nature of educational evaluation. My discussion employs investigations in areas too long ignored by educators. By bringing new perspectives to bear, I hope to illuminate alternatives to the very limited models we now employ. For example, my discussion often draws upon research on the question of "deviance." It seems that schools act to create certain student roles and expectations; groups of students either fill these and "make progress at school" or do not fill them and thus are channeled into other paths, in much the same way that deviants are created and are treated by other social institutions. Evaluation may play an interesting part here. Research on deviance is also critical in examining the place occupied by psychological language and research, and educational evaluation based on them, in upholding bureaucratic and institutional rather than interpersonal and situational norms and values.

This chapter, then, is meant to serve a number of functions: to raise serious questions in the reader's mind concerning educational evaluation; to point to ideological, methodological, epistemological, and ethical issues raised by the current emphasis on evaluation and accountability; and, at least partly, to reorient educational evaluation to what might be called *institutional evaluation* rather than evaluation of "learning."

HISTORICAL INTERPRETATION

In the scientific disciplines, new paradigms emerge to offer more fruitful disciplinary matrices for reorganizing and reconstructing previously accepted explanations.[3] Similar "revolutions" occur in other fields of study. Among the foremost of these is the recent revisionist perspective in the history of American education. Critically oriented history has begun to raise a number of potent objections to our usual understanding of the past and the roles schooling and evaluation have played in it.

Educators' interpretations of their history have often reflected a belief that schools have "liberated the individual and opened up opportunities for social mobility to the disadvantaged."[4] Furthermore, the interpretation holds that, while schools have had their problems, they have been steadily moving toward a more egalitarian ethic and have contributed to and been a part of lasting social and institutional reforms. The accepted view sees testing and evaluation in a similar light, taking for granted the notion that they have led to more humane educational environments and will continue to do so in the future.

However, much of this interpretation is changing and cannot be quite so readily accepted anymore. Historian Michael Katz, for instance, states that the structure of schooling has remained basically the same for decades, a fact that is given more warrant by studies such as Sarason's recent investigation of the process of change in schools.[5] Katz argues that the past "moments" of schooling have reflected "not the great democratic engines for identifying talent and matching it with opportunity," but rather a treatment of "students as units to be processed into particular shapes and dropped into slots roughly congruent with the status of their parents."[6] Schools, therefore, have been instrumental in confirming the existing distribution of knowledge and power in the United States.

Reassessment of the latent social outcomes of education has not been limited to the broad structural characteristics of schools and society. The focus has increasingly come to rest on basic but quite specific aspects of school life. This historical reappraisal has included the process of evaluation. It is possible to interpret the history of the testing and evaluation movement through just such a revisionist framework. In other words, the quest for efficiency and quantitative "output measures" that the movement embodies has mirrored social interests in stability, human predictability, and ultimately social control, and may continue to mirror these interests today.[7] As Karier puts it:

> Whether it was Terman calling for special education for the gifted, or Conant calling for "national educational assessment," or E.T.S. striving to develop, in the name of "accountability," performance-based teacher tests, all served as part of a broader efficiency movement to classify, standardize, and rationalize human beings to serve the productive interests of a society essentially controlled by wealth, privilege, and status.[8]

Evaluators and other school people may find themselves quite disconcerted by such a reconstruction of their past. However, they must not dismiss it casually. A primary reason for taking this perspective seriously is the fact that education is through and through a valuative enterprise. The proposals educators make for organizing and evaluating school activity are usually derived from slogan systems (such as structure of the disciplines, life adjustment, or social efficiency) with identifiable ideological and epistemological presuppositions.[9] Given this fact, educators really cannot afford to be less than fully aware of the latent tendencies in their work.

Let us take one example. The current goal of assessing "affective" educational programs is usually viewed as a meritorious aim, one that enables school personnel to instill in students respect for self and others, to better teach values concerning human relations, and so on. However, given the reality of schools as bureaucratic institutions, the possible latent function of such programs and the measurement of their outcomes should be clear. They have tended and will tend to bring under the purview of public institutions like schools even the most private of students' dispositions and personal meanings, thereby contributing to their rationalization by placing them under the custodial function of the school. Public behavior replaces private meaning.

This interpretation receives historical credibility from the fact that, by the early part of this century, the increasing industrialization and urbanization of American society "had severely eroded the influence of the family, church, and community on individual behavior." While the potency of these institutions weakened, another—the school—received attention as a critical institution of social control. It

became *the* agency charged with the responsibility of maintaining social order and cohesion and of instilling individuals with codes of conduct and social values that would insure the stability of *existing* social relationships. Although a preserving institution, the school was viewed as a form of internal control—and therefore more in the "democratic" tradition than such external forms as law, government, and police.[10]

Thus, in response to the conflicts created by the perceived disorder of an expanding industrial economy and a steady flow of immigrants, the school expanded its responsibilities to maintain a social order that seemed to be threatened. It became responsible for the "whole child," increasing its custodial functions to include all of a child's social life,[11] and attempting to homogenize social reality and the different perceptions of disparate groups.

Coupled with the interest in maintaining the stability of the existing market system and social hierarchy was a strong and widespread racist element running through the testing movement and the tests themselves. Early proponents often looked on testing as a truly "scientific" mode by which the "scientific expert could control the evolutionary progress of the race."[12] Thus, another strikingly conservative factor can be uncovered in the roots of evaluation.

If this revisionist interpretation is correct, that the testing movement— the historical roots of the current emphasis on evaluation—often served rather conservative social and economic interests, that it was consistently biased against students who were somehow "different" according to existing institutional labels, and that it acted as an important implement of social control, then school people must examine quite carefully the effects it has today when the movement is supposedly motivated by more "enlightened" sentiments. If these social interests are deeply embedded in the history of evaluation and testing, does use of the methodological fruits of that tradition unconsciously compel educators to appropriate its ideological positions as well? This is a question that cannot be taken lightly, especially when, as I shall note later in my discussion, the logic of the methodologies usually employed in educational research may rest on similar conservative foundations.

EVALUATION AND IDEOLOGICAL PERSPECTIVES

Process-Product Reasoning

One of the tasks of the committed educator is to recognize his own perspective and locate this and its latent implications in relation to competing perspectives extant not only in the past but also now.[13] This task is no less important for those interested in evaluation than for other policy-minded educators.

In order to accomplish this, we should realize that evaluation itself is a process of *social valuing*. It involves one or more groups of people *assigning* values to activities, goals, and procedures done by others, such as students. Furthermore, it involves some particular conception of the types of values to be placed on these activities, goals, and procedures. This sounds rather obvious, but it is especially significant, because it implies that the act of and research in evaluation are not neutral.

Evaluation actually connotes the *placing of value* on a specific set of acts or objects. It not only deals with a form of social valuing but also implies a *choice* among a range of value systems that might give meaning to educational activity. For instance, we can value an activity for its efficiency (its ability to get a student from point A to point B quickly and inexpensively)—a process of valuing that unfortunately is considered the sine qua non of educational evaluation today— or for its human qualities (the extent to which it is an experience that has beauty and form), or for its embodiment of conflict, ambiguity, and uncertainty (its fulfillment of the uniqueness of the human condition).[14] It is also possible to evaluate educational experience politically (the extent to which it increases the power of individuals or groups to make determinations about their own present and future actions). Hence, it is not naturally predetermined that education should be valued only for its ability to reach our goals adequately and efficiently. This is, in fact, a process-product rationality, which Kliebard has shown is actually a factory metaphor.[15] The dominance of this outlook is one of the inherent problems confronting individuals concerned with evaluation.

Let us examine it a bit closer. Evaluation usually fits into a systems management model that looks something like this: we define a program's educational objectives (preferably in measurable terms); proper experiences are developed and organized to bring the student from point A to point B (from not meeting objectives to meeting them); evaluation occurs along the way and at the completion, comparing results to other programs or to the discrepancy between goals and performance; and this evaluation gives feedback to make the system function more smoothly and efficiently. In essence, it is an industrial production model of schooling. However, when systems approaches such as these are applied to education, they bring about political and educational quiescence in a variety of ways. They defuse the important process of political argumentation over what goals educators should be striving for, and they are quite often epistemologically and politically conservative.[16] This conservatism is strengthened by the common sense of evaluation.

Much of the discourse surrounding educational evaluation has been concerned with the development of means to measure the outcomes of schooling. Taken by itself, this is certainly needed. However, the discourse has also been strikingly apolitical (though the way evaluation functions has not), as if the means and ends of education were not context-bound and linked to a specific nexus of institutions, economic interests, and political power.

For instance, the predominance in advanced industrial societies of attempts to rationalize all aspects of intersubjective behavior may lie at the heart of a good deal of evaluation in education. Educators share an unconscious commitment to a form of reasoning that assumes that considerations of instrumental effectiveness when confronting human action are the only ways of generating decisions. In this regard, the current emphasis on systems management, the more vulgar forms of accountability, and the place of evaluation in each are not only "tools toward a more effective educational system," but also symptoms of the absence in our commonsense thought of any appreciation of the necessity of certain factors that are embodied in the human condition. Awe and mystery, uncertainty and ambiguity, conflict and the dialectic of stability and change—all of these are difficult to deal with using an industrial logic, yet all are essential if educators are to appreciate the complexity of their dilemmas and to create institutions that respond to the tension between institutional history and personal biography.

There are a number of difficulties associated with a process-product perspective on schooling. I cannot hope to discuss each fully, nor can I even be exhaustive in listing them in a chapter this size. It is essential, however, that I at least illuminate several of the problematic aspects, so that educators can confront them honestly.

There are two principal problems, one "educational," the other "ideological." First, process-product reasoning can and quite often does lead to consideration of people as "things"—manipulatable abstractions. There is a significant danger in coming to conceive of one's fellow persons as objects: one may begin to treat them as they are conceived.[17] This is a very real problem in schools today and one that is heightened by a number of aspects of evaluation. Along with the possible objectification of individuals, instrumental rationales lead to what sociologists like to call *goal displacement*. For example, efficient institutions obviously should exist for educational purposes; but efficiency may soon become a goal in itself rather than only one consideration in ascertaining the educational worth of an activity. Thus, those items on an educational agenda that are more easily identified and reached seem naturally to become the focus and the actual goals of the institution, although they may be much less important than others.

It is crucial to recognize this danger of efficiency becoming the most important outcome of schooling—the reification of means into ends. It was perhaps best noted by Dewey, who went even further in linking it to the importance of aesthetic experience in any educative event worthy of its name. Bernstein puts it this way:

[Dewey] emphasizes the esthetic consumatory dimension of experience. He criticizes educational and social institutions and practices for neglecting this esthetic dimension of experience. This is evidenced in the separation of means and ends in our educational and social thinking. The quality and content of ends-in-view which we strive to attain depend upon the quality of the means that we use to attain them. When we separate ends and means, when we think of means as *mere* means to some . . . goal, we are in danger of destroying the efficacy of our means and the potency of our ends. Means and ends, whether in education, moral, or political life designate the same experience viewed from different perspectives. Our task is to make all experience more esthetic, funded with meaning, and fulfilling.[18]

One can value, say, predetermined behavioral objectives for their supposed ability to lead to measurable outcomes (their efficiency as means to reach previously chosen ends); however, the very notion that such reductive and atomistic curricular formulations are worthwhile educationally in themselves is an arguable assertion to say the least. It can certainly be argued that they embody an ideology of control, that they place much too high a value on certainty above all else, that they are inaccurate representations of and trivialize the processes of inquiry, and that they are psychologically and philosophically naive.[19] Thus, here as elsewhere, the idea that means are mere instruments to meritorious ends is too limited a concept. This becomes clear if it is examined more carefully than educators are apt to do.

Just as significant a problem with process-product reasoning in education is its ability to hide from school people the political and ethical nature of their acts. It is not an effective language system for disclosing the ideological character of educational valuing. In calling the normal modes of evaluation in schools ideological, I do not wish to debunk entirely the usual means by which professional educators place value on their activity. Rather, my point is to bring into clearer focus the taken-for-granted nature of much that school personnel and others do. An ideology can be defined as a taken-for-granted perspective held by a specific social group. The perspective is not necessarily wrong, but it is necessarily partial and incomplete, just as any accepted perspective is limited.[20] One of my points throughout this chapter will be to argue exactly that—that evaluation as it is currently practiced can give only a decidedly partial perspective on the worth of educational events.

Evaluation is ideological in other ways besides its limited perspective on valuing. In the main it has tended to be quite conservative with regard to existing institutional structures of education. In his discussion of the latent conservatism of structural-functional social theory and the brand of systems analysis that has grown out of it, Gouldner describes rather clearly the nature of a conservative posture.

What makes a theory conservative (or radical) is its posture toward the institutions of its surrounding society. A theory is conservative to the extent that it: treats these institutions as given and unchangeable in essentials; proposes remedies for them so that they work better, rather than devising alternatives to them; foresees no future that can be essentially better than the present, the conditions that already exist; and, explicitly or implicitly, counsels acceptance or resignation to what exists, rather than struggling against it.[21]

This is an apt description of the latent workings of even rather well intentioned and change-oriented evaluation.

Evaluation as a Social Construct

I should begin by stating that certain types of performance, certain forms of knowledge, certain dispositions, achievements, and propensities are not necessarily good in and of themselves. Rather, they are made so because of specific taken-for-granted assumptions. Thus, their values are relative and temporally conditioned. In order to make this clear, a rather significant but often unrecognized fact should be mentioned here. The guiding principles of evaluation—conceptions of achievement, of success or failure, and so on—are *social constructs*. They are not inherent in individuals or groups of people. Instead, they are instances of the application of identifiable social rules about what is to be considered good or bad performance. Such conceptions are similar to the notion of ''deviance'' in that just as other people must define an individual's behavior as ''out of line'' or ''abnormal'' for it to be deviant, people other than the student define his educational activity as good or bad.

Becker clarifies this in his discussion of deviant behavior.

Social groups create deviance by making rules whose infraction constitutes deviance, and by applying these rules to particular people and labeling them as outsiders. From this point of view deviance is *not* a quality of the act the person commits, but rather a consequence of the application by others of rules and sanctions to an "offender." The deviant is one to whom that label has successfully been applied; deviant behavior is behavior that people so label.[22]

This has important consequences for any analysis of evaluation, since it implies that a complete understanding of evaluation necessitates an investigation into not only the groups of children and programs being evaluated but also the socially accepted rules and assumptions that make certain things important (e.g., demonstration of competence on certain school tests) and other forms of knowledge relatively unimportant. Hence, our focus must be on "evaluating" the school as an institution that embodies these social rules and assumptions as well as on "evaluating" the recipients, the students.[23] Educators must examine the ideological and political *uses* of evaluation and the place of the school in a larger social setting if they are to uncover what evaluation is actually about. And they must engage in the prior examination of what is considered valuable knowledge both overtly and covertly in school settings, why this is considered valuable knowledge, and how this conception of valuable knowledge is linked to institutions in the larger society. I shall sketch some areas that may be worthy of such investigation by examining a number of points: (1) that evaluation is a political language that prevents rather than fosters the questioning of school procedures by people other than professionals; (2) that the power of the evaluation expert is distinctly limited in dealing with organizations like schools by the definition of his role; (3) that the basic clinical perspective of experts contributes to the conservatism of evaluation; and (4) that the interests underlying the basic methodologies evaluators employ may foster the ideology of strict control of human action that guides a good deal of educational policy making.

The Process of Political Quiescence

Any analysis of the political meaning of educational research (and educational evaluation *has* political meaning in terms of the distribution of power in institutions) must occur on at least two levels. First, it needs to examine how evaluation activity gets some groups the tangible results they want, at the expense of others. In the competition for public money, for instance, measurable results are exceedingly important if an institution wants to generate funding. Secondly, the analysis must explore what this research and its results mean to the public at large, and how the general public is "aroused" or "placated" by it.[24] One might want to ask *how and by whom* evaluation data are used. In many cases, evaluation is a means to deflect potent criticism away from the fundamental policies of bureaucratic structures.

It is not too odd a position to argue that the language used for major aspects of evaluation—e.g., accountability, cost-effectiveness, systems analysis, effective schooling—may act to reassure the public that serious changes need not occur in educational settings. This may be especially true in inner-city areas. Like abstractions such as democracy and justice, they are reified by and become identified with existing institutions. The terminology becomes what Edelman has called a "socially pathic" language, a form of language that tends to encourage attachment to existing institutional structures that may actually "deny [individuals] values they prize."[25] That is, because of the bureaucratic complexity and traditional character of the regularities of schooling, it is possible that significant alterations in the structural characteristics of schools and the relative distribution of power to individuals in schools (for example, greater student autonomy and responsibility) must occur if the institution is to perform many of the functions expected of it. In fact, as will be argued later on, it is not inconceivable that schools may effectively create a number of the difficulties they are supposed to solve.

The linguistic metaphors associated with evaluation may act to hide this possibility from the public and especially from minority and culturally diverse groups. By seeming to show the public the undoubtedly real concern of school people to change many ineffective practices in schools, evaluation terminology keeps the populace from seeing the uncomfortable fact that significant alterations in the school environment have been rare and short-lived. Thus, the knowledgeable criticism of a concerned citizenry is deflected.

The Role of the Expert

Not only does evaluation contribute to an often unwarranted sense of well-being on the part of the public, but all too often such research is used to legitimate educators' own commonsense activity rather than to challenge it. This occurs primarily because its practitioners do not very often step back and look at what stands behind their work. Evaluators should be rather cautious about accepting their work at face value for a number of reasons. One of the more important is their failure to see that by committing themselves to the study of officially defined goals and procedures using official categories they may also be giving the rhetorical prestige of science to extant bureaucratic regularities.[26] This offers a prime example of the less than neutral effects of educational evaluation.

An evaluator's or other researcher's basic perspective is quite strongly influenced by the dominant values of the collectivity to which he belongs and the social position he occupies in it. These dominant values *necessarily* affect his work.[27] In fact, his outlook is already sedimented into the forms of language and implicit perspectives found in the social role an evaluator fills. Linguistic, programmatic, methodological, and conceptual tools, and expectations of how they are to be used, are built into his job.[28] It is not very common for evaluators to turn their backs on the institutionalized goals, procedures, and norms that already exist and the storehouse of knowledge serving these official goals that has been collected over the years in the evaluation field.

This congerie of accepted wisdom and value is reinforced by the need of institutional managers for special types of expert advice. This is an exceptionally important point. Educational evaluators are "experts for hire." I do not mean to denigrate the important position they fill. Rather, I wish to stress that the role of the expert in American society is unique and leads to certain expectations that are themselves problematic in educational settings.

Experts are under considerable pressure to present their findings as scientific information, as knowledge that has a significant scientific warrant and, therefore, an inherent plausibility.[29] Not only are experts expected to couch their arguments in scientific terms, but also, because of their very position in the social system, their data and perspectives are perceived as authoritative. The weight and prestige given to their expertise is considerable.[30]

It should be clear, however, that in general educators have appropriated the reconstructed logic of science rather than the logic-in-use of scientific investigation.[31] Their view of scientific activity as the expert and efficient means to guarantee certainty in results has been fundamentally inaccurate. It represents a picture drawn from technological models of thought, whereas accounts of significant scientific investigations show a more sophisticated posture, in which the complex blend of technique, art, and personal commitment is highly evident. This appropriation of an inaccurate model produces considerable difficulty. It leads educators to practice poor research, and, most importantly, it is a major component of their tendency to confirm the conceptual paradigm under which they are working even though substantive progress may require a new disciplinary matrix in place of the current one.[32] The numerous findings of "no significant difference" might just point to this conclusion.

The use of a quasi-scientific or technological perspective is quite unfortunate in other ways. The process of education and the evaluation of educational settings are much too complex human endeavors to ever be totally subsumed under the rubric of science, especially a poor representation of scientific activity. Rather, they can also be illuminated through ethical and aesthetic perspectives and indeed cannot be understood without using these perspectives, if the field is not to lose all sight of the fact that the educational process always ends in a particular act of personal knowing. Walsh puts it well in his discussion of "poetic intelligence" in giving value to educational events.

In the act of knowing . . . we find engaged two distinct impulses of the mind which are related by a mutual tension and support. They are an eagerness to light on the highest degree of individuality of things and a concern to generalize, to establish an order among the particulars. On the intimacy of union of these two, the richness of the first, the relevance and adequacy of the second, depends the completed act of understanding. It is the nature of poetic intelligence . . . to give us the wholeness of the act of knowing. It is this which makes it so salutory a corrective in education where we fall continually into the error of identifying understanding . . . with one component of understanding, the generalizing, systematizing element, and neglect what it should be grounded in, a sense of the particular, as well as what it should return to, a still more heightened sense of the particular.[33]

The field's use of outdated positivistic models of science to define out of existence these other forms of giving meaning to and evaluating education is indicative of a similar technological orientation throughout other areas of industrialized nations. However, even if we accept the critical power of an elaborated, not reconstructed, scientific rationality to illuminate the consequences of education, giving too strong a scientific warrant to much expert evaluation data does not do justice to the conceptual difficulties that abound beneath the overt assumptions educators make to organize their research. For one example, educators have little cumulative knowledge and only a partial understanding of the process psychologists label "learning." Yet a good deal of evaluation purports to assess this very aspect of human activity. This problem is heightened by the fact that the training of experts in education is usually deep but quite narrow. They are trained to believe in the efficacy of their technical expertise. Thus alternative models of examining problems, models that may come from distinctly different conceptual traditions, are not often considered. Therefore, basic problems with the accepted expertise itself remain unchallenged even when the results of using this framework are poor.

While there are considerable conceptual and technical difficulties with the usual view of what important research looks like, one thing is obvious. Even given these difficulties, school people and decision makers do perceive the information they get from evaluational researchers as "worthy," again because it comes from those who hold the title of expert.

One of the tasks of the expert (read evaluator) is to furnish administrative leaders of an institution with the special knowledge they require before decisions are made. The bureaucratic institution, not the expert, furnishes the problems to be investigated. Hence, the type of knowledge that the expert is to supply is *determined in advance*. Since the expert bears no responsibility for the final outcome of a program, his activities can be guided by the practical interests of the administrative leaders. And what administrators are *not* looking for are new hypotheses or new interpretations that are not immediately and noticeably relevant to the practical problems at hand—the teaching of reading, say. The fact that the expert is expected to work on the practical problems as defined by the institution and not to offer advice outside these boundaries is of considerable moment. It has become increasingly evident that, for whatever reasons (socialization into a position, timidity because of political pressure, a belief that engineering techniques will solve all of our problems, and so forth) the administrative leadership of a large educational organization seeks and is probably supposed to seek to reduce the new and uncertain elements of each complex situation to a practical, safe combination of "old and certain truths" about the processes of schooling.[34] However, there are very few things as conceptually, ethically, and politically complex as education, and educational scholarship has hardly scratched the surface of its intricacies. The fact that these old and certain truths may be less than efficacious, given the complicated nature of educational problems in cities and elsewhere, is not often considered by practical decision makers, for, after all, it is the role of the expert to deal with this complexity. But, as we saw, the knowledge expected of the expert is predetermined; thus, we are caught in a double bind. The evaluator is expected to provide expert advice and services to help solve the institution's problems; however, the range of issues and the types of answers that are actually acceptable are limited by what the administrative apparatus has previously defined as "the problem." In this way the circle of inconsequential results is continued.

This is certainly not new. Expertise has been used by policy makers for quite a long time. It should be clear, though, that from the very beginning, when statistical skills were used to assess social programs, the bulk of official statistics such as evaluation data were policy-oriented, not descriptive. Just as important, these data were determined primarily by and in support of the political goals of officials,[35] often at the expense of an institution's responsiveness to its clientele.

This raises a rather provocative question. Can one study the real outcomes and processes of educational programs when one's research uses categories and data derived from and serving the institution itself, without at the same time giving support to the bureaucratic apparatus these categories and data serve? Can one truly evaluate an institution or a program using such a procedure? If an evaluator's work does latently provide such support on this level, is it possible that other things—the attitudes of researchers and the ameliorative and, especially, clinical perspective that guides them—do likewise?

Clinical Assumptions and Bureaucratic Support

A careful examination of, say, programs to raise the achievement levels of inner-city students might reveal that evaluators have internalized a clinical model. From the outset, three things seem to be striking about this model: (1) the research accepts as given the basic values of the institution that has called these children "under-achievers"; (2) the blame is often put on the person or group rather than the institution; and (3) action is taken to change the individual rather than the fundamental structure of the social setting.

In her discussion of the process of labeling groups of mental patients, Mercer makes these points even more cogently.

[The clinical viewpoint] is readily identified by several distinguishing characteristics. First, the investigator accepts as the focus for study those individuals who have been labeled deviant. In so doing, he adopts the values of whatever social system has defined the person as deviant and assumes that its judgments are the valid measures of deviance . . . without serious questioning.

A second distinguishing characteristic of the clinical perspective is the tendency to perceive deviance as an attribute of the person . . . as a lack to be explained. This viewpoint results in the quest for etiology. Thus, the clinical perspective is essentially a medical frame of reference, for it sees deviance as individual pathology requiring diagnostic classification and etiological analysis for the purpose of determining proper treatment procedures and probable prognosis.

Three additional characteristics of the clinical perspective are the development of a diagnostic nomenclature, the creation of diagnostic instruments, and the professionalization of the diagnostic function.

When the investigator begins his research with the diagnostic designations assigned by official defining agents, he tends to assume that all individuals placed in a given category are essentially equivalent in respect to their deviance. . . . Individuals assigned to different categories of deviance are compared with each other or with a "normal" population consisting of persons who, for whatever reason, have escaped being labeled. The focus is on the individual [rather than on the defining agents].

Another characteristic of the clinical perspective is its assumption that the official definition is somehow the "right" definition. . . . Finally when deviance is perceived as individual [or group] pathology, social action tends to center upon changing the individual, or, that failing, removing him from society.[36]

All these characteristics, in varying degrees, act in subtle ways to prevent evaluators and the managerial recipients of their information from raising serious questions about the basic qualities of educational life in schools. The phenomenon of mass testing based on unexamined institutional assumptions, the "treatment" language of educators, the acceptance of institutional definitions of normality and deviance all contribute to the problem.

Evaluation expertise, thus, often serves as an administrative procedure that is relatively ineffective in bringing about significant changes in educational processes. To the extent that evaluation fits within the existing factory model of schooling—an input-output model ideally suited to maintain the bureaucratic regularities of educational institutions—it is less than helpful in adequately treating the profound ethical, political, and educational issues confronting educators today. For instance, evaluation as it is practiced does not bring us significantly closer to the answer to one complex educational dilemma school people face: how to design environments that strike the difficult and tenuous balance between a student's desire for a setting that is personally responsive and the professional educator's need to school and control large masses of students. This is as much a moral problem as it is an engineering one.

Large-scale evaluation can in fact be interpreted as one means, latent to be sure, of stereotyping large groups of people. Much evaluation research has had the effect of labeling *students* as the cause of achievement problems and the like, rather than placing a significant portion of the blame on the social rules and assumptions of the institutions that create and impute these labels. By employing testing on a large scale, the educational bureaucracy can maintain a significant social distance from individual students and their perceptions. This is of no small moment, since the greater the social distance between the people doing the stereotyping (with labels such as slow learners, remedial problems, and underachievers) and those having the labels put on them, the broader the type can be, the less evidence educators need to support it, and the more quickly it can be applied.[37] Thus, under the guise of trying to evaluate programs to make them more effective for students, professionals avoid ever having to face large portions of the student population and their specific realities.

This mode of operation, especially as it is carried on in areas drawing, as evaluation does, on psychological and social psychological models of research and practice, has received other pointed criticisms besides those concerning its support of institutional values, its homogenizing effect, its tendency to impute culpability to the individual or the group rather than the defining institution, and so on. Thomas Szasz, for instance, argues that the very perspective of this model of research and practice, when used in large institutions such as mental institutions, clinics, and schools, ultimately serves to harm rather than help those people who are the focus of the particular ameliorative social program.[38] The history of many programs that have sought to improve institutions dealing with youth is instructive. It documents the fact that the social and educational remedies that were supported by research similar to current evaluation practices seemed to aggravate rather than alleviate problems.[39] It is also interesting to note that these remedies almost invariably led to further layers of institutional hierarchy. Hence, the question of giving research support to programs that may have deleterious effects in the long run needs continual scrutiny by evaluators. Without such continual scrutiny, they may indeed be performing merely as data collectors in support of problematic institutional contexts.

One possible interpretation should not be closed off here. Social institutions such as schools may actually be organized to tacitly maintain, if not promote, the problems of achievement and performance that evaluators are called on to examine.[40] The size, relative anonymity, and complexity of the school may prevent meaningful inroads from being made on these issues. This same size and the amount of economic support committed to schools in our society make it less than easy for there to be alternative paths to the goals school people talk about. As long as this set of institutions provides the only real avenue of access to knowledge and power in American society, it may very well be that the problems educators confront not only will not be solved, but also will be continually *created* by schools. This is a hypothesis that must not be overlooked. The social definitions prevailing in schools create the categories that define deviance from educational achievement norms. Evaluation, hence, can be interpreted as giving legitimacy to categories of performance, all too frequently without raising questions about the efficacy of the social definitions themselves.

That we do not see the political nature of this kind of professional work can be partially explained by Mannheim's argument that "the growth of rational bureaucracy decreases the political rationality of the ordinary person employed within a bureaucracy." The same holds true for individuals such as evaluators whose work is generated out of the process-product thought of schools. As Mannheim put it, "the growth of functional rationality decreases substantive rationality."[41] By placing themselves in a position of upholding policy decisions within an administratively predefined context of deliberation, and without also stepping back to examine carefully the possible implications of the position they hold, evaluators are taking a political stance without being aware of it. To paraphrase Mannheim, they run the risk of substituting the search for a smoothly running factory for the critically important debate over the purposes and means of the institution.

The Logic of Research and the Ideology of Control

Not only does a good deal of evaluation research in education often accept institutional assumptions as given and serve as rhetoric to support them, but an even more subtle consequence also occurs. The very logic behind the methodologies employed in educational research may limit us to merely accepting the existing institutional definitions of situations.

The work of the German social theorist Jürgen Habermas illuminates the problem. Modern consciousness in advanced industrial societies centers around forms of logic that tend to make people treat their major problems as technical puzzles that can be solved by the application of an engineering rationality. That is, process-product reasoning, or what Habermas calls *purposive-rational action,* dominates to such an extent that political and especially ethical questions are treated as somehow "metaphysical" or are defined out of existence in some way.[42] They are redefined in terms of the categories of instrumental logic so that they can be made into technical concerns demanding a solution based on the application of what Ellul has so nicely called *technique*—standardized means to get to previously chosen ends. This effectively vitiates the ethical and political elements involved in argumentation.

Habermas argues that the orientation of purposive-rational action is guided by certain prereflective (or unconscious) cognitive interests. These include a fundamental interest in *control* and *certainty.* In the physical sciences, for instance, this is evident in our attempt to understand and hence control physical forces and phenomena. However, in the human sciences, the orientation seems to lead to a basic interest in gaining certainty in the interaction among human beings and attempting to control (in the strong sense of the term) the environment to guarantee this certainty. The entire orientation seeks to eliminate the ambiguity and uncertainty that makes human action a personal statement, thus also effectively depersonalizing human interaction. Habermas goes on to argue that such interests, which dominate advanced industrial society and the knowledge-producing sciences that support it, tend to break down the symbolic ties that bind individuals together, lead to alienation and anomie, and ultimately prevent potent ethical and political dialogue from evolving.

Politics then becomes a way of manipulating people, rather than a primary way in which individuals engage in reshaping their institutions so that these structures are more mutable. Educational thought becomes an ideology of manipulation rather than a means for providing varied structures that can be made responsive to the needs of intellectual traditions, social beliefs, and student sentiments. The growth of the "educational engineering" approach of behavioral objectives and criterion-referenced measures is indicative of these ideological configurations.[43]

Habermas's work is exceptionally abstract, and this is unfortunate.[44] But his points are quite provocative and merit much further investigation by educators. Educational research has indeed drawn its modes from behavioristic sociology and psychology, fields that have sought to pattern themselves after the strict sciences and that are increasingly under attack for providing support for corporate and bureaucratic interests under the guise of neutrality.[45] Educational research, thus, has adopted the cognitive interests that cohere with these research traditions, those of bringing as many aspects of human activity as possible under technical control and assuring that educators can have surety in dealing with the complex processes of human action.[46] Yet, in the search for certainty of outcome in schools, there is a tendency both to eliminate (or at least not give substantial support to) those portions of student conduct that may somehow threaten the taken-for-granted regularities of the educational setting and to dissolve the elements of argumentation and conflict that enable substantive educational change to evolve.[47]

In saying, then, that a major segment of the educational evaluation that goes on is conservative, the following points should be noted about its latent position. First, there is a tacit advocacy of order and certainty, with little appreciation of the value of conflict and disorder. Evaluation, thus, often can do no more than accept the kind of institutional order it currently finds. Secondly, it has been disposed to put its technical expertise in the service of solving officially and bureaucratically defined problems, even when the official problems offer too limited a perspective. (This disposition may be changing considerably now, however.) Thirdly, it has comported itself in what might be called a quasi-neutral fashion, persistently shying away from social dissent and criticism. It thereby latently gives support to the view that social dilemmas can be dealt with effectively through the application of "modest inputs of centralized administration, along with expert services, research, and advice."[48] This vision of educational issues as modest engineering or technical difficulties does not do justice to the complexity we face in the real world of education. This one-sided vision, though, is not limited to the field of education but is generic to advanced industrial societies. Therefore, any serious criticism of the process-product rationality that stands behind so much evaluation literature must also analyze the economic and political foundations of this commonsense perspective. While that is beyond the scope of this chapter, it is one of the wide-ranging issues educators and others must begin to face.

ANALYTIC QUESTIONS

Aside from the ideological issues I have sought to raise, there are certain analytic problems that must be considered when one seriously grapples with the nature of evaluation in educational settings. What one *means* by evaluation is not easily answered when one is pushed beyond surface concepts and slogans. Here I shall note but a few of the more important conceptual difficulties that represent a sample of topics in need of closer scrutiny.

One exceptionally important analytic issue lies at the very heart of evaluation. Educational evaluators are asked to assess "learning," a concept drawn from and warranted by psychology. In fact, much of the entire educational structure and our everyday activities in it rest on such commonsense concepts as reinforcement, feedback, learning, and conditioning. This puts education in a rather difficult position. These are psychological constructs that gain their efficacy within the psychological community. Thus, they can be criticized and corrected by the tradition of scholarly argumentation that exists in that field as in any discipline. However, by borrowing these explanatory constructs, educators take them out of their self-correcting context. They thus risk reifying and misusing them and run the even greater risk of appropriating outworn, surface, or problematic concepts and techniques.[49]

This difficulty is particularly important. Many of the concepts that educators employ are, in fact, being radically challenged within their original communities. Education, without a tradition of careful scrutiny of borrowed constructs, is left out of the discourse that may be crucial to its search for better tools to explain the dynamics of interaction in school settings. Significant examples being questioned include the notion of reinforcement, the basic value of a behavioristic position on human action, and the very concept of learning itself.[50] Hence, evaluation rooted in psychological constructs stemming from these concepts in the long run may be on rather shaky ground. This points to the utter necessity of further philosophical and analytic study of educational problems if we are to make significant progress.

It has become rather commonplace to state that evaluation often deals with those things that can be most readily measured. To be sure, many educational evaluators recognize the problem and seek to rectify it by becoming more technically sophisticated. However, it may also be the case that we are at present dealing with only a limited representation of "knowledge" in more ways than our tendency to stress what can be easily measured. The provocative work of the noted philosopher of science Michael Polanyi seems to indicate that there is a substructure of *tacit knowing* that serves as a foundation for the more explicit types of activities we usually talk about. In fact, tacit knowledge may be more important than explicitly formulated knowledge. This suggests the necessity of a considerable expansion of our investigation of the powers of human comprehension.[51] It also suggests that it may be necessary to reconsider the current emphasis in evaluation on explicit knowledge—an emphasis that can effectively destroy the act of personal knowing that Polanyi argues is the fundamental property of scientific and aesthetic awareness. In our stress on quantifiable achievement we may be negating the very element that makes anything worth knowing.[52]

In addition, the theory of knowledge that underpins curriculum thought, and therefore the aspects of evaluation that are generated out of it, need to be carefully scrutinized in light of positions such as Polanyi's. The basic problems confronting curriculum specialists and other educators may be epistemological as well as methodological, political, and ethical. If it is correct that explicit knowledge is less important than the processes of tacit knowing, then our evaluation efforts are, to a significant extent, misdirected.

Finally, conceptual examinations of the nature of dispositions, propensities, and so forth are of considerable moment in evaluation. If educators are concerned with more than the teaching of information, they have much to learn from investigations that point to the difficulty and danger of reducing these modes of action to atomistic and measurable elements.[53]

INSTITUTIONAL EVALUATION

I have said that, while evaluation is considered to be "merely" a technical problem by many educators, it is just as clearly an ethical concern. That is, evaluation cannot be simply a question of assessment, as some might argue. The statement: "After all, didn't this group average such and such a 'score' on our instruments compared to the other group's performance?" simply ignores the fact that the choice of *what* one is to assess is itself a valuative decision. Often this decision is made on practical grounds: "These instruments are available; they may be partial but they are better than not getting any information at all." Or it may be an "ideological" decision: "These are the things we must evaluate because they are exceptionally important in the context of an advanced industrial economy such as our own." These concerns derive mainly from an efficiency rationale that may be important in and of itself but is too limited a rubric to deal with the fact that education is not "just" an interaction among traditions and students but also a profoundly interpersonal act of influence. It, thereby, must be held accountable and evaluated according to ethical norms as well as considerations of instrumental effectiveness. Let us examine what this might mean in terms of reorienting a major aspect of educational evaluation.

All too often, what is ignored in evaluation is what has been called *institutional evaluation,* that is, the assessment of the "quality of life" students experience in schools.[54] The lack of consideration for this quality of life is at least partly due to a factor I pointed to in my discussion of the constitutive interests underlying the dominant forms of consciousness in modern societies. The "goodness" of an educational environment is an *ethical* question; it embodies disparate views on how a group of individuals may treat and influence a younger group. However, the orientation that predominates in much of public policy discourse, and educational discourse in particular, tends to redefine just such a moral question into a technical puzzle, so that it may be dealt with in a means-ends schema, thereby making it less potent.

This obstacle to institutional evaluation could be partially overcome if questions such as the following were raised seriously: Does the basic style of interaction in this institution reflect a commitment to treat individuals *justly*? If roles were reversed and educators were to become students, would they (the educators) consider the basic forms of activity to be morally responsible? These are exceptionally difficult issues and no doubt will lead to only situational rather than general answers.[55] Yet the very posing of the question points out the inherent dilemma of serious educational evaluation. For instance, if it is found that the human engineering techniques of behavior modification and operant conditioning "work" for certain types of "training," will it then be argued that they *should* be used as a primary mode of education? If so, is this ethically justifiable? In other words, what are the moral limits on control of individuals in the name of "efficient" instruction? Here, one is hard pressed to separate the evaluation from the consequences.

Raising questions of this type as a form of institutional evaluation obviously would not require a more rigorous empirical methodology (though such rigor is important, to be sure); rather, it requires a legal and philosophical sophistication that is sorely lacking in the educational community.[56] There are areas of institutional evaluation, however, where a broadened and more sophisticated empirical foundation would be quite helpful. Evaluative research in these areas can be instituted fairly readily.

Among the questions institutional assessment would be called on to investigate here would be the abridgment of legal and constitutional rights of students in schools. The Supreme Court has ruled that students do not lose their rights as citizens upon entering educational institutions, and, hence, anything that is done inside these establishments must be within the bounds of constitutional guarantees.[57] The area of student rights can be a potent focus for evaluation of the patterns of interpersonal interaction in schools.

Norms of institutional evaluation such as these make it desirable that educators engage in much greater descriptive analysis, rather than the means-end model so often employed. For example, we should examine what Goffman[58] has called the "moral career" of a child to see what effect, say, the labeling process has on his or her life in that specific educational setting. This may tell us much more about what actually occurs in schools and what schools really do value in their day-to-day patterns of interaction than we can presently ascertain using our conventional models of evaluation. This is one reason why anthropological approaches similar to those employed by Jules Henry,[59] Philip Jackson,[60] and others are so important to a serious and *complete* evaluation of an educational program or total institution.

For example, it should be obvious that a fair proportion of what is effectively "taught" in schools cannot be illuminated through our usual process-product forms of evaluation. The literature on the hidden curriculum has made the significant point that many of the dispositions, propensities, and achievements that may make a critical difference in a person's life are internalized by students in the very act of living within an institutional framework for a number of years. The institutional structure itself mirrors and redundantly communicates to students lasting norms, basic ideological assumptions, and models of human interaction.[61] "Teaching" of this sort—and it is effective teaching—may necessitate a searching reappraisal of our accepted evaluation efforts and, perhaps, the training of a different type of educational evaluator.

The implications of the arguments in this section point clearly in one direction. They require an advocacy framework for evaluation, rather than the quasi-neutral approach that has dominated the field throughout much of its history. This need not replace the models now in use, but may be a complementary and essential counterbalance to them. Clearly an advocacy position will lead to extensive conflict and debate in the field. Yet, as I noted earlier, such argumentation is essential if we are to do more than serve the existing and often questionable practices of bureaucratic institutions.

One final point should be made. Shifting the focus at least partly to the institution rather than concentrating on "learning" enables us to see what effect evaluation has on the school and what use the institution makes of evaluative data. Often the data may serve as an excuse to try a program similar to the one first completed but with some slight variation; or they may serve as a socially pathic language, merely to signify to the community that something is being done to change conditions in the schools. If we find that either of these is the outcome, we will have learned a good deal about the role evaluation plays in the process of change. We may be rather disheartened by what we learn.

THE PERSONAL RESPONSIBILITY OF EVALUATORS

What I have been asking throughout this chapter is that evaluators and other educators suspend their judgment of what they usually accept unquestioningly and question what they generally assume as given. In so doing, all of us might begin to shed light on the implications of our activities.

The tendency in the face of the all-too-usual finding of "no significant difference" is to argue for better teacher training, for better science materials, for more sophisticated administrative systems designs, and the like. However, it may well be that more basic questions must be asked, that even the obligatory nature of the institution of schooling may need questioning, or that educators are asking the wrong kinds of questions.

For example, much low achievement on the part of many students could be attributable to a symbolic dismissal of the school itself as a meaningful institution. These students may perceive schools as relatively unresponsive to human sentiments. This is not to argue that schools should be done away with; to take such a position in a knowledge-based economy is somewhat unrealistic. It does signify, however, that educational problems are considerably more fundamental than educators may suppose, and it places responsibility on the individual educator to examine his or her own professional activity in a wider social and political context.

This requires some rather difficult searching, of course. Issues such as the following need to be faced. Why is it important that students learn these particular what's, how's, and to's? Is the reason we continually find little significant difference in our comparative evaluations due to epistemological and analytic as well as methodological problems? What are the *actual* functions of evaluation in educational institutions? What social group does this research support? A final and critically important ethical question can act as a summary of a number that have preceded it: Is my work truly contributing to the reconstruction of educational institutions so that they are more just and responsive?

Only by raising queries of this sort and taking the search for their answers as a personal responsibility can we begin to assume a title that should not be easily bestowed, that of educator.

NOTES

1. Israel Scheffler, *The Language of Education* (Springfield, Ill.: Charles C. Thomas, 1960), p. 36.

2. Stephen Toulmin, *Human Understanding: The Collective Use and Evolution of Concepts* (Princeton, N.J.: Princeton University Press, 1972), p. 84.

3. Thomas S. Kuhn, *The Structure of Scientific Revolutions* (Chicago: University of Chicago Press, 1970).

4. Stephan Thernstrom, Foreword to Michael Katz, *Class, Bureaucracy, and Schooling* (New York: Praeger, 1971), p. x.

5. Seymour Sarason, *The Culture of the School and the Problem of Change* (Boston: Allyn and Bacon, 1971).

6. Katz, *Class, Bureaucracy, and Schooling,* p. xviii.

7. Clarence Karier, "Liberal Ideology and the Quest for Orderly Change," in Clarence Karier, Paul Violas, and Joel Spring, *Roots of Crisis* (Chicago: Rand McNally, 1973), p. 90.

8. Clarence Karier, "Testing for Order and Control in the Corporate Liberal State," in Karier, Violas, and Spring, *Roots of Crisis,* p. 136.

9. James McClellan and B. Paul Komisar, "The Logic of Slogans," in B. Othanel Smith and Robert Ennis (eds.), *Language and Concepts in Education* (Chicago: Rand McNally, 1961); Michael W. Apple, "Models of Rationality and Systems Approaches," in Albert H. Yee (ed.), *Perspectives on Management Systems Approaches in Education* (Englewood Cliffs, N.J.: Educational Technology Publications, 1973), p. 107.

10. Joel Spring, "Education as a Form of Social Control," in Karier, Violas, and Spring, *Roots of Crisis,* p. 30.

11. *Ibid.,* p. 33.

12. Karier, "Testing for Order and Control," p. 112. See especially his discussion of the close link between the testing movement, eugenics, and scientific racism.

13. John Horton, "Order and Conflict Theories of Social Problems as Competing Ideologies," in James E. Curtis and John W. Petras (eds.), *The Sociology of Knowledge* (New York: Praeger, 1970), p. 606.

14. An insightful discussion of various modes of placing value on educational events can be found in Dwayne Huebner, "Curricular Language and Classroom Meanings," in James B. Macdonald and Robert R. Leeper (eds.), *Language and Meaning* (Washington, D.C.: Association for Supervision and Curriculum Development, 1966), pp. 8–26.

15. Herbert M. Kliebard, "Bureaucracy and Curriculum Theory," in Vernon F. Haubrich (ed.), *Freedom, Bureaucracy and Schooling* (Washington, D.C.: Association for Supervision and Curriculum Development, 1971), pp. 74–93.

16. Michael W. Apple, "The Adequacy of Systems Management Procedures in Education," in Yee, *Perspectives on Management Systems,* pp. 3–31. Even such systems procedures as creating pools of goals among which one can "democratically" choose are quite inadequate. See Louis Fischer and Robert Sinclair, "Behavioral Objectives, Performance Contracting, Systems Management and Education," in Yee, *Perspectives on Management Systems,* pp. 82–98.

17. Robert W. Friedrich, *A Sociology of Sociology* (New York: Free Press, 1970), pp. 172–73.

18. Richard J. Bernstein, *Praxis and Action* (Philadelphia: University of Pennsylvania Press, 1971), p. 213.

19. For a more detailed treatment, see Apple, "The Adequacy of Systems Management Procedures"; William E. Doll, Jr., "A Methodology of Experience: An Alternative to Behavioral Objectives," *Educational Theory* 22 (Summer 1972): 309–24.

20. Nigel Harris, *Beliefs in Society: The Problem of Ideology* (London: C. A. Watts, 1968), p. 22.

21. Alvin W. Gouldner, *The Coming Crisis of Western Sociology* (New York: Basic Books, 1970), p. 332.

22. Howard Becker, *The Outsiders* (New York: Free Press, 1963), p. 9.

23. See Edwin M. Schur, *Labeling and Deviant Behavior* (New York: Harper and Row, 1971), pp. 12–13.

24. Murray Edelman, *The Symbolic Uses of Politics* (Urbana: University of Illinois Press, 1964), p. 12.

25. *Ibid.,* p. 190.

25. Jack D. Douglas, *American Social Order* (New York: Free Press, 1971), pp. 70–71.

27. Curtis and Petras, Introduction to *The Sociology of Knowledge,* p. 48.

28. Peter L. Berger and Thomas Luckmann, *The Social Construction of Reality* (New York: Doubleday, 1966), pp. 34–46.

29. Jack D. Douglas, "Freedom and Tyranny in a Technological Society," in Jack D. Douglas (ed.), *Freedom and Tyranny: Social Problems in a Technological Society* (New York: Alfred A. Knopf, 1970), p. 17.

30. See the discussion of the role of the expert in Alfred Schutz, "The Well-informed Citizen: An Essay on the Social Distribution of Knowledge," in *Collected Papers II: Studies in Social Theory* (The Hague: Martinus Nijhoff, 1964), pp. 120–34.

31. See, for example, Michael Polanyi, *Personal Knowledge* (New York: Harper and Row, 1964). Compare this vision of science as explicated by a member of that "society of explorers" with the sterile and unimaginative reconstruction of it in the field of education.

32. See Michael W. Apple, "School Reform and Educational Scholarship: An Essay Review of *How Effective is Schooling?" Journal of Educational Research* 66 (April 1973): 368, 373, 380–81. An alternative research program is suggested in Michael W. Apple, "Common-sense Categories and Curriculum Thought." Paper presented at a conference entitled "Toward the Reconstruction of the Curriculum Field," Philadelphia, May 10–11, 1973.

33. William Walsh, *The Use of Imagination* (New York: Barnes and Noble, 1959), p. 124.

34. Florian Znaniecki, *The Social Role of the Man of Knowledge* (New York: Harper and Row, 1968), pp. 45–49.

35. Douglas, *American Social Order,* p. 49.

36. Jane R. Mercer, "Labeling the Mentally Retarded," in Earl Rubington and Martin S. Weinberg (eds.), *Deviance: The Interactionist Perspective* (New York: Macmillan, 1968), p. 77.

37. Rubington and Weinberg, "Introduction to the Social Deviant," in *Deviance,* p. 10.

38. Thomas Szasz, *Ideology and Insanity* (New York: Doubleday, 1970).

39. See the excellent treatment of the history of the ameliorative reforms of the juvenile justice system in Anthony M. Platt, *The Child Savers: The Invention of Delinquency* (Chicago: University of Chicago Press, 1969).

40. Schur, *Labeling and Deviant Behavior,* p. 147.

41. Mannheim as quoted in Norbert Wiley, "America's Unique Class Politics, " in Hans Peter Dreitzel (ed.), *Recent Sociology I* (New York: Macmillan, 1969), p. 200.

42. See, e.g., Jürgen Habermas, *Knowledge and Human Interests* (Boston: Beacon

Press, 1971); Michael W. Apple, "Scientific Interests and the Nature of Educational Institutions." Paper presented at a symposium entitled, "Oppression and Schooling," American Educational Research Association, Chicago, 1972.

43. It should be clear that these are not necessarily "scientific" procedures, but instead *are* ideological elements to a large extent. See Apple, "The Adequacy of Systems Management Procedures."

44. See Trent Schroyer, "The Dialectical Foundations of Critical Theory," *Telos* 12 (Summer 1972): 113.

45. Gouldner, *Crisis of Western Sociology.*

46. That action, not behavior, cannot be adequately known beforehand, nor can we have nor should we want certainty concerning it, is discussed quite fully in Hannah Arendt, *The Human Condition* (New York: Doubleday, 1958). See also her discussion of the dangers of attempting to reduce, as educators try to, all aspects of human action to forms of overt behavior.

47. A more complete analysis of this can be found in Apple, "The Adequacy of Systems Management Procedures."

48. Gouldner, *Crisis of Western Sociology,* pp. 161, 335–36.

49. Dwayne Huebner, "Implications of Psychological Thought for the Curriculum," in Glenys Unruh and Robert R. Leeper (eds.), *Influences in Curriculum Change* (Washington, D.C.: Association for Supervision and Curriculum Development, 1968), pp. 28–37; Apple, "The Adequacy of Systems Management Procedures."

50. See Charles Taylor, *The Explanation of Behavior* (New York: Humanities Press, 1964); Maurice Merleau-Ponty, *The Phenomenology of Perception* (London: Routledge and Kegan Paul, 1962); idem, *The Structure of Behavior* (Boston: Beacon Press, 1963); Karl U. Smith and Mary Smith, *Psychological Principles of Learning and Educational Design* (New York: Holt, Rinehart and Winston, 1966).

51. Michael Polanyi, *The Study of Man* (Chicago: University of Chicago Press, 1959), p. 23.

52. It is important to point out that this is *not* a romantic notion or a "do your own thing, kids, with no interference" position. See Polanyi's excellent discussion óf the nature of apprenticeship to a scientific tradition in *Personal Knowledge.*

53. Donald Arnstine, *Philosophy of Education: Learning and Schooling* (New York: Harper and Row, 1967).

54. Gary Wehlage, Thomas S. Popkewitz, and H. Michael Hartoonian, "Social Studies Assessment in Wisconsin Public Schools," *Social Education,* in press.

55. For other types of questions institutional evaluation might begin to explore, see the interesting but sometimes analytically troublesome discussion in *ibid.*

56. The concept of *justice* is critical here. The best recent exploration of the idea in relation to policy making can be found in John Rawls, *A Theory of Justice* (Cambridge: Harvard University Press, 1971).

57. For a more complete discussion of the complex topic of student rights, see Vernon Haubrich and Michael W. Apple (eds.), *Schooling and the Rights of Children* (Berkeley, Calif.: McCutchan Publ. Corp., 1975).

58. Erving Goffman, *Asylums* (New York: Doubleday, 1961).

59. Jules Henry, *Culture against Man* (New York: Random House, 1963).

60. Philip Jackson, *Life in Classrooms* (New York: Holt, Rinehart and Winston, 1968).

61. See Michael W. Apple, ''The Hidden Curriculum and the Nature of Conflict,'' *Interchange* 2 (No. 4, 1971): 27–40.

CHAPTER 5

How Should the Curriculum Be Changed?

One principle of education which those men especially who form educational schemes should keep before their eyes is this—children ought to be educated, not for the present, but for a possibly improved condition of man in the future; that is, in a manner which is adapted to the idea of humanity and the whole destiny of man. This principle is of great importance. Parents usually educate their children in such a manner that they may be adapted to the present conditions, however degenerate the world may be. But they ought to give them a better education, in order that a better condition of things may thereby be brought about in the future.

Immanuel Kant
"Pedagogical Principles"

In education, as in other fields of professional practice, there is continuing emphasis on the improvement of practice. What curriculum changes are desirable and how to bring about these changes in the schools are subjects of continuing debate and, in a rapidly changing society, take on increased importance. Alternate directions for curriculum improvement are explicit in the variety of responses to questions already discussed. Organizing school and community for curriculum change poses numerous additional problems, for example: (1) how to deal with societal forces acting against and toward change; (2) how to mobilize material and human resources in school and community; and (3) how to provide for the participation of interested groups such as students, educators, and laymen.

495

Historically, leading spokesmen in the curriculum field have urged change; sponsored change, and even worked for change in the school curriculum, but, more often than not, they are left puzzled by the curious resistance to change they have experienced. Implied in this phenomenon is the notion that any serious study of the issue of curriculum change must include its counterpart—stability. The question, therefore, is not simply how should the curriculum be changed, but what are the roots of the curriculum as we know it and what are the forces that sustain it. These questions invite consideration of how the curriculum is established and maintained as a crucial ingredient in the question of how it should change.

In reading #28, the noted philosopher Israel Scheffler delineates two senses of justification and then analyzes these levels of justification in terms of certain principles guiding curriculum decisions. Reading #29, by John Goodlad and Maurice Richter, also considers the process of curriculum decisionmaking through an elaboration of Ralph Tyler's work. The principal concern of this reading, drawn from a larger study, is the levels at which certain curriculum decisions are made.

The first of Eric Hoyle's two-part article (reading #30) considers the relationship between social change and curriculum change as well as the question of how curriculum innovations become diffused. The second part treats the school as the setting for curriculum change as well as the deliberate planning of change. Michael Kirst and Decker Walker analyze in reading #31 the ways in which curriculum policymaking proceeds in this country. Their analysis includes a consideration of the influence exerted by such agencies as state legislatures, school boards, accrediting associations, and private interest groups. The next reading (#32), a chapter from Seymour B. Sarason's perceptive book, *The Culture of the School and the Problem of Change,* focuses on the particular "regularities" that occur within a school setting. This aspect of the school's culture is critical in the consideration of changes that may be introduced.

The final two articles are concerned with the ways in which language may be used to justify curriculum practice. Both draw on historical sources for their argument. Elizabeth Vallance (reading #33) examines nineteenth century developments to consider how the so-called "hidden curriculum" became ensconced in American schools. Herbert M. Kliebard in reading #34 then looks at early twentieth century developments with a view to tracing the growing acceptance of a central curriculum metaphor.

28. JUSTIFYING CURRICULUM DECISIONS*

Israel Scheffler

Decisions that confront educators are notoriously varied, complex, and far-reaching in importance, but none outweighs in difficulty or significance those decisions governing selection of content. In view of recent talk of "teaching children rather than subject matter," it is perhaps worth recalling that teaching is a triadic relation, describable for the form "*A* teaches *B* to *C*," where "*B*" names some content, disposition, skill, or subject. If it is true that no one teaches anything unless he teaches it to someone, it is no less true that no one teaches anybody unless he teaches him something.

We do not, moreover, consider it a matter of indifference or whim just what the educator chooses to teach. Some selections we judge better than others; some we deem positively intolerable. Nor are we content to discuss issues of selection as if they hinged on personal taste alone. We try to convince others; we present ordered arguments; we appeal to custom and principle; we point to relevant consequences and implicit commitments. In short, we consider decisions on educational content to be responsible or justifiable acts with public significance.

If these decisions are at once inescapable, important, and subject to rational

SOURCE. *School Review* 66 (Winter, 1958), pp. 461–72. Published by The University of Chicago Press. Copyright © 1958 by the University of Chicago.

*Originally prepared for the Committee on Curriculum Exploration of the Harvard Graduate School of Education in 1957. The discussion of justification is based on my article "On Justification and Commitment," *Journal of Philosophy* 51 (1954): 180–90.

critique, it is of interest to try to clarify the process of such critique, to state the rules we take to govern the justifying of curricular decisions. Such clarification is not to be confused with an attempt to justify this or that decision; rather, the aim is to make the grounds of decision explicit. Furthermore, clarification cannot be accomplished once and for all time but is rather to be seen as a continuing accompaniment to educational practice.

It is the task of clarification that I shall consider here. I shall offer an analysis of the process of justification along with suggestions for justifying decisions on curriculum.

What is subject to justification? A child may be asked to justify his tardiness, but he would never be asked to justify his cephalic index. Fiscal policies and choices of career are subject to justification, but typhoons and mountain ranges are not. Justifiability applies, it seems, only to controllable acts, or *moves,* as they will henceforth be called.

In this respect, justifiability is paralleled by the notion of responsibility, with which indeed it is intimately related. If I am held responsible for violating a traffic regulation, I expect to be subject to the demand that I justify my violation. Conversely, the child who is called on to justify his late arrival for dinner is being held responsible for tardiness. The child may escape the need to justify his lateness by denying his responsibility for it. He can deny his responsibility by denying that his lateness was a move at all, by claiming that it could not be helped, was not deliberate or subject to his control.

Now that I have asserted that only moves are justifiable, I must immediately add one qualification. In ordinary discourse, we do not limit justifiability to moves. A city-planning group may debate the justifiability of a projected highway. However, the issue here can ultimately be construed as the justification of moves calculated to produce the highway in question. In general, ostensible reference to the justifiability of non-moves may be construed as a shorthand reference to the justifiability of moves appropriately related to non-moves. Where such moves are lacking, the justification of non-moves fails to arise as an issue. Thus, while we may speak of highways and courses of study as justifiable, we do not inquire into the justification of comets or rainbows. Justifiability may, then, be taken as a universal property of moves; and those that are, in fact, justified comprise a subclass of moves with a certain authority in our conduct.

How are moves justified? If the justified moves represent a subclass of all moves, then to justify a particular move requires that we show it to be a member of this subclass. If no further specification of this subclass is given, we have a relative sense of justification.

Consider chess: we have a board and the standard pieces. We understand what constitutes a move, and we have rules that permit only certain moves. These rules, in effect, define a subclass of all moves. For a player to justify his move as a chess move requires that he show that it belongs to the chess subclass. Such justification is strictly limited, for it depends clearly on the set of rules that define chess. There are an indefinite number of other rule-sets singling out alternative subclasses of moves. A move justified for chess may not be justified for checkers and vice versa. A chess player justifying his move is not implying that chess is superior to checkers. He is only showing that his move conforms to the rules of chess. Hence we cannot speak, strictly, of a move on the board as justified in general or in the abstract; we have to specify also the operative rules.

Some processes of justification resemble the justification of moves in chess and in other formal games. These processes have a well-specified set of rules defining appropriate moves. Justification consists in showing that a move conforms to these rules, that is, belongs to the subclass singled out by them. There is no thought of justifying the set itself as against alternatives. Though it may not be explicitly stated, it is evident that moves are being justified only relative to this set. These conditions seem to apply when, for example, we consider Smith's driving on the right side of the road (in Massachusetts) to be justified. Driving on the right conforms to Massachusetts traffic rules. We are by no means claiming that these rules are unique or superior or alternative rules; for example, rules of countries where driving on the left is prescribed. What is involved here is relative justification. Traffic regulations are, in an important sense, like chess rules or games in general. For one reason or another we may be interested for the moment in playing a certain game or in seeing what the game demands in a particular case. But the existence of alternative games fails to upset us, nor is the comparative justification of the games as such in question.

Relative justification is not limited to such clear cases as traffic control. Much of our conduct falls within the range of less well-defined rules, or social practices and traditions. Much of the time, we justify this conduct simply by appeal to conformity with established practice. Nor should it be supposed that such justification is always as uncomplicated as that of our traffic illustration. Often a move is justified by appeal to a rule, and that rule by appeal to another. For example, Smith's right-hand driving may be justified by a demonstration of its conformity with Massachusetts law and this particular law by conformity with traditional legal practice throughout the United States. Though various levels are distinguishable, it is still true that the justification as a whole is here carried out in relation to American practice. That is, such practice sanctions a class of certain subclasses of moves, one subclass of which includes the move in question. In effect, one "game" is justified by showing its embeddedness in another, larger "game."

The relative sense of justification is, however, not exhaustive of the types of justification that one uses and, in itself, is hardly satisfactory for many purposes, since every move is both justified and unjustified in relation to appropriately chosen sets of rules. If I am not, as in a game, asking what move I ought to make in order to comply with some particular set of rules, but am asking what move I ought to make at all, the relative sense of justification will be of no help whatever. At best, it can lead me to another query of the same sort on a new level and leave me equally undecided there. The nonrelative, or general, request for justification is, furthermore, one we often make or imply, and in the most important departments of life—belief, social relations, individual choices.

When we decide broad educational issues, we are often asking not merely what jibes with American practice, past or present, but what is generally justified, whether or not it is sanctioned by practice. The desire to evade this general question is understandable because it is difficult. But this evasion, I think, is responsible for much of the inadequacy of value-decisions in education. Two tendencies seem to develop. A move is defended on grounds of its conformity with American practice, and the question of the justification of this practice itself is not considered at all. Or it is flatly asserted that it is the duty of the teacher to conform to the educational practices of his society, an assertion that, besides calling on a nonrelative notion of duty that is itself uncriticized, seems to many schoolmen to be far from obvious.

Both the nature of this general request for justification of acts or moves and the possibilities for dealing with it may be illuminated by comparison with belief. To know that a belief is justified in relation to certain evidence does not provide general justification unless we have confidence in the evidence to begin with. With this initial confidence or credibility, we can proceed to provide ground for our belief. Roughly speaking, what we seem to do is to justify beliefs that not only hang together logically but also, as a family, preserve this initial credibility to the highest degree. We judge the belief in question by its general impact on all other beliefs in which we have some confidence. No matter how confident we are of a particular belief, we may decide to give it up if it conflicts with enough other beliefs in which we have a higher degree of confidence.

In practical situations, of course, we do not actually take all our beliefs into account. We concern ourselves, rather, with a limited domain of beliefs that we feel are interdependent. Furthermore, we do not make piecemeal estimates of the impact of each belief on the credibility of that mass of our beliefs in this domain. Instead, we use summary rules of varying generality. These rules are quite different from the rules of chess, however. They are not simply chosen at will but mirror, in a systematic and manageable form, our confidence in particular beliefs, classes of beliefs, and combinations of beliefs. Theoretically, there is no control (except perhaps that of the demand for consistency) over the design of games, no external requirements they need meet. The rules we use in general justification of belief are subject to the requirement that they be true to our credibilities on the whole. If a rule conflicts with our credibilities, it will be scrapped. We may say that rules are justified if they adequately reflect our credibilities by selecting those groups of beliefs that rank highest in this regard.

A particular belief, then, is justified if it hangs together with that family of beliefs that as a whole commands our highest degree of confidence.

Formal logic as a code of valid inference provides an instructive example. People judged good and bad arguments long before the Aristotelian code. The latter was intended to systematize individual judgments and derives its authority from its adequacy as a systematization. When we now refer the justification of a particular inference to the ruling of Aristotle, our procedure depends on our confidence in this adequacy. It is a shorthand way of seeing whether or not the inference belongs with the mass of inferences we find most acceptable. Theoretically, no element in our procedure is free from future reappraisal. If, at some future time, we find that the existing code demands the abandonment of an inference that we value or the acceptance of an inference that we detest, we may alter the code. If an inference we are attached to conflicts with our code, we may give up the inference. There is a mutual adjustment of rules and instances toward selection of that family of instances that, as a whole, has the highest claim on our acceptance. An instance or rule that interferes with such selection is subject to rejection.

Codes of deductive or inductive logic may be construed as definitions of valid inference, not in the sense in which definitions may be used to introduce coined terms, but rather in the sense in which we set about defining a term already in common use, where this use controls our definition. The man who invented Scrabble was defining the game in the first sense by laying down rules that were labeled "Scrabble Rules." On the other hand, if a man from Mars were to arrive in the midst of a Scrabble tournament, without benefit or prior study of the official rules, and were asked after some hours to define the game, his task would be considerably different from that of the inventor. He would have to observe, guess, and test, to determine whether his proposed list of defining rules actually squared with the moves of the players. He would be attempting a definition in the second sense.

Even this task would be simpler than that of defining valid inference or, indeed, of defining any term in general use. For our man from Mars could always, as a final resort, check his definition against the official rule book. But for valid inference as for other notions in general use there is no official rule book at all. We start by proposing a definition that will serve as a simplified guide to usage but continue to check our proposal against actual use. We justify a particular use of a term by appeal, not just to any definition, but to one that we feel is itself justified by adequate codification of usage. In effect, we justify a particular use by checking it, through adequate definitions, against all our other uses.

These examples illustrate what we may expect and what we may hope to accomplish in the general justification of moves. Justification in relation to a given set of rules is useless unless the latter are themselves justified. But further relative justification by reference to other sets of rules is fruitless. Somewhere there must be control of rule-sets by initial commitments to moves themselves. The rules we appeal to in justifying social moves are rules that we hope are themselves adequate codifications of our initial commitments. The rules we appeal to select those families of moves that, as wholes, command our acceptance to the highest degree. Without initial commitments there can be no general justification, any more than there can be real or controlled definition without initial usage. But the fact that we are attached to a particular move does not mean that we cannot check it against all others we are committed to (by way of rules), any more than our attachment to a particular locution means that we cannot check it against others we hold proper (by way of controlled definitions). Our legal and moral rules serve, indeed, to guide the making of particular moves, but their guidance depends on their presumed adequacy in codifying our initial commitments to moves, on the whole.

In accordance with the two senses of justification just discussed, we may distinguish two levels of justification of educational decisions. On one level, justification involves conformity with a set of rules, reference to which may be implicitly understood. Here the issue is relative. We ask, "Is such-and-such decision justified according to rule-set S?" For many purposes, the question is legitimate and important, but the answer is often far from simple, even when the rules are fairly well defined. Relative justification is often a highly complicated, intellectually engaging business. To appreciate this fact, one need only recall that there is a whole profession (law) devoted to solving just such questions as the conformity of cases to rule. In education, such justification seems to relate not to specific laws but to broad social practices and traditions, the formulation of which has to be abstracted from our history and is itself a difficult job. Still, such traditions are often cited and used as a level for changing laws as well as individual decisions.

Yet, legitimate as relative questions are, they do not exhaust our queries in educational contexts. We are not always interested merely in knowing that an educational move conforms to some code. We want to press the issue of deciding among codes. We ask that our moves be justified in terms of some justified code. If our previous analysis is correct, we are seeking justification by rules themselves controlled by the mass of our initial commitments. Of the two levels of justification in educational contexts, the relative type is familiar. The practical issues here may be complicated, and one factor often adds to the complexity: ostensible questions of relative conformity to a given rule may be decided, partly at least, on independent moral grounds. Yet, many of these issues seem familiar in outline. The understanding of general justification presents a more formidable task, since the formulation of relevant rules is of the difficult variety illustrated by the attempt of the man from Mars to codify the rules of a game by watching the play. We need to do something of this sort, but far more complex, since the activity involved is our own and touches on our fundamental commitments.

What rules do we appeal to in general justification of educational decisions on content? The answer to this question consists of a set of rules, not assertions, but the process of compiling an adequate set of rules is as empirical a task as can be imagined. Definitions are not assertions; but to compile a set of definitions one needs to call on all sorts of information, hypotheses, hunches—and the resulting set is always subject to recall, if not to falsification. It is with such qualifications that I offer my list of rules relating to decisions on curriculum. This list should be construed as a hypothesis, tentatively offered and inviting criticism. If it proves wrong, the process of correcting it will itself help clarify the ground of our curricular decisions.

To simplify our considerations, let us avoid, at least at the outset, the problem of formulating special, complicated rules for deciding on content to be taught at a particular time and in particular circumstances. Let us consider instead all the content to be learned by a child during his formal schooling. Without worrying, for the moment, about the functions of particular segments of this content, let us ask instead what we expect of the content as a whole. Let us, further, state our rules in terms broad enough to allow for practical judgment in applying them to cases.

The guiding principle underlying the following rules is that educational content is to help the learner attain maximum self-sufficiency as economically as possible.

Presumably, self-sufficiency can be brought about economically or extravagantly; content should be selected that is judged most economical. Three types of economy are relevant. First, content should be economical of teaching effort and resources. Second, content should be economical of learners' effort. If a very strenuous way and a very easy way of learning something are otherwise equal, this rule would have us select the easier course. Some such principle seems to figure often in educational discussion. For example, the linking of subject matter to children's interests is often defended on grounds that this technique facilitates learning, and even opponents of this approach do not argue that these grounds are irrelevant. It is important, however, to specify that our rules all contain a tacit clause: "other things being equal." It may be argued, for example, that the strenuous course makes for perseverance and other desirable habits, as the easy course does not. Here, however, other things are not equal, and the present rule fails to apply. Criticism of extremism in progressive education, for instance, may be interpreted as insisting that the "interest" principle never stands alone but is always qualified by the clause "other things being equal.'' Once qualified, the rule stands, in my opinion. There is no positive virtue, in unnecessarily taxing the learner; his energy may better be saved for other tasks.

Finally, we must consider economy of subject matter; content should have maximum generalizability or transfer value. The notion of generalizability is, however, ambiguous. Accordingly, two types of subject-matter economy need to be distinguished. First, is there an empirically ascertainable tendency for the learning of some content to facilitate other learning? Presumably, this sort of question was at issue in the controversy over classics, and it was discussed in terms of empirical studies. Second, is the content sufficiently central logically to apply to a wide range of problems? This is not a psychological question but one that concerns the structure of available knowledge. Nevertheless, it is through some such principle of economy, in the logical sense, that we decide to teach physics rather than meteorology, for instance, where other considerations are balanced.

The most economical of contents in all the aspects described must still meet the requirements of facilitating maximum self-sufficiency. It should be obvious that we do not necessarily, or ever, apply first the rules of economy and then the rules of self-sufficiency. These rules represent, rather, various requirements put on content, and we may apply them in various orders or simultaneously. We turn now to the rules of self-sufficiency.

Content should enable the learner to make responsible personal and moral decisions. Self-awareness, imaginative weighing of alternative courses of action, understanding of other people's choices and ways of life, decisiveness without rigidity, emancipation from stereotyped ways of thinking and perceiving—all these are bound up with the goal of personal and moral self-sufficiency. The problem of relating school subjects to such traits is an empirical one, but I think it extremely unlikely that a solution is to be found in the mechanical correlation of each subject to some one desired trait. Rather, the individual potentialities of each subject are likely to embrace many desired habits of mind. The use of literature to develop empathy is often noted. But to suppose that this function is restricted to literature is to impoverish our view of the potentialities of other subjects. Anthropology, history, and the other human sciences also offer opportunities to empathize. But even the natural sciences and mathematics may be seen not merely as technical equipment but as rich fields for the exercise of imagination, intuition, criticism, and independent judgment.

The making of responsible personal and moral decisions requires certain traits of character and habits of mind, but such decision-making also requires reliable knowledge, embodied in several areas of study. Psychology, anthropology, and other human studies illumine personal choice; history, political science, economics, sociology and related areas illumine the social background of choices of career and ideology.

We have spoken of personal and moral self-sufficiency, but this is not enough. Since personal and moral decisions are not made in a vacuum, their execution requires technical skills of various sorts. Content should thus provide students with the technical or instrumental prerequisites for carrying out their decisions. What this goal may require in practice will vary from situation to situation; but, speaking generally, mathematics, languages, and the sciences are, I believe, indispensable subjects, while critical ability, personal security, and independent power of judgment in the light of evidence are traits of instrumental value in the pursuit of any ends. In creating curriculums, the notion of technical or instrumental self-sufficiency provides a counterbalance to emphases on the child's interest. For subjects unsupported by student interest may yet have high instrumental value for the students themselves. To avoid teaching them such subjects is, in the long run, to hamper their own future self-sufficiency, no matter what their future aims may be. Thus, it is misleading to label as an imposition of adult values the teaching of instrumentally valuable subjects.

Finally, beyond the power to make and to carry out decisions, self-sufficiency requires intellectual power. Content, that is, should provide theoretical sophistication to whatever degree possible. Here we may distinguish between logical, linguistic, and critical proficiency—the ability to formulate and appraise arguments in various domains, on the one hand, and acquaintance with basic information as well as with different modes of experience and perception, on the other. The danger here, a serious risk of general education programs, is that of superficiality. But ignorance is also a danger. How to avoid both ignorance and superficiality is the basic practical problem. I should hazard the opinion that the solution lies not in rapid survey courses but in the intensive cultivation of a small but significant variety of areas.

29. DECISIONS AND LEVELS OF DECISION-MAKING: PROCESSES AND DATA-SOURCES

John I. Goodlad with Maurice N. Richter, Jr.

Rational curriculum planning seeks to produce valid and justifiable intended learnings. On what grounds valid? On which bases justifiable? Validation and justification call for data-sources and processes of inquiry. . . . A *data-source* is a general category of phenomena or category by which phenomena are classified from which data are extracted or might be extracted.

Knowing which data-source to consult when faced with the need for data is prime knowledge in human activity. One turns to psychology for general information about individual differences in human learning but to the learners themselves to find out about individual differences in a class to be taught. One turns to politics for principles of government but to the people for insight into how they wish to be or believe they are governed. In curriculum planning, one needs to determine at various times what is possible, what is believed, what is being done, what is happening as a result of what is being done, what is desirable, what is thought to be desirable, and so on. One consults a different data-source in each instance. In curriculum, there has been relatively little exploration of the relevant data-sources to be consulted in seeking to answer the various curricular questions of ends and means.

Curriculum inquiry, like other inquiry, requires two modes of investigation,

SOURCE. In *The Development of a Conceptual System for Dealing with Problems of Curriculum and Instruction.* Cooperative Research Program. Office of Education, 1966, pp. 24–39. ED01 0064.

each at its own time and each in its own place: the theoretical-deductive and the empirical-inductive.[1] In making curricular decisions of ends and means, there are times and places for logically-determined reasons and times and places for empirically-determined conclusions. But there has been little systematic differentiation of the two in curriculum planning.[2]

The preceding section implies that rational curriculum planning involves the derivation of educational aims from values, educational objectives from educational aims, and learning opportunities from educational objectives. The first is a prime data-source for the second, the second for the third, and the third for the fourth. But to assume that curricular ends and means are determined solely by a process of derivation or logical deduction from values is to oversimplify. Other data-sources, together with empirical-inductive inquiries, are called for.

The process of deriving educational aims goes back first to selection among values. Logicians can help us see contradictions among values. The predictions of population specialists, geographers, and others may reveal that unchecked "freedom for the individual" to populate the earth, pollute the air, and exhaust the water supply call for espousing values pertaining to the welfare of all mankind as well as to the welfare of each individual. With values selected, analyses of society may reveal that educational institutions have little contribution to make to the achievement of certain values, or that one kind of institution is much better suited than others to the attainment of some educational aims. Analysis of students in a program might show that they possessed the behavior implied in an objective before they came; students for whom such an objective would be appropriate never come to the institution. Studies might reveal that attainment of a given objective is desirable but quite unrealistic, given the time available for acquiring the behavior sought. Or, a learning opportunity might be dropped because it is seen to be in direct contradiction to the tenets of the religious group controlling the institution.

The ultimate derivation of learning opportunities does, indeed, involve a deductive justification from educational objectives, they in turn from educational aims, and aims from values. But the process is neither direct-line deduction nor deduction alone. A number of data-sources, as illustrated above, and empirical data derived from them are consulted in selecting and choosing at each successive level in the process. Further, values are not ignored after educational aims have been determined. In the final example above, a learning opportunity came into question because it conflicted with certain accepted values.

One could argue that this last happening could not occur in a fully rational process of curriculum planning. True. But we already have expressed the doubt that curriculum planning ever will be fully rational; we hope only for a considerably higher level of rationality than currently exists. No matter how carefully any rationale is set forth, human frailty will prevail to some degree in constructing the rationale itself as well as in following it in curriculum planning.

The first curricular question set forth in the Tyler rationale[3] is one of aims or objectives. (He does not differentiate between these two levels of generality.) It is an "ought" question: What educational purposes should the school seek to attain? Tyler proposes that this question be answered by systematically consulting three data-sources for suggestions: society, learners, and subject-matter specialists. Then, recognizing that some of the tentative statements of objectives so developed will be undesirable, contradictory, or unattainable, he proposes the use of two "screens"—philosophy and psychology—through which the statements must pass if they are to remain in the list.

Tyler does not propose turning to values first, as we do. Rather, after a tentative list of objectives has been formulated by consulting his three data-sources, they are validated against questions pertaining to the good life in the good society, what knowledge is of most worth, and so on, or against a carefully formulated philosophical system within which answers to such value questions already have been formulated. We propose turning to values as the primary data-source in selecting purposes for the school and as a data-source in making all subsequent curricular decisions.

It is becoming increasingly clear in all fields of inquiry that a completely value-free position is impossible. One must make a beginning, and to make a beginning is to accept certain assumptions; values are imbedded in assumptions. When one turns to an examination of the characteristics of society in seeking to formulate educational objectives, one's values are likely to guide him to some characteristics and not to others. Therefore, it is desirable to admit to these value positions at the outset. (In making such a statement, of course, we take a value position with respect to curriculum development.)

None of the above is intended, however, to reject the value of a philosophical screen in selecting from among possible educational objectives. It is, in fact, a useful way of checking on the amount of "slippage" or irrationality that might have occurred in the supposedly rational process of deriving educational aims from values and educational objectives from these aims, a process not specifically identified by Tyler which we think to be central in curriculum planning. Values and philosophical positions inevitably enter into all steps in curriculum planning; many alternatives already will have been consciously or subconsciously ruled out by the time of Tyler's proposed screening. Therefore, we recommend similar formal and informal checks at all major decision-making points so that, hopefully, the selection of ends and means will be compatible with the values initially espoused. Curriculum planning involves more than seeking data. It involves, rather, the sensitive utilization of values and data simultaneously.[4]

It is within the above context that the concept "evaluation" takes on rich meaning. *Evaluation* is essentially a process of checking on values, as suggested above. This is why evaluation in curriculum is more than administering a test to students. Student performance is as much a product of curricular rationality as of student rationality, given a test that is truly valid in the sense of seeking to elicit from the students the behaviors sought in the curriculum.

Evaluation is a means of checking each step in the curriculum planning process; it is not just a terminal process of checking student performance. Once a curriculum is constructed, evaluation becomes a process of checking backwards on how and how well preceding decisions were made. Sound evaluation assesses learning opportunities in relation to educational objectives, objectives in relation to educational aims, and aims in relation to values. It contributes to rationality through revealing that otherwise attractive learning opportunities simply do not provide for practice of the behavior implied in the objective; that other objectives pertaining to stated aims might have been formulated; or that certain values selected initially are mutually incompatible. Careful evaluation forces validation and justification where none might have occurred otherwise.

LEVELS OF CURRICULUM DECISION-MAKING

It is conceivable and feasible that one individual could plan a curriculum for a student or group of students or, for that matter, that an individual could plan a curriculum for himself. In fact, both frequently occur. The planning—from selection of values, to formulation of aims, to refinement of objectives, to selection of learning opportunities, and finally to the creation of organizing centers for learning—if rationally conducted, would reveal clearly some of the derivations and appropriate data-sources, the whole unencumbered by political machinations and the need for consensus.

Curriculum planning in primitive cultures is similarly unencumbered. Immediate relatives or members of the tribe initiate neophytes into tribal customs and provide direct training in the skills needed for survival. Sometimes, the elders of the tribe select a few values for inculcation through training and assign responsibility for this training to a member of their group. He assumes a position comparable to the curriculum maker—be he superintendent of schools, curriculum director, supervisor, or teacher—in modern society.

But life in modern society is not this simple, and grows less simple by the hour. Curriculum construction by individuals or as depicted for primitive societies does not provide adequate models for the world we know and will increasingly know. The United States of America, the Soviet Union, Great Britain, Sweden, and any number of other nations would provide better examples.

We believe that the subsequent analysis is relevant, with various modifications, for most relatively large-scale curriculum planning activities, whether for private or public and whether for elementary, secondary, higher, adult, or professional education. It is particularly relevant, we think, to curriculum planning in the United States.

In Section I, we observed that curriculum planning occurs at several levels of remoteness from the learner. We used the term *instructional* to define the level closest to the learner. Here, two steps are involved: the very precise delineation of educational objectives and the selection of organizing centers for learning. Often the two are almost indistinguishable one from another; the child is to be able to use a table of contents, he looks up stories by finding their page numbers in the table of contents; the student is to learn to distinguish the gender of French nouns, he reads aloud a long list such as le mer, la chaise, le chien, la porte.

The organizing center is, in effect, a description of the stimulus to which the student is to respond. It involves so direct a derivation from the educational objective that it literally produces in the student a segment of the behavior called for in the objective. A behavior such as a psychomotor skill is displayed before one's very eyes. But many cognitive and affective behaviors are so subtle that reactions simply are not visible to the observer. Therefore, it becomes necessary to create an evaluative situation in which some form of terminal behavior is revealed and the success or failure of the organizing center demonstrated.

Selecting the organizing center involves more than deduction from the objective. Usually, many organizing centers can be deduced from one educational objective. The final selection of a few is determined from examination of other data-sources: the learners for evidence as to readiness, instructional materials as to authenticity of content, psychology for appropriate learning principles to employ, self (if the teacher is a human one—although even robots are now being programmed with alternatives) for selection from a pedagogical repertoire, values for clues as to appropriateness, and so on. But one begins by "squaring" the organizing center with the objective. Objectives constitute the primary data-source for the selection of organizing centers.

Just as the organizing center represents a direct derivation from the educational objective, so the latter is a derivation from educational aims set by the institution's *controlling agency*. Usually this is a board selected by or appointed for a larger group serving as the institution's *sanctioning body*. In Section I, we used the term *societal* for the decisions made by such boards representing themselves or their larger constituency. The derivative jump from teachers (human or robot) at the instructional level to boards at the societal level reflects a simple society more than a complex, modern one.

Usually, a board is responsible for a large institution, or for many, and employs many teachers. It cannot check on the derivation processes of teachers to see whether the learning fare they set forth in their classrooms represents the true interest of the selected educational aims. But even in the case of a small institution, when individual checks on teachers might be possible, a wise board—usually serving only part-time and possessing little personal competence among its members regarding the derivative processes involved—delegates this responsibility to a manager or administrator.

A level of decision-making between instructional and societal is thus introduced: . . . the *institutional* level. The interposition of this level complicates the derivative processes we have been describing. In effect, a transaction has occurred between the board and its manager—and just what has been transacted often is far from clear. Another transaction must now occur between manager and teachers—and, in a large system of institutions, layers of personnel between manager and teachers. Again, just which is to be transacted usually is not made clear.

. . . The kinds of curricular decisions that should occur at this institutional level are the formulation of educational objectives and the selection of illustrative learning opportunities. It is unrealistic and undesirable for boards to formulate precise educational objectives. The task is extremely difficult (if it were not, it would be performed more often!) and demands specialized knowledge. For example, a board might well propose that children in the elementary schools learn to read and write French when research—of which they probably would be unaware—might suggest the desirability of learning to speak French in the early years, with reading and writing following in the secondary schools. It is more rational, we think, for boards to concern themselves with more general aims and functions of their schools. But to maintain a level of generality desirable for boards is to create a most difficult problem of derivation for teachers.[5] Not only is logic involved but, in addition, there is need for highly specialized knowledge pertaining to the structure of the academic disciplines, the nature of learning, techniques of programming, and so on.

Unless there are well-established processes of rational curriculum decision-making at a level between boards of education and teachers—that is, at the institutional level—it is unlikely that rational processes for translating societal decisions into institutional decisions will exist. And into the gulf will come pressure groups of all kinds promoting this essay contest or that fund drive in the name of some value that may be highly significant but of little relevance to education or the functions to be performed by specific institutions. The ends and means of education, of schools, of teachers, and of students are thus determined outside of the structure formally charged with such responsibility.[6]

We see, therefore, the need for ends and means to be stated at a level of generality that, on one hand, conveys to the board assurance that provision is being made for attainment of each major aim and that, on the other, provides teachers with the general categories of behavior and substance from which the specifics of instruction are to be derived. Serving both masters adequately may call for two or more sub-levels of ends-means derivations at the institutional level. Thus, for example, the Montgomery County (Maryland) Board of Education—employing part of the conceptual system for curriculum decision-making set forth in this document—approved a rather general set of purposes (more specific than aims but not expressed behaviorally) for its schools. But a highly skilled curriculum staff for the school system as a whole, with the help of consultants, found it necessary to translate these into an overall design for the curriculum as a whole and then separate designs for each subject taught in the schools. The ends and means set forth at each subsequent level of decision-making were derived from previous, more general decisions of ends and means.[7]

It might be useful to designate the possible sub-levels of institutional decision-making with a hierarchy of new terms for ends and another for means instead of employing simply "objectives" and "learning opportunities" for several sub-levels of generality of specificity. It might be preferable, also, to use the word "purposes" for objectives at the institutional level, since we use "objectives" at the instructional level. In regard to the former suggestion, however, we see little possibility of creating sub-levels to cover all circumstances and the creation of still more terms implying "objectives" and "learning opportunities," we believe, would lead to confusion. In regard to the second, we prefer to reflect popular practice. The term "objectives" is used to cover many levels of generality, even when used to define student behavior. We view the categories and their sub-divisions set forth in the taxonomies prepared by Bloom and his associates and by Krathwohl, Bloom, and Masia as representing the kinds of distinctions and formulations required at the institutional level, and the refinements of Mager as representing what is needed at the instructional level.

We return now, briefly, to the societal level.[8] The sanctioning body—that is, the total group of persons responsible for bringing into existence and maintaining one or more educational institutions (in the United States, the taxpayers of a school district would be such a group)—must assume responsibility for selecting among values and formulating educational aims for the attainment of these values. In modern societies, this responsibility is delegated to an elected or appointed body or usurped by a dictator. (We shall ignore the latter possibility for purposes of this discussion.)

Again, a transaction has occurred. And, again, the key question pertains to the precise nature of this transaction.

In rational curriculum planning, we think, the board assumes, through a transaction between it and the sanctioning body, responsibility for continuously seeking consensus as to what the educational institutions are for. The board is now—until removed from office—the controlling agency for these institutions. It should devote its energies primarily to maintaining a dialogue about and promoting inquiries designed to define educational ends.[9] Because this is a tremendously difficult task and because the "wrong" consensus may result in lost votes, elected board members, in the United States at least, devote most of their time to more immediately practical pursuits. As a consequence, educational personnel at both institutional and instructional levels of decision-making usually have no clear directives, no data in the primary data-source, to guide their daily actions. Ironically, the blame for this omission more often than not falls upon the educators, usually in the form of criticism of certain school practices. Sometimes, blame or praise, depending on the values of the viewer, falls upon highly visible individuals outside of the formal, official hierarchy who are seen as influential because of their speaking, writing, or other activity.

In a complex society, the societal level of curricular decision-making usually can be divided into sub-levels. In the United States, these levels are local, state, and federal, although many persons would question the right of the third of these to make decisions of the kind discussed here. Nonetheless, the federal level does, indeed, make significant curricular decisions either directly or indirectly through Congress, and administers them through the United States Office of Education, the National Science Foundation, and other federal offices.

Analyses of the actual or desirable roles of these societal sub-levels in American life are only beginning to appear.[10] Relatively little attention has been given to the respective responsibilities of each. It is traditionally (and perhaps anachronistically) assumed that local school districts are responsible for determining what their schools are for. But examination of state courses of studies and the enactments of state legislators reveals that controlling agencies at this level assume designation of the ends of education as their responsibility, too. And curriculum materials prepared by remote projects financed by the National Science Foundation bring into schools ends that often are not subjected to diligent local scrutiny.

The desirability or undesirability of these specific practices is not the question that concerns us here. Rather, we are concerned about the fact that actual practices are not adequately described or understood and about the fact that little attention has been given to questions of which levels should do what in curriculum planning. In effect, we are concerned that so little rationality enters into practices of such far-reaching significance.

In any society, the transactions indicated here inevitably are to a considerable degree political in character. In fact, in contrast to the derivative decisions set forth, which are substantive in character, the transactions between sanctioning bodies and controlling agencies, controlling agencies and administrators, administrators and teachers, are political decisions, in both the best and the worst sense of that term. All the known talents of persuasion, negotiation, compromise, and influence come into play.

Participants in these transactional processes turn to logical deduction, "hard" and "soft" research data, and various persons "outside" of the context of immediate negotiations—scholars, charismatic figures, and various "names" thought to carry influence. The first and second of these data-sources already have been identified and discussed. Our concern with them is that the logic be sound and the data both hard and appropriate to the question at hand. The third introduces a fourth category or level of curriculum decision-making which we designate here as *ideological*.[11]

The ideological level involves none of the transactions pertaining to the other three. But the ideological determination of ends and means rationally and not through idle speculation involves precisely the theoretical-deductive and empirical-inductive derivations proposed in this document. In fact, ideological formulation of the categories and decisions of curriculum construction, the subsequent simulation of alternative curricula from alternative value premises, and ensuing derivations represent *curriculum* in its purest form, curriculum as a form of inquiry uncontaminated by the vagaries of actual practice. In keeping with the ground rules set forth for a conceptual system in Section I, however, we have chosen always to test our abstract categories against the realities of curricular practice, particularly in the United States, so far as immediately preceding pages are concerned.

At the ideological level, as at all other levels, we are concerned with rationality and, therefore, with a set of rules for a human game that is to be played effectively. Therefore, we are not interested, except as examples of what we do not endorse, in idle speculation concerning intended learnings of the kind expressed at one time or another by human beings. We require of ideological curriculum discourse that definitions, decisions, data-sources, and derivations be set forth rigorously by participants in the game; that is, that they set forth and play by a set of ground rules reflecting at least the substantive realities of what is involved in rational curriculum planning. Unfortunately, few pronouncements—even most of those gaining considerable currency in the curricular market place—relative to curriculum by prestigious persons satisfy the criteria of rigor that must be applied if ideological curricula are to serve as data-souces in ongoing curriculum planning.[12]

In foregoing discussions of derivations, we have perhaps implied over-emphasis on logical to the detriment of empirical derivations, even though at least some disclaimers have been stated. Actually, we are very much concerned with empirical-inductive processes and with the hard data of research. The subsequent section helps to correct any apparent imbalance. However, the kinds of research data needed for more rational curriculum planning are lacking. The conceptualizations set forth here are designed to contribute to the correction of this situation through stimulating theoretical inquiry and subsequent cumulative research.

NOTES AND REFERENCES

1. Conant (James B. Conant, *Two Modes of Thought* (New York: Trident Press, 1964)) states the following as his credo: "A free society requires today among its teachers, professors and practitioners two types of individuals: the one prefers the empirical-inductive method of inquiry; the other the theoretical-deductive outlook. Both modes of thought have their dangers; both have their advantages. In any given pro-

fession, in any single institution, in any particular country, the one mode may be under-developed or overdeveloped; if so, the balance will need redressing. Above all, the continuation of intellectual freedom requires a tolerance of the activities of the proponents of one mode by the other'' (p. xxxi).

2. Some promising inquiry into certain logical operations in teaching is now underway. See, for example, B. Othanel Smith and Milton O. Meux, *A Study of the Logic of Teaching* (Urbana: Bureau of Editorial Research, University of Illinois, 1963).

3. Ralph W. Tyler, *Basic Principles of Curriculum and Instruction* (Chicago: University of Chicago Press, 1950), p. 1. The reader is urged to turn to this basic reference now. The present authors accept in general the questions and data-sources set forth but do not repeat them here except as necessary to their purposes. We choose, rather, to attempt certain clarifications, modifications, and additions. In the process, some differences in the present approach and Tyler's approach become apparent. By putting the two together, perhaps a third, improved rationale for curriculum planning might result.

4. The Project on Instruction of the National Education Association made much of this point. See Schools for the Sixties (and supporting volumes in the series) (New York: McGraw-Hill Book Co., 1963).

5. Responsibility for almost autonomous derivation of ends and means by university professors is the standard situation in higher education, on the assumption, presumably that they know their subjects best and, therefore, what should be taught to their students. This is a serious over-simplification of what is involved in and needed for rational curriculum planning, however, and is largely responsible, we think for the chaotic condition of college curricula. Highly-specialized college professors may be among the least interested and poorest qualified persons to whom to entrust the overall questions of ends and means in matters, for example, of general education.

6. The report of John I. Goodlad (with M. Frances Klein and Renata von Stoephasius) of current curriculum reform in the United States (*The Changing School Curriculum* (New York: Fund for the Advancement of Education, 1966)) reveals that many objectives of elementary and secondary schools are determined by remote curriculum planners, coming into the classrooms via their materials.

7. Edmund S. Hoffmaster, James W. Latham, Jr., and Elizabeth D. Wilson, "Design for Science," *Science Teacher* 31 (November, 1964).

8. One is struck with the similarity between our levels of curriculum planning and Parsons' four levels of structural organization of a complex social system: *technical* (which would correspond to our instructional); *managerial* (which is essentially our "institutional," although we might readily use his term to designate the role of administrators as an institutional sub-level); *institutional* (represented by a board; here we use the term, "societal"); and *societal* (political leaders and authorities, corresponding to at least one sub-level in our use of the same term). See Talcott Parsons, "General Theory in Sociology," in Robert K. Merton, Leonard Broom, and Leonard S. Cottrell, Jr. (eds.), *Sociology Today* (New York: Basic Books, Inc., 1959). See especially pp. 12–16.

9. The supporters and the recipients of education constitute a significant data-source for determining what various sub-publics expect of schools or other educational institutions and, therefore, for determining what values various groups wish to maintain or strengthen through education. For use of this data-source, see Lawrence W. Downey, "The Task of the Public School as Perceived by Regional Sub-Publics," unpublished

doctoral dissertation, University of Chicago, 1959; Roger C. Seager, "The Task of the Public School as Perceived by Proximity Sub-Publics," unpublished doctoral dissertation, University of Chicago, 1959; and Allen T. Slagle, "The Task of the Public School as Perceived by Occupation and Age Sub-Publics," unpublished doctoral dissertation, University of Chicago, 1959.

10. For discussion of many issues of respective responsibilities of governmental levels for education, see Seymour E. Harris (ed.), *Education and Public Policy* (Berkeley, Calif.: McCutchan Publishing Corp., 1965).

11. The four levels of curriculum discussion-making set forth here—instructional, institutional, societal, and ideological were first formulated for purposes of structuring a review of pronouncements, theoretical formulations and research pertaining to curriculum construction; see John I. Goodlad, "Curriculum: State of the Field," *Review of Educational Research* 30 (June, 1960), pp. 185–198 (prepared with the assistance of Margaret P. Ammons). Subsequently, Goodlad used the first three in an analysis of and recommendations regarding the organization of curriculum in the United States; see *Planning and Organizing for Teaching*. Project on the Instructional Program of the Public Schools (Washington: National Education Association, 1963). Also, the "levels" concept has been used as part of the guiding rationale for at least two doctoral dissertations conducted under guidance of the principal investigator: Margaret P. Ammons, "Educational Objectives: The Relation between the Process Used in Their Development and Their Quality," unpublished doctoral dissertation, University of Chicago, 1961; Robert M. McClure, "Procedures, Processes, and Products in Curriculum Development," unpublished doctoral dissertation, University of California, Los Angeles, 1965.

12. Carl Tjerandsen, "The Adequacy of Current Treatments of General Education in the Social Sciences," unpublished doctoral dissertation, University of Chicago, 1958, concluded from an analysis of curricular pronouncements and recommendations in the social sciences that very few writers sought to answer any reasonably complete series of curricular questions in rigorous fashion. Most writers contended themselves with a few polemics pertaining to only one or two of a much larger number of relevant questions. Their ideological curricula could scarcely be defined as curricula at all; nor could their discourse properly be termed curriculum inquiry.

30. HOW DOES THE CURRICULUM CHANGE? PART 1: A PROPOSAL FOR INQUIRIES

Eric Hoyle

INTRODUCTION

Curriculum change is a variety of educational change which, in turn, is one form of social change. By and large sociologists have been more successful in carrying out static analyses of social institutions, focusing upon the "functional" contributions which the parts make to the whole, than in analyzing their dynamic aspects. One student of social change has commented with some justification that the study of social change is an area "where only fools rush in and authentic angels have not yet trod,"[1] and it must be conceded that the sociological study of education has concerned itself with change neither more nor less than other branches of sociology. The contribution which sociologists have made so far has been to analyze changes in the structure of education rather than in the content of education (although this is not a true dichotomy). The emerging curriculum movement is thus a challenge to the sociologist of education not to found a new subdiscipline which might be termed "the sociology of the curriculum," but to extend current modes of sociological analysis to a new set of problems.

The term *curriculum change* in the title has been deliberately preferred to the more common term *curriculum development* since the sociologist is not only concerned with the rational processes of curriculum planning which are implied

SOURCE. Part 1: *Journal of Curriculum Studies* 1 (No. 2, May 1969), pp. 132–41; Part 2: *Journal of Curriculum Studies* 1 (No. 3, November 1969), pp. 230–39. Published by William Collins and Sons Ltd., London and Glasgow.

in the term *development,* but also with the relatively unplanned and adaptive "drift" which has characterized so much curriculum change in the past, and still remains a significant form of change. The following are some of the aspects of curriculum change which are of interest to the sociologist:

The relationship between socio-economic change and curriculum change.
The determinants of long-term evolutionary change in the curriculum.
The cumulative and/or cyclical nature of curriculum change.
The strategies of planned curriculum development.
The diffusion of innovation in education.
The school's response to outside pressures for curriculum change.
The factors which generate an impetus towards change within a school.
The short-term and long-term effects of curriculum change—both intended and unintended.

He is thus concerned with the large-scale and the small-scale, the evolutionary and the planned, the past and the present. He may also play a role at some point on a continuum which stretched from detached analysis to active involvement where the sociologist himself acts as an agent of change.[2]

It would be impossible in two short articles to discuss all the potential areas of sociological research into curriculum change. Four topics have therefore been selected for consideration. This article will discuss (*a*) the relationship between social change and curriculum change, and (*b*) the diffusion of innovation in education. A subsequent article will discuss (*a*) factors determining the innovativeness of the school, and (*b*) strategies of planned curriculum change. In discussing different levels of analysis, patterns of interaction, and clusters of variables, reference will be made to the following diagram:

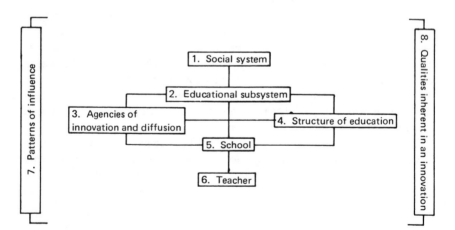

It must be emphasized, however, that this diagram cannot be regarded either as a model or a paradigm. The lines which connect the boxes indicate a reciprocal relationship, but not the direction of the flow of influence. Models could be constructed to indicate the systematic relationship between some of the variables suggested, but we know too little at the present time about the process of educational innovation to construct a single overarching model.

SOCIAL CHANGE AND CURRICULUM CHANGE

Society (represented here in Box 1 as *the* social system)[3], has two major dimensions:

(*a*) *institutional*—consisting of economic, political, religious, educational and other institutions,

(*b*) normative—consisting of the values and norms which pervade the social system and its institutions.

The degree of "necessary" integration between the different institutions of society, and the "necessary" degree of value consensus within society, are fundamental questions still very much in dispute amongst sociologists. But it is sufficient for our purpose here to affirm the relationship between education (represented in Box 2 as a subsystem) and other institutions of society, and between the values pervading education and the values pervading other parts of society. We know little about the nature of these relationships, yet they are crucial for an understanding of the process of curriculum change. Potentially, the role of education can range from *initiation* to *adaptation* on both the normative and institutional dimensions, and these possibilities suggest a number of important questions, e.g.:

Is education inevitably adaptive to economic and technological change, or can education itself generate change in these areas?

Does the class structure inevitably shape the structure and content of education, or could educational change alter the class structure?

If, at the present time, we are experiencing a shift from élitist to egalitarian values, and from ascriptive to achievement values in education, to what extent is this a reflection of such value shifts in society as a whole? And are these normative shifts themselves a response to economic and technological pressures?

To what extent are changes in educational philosophy generated within the educational system independently of broader normative and institutional changes? What, for example, is the relationship between the growing emphasis on flexibility and open-endedness in the curriculum and the economic demand for flexible and creative manpower? Are these trends independent and their complimentariness a happy coincidence? Or is the economic demand being exploited by educationists as an argument for institutionalizing ideas which have long appealed to progressives, but which have not been institutionalized hitherto because they have offered no economic pay-off?

The answers to such questions can only emerge from a careful analysis of institutional and normative change in society and in education.

Contributions to the analysis of social change and curriculum change have come from many sources. British sociologists have tended to concentrate their attention upon institutional structures, and have produced excellent case studies of the relationship between socio-economic factors and the social function of different sorts of educational institutions. Clearly structure and content are very closely related and studies such as those of Banks[4], Cotgrove,[5] Halsey,[6] Taylor,[7] and Blyth[8] have considerable significance for the understanding of curriculum change in the different institutions with which each one deals. There have been a number of attempts, especially in the United States, to take a broad view of curriculum development which have included a consideration of sociological influences on the curriculum, e.g., Smith, Stanley and Shores,[9] Taba,[10] and Saylor and Alexander.[11] Another approach, especially strong in the United States, has been through the analysis of the values pervading society and their influence upon the content of the curriculum, e.g., Riesman,[12] Spindler, [13] Getzels,[14] Callahan,[15] and Hofstadter.[16] A fourth approach, which is being strongly pursued in both this country and the United States, is through the study of the social determinants of educability. Clearly socially-induced handicaps to learning must enter into any consideration of curriculum objectives or teaching methods. Studies have been made of the ecological, material and cultural correlates of educability, e.g., Bernstein,[17] Wiseman,[18] Douglas,[19] Swift,[20] Kahl,[21] Turner,[22] Herriott and St. John, [23] and there is a growing number of American studies which deal in a pragmatic way with the educational problems of deprived social groups, e.g., Reissman, [24] Passow,[25] and also the British Plowden Report.[26]

The relationship between educational change and social change is a highly complex one and there is a variety of different ways of approaching the problems involved. It is incumbent upon those who are engaged in curriculum development to draw appropriate inferences from the institutional studies of the sociologists of education and to relate these to their own pursuit of objectives and strategies of change. For their party, sociologists of education can make further contributions to curriculum development by increasing the attention which they pay to the sociological determinants of the *content* of education. This presupposes the existence of a theory of educational change which we do not yet have. However, a recent attempt has been made by McGee[27] to develop a paradigm for identifying the nature of educational change which is a useful starting point. He proposes a distinction between education as an *agent* of social change (i.e., where social changes are brought about through education), as a *condition* of change (i.e., where changes in education are necessary to broader social changes), and as an *effect* of change (i.e., where educational institutions adjust to changes occurring in other social institutions). He also proposes that these different functions of education in the process of social change should each be related to three major factors: economic, technological and ideological. The categories in this paradigm do not, of course, occur independently, but the analytical distinction can be made in the interests of collecting the data on educational change upon which a theory might be built.

THE DIFFUSION OF CURRICULUM INNOVATIONS

In this section we turn from the general relationship between social change and educational change to one aspect of the change process itself, i.e., how new ideas and practices spread. Innovation is defined as:

(1) acceptance, (2) over time, (3) of some specific item—idea or practice, (4) by individuals, groups or other adopting units, linked by (5) specific channels of communication, (6) to a social structure, and (7) to a given system of values or culture.[28]

An analytical distinction can be made between *innovation* and *diffusion*. An *innovation* is an idea or practice which is perceived as new by the potential adopting unit. *Diffusion* is the process whereby this new idea or practice spreads through a social system. It must be admitted, however, that the term *innovation* is also frequently used to indicate the process as well as the idea or practice. An innovation is always a development of some existing form, and it is not easy to trace cases back to the point of creation. Undoubtedly many new ideas originate with creative teachers who develop them to meet their own particular problems, and are then diffused through informal channels of communication via teachers, headteachers, local inspectors, college lecturers and others, and perhaps in a more formalized way through locally-sponsored courses or through articles in the teachers' journals. Other innovations, especially those requiring capital outlay, are developed outside the schools and promoted amongst teachers through a variety of organizations. We know almost nothing about the sources of new ideas in education, whether these are largely conceived in the schools to be taken up or promoted by outside bodies, or whether most of the new ideas in education are generated outside the schools. Although the creation of new materials, methods, teaching aids, forms of organization and curriculum content is rapidly becoming institutionalized with the progress of the curriculum development movement, it would be worthwhile to study not only these institutionalized forms, but also the sources and pathways of other useful innovations.

The institutional agencies of innovations and diffusion are represented in Box 3 of Figure 1. They include:

The Schools Council
Private foundations
Commercial agencies (e.g., publishers)
Research units (e.g., N.F.E.R., university units)
Teacher-training institutions
In-service training institutions (e.g., university courses, L.E.A. courses)
Professional organizations (e.g., Science Masters' Association, the Physical Education Association)
Her Majesty's Inspectorate
L.E.A. Inspectors and advisers
Examining bodies
Teachers' unions

These agencies differ, of course, in the degree to which they are concerned with innovation and/or diffusion, but in the absence of detailed case studies one cannot range them along this continuum.

These agencies might be studied in the following ways:

(a) The overall analysis of the functions of interorganizational cooperation in curriculum development. Clark[29] has made an approach to this form of study and has summarized the American pattern as follows:

The pattern of influence sums up as follows: it was set in motion from the top, by a Federal agency and a private national committee. Its object was to affect grass roots educational practice which was seen as a national weakness. This flow of influence is downward, through a chain of independent groups and organizations who find it in their interest to enter the alliance or compact. A federal agency provides the funds; a private non-profit group receives the money and develops a new course; commercial firms carry the new materials to all corners of the existing decentralized structure; dispersed universities and colleges train teachers in all regions of the country to the new materials; existing local authorities adopt the materials and allow their teachers to reshape the local courses. Decision-making in this pattern, right down the line, is heavily influenced by the prestige of expertise. The National Science Foundation was expert and prestigeful; so were the committees, the Institutes, the teachers training in the new materials. The very materials themselves travelled under the same aura.

There are obvious affinities with the major patterns of diffusion in Britain, and there is considerable scope for studies of the relationships between the various agencies involved in the promotion of curriculum innovation, e.g., between commercial firms and the foundations, between curriculum development units and the teachers' unions.

(*b*) Studies of the structure and functions of the agencies of innovation and diffusion. A welcome starting point here would be careful descriptions of the work of these bodies using a case approach[30] and beyond this the application of the concepts and techniques of organizational analysis (see on this topic Wilson,[31] Etzioni,[32] Hoyle[33]).

(*c*) Studies in the key roles in the process of innovation through the use of the concepts and techniques of role analysis (see on this topic Gross, Mason and McEachern, 1958[34]; Gross and Herriott, 1965[35]). Interest might center upon the role played by particular "product champion" or upon a role category, e.g., the problems besetting the H.M.I. as a promoter of curriculum change as he seeks to overcome the non-motivating "punishment-centered" perceptions of his role.

(*d*) Surveys of the attributes, e.g., age, sex, qualifications, experience, professional mobility, professional aspirations, etc. of those teachers who become involved in curriculum development either as leaders or as consumers.

(*e*) Sociometric studies of the pathways of innovation in local areas.

Box 4 in Figure 1 represents the structure of education—local, national, and private. Although L.E.A.'s are both "target systems" for innovation and also agencies of diffusion, the different levels of the educational structure (and their financial policies, decision-making structures, etc.) are treated here also as an independent cluster of variables. Major questions in this area center upon the integration of local and governmental authorities in the area of curriculum innovation, the significance of the size of the local authority in relation to its innovativeness, and the relative innovativeness of the public and private sectors of education.

Boxes 7 and 8 represent clusters of variables which are significant at all stages of the diffusion process and can be treated as independent.

Box 7—Patterns of influence—represents a variety of techniques which individuals and groups can employ in order to facilitate the adoption of an innovation by others. One would be concerned here with the functions of different forms of authority, power, and interpersonal influence, and with the role of the mass media in encouraging the adoption of curriculum innovation. Box 8 represents a recognition of the fact that there are qualities inherent in an innovation which make it acceptable or otherwise to adopting systems. Carlson[36] found differential rates of adoption for different innovations, e.g., modern maths was adopted more readily than foreign language programs, and although educationists rated team teaching as potentially more diffusible than programmed instruction, this was not found to have happened. Miles,[37] reviewing the literature in this area, found that cost, congruence between the innovation and the values of the adopting system, degree of technical expertise required, availability of supporting teaching materials to be some of the significant factors.

The sociological study of the diffusion of innovation is a relatively underdeveloped field at the present time. The major work of reference is that of

Rogers[38] which discusses concepts and techniques, and reports many substantive studies of the diffusion of new ideas and practices in agriculture, industry, medicine, and education. He reports that typically, where adopting units are categorized on the basis of standard scores, the distribution of adopters over time approaches normality, and that cumulative frequencies conform to an S-shaped curve (thus mirroring the learning curve for individuals). The "innovativeness" of adopting units, as assessed by their position within the distribution, can be taken as an independent variable and related to a whole variety of correlates. Rogers concludes his work with fifty-two generalizations about the diffusion of innovation based upon the researches of himself and others. A further source of generalizations about the diffusion of innovation, is the work of Lionberger.[39]

A larger number of studies of the diffusion of new ideas in education has been undertaken by the late Paul Mort[40] and his colleagues at Teachers College, Columbia University (Ross[41]). This work on the adaptability (i.e., innovativeness) of school systems (i.e., local units of educational administration) revealed a very slow rate of diffusion. It was found that typically there was a fifty-year lag between a felt need and the appearance of an innovation to meet that need, a further period of fifteen years before the innovation was adopted by three percent of school systems, and then a rapid period of adoption followed by a period of deceleration until near-complete diffusion had been achieved. Mort's studies were focused upon financial rather than on sociological variables, and whilst there is no doubt that for some innovations—though not all—financial provision is a fundamental facilitating or inhibiting factor, to focus upon this factor is to omit from consideration the factors which determine curriculum innovations which cost little, and also the factors which lead to the utilization of what financial resources are available (e.g., the school's capitation allowance) for changing rather than maintaining the existing curriculum.

Carlson,[42] unhappy with the approach of Mort and his colleagues, undertook a study which concentrated upon sociological variables. He sought to relate the rate at which school systems adopted certain innovations (foreign language teaching, modern maths, accelerated programs, team teaching, language laboratories, and programmed instruction) to the social characteristics of the superintendents of those systems. He was able to demonstrate that the early adopting systems had superintendents who had a high social network involvement with other superintendents who also had a high social status vis à vis other superintendents. Eichholz (1963;[43] Eichholz and Rogers, 1964[44]), working within the sociological tradition but taking the teacher as the adopting unit, carried out a study of the rejection of electro-mechanical teaching aids. He identified five major forms of rejection (ignorance, suspended judgment, situational, personal, and experimental) and linked these with the state of the rejecting teachers (e.g., uninformed, anxious, guilty, doubtful), and their responses.

In order to proceed further with the explanation of the process of diffusion in education, the ordering of data is dependent upon the existence of a viable theory. Guba and Clark put forward the following paradigm for the identification of the different stages of the diffusion process:[45]

Guba-Clark Scheme for Change in a Social Process Field

	Research	Development	Dissemination	Demon-stration	Implemen-tation
Objective	To advance knowledge	To apply knowledge	To distribute knowledge	To build conviction	To facilitate action
Criteria	Validity of knowledge produced	1. Feasibility 2. Perform-ance	1. Intelligibility 2. Fidelity 3. Compre-hensiveness 4. Pervasive-ness	Credibility	1. Effective-ness 2. Efficiency
Relation to change	Provides basis for innovation	Produces innovation	Informs about innovation	Promotes innovation	Incorporates innovation

Finally, Bohla[46] has proposed a theory of diffusion which is intended to have both explanatory and predictive power. This theory can be symbolized as:

$$D = f(CLER)$$

Thus diffusion (D) is a function of configurational relationships (C) between initiators and targets (where configurations include individuals, groups, institutions, and cultures), the nature and extent of the linkages (L) between and within these configurations, the environments (E) in which the configurations are located, and the resources (R) of both initiator and target configurations. Bohla discusses at length the connotation of the concepts used in this theory, ways in which they might be operationalized, and a number of hypotheses which it generates and which might be tested.

Theories of diffusion seek to articulate innovators and targets, and where these targets are schools one can draw upon a wider range of research relating to the nature of schools as social systems and particularly their potentialities as adopting units. These characteristics will be considered in a subsequent article.

NOTES

1. W. Moore, *Social Change* (Englewood Cliffs, N.J.: Prentice Hall, 1963).
2. W.G. Bennis, "A New Role for the Behavioural Sciences: Effecting Organizational Change," *Administrative Science Quarterly* 8 (1962).
3. T. Parsons, *The Social System* (London: Routledge and Kegan Paul, 1951).

4. O. Banks, *Parity and Prestige in English Secondary Education* (London: Routledge and Kegan Paul, 1955).

5. S. Cotgrove, *Technical Education and Social Change* (London: Allen and Unwin, 19__).

6. A. H. Halsey, "The Changing Functions of Universities," in A. H. Halsey *et al., Education, Economy and Society* (New York: Free Press, 1961).

7. W. Taylor, *The Secondary Modern School* (London: Faber, 1963).

8. W. A. L. Blyth, *English Primary Education* (London: Routledge and Kegan Paul, 1965).

9. B. O. Smith, W. O. Stanley, and J. H. Shores, *Fundamentals of Curriculum Development* (New York: World Books, 1957).

10. H. Taba, *Curriculum Development: Theory and Practice* (New York: Harcourt, Brace, World, 1962).

11. J. G. Saylor and W. M. Alexander, *Curriculum Planning for Better Teaching and Learning* (New York: Rinehart, 1954).

12. D. Riesman, *Constraint and Variety in American Education* (New York: Harper, 1958).

13. G. D. Spindler, "Education in a Transforming American Culture," *Harvard Educational Review* 25 (1955).

14. J. Getzels, "Changing Values Challenge the Schools," *School Review* 65 (1957).

15. R. E. Callahan, *Education and the Cult of Efficiency* (Chicago: University of Chicago Press, 1962).

16. R. Hofstadter, *Anti-intellectualism in American Life* (London: Cape, 1964).

17. B. Bernstein, "Social Class and Linguistic Development: A Theory of Social Learning," in A. H. Halsey *et al., Education, Economy and Society* (New York: Free Press, 1961).

18. S. Wiseman, *Education and Environment* (Manchester: Manchester University Press, 1964).

19. J. W. B. Douglas, *The Home and the School* (London: McGibbon and Kee, 1964).

20. D. F. Swift, "Family Environment and 11+ Success: Some Basic Predicters," *British Journal of Educational Psychology* 37 (No. 1, 1967).

21. J. Kahl, "The Educational Aspirations of 'Common Man' Boys" in A. H. Halsey *et al., Education, Economy and Society* (New York: Free Press, 1961).

22. R. H. Turner, *The Social Context of Ambition* (San Francisco: Chandler, 1964).

23. R. E. Herriott and N. H. St. John, *Social Class and the Urban School* (New York: Wiley, 1966).

24. F. Reissman, *The Culturally Deprived Child* (New York: Harper, 1962).

25. A. H. Passow, *Education in Depressed Areas* (New York: Teachers College, Columbia University, 1966).

26. H.M.S.O., *Children and their Primary Schools* (London, 1967).

27. R. McGee, "Education and Social Change," in D. A. Hansen and J. E. Gerstl, *On Education: Sociological Perspectives* (New York: Wiley, 1967).

28. E. Katz, M. L. Levin, and H. Hamilton, "Traditions of Research on the Diffusion of Innovation," *American Sociological Review* 28 (No. 2, 1963).

29. B. R. Clark, "Interorganizational Patterns in Education," *Administrative Science Quarterly* 10 (No. 2, 1964).

30. M. B. Miles, *Innovation in Education* (New York: Teachers College, Columbia University, 1964), Section I. M. B. Miles and E. V. Lake.

31. B. R. Wilson, "Institutional Analysis," in A. Welford *et al., Society: Problems and Methods of Study* (London: Routledge and Kegan Paul, 1961).

32. A. Etzioni, *A Comparative Analysis of Complex Organizations* (New York: Free Press, 1964).

33. E. Hoyle, "Organizational Analysis in the Field of Education," *Educational Research* 7 (No. 2, 1965).

34. N. Gross, W. S. Mason, and A. W. McEachern, *Explorations in Role Analysis* (New York: Wiley, 1958).

35. N. Gross and R. E. Herriott, *Staff Leadership in Public Schools* (New York: Wiley, 1965).

36. R. O. Carlson, *Adoption of Educational Innovations* (Eugene, Oregon: Center for the Advanced Study of Educational Administration, University of Oregon, 1965).

37. M. B. Miles, *Innovation In Education* (New York: Teachers College, Columbia University, 1964).

38. E. M. Rogers, *Diffusion of Innovations* (New York: Free Press, 1962).

39. H. F. Lionberger, *Adoption of New Ideas and Practices* (Ames, Iowa: Iowa State University Press, 1960).

40. P. Mort, "Studies in Educational Innovation from the Institute of Administrative Research: An Overview," in M. B. Miles (ed.), *Innovation in Education* (New York: Teachers College, Columbia University, 1964).

41. D. H. Ross, *Administration for Adaptability* (New York: Teachers College, Columbia University, 1958).

42. R. O. Carlson, "School Superintendents and the Adoption of Modern Maths," in M. B. Miles (ed.), *Innovation in Education* (New York: Teachers College, Columbia University, 1964). See also Carlson (1965), *op. cit.*

43. G. C. Eichholz, "Why Do Teachers Resist Change?" *Theory into Practice* 2 (No. 5, 1963).

44. G. C. Eichholz and E. M. Rogers, "Resistance to Adoption of Audio-visual aids by Elementary School Teachers," in M. B. Miles, (ed.), *Innovation in Education* (New York: Teachers College, Columbia University, 1964).

45. E. G. Guba, "From Research into Action." Address given at the annual meeting of the Educational Research Association of New York State, October, 1964 (cited by Bohla, see note 46).

46. H. S. Bohla, "A Configurational Theory of Innovation and Diffusion," *Indian Educational Review* 2 (No. 1, 1967).

HOW DOES THE CURRICULUM CHANGE?
PART 2: SYSTEMS AND STRATEGIES

An earlier article in this journal[1] discussed two aspects of curriculum change: the relationship between social change and educational change, and the diffusion of innovation in education. The present article focuses upon two further aspects of curriculum change: the innovativeness of schools and strategies of planned curriculum change.

THE INNOVATIVE SCHOOL

For any curriculum innovation to become an effective improvement on an existing practice it must "take" with the school and become fully institutionalized. Genuine innovation does not occur unless teachers become personally committed to ensuring its success. Unless this commitment occurs, new methods and materials may eventually be permanently relegated to store-cupboards, or used only in an unsystematic manner. Organizational innovations are less likely to fall into disuse because the number of people involved ensures some continuity, but these can remain ineffective even when they are nominally operative. Mixed ability grouping is a case in point; for this to be fully effective the teacher must be committed to its success otherwise it is unlikely to be more effective than grouping by ability. The rather ambiguous results of research on the effects of mixed ability grouping are perhaps a reflection of the fact that researchers have focused their attention only upon the structure of the school and not upon its climate. Yet it is clear that de-streaming introduced by fiat and without the commitment of the teachers is likely to prove ineffective.

This section is concerned with those characteristics of a school which pre-dispose it to innovativeness. This does not assume that innovative schools will indiscriminately adopt anything which is new, but that they will adopt some innovations and reject others dependent upon their relevance to the particular needs of the school at a given time. It does assume, however, that some schools are more open to new ideas than others. It also assumes that schools have a collective quality of innovativeness. Ultimately the individual teacher is the "adopting unit" who will determine the effectiveness of an innovation, and some teachers have more "open" minds than others as a function of their cognitive, perceptual and creative skills. But the focus of this paper will be upon the school as the adopting unit partly because many curriculum innovations are school-wide both in their extent and in their consequences, and partly because the behavior of individual teachers is influenced by the institution in which they work.

In an important contribution to the discussion of the innovative school Miles has used the concept of *organizational health* to denote "a school system's ability not only to function effectively, but to develop and grow into a more fully-functioning system."[2] A school in good organizational health is likely to be characterized by an awareness of potential innovation, a continuing willingness to examine its own procedures, and a capacity to adopt innovations in a way which ensures their full effectiveness. Miles makes the following point:

> It seems likely that the state of health of an educational organization can tell us more than anything else about the probable success of any particular change effort. Economy of effort would suggest that we look at the state or an organization's health as such, and try to improve it—in preference to struggling with a series of more or less inspired short-run change efforts.

Extending Miles' medical metaphor we can say that the central problem facing the curriculum development movement is the avoidance of *tissue rejection* whereby an innovation does not "take" with a school because the social system of the school is unable to absorb it into its normal functioning.

Any appreciation of the innovative potential of a school is dependent upon an understanding of its nature as a social system which includes such dimensions as its formal structure, administrative processes, informal structures and activities, and culture. Little research exists at the present time which would enable us to predict the likelihood of a school being receptive to curriculum innovation nor the strategies which it could employ to induce a greater innovativeness. However, useful inferences can be drawn from the research based upon Halpin's Organizational Climate Description Questionnaire.[3] A factorial analysis of responses to a questionnaire containing items relating to administrative relationships in the school revealed eight major dimensions—four referred to staff behavior and four to the principal's behavior. Further analysis revealed that these dimensions yielded six distinct school profiles which are referred to as *organizational climates*. Halpin ranged these climates on a continuum from "open" to "closed" which he concedes is based upon his own value preferences. The climates can be briefly summarized as follows:

Open

The head is a leader who works hard himself and thus sets an example. He establishes rules and procedures and is prepared to be critical, but he is also flexible and to a large extent meets the social needs of his staff. He does not monitor the teacher's work too closely and allows leadership acts to emerge from his staff. Morale is high owing to a feeling of accomplishment by the staff and their experience of good personal relationships.

Autonomous

The head gives greater autonomy to his teachers than the "open" climate head, but does not give them the same degree of positive leadership nor meets their social needs satisfactions to the same extent. He is aloof but gives a free hand, and all the teachers experience a sense of task accomplishment.

Controlled

The head is an authoritarian who controls his staff closely, works them hard, and provides for little social satisfaction. Nevertheless, the staff respond to this militant behavior and derive satisfaction from their task achievement.

Familiar

The head is centrally concerned with creating a happy family atmosphere in the school. Hence he exerts little leadership or control and is disinclined to be critical. The staff enjoy friendly relationships but their morale is diminished through having little sense of task achievement.

Paternal

The head tries to exert control over his staff with little effect. He is constantly busy within the school but this is regarded as interference rather than leadership. The teachers pay little heed and rather little is achieved. The head also attempts to fulfill the social needs satisfactions of his staff, but this is characterized in Halpin's terms as a "seductive oversolicitousness" which is regarded as non-genuine and is therefore non-motivating.

Closed

The head is aloof, controlling, impersonal, arbitrary and unconcerned with teachers as people. He gives no leadership and provides no example. The teachers gain little satisfaction from either their social relationships or their achievements.

Halpin now concedes that this climate dimension is not necessarily linear but feels that at least the open-closed dimension is meaningful.[4] It would appear from Halpin's description of the "open" climate that such a school could be said to be in a state of "organizational health" and hence innovative. But in his review of the state of research on school climates he states: "The blunt truth is that we do not yet know very much about how to change a climate."

Clearly the willingness of a school to institutionalize curriculum development is very much dependent upon the manner in which the head teacher performs his leadership role; whether he is, in fact, a *leader* in the sense that he attempts to keep the school moving rather than simply ticking over. It is also dependent upon the administrative structure which he creates since communication and decision-making patterns of a school can clearly be motivating or otherwise. Revans,[5] for example, has shown how a measure of pupils' involvement in their school work is correlated with administrative relationships in the school. We are not in a position to say what are the patterns of communication and decision-making which are likely to maximize teacher commitment to curriculum innovation. Sharma[6] reports that teachers' moral is high when there is a close relationship between *desire* for involvement and *actual* involvement, and that teachers express a particular desire for participation in decision-making in the area of the curriculum. As a broad generalization it is probably true to say that schools would be more innovative if teachers played a greater part in decision-making than at present, but there are incompatibilities between certain of the goals of decision making.[7] For example the goals of motivation, quality of decision, and training might point to extended participation. Teachers want to be involved in decisions about the curriculum, but for many at the present time their only participation in decision-making is limited to basic organizational arrangements, with such questions for example, as how best to prevent pupils going "up the down staircase." Undoubtedly the curriculum movement itself is creating situations in which teachers are taking more responsibility for decision-making, but the effectiveness of the various structures of decision-making which are emerging in schools have yet to be evaluated.

The effectiveness of any complex organization such as a school is dependent upon *differentiation* (whereby individuals are allocated specialized functions) and *coordination* (whereby these functions are integrated in the service of a common purpose). The coordination of the activities of the personnel of a school requires a balance between order and initiative. Since Max Weber outlined his model of a bureaucracy—characterized by an emphasis on hierarchy, procedures, and predictability—sociologists have been concerned with the validity of this model for different types of organization. This is probably not the place to discuss the degree to which schools can be said to be bureaucracies, but it can be noted that a bureaucratic mode of organization perhaps has certain dysfunctions for schools, particularly in its emphasis on rule-following rather than creative and innovative behavior. Bidwell[8] has pointed out that schools are characterized by a mixture of authority and autonomy. Within his classroom the teacher has a high degree of autonomy if not over what he teaches at least how he teaches it, but in terms of the overall policy of the school he has relatively little influence. A major problem in all organizations is the prevention of ends becoming superseded by means. This is a particularly potent threat in educational organizations owing to the diffuseness of cultural goals and the great difficulties involved in evaluating procedures. Organizations with diffuse and diverse goals are liable to scale down these goals and sometimes to transform them into much more limited commitments largely concerned with maintaining the school in good running order, the substitution of discipline for education. It is perhaps too much to expect the head to promote a Maoist cultural revolution and shatter his own bureaucracy in the services of promoting the goals of education, but the good head will seek to prevent the structure of his organization repressing the innovativeness of teachers. Corwin[9] has pointed out that teachers can perform their role on a continuum which extends from an *employee* model to a *professional* model. The *employee* teacher follows fixed rules and procedures, his work is characterized by uniformity and lack of innovation, he is primarily concerned with narrow teaching techniques, has a personal commitment to his school and its existing structure and functions, and participates in a "punishment-centered" administration. The *professional* teacher on the other hand emphasizes the uniqueness of problems which he faces, is flexible within the broad policy of the school, adapts readily to changes, emphasizes the importance of curriculum knowledge, gives his loyalty to the wider profession and takes its innovators as his reference group, and participates in a "representative" administration. Corwin's typology has much in common with Gouldner's distinction between *locals* and *cosmopolitans*.[10]

What sort of teacher-role is most appropriate to curriculum development? Employee? Or professional? Or is there an optimum balance between the two? Arguments have been advanced in favor of a "teacher-proof" curriculum whereby the class teacher simply accepts a prepared package and goes through teaching procedures in a more or less bureaucratic way.[11] On the other hand there is a strong argument for extending the professionalism of teachers since solutions to educational problems cannot be fully standardized and require the flexibility, adaptability and insight of the profession. The problem ought not, perhaps, to be framed in this way, since it is predicated upon a model of a school and the role of the teacher within it which may be disappearing. Eggleston[12] has pointed out that "English educational organizations are moving from a situation where their *differentiated* nature is the paramount determinant of the roles of their personnel, to one where their part in the differentiating process is paramount." This change is attributed to a number of changes within industrialized society including the breakdown in the traditional distinction between academic and practical curricula, the demand for the generation of new knowledge, the "personalization" of goals, changes in the concept of ability, societal demand for increasing numbers of personnel with extended education, and the reorganization of institutions to embody these changes. The power of the client is becoming more pronounced and leading to individualized instruction and teacher-pupil roles based upon cooperation. These changes in organization have much in common with Bernstein's[13] model of an "open school" characterized by a non-bureaucratic structure, achieved (rather than ascribed) teacher and pupil roles, and cooperation between teachers. This form of school organization is fully congruent with current curriculum trends. In fact, although we do not yet know the educative power of the school organization, one can hypothesize that to some extent "the organization is the message" in that the structure and climate of the school have an impact upon the child which is relatively independent of the content of the curriculum and the influence of individual teachers. Yet there remain certain problems to be faced and questions to be answered before it can be affirmed that the open-school and associated curriculum trends can become fully effective. One such question is whether lower working class children are able to profit from a system which is relatively unstructured and throws an increased responsibility for decision-making upon pupils and parents. Evidence from many sources on the socialization of lower working class children suggests that extremely careful strategies will be needed to ensure that these children will gain the presumed benefits of the open school. A similar problem exists for the teachers. The stratification of the teaching profession in recent years has perhaps been antithetical to the open school. Status distinctions, the vested interests of subject teachers, the need to demonstrate personal superiority in order to achieve promotion, and the tendency of many teachers to aspire to posts outside the classroom may tend to inhibit the beneficial aspects of the open system. Perhaps our thinking about the flexible school needs to be coupled with a reconsideration of the career structure in education.[14]

STRATEGIES OF CHANGE

As Hilda Taba[15] has pointed out, to change the curriculum implies changing people and institutions. The implication of this is that curriculum change cannot be considered independently of planned organizational change founded upon adequate theories derived from the social sciences. This was recognized long ago in a pioneering work edited by Benne and Muntyan[16] which applied some of the extant findings in the area of group dynamics to the problems of curriculum change. Group dynamics is not, however, the only approach to the social science of curriculum change. Chin[17] has grouped strategies of planned organizational change into three broad categories. *Power-coercive* strategies are, as the term implies, based upon the use of power to alter the conditions within which other people act by limiting alternatives, shaping the consequences of acts and by directly influencing actions. This is currently perhaps the most common form of administrative intervention to secure change. But within education there is a strong sentiment against such strategies founded on the assumption that because of their very nature educational ends cannot be achieved without the commitment of the participants, both teachers and taught. Chin notes that any major innovations which alter the forces in a school will inevitably also alter the power relationships and that the conflict is a normal state of affairs and must be recognized as such. But he also notes that: "The concurrent strategy of converting these types of conflicts into problem-solving ones is one phase under way in educational circles." *Normative-re-educative* approaches to effecting change are defined as making use of direct interventions based upon a theory of change and applied to individual behavior in small groups, organizations and communities. Two main approaches can be identified within this group. One is the problem-solving method in which change strategies are concerned with "activating forces within the system to alter the system," and in terms of curriculum development this implies a prior self-study of the school as a social system with the object of identifying and solving the problems associated with change. The other approach is the process of attitude change through a study of how one's behavior impinging on others leads to a greater sensitivity and hence to collaborative behavior in the change situation. The disciplinary basis of *normative-re-educative* approach is social psychology and owes much to the pioneering work of Kurt Lewin. Currently its major procedures include T-groups, human relations laboratories, and curriculum laboratories. *Empirical-rational* approaches make an intellectual appeal through the demonstration of the greater effectiveness of some new idea or practice over existing ones. Basically the method involves linking innovative processes with research and development[18] often utilizing consultants to establish the link between knowledge and change. This has perhaps been the major approach to curriculum development in this country except that consultants have been largely concerned with the *content* of change rather than with the change mechanisms themselves and have not usually become involved in the change processes *within* the schools.

One of the most explicit statements on the potentiality of planned organizational change is that of Miles[19] who proposes the following six types of intervention: *team training* (i.e., an intact work group such as a school department meets away from the school setting to discuss common problems with the central objective of improving relationships); *survey feedback* (i.e., the use of research on the school as an organization including the attitude and opinions of staff as a basis for decision-making); *role-workshop* (i.e., where the incumbents of a particular role—such as head teachers—meet to discuss, on the basis of questionnaire data, the problems associated with the role with a focus on role clarity and an improved fit between role and personality); *target-setting* (i.e., regular meetings between, say, the school head and individual members of his staff to arrange "targets" for the subordinate's work for periods of about six months when a review takes place); *organizational diagnosis* (i.e., residential meetings of a work group focused less upon improving interpersonal relationships—as in *team-training*—but more upon specific problems and their solutions via established or new procedures); *organizational experiment* (i.e., the conduct of an experiment designed to evaluate some particular innovation and the use of resultant data as a basis for further decision-making). These strategies combine the three approaches outlined above. Miles notes that certain common threads flow through them: self study, an emphasis on personal relationships, increased data flow, norms as a change target, a temporary systems approach and the use of expert consultants. Miles has written at great length about the temporary systems approach.[20] Basically his view is that it is the group which is the unit of change rather than the individual and that one can only change groups by having them meet away from the normal work setting with its pressures, vested interests and specific power relationships. When one considers the phenomenon of the individual who returns from some course or workshop highly enthusiastic about some innovation only to be met by the stony apathy of colleagues who have not shared his experience, one can appreciate the value of Miles' proposal to work through complete work groups preferably in a setting conducive to interaction.

The use of consultants or change agents in the process of curriculum development is likely to meet with considerable resistance in British education owing to the power traditionally exercised by the head and the classroom autonomy of the teachers. Nevertheless, it will perhaps be clear from the discussion so far that not only the curriculum consultants but also behavioral scientists can play a useful role in the induction of innovation. Organizational analysis, theory development, experimentation and evaluation, group leadership, etc. are specialized tasks which are nevertheless important in the change process. The potentialities of a change-agent role have yet to be worked out for the British context. These are currently occurring at the practical level as in the North West Curriculum Development Project, but there is also the need to consider the role of the change-agent in education from a more theoretical standpoint utilizing the perspectives of behavioral scientists who have been working in these areas in educational and non-educational settings.[21]

CONCLUSION

One of the striking features of British education at the present time is the institutionalization of innovation. It is now widely accepted that education can never be in a steady state but must constantly be seeking new solutions as new problems are generated by social and educational change. New structures are being developed for the creation and diffusion of innovation, but one of the most pressing problems at the present time is to develop strategies whereby schools are transformed. Miles has rightly pointed out that one-shot innovation is not likely to be successful unless the school is in sound "organizational health." Curriculum development is exerting a pressure towards a more open and flexible school with greater freedom for the teacher, perhaps, paradoxically, the freedom to co-operate with other teachers in the organization of his teaching. This process might be accelerated by means of carefully designed change strategies having their initiative both within the school and outside. Again a paradox is apparent in that the initiative which would seek to maximize the creativity of teachers could come from outside intervention. But the paradox is more apparent than real in that it is basic to the theory of consultancy that it is a co-operative relationship in which the consultant helps to remove barriers to changes which the clients themselves come to see as desirable during the analysis of a problem. There is no question of an external agent imposing change upon an unwilling client, both change-agent and client system work together towards a solution to a problem with each party having equal power to influence the other.

In conclusion it should be pointed out that although this paper has been concerned with change it has not been the intention to convey the view that change for its own sake is a good thing. Resistance to change is a natural response and any attempt to force change upon unwilling teachers would bring no benefit to education. Planned change should itself be regarded as an educational enterprise which is essentially a dialogue. One can end with the following point made by Andrew Halpin:

Social change takes place slowly. To force its growth "out of phase" is to invite unanticipated social consequences that can be damaging. For political reasons some of us may be forced to make rhetorical declamations about change and its happy consequences for everybody. These declamations are like T.V. commercials. I suggest that we recognize such rhetoric for what it is, but that we do not confuse it with reality.[22]

NOTES

1. E. Hoyle, "How Does the Curriculum Change? I. A Proposal for Inquiries," *Journal of Curriculum Studies* 1 (No. 2, 1969).

2. M. Miles, "Planned Change and Organizational Health: Figure and Ground" in *Change Processes in the Public Schools* (Eugene, Oregon: Center for the Advanced Study of Educational Administration).

3. A. W. Halpin, *Theory and Research in Educational Administration* (New York: Macmillan, 1966).

4. A. W. Halpin, "Change and Organizational Climate, *Journal of Educational Administration* 5 (No. 1, 1967).

5. R. W. Revans, "Involvement in School," *New Society* 6 (No. 152, 1965).

6. C. L. Sharma, "Who Should Make Decisions?" *Administrators Notebook* 3 (1955).

7. W. R. Dill, "Decision-making" in *Behavioral Science and Educational Administration,* 63rd Yearbook of the National Society for the Study of Education. Part II (Chicago: University of Chicago Press, 1964).

8. C. Bidwell, "The School as a Formal Organization," in J. G. March (ed.), *Handbook of Organizations* (New York: Rand McNally, 1965).

9. G. Corwin, *A Sociology of Education* (New York: Appleton-Century-Croft, 1965).

10. A. W. Gouldner, "Cosmopolitans and Locals: Towards an Analysis of Latent Social Roles," *Administrative Science Quarterly* 2 (1957–58).

11. S. Wayland, "The Rôle of the Teacher," in A. H. Passow, *Curriculum Cross-roads* (New York: Teachers College Press, Columbia University, 1965).

12. J. S. Eggleston, "Convergences in the Rôles of Personnel in Differentiated Educational Organizations." Paper presented to the European Seminar on Sociology of Education, Noordwijk van Zee, The Netherlands, September 1968 (forthcoming).

13. B. Bernstein, "Open Schools, Open Society?" *New Society* 10 (No. 259, 1967).

14. E. Hoyle, "Rôle Differentiation and Professional Stratification in Education," *Pedagogica Europaea* 1969 (forthcoming).

15. H. Taba, *Curriculum Development: Theory and Practice* (New York: Harcourt Brace World, 1962).

16. K. D. Benne and B. Muntyan, *Human Relations in Curriculum Change* (New York: Dryden Press, 1951).

17. R. Chin, "Basic Strategies and Procedures in Effecting Change," in E. L. Morphet and C. O. Ryan, *Designing Education for the Future*. No. 3 (New York: Citation Press, 1968).

18. M. Young, *Innovation and Research in Education* (London: Routledge and Kegan Paul, 1967).

19. M. B. Miles, *op. cit.*

20. M. B. Miles, "On Temporary Systems" in M. B. Miles (ed.), *Innovation in Education* (New York: Teachers College Press, Columbia University, 1964).

21. See W. G. Bennis, K. D. Benne and R. Chin, *The Planning of Change* (New York: Holt, Rinehart and Winston, 1966); G. Jones, *Planned Organizational Change* (London: Routledge and Kegan Paul, 1969); R. Lippett, J. Watson, and B. Westley, *The Dynamics of Planned Change* (New York: Harcourt, Brace, 1958).

22. A. W. Halpin, "Change and Organizational Climate," *Journal of Educational Administration* 5 (No. 1, 1967).

31. AN ANALYSIS OF CURRICULUM POLICY-MAKING

Michael W. Kirst and Decker F. Walker

Any organization or institution with purposes of its own develops policies—
"a body of principles to guide action [Lerner and Lasswell, 1951, p. ix]"—for
dealing with recurring or crucial matters. Schools normally formulate policies on
a variety of matters including promotion of students, grading, grouping of
students for instruction, and dress for students. Schools also implement policies
formulated by other bodies, most notably policies of the district administration,
the state and local board of education, and the U.S. Congress. The policies
executed by schools include specifically educational policies as well as others
which, while they may have educational aspects, are not unique to schools or
even characteristic of them. Among the most important of the specifically
educational policies of schools are those pertaining to what children study in
school. Children in school are normally required to study certain subjects and
forbidden to study others, encouraged to pursue some topics and discouraged
from pursuing others, provided with opportunities to study some phenomena but
not provided with the means of studying others. When these requirements and
pressures are uniformly and consistently operative they amount to policy,
whether we intended so or not. We shall call such explicit or implicit "guides to
action" *curriculum policy* and the process of arriving at such policy we shall call
curriculum *policy-making*.

Our purpose in this paper is to explore what is known about curriculum
policy-making in the public schools of the United States, relying whenever

---

SOURCE. *Review of Educational Research* 41 (No. 5, December 1971), pp. 479–509.
538

possible on the demonstrable conclusions of formal studies, but resorting when necessary to conventional wisdom, common sense, personal experiences, and outright speculation. We do not intend to give an historical account of the development of either the policy-making process or the policies produced by it. Rather we are primarily interested in the present status of the policy-making process. For this reason we direct our attention exclusively to works published since 1950. Even though we are aware of many interesting and informative earlier treatment of parts of this topic (e.g., Lippmann, 1928; Counts, 1928; Nelson and Roberts, 1963; Krug, 1964), limitations of time, space, and energy forbid a more historical approach. The reader should also keep in mind that treating such a broad topic in a paper of this size means that we have to deal in national-scale generalizations without mentioning the numerous exceptions that can be found in the country's diverse regions, states, and 19,300 school districts. We hope that the perspective for future research directions such an approach provides on the problems of curriculum policy-making will compensate for the exception cases that, despite our best efforts, we overlooked.

In this country school policy, including curriculum policy, is determined at many levels. State legislatures require the study of some subjects. State and local boards of education commission and endorse courses of study, specifying the content to be included in these courses. The professional employees of the school districts, from the superintendent to the teacher's aide, have varying degrees of influence in the determination of courses of study, textbooks, supplies, allotments of time, etc. which embody curriculum policy. Given a complex system of public policy-making, an unfamiliar observer might expect curriculum policy-making to be the scene of conflict and uneasy accommodation, as are most political issues in our democracy. And, indeed, we do find signs of powerful influences of political and social events on curriculum policy-making. For example, in a survey of professional discourse in the field of curriculum—the periodic policy statements of the Educational Policies Commission, the yearbooks of the National Society for the Study of Education, the publications of professional scholars, and their influential publications in the curriculum field— Pilder (1968) found that this literature reflected most of the major national political tensions in the period he studied (1918-1967). When immigration was a national issue, Americanization was a curriculum issue. When totalitarianism posed a threat to democracy, education for democratic life was a concern in curricular discourse. When World War II created a shortage of trained workers, manpower training became an important theme in writing on curriculum. When Sputnik shocked the nation, the softness of existing curricula was cited as a major contributing factor in our national decline. The school curriculum was entangled in these national political issues even though the federal government was formally and in theory not a party to educational questions, especially curriculum questions.

Such evidence as this indicates that the determination of the public school curriculum is not just influenced by political events; it is a political process in important ways. By "political" here and elsewhere in this article we refer not merely to the processes by which we are governed or govern ourselves. Throughout curriculum policy-making, political conflict is generated by the existence of competing values concerning the proper basis for deciding what to teach. The local school system and the other public agencies responsible for these decisions must allocate these competing values in some way, even though this means that some factions or interests win and others lose on any given curriculum issue. The inevitability of conflicting demands, wants, and needs is responsible for the necessarily political character of curriculum policy-making, a character which cannot be avoided even by the adoption of some mathematical decision-procedure. Some legitimate authority must decide (and perhaps bargain and compromise) among the conflicting policy viewpoints.

Yet when professional educators write about or study the curriculum, they rarely conceive of their subject in political terms. The words "policy," "politics," and "political" do not even appear in the indices of any of the major textbooks in the field (Tyler, 1949; Smith, Stanley, and Shores, 1950; Gwynn, 1960; Taba, 1962; Saylor and Alexander, 1966). These authors treated conflict always as conflict among ideas, never as conflict among individuals, interest groups, or factions within school system bureaucracies. One finds consistent acknowledgement of the existence of political influence on curriculum, but no mention of policy or policy-making, nor any attempts to compare or contrast curriculum policy-making with other types of public or private policy-making. Instead, terms such as "decision-making," "planning," "development," and "management" were used. National, state, and local political figures, as well as parents, taxpayers, and other interested parties and the organizations that represent their interests were treated as "influences" on curriculum "decision-making." These terms and the ideas that accompany them embody an image of curriculum determination that plays down—if it does not altogether ignore—the conflict and accommodation characteristic of policy-making in all but the most monolithic institutions. Consistently followed, this image leads the investigator to search for some sort of mechanism for deciding "scientifically" what children should study in school. More important for present purposes, this ideal sidesteps the political questions of who should have a say in determining curriculum at what stages in which ways with what impact. Instead, it holds out the promise of resolving competing claims at the level of principle. Here is one clear statement of this position.

If curriculum development is to be a rational and a scientific rather than a rule-of-thumb procedure, the decisions about these elements [of the curriculum] need to be made on the basis of some valid criteria. These criteria may come from various sources—from tradition, from social pressures, from established habits. The differences between a curriculum decision-making which follows a scientific method and develops a rational design and one which does not is that in the former the criteria for decisions are derived from a study of the factors constituting a reasonable basis for the curriculum. In our society, at least, these factors are the learner, the learning process, the cultural demands, and the content of the disciplines. Therefore, scientific curriculum development needs to drawn upon analyses of society and culture, studies of the learner and the learning process, and analyses of the nature of knowledge in order to determine the purposes of the school and the nature of its curriculum [Taba, 1962, p. 10].

Once such an ideal has been adopted, it is difficult to avoid disapproval of political resolutions of curriculum questions. And, once political solutions to curriculum questions are seen as deficient or inferior, the tendency is to lump all the complex and varied means by which personal and group interests are defended and advanced in curriculum issues under the vague and somewhat sinister term "influences" and to treat them as aberrations rather than as normal and necessary, if not altogether desirable, aspects of public policy-making.

In this review we treat the determination of the public school curriculum as a process of public policy-making which is necessarily political in character. We choose not to concentrate on the interaction of strictly political (in the narrow sense of political) and educational institutions. Our concern is with the whole range of processes which eventuate in the curriculum of the local public schools. Since local districts have ultimate authority and responsiblity for carrying out curriculum policy, and much authority for determining it, we focus our attention on the curriculum decisions of local schools and the activities of individuals and groups in local school systems as they engage in these collective decisions. Inevitably this focus draws us into a consideration of the state, regional, and national factors—governmental and private—that condition and constrain local decision-makers. In light of these aims this paper is perhaps most accurately described as an exploratory review of the literature—exploratory not because the topic is new, but because it has not been treated in this way before.

VALUE BASES

For most of their recorded history, schools have regarded their curricula as fixed quantities, not variables to be adjusted in the interest of achieving some goal. The Latin root for the word "curriculum" means "race course" and the virtue of a race course is that it is fixed and standard. For centuries the European curriculum was fixed, bounded by the study of the trivium and the quadrivium. Moreover, for most of the last three hundred years the curriculum in Western schools has changed slowly, consisting of literacy training in the vernacular and in arithmetic, supplemented with Bible study for most of those who got any education, and study of the "disciplines"—higher mathematics, history, the national literature, languages, philosophy, and increasingly, the natural sciences—for the intellectual elite. So long as the curriculum changed only slowly there were few occasions for conflict and little use for political processes.

But the image of the race course has not really been an accurate one for the curricula of the schools in Western civilization since the 17th century. The race itself would be a more accurate symbol of the increasingly agitated jockeying for position in the curriculum that has characterized the last three hundred years. First the vernacular languages, then the physical sciences, then the biological sciences, the applied sciences, engineering, and most recently, the social sciences successively fought their way into the curriculum at the upper levels of the educational system, from whence they have exerted pressure for entry into the curricula of the lower schools. In the lower schools other pressures to include more immediately useful material in the curriculum, dating from at least the 1850's (Spencer's *Education: Intellectual, Moral and Physical* (1870) is an early landmark), eventually produced such curricular offerings as home economics, the agricultural and industrial arts, physical education, driver training, and sex education.

These developments have reached their logical (and absurd) conclusion in the present situation of the elementary schools where teachers may be expected to teach children to learn reading, writing, several varieties of arithmetic, geography, spelling, science, economics, music, art, foreign languages, and history at the same time that the children are supposedly helped to develop physically, morally, and intellectually, and are molded into good citizens. Furthermore, if the school is to take advantage of the millions of dollars invested in national curriculum development, each of these matters must be addressed independently with specially developed and packaged materials in the hands of specially trained teachers. Things are hardly less chaotic in secondary schools.

All this confusion has provoked continued conflict over the proper bases for deciding what to teach. Should schools teach those things that are likely to be immediately useful in life outside the school or should they teach those things that are most fundamental to an understanding of organized knowledge? Should they emphasize the development of individuality or the transmission of the cultural heritage? What are schools *for*, anyway? So long as there is disagreement on the proper bases for assessing the worth of the curriculum, there are bound to be conflicting views concerning its composition. The authoritative allocation of these value conflicts is the essence of what we mean by the political process in curriculum decision-making. We would identify as salient over the last several decades four broad bases for assigning value to curriculum elements—tradition, community, science, and individual judgment. These value bases are positions around which people's preferences tend to congregate. They are neither mutually exclusive nor exhaustive, but they do represent major streams of thought and feeling among individuals and groups concerned with the school curriculum.

The appeal to tradition, exemplified in recent times by the Great Books program and the Council for Basic Education, rests on the assumption that those subjects of study that have survived the test of time are in the long view most beneficial and therefore should receive the highest priority in the curricula. The appeal to science, the newest and probably the fastest growing basis for curriculum decision-making, has received strong support from many influential groups including the U.S. Office of Education. This appeal rests on the assumption that educational and psychological research will reveal those capabilities that are essential to the performance of the activities which the school is responsible for cultivating. In this view the school curriculum should give first priority to the development of these scientifically identified capabilities. The appeal to community presupposes that every school is part of a community of association and interest in which resides the ultimate criterion of usefulness, relevance, and beneficiality of any curriculum element. Therefore, those matters which deserve first priority in the curriculum are to be determined by the community, either directly or via its representatives or by studies of the community. The appeal to individual judgment amounts to a skeptical denial of any rational value basis for curriculum-making beyond the student's own values, needs, and desires as these are manifested in his own considered judgments. Adherents of this position argue that any basis for curriculum that purports to provide general, impersonal answers to Spencer's (1860) question "What knowledge is of most worth?" is doomed to failure.

Each value basis has its supporters and detractors who use political techniques to bolster their position. There are schools that stand primarily and reasonably consistently on only one basis. The curriculum of St. John's University in Annapolis is based largely on the appeal to tradition as are the curricula of a number of private "Latin" schools; several medical schools have reorganized their curricula along predominantly scientific lines (Henderson, 1969), and experimental programs with a scientific basis are widespread, most visibly in preschool and primary shool programs (Pine, 1968; Bereiter and Engelman, 1966); many so-called free schools and free universities across the country as well as "progressive" or "radical" schools base their programs on a particular community or on the free choices of individual students (Stretch, 1970). But by and large public school programs seem to be a heterogeneous mixture of these different bases reflecting political compromises among the heterogeneous values in any state or local district. A study of the value bases for various elements in the school curriculum and the groups who advance and defend each basis would add considerably to our understanding of curriculum policy-making.

THE USE OF DECISION TOOLS: DISJOINTED INCREMENTALISM

The acceptance of any definite value basis, when this is possible, simplifies the determination of the curriculum considerably by providing a limited and well-defined set of criteria for narrowing the bewildering array of curricular choices. But adopting a single clear and consistent basis of value does not entirely resolve the political conflict in curriculum policy-making. Those who agree that the truths honored in our tradition should be the primary curriculum elements may still disagree over whether certain classics should be taught in English translations, Latin translations, or the original Greek. They may argue whether to include Vergil together with Tacitus and Julius Caesar in a fixed time of study. They may differ over the amount of time to be allotted to the Bible and other more strictly oriental texts. The resolution of such problems requires a decision procedure in addition to a value basis.

The oldest and simplest solution to this problem is to endow an individual or small group with the authority to make these decisions by exercising professional and presumably expert judgment. This decision-making body can be related to the community that gives it power as a government is related to its constituency (traditional school boards), as the management of a firm is related to its customers (voucher systems), or in any of a number of other ways ranging from tight control of decision-makers by the community to virtual independence.

But this only pushes our search one step further. What sort of decision procedures do these groups follow? They adopt what Lindblom and Braybrooke (1963) called a strategy or disjointed incrementalism. Disjointed incrementalism is a name for a collection of "relatively simple, crude, almost wholly conscious, and public" strategies for decision-making which "taken together as a mutual reinforcing set . . . constitute a systematic and defensible strategy [Lindblom and Braybrooke, 1963, p. 82]." The major features of disjointed incrementalism are (a) acceptance of the broad outlines of the existing situation with only marginal changes contemplated, (b) consideration of a restricted variety of policy alternatives excluding those entailing radical change, (c) consideration of a restricted number of consequences for any given policy, (d) adjustment of objectives to policies as well as policies to objectives, (e) willingness to formulate the problem as data becomes available, and (f) serial analysis and piece-meal alterations rather than a single comprehensive attack. In short, curriculum decision-makers use informal methods of decision-making.

This is no surprise considering the history of the field, the state of the art of formal decision-making methods, the complexity of the school as a phenomenon, and the paucity of reliable data about the events taking place within the classroom and their effects on children. This absence of formal decision-making procedures complicates the task of comprehending the political processes involved in decision-making since informal methods are more complex, diffuse, and irregular. There are indications that modern decision-making tools may eventually be used to decide what to teach, however, and before looking more carefully at the existing decision processes it is interesting to glance at three of the most promising of the developing formal procedures.

The first sort of formal procedure to be employed still does not have a name, although several of the operations that make it up are named. For convenience let us call it behavioral analysis. This method, an educational application of techniques developed in the time-and-motion studies of the early 1900's (see Taylor, 1911; Gilbreth, 1914), begins with the activities students are being trained to engage in. It consists of analyzing these activities into a hierarchy of prerequisite capabilities, i.e., performances such that success at a higher-level performance implies the ability to succeed at all the lower-level performances which together constitute the prerequisites of the higher-level performance. After this "task analysis" has been completed, instructional sequences are designed which lead students step-by-step up the hierarchy to more and more complex performances. For examples of behavioral analysis see Gagné (1965), Lewis and Pask (1965), and Miller (1962).

Like behavioral analysis, which was developed by psychologists engaged in military and industrial training, the next cluster of related techniques have been taken from military and industrial contexts and applied to educational problems. These techniques go under various names, e.g., Program Planning and Budgeting Systems (PPBS), cost-effectiveness analysis, and systems analysis. We need not describe these widely known methods, but their educational applications may not be familiar and therefore merit a few words. The first step in all these methods is to specify either the complete set of achievements desired of students or a representative sub-set of these. Measures are then constructed of these educational outputs. Measures are also taken of the costs of the inputs used in teaching students to succeed in achieving these goals. Then the relative costs and benefits of different educational programs are compared quantitatively. For examples of these methods applied to education see Levin (1970), Ribich (1968), Kaufman (1967), and Joint Economic Committee (1969).

The third method of formal curriculum decision-making might be called empirically-derived computer-based decision-making. It consists of identifying a large number of content units, each containing a large number of specific desired competencies. Students and teachers are asked to complete questionnaires, and these, together with aptitude and achievement information on each student, are stored in a computer. The machine uses this information to make initial content decisions for each student. Achievement test information and student and teacher reactions are fed into the machine and it, in theory, at least, automatically changes its decision-rules to optimize achievement subject to constraints of interest and involvement. No such system is in full operation now, to our knowledge, but simpler versions are (Harnack, 1969), and there is no reason to doubt that fully operational systems will be available presently.

These are tentative first steps toward more formal procedures for designing curricula. Whether further significant steps will follow quickly or at all is a moot question. The methods outlined above are relatively simple applications of simple ideas, almost certain to prove less than fully adequate. Curriculum decision-making presents a severe test for any formal decision-making tool. There is no clear and simple criterion of success such as profit or number of enemy dead. Each of the methods sketched above relies on behavioral objectives as criteria of value. That is, the users of each method assume they have been supplied with a complete list of the "behaviors" desired by the school and that all the school's real objectives can be expressed in the form of these behaviors. This point is vigorously disputed in the professional literature. For examples, see Atkin (1963), Eisner (1967), Eisner (1969), Jackson and Belford (1965), and Moffett (1970). Some individuals and groups strongly oppose even the attempt to define such criteria on the grounds that they would necessarily leave out the more evanescent benefits of education. Indeed, we are hard-pressed to specify the educational benefits of, for example, play for children even though most of us believe that play can and does have educational value.

Even if we could get wide agreement on operational goals, however, the most significant goals are likely to take a long time to achieve and the assessment of the beneficial effects of a complex treatment on a distant objective is a presently insoluble technical problem. An even more elementary problem is to find satisfactory measures of the subtle effects we want, such as the ability to apply what is learned to unfamiliar situations, the ability to learn new things quickly and surely, and the ability to decide what knowledge is appropriate to a given problem. It will be interesting to see how far we are able to get toward a solution of these difficulties in the last third of the twentieth century.

And finally, these formal decision-making procedures leave open the political questions of who will determine the goals and the decision-rules and in whose interest. It seems reasonable to suppose that if the staff of the school—teachers and administrators—make the determinations the results would reflect their value bases. Are their bases substantially different from those of the public at large? Even assuming they are not, is it not possible that they would become different in the future? And is it not virtually certain that the goals and decision-rules adapted will differ markedly from the preferences of some substantial groups or interests in the larger society? How will the conflicts generated in these situations be resolved?

In summary, curriculum decisions are not based on quantitative decision techniques or even on a great deal of objective data. This leaves a great deal of latitude for deliberation and for complicated political processes to resolve conflicts of values among various groups and individuals. As we will see, these value conflicts are resolved through low profile politics, but, even so, there is a considerable amount of overt political interaction.

MAJOR INFLUENCES ON CURRICULUM POLICY

At this point we would like to turn our attention to the structure and process of political influence in the making of local school district curriculum policy. By influence we mean the ability to get others to act, think, or feel as one intends (Banfield, 1961). A school superintendent who persuades his board to install the "new math" is exercising political influence on a curriculum issue. A related concept is what Gergen (Bauer and Gergen, 1968) called points of leverage— individuals or institutions that have the capacity to effect a substantial influence on the curriculum output of a school system. An individual or group that has leverage is one that can make a big difference in the outcome of conflicts over curriculum policy. Our focus here is on the content of curriculum policy rather than the priority curriculum receives in budget allocations, etc. Our perspective is that of the local school system and our focus is on the decisions of what to teach to children.

A mapping of the leverage points for curriculum policy-making in local schools would be exceedingly complex. It would involve three levels of government, and numerous private organizations including foundations, accrediting associations, national testing agencies, textbook-software companies, and interest groups (such as the NAACP or the John Birch Society). Moreover, there would be a configuration of leverage points within a particular local school system including teachers, department heads, the assistant superintendent for instruction, the superintendent, and the school board. Cutting across all levels of government would be the pervasive influence of various celebrities, commentators, interest groups, and the journalists who use the mass media to disseminate their views on curriculum. It would be very useful if we were able to quantify the amount of influence of each of these groups or individuals and show input-output interactions for just one school system. Unfortunately, this is considerably beyond the state of the art, and we must settle for a less precise discussion. (For a critique of such concepts as political influence for constructing empirical political theory see James G. March, "The Power of Power," in Easton (1969).)

We distinguish three ways in which national or regional agencies affect state and local curriculum policy-making: by establishing minimum standards, by generating curricular alternatives, and by demanding curriculum change. We treat these three types of effect on policy-making separately, even though some groups affect policy-making in more than one of these ways.

Groups That Establish Minimum Curriculum Standards

From the vantage point of a local public school system, flexibility in determining curriculum content is constrained greatly by several outside groups. The political culture of this country has emphasized "local control" and played down the role of the national government. The curriculum area has been singled out as one where a uniform national standard and substance should be avoided. Federal aid to education was stalled for years, in large part because of a fear that the federal dollar would lead to a uniform national curriculum (Sundquist, 1969). Visitors from abroad, however, are usually surprised by the coast to coast similarity of the curriculum in American public schools. In effect, we have granted political influence over curriculum to national *nongovernment* agencies that demand a minimum national curriculum standard below which few public schools dare to fall.

A good example of this is the leverage on curriculum that private accrediting associations display. State governments also accredit but it is the private regional accrediting organizations that really concern the local school officials. These accrediting agencies define specific curriculum standards and criteria required for their stamp of approval. The largest of the regionals, the North Central Association, used written reports for their judgments, but others employ site visitors. The accrediting agencies' curriculum standards are highly detailed. For instance, a sample recommendation included in the *Visiting Committee Handbook* of the Western Association of School and Colleges (1965) provides "that written criteria be set up for the evaluation and selection of textbooks [p. 20]," "that continuing study be given to offering four years of language [p. 22]," and "that broader use of the audio-lingual approach be explored [p. 21]."

The political influence of the accrediting agency is based on the faith other people have in the accreditation. Since loss of accreditation is dreaded by every schoolman, these accrediting agencies can bring almost irresistible pressure on the curriculum offerings of a local school. The accrediting agencies often are a force for supporting the traditional curriculum and resisting radical changes (Koerner, 1968). In effect, accrediting agencies make value judgments about what should be taught while their credo stresses professional judgments.

Testing agencies in the United States are also largely in private hands and exert a "standardizing" influence on curriculum. Educational Testing Service, for instance, has an income of about $20,000,000 a year from its tests. Over one million students take the College Boards and seven hundred institutions require it. Consequently, local schools do not have a choice as to whether or not they offer the dozen subjects covered by the achievement exams of the College Boards. These tests do not entirely determine the detailed content of the curriculum but they do limit what teachers can spend their time doing. Moreover, national standardized reading or math tests given in the pre-high school grades may determine a great deal of the specific content of the reading or math curriculum. Local schools want to look good on these nationally normed tests.

While the testing agencies and their panels of expert advisers largely determine the content of the standard tests used in elementary and junior high schools, in high schools the tests tend to be dictated largely by the colleges and universities. The tests follow guidelines presented by colleges as part of their entrance requirements. For those students who take a college-preparatory course, the high school curriculum is determined almost entirely by college entrance requirements. And the prestige accorded to the subjects required for entrance by colleges undoubtedly influences many non-college-bound students (probably via their parents) to take these courses. The tyranny of college entrance requirements over the secondary school curriculum has been a persistent complaint of high schools. In the late thirties the Progressive Education Association sponsored a study, called the Eight Year Study (Aikin, 1942), of the secondary school curriculum in which they asked for and received permission to waive entrance requirements for the students in the experimental schools. Students from these schools were not required to have so many units of English, history, etc. in order to be admitted to college; only a recommendation from their principal was needed. An evaluation of the performance of these students in college showed them to be equal to students in similar schools in every respect and superior in many (Chamberlin, 1942). The design of this study has been criticized (see Travers and Wallen, 1963, pp. 472–493), but no one has attempted to replicate it, and entrance requirements remain.

State Departments of Education and State Boards of Education have also had a traditional role in setting and enforcing minimum curriculum standards. This role has varied enormously depending on whether the political culture of the state supported what Elazar (1965) called a centrist or localist policy. In New England, the local schools enjoy an autonomy from state controls that goes back to the hatred of the English royal governor, while some Southern states often mandate textbooks and courses of instruction. Most states do not mandate the school curriculum to any great extent. A 1966 survey (Conant, 1967) revealed that the great majority of states mandated courses in the dangers of alcohol and narcotics, only half required work in U. S. History and physical education, and less than half (ranging from 46 percent to 2 percent of the states) required instruction in other specific subjects. Although California and Iowa had over 30 curriculum prescriptions, over half the states had fewer than ten. Enforcement of state board curriculum mandates was very spotty, and local districts with strong views were able to circumvent the weak enforcement machinery.

It is often the newer subject areas (vocational education, driver training) that have used state law to gain a secure place in the curriculum. These subjects were introduced into the curriculum after 1920, amid great controversy, whereas mathematics and English never had to use political power to justify their existence in the school curriculum. Consequently, the "standard" subjects are less frequently mandated by state law.

Associations of teachers and special subjects can be very influential at the state level and use their power base for preserving state curriculum requirements. Vocational education, physical education, and home economics teachers use their NEA state affiliate to ensure that their specialities are stressed in the local schools. They are also supported by the manufacturers of sports equipment and home appliances. The driver education teachers are a new state lobby, but so effective that almost all states mandate driver education.

Ironically, teachers of academic subjects are usually poorly organized and not united at the state level. Nobody consults them and their minimal influence is indicated by the national trend to require less professional training for teaching licenses in physics, math, or history than for home economics or industrial arts (Conant, 1967). The impact on curriculum policy of these organizations that set minimum standards that tend to support the status quo was summarized by Koerner:

Suppose a local board, aware of the obsolescence and flaccidity of much that passes for vocational training . . .decides to reduce its program in these areas. In theory this is one of its sovereign rights. In practice several things occur to change its mind. First, the vocational education lobby goes to work on other members of local government and on the state legislature or state department of education to protect the extensive interests of vocational education teachers. Second, the regional accrediting association comes to the aid of the status quo and makes threatening noises, suggesting and then perhaps demanding, on pain of disaccreditation . . .that the board rescind its decision. Third, the NEA state affiliate "investigates" and through its considerable power "persuades" the board to a different view [1968, pp. 126–27].

Alternative Generators

Operating in the political environment of the local school are several organizations and individuals who provide alternatives with respect to curriculum. The range and nature of the curriculum alternatives proposed by these organizations is restricted by the minimum standards and requirements discussed in the prior section.

Most curriculum decisions are made at the local level; outside agencies can only provide alternatives to choose from. School boards, superintendents, directors of curriculum, principals, department chairmen, and teachers must take the final steps in deciding what to teach. As we have seen, state officials and the state legislature usually prescribe certain rather broad limits. The power of local officials to select is also bounded, however, perhaps more severely than by state laws, by the decision-alternatives available to them. If, 10 years ago, a school had wanted to teach a history of America that gave the black man a place in it, the teachers would have had to write the textbook themselves. Some schools attempt such things, but most do not. Teachers do not feel able to do the job, and the board has little money for released time or research assistants. So, until recently, most schools could not opt for an integrated history even if they were so inclined. It is only now becoming possible for schools to teach a reasonably balanced account of the wresting of this continent from its aboriginal inhabitants. Until 1960 it was not possible for a school to teach modern physics unless it was blessed with a truly outstanding teacher.

The bald fact is that most teaching in our schools is and must be from a textbook or other curriculum package. We do not trust teachers to write their own materials, we do not give them the time or money, and we insist on standardization. So long as this is true, the suppliers of teaching materials will have a potentially powerful effect on the curriculum.

Who supplies decision-alternatives to local schools? Until 10 years ago the unequivocal answer to this question would have been "textbook publishers." But a lot has happened in the interim. Textbook publishing has become part of an enlarged education industry which produces all sorts of printed, electronic, and mechanical devices for classroom use. Also, the federal government, private foundations, and various nonprofit organizations of scholars, teachers, and laymen have taken a more active role in producing curriculum materials. Nevertheless, the textbook is undoubtedly still the most widely used piece of educational technology and textbook publishers are still powerful influences on the curriculum. It was estimated in Texas that 75 percent of a child's classroom time and 90 percent of his homework time is spent using textbooks (Governor's Committee on Public Education, 1969). Thus the publisher's control of the content of the textbook is virtual control over the curriculum.

But the power of the textbook publishers is a brittle sort of power that cannot stand up against serious opposition from any large segment of the population. Some publishers still put the unit on evolution in the center of the biology textbook so that the books destined for Southern and Western schools can readily be bound without those pages. Sections on "Negro history" were once added in the same way. Publishers cannot (or will not, which amounts to the same thing) stand against the demands of their customers. Nor can publishers spend millions of dollars developing materials for one course in the way the National Science Foundation has supported projects in the sciences and mathematics. Apparently, in spite of their potential power, publishers have not been able to operate as independent agents. Instead, they reflect the conflicting desires of their customers, i.e., the local schools and in some areas the state authorities. (Black (1967) offered an account of this process, but more careful and systematic studies of the influences (in this context the term is useful and accurate) on textbook content are needed.

Research is also needed on the relative efficacy in determining what is actually taught in classrooms of textbooks and various other factors such as teachers guides, courses of study, and the teachers' own views. Most studies of the curriculum assume that what appears in the textbook or course of study is what is taught. But a few observational studies of science teaching (Gallagher, 1967; Smith, 1969; Kaiser, 1969) seem to show that teachers do not simply reflect the views of the curriculum writers. The teachers in these studies projected a conception of their subject and of teaching that was different in important ways from the conception embedded in the phalanx of curriculum materials they were using. We should exercise extreme caution in interpreting the results of studies of curriculum policy-making which assume that policies formulated outside the classroom make their way undistorted to the pupil. Studies which describe the kinds of change which policies tend to undergo in filtering through the school staff to pupils would be extremely valuable.

Where there is state adoption, the State Department of Education seems to exercise considerable leverage. In Texas the State Commissioner nominates members to serve on the State Textbook Committee and must approve books recommended by the Committee. Texas State Department specialists draw up the detailed criteria for the publishers' bids including the topics to be covered. The selected books are distributed at state expense to every school room, but the same textbook must stay in service for six years. Districts who want to "stay on top of things" must do so at their own expense (Governor's Committee, 1969).

The U.S. Government has become a very powerful influence on the curriculum in the past 10 years. Because of the fragmented federal budgeting of monies for curriculum development it is not possible to determine exactly how much the government, mainly through the National Science Foundation and the Office of Education, has spent on curriculum development over the past 10 years. This figure is very large, however, and dwarfs all previous curriculum development efforts by states, regions, localities, and private enterprise. As an index of the impact of government-sponsored courses, it was estimated that over 50 percent of our schools use the new physics and chemistry programs while 65 percent use the new biology (Koerner, 1968).

Federal agencies have not sponsored the development of controversial curricula. The National Science Foundation, in particular, perceives its role as one of "course improvement," not the creation of new courses (Campbell and Bunnell, 1963). Therefore, almost all of the money allocated to curriculum development by the federal government has gone to up-date and improve the existing curriculum. Thus we have new math, new physics, new biology, new social studies, and new English, but not psychology, sociology, economics, philosophy, problems of modern living, interpersonal relationships, sex education, or film-making and -viewing. But federal agencies have decided which proposed "improvements" to finance and they have exerted certain pressures on the staffs of projects they finance, including pressure to state objectives and to conduct evaluations using these objectives. See Grobman (1969) and Marsh (1963) for accounts of the interactions between project staffs and federal agencies. Will these federal agencies continue this pattern, will they expand their efforts to genuinely new courses, or alternatively, will they cut back on their funds for curriculum development in disillusionment over the failure of test results to show definite superiority of the new curricula?

No one can foresee the path federal curriculum policy will take in even the next few years. Agencies of the federal government jumped from virtually no influence to a place of preeminence at one stroke when the National Defense Education Act was signed into law. President Nixon proposed the creation of a National Institute of Education. He also inaugurated a "right to read" campaign to encourage emphasis on reading in elementary and junior high schools. "Sesame Street," a nationally televised preschool program, has been produced under the auspices of the U. S. Office of Education. Until now, the federal government's influence has been a conservative one, educationally speaking; but the government's role has been an important one, and when the right circumstances arise we have every reason to believe that federal agencies will seize the initiative in curriculum matters.

Another set of powerful agents in curriculum-making are the foundations. Over the past 10 years they have generally seen their role as one of supplementing and balancing the efforts of the federal government. When the federal government was financing only projects in mathematics, science and foreign languages, the foundations were financing projects in the arts and social sciences. The foundations have also been bolder in funding efforts in non-standard courses including psychology, economics, and photography, among many others. All that is known of the policies of the foundations that have supported curriculum development over the past decade—chiefly the Ford, Rockefeller, Carnegie and Kettering foundations—are their declarations. We have not been able to locate a single study or evaluation of the foundations' effects on curriculum. We can understand the difficulty of studying this problem, but in view of its importance one might expect at least a case study. The foundations, like the federal government, are relatively new to curriculum development, and also must rely on local or state education authorities to accept the new materials or on interest groups to present political demands for change to such authorities.

Although the two major sources of funds for curriculum planning in this country are relatively new and therefore not fully dependable, there are steadier, if less copious, sources. Professional associations of scientists, engineers, and business and professional men have supported curriculum development efforts related to their professional interests. They will no doubt continue to do so as long as they can be convinced of the need for new curricula in their special field. Local school districts provide a modest amount of money for updating their schools' curriculum. We have no dependable estimates of the amount of money spent by individual school districts on curriculum but the figure must surely be quite small for individual districts. Occasionally regional or statewide curriculum development projects have been funded well enough and long enough to permit thorough substantial efforts. The state of New York through its Board of Regents has been outstanding in this respect. And, of course, private businesses (chiefly textbook publishers in the past, but increasingly amalgams of publishing and electronic firms) spend nobody knows how much for curriculum development. Curriculum development will likely be forced to rely chiefly on these traditional sources of money in the next decade, since the pressing problems of foreign involvement and noneducational domestic issues such as race relations, the environment, and poverty will leave at best a moderate priority for educational concerns unrelated to such issues.

But sources of money are not the only factors influencing the alternatives placed before the local decision-maker. Sources of ideas and expertise are also crucial. The major source of ideas for curriculum change has always been the college or university. The last 20 years have seen an intensified reliance on college and university professors in the form of national curriculum commissions and university-based projects. In most cases the participation of professors has been as subject-matter experts, e.g., scientists, mathematicians, or historians. But a few psychologists have been employed to advise projects on methods. Education faculty have not been heavily involved in projects.

University professors do not, of course, constitute anything like a unitary block of opinion on curriculum questions. In fact, they have been a major source of much-needed diversity in the once seemingly stagnant curriculum of the American school. Nevertheless, university professors tend to regard education as an entirely intellectual affair, whereas long tradition in this country and, indeed, the Western world, emphasizes moral, physical, and aesthetic concerns. Many of the scholars who became involved in the public school curriculum through the federal-government-supported national curriculum projects shared MIT physicist Jerrold Zacharias' view that "our real problem as a nation was creeping anti-intellectualism from which came many of our educational deficiencies [Koerner, 1968, p. 62]." This value orientation differs significantly from that of the general public which, if it chose, could reassert the claims of less intellectual matters for attention in the curriculum.

If university faculty do not represent any organized body of opinion, their professional associations sometimes do, and when they do they can be extremely influential. The role of the American Association for the Advancement of Science and the American Institute for Biological Sciences in getting evolution into biology books over the strong objections of fundamentalist Christians (Grobman, 1969; Black, 1967), shows that these associations can be influential when they are united and determined. The American Mathematical Society sponsored the School Mathematics Study Group (SMSG) until the Sputnik-induced National Defense Education Act authorized the National Science Foundation to finance SMSG as an independent enterprise. As Turner (1964) described its activities, the American Council of Learned Societies was extremely influential in recent revisions of social studies curricula. This organization urged its constituent societies to see what they could do about revising the curriculum in their disciplines; it commissioned nine scholars in various social sciences to investigate the relations between the social sciences and the social studies (National Council for the Social Studies, 1962); it conducted a survey to determine what the constituent societies were doing about curriculum questions; it sponsored a conference of scholars and educators to formulate a K-12 design in the humanities and social sciences; and, finally, it commissioned a study of the present state of the social studies curriculum. How effective were these actions? We cannot say without further research.

In addition to universities and professional associations, private firms harbor vital curriculum expertise. Publishers use their sales organizations to ferret out the likes and dislikes of the schoolmen who buy their books and they "edit" the books with one eye on this information (Black, 1967). Strangely enough this network of salesmen is the only reasonably dependable comprehensive mechanism for compiling the preferences and prejudices of local schools on curriculum matters. This part of the curriculum policy-making process badly needs careful study.

Twenty years ago the contribution of private firms to curriculum decisions was restricted to textbooks. But not anymore. IBM has bought SRA, Xerox has bought American Educational Publications, GE and Time have formed General Learning, RCA has bought Random House, and CBS has bought, Holt, Rinehart and Winston. These firms can produce curriculum alternatives in the form of text materials, programmed sequences, films, software and hardware for use in computer-assisted instruction, and similar devices which have potentially powerful effects on the school curriculum, and which few other agencies have the resources or expertise to produce. The new notions of performance contracts and vouchers are supported by both federal agencies and private firms, but the corporations will formulate the specific curriculum packages and contract with local districts who have federal money.

Finally, we cannot conclude this discussion of groups that generate curricular alternatives without considering professional educators themselves. Teachers, former teachers, supervisors, and administrators write textbooks and devise curriculum materials. Their ideas, published in professional journals and school district publications, constitute a constantly renewing pool of alternatives from which they and their colleagues can draw in making curriculum decisions. Frequently, however, teachers' contributions are specific practices rather than general principles. But teachers often produce the teachers' guides and courses of study that embody the details of district curriculum policy. Furthermore, teachers served on the staffs of the major curriculum development projects which have powerfully affected the public school curriculum in recent years. The published accounts of these projects (Marsh, 1963; Merrill and Ridgway, 1969; Wooten, 1965; Grobman, 1969) raise some doubts about the importance of teachers in the decision-making that took place in these projects. For the most part it seems that teachers were assigned the role of commenting on the "teachability" of the ideas generated by university scholars. It is a measure of the depth of our ignorance that we cannot cite any reasonably hard evidence pertaining to the kind and degree of power teachers have in curriculum policy-making at any level.

Groups Demanding Curriculum Change

Most of the groups generating curricular alternatives are also important sources of demands for curriculum change. Foundations are concerned mainly with inducing certain kinds of changes in schools. They supply money to finance individuals willing to generate alternatives that show promise of encouraging these changes. The U. S. Office of Education has in recent years taken a more active stance in dispensing funds for research, development, demonstration, and dissemination. They stated that "the goal of these efforts is to generate alternatives to current educational practices that schools may adopt in whole or part as they see fit [United States Office of Education, 1969, p. i]." But they seem more and more to see their role as one of producing change, rather than simply making change possible. Some organizations demand curriculum changes but do not concern themselves with creating additional options. Rather, such groups support one of a number of existing competing alternatives. An example of this sort of organization is the Council for Basic Education (CBE). The CBE has lobbied consistently for greater emphasis on the fundamental intellectual disciplines.

CBE's credo is the following:

That school administrators are encouraged and supported in resisting pressures to divert school time to activities of minor educational significance, to curricula overemphasizing social adjustment at the expense of intellectual discipline, and to programs that call upon the school to assume responsibilities properly belonging to the home, to the religious bodies, and to other agencies. (Descriptive Leaflet, "Council for Basic Education," p. 4.)

CBE attempts to influence curriculum policy-makers through publications, conferences, and other uses of the media. It does not produce curriculum materials but it lobbies for existing materials consistent with its views. The organization does not have local chapters. It is an example of an interest group operating entirely through journalism and popular writing to influence board members, PTA's, and voters to demand curriculum change in their locality.

Most large national organizations, e.g., the Chamber of Commerce, the National Association of Manufacturers, the John Birch Society, and the AFL-CIO, have attempted at one time or another to influence curriculum policy on particular nationwide issues. In fact, such a variety of powerful national interest groups can enter the arena on any given disputed question that it is probably desirable to think of two separate policy-making processes—normal policy-making and crisis policy-making. These not specifically educational interest groups would probably be relatively weak forces in normal policy-making, but extremely powerful in crisis policy-making. The relevant literature on crisis policy-making is much too large to review here. It includes many, if not most, of the references cited already. Crises occur at such short intervals in the history of American education—immigration, the great Red scare, war depression, war again, Sputnik, racial violence, war again—that crisis policy-making is normal and normal policy-making exceptional. What seems to be needed in this area is theory which would distill some useful generalizations from the details presented in the numerous case studies and historical and journalistic accounts.

In summary, when a school district faces the problem of putting together a course they have only three basic choices. The whole problem can be left to individual teachers; groups of teachers can make the plans and devise teaching materials for the whole school; or materials can be purchased. American public schools increasingly favor the last approach. Therefore the sources of these materials are, and will probably remain, important determinants of the curriculum. The sources we have identified are the projects financed by the federal government and private foundations, college and university faculties, professional associations, private business, and organizations of laymen. But the fact of the matter is that any group with sufficient talent and resources can prepare curriculum materials and possibly start a trend that will sweep these other sources either aside or along.

THE LOCAL COMMUNITY AND CURRICULUM POLICY

Pellegrin surveyed the whole field of innovation in education and concluded:

The greatest stimuli to changes in education originate in sources external to the field. What I have shown is that the sources of innovation lie largely outside the local community, and in most instances outside the education profession [Pellegrin, 1966, p. 15].

This statement would appear to apply to curriculum and to refer to the organizations and individuals (discussed in the previous sections) which provide most of the ideas, alternatives, and value orientations adopted by school officials. Today we see a good example of this in the teamwork of corporations and the federal government to implement performance contracts. The role of the local lay community in curriculum change, however, appears minimal. In the local community, it is primarily actors within the school system that decide whether a break is to be made with the traditional curriculum. The mayor and city council have no influence.

The minimal political leverage of the community was demonstrated by a nationwide Gallup poll (Gallup, 1969) which showed that the public knew almost nothing about the substance of education and was not involved with broad curriculum issues. Gallup reported that most of the information that the public received about schools concerned "happenings"—the hard news—reported in the newspapers or other media. Gallup concluded, "knowledge about education is very limited, at least the kind of knowledge that has to do with curriculum and goals of education." When asked to tell on what they would judge a good school, the public replied, first, qualified teachers (vaguely defined by most respondents), second, discipline, and third, physical equipment. Discipline was considered the "biggest" problem of the public schools (26 percent) while only 4 percent saw curriculum as the biggest problem. Gallup observed that this lack of information did not stem from a lack of public interest:

When asked specifically what kind of information they [the public] would like to have, the answers deal to a large extent with the courses taught—the curriculum—innovations being introduced and why—college-requirements—and the like. Significantly there is great interest in the very areas that most school publicity presently neglects—the content of courses and the educational process versus school operations [Gallup, 1969, p. 9].

This limited public role undoubtedly stems in large part from the point made at the outset of this paper, i.e., curriculum is considered an issue to be properly settled by professional educators trained in these matters. Of course, the community does get involved in curriculum issues on occasion. Martin (1962) surveyed a large sample of suburban citizens, mayors, presidents of Leagues of Women Voters, and officials of local Chambers of Commerce and concluded:

These areas (curriculum, textbooks, subversive activities, personalities, athletics, race relations) provide a reservoir for what we have called episodic issues—issues which emerge under usual or special conditions and shortly subside. Thus, it is not textbooks which cause concern, but a particular textbook under a special set of circumstances [Martin, 1961, p. 55].

Martin and other writers conclude that community influence seemed most often to be a negative action such as the defeat of a bond issue, tax increase, school board member, or the termination of controversial curriculum offerings like sex education. On the other hand, Gittell et al. (1967) in a study of six cities concluded:

innovation can only be achieved as a result of strong community participation with power to compel both new programs and expenditure increases necessary to finance them. The brief experience in Philadelphia under Dilworth suggests that substantial community involvement provides both the pressure for change and a community atmosphere favorable for obtaining the necessary financing [Gittell, 1967, p. 212].

Gittell et al. were referring to innovations of all types and it is not clear to what extent their findings are relevant to curriculum. All the studies demonstrate, however, that the historic separation between education and general government has left minimal influence to the mayor and the city council in curriculum (Salisbury, 1967; Gittell et al., 1967; Martin, 1962; Rosenthal, 1969; Saxe, 1969). Saxe (1969) in his survey of 50 mayors noted a traditional "separation of functions" between schoolmen and city officials epitomized in one mayor's comment that "I do not intend, however, to become involved in school issues such as curricula, busing of students, and matters of that type, since this is clearly the responsibility of another agency [p. 249]''; however, Saxe noted that ''a majority of the mayors cooperating in this survey (20 out of 32. . .). . . [were] reconsider[ing] their 'hands off' attitude [p. 250].''

At the local level, then, curriculum decisions have been very much an internal issue to be decided by school professionals. Indeed we have some evidence that decisions on curriculum in middle-sized and large systems are often made within the school bureaucracy beneath the superintendent. The formal institutional description of powers and prerogatives would lead one to believe that the school board plays a more decisive role in curriculum policy-making than it seems to play. Indeed, research has shattered the myth of lay control of schools, at least in the area of curriculum.

The School Board

The limited influence of the school board deserves further examination. Curriculum decisions require an analysis of the philosophy and substance of education. Lay school boards usually have no expert or even part-time staff independent of the school bureaucracy. Board members are also part-time officials who meet at night once or twice a week after a full day in a responsible position. These busy laymen are usually not presented with performance criteria or test data upon which to question the curriculum judgments of the superintendent and his staff. Curriculum proposals are rarely related to measurable objectives nor do they undergo systematic analysis, as we saw in the first section. The use of disjointed incrementalism for curriculum decisions does not assist a lay board in playing a crucial decision-making role.

The method of school board elections also limits the board's perspective on curriculum matters. The Gallup poll indicates that curriculum issues are usually not presented to the voters as election mandates. Moreover, as Salisbury (1967) pointed out, traditionally the board has the same viewpoint as the superintendent as far as representation of wards or ethnic groups is concerned: ''regardless of ethnic, racial, religious, economic, or political differences in other areas of urban life, education should not legitimize those differences. Education is a process that must not be differentiated according to section or class, and the city is a *unity* for purposes of the school program [Salisbury, 1967, pp. 408–424].'' Consequently, school boards and superintendents have historically resisted a differentiated curriculum for Italians, Irish, blacks, chicanos and other ethnic, racial, or religious groups.

The Superintendent

To date, very few studies have differentiated political influence and leverage within the school bureaucracy. There has been a tendency to treat the superintendent and his bureaucracy as one actor and to compare their role to that of school boards, city officials, community interest groups, etc. Those studies of large school systems that examined the bureaucracy found that it wields substantial influence.

Superintendents have guarded curriculum decisions as an area of their professional competence, and have been viewed by many researchers as the key figures in the innovation process (see Carlson, 1965; Mackenzie, 1964). As Martin (1962) concluded:

> he (the superintendent) is as much a policy maker as he is a manager in the narrow sense; for he enjoys an expertise, a professional reputation, and a community position which combine to give him an almost irresistible voice in school affairs [p. 61].

In his study of Allegheny County, Pennsylvania and the state of West Virginia, Carlson (1965) found that superintendents were the "agricultural extension agent" as well as the "experimental station" for the new math. The superintendents who adopted new curricula interacted frequently with a peer group of other superintendents who were also innovators. In short, a group of professional friends spread the new math to each of the members of the group. There were certain key superintendents in these counties who were viewed by other superintendents as good advisors and opinion leaders on curriculum. In West Virginia, however, the State Department's advice was often sought. Looking at Carlson's data from another vantage point, superintendents who did *not* adopt curriculum reform programs (a) has less formal education, (b) received fewer friendship choices among local superintendents, (c) knew well fewer of their peers, (d) participated in fewer professional meetings, (e) held less prestigious superintendencies, (f) perceived less support from their school boards, and (g) relied more on local sources for advice and information [Carlson, 1965, p. 64]. It is worth noting that the innovations Carlson explored were developed by the federal government and foundations. In effect, the superintendent mediates between outside demands for change and the local population.

Since Carlson's study, a new group of federally supported regional educational laboratories have sprung up and very little is yet known about their role. But a recent study in the San Francisco Bay area (Hamrin, 1970) found that ideas for curriculum change were derived generally from the literature and from awareness of changes occurring in other schools.

The School Bureaucracy

While a superintendent can, if he chooses, block most internal demands for changes in official district-wide curriculum policy (other than "episodic issues" like sex education), it is not clear, especially in large cities, whether he is closely involved in many important curriculum decisions. The key bureaucratic officers appear to be Assistant Superintendents for Instruction and Department Chairmen (Hamrin, 1970; Carlson, 1965) who work in committees with groups of teachers.

These committees of curriculum administrators and teachers employ a decision procedure of disjointed incrementalism and mutual adjustment. In effect, many curriculum policies are made on a piece-meal basis—academic department by department—and they may not be reviewed or changed for many years through any formal decision by the superintendent or anyone else. We know very little about this bureaucratic bargaining and conflict.

We are more certain that the influence of the principal seems small because, as Pellegrin (1966) noted, "he is burdened with such a multitude of managerial activities that it is extremely difficult for him to devote the time and effort required for innovation on a substantial scale (p. 9)." In effect, the principal is too bogged down in day-to-day management to be more than a middle man between the teacher and the central office for the implementation of curriculum. This is despite the stress the formal job description of the principal puts on curriculum leadership.

Teachers

It may seem somewhat odd to leave detailed consideration of the teacher until so near the end of a paper on curriculum policy-making, but we have been concerned with curriculum policy that affects several teachers (e.g., the entire English department). Teachers have autonomy with regard to the mode of presentation of material within their own classroom. The teacher regulates her own schedule and methods of instruction. But studies dealing with curriculum innovation at the classroom level find "teachers seldom suggest distinctly new types of working patterns for themselves [Brickell, 1964, p. 528]." Another study put it this way:

It is a unique school indeed in which teachers discuss their classroom problems, techniques, and progress with one another and with their principal. In most sci·ools teachers practice their own methods—rarely hearing, or even caring, if one of their colleagues is experimenting with some new teaching device or technique [Chesler et al., 1963, p. 76].

Teachers are increasing their control of salary, promotions, and working conditions through collective bargaining. But surveys reveal that the political energies of teachers at this time are focused on "bread and butter" issues, such as pay, class size, and relief from noninstructional duties. To date, their influence or bargaining rarely extends to curriculum. James (1966) found that demands from teacher organizations in 14 cities related to staff benefits and not to curriculum. It is quite possible, however, that curriculum will become a concern of future teacher negotiations. Curriculum issues are beginning to appear among the contract demands of teacher organizations but as yet these have not been central issues, issues over which a strike might occur. Perhaps as differentiated staffing arrangements bring teachers together over curriculum concerns, curriculum issues will receive more attention from teacher organizations. The accountability movement may result in curriculum performance standards in teacher contracts.

Students

Students have no influence in any formal sense over what they learn. This is so obvious a fact that research to establish it would be superfluous. Of course, decision-makers sometimes take students' views into account, but not usually. Even surveys to assess student opinion are rare. But students, to the distress of parents and school officials, vote with their feet on major curriculum questions. Enrollments in high school physics are declining even faster since the new physics began to be taught. It is only speculation, but perhaps the increased interest among students in "free schools" is a reaction to a curriculum over which they have little control and which they see as overly rigid and intellectualized. This is a matter that needs further study.

What we have described as the actors and organizations that influence curriculum policy-making are presented in Table 1.

TABLE 1
Influences on Curriculum Policy-Making

	National	State	Local
General legislative	Congress	State legislature	(City Councils have no influence)
Educational legislative	House Committee on Education and Labor	State school board	Local school board
Executive	President	Governor	(Mayor has no influence)
Administrative	HEW-USOE	State Department	School superintendent
Bureaucratic	OE (Bureau of Research), National Science Foundation (Division of Curriculum Improvement	State Department (Division of Vocational Education)	Department chairmen, Teachers
Professional association	National testing agencies	Accrediting associations, NEA State Subject Matter Affiliates	County Association of Superintendents
Other private interests	Foundations and business corporations	Council for Basic Education	John Birch Society NAACP

DISTINCTIVE FEATURES OF CURRICULUM POLICY-MAKING

It might be useful as a summarizing device to compare curriculum policy-making with other types of policy-making. For several reasons economic policy provides a fairly close analogy to educational policy. In our economic system everyone's decisions to buy and sell ultimately shape the economy. In our educational system the decisions of thousands of local boards shape educational policy. Economic questions are usually considered too complex to permit direct voting. For this reason some economic decision-makers are insulated from the electorate and those who are not insulated usually confine their economic campaign positions to being against inflation and recession, although they will take stands on particular "hot" issues such as the oil-depletion allowance or wage-price controls. Similarly, although to a lesser degree, parents are not expected to understand or to vote on the new math or the new social studies. Nor do candidates for election to local school boards normally take campaign stands on curriculum issues, except on particular "hot" issues such as sensitivity training and sex education.

But the analogy between economic policy and curriculum policy cannot be carried very far. Curriculum policy is primarily and traditionally the concern of the states and localities, even though the federal government's role is rapidly expanding. And when curriculum policy is determined it is still a long way from being implemented. Supposing that a policy decision survives emasculation by the administrative hierarchies of federal agencies and state and local officials, it still faces a pocket-veto by 2,000,000 classroom teachers. So long as teachers consider themselves professional agents with some autonomy in curriculum questions by virtue of their professional expertise, policy implementation will be a matter of persuasion rather than direction. Of course it is possible that teachers will be replaced by mechanical and electronic devices. Or they may be so cowed as to make them dependable implementers of administrative policy. But the increasing unionization of teachers indicates that they will at least have a say in the determination of the policies they are asked to carry out.

Not only classroom teachers stand between policy-makers and their goals, however. Numerous other agencies such as the College Entrance Examination Board, the national accreditation committees, scholarly, scientific, and professional organizations, as well as specifically educational pressure groups, vie for a voice in curriculum policy-making. It seems highly unlikely that any one agency, even the federal government, could wrest policy-making autonomy from so many hands. But the example of Sputnik has shown that if national emergency is frightening enough, centuries-old traditions can be swept aside in one session of the Congress; the possibility of national educational planning for the U.S. should not be ruled out.

Even assuming that curriculum policy could be successfully formulated and consistently carried out, several barriers to the attainment of policy objectives remain that are inherent in the educational enterprise. One of these is the necessarily long-range nature of educational goals. A significant and stable change in the reading level of junior high school cannot be obtained in less than a year and will probably take three or four years to appear, assuming we know how to get it. Learning anything important takes time and therefore results are delayed. When results appear it is difficult to counter the argument that other forces than the policy change account for the results. For example, Tuddenham (1948) found evidence of a striking increase (a full standard deviation) in the mean absolute score of the Army Alpha intelligence test between World Wars I and II. Schaie and Strother (1969) reported a similar finding in a study comparing the differences in the tested mental ability among cohorts (generations) with the changes in score due to aging. He concluded that "a major proportion of the variance attributed to age difference (i.e., to aging) [on tests of basic mental abilities] must properly be assigned to differences in abilities between successive generations [p. 679]." Both investigators speculated that improved education of later generations was largely responsible for the apparent increase of scores on tests of mental ability. No propensity to assign this effect to the efforts of the public schools has yet appeared in or out of educational circles, but might they not be responsible? But then the result could be due to TV or to the training programs of industry or to the armed forces efforts. The question seems academic in any event. How could one determine the extent to which this increase in scores was due to the continually shifting practices of public schools over a quarter century?

Another difficulty of making, executing, and evaluating curriculum policy is the necessary ambiguity and generality of educational goals. Some educational goals are unnecessarily ambiguous. Such blatant examples as "appreciation" and "understanding" are notorious among students of education. But when these gratuitous sources of ambiguity have been eliminated, considerable additional ambiguity remains. This is necessarily so for at least two reasons. First, because of the necessarily long interval between teaching and the adult use of the thing taught, together with the rapid rate of change in society generally, we must prepare students for a world whose outlines can be seen dimly at best. The age group with the largest responsibility for running the world today is, let us say, about 50 years old. They began school in 1926 and graduated from high school in 1938. Could we reasonably expect the educational planners of that period to have anticipated the specific knowledge, skills, and attitudes that would have begun to prepare these people for their lives today—for urban decay, television, atomic power, cold war, guerilla war, computers, pollution, future shock, and the knowledge explosion? If we make curriculum policy we must either make it concretely and in detail, with virtual certainty that much of the plans will be rendered useless by unexpected change, or make it somewhat general and loose in the expectation that in this way our students will be prepared for a greater variety of possible futures. It is somewhat like the difference between training an athlete for the decathlon and training him for a single event. If you don't know what events will appear in the games you can either train for one event and hope it appears or train for the decathlon and hope your athletes can bone up on their best event when they find out which events are scheduled.

A second barrier to precise, detailed curriculum policy-making is our meager knowledge of the phenomena of schooling. An elaborate argument to substantiate our ignorance is out of place here. Suffice it to say that trying to construct a complete school curriculum according to the currently accepted principles of behavioral science would appear to be roughly equivalent to trying to create a living plant with the principles of the 17th century alchemy.

In spite of the difficulties of systematic curriculum policy-making, efforts in this direction are virtually certain to increase. The steadily increasing role of federal and state governments, the increasing willingness of elected officials to speak out on educational questions, the increasing willingness of mass media to publish achievement test scores of local schools, National Assessment (which will provide detailed information on the educational attainment of American youth), and demands for community control are portents of an increasingly political approach to curriculum questions on the part of the general public. As one observer noted: "It seems to me that, at least in the giant cities, it is academic to debate closer educational-political cooperation. Whether we like it or not, the events of the day will not permit a fragmented approach to education in the city (Saxe, 1969, p. 251)." This development, whether one anticipates it with eagerness or dread, merits careful attention from educational scholars and researchers.

REFERENCES

Aikin, W. *The Story of the Eight-Year Study* (New York: Harper, 1942).

Atkin, J. "Some Evaluation Problems in a Course Treatment Project." *Journal of Research in Science Teaching* 1 (1963): 1.

Banfield, E. *Political Influence* (New York: Free Press, 1961).

Bauer, R., and Gergen, K. *The Study of Policy Formation* (New York: Free Press, 1968).

Bereiter, C., and Engelmann, S. *Teaching Disadvantaged Children in the Preschool* (Englewood Cliffs, N. J.: Prentice Hall, 1966).

Black, H. *The American Schoolbook* (New York: Morrow, 1967).

Brickell, H. M. "State Organization for Educational Change." In M. Miles (ed.), *Innovation in Education* (New York: Teachers College Press, 1964).

Campbell, F., and Bunnell, R. A. *Nationalizing Influences on Secondary Education* (Chicago: Midwest Administration Center, 1963).

Carlson, R. O. *Adoption of Educational Innovations* (Eugene: University of Oregon, 1965).

Chamberlin, C. D. *Did They Succeed in College?* (New York: Harper, ·1942).

Chesler, M., *et al.* "The Principal's Role in Facilitating Innovation." *Theory Into Practice* 1 (1963):2.

Conant, J. B. *The Comprehensive High School: A Second Report to Interested Citizens* (New York: McGraw-Hill, 1967).

Counts, G. *School and Society in Chicago* (New York: Harcourt, Brace, 1928).

Easton, D. (ed.) *Varieties of Political Theory* (Englewood Cliffs, N.J.: Prentice-Hall, 1969).

Eisner, E. W. "Educational Objectives: Help or Hindrance?" *School Review* 73 (1967):3.

————. "Instructional and Expressive Educational Objectives: Their Formulation and Use in Curriculum." In American Educational Research Association, *Instructional Objectives* (Chicago: Rand McNally, 1969).

Elazar, D. *American Federalism* (New York: Crowell, 1965).

Gagné, R. M. "The Analysis of Instructional Objectives for the Design of Instruction." In R. Glaser (ed.), *Teaching Machines and Programmed Learning. II: Data and Directions* (Washington: National Education Association, 1965).

Gallagher, J. J. "Teacher Variation in Concept Presentation in BSCS Curriculum Program." *BSCS Newsletter* (No. 30, 1967).

Gallup, G. *How the Nation Views the Public Schools* (Princeton, N.J.: Gallup International, 1969).

Gilbreth, F. B. *Primer of Scientific Management* (New York: D. Van Nostrand, 1914).

Gittell, M., *et al.* "Investigation of Fiscally Independent and Dependent School Districts." Cooperative Research Project No. 3237 (Washington, D.C.: Office of Education, 1967).

Governor's Committee on Public Education. *Public Education in Texas* (Austin: Texas Education Agency, 1969).

Grobman, A. *The Changing Classroom.* BSCS Bulletin No. 4 (Garden City, N.J.: Doubleday, 1969).

Gwynn, O. M. *Curriculum Principles and Social Trends.* 3rd ed. (New York: Macmillan, 1960).

Hamrin, G. "An Analysis of Factors Influencing Educational Change." Ph.D. dissertation, Stanford University, 1970.

Harnack, R. S., *et al. Computer-based Resource Units in School Situations* (Buffalo: State University of New York, 1969).

Henderson, A. D. "Innovations in Medical Education." *Journal of Higher Education* 40 (1969):7.

Jackson, P., and Belford, E. "Educational Objectives and the Joys of Teaching." *School Review* 73 (1965):3.

James, H. T., *et al. Determinants of Educational Expenditures in Large Cities in the United States* (Stanford, California: School of Education, 1966).

Joint Economic Committee. "The Analysis and Evaluation of Public Expenditures: The PPB System," 91st Congress of the United States, 1969.

Kaiser, B. "Development of a Teacher Observation Instrument Consistent With the Chemical Education Material Study." Ph.D. dissertation, Stanford University, 1969.

Kaufman, J. "An Analysis of the Comparative Costs and Benefits of Vocational versus Academic Education in Secondary School." Contract OEG-1-6-00512-0817, U.S. Office of Education, 1967.

Koerner, J. *Who Controls American Education?* (Boston: Beacon Press, 1968).

Krug, E. *The Shaping of the American High School* (New York: Harper and Row, 1964).

Lerner, D., and Lasswell, H. D. (eds.) *The Policy Sciences: Recent Developments in Scope and Method* (Stanford: Stanford University Press, 1951).

Levin, H. M. "A Cost Effectiveness Analysis of Teacher Selection." *Journal of Human Resources* 5 (1970):1.

Lewis, B. N., and Pask, G. "The Theory and Practice of Adaptive Teaching Systems." In R. Glaser (ed.), *Teaching Machines and Programmed Learning. II: Data and Directions* (Washington, D.C.: National Education Association, 1965).

Lindblom, C., and Braybrooke, D. *A Strategy of Decision* (New York: Free Press, 1963).

Lippman, W. *American Inquisitors* (New York: Macmillan, 1928).

Mackenzie, G. N. "Curricular Change: Participants, Power, and Process." In M. Miles (ed.), *Innovation in Education* (New York: Teachers College Press, 1964).

Marsh, P. "The Physical Science Study Committee: A Case History of Nationwide Curriculum Development." Ph.D. dissertation, Harvard University, Graduate School of Education, 1963.

Martin, R. *Government and the Suburban School* (Syracuse, N.Y.: Syracuse University Press, 1962).

Merrill, R. J., and Ridgway, D. W. *The CHEM Study Story: A Successful Curriculum Improvement Project* (San Francisco: W. H. Freeman, 1969).

Miller, R. B. "Analysis and Specification of Behavior for Training." In R. Glaser (ed.), *Training Research and Education* (Pittsburgh, Penn.: University of Pittsburgh Press, 1962).

Moffett, J. "Misbehaviorist English: A Position Paper." In J. Maxwell and A. Tovatt (eds.), *On Writing Behavioral Objectives for English* (Champaign, Ill.: National Council of Teachers of English, 1970).

National Council for the Social Studies. *The Social Studies and the Social Sciences* (New York: Harcourt, Brace, and World, 1962).

Nelson, J., and Roberts, G. *The Censors and the Schools* (Boston: Little, Brown, 1963).

Pellegrin, R. J. *An Analysis of Sources and Processes of Innovation in Education* (Eugene, Ore.: Center for the Advanced Study of Educational Administration, 1966).

Pilder, W. "The Concept of Utility in Curriculum Discourse: 1918–1967." Ph.D. dissertation, Ohio State University, 1968.

Pine, W. "Where Education Begins." *American Education* 4 (1968):14.

Ribich, T. I. *Education and Poverty* (Washington, D.C.: Brookings Institution, 1968).

Rosenthal, A. *Pedagogues and Power* (Syracuse, N.Y.: Syracuse University Press, 1969).

Salisbury, R. H. "Schools and Politics in the Big City." *Harvard Educational Review* 37 (1967):3.

Saxe, R. W. "Mayors and Schools." *Urban Education* 4 (1969):3.

Saylor, J. G., and Alexander, W. M. *Curriculum Planning for Modern Schools* (New York: Holt, Rinehart and Winston, 1966).

Schaie, K. W., and Strother, C. R. "A Cross-Sequential Study of Age Changes in Cognitive Behavior." *Psychological Bulletin* 70 (1969):6.

Smith, B. O., Stanley, W. O., and Shores, J. H. *Fundamentals of Curriculum Development* (New York: World Book, 1950).

Smith, J. "The Development of a Classroom Observation Instrument Relevant to the Earth Science Curriculum Project." Ph.D. dissertation, Stanford University, 1969.

Spencer, H. *Education: Intellectual, Moral, and Physical* (New York: D. Appleton, 1860).

Stretch, B. B. "The Rise of the 'Free School.' " *Saturday Review,* June 20, 1970.

Sundquist, J. *Politics and Power* (Washington, D.C.: Brookings Institution, 1969).

Taba, H. *Curriculum Development: Theory and Practice* (New York: Harcourt, Brace and World, 1962).

Taylor, F. W. *Principles of Scientific Management* (New York: Harper, 1911).

Travers, R. M. W., and Wallen, N. E. "Analysis and Investigation of Teaching Meods," In N. L. Gage, *Handbook of Research on Teachings* (Chicago: Rand McNally, 1963).

Tuddenham, R. D. "Soldier Intelligence in World Wars I and II." *American Psychologist* 3 (1948):2.

Turner, G. B. "The American Council of Learned Societies and Curriculum Revision." In R. W. Heath (ed.), *New Curricula* (New York: Harper and Row, 1964).

Tyler, R. *Basic Principles of Curriculum and Instruction* (Chicago: The University of Chicago Press, 1949).

United States Office of Education, Bureau of Research. "Support for Research and Related Activities." April 1969.

Werle, H. D. "Lay Participation in Curriculum Improvement Programs." *Dissertation Abstracts* 25 (1964):5081.

Western Association of Schools and Colleges. *Visiting Committee Handbook,* Upland, California, 1965.

Wooten, W. *SMSG: The Making of a Curriculum* (New Haven, Conn.: Yale University Press, 1965).

32. PROGRAMMATIC AND BEHAVIORAL REGULARITIES

Seymour B. Sarason

The attempt to introduce a change into the school setting makes at least two assumptions: the change is desirable according to some set of values, and the intended outcomes are clear. In this chapter we shall be concerned with the clarity of the intended outcomes.

The new math illustrates the problem of intended outcomes clearly. Was one of its intended outcomes to demonstrate that children could learn the new math to certain criterion levels? Was another outcome to show that children would enjoy the new math more than children enjoyed learning the old math? Was it an intended outcome that exposure to the new math would have some demonstrable effect on how children thought about other subject matter in school? Was it an intended outcome that the new math would affect the thinking and activities of children outside of school, more than the old math did? Was it an intended outcome to change in any way the nature of relationships between teacher and child? Was it an intended outcome to change the quantity and quality of questions that children asked about numbers and problem solving? Was it an intended outcome that children would learn that the principle that a particular thing (e.g., a number) can have different significances, is a principle equally applicable to other kinds of events, such as those they study in history?

SOURCE: *The Culture of the School and the Problem of Change* (Boston: Allyn and Bacon, Inc., 1971), pp. 62-87. Copyright © 1971 by Allyn and Bacon, Inc. Reprinted with permission of the publisher.

Undoubtedly, one can ask about other possible intended outcomes. Neither in the specific case we described nor in the general literature is it clear what outcomes were intended, whether or not there was a priority among outcomes, and what the relationship is between any outcome and the processes of change leading to it. As a colleague remarked: "In a way this is a happy state of affairs. You don't have to think about important problems, you have little or nothing to evaluate, and faith and personal opinion carry the day." But more than the new math is at stake, and we cannot allow ourselves to be content with studying states of illusory happiness.

THE EXISTING REGULARITIES

Let us approach the general problem of outcomes by indulging in a fantasy. Imagine a being from outer space who finds himself and his invisible space platform directly above an elementary school. Being superior to earthly beings he is able to see everything that goes on in the school. But he does operate under certain restrictions: he does not comprehend the meaning of written or spoken language, and it can never occur to him that things go on inside of what we call heads. He can see and hear everything and, being an *avant garde* outer-spacer, he, of course, possesses a kind of computer that records and categorizes events on any number of dimensions, allowing him to discern what we shall call the existing regularities. (Let me anticipate the discussion of the latter part of this chapter by advancing the hypothesis that *any attempt to introduce change into the school setting requires, among other things, changing the existing regularities in some way. The intended outcomes involve changing an existing regularity, eliminating one or more of them, or producing new ones.*)

Let us start with one of the more obvious regularities. Our outer-spacer will discern (but not understand) that for five consecutive days the school is densely populated while for two consecutive days it is devoid of humans. That puzzles him. Why this 5-2 pattern? Why not a 4-3 or some other kind of pattern like 2-1-2-1-1?

What if the outer-spacer could talk to us and demanded an explanation for this existing regularity? Many of us earthlings would quickly become aware that we have a tendency to assume that the way things are is the way things should be. But our outer-spacer persists. Is this the way it has always been? Is this the way it is in other countries? Is it demonstrably the best pattern for achieving the purposes of schooling? Does the existing regularity reflect non-educational considerations like religion, work patterns, and leisure time? Is it possible that the existing regularity has no intrinsic relationship to learning and education?

The significance of an existing regularity is that it forces, or should force, one to ask two questions: *What is the rationale for the regularity? and What is the universe of alternatives that could be considered?* Put in another way: Can the existing regularity be understood without considering its relationship to the alternatives of which it is but one possibility?[1] I would suggest that if we could peruse this issue in the case of the 5-2 pattern we would become increasingly aware not only of the universe of alternatives but also of the degree to which the existing pattern reflects considerations that have little or nothing to do with the intended objectives of schooling.

Let us take another "population" regularity. After a period of time our outer-spacer notes that at regular intervals (what earthlings call once a month) a group of people come together at a particular time in the evening. No small people are there, only big people. With few exceptions, the big people tend not to have been seen in the school during the day. The exceptions are those who during the day are in rooms with small people.

At this meeting most of the people sit in orderly rows, very quietly, and rarely say anything. When someone in these rows says something it is most frequently preceded by the raising of his right hand. There are a few people who do most of the talking and they sit in front at a table.

Several things puzzle the outer-spacer. For example, his computer tells him that there is no relationship between this meeting and any existing regularity during the day; that is, any existing regularity during the day is in no way affected by the occurrence of these meetings. This puzzles the outer-spacer because there are obvious similarities between the evening meeting and what goes on in the daytime. For example, at both times most people sit quietly in orderly rows—in the evening big people sit quietly, while during the day it is the little people who sit quietly. At both times it is the big people "in front" who do most of the talking—in the evening there is one big person who talks the most, while during the day it is the only big person in the room who does most of the talking. What complicates matters for the outer-spacer is that he has seen that in both instances as soon as the people leave their rooms they speak much more, and they have a much greater variety of facial expression.

How do we respond to our celestial friend when he learns English and demands explanations for these regularities and similarities? What do we say to him about why there is no apparent relationship between what goes on at a PTA meeting and anything else that goes on at the school? What do we say when he demands that we tell him the alternative ways that were considered for organizing a PTA meeting or classroom, and the basis used for making a choice?[2]

Earlier in this chapter I said that "any attempt to introduce change into the school setting requires, among other things, changing in some way the existing regularities." At this point I would further suggest that this statement should be preceded by the statement that *the attempt to introduce a change into the school setting usually (if not always) stems from the perception of a regularity that one does not like*. We, like the outer-spacer, are set to see regularities, but unlike the inhabitant of the space platform we are not set either to observe the tremendous range of existing regularities or to inquire naively about the rationale for any one of them and the nature of the universe of alternatives of which the existing regularity is but one possibility.

Let us now leave both fantasy and heavenly friend and take up several existing regularities that not only illustrate the fruitfulness of this approach for understanding the school culture but also help clarify the problem of how to state intended outcomes in ways that are testable.

THE PHYSICAL EDUCATION PROGRAM

In most schools there is a place, usually large, where physical education programs are conducted. Those who conduct these programs are expected to have special training.

What happens when, as I have done in numerous occasions, I say to groups of teachers that I simply do not comprehend why there should be physical education programs in the schools? As you might imagine, the most frequent response is staring disbelief followed by a request to reformulate the statement. Without going into the details of the discussion—which is usually quite heated—I shall indicate the significances I attribute to the initial response and the ensuing discussion. First, there is the implicit recognition both by the teachers and myself that we operate in different worlds, i.e., I perceive them and they perceive me as having different backgrounds and experiences. Second, it is inconceivable to the teachers that a school could or should be without a physical education program. They have a conception of a school which, if changed or challenged, they strongly defend. Far from being indifferent to the conception they defend it to a degree which illuminates how their sense of identity is related to their conception. Third, they justify the physical education program in terms of what they think children are and need. Put in another way, their justification is psychological and philosophical.[3]

One of the most frequent responses to my question is that children need an opportunity ''to get rid of all that energy which they have in them.'' This energy cannot be discharged by sitting and doing work in classrooms. (It is interesting to note that in the minds of teachers this response is much more applicable to boys than to girls.) This response seems to assume that at least three things are true: (1) the greater the amount of continuous time a child spends in a classroom the more restless he becomes: (2) much energy is discharged in gym activities, and (3) following the discharge of energy the child's restlessness in class is discernibly less than before gym.

As to the first assumption I am not aware that anyone has demonstrated that increased restlessness is a function merely of time. I have seen classrooms where I could discern no increase in restlessness, and I have seen other classrooms where the increase was predictably related to subject matter interacting either with teacher interest or adequacy, or with style. Teachers responding to my question in a group do not say what many have said to me when I have talked with them alone while their classes were in gym: *the gym period is one during which the teacher can recoup his or her energy losses, or get some paper work done.*

As to the second assumption, I do not doubt that there is much energy discharged in gym. But I do doubt, as do many teachers, the third assumption. *Observation rather compellingly suggests that following gym there is frequently an increase in restlessness and listlessness that interferes with class work. The intended outcome does not seem to occur; in fact the reverse of it may be the modal consequence.* In connection with outcomes my observations suggest that the level of class restlessness before gym is highly related to level of restlessness after gym.

The rationale for the regularity of gym frequently includes intended outcomes other than the ones given above. Increasing motor skill, teaching cooperation in group or team effort, and preparing children for productive use of leisure time are some intended outcomes advanced to justify gym programs. Although these are statements about intended outcomes they do not in any clear way tell me how existing behavioral regularities of children are changed or new ones are added.

For example, I know of several suburban school systems in which the major gym activities of girls during the fall and spring are field hockey and a variety of kickball games. If *one* of the intended outcomes of such activities is to influence leisure time behavioral regularities (types of physical activities, their frequency, etc.), I must report the fact that I have never seen girls engage in these activities outside of school. But, one can maintain, there are other and perhaps more important outcomes for out-of-school activities. Agreed; but without knowing the out-of-school behavioral regularities one cannot determine what effects, if any, gym activities have on them.

What *would* happen if gym programs ceased? This alternative would probably arouse reactions similar to those that surrounded the withdrawal of certain universities from intercollegiate football competition. But these universities have suffered no baleful effects.

Physical education personnel are not likely to believe that I have no strong feelings for or against their programs. My purpose in discussing these programs has been to make several points: first that they represent a programmatic regularity in the school culture; second, that any programmatic regularity, explicitly or implicitly, describes intended outcomes that involve either new behavioral regularities or the changing of old ones; third, that there are alternatives to the existing programmatic regularity; and, fourth, that any challenge to a programmatic regularity is more likely to engender feeling than reason. This last point is certainly not peculiar to the school culture.

It has not been my intention here, nor will it be in the later pages, to convey the impression that I am demanding proof or justification for the programmatic regularities that exist in the school culture. The absence of proof does not mean that the underlying rationale is invalid. Even where there is apparently disconfirming evidence we must be clear as to whether the rationale is being relevantly tested. My position in these pages is that the intended outcomes for programmatic regularities can and should be stated in terms of overt behavioral regularities that the dispassionate observer can record. To state intended outcomes in any other way increases the chances that we will be dealing with all the confusion and controversy produced by what Hook has called the unanalyzable abstraction.

THE ARITHMETIC-MATHEMATICS PROGRAMMATIC REGULARITY

We turn to the arithmetic-mathematics regularity in order to help the reader see how easy it is to assume that the way things are is the way they should be, and to help him grasp how difficult it is to examine what I have called the universe of alternatives. In an earlier chapter [Sarason, *The Culture of the School and the Problem of Change*, chap. 4], I alluded to the following programmatic regularity: beginning in the first grade and on every school day thereafter until graduation from high school the child receives instruction and drill in the use and understanding of numbers. Like eating and sleeping that is quite a regularity, and one may assume that this degree of regularity reflects considerations vital to the development of children.

The naive person might ask several questions: Would academic and intellectual development be adversely affected if the exposure was for four days a week instead of five? Or three instead of five? What would happen if the exposure began in the second or third grade? What if the exposure was in alternate years? Obviously, one can generate many more questions, each of which suggests an alternative to the existing programmatic regularity. From this universe of alternatives how does one justify the existing regularity?

Before taking up this question we must first deal wih the emotional reactions I have gotten when on numerous occasions I have asked different groups (e.g., educators, psychologists, and parents) questions that challenge what exists and implicitly suggest that there may be other ways of thinking and acting. I focus on the emotional reactions because they reveal the distinctive characteristics of the culture more than other ways of understanding the setting, particularly if one is or has been a member of that setting. Because we have spent so much of our own lives in schools, and watched our own children in school, we may never be aware of the process whereby we uncritically confuse what is with what might be. In fact, in diverse ways, one of the most significant effects of school on children is to get them to accept existing regularities as the best and only possible state of affairs, although frequently this is neither verbally stated nor consciously decided.

The first response to my statement of alternatives is essentially one of humor; that is, the listener assumes that I intended something akin to a joke and it was funny.[4] Having established myself as a comic, however, I usually persist and insist that I am quite serious. To keep the discussion going I then say the following:

Let me tell you the results of an informal poll I have been conducting among friends and colleagues, and I will take this opportunity to get your answers to this question: When you think back over the past few months, how many times have you used numbers other than to do *simple* addition, subtraction, multiplication, and division? The results of the poll are clear: highly educated, productive people very rarely use numbers other than in the most simple ways, leaving aside, of course, those individuals whose work requires more advanced number concepts (e.g., mathematicians). On what basis is it illegitimate to suggest that these results have no significance for the fact that a large part of what children learn in twelve years of arithmetic and mathematics is content other than the simple computations? Incidentally, I have also polled many far less educated individuals and, needless to say, the results contain no exception to the use only of simple computations.

And now the fur begins to fly. Among the more charitable accusations is the one that I am anti-intellectual. Among the least charitable reactions (for me) is simply an unwillingness to pursue the matter further. (On one occasion some individuals left the meeting in obvious disgust.) One can always count on some individuals asserting that mathematics "trains or disciplines the mind" and the more of it the better, much like Latin used to be justified as essential to the curriculum.[5]

The fact is that whenever I have presented these thoughts I have been extremely careful to state them so that the words and sentences I employ do not contain any preference for any alternative, *simply because I have no adequate basis for choosing among the universe of alternatives*—and neither do the audiences. The intent of the thoughts is twofold: to indicate that there is always a universe of alternatives from which to choose, and to show that when any programmatic regularity is no longer viewed in terms of that universe of alternatives, rational thought and evaluation of intended outcomes are no longer in the picture, overwhelmed as they are by the power of faith, tradition and habit.

BEHAVIORAL REGULARITIES

Thus far in this chapter we have discussed two examples of regularities to which all within the school must adapt, since there is little or no element of individual choice. They are predetermined characteristics of the setting. Let us now turn to what might be termed behavioral regularities, which have to do with the frequency of overt behaviors. Laughing, crying, fighting, talking, concentrating, working, writing, question-asking, question-answering, test behavior and performance, stealing, cheating, unattending—these are *some* of the overt behaviors that occur with varying frequency among children in school. That they occur is important to, and expected by, school personnel. But what is equally important is that they are expected to change over time. *Behavioral regularities and their changes represent some of the most important intended outcomes of programmatic regularities. Deliberate changes in programmatic regularities are intended to change the occurrence and frequency of behavioral regularities.*

In 1969, the time this chapter was being written, newspapers and other media daily reported how our schools and universities were changing programmatic regularities in an effort to change the overt behavioral regularities of students. That these reports reached us through public channels of communication reflects the fact that the programmatic changes were themselves a result of changes in the overt behavior of students; that is, the existing programmatic regularities were no longer achieving their intended outcomes. Changes due to open conflict are probably less numerous than changes (as in the case of new math) that were initiated by those at the administrative or supervisory levels. Although in both conflict and nonconflict situations of change, programmatic changes are intended to effect changes in behavioral regulations, there seems to be much greater clarity about intended outcomes in conditions of conflict than in the modal process of change. This should not be surprising because "revolutionary situations," almost by definition, are those in which issues and outcomes have become sharpened and polarized.

Some behavioral regularities are concerned with individual pupils while others reflect pupil-pupil interactions, such as boys with girls, older pupils with younger pupils, and black with white. As important as any of these are the behavioral regularities characterizing teacher-pupil interactions. We shall take up now a teacher-pupil behavioral regularity fateful for the intended outcome of any change in programmatic regularities.

QUESTION-ASKING: A BEHAVIORAL REGULARITY

As in our discussion of programmatic regularities I shall not start with questions about assumptions, values, intended outcomes, or alternative patterns, but rather with the discernible regularity. It is, I think, only when one is confronted with a clear regularity that one stands a chance of clarifying the relationship between theory and practice, intention and outcome. Let us, therefore, start by asking two questions: At what rate do teachers ask questions in the classroom? At what rate do children ask questions of teachers?

From a theoretical and practical standpoint—by which I mean theories of child development, intellectual growth, educational and learning theory, techniques of teaching, presentation and discussion of subject matter—the importance of question-asking has always been emphasized. It is surprising, therefore, that there have been very few studies focusing on this type of behavior. Susskind (1969) recently did a comprehensive review of the literature. He expresses surprise that a type of behavior considered by everyone to be of great importance has hardly been investigated. However, he points out that although the few studies vary greatly in investigative sophistication, they present a remarkably similar state of affairs. But before we summarize the findings, the reader may wish to try to answer Susskind's question:

Before exploring the research literature we suggest that the reader attempt to estimate the rates of two classroom behaviors. Imagine yourself in a fifth grade, social studies classroom in a predominantly white, middle-class school. During a half-hour lesson, in which the teacher and the class talk to each other (there is no silent work), how many questions are asked (a) by the teacher, (b) by the students? How do the two rates correlate?[6]

The first two questions are deceptively simple because, as Susskind has made clear, there are different types of questions, and there are problems as to how questions (and which questions) are to be counted. For example, if the teacher asks the same question of five children should it be counted once or five times? Susskind has developed a comprehensive, workable set of categories, and the interested reader is referred to his work. We will now summarize the answers to the above questions in light of existing studies, including the very recent ones by Susskind, whose findings are very similar to those from older studies.

1. Across the different studies the range of rate of teacher questions per half-hour is from 45–150.

2. When asked, educators as well as other groups vastly underestimate the rate of teacher questions, the estimated range being 12–20 per half hour.

3. From 67 to 95 percent of all teacher questions require "straight recall" from the student.

4. Children ask *fewer* than two questions per half hour. That is to say, during this time period two questions by children will have been asked.

5. The greater the tendency for a teacher to ask straight recall questions the fewer the questions initiated by children. This does not mean that children do not have time to ask questions. They do have time.

6. The more a teacher asks "personally relevant" questions the higher the rate of questioning on the part of children.

7. The rate of questions by children does not seem to vary with IQ level or with social-class background.

These statements derive from existing studies, but, as Susskind points out, scores of people have come to similar conclusions from informal observations.

We have here a clear behavioral regularity. How should we think about this? Is this behavioral regularity an intended outcome? Put in another way, this is the way things are; Is this the way things should be? I know of no psychological theory or theorist, particularly those who are or have been most influential on the educational scene, who would view this behavioral regularity as a desirable outcome, that is, as one kind of barometer indicating that an organized set of conceptions are being consistently implemented. In addition, I have never read of or spoken to curriculum specialists and reformers who would not view this behavioral regularity as evidence that their efforts were being neither understood nor implemented. Finally, the fact that teachers and other groups vastly underestimate the rate of teacher-questioning (in Susskind's study teachers were quite surprised when confronted with the rates obtained in *their* classrooms) suggests that this behavioral regularity is not an intended outcome according to some part of the thinking of teachers.[7]

We have, then, an outcome that practically nobody intends, a situation that would not be particularly upsetting were it not that practically everybody considers question-asking on the part of teachers and children one of the most crucial means of maintaining interest, supporting curiosity, acquiring knowledge, and facilitating change and growth.

In an earlier chapter [Sarason, *The Culture of the School and the Problem of Change*, chap. 4], where we used the new math to illustrate the modal process of introducing change into the school culture, we emphasized the point that the curriculum reformers seemed quite aware that they wanted to do more than merely change textbooks; they realized that classrooms tended to be uninviting and uninspired places in which teachers were active and children passive. Their intended outcome was to change, among other things, behavioral regularities such as the one we are here discussing. But this intended outcome was never systematically discussed (or even written about) or stated as a criterion by which the new curriculum was to be judged. Certainly the teachers who underwent retraining could not focus on this issue, if only because they were in the same passive role that characterized, and would continue to characterize, their own students.

For our purposes here the generalization that required emphasis is that *any change in a programmatic regularity has as one of its intended outcomes some kind of change in existing behavioral regularities, and these behavioral regularities are among the most important criteria for judging the degree to which intended outcomes are being achieved.* At this point I am not interested in whether or not one likes or agrees with the programmatic change but rather in the fact that these changes require changes in some kind or kinds of behavioral regularities. It is almost always true that changes in the behavioral regularities will be assumed to be effected or mediated by internal emotional and cognitive processes and states, but the behavioral regularities remain as our most secure, albeit not infallible, criterion for judging what we have achieved. In fact (and the question-asking regularity is a good example), behavioral regularities are probably our best means for inferring internal cognitive and emotional states.

It is the rare observer of classrooms who has not inferred from the overt behavior of children and teachers that the great majority of children seem "inside" to be neither strongly interested in, curious about, nor feeling satisfaction in regard to what they are doing or what is going on. They are, in short, not having a particularly good time. But, someone can say, this is an inference, and it may frequently be a wrong one, which of course, is true. To what behavioral regularities can we look that could serve as a kind of check on these inferences?

One of them, of course, requires asking children to respond to relevant questions about what they are feeling, but this will be regarded as either too obvious or naive because of the frequently held assumption that what people, particularly children, report about what they feel should not be given much weight. But what if we were to look at the behavior of children in the hall *immediately* after they leave one classroom to go to another, as is the case in junior and senior high? How does one account for the noise level, the animated talking, running, and formation of groups, and the absence of talk about the intellectual substance of what they had just experienced? *Why is it that one of the most trouble-producing (from the standpoint of school personnel) times in the school day is when students are in the halls going from one room to another?* When the behavioral regularities in the hall are ascertained, I have no doubt that they will be found to be related to regularities in the classroom in a way that confirms inferences made about the internal states of children in the classroom.

But we cannot understand the question-asking regularity without briefly trying to understand what aspects of the school culture contribute to a state of affairs that few, if anyone, feel is the way things should be.

1. *Teachers tend to teach the way in which they themselves were taught.* I am not only referring to the public schooling of teachers but to their college experiences as well—and I am not restricting myself to schools of education. In general, the question-asking regularity we have described does not, in my experience, differ markedly from what goes on in college classrooms. The culture of the school should be expected to reflect aspects of other types of educational cultures from which the teachers have come. As suggested in an earlier chapter [Sarason, *The Culture of the School and the Problem of Change*,

chap. 3], the university critic of the public schools frequently is unable to see that his criticisms may well be true of his educational culture. It would indeed be strange if teachers did not teach the way they had been taught.

2. *In their professional training (courses, practice teaching) teachers are minimally exposed to theories about question-asking and the technical problems of question-asking and question-producing behavior—the relationship between theory and practice.* To the reader who may be surprised at this, I would suggest he consult the most frequently used books in educational psychology, learning, or child development courses. Such a reader may conclude either that it is not an important question or that the obvious is being overlooked.[8]

3. *Whatever educational help or consultation is available to the teacher (principal, supervisors, workshops, etc.) does not concern itself directly with the question-asking regularity.* Particularly in the earliest months and years of teaching the primary concern of everyone is "law and order," and the possibility that discipline may be related to, or can be affected by, the question-asking regularity is rarely recognized. The anxiety of the beginning teacher about maintaining discipline too frequently interferes with his sensitivity to, and desire to accommodate to, the questions and interests of his pupils.

4. *The predetermined curriculum that suggests that teachers cover a certain amount of material within certain time intervals with the expectation that their pupils as a group will perform at certain levels at certain times is responded to by teachers in a way as to make for the fantastic discrepancy between the rate of teacher and student questions.* This factor touches on a very complicated state of affairs. From the standpoint of the teacher the curriculum is not a suggestion but a requirement, for if it is not met the principal and supervisors will consider the teaching inadequate. In addition, the teacher whom the pupils will have in the next year will consider them inadequately prepared. Therefore, the best and safest thing to do is to insure that the curriculum is covered, a view that reinforces the tendency to ask many "straight recall" questions.

From the administrator's standpoint the curriculum is only a guide, and the trouble arises because teachers are not "creative"; that is, the problem is not the curriculum but the teacher. As many administrative personnel have said, "We *tell* them to be creative but they still stick slavishly to the curriculum as if it were a bible." To which teachers reply, "What they want to know at the end of the year, and what I will be judged by, are the achievement test scores of my children."

Although both sides *correctly* perceive each other's behavioral regularity, the administrator feels unable to change the state of affairs—that is, he is of no help to the teacher—and the teacher continues to feel unfree to depart from the curriculum. In short, we are back to a familiar situation in which no one sees the universe of alternatives to current practices.

There are, of course, alternatives. For example, as Susskind's studies show, there is variation among teachers in the question-asking regularity; some teachers can utilize a curriculum without being a question-asking machine and without requiring pupils to respond primarily to "straight recall" questions. In addition, and a source of encouragement, Susskind obtained data suggesting that when a group of teachers were confronted with the question-asking regularities in their classroom, and this was discussed in terms of theory and intended outcomes, the teachers as a group were able to change the regularity. *But here one runs smack into the obstacle of another characteristic of the school culture: there are no vehicles of discussion, communication, or observation that allow for this kind of variation to be raised and productively used for purposes of help and change.* Faculty meetings, as teachers are acutely aware, are not noted for either their intellectual content or their sensitivity to issues that may be controversial or interpersonally conflictful. (As our man from outer space could well have discerned, the classroom, the PTA meeting, and the faculty meeting, are amazingly similar in the question-asking regularity.)

For our purposes here what is most important is not the particular behavioral regularity or the factors that may account for it, but the obvious fact that within the school culture these regularities, which are in the nature of intended outcomes, are not recognized, and it is not traditional to have means for their recognition. What is not recognized or verbalized cannot be dealt with, and if it is important and not recognized, efforts to introduce substantive change, particularly in the classroom, result in the illusion of change.

WHAT IS THE INTENDED OUTCOME?

We will now take up something that is not the usual behavioral or programmatic regularity, although it has features of both. It is a regularity that will not be found in all schools; in fact, it may be rather infrequent. The first justification for presenting it is that it illustrates well the fruitfulness of discerning regularities, using them to determine their intended outcomes, and squaring these outcomes with what actually happens. The second justification is that the data we possessed were surprising to all concerned. I should add that these data were gathered in relation to a study (Sarason, Hill, and Zimbardo, 1964; Hill and Sarason, 1966) tangential to the purposes of this book, and it was not until we experienced "surprise" at some findings that we examined the purposes of the regularities in terms of intended and actual outcomes.

In the two junior high schools of a suburban school system, when a student considered capable of good work is doing poorly in any subject, an "interim" is sent to his home indicating that he is in danger of failing the course. The student may be doing failing work or the level of his performance may be significantly below expectations. If the low or failing performance is considered a true indication of the student's intellectual capacity no interim is sent. Since the average IQ in these schools is discernibly above the national average (not surprising in light of the predominantly middle-class composition of the community), there are relatively few students who do not possess the capacity to get passing grades in their courses. In the bulk of instances when an interim is sent home the student is in danger of getting an F or a D for that marking period.

The study we were doing involved two large samples of children. We had been following one sample since they were in Grade 1; the other since they were in Grade 2. There was no reason to believe that each sample was not representative of all children in that particular class. One question in which we were interested was what happened to these children in their first year of junior high school?

One could say that we were dealing with a behavioral regularity in which the failing or near-failing performance of certain students gave rise to a certain action on the part of school personnel resulting in a standard written message being sent to the home. What was the intended outcome of the relationship between performance and school action? Was it merely *to inform* the home? If that were the sole intended outcome, then one could expect the parents to treat the information in much the same way as they would if they had been informed about the exact height of their children; there would be no intention that the parents act on the information. It is not violating the canons of reflective thinking to say that the intended outcome was to raise the level of the student's performance by actions that parents would take on the basis of the message from school. That, of course, is what school personnel explicitly expected.

Our surprise began when our data indicated that receiving interims was by no means infrequent. Forty-seven percent of the boys in one sample, about 49 percent in the other sample, received at least one interim during the four marking periods. For girls in the same samples the figures were 33 and 32 percent, respectively.

We then asked what happened to the student's grade in the subject in which he had received an interim—did his grade increase, decrease, or remain the same compared to the grade in the previous marking period? Since the previous grade was typically a D or F it was obvious that for many students they had only one direction in which to go, and that was up. *What the data clearly revealed was that in half the cases the grade remained the same, in 38 percent the grade went down, and in 12 percent the grade went up.* If the intended outcome of this procedure was to raise grades it clearly was not successful. School personnel were unaware of these actual outcomes, and when they were made aware of them they were surprised at the discrepancy between intended and actual outcomes.

We then asked the following question: in the three major courses (English, Social Studies, Mathematics) what was the frequency and pattern of interims over the four marking periods? We expected, as did the school personnel, that mathematics would have the highest frequency in each marking period. *To the surprise and consternation of everyone, social studies was far and away the subject matter in which the most interims were received in each marking period, with English and mathematics following in that order.*

Number of Interims in Relation to the Marking Period
(All Boys and All Girls From the Two Samples In the Two Schools)

	Boys				Girls			
	Marking Period				Marking Period			
	I	II	III	IV	I	II	III	IV
English	50	78	62	74	21	27	28	13
Social Studies	80	91	65	86	54	40	54	29
Math	40	66	72	64	23	20	20	19

One of the major advantages of viewing the school culture in terms of regularities and intended outcomes is that it requires one, at least temporarily, to suspend or control the role of opinion, values, or bias. As we shall see in later chapters, viewing the school culture in this fashion is but one way of understanding it, and I have been emphasizing and illustrating this way because so much of what is written about the school culture centers around issues of values and objectives without relating them to existing regularities or defining new regularities by which to judge the consistency between intent and outcome.

A second advantage of viewing the school culture in terms of existing regularities and intended outcomes is that one frequently comes up with unanticipated findings that further illuminate the existence of other kinds of regularities, and one's understanding of the setting deepens. For example, why should social studies have the greatest number of interims? Why is it apparently difficult for so many students in the first year of junior high school?

DISCONTINUITIES AND SOCIAL STUDIES

When so large a number of first year junior high school students in a middle-class, suburban community receives at least one interim in major subjects, and in very few instances can intelligence level be a factor, one is forced to speculate about possible explanations. Consistent with our approach in this chapter (the outer spaceman approach) we can begin by comparing the elementary and junior high school settings on the more obvious regularities.[9] For example, in contrast to the elementary schools the junior high schools are physically larger and contain more people. The students come from more than one neighborhood, they move more frequently from room to room, they have more teachers, and they have more freedom in that there is not one teacher who is *their* teacher and whose responsibility it is to oversee them. In light of these and other differences there is a host of new rules and regulations that the students must observe. The students are like people who have spent their lives in a small town and suddenly find themselves in a large, unfamiliar city.

There are many discontinuities between elementary and junior high schools that require a good deal of unlearning or learning on the part of young people, and if one had to make any prediction it would be that many children would respond maladaptively. This expectation is reinforced by the fact that the usual orientation exercises are brief and ritualistic. I have sat through some of these exercises, and I have read the materials provided the children, and I can only conclude that the intended outcome was to impress on the new students that there was much to learn about socially navigating in this culture and most of that was what not to do.

But now let us ask some ''regularities'' questions. What information is provided the junior high about the new students? Who provides this information? What is done with the information? What we found out was that the elementary school record, including personality and academic evaluation by the student's last teacher, is sent ahead. We also found out that the teachers who made the evaluations were (a) resentful of the fact that junior high personnel never spoke to them or sought their advice, particularly in relation to children with one or another kind of problem; and (b) they were puzzled at the number of children who had not been any kind of problem in elementary school but who had various difficulties in junior high. As best as we could determine, the information sent on to the junior high was read and filed. It was the truly rare instance when junior high personnel (e.g., guidance counselors) acted on the information before the child showed up or shortly after. *Our study revealed that the single best predictor of the occurrence of academic or personality problems in the first year of junior high school was the evaluation of the last teacher the children had in elementary school.*[10]

If the intended outcome of this record keeping and its transmittal to the junior high was to *anticipate* problems with the aim of taking action to prevent their reoccurrence or to lessen their consequences, it clearly was not achieved. When this was discussed with junior high personnel it was pointed out to us that the size of the freshman class simply did not allow effective use of the information, a fact that concedes the argument that the major intended outcome was not achieved. Whatever the reason, the fact remains that these record-keeping regularities were not serving their intended purposes.

As I indicated earlier, discerning and examining regularities in relation to intended outcomes frequently lead one to questions, issues, or other observations that illuminate important aspects of the school culture. For example, in the process of doing this study—spending time in the elementary and junior high schools, talking to teachers, principals, and other administrative personnel—we became increasingly aware that junior high personnel view the new student in

September rather differently than elementary school personnel did in the previous June. Whereas in June the elementary school viewed him as a *child,* in September the junior high viewed him as a *young adult.* These different views result in different expectations and are an important aspect of the discontinuity between the structure and organization of the two settings. I am, of course, suggesting that meeting these different expectations is frequently difficult for some children, even for many who manifested no problems in elementary school. (Anyone who has any knowledge of, or experience with, college freshmen will not be surprised by this explanation.)

There is another aspect to this problem that is illuminating of the school culture: *the differences in the ways in which pupils are viewed by elementary and junior high personnel are reflections of the differences in the ways in which these personnel view each other.* Many (by no means all) junior high school teachers view themselves as "specialists" in a particular subject matter, while they view the elementary school teacher as a somewhat superficial generalist—much like the differences between the general practitioner and specialist in medicine. Put in another way, the junior high teacher tends to view himself as "higher" and, therefore, better than the elementary school teacher.[11] Although less true today than in previous decades, there is still a tendency for junior and senior high personnel to receive higher salaries than those in the elementary schools. The fact that there are far more men teachers in the junior high school than in the elementary school is undoubtedly a reflection of the view that the elementary school pupil is a child (taken care of by child-care kinds of teachers) while the junior high school pupil (who two months before was in elementary school) is a beginning young adult. These differences in views and expectations sharpen the discontinuities between the two settings.

But why should social studies (in these two junior high schools, at least) be so difficult in the first year? We looked into the curriculum manual and guide (a heavy and imposing document of two hundred or more pages), talked to teachers, and sat in classrooms. I do not pretend to know and understand all the factors that would comprise an answer, but I can point to two related factors that seemed important. The first of these factors is that the student was frequently required to engage in projects for which he had to read in different sources, use the library (school and community), and organize readings and materials. Many of the pupils were simply not able to take on this kind of independent responsibility. The task was not made easier by the fact that the degree and content of direction given by the teacher seemed to assume an amount of previous experience with such a task that struck us as unrealistic.

Two years after the above observations I conducted a college senior seminar for the first time in my teaching life. Up to that time I had only taught graduate students. My attitude had been that parents who sent their sons to Yale had a right to expect that they would be given an excellent education, but it did not follow that I had to participate in that education. (Elementary school pupils = undergraduates; junior high school pupils = graduate students.) Midway through the seminar I was aware that I was frustrated and annoyed. Why do *they* know so little? Why is it that when I assign a paper, with a brief but commendably clear explanation of its purpose and scope, I get a barrage of questions (during and after class, in person and on the phone) about what I mean and want? Why are they so dependent and fearful or exercising independent judgment? Where have they been for three years? Who was spoon feeding them? The principle underlying these thoughts of a teacher is quite similar to that enunciated by Professor Higgins in *My Fair Lady* when he compares men and women and concludes "We are a marvelous sex!"

The second factor I can point to in regard to the social studies finding is that the pupils were required *to organize and write* papers and many of them clearly were inadequate to the task—and I must remind the reader that this population was discernibly above average in ability. This raised questions: In the last year (sixth grade) of elementary school how many times were pupils required to write a paper? How many times did a teacher sit down with a child and go over what he had written? My informal polling indicated that some teachers required as few as two "papers" and some required more than four.[12] Although I polled far more children than teachers, I did not hear of a single instance in which a teacher had sat down with a child to go over what he had written. When papers were returned to the children there were usually comments, pro and con, written on them, but the matter ended there.

At this point in our discussion it is not relevant to go into explanations of this state of affairs or to explore the universe of alternatives. I have used social studies for the purpose of illustrating how one regularity (i.e., interims) leads one to another regularity (i.e., social studies), the examination of which can be extremely productive toward one's understanding of aspects of the school culture.[13]

The purposes of this chapter were to state and illustrate the following:

1. There are regularities of various kinds.

2. Existing programmatic and behavioral regularities should be described independent of one's own values or opinions.

3. Regularities exist because they are supposed to have intended outcomes.

4. There are at least two characteristics to intended outcomes: (1) aspects of them are discernible in overt behavior or interactions, and (2) they are justified by statements of value (i.e., what is good and what is bad).

5. There are frequent discrepancies between regularities and intended outcomes. Usually, no regularity is built into the school culture to facilitate the recognition of such discrepancies.

6. The significance of any regularity, particularly of the programmatic type,

cannot be adequately comprehended apart from the universe of "regularity alternatives" of which the existing regularity is but one item. The failure to consider or recognize a universe of alternatives is one obstacle to change occurring from within the culture, and makes it likely that recognition of this universe of alternatives will await events and forces outside the culture.

7. Any attempt to introduce an important change in the school culture requires changing existing regularities to produce new intended outcomes. In practice, the regularities tend not to be changed and the intended outcomes, therefore, cannot occur; that is, the more things change the more they remain the same.

8. It is probably true that the most important attempts to introduce change in the school culture *require* changing existing teacher-child regularities. When one examines the natural history of the change process it is precisely these regularities that remain untouched.

The more our discussion has proceeded the more evident it has become that a central problem to the understanding of the school culture is how to describe it so that the regularities that characterize it can become apparent. I have already suggested that our usual theories and ways of thinking about individuals are far from adequate for our purposes.

NOTES

1. It is an interesting digression to suggest that one of the major sources of the conflict between generations is that the younger generation has the annoying ability not only to discern existing regularities but also to force the older generation to the awareness that there are alternative regularities. This, of course, the older generation finds difficult to accept because of the tendency to confuse the way things are with the way things should or could be. I remember as a child being puzzled and annoyed that no one could satisfactorily explain to me why one could not eat fried chicken for breakfast. It was obvious what the existing breakfast regularities were but I could not understand why the alternative of chicken aroused such strong feeling.

2. Most readers will be aware that a good part of the controversy surrounding large urban school systems arises precisely because some community groups are pushing for an alternative way of implementing "community control," a way that would presumably change, if not eliminate, some of the PTA and classroom regularities described above. I say "presumably" because I have neither seen nor heard nor read anything to indicate that aside from changing the curriculum (as in the case of new or old math) there is any intent to change the most significant existing regularities in the classroom, for example, the passivity of the learner or the teacher as talker and question-asker. My reservation may become more clear later in this chapter when we take up in detail some of the existing regularities in the classroom. The point I wish to emphasize here is that those who are in favor of "community control" state their intended outcomes for the classroom, when they state them at all, in terms so vague and virtuous that they would

defy subsequent attempts at evaluation—quite in contrast to the specificity of intended outcomes as to the role of parents in decision-making.

3. S. B. Sarason, "The School Culture and Processes of Change." In S. B. Sarason and F. Kaplan (eds.) *The Yale Psycho-Educational Clinic: Collected Papers and Studies* Monograph Series (Boston: Massachusetts State Department of Mental Health, 1969), p. 6.

4. This reminds me of the suggestion that a former colleague, quite eminent, made in the course of a discussion about how a university could get rid of tenured professors who were "dead wood" (i.e., whatever contribution they made was a long time ago and there was no reason to believe that they served any function other than to stand in the way of younger men). His suggestion was that all beginning instructors be given tenure and as they get promoted (from assistant, to associate, to full professor) they have increasingly less tenure so that when they become full professors they have no tenure at all. The suggestion, of course, was treated as a joke and no one (including myself) considered for a moment that there *were* alternatives to the existing structure (the way things are is the only way things should be) even though no one had examined our thought through the universe of alternatives in terms of intended outcomes.

5. It is important for an understanding of the school culture, although it certainly is not peculiar to it, that one not assume that the *public* positions taken by groups within that culture are those held *privately* by all or most individuals comprising those groups. Many within the school culture question many aspects of programmatic regularities and are willing to consider the universe of alternatives. However, several factors keep this seeking and questioning a private affair. First, there is the untested assumption that few others think in this way. As we have said elsewhere (Sarason, *et al.*, 1966) "teaching is a lonely profession" despite the fact that the school is densely populated. Second, existing vehicles for discussion and planning within the school (faculty meetings: teacher-principal contacts, teacher-supervisor contacts, etc.) are based on the principle of avoidance of controversy. Third, at all levels (teacher, principal, administrator) there is the feeling of individual impotence. Fourth, there is acceptance of another untested assumption: that the public will oppose any meaningful or drastic change in existing regularities. In short, these and other factors seem to allow almost everyone in the culture to act in terms of perceived group norms at the expense of the expression of "deviant" individual thoughts, a situation conducive neither to change nor to job satisfaction. It was only after I had worked intensively for months in schools, and had developed a relationship of mutual trust with school personnel, that I came to see that there was a difference between public statements and private positions.

6. E. C. Susskind, "Questioning and Curiosity in the Elementary School Classroom," Ph.D. dissertation, Yale University, 1969, p. 38.

7. Children are the one group who realistically estimate or know the behavioral regularity. My informal poll of scores of children leaves no doubt in my mind that they view the classroom as a place where teachers ask questions and children provide answers.

8. How the obvious can be overlooked can be illustrated (Sarason, Blatt, Davidson, 1962), by looking at a function that all teachers perform, are expected to perform, and must perform—talking to parents. Yet, I know of no teacher-training (some may exist) that gives the prospective teacher five minutes of training in this function, a situation that can be justified only by assuming that God singled out teachers to have the special gift of

how to talk to parents meaningfully and productively. Reality, as we shall see later, does not support this assumption.

9. We are apparently in an era when the term junior high is somewhat in disrepute and the more fashionable term is "the middle school." In some communities the pupil comes to the middle school at a somewhat earlier age and remains there somewhat longer than was the case with the junior high. Typically, the building remains the same but the label changes. This is like the elementary school whose principal prided himself on the initiation of ungraded classes. I was impressed until I strolled through the halls and saw that each door contained grade signs (e.g., Grade 1, Grade 2). Observation in the classrooms provided no good evidence that they should be viewed as other than traditionally organized units.

10. In this study we were given the names of all first year junior high children who were referred to any administrator because of a problem, or who had received an interim. We were then able to see the relationship between what the child's last teacher in elementary school had said (and implicitly predicted) and how many and what kinds of problems were recorded in his folder. For two successive years the evaluation of the child's last teacher was the best predictor of the occurrence of problems in the first year of junior high school.

11. This is, of course, identical to the situation in universities where those who teach only graduate courses tend to view themselves as doing a more important, more worthy, or more difficult task than the instructor who only teaches undergraduates. In the public schools, as well as the universities, it is as if the worth of a teacher is determined in part by the age of his students.

12. When my daughter was in the sixth grade in an elementary school (in an adjacent community) that had the best reputation of any school in our metropolitan area, she was required to write only *one* paper.

13. The reader will recall that we and school personnel were surprised that mathematics did not produce the largest number of interims. One reason for this may be that mathematics teachers *expect* children to have difficulty and, therefore, either they proceed more slowly or they are more lenient in their grading and evaluations. I present this possible explanation in order to make the point that our understanding of the school culture requires that we try to understand why an expected regularity (or pattern of regularity) does not occur.

REFERENCES

Hill, K., and Sarason, S. B. "A Further Longitudinal Study of the Relation of Test Anxiety and Defensiveness Test and School Performance over the Elementary School Years." *Monographs of the Society for Research on Child Development* 31 (No. 2, 1966).

Sarason, S. B., Hill, K., and Zimbardo, P. "A Longitudinal Study of the Relation of Test Anxiety to Performance on Intelligence and Achievement Tests." *Monographs of the Society for Research on Child Development.* No. 98 (1964).

Sarason, S. B., Levine, M., Goldenberg, I. I., Cherlin, D. L., and Bennett, E., *Psychology in Community Settings* (New York: John Wiley & Sons, Inc., 1966).

33. HIDING THE HIDDEN CURRICULUM: AN INTERPRETATION OF THE LANGUAGE OF JUSTIFICATION IN NINETEENTH-CENTURY EDUCATIONAL REFORM

Elizabeth Vallance

There is a curious discontinuity in the history of educational rhetoric, one that to my knowledge has not yet been seriously explored. The discontinuity appears toward the beginning of the twentieth century as a sudden shift in the ways that school people and others have justified public schooling in America. Exploring this shift may shed considerable light on a current issue in education, the issue of the schools' "hidden curriculum."

Recently we have witnessed the discovery—or, rather, we have heard the allegation, for the issue is cast most often as criticism—that schools are teaching more than they claim to teach, that they are doing it systematically, and doing it well. A pervasive hidden curriculum has been discovered in operation. The functions of this hidden curriculum have been variously identified as the inculcation of values, political socialization, training in obedience and docility, the perpetuation of traditional class structure—functions that may be characterized generally as social control. Critics allege that, although this function of social control is not acknowledged openly, it is performed nevertheless, perhaps more effectively than the deliberate teaching of intellectual content and skill, the function in whose name we explicitly justify schooling.

But if social control is now called a hidden function of the school, it cannot be called an unfamiliar one. Even the recent literature of discovery and exploration

SOURCE. *Curriculum Theory Network* 4 (No. 1, 1973/74), pp. 5–21.

(e.g., Overly, 1970) conveys no astonishment at what it has found. The functions of the hidden curriculum are performed openly, sometimes by the most mundane and venerable practices of the schools. If these practices constitute a hidden curriculum, it is hidden only in the sense that the function of social control goes unacknowledged in current rationales for public education. The schools' social control function has been hidden from the language of justification. Indeed, it has vanished from that language, for much that is today called a hidden function of the schools was previously held to be among the prime benefits of schooling. Until the end of the nineteenth century, American educators argued the case for public education precisely in terms of social control.

This paper is an attempt to understand the hidden curriculum from a historical perspective through a survey of the language of justification for schooling in America. I shall attempt to demonstrate by sketching the development of reform rhetoric up to the end of the nineteenth century that the function of the hidden curriculum had been explicit from the beginning, that it gained in salience as formal education became legitimatized and institutionalized, and that it went underground only when schooling as a social institution was secure enough to turn for its justification from the control of groups to the welfare of individuals. The hidden curriculum became hidden only when school people were satisfied that it was working.

The question is, then: When did reference to the function of the hidden curriculum drop out of the public rationales for schooling and what contributed to this apparent shift in focus? What hid the hidden curriculum?

THE CONCEPT OF THE HIDDEN CURRICULUM

The great deal of attention given in recent years to the hidden curriculum has done more to establish the legitimacy of the concept than to clarify its specific referents. That the concept itself is still somewhat loose is apparent in the number of satellite labels that attach themselves to it—including the "unstudied curriculum," the "covert" or "latent" curriculum, the "non-academic outcomes of schooling," the "by-products of schooling," the "residue of schooling," or simply "what schooling does to people" (Overly, 1970; Vallance, 1972a). Each label carries a set of connotations as to what the hidden curriculum is presumed to mean. Let me suggest three dimensions along which these various labels may be read: (1) Hidden curriculum can refer to any of the *contexts* of schooling, including the student-teacher interaction unit, classroom structure, the whole organizational pattern of the educational establishment as a microcosm of the social value system. (2) Hidden curriculum can bear on a number of *processes* operating in or through schools, including values acquisition, socialization, maintenance of class structure. (3) Hidden curriculum can embrace differing *degrees of intentionality*, and of depth of "hiddenness" as perceived by the investigator, ranging from incidental and quite unintended by-products of curricular arrangements to outcomes more deeply embedded in the historical social function of education. The position that any given conception occupies along these or other continuums will likely reflect the academic discipline from which the investigator comes and, not infrequently, his or her political orientation as a critic.

The notion of hidden curriculum used here is a composite of some of the more salient perspectives on the topic. Dreeben (1967, 1968, 1970) focuses on "what is learned in school" as a function of the social structure of the classroom and of the teacher's exercise of authority. Kohlberg (1970) identifies the hidden curriculum as it bears on moral education and the role of the teacher in transmitting moral standards. Jackson (1970) distinguishes the "secondary consequences" of schooling, the broad range of outcomes that the formal curriculum may hope to bring about, from the "primary consequences," the lasting impressions that children pick up from the school environment as though by osmosis. Henry (1955, 1957) attends to the relationship between student and teacher, the rules governing it, and the role of these rules in "educating for docility." Social critics such as Goodman (1960, 1964), Friedenberg (1965, 1966, 1970), Reimer (1971), and Illich (1971) use a conception of the hidden curriculum in order to identify and account for the schools' reinforcement of the class structure and of certain social norms. Bowles (1971) draws similar inferences with reference to Cuban society. The notion of hidden curriculum used here borrows from each of these accounts, as well as from other similar accounts of schooling that do not treat the issue of the hidden curriculum directly (Vallance, 1972*a*). In general, I use the term to refer to those nonacademic but educationally significant consequences of schooling that occur systematically but are not made explicit at any level of the public rationales for education. This usage is intended to include, for example, both the "Pygmalion effect" of teacher expectations (Rosenthal and Jacobson, 1968) and coming to believe that art is something one does only on rainy days. It refers broadly to the social control function of schooling.

It is difficult, then—and perhaps unwise in the earliest stages of investigation—to be too precise about the meaning of "the hidden curriculum." The very fluidity of the notion offers a rich perspective from which to analyze the phenomenon of schooling. The idea of a hidden curriculum functions most usefully as a device for identifying those systematic side effects of schooling that we sense but which cannot be adequately accounted for by reference to the explicit curriculum. To grapple with the notion at all is to adopt a critical attitude toward schooling and to allow ourselves to ask what the institution's nonacademic functions and effects really are.

THE LANGUAGE OF JUSTIFICATION: A HISTORICAL OVERVIEW

There are three major reasons for the focus here on nineteenth-century rationales for schooling: (1) The nineteenth century offers in microcosm the range of social conditions that have characterized American society from its beginnings to the modern era; it witnessed the shift from a predominantly rural to a highly urbanized industrial society. (2) More specifically, the century was an urbanizing one and the history of the hidden curriculum appears to be closely tied to the changing demands of an urban society. (3) Since, as I shall try to demonstrate, the hidden curriculum went underground around the turn of the century, it is important to trace developments up to that time. Because the hidden curriculum can be traced even farther back, I shall make frequent reference to its background in the colonial period. I leave it for another study to trace the career of the hidden curriculum during the twentieth century.

The history of public education in America can be divided roughly into periods. Those established here correspond approximately to quantitative differences in the sheer size of the educational establishment, to significant shifts in patterns of organization, and most pertinently to corresponding shifts in the rhetoric of reform efforts. These periods are: (1) *Prior to the 1830s:* This embraces the colonial period and continues through the era of the common school crusade, when the form of public education was irregular. Schooling was predominantly a rural institution, it was not universal nor compulsory, and it served a very limited population. (2) *Mid-nineteenth century:* The period from the 1830s to the Civil War included the common school reform movement, and the extension of the village school pattern across both the rural society and the gradually growing towns and cities where large numbers of immigrants had begun to settle. The pattern of the district school developed and was extended into the context of cultural diversity that was developing in the cities. (3) *Post-Civil War:* The period from the end of the Civil War to 1900 saw vast industrial expansion and the swelling of the cities by both rural migration and a second wave of immigrants from abroad. During this period the urban school systems became centralized and their control was shifted from the community to the professionals. During this period too the high school began to come into its own. I shall examine in turn the rationales for schooling characteristic of each period.

Prior to the 1830s: From the Colonial Period

America in the long period preceding and the period immediately following the Revolution was a rural society organized around self-sufficient farms and villages. Its social structure was tied to the small local community struggling for survival in virgin territory; social organization of the territory was without a center. Within each community the burden of socialization fell heavily on the family unit tightly bound by local mores. Formal education in the early part of the period was extremely limited; moral standards and the necessary skills for survival were transmitted through the institutions of family and church. Formal schooling was unsystematic, a rare elite function restricted to the upper classes and reflecting most often the classical and nonutilitarian orientation of the private academy, as in New England, or of the tutor system, as in the South. *Public* schooling did not exist.

Yet the beginnings of a need for social control were there. Bailyn (1960) argues that the stable socializing family structure began to break down not long into the colonial period. The wilderness setting proved inadequate to maintain the constraints that had held European society together. In the course of adjusting to new demands, the family structure shifted. Children gained a measure of independence, and changing work patterns and the rising status of women tended to reduce the traditional authority of the male-dominated family unit. Socialization by family and church weakened as the pattern of social contact shifted from the patriarchal kinship group to the more heterogeneous and functionally differentiated village community. By the end of the colonial period, Bailyn maintains, the "once elaborate interpretation of family and community [had] dissolved" and the child's transition from family to society had lost its "naturalness" (Bailyn, 1960, p. 25). Socialization as a smooth, automatic process had lost its traditional base; family and community as educational institutions were no longer adequate.

Early rationales for public schooling were phrased in these terms. Public education was urged as an antidote to this breakdown in the socialization process. Increasing economic complexity made skill learning imperative, and a pattern of independent village schools emerged as a functional response to the needs for socialization and mastery of the three Rs—mastery through the explicitly moral medium of the Bible and the social catechisms of spellers and readers (Johnson, 1963; Tyack, 1967a).* Thus the 1642, 1647, and 1648 education laws of Massachusetts were an attempt to fill the gap created by rapid social changes in the colony; the "ould deluder Satan" had disrupted a heretofore stable social pattern and created new needs. Because of "the great neglect of many parents and masters in training up their children," and amid allegations of excessive indulgence (*TP*, pp. 14–16), public schools were established to restore the pervasively educational climate that children had traditionally enjoyed. Schooling was clearly closing a breach. The earliest public—and denominational—schools in the colonies were largely an adaptive response to recently developed gaps in the traditional process of education.

---

*Hereafter all references to David B. Tyack's *Turning Points in American Educational History* (1967a) are indicated by the abbreviation *TP*, followed where necessary by a page number.

By mid-eighteenth century the spirit of nationalism was growing and schooling was coming to be seen as more than a stopgap measure. In addition to assuming the socialization responsibilities borne previously by family and church, schools were called upon to actively form a national character (*TP*). The language of educational reform preached by those leaders attempting to define and consolidate a new nation was dominated by reference to the need to inculcate a spirit of nationalism, and thereby to establish social control from above. If the states and local communities had earlier seen the need to fill a gap, those intent on creating from these communities a single unified nation saw a broader need. More than simply supplementing the traditional training of the young, the function of education was to actively create what Benjamin Franklin called a "Publick Religion" (*TP*, p. 75). The generation spanning George Washington, Thomas Jefferson, Benjamin Rush, Benjamin Franklin, and Noah Webster, deliberately engaged in unifying an ethnically and socially diverse population, turned to education for the creation of a homogeneous American public.

Homogeneity was explicitly cited as a goal. Washington advocated public higher education on the grounds that "the more homogeneous our citizens can be made . . .the greater will be our prospect of permanent union" (*TP*, p. 85). Jefferson argued against foreign education of Americans, preferring a system that would "educate men to manners, morals, and habits perfectly homogeneous with those of the country" (*TP*, p. 85). Benjamin Rush of Pennsylvania sought to reinforce the "prejudices in favor of our country" through his proposed "one general and uniform system of education" that would "render the mass of the people more homogeneous, and thereby fit them more easily for uniform and peaceable government" (*TP*, p. 103). This demand for the free and uniform republican citizen was echoed by Noah Webster who called for an education that would produce an "inviolable attachment" to country.

Insofar as it embodied the intent of these educator-statesmen, the pattern of American schooling prior to the 1830s was designed to serve two purposes. First, it was intended to transmit the traditional culture. But the need to perform such a function had become apparent only in the light of unsettling changes in the social structure; family and church were no longer carrying their old share of the educational burden. The pattern of schooling that had been urged as a remedy to this breakdown of the socialization process represented an adaptive, but also a conservative, response. Second, the pattern of schooling had come to serve as a means of creating a specifically national and uniform culture. Schools as agencies of social reform were to inculcate the standards of a public morality and to reinforce the legitimacy of established authority.

Interestingly, this seeking after a homogeneous national character was not seen to demand a levelling of the class structure. In fact, it often sought specifically to maintain what was presumed an inevitable pattern of class differences, but to maintain it peaceably. The rhetoric of justification did not refer to individual betterment as such, nor to the amelioration even of so gross a social difference as that between the aristocracy and the laboring classes. With the provisions of his bill for the greater diffusion of knowledge, Jefferson hoped to "rake a few geniuses from the rubbish" while providing the laboring classes with the basic three Rs. Although a public academy had been established by Franklin to foster the mobility of lower-class youth, its curriculum maintained implicitly the distinction between the practical education that it offered its students and the classical one customarily offered the upper class. Class structure, though acknowledged, was not an issue, and the language of justification could effectively remain at the undifferentiated level of a public morality applicable to all. The rationale for schooling invoked the welfare not of individuals but of the public at large.

Mid-Century: The Common Schools and Beyond

The period from the 1830s to the Civil War marks the beginning of urban education in America and, as the era of the Common School crusade and the establishment of public school systems, it fixes the emerging rhetoric of the hidden curriculum in the context of a more systematic policy.

This was the era when urban growth became problematic. During the 1830s, the first great wave of post-Revolutionary immigration profoundly changed the established social fabric. The spirit of nationalism engendered in the period of the Revolution (and propounded, as some allege [Beard and Beard, 1935], largely by the elite and educated classes anyway), was threatened by new social turbulence. The patchwork pattern of educational institutions—some supported publicly, some by religious institutions, others by charitable "free school societies" and private enterprise, and all reflecting the division between elite classical and quasi-public functional schooling—appeared too fragile in the eyes of the 1830s reformers to deal with the new and conflicting needs. The drive to create truly common schools, a move that was to define the system of nationwide public education, began in the settled regions of the East where the threat of conflict and diversity was most keenly felt.

Whereas the Revolutionary generation had felt a need to create a national character, the reformers of the mid-century period were not at all sure that this national character could withstand the onslaught of cultural diversity. It was clear to the Common School crusaders that the national character was basically "Anglo-American" (*TP*); the problem facing that character was now one of self-preservation. "To sustain an extended republic like our own," wrote Calvin Stowe in 1836, "there must be a *national* feeling, a national assimilation. . . . It is altogether essential to our national strength and peace that the foreigners should cease to be Europeans and become Americans. Let them be like grafts which become branches of the parent stock" (*TP*, p. 149). Dr. Daniel Drake described the schoolhouse hopefully as "the crucible of social amalgamation" (*TP*, p. 150). Conservative support of the common school saw education as a peacekeeping agency, "a wise and liberal system of police, by which property, and life, and the peace of society are secured," thereby purifying "the whole moral atmosphere" (*TP*, p. 126).

There certainly was concern for the individual child. During this period a genuine compassion for the victims of social inequities appears in the rhetoric for the first time. Horace Mann's passionate humanism and his devotion to the plight of the urban workers is unquestionable (Curti, 1959; *TP*). His abiding dedication to equality of opportunity and to the inherent "capability of man for self-government" was a motivating force behind the common school movement. But the persuasive arguments for free public education were presented less on grounds of compassion for individuals than on the basis that the alternative to free public education was a general moral degeneracy and loss of the public peace. Mann himself "overemphasized the effectiveness of morality implanted by education" and "entirely approved of indoctrination" that would prevent the masses from resort to violence; he was "hardly free to think out either an educational or a social philosophy that could challenge the status quo in any fundamental way" (Curti, 1959, pp. 125–31). Though he welcomed diversity, at the same time he feared "the mob" and the accompanying conflict of values (*TP*). His work was a move against what he perceived as two dangers, ignorance and vice, and in its course he hoped to stave off the "increasing darkness and degeneracy" threatened by the complex new national situation.

Henry Barnard, after Mann the second great reformer for the cause of the common school, was even less equivocal in his view of its moral function which he saw as "the first essential" of education (Curti, 1959, p. 142). He, too, believed "that the status quo might be preserved if the worst abuses were removed" and seems to have sanctioned "what was virtually the indoctrination of the teachers of youth with capitalistic theory" (Curti, 1959, pp. 147–54). Whether these and other reformers genuinely desired the "well-being of the masses" is not at issue here; what is significant is the tone of the language in which the case was argued.

The rationales of the common school reformers in these decades around mid-century were at least in part a call, in the name of self-preservation, to assimilate aliens into the national character. The language of justification in this era both continued and extended that of the Revolutionary generation. School was still seen as a supplementary nurturing institution; but it was seen also, now that a national character could be identified, as an active socializing agent to guarantee stability in the face of the growing diversity of the populace. A society newly in conflict over its own identity could respond to such an appeal. Education continued to be justified more as a means of social control than as an instrument of individual betterment.

Post-Civil War: Urbanism and Centralization

The Common School crusade won its major battle, of course, and by the period following the Civil War the district-school pattern had become, as much as anything could, a nationwide institution (Cubberley, 1914). It was carried from New England westward in virtually the same form it had known in its northeastern origins.

It should be remembered, however, that assertive socialization remained a more prominent feature of urban than of rural schooling. In the simpler and less diverse rural communities, control of the schools still lay largely in the hands of the communities; social control was not commonly cited as a rationale for reform until later in the century, when nostalgia for a vanishing ruralism would prompt educators to advocate consolidating the schools as a means of preserving the rural tradition. A concern for moral conservation continued to dominate rationales for rural schooling.

In urban areas the situation was quite different. The village-school pattern emerging from the previous reform era had been transposed into urban areas as well, and here community control meant immersion of the schools in the baroque machinations of ward politics (Katz, 1971; Schrag, 1967; Tyack, 1967b, 1972a). Precisely at the moment when there again seemed an urgent need to Americanize and assimilate, local control in urban areas spelled control by ethnic and special interest factions. The cities were a patchwork of ethnic groupings living under volatile slum conditions (Riis, 1957). A generation of reformers nurtured in the production ethic and confronted by the success of bureaucratic organization in industry found the local politics of urban education maddeningly inefficient. City school boards were vast operations with memberships numbering into the hundreds (Tyack, 1972a, b); they assumed such diverse responsibilities as responding to constituent interests, controlling policy, appointing teachers and making purchases (Schrag, 1967; Tyack, 1972a, b).

As the sheer size and complexity of urban educational machinery continued to increase, the language of educational reform began to focus more on the organizational structure than on the moral content of schooling. Moral concern itself remained undiminished certainly. But in counterpoint with the deliberate Americanizing of the textbooks and the literal washing of the unwashed immigrants, there was a vigorous structural move to centralize. Tyack (1967b, 1972a, b), Schrag (1967) and Katz (1971) have amply documented this movement toward centralization in cities in every corner of the country; by the 1870s and 1880s the pattern was virtually fixed from Portland to Boston.

Implications of centralization. Centralization had clear implications for the curricular and social experiences offered to the children. It is evident from muckraking reports of that era, from reports by the children themselves (Tyack, 1972b) and from public documents on educational policy that the standardization and efficiency of both process and product that dominated the public rhetoric had to filter down to affect the classroom experience. Superintendent John Philbrick of Boston, leading an army of vociferous professionals in centralizing and professionalizing the schools, had asserted in 1885 that "the best is the best everywhere" and that movement toward greater centralization would surely be "in the direction of progress and improvement" (Philbrick, 1885, p. 19). The quest for the one best system precluded any acknowledgement of local differences and aspired instead to a uniformity of experience.

That the standardization of organizational structure was parallelled by a focus on homogeneity, efficiency, and obedience to authority is clear in an 1874 statement describing the theory and practice of American education. The statement was signed by seventy-seven leading educators, and it held that: (1) a system of public education was necessary to the existence of the "modern industrial community," because (2) the "peculiarities of civil society" in America weaken the family's role in initiating the young into society and "the consequence of this is the increased importance of the school in an ethical point of view," (3) the functions of the school therefore include the development of discipline and the "moral phase" of education "in order to compensate for lack of family-nurture," and finally (4) this moral education must necessarily coincide with "the commercial tone prevalent in the city" which stresses "military precision in the maneuvering of classes. Great stress is laid on punctuality, regularity, attention, and silence, as habits necessary through life" for success in an industrial civilization (*TP*, pp. 325–26). The schools, under this description, offered skill training and initiation into the prevailing mode of social organization. Socialization into the industrial mode was the express purpose of the curricular and organizational structure of schools and remained so through the end of the century. In 1891 the Commissioner of Education, William Torrey Harris, frankly admitted that a major purpose of schools was to teach respect for authority and that forming the "habits of punctuality, silence, and industry" was more important than understanding the reasons for good behavior (Curti, 1959, p. 334).

That the production-model approach to cultural assimilation did prevail is crucial. Its success is indicated in the numerous muckraking reports issued toward the end of the century as well as in the criticisms of over-standardization made by educators a decade later. Writing in the 1890s, Joseph Mayer Rice vigorously attacked the automatized, regimented, and dehumanized instruction carried out in classrooms dominated by a compulsion to "save the minutes" where children responded in rote manner to a teacher who stood as the unquestioned source of wisdom "giving the child ready-made thoughts"; Rice described the schools of New York as places of mechanical drudgery where "the laws of mental development are entirely ignored" (*TP*, pp. 329–32). By 1916, the critics of Ellwood P. Cubberley's generation could decry the outcome of this orientation. In that year Cubberley described the Portland public school system as one offering a "rigidly prescribed, mechanical" schooling in which "all must be made as nearly alike as possible" (*TP*, p. 333).

The painful accounts by social critics and parents at the end of the nineteenth century, and later recollections by students, indicate the bitterness of the conflict induced by the moral domination of the school's culture over the traditional European family norms. Americanization was difficult but it was levelling out some of the differences and wrenching children away from the inefficiency of cultural diversity. Both those children who hoped only to survive in the public schools and those who actively sought to succeed and thrive followed the schools' dicta and adapted to the norms of obedience. Homogeneity was as much a goal of schooling as it had been over a century before; it was now buttressed by a standardized organizational mode that strengthened the means to that end.

Some Generalizations

At this point let me offer four generalizations about the arguments for education during the period when the present urban orientation of schooling was established. First, public schooling evolved as a response to the declining role of the family and local community. The weakening of traditional educative processes had been the initial impetus to public schooling; rhetoric throughout the nineteenth century continued to claim that training in the home was inadequate and consequently that the school must assume a compensatory burden. Second, the notion of schooling as supplementary socialization becomes altered with reference to the Revolutionary generation. During that period educator-statesmen turned to the schools less to maintain a stable traditional value system than to create a national character where none had existed. In both arguments, the function of education is still cast in moralistic terms. Schools are an agency of undifferentiated social control. Third, the prevalence of social over individual concerns runs consistently through the nineteenth-century language of justification, emerging most strongly in response to the urban developments of that century. The great waves of immigration during the 1830s, the 1880s and the 1890s produced enormous strains in the cities both on the immigrants themselves and on the Anglo-American "character" they encountered. Cultural diversity was seen as a problem in both periods of immigration. In both periods schooling was called on actively to socialize and assimilate. But, fourth, as Tyack suggests (1972*a*), the bodies of rhetoric in the two immigration periods were different in tone. Though the reformers of the 1830s were more actively oriented toward assimilation and imposition than the Revolutionary generation had had to be, schooling was still viewed as a nurturing agency. By the end of the century the language of justification had become more strident; the element of coercive detention had been added.

Thus the nineteenth century is a significant period in the history of the hidden curriculum. One major characteristic of the period—the growing diversity of cultural and political structures—pushed educators to resume with renewed vigor the language of social control and homogenization that had dominated educational rhetoric from the earliest colonial period. The language of the hidden curriculum was never more explicit than in this period when the rationales for education began shifting focus from an emphasis on supplementary nurture to one on active molding and imposition of values.

Yet the other major characteristic of the period, the growth of a commercial and industrial production ethic and of a cult of rationalism and efficiency, meant that a concern with inculcating values was no longer enough. In the fragmented political structure of the cities, and therefore also of education, the reform rhetoric discovered a salient new need. To assertive socialization was added a focus on organizational efficiency. The language of production, economic models, and bureaucratic skills came to dominate the educational reform movements that had the greatest effect on schooling at the time. The rationale for change shifted from moralism to functionalism.

At the same time, of course, functionalism became a demand not only of the educational organizers but of society as a whole. The pressures of modernization and industrialization in this post-Civil War period produced new demands for skill training and practical learning. The functionalism and means-ends orientation of the educational reformers reflected a mode that permeated most of American urban society at the time. The changes of the industrial era demanded more than training in American morals. For if Horace Mann had seen the school as fashioning a stable social order, the generation of William T. Harris had to confirm this social order in the face of threats from without and from within. As apologists for industrialism the late-century reformers had to begin dealing with providing specific skills to large numbers of people, developing the capabilities that would assure survival of the industrial order. Americanize they must, and organizational reform helped to standardize the product.

But now for the first time educators began talking of an education that would "fit" the child "for the active life." The curriculum itself had to be product-oriented, practical, and useful. Schooling became a functional creature not only organizationally but in intent. The goals became less unitary.

HIDING THE HIDDEN CURRICULUM

It was at this point, when the rationale for schooling began to be argued in functional as well as moral terms, that what we now call the hidden curriculum could safely lose its saliency in the rhetoric. With a shock of recognition we note today that the schools are educating "for docility" (Henry, 1955), or that they operate to reinforce a rigid class structure (Illich, 1971; Reimer, 1971), or that teaching methods and curriculum content are saturated with a middle-class value bias (Kohlberg, 1970). These are precisely the grounds on which American schooling was initially justified.

I suggest that the hidden curriculum became hidden by the end of the nineteenth century simply because by that point the rhetoric had done its job. Schooling had evolved from a supplementary socializing influence to an active impositional force. By the turn of the century it could be taken for granted that the schools offered an experience sufficiently homogeneous and regimented. The hidden curriculum was well ensconced. Only when the view of schooling as molder of a common character was at its height did functionalist reforms in organization open the door to a new rhetoric of justification. Only at this point could the need to provide individuals with the tools of economic and social survival offer a rationale for schooling that would rival, and eventually displace, the need to create a homogeneous populace.

A Parallel Development: The Growth of the High School

The clearest confirmation of this process of hiding the hidden curriculum may be a concurrent phenomenon, the rise of public secondary education. Secondary education had not been a major concern of the early nineteenth-century reformers. Jefferson had never intended that the working classes have more than three years of basic schooling. The reformers of Mann's generation spoke in more egalitarian terms, but the scope of their interest was limited nevertheless and did not extend far beyond the goals of basic literacy. In the 1870s William T. Harris boasted that the greatest achievement of the common schools had been their "transformation of an illiterate population into a population that reads the daily newspapers" (Tyack 1972a)—in addition to imparting the necessary urban discipline. As long as schooling was seen primarily as a source of social harmony and stability, and only secondarily as a means of personal advancement, extended education was not only unessential but, insofar as it was oriented to the classical curriculum, not even very useful. In his comprehensive study of the high school, Edward Krug (1964) documents the sudden growth of public secondary education in the decades following 1880. Both Krug and Cremin (1961) trace the development of a demand for the "practical" in public education. I offer here only a very brief synopsis of this story.

At the end of the century secondary education was by no means widespread. Krug reports that in 1889 the total number of students enrolled in institutions of secondary education, academies and public high schools alike, was less than one percent of the total population; though within a decade the number had increased by a factor of two and a half, the numerical reach of secondary education was still very restricted. Changes in the patterns and balance of secondary schooling in this period are, however, quite significant, for they reflect important shifts in the public conception of the functions of public education.

Attendance at the private academies had been limited, for the most part, to the children of those who could afford the luxury; and public secondary schooling had not accumulated much momentum, even though the first public high school had opened in Boston as early as 1821. Confined as it was to urban areas where longer schooling could be justified, secondary education retained a flavor of elitism simply by virtue of its limited numbers. In 1890 Harvard President Charles W. Eliot reported that "the mass of the rural population—that is to say three-quarters of the American people—is unprovided with secondary schools" (*TP*, p. 354). Of the one-quarter that was suitably provided, very few availed themselves of the chance. And though even fewer actually went on to college—less than 10 percent of secondary students—college preparation strongly influenced the curriculum; a secondary education was scarcely a practical one.

In the post-Civil War era, however, there arose a demand for practical education which a few decades later would reach much greater proportions. In this period, vocationalism as such was not yet a major theme in education but it was emerging significantly in the establishment of manual training and agricultural programs beginning in the late 1870s, as well as in the growing demand for high school programs offering commercial courses. The public high school grew partially in response to the sheer increase in numbers of children who could afford to extend their education, and partially therefore in response to a need for a more practical education than either the elementary school or the classically oriented secondary curriculums could provide.

The high school developed as an urban institution. It was a creature of late-nineteenth-century urbanization and the new demands it created. By the 1880s public high schools began to outnumber the academies as institutions of secondary education, increasing in number from 2,520 in 1890 to 6,005 ten years later (Krug, 1964). Reasons for the rise of the high school in this period are varied. One was the sheer increase in urban population as a function of rural migration. Another was the growth of technology and its demand for more advanced occupational skills. The inability of the elementary schools to fully equip students for assimilation into the urban situation was clear; and it is possible that the elementary school's emphasis on homogeneity, and its consequent disinclination to acknowledge individual needs and interests by differentiating its programs, provided the necessary impetus for the growth of secondary education. The explicit social control function assigned to the elementary schools meant both that their curriculum was necessarily standardized and uniform, and that (a) the products of these schools could be assumed to have certain backgrounds in common, and (b) any necessary specialized training would have to be provided by an institution other than the elementary school.

Thus the high school, as a relatively novel element in the educational structure, was able to evolve its own rationale. In the role of "the people's college" it assumed responsibilities attendant on it as the highest level of education to which most people could aspire. As chief agent of social mobility it had to be able both to prepare students for higher education and also (mainly) to "prepare for the duties of life," performing "the two-fold function of the 'fitting' and the 'finishing' school" (*TP*, p. 390). It was thus forced to diversify its curriculum to meet the needs of diverse groups of students. In 1892 Eliot's Committee of Ten, although allegedly prompted by a concern for the lack of articulation between secondary schooling and the colleges, proposed a package of four separate curricula for high schools (Krug, 1964). The high school was compelled to be responsive to diversity in a way that the elementary school had never been. It became, in a sense, a vehicle by which the explicit curriculum came to be tailored to the needs of the individual. The demands placed on the late-nineteenth century high school offered a starting point for orienting education as much to the demands of the individual as to the undifferentiated need for societal homogeneity and uniform social control. The high school was made necessary partly, I suggest, by the effectiveness of the hidden curriculum at the elementary level. It was the vehicle for the progressive individualization of the curriculum. As such it helped to accomplish the hiding of the hidden curriculum.

With the rise of public secondary education around 1900, then, we see the clearest indication of the nineteenth-century shift in the rationale for schooling. Education came to be justified less from the top down than from the bottom up. The burden of the argument began to shift from the need to impose homogeneity to the social needs of the individual. Social control was not abandoned as an aim; it simply shifted its visibility as the goals of education came to be phrased in terms of individual development *within* the social context.

Though direct reference to social and moral shaping has occasionally re-emerged in the period since 1900—the public reaction to the Red Scare and McCarthyism is but one example—a progressive personalization of the curriculum and of the goals of education has continued to saturate the language of justification since the turn of the century. By 1918 the Committee on the Reorganization of Secondary Education could state that "education in a democracy . . . should develop in each individual the knowledge, interests, ideals, habits and powers whereby he will find his place and use that place to shape both himself and society toward ever nobler ends" (*TP*, p. 399). Social control is there, but hidden through reference to the individual. The shift in emphasis is enormous; I suspect it would have been impossible if the hidden curriculum had not been taken for granted.

REDISCOVERY

It is beyond the scope of this paper to develop the notion that the language of justification of modern education has been phrased increasingly in terms of the welfare of individuals. Some sketchy evidence for the altered emphasis appears in the thrust, and in the very names, of those movements, campaigns, and enthusiasms that have marked the progress of twentieth century education—the child-study movement and the measurement of individual differences, Progressive Education and the child-centered school, the development of a psychology of learning, and individualized instruction. Surely the individual has come into his or her own. In 1961 the Educational Policy Commission stated the goals of American education in these terms: "to foster that development of individual capacities which will enable each human being to become the best person he is capable of becoming. . . . The general morality depends on choices made by individuals" (*TP*, pp. 408–9). The four major goals of schooling were given as "self-realization, human relationship, economic efficiency, and civic responsibility," in that order—which is a long way from creating the "homogeneous American."

That Reimer, Goodman, Friedenberg, and Henry, to name a few, are now criticizing the schools for having succeeded in the very purposes they initially set for themselves is perhaps ironic. But in a sense it is not surprising that growing attention to the individual, and to the role of the social environment in individual growth, should be accompanied by the discovery that a hidden curriculum is operating in the schools. It is tempting to suggest that it was not until the effectiveness of the hidden curriculum could be taken for granted that educators were able to turn their attention to other matters and begin to understand and respond to the unique problems of the learning process itself. That the schooling experience might not be the same for every child was perhaps a discovery that could not have been made until the context of learning had been sufficiently standardized to make such comparisons pertinent. This is not to say that the hidden curriculum's effectiveness was a good thing. It is simply to suggest, and only very tentatively, that there may be a line of development in fact from the explicitness of nineteenth-century educational rhetoric, to its success in establishing social control and a uniform learning context, to the subsequent dropping of the social-control function from the rhetoric, and to the rediscovery of it as an explanation for the peculiarly systematic, though allegedly unintended, outcomes of schooling. These outcomes may not be nearly as unintended as we think. They may be hidden from the rhetoric precisely because they do work.

What to do with the hidden curriculum now that we have found it is an open question. We can embrace it wholeheartedly once again, attempt to expunge it altogether, or most likely something in between these two extremes. This survey of the language of justification of school reform suggests that the hidden curriculum is so deeply embedded in our whole conception of schooling that while it no longer needs to be made explicit, neither can it merely be washed away. The history of the language of justification throughout the nineteenth century should give us a better idea of what modifying the hidden curriculum might entail.

REFERENCES

Bailyn, Bernard. *Education in the Forming of American Society: Needs and Opportunities for Study* (Chapel Hill: University of North Carolina Press, 1960).

Beard, Charles, and Beard, Mary. *An Economic Interpretation of the Constitution of the United States* (New York: Free Press, 1935).

Bowles, Samuel. "Cuban Education and the Revolutionary Ideology." *Harvard Educational Review* 41 (No. 4, November 1971): 472–500.

Cremin, Lawrence. *The Transformation of the School: Progressivism in American Education* (New York: Random House, 1961).

Cubberley, Ellwood P. *Rural Life and Education* (New York: Houghton-Mifflin, 1914).

Curti, Merle. *The Social Ideas of American Educators* (Paterson, N.J.: Littlefield, Adams, 1959).

Dreeben, Robert. "The Contribution of Schooling to the Learning of Norms." *Harvard Educational Review* 37 (No. 2, Spring 1967): 211–37.

―――. *On What Is Learned in School* (Reading, Mass.: Addison-Wesley, 1968).

―――. "Schooling and Authority: Comments on the Unstudied Curriculum." In Norman Overly (ed.), *The Unstudied Curriculum* (Washington, D.C.: Association for Supervision and Curriculum Development, 1970).

Easton, D., and Dennis, J. "The Child's Acquisition of Regime Norms: Political Efficacy." *American Political Science Review* 61 (No. 1, 1967): 25–38.

Friedenberg, Edgar Z. *Coming of Age in America: Growth and Acquiescence* (New York: Random House, 1965).

―――. "New Value Conflicts in American Education." *School Review* 74 (No. 1, Spring 1966): 66–94.

―――. "Curriculum as Educational Process: The Middle Class Against Itself." In Norman Overly (ed.), *The Unstudied Curriculum* (Washington, D.C.: Association for Supervision and Curriculum Development, 1970).

Goodman, Paul. *Growing Up Absurd* (New York: Random House, 1960).

―――. *Compulsory Mis-education* (New York: Horizon Press, 1964).

Hays, Samuel P. "The Politics of Reform in Municipal Government in the Progresssive Era." *Pacific North-West Quarterly* 55 (October 1964): 157–69.

Henry, Jules. "Attitude Organization in Elementary School Classrooms." *American Journal of Orthopsychiatry* 27 (1957): 117–33.

―――. "Docility, or Giving Teacher What She Wants." *Journal of Social Issues* 2 (No. 2, 1955): 33–41.

―――. *Culture Against Man* (New York: Random House, 1963).

Hess, Robert D., and Easton, David. "The Role of the Elementary School in Political Socialization." *School Review* 70 (Autumn 1962): 257–65.

Hess, Robert D., and Torney, Judith V. *The Development of Political Attitudes in Children* (Chicago: Aldine, 1967).

Illich, Ivan. *De-Schooling Society* (New York: Harper and Row, 1971).

Jackson, Philip. "The Way Teaching Is." In C. Hitchcock (ed.), *The Way Teaching Is* (Washington, D.C.: Association for Supervision and Curriculum Development, 1966).

——. "The Consequences of Schooling." In Norman Overly (ed.), *The Unstudied Curriculum* (Washington, D.C.: Association for Supervision and Curriculum Development, 1970).

Johnson, Clifton. *Old-Time Schools and School-Books* (New York: Dover, 1963).

Katz, Michael. *Class, Bureaucracy and Schools: The Illusion of Educational Change in America* (New York: Praeger, 1971).

Kohlberg, Lawrence. "The Moral Atmosphere of the School." In Norman Overly (ed.), *The Unstudied Curriculum* (Washington, D.C.: Association for Supervision and Curriculum Development, 1970).

Krug, Edward A. *The Shaping of the American High School* (New York: Harper and Row, 1964).

Overly, Norman (ed.), *The Unstudied Curriculum: Its Impact On Children* (Washington, D.C.: Association for Supervision and Curriculum Development, 1970).

Philbrick, John D. *City School Systems in the United States.* 1885. Reprint. U.S. Bureau of Education, Circulars of Information, No. 1 (Washington, D.C.: U.S. Government Printing Office).

Reimer, Everett. *School is Dead: Alternatives in Education.* 1st ed. (Garden City, N.Y.: Doubleday, 1971).

Riis, Jacob. *How the Other Half Lives* (New York: Hill and Wang, 1957).

Rosenthal, Robert, and Jacobson, Lenore. *Pygmalion in the Classroom: Teacher Expectation and Pupils' Intellectual Development* (New York: Holt, Rinehart and Winston, 1968).

Schrag, Peter. *Village School Downtown: Politics and Education* (Boston: Beacon Press, 1967).

Tyack, David. *Turning Points in American Educational History* (Waltham, Mass.: Blaisdell, 1967). (*a*)

——. "Bureaucracy and the Common School: The Example of Portland, Oregon, 1851–1913." *American Quarterly* 19 (No. 3, Fall 1967). (*b*)

——. *From Village School to Urban System: A Political and Social History* (Washington, D.C.: United States Office of Education, 1972). (*a*)

——. "City Schools: Centralization of Control at the Turn of the Century." In Jerry Israel (ed.), *The Organizational Society* (New York: Free Press, 1972). (*b*)

——. "Views from Below." Colloquium on History of American Urban Education, Ed. 302, Stanford University. Mimeographed.

Vallance, Elizabeth. "Introduction to the Bibliography: Conceptualizing the Hidden Curriculum." Unpublished manuscript. 1972. (*a*)

——. "The Later Case for Consolidation: Romanticism in Rural School Reform." Unpublished manuscript. 1972. (*b*)

34. BUREAUCRACY AND CURRICULUM THEORY*

Herbert M. Kliebard

Historians of education agree that American Education went through a kind of metamorphosis after the turn of this century, but the nature and effect of the changes are in some dispute. In the popular mind, the reforms that were wrought during that period—indeed the whole first half of the 20th century—have become associated with a broad and loosely defined "progressive education" movement. John Dewey is seen as the dominant force in American educational practice with an undisciplined child-centered pedagogy dubiously ascribed to him. Even a cursory examination of the work of educational reformers during this period, however, indicates that influential leaders differed widely in the doctrines they espoused and in the pedagogical reforms they advocated. Clearly, the educational ideas of a David Snedden or a Franklin Bobbitt differed enormously from those of a John Dewey or a Stanwood Cobb. There is no doubt that this was a period of ferment in education, with new ideas filling the void being created by the steadily declining theory of mental discipline.

The picture that emerges from the apparently frenetic educational activity

SOURCE. In Vernon F. Haubrich (ed.), *Freedom, Bureaucracy, and Schooling*. 1971 Yearbook (Washington, D.C.: Association for Supervision and Curriculum Development, 1971), pp. 74–93. Copyright © 1971 by the Association for Supervision and Curriculum Development. All rights reserved.

*I am grateful to the Research Committee of the Graduate School, University of Wisconsin, for granting the summer research leave which made it possible for me to conduct the research reported here in part.

during the first few decades of this century seems to be one of growing acceptance of a powerful and restrictive bureaucratic model for education which looked toward the management techniques of industry as its ideal of excellence and source of inspiration. The dominant metaphor for educational theory in the early 20th century was drawn not from the educational philosophy of John Dewey or even from romantic notions of childhood, but from corporate management. As Ellwood Cubberley explicated that model in 1916,

Every manufacturing establishment that turns out a standard product or a series of products of any kind maintains a force of efficiency experts to study methods of procedure and to measure and test the output of its works. Such men ultimately bring the manufacturing establishment large returns, by introducing improvements in processes and procedure, and in training the workmen to produce larger and better output. Our schools are, in a sense, factories in which the raw products (children) are to be shaped and fashioned into products to meet the various demands of life. The specifications for manufacturing come from the demands of twentieth-century civilization, and it is the business of the school to build its pupils according to the specifications laid down. This demands good tools, specialized machinery, continuous measurement of production to see if it is according to specifications, the elimination of waste in manufacture, and a large variety in the output.[1]

SCIENTIFIC MANAGEMENT

The context for the bureaucratization of the school curriculum that was to take place in the 20th century was manifest in the general social and intellectual climate of American society at the turn of the century. The late 19th century saw the breakdown of a community-centered society and with it the ideal of the individual as the unit element in social life. The press of corporate expansion and urbanization made the individual merely a cog in a great machine. Whereas the individual retained a measure of recognition in a community-centered society, the vast new social and economic units robbed him of his identity. Responses to this fundamental change in American society ranged from the economic radicalism of Henry George to the utopian socialism of Edward Bellamy. But "the ideas that filtered through and eventually took the fort," according to Wiebe, "were the bureaucratic ones peculiarly suited to the fluidity and impersonality of an urban-industrial world."[2]

The particular response that captured the imagination of Americans at the turn of the century was a form of idealized bureaucracy known widely as scientific management. Its principal spokesman was Frederick W. Taylor, and its watchword was efficiency. Taylorism differs from classical conceptions of bureaucracy (for example, Weber) in its emphasis on sheer practical efficiency rather than analysis of complex lines of power and influence within organizations. Under Taylor's concept of scientific management, productivity is central, and the individual is simply an element in the production system. Basic to Taylor's conception of scientific management was the assumption that man is motivated by economic gain and would sacrifice much in the way of job satisfaction and physical ease in order to achieve such gain. Yet scientific principles had to be applied to the workman as well as to the work, and this involved careful study of the workman's "own special abilities and limitations" in an effort "to develop each individual man to his highest state of efficiency and prosperity"[3] (anticipating, in a way, the modern guidance movement in schools).

One of Taylor's proudest accomplishments was to inveigle a man he called Schmidt into increasing his handling of pig iron at a Bethlehem Steel plant from 12½ tons a day to 47 tons. Schmidt was selected after careful observation and study of 75 men, partly because he was observed to trot home in the evening about as fresh as when he trotted in to work in the morning and partly because inquiries revealed that he was "close with a dollar." Taylor even gives an extended verbatim account of his discussion with Schmidt:

> "Schmidt, are you a high-priced man?"
> "Vell, I don't know vat you mean."
> "Oh, yes you do. What I want to know is whether you are a high-priced man or not."
> "Vell, I don't know vat you mean."
> "Oh, come now, you answer my questions. What I want to find out is whether you are a high-priced man or one of these cheap fellows here. What I want to find out is whether you want to earn $1.85 a day or whether you are satisfied with $1.15, just the same as all those cheap fellows are getting."
> "Did I vant $1.85 a day? Vas dot a high-priced man? Vell, yes, I vas a high-priced man."
> "Oh, you're aggravating me. Of course you want $1.85 a day—everyone wants it! You know perfectly well that that has very little to do with your being a high-priced man. For goodness' sake answer my questions, and don't waste any more of my time. Now come over here. You see that pile of pig iron?[4]

Using this economic motivation, Taylor proceeded to instruct Schmidt in the efficient performance of every stage of the operation. Schmidt's step must have been a little heavier as he trotted home that night.

Thus, the individual under Taylorism was not ignored; on the contrary, he was made the subject of intense investigation, but only within the context of increasing product output. Through time and motion studies, the worker's movements were broken down into minute operations and then standards of efficiency were developed for each of the operations. The rules of scientific management and psychological principles were then applied to the worker to bring him up to the appropriate level of efficiency. As Mouzelis summarizes the individual's role under Taylorism, "The organisation member was conceived as an instrument of production which can be handled as easily as any other tool (provided that one knows the laws of scientific management)."[5] The essence of scientific management was the fragmentation and analysis of work and its reordering into the most efficient arrangement possible.

One of the attractions of Taylorism was that it carried with it an ethical dimension which bore a superficial resemblance to some of the tried and true virtues of the 19th century. Taylor's first professional paper, for example, delivered in 1895 at a meeting of the American Society of Mechanical Engineers, made the case for a "piece-rate system" partly on moral grounds. The minimum time for each operation would be computed and the worker would be paid for his performance relative to that fixed performance level. In this way, the workman's interest would coincide with that of his employer and "soldiering" (loafing on the job) would be eliminated. Once the work load was broken down into elementary operations, an "honest day's work" could be scientifically computed.[6] "If a man won't do what is right," Taylor argued, "*make* him."[7] Since scientific rate-fixing could be used to outline the dimensions of virtuous activity, industry could be rewarded and sloth punished.

The appeal of Taylor's doctrine of scientific efficiency was not limited to an elite corps of business leaders. The rising cost of living in the early 20th century was a matter of great concern to the broad American middle class, and scientific management promised lower prices through increased efficiency. The wide publicity given the Eastern Rate Case of 1910-11 also drew much popular attention to the cause of efficiency. Railroads were asking an increase in freight rates, and, arguing against their position, Louis Brandeis claimed that scientific management could save the railroads a million dollars a day. In support of his contention, he brought forward a series of witnesses in the form of efficiency experts. As Haber summarized the effect of their testimony, "The Eastern Rate Case was transformed into a morality play for up-to-date middle-class reformers"[8] which eventually culminated in an orgy of efficiency affecting millions of Americans. The effect on the schools was not long in coming.

BUREAUCRATIC EFFICIENCY IN SCHOOL MANAGEMENT AND CURRICULUM THEORY

The bureaucratic model for curriculum design had a rather unremarkable birth. School administrators simply reacted to the influence of the scientific management movement in industry by interpolating those methods to the management of schools. Managers of schools patterned themselves after their counterparts in industry and took pride in adapting the vocabulary and techniques of industry to school administration.[9] Cost accounting and maximum utilization of school plants were among their paramount concerns. The period, in fact, may be regarded as one in which the "transition of the superintendent of schools from an educator to a business manager" took place.[10]

The efficiency movement, however, was to affect more than just the administration of schools. Its most profound effect was on curriculum theory itself. Among the early prophets of the new efficiency in school administration was the man who later was to become the preeminent force in curriculum reform, and, indeed, the man who gave shape and direction to the curriculum field, John Franklin Bobbitt.

Bobbitt's early work essentially followed the main line of adapting business techniques for use in schools. In 1912, for example, Bobbitt took as his model of efficiency the operation of the Gary, Indiana, schools. "The first principle of scientific management," he announced, "is to use all the plant all the available time."[11] Although the typical school plant operates at 50 percent efficiency, the "educational engineer" in Gary set as his task the development of a plan to operate at 100 percent efficiency during school hours. Although a relatively high level of efficiency of school plant operation was achieved by creating regular and special periods of activity, perfect efficiency was thwarted by the fact that the school plant was used only five days a week. "That an expensive plant should lie idle during all of Saturday and Sunday while 'street and alley time' is undoing the good work of the schools," Bobbitt complained, "is a further thorn in the flesh of the clear-sighted educational engineer."[12] He also mourned the closing of the school plant during the summer, "a loss of some 16 percent, no small item in the calculations of the efficiency engineer."[13]

Bobbitt's second principle of scientific management, "to reduce the number of workers to a minimum by keeping each at the maximum of his working efficiency,"[14] reflected the need for division of labor and job specialization in the school. His third principle simply involved the elimination of waste. Here, Bobbitt commented on the wasteful concomitants of "ill-health and lowered vitality" and commended Superintendent Wirt's efforts to provide appropriate recreational facilities for the students in the Gary schools.

Bobbitt's fourth principle of general scientific management made the leap from the areas of simple plant and worker efficiency into the realm of educational theory itself:

Work up the raw material into that finished product for which it is best adapted. Applied to education this means: Educate the individual according to his capabilities. This requires that the materials of the curriculum be sufficiently various to meet the needs of every class of individuals in the community; and the course of training and study be sufficiently flexible that the individual can be given just the things he needs.[15]

This extrapolation of the principles of scientific management to the area of curriculum made the child the object on which the bureaucratic machinery of the school operates. He became the raw material from which the school-factory must fashion a product drawn to the specifications of social convention. What was at first simply a direct application of general management principles to the management of schools became the central metaphor on which modern curriculum theory rests.

"Educate the individual according to his capabilities" has an innocent and plausible ring; but what this meant in practice was that dubious judgments about the innate capacities of children became the basis for differentiating the curriculum along the lines of probable destination for the child. Dominated by the criterion of social utility, these judgments became self-fulfilling prophecies in the sense that they predetermined which slots in the social order would be filled by which "class of individuals." Just as Taylor decided that "one of the first requirements for a man who is fit to handle pig iron as a regular occupation is that he shall be so stupid and phlegmatic that he more nearly resembles in his mental makeup the ox than any other type,"[16] so it was the schools that now were to determine (scientifically, of course) what biographical, psychological, or social factors in human beings fit them to be the hewers of wood and the drawers of water in our society. Although still in undeveloped form, this conception of the work of the school in relation to the child and his studies became a central element in Bobbitt's influential curriculum research and theory a decade or so later. The ramifications of this central production metaphor in educational theory are now widely felt.

Through the first quarter of the 20th century, Bobbitt continued to take the lead in reforming the administration of public schools along the lines of scientific management advocated by Taylor. One such recommendation, for example, took the Harriman railroad system as the model of efficiency. Bobbitt pointed out how that massive enterprise had been divided into 30 autonomous divisions, each with its own specialized staff, resulting in a high rate of efficiency. Extrapolating from this and other examples, Bobbitt went on to comment on the functions of specialized supervisors in schools in determining "proper methods" and "the determination of more or less definite qualifications for the various aspects of the teaching personality."[17] The supervisor of instruction occupied that middle-management function roughly comparable to the foreman in industry.

Increasingly, however, Bobbitt was moving from the mere translation of general principles of scientific management to the management of schools into the domain of curriculum theory. As a kind of quality control, Bobbitt advocated that "definite qualitative and quantitative standards be determined for the product."[18] In the railroad industry, he pointed out, each rail "must be thirty feet in length, and weigh eighty pounds to the yard. It must be seven and three-eighths inches in height, with a head two and one-sixty-fourth of an inch in thickness and five inches deep, and a base five inches wide."[19]

Based on studies by Courtis and others and using standard scores, Bobbitt concluded that:

The third-grade teacher should bring her pupils up to an average of 26 correct [arithmetic] combinations per minute. The fourth-grade teacher has the task, during the year that the same pupils are under her care, of increasing their addition speed from an average of 26 combinations per minute to an average of 34 combinations per minute. If she does not bring them up to the standard 34, she has failed to perform her duty in proportion to the deficit; and there is no responsibility upon her for carrying them beyond the standard 34.[20]

Two years later, Bobbitt was to apply principles of cost accounting in business organizations to school subjects. This brought the heart of the school curriculum, the subjects, into the orbit of bureaucratic efficiency. Bobbitt continued to be impressed by standardization in relation to efficiency in railroad administration. He pointed out, for example, that railroad companies know that "locomotive repair-cost should average about six cents per mile-run" and that "lubricating oils should cost about eighteen cents per hundred miles for passenger locomotives, and about twenty-five cents for freight locomotives."[21] Using cost per 1,000 student-hours as his basic unit, Bobbitt was able to report, in terms comparable to those of industry, that the cost of instruction in mathematics in his sample of 25 high schools ranged from $30 to $169 and that Latin instruction was, on the average, 20 percent more expensive than mathematics instruction. The implications of such an accounting procedure were developed later by Bobbitt, his colleagues, and his present-day intellectual heirs.

STANDARDIZATION AND THE WORKER

The great bane of bureaucracy is uncertainty. The inevitable course of the bureaucratization of the curriculum, therefore, was in the direction of predictability. As in industry, this was accomplished mainly through the standardization of activity or work units and of the products themselves. In the curriculum field, vague conceptions of the purposes of schooling became intolerable, and "particularization" of educational objectives became a byword. "An age of science is demanding exactness and particularity," announced Bobbitt in the first modern book on curriculum.[22] The curriculum became something progressively to be discovered through the scientific analysis of the activities of mankind. Just as scientific management became associated with virtue, so the incipient field of curriculum looked to scientific curriculum making as the source of answers to the great value questions that govern the purposes of education.

The process had a commonsensical appeal. "The curriculum-discoverer will first be an analyst of human nature and human affairs."[23] He would go out into the world of affairs and discover the particular "abilities, attitudes, habits, appreciations, and forms of knowledge" that human beings need. These would become the objectives of the curriculum. When these multitudinous needs are not filled by "undirected experiences," then "directed experiences" would be provided through the curriculum. Bobbitt set forth the basic principle: *"The curriculum of the directed training is to be discovered in the shortcomings of individuals after they have had all that can be given by undirected training."* [24] The curriculum was the mechanism for remedying the haphazard effects of ordinary living, for achieving the standard product which undirected socialization achieved so imperfectly.

One major concomitant of such a conception of the curriculum was the broadening of its scope into the boundless domain of human activity. Instead of being merely the repository of man's intellectual inheritance, the curriculum now embraced the gamut of human experience, "the total range of habits, skills, abilities, forms of thought, valuations, ambitions, etc., that its members need for the effective performance of their vocational labors; likewise, the total range needed for their civic activities; their health activities; their recreational activities; their language; their parental, religious, and general social activities." [25] The standard product would be designed and particularized in every detail.

A lonely voice of opposition to the "blight of standardization" was that of the president emeritus of Harvard University and the chief architect of the Committee of Ten report, Charles W. Eliot. Eliot, then 89 years old, pointed out that while standardization of the worker's movements in industry may have resulted in increased productivity, "the inevitable result was the destruction of the interest of the workman in his work." Standardization, he argued, was also having the same effect in education. What is more, it was antithetical to the true process of education as he saw it. "The true educational goal," he said, "is the utmost development of the individual's capacity of power, not in childhood and adolescence alone, but all through life. Fixed standards in labor, in study, in modes of family life, are downright enemies of progress for the body, mind, and soul of man." [26] Clearly, the temper of the time would not support such an anachronistic conception of education.

STANDARDIZATION AND PRODUCT DIVERSIFICATION

Apart from its implications for the individual as producer, the production metaphor in curriculum theory carries with it important implications for the individual as product. By the 1920's, a massive effort was under way to reform the curriculum through product standardization and predetermination. As usual, Bobbitt set the tone:

In the world of economic production, a major secret of success is predetermination. The management predetermines with great exactness the nature of the products to be turned out, and in relation to the other factors, the quality of the output. They standardize and thus predetermine the processes to be employed, the quantity and quality of raw material to be used for each type and unit of product, the character and amount of labor to be employed, and the character of the conditions under which the work should be done. . . . The business world is institutionalizing foresight and developing an appropriate and effective technique.

There is a growing realization within the educational profession that we must particularize the objectives of education. We, too, must institutionalize foresight, and, so far as conditions of our work will permit, develop a technique of predetermination of the particularized results to be obtained.[27]

The technique that Bobbitt referred to, the analysis of man's activities into particular and specialized units of behavior, came to be known as activity analysis.

By the 1920's, Bobbitt had been joined in his campaign to reform the curriculum along the lines of the bureaucratic model by such extraordinarily influential education leaders as W.W. Charters and David Snedden. In the main, the reform in the 1920's took the form of using activity analysis to strip away the nonfunctional, the "dead wood" in the curriculum. Increasingly, this was being done with reference to particular groups in the school. "The curriculum situation has become acute," Charters declared in 1921. "The masses who send their children to school are growing restive under what they consider to be the useless material taught in the grades."[28]

Besides his concern for the masses, Charters went on to show how a curriculum could be developed for another identifiable group, women. He developed a curriculum particularly for women as part of the famous study he conducted for Stephens College of Columbia, Missouri. Charters' task was to develop a program which would provide "specific training for the specific job of being a woman."[29] What constitutes being a woman, of course, was determined through activity analysis. Women all over the country were asked to write a complete statement of what they did for a week, and 95,000 replies were received. The replies were then analyzed into about 7,300 categories such as food, clothing, and health. Using these activities as his base, Charters developed the curriculum for Stephens College.

Just as Taylor found it necessary to identify discrete units of work, so were the educational leaders of the period embarking on the task of identifying the units of all human activity as the first step in curriculum planning. As Charters expressed it, the job is one of "finding out what people have to do and showing them how to do it."[30] The possibilities were limitless. Once women were identified and trained to be women, so could almost any other identifiable group in our society be trained for its role. To be sure, all persons would be trained to perform some activities in common, such as some of those involved in maintaining physical efficiency, but their differentiated roles in society could be programmed as well. As in current proposals, such programs could be advertised under the slogans of curriculum flexibility and individualized instruction.

Paradoxically, the effort to diversify the product along the lines of probable destination called for an even greater effort to standardize the units of work than before. Product diversification was not to be accomplished by diversifying work and creating variety in school activity, but by arranging the standard units of work into the most efficient arrangement for manufacturing the particular products. The man who took the lead in this aspect of the social efficiency movement was David Snedden. In 1921, Snedden had written that, "By 1925, it can confidently be hoped, the minds which direct education will have detached from the entanglements of our contemporary situation a thousand definite educational objectives, the realization of which will have demonstrable worth to our society."[31] Snedden devoted the next few years to the realization of that prediction, and also differentiating the curriculum so that the right objectives were applied to the right "case groups."

Case groups were defined as "any considerable group of persons who in large degree resemble each other in the common possession of qualities significant to their school education."[32] Objectives, therefore, would not be applied indiscriminately, but only with reference to the raw material. This was a particular problem, according to Snedden, in the junior high school where "differences of abilities, of extra-school conditions, and of prospects will acutely manifest themselves, forcing us to differentiate curricula in more ways, probably, than as yet suspected."[33] Such a division of the school population into appropriate case groups, in Snedden's mind at least, required sustained attention to the standardization and atomizing of the curriculum. His smallest curriculum unit, the "peth," is probably best illustrated by a single spelling word.[34]

Peths, however, had to be assembled in relation to "strands," classifications of "adult life performance practices" such as "health conservation through habitual safeguarding practices" for which Snedden estimated 50 to 100 peths, and "moral (including fellowship) behaviors" for which the same number was estimated. The vocational participations strand, however, necessitated differentiated numbers of peths, a streetcar motorman requiring only 10 to 20 while a farmer or a homemaker would call for 200 to 500 peths. A "lotment," in turn, was "the amount of work that can be accomplished, or ground covered, by learners of modal characteristics (as related to the activity considered) in 60 clock hours."[35] Thus, as in Taylorism, standards of efficiency were set for individual units of work in line with idealized performance levels. Actually, much of Snedden's work parallels the work of one of Taylor's major disciples, Frank Gilbreth, who identified 18 units of motion which he called "therbligs," thereby immortalizing his name in reverse.[36]

Yet the quaint obscurity of the educational terminology of the period tends to mask the underlying serious implications of the bureaucratic model applied to curriculum theory. The schoolchild became something to be molded and manipulated on his way to filling his predetermined social role. Guidance departments probed his inner resources in order to determine which of his potentialities were worth mining. Usually, these policies were followed in the name of bringing the outmoded academic curriculum into line with the new high school population, now dominated by the great unwashed. The curriculum was simply being made more democratic; but as Ellul has pointed out, the individual potentialities that were identified tended to coincide, as if by magic, with the needs of modern industrial society.[37] As the raw material was processed through the curriculum on its way to its ultimate state, simple efficiency dictated a differentiated curriculum in order to achieve the diversification of human labor that a modern industrial society demanded.

Snedden's ideal curriculum of minute standardized work units organized into the most efficient combinations for distinctive case groups was, of course, never achieved. The influence of such a conception of the curriculum was, nevertheless, widely felt. As early as 1923-24, when George S. Counts was conducting his classic study of the high school curriculum, the multiplication of different types of curricula designed for different population groups within the schools was evident. Of the 15 city school systems studied, only two, Detroit and Kansas City, used a system of constants and electives in their high school programs rather than a series of labeled curricula. Los Angeles, where Bobbitt's influence was undoubtedly strong in this period, maintained 18 different curricula in its high schools. Newton, Massachusetts, for example, listed the following 15 differentiated curricula:[38] Classical, Scientific, General, Business, Stenographic, Clerical, Household Arts, Agriculture, Printing, Electricity, Machine Work, Cabinet and Pattern-Making, Drafting, Automobile, and Carpentry. The principle of predetermination was in this way applied to differentiated vocational roles in addition to one's role as a citizen, parent, church member, and so on.

In the 1923-24 school year, also, the Lynds found in Middletown a "manifest concern . . . to dictate the social attitudes of its young citizens."[39] This was in part reflected in a host of required courses in civic training designed to support "community solidarity against sundry divisive tendencies."[40] The inculcation of appropriate civic attitudes was second only in emphasis to vocational preparation. Upon entering high school, the Middletown student chose among 12 courses of study, 8 of which were distinctly vocational. Education in Middletown was clearly becoming specific preparation for certain community-sanctioned adult roles.

By the mid to late 1920's signs began to appear of a decline in efficiency as the predominant educational ideal and social control as a major function of the schools. Bobbitt's contribution to the influential Twenty-Sixth Yearbook of the National Society for the Study of Education represents a curious denial of some of the basic curriculum tenets he had proposed in his most popular book, published only two years before. In *How To Make a Curriculum,* Bobbitt set forth as one of his major premises that, "Education is primarily for adult life, not for child life. Its fundamental responsibility is to prepare for the fifty years of adulthood, not for twenty years of childhood and youth."[41] It was on this fundamental assumption that Bobbitt based his case for the analysis of adult activities as the source of curriculum objectives. The efficient performance of adult activities of all kinds was the ideal toward which the whole curriculum was directed. In 1926, however, Bobbitt was to declare:

Education is not primarily to prepare for life at some future time. Quite the reverse; it proposes to hold high the current living, making it intense, abundant, fruitful, and fitting it firmly in the grooves of habit. . . . In a very true sense, life cannot be "prepared for." It can only be lived.[42]

Such a declaration can only mean a rejection of the production model of curriculum theory, since it denies such central concepts as predetermination and predictability. When, in 1934, Bobbitt was asked to prepare a statement summarizing his curriculum theory, his rejection of his former work was clearly evident and nearly complete.[43] In the 1930's, the ideal of social efficiency in education and the production metaphor as the basis for curriculum theory were obviously in a period of decline, a decline which, however, proved to be only temporary.

THE CONTEMPORARY REVIVAL

Just as the first great drive toward standardization, predetermination, and fragmentation in the school curriculum came about in the aftermath of the first industrial revolution, so the renewal of those curriculum tendencies has come about in the aftermath of the second one—what is sometimes called the electronic or technological revolution. To be sure, some differences are evident. In the first place, the theory of behaviorism has been raised to the status of canon law in the social sciences, and so we are admonished to state the design specifications which set forth how a student will turn out in terms of observable behaviors. Second, the 1920s' doctrine of social efficiency has been overlaid with a thin veneer of academic respectability, and so the modern design specifications tend to call for a student to identify certain points on a map or to reel off the valences of a set of chemical elements instead of emphasizing practical, nonacademic activities.

Given these qualifications, Snedden's bureaucratic ideal of a thousand educational objectives to be used as a blueprint for shaping the educational product is now closer to realization than ever before. Teachers may now order from a catalog 96 objectives in language arts 7-9 for $3.00 or 158 objectives in social science (geography) K-9 for $4.00, or 25 objectives in English literature 10-12 for $3.00.[44] Snedden would have considered these a bargain at twice the price. These new objectives, furthermore, are evidently being formulated with such precision and wisdom that one major proponent of the new bureaucracy was led to observe of the period preceding the present millennium: "American educators have generally engaged in the same level of discourse regarding the specification of educational goals that one might derive from the grunts of a Neanderthal."[45] One can only sympathize," he reflected, "with the thousands of learners who had to obtain an education from an instructional system built on a muddle-minded conception of educational goals."[46]

One can avoid muddle-mindedness, apparently, by overcoming a preoccupation with means or process in favor of a focus on outcomes.[47] Current curriculum practice seems to take the form of drawing up endless lists of minute design specifications in behavioral terms and then finding the right "media mix" by which the product can be most efficiently manufactured. "Judgments about the success of an instructional procedure," we are told, "are made exclusively on the basis of results, that is, the changes in learner behavior which emerge as a consequence of instruction. Only if the hoped-for changes in learner behavior have been attained is the instructional process considered successful."[48] The efficient achievement of the end product becomes the criterion by which the means are selected.

Such a sharp dichotomy between ends and means is precisely what resulted from the introduction of the assembly line in the first industrial revolution. Work became important only insofar as it was instrumental in achieving the desired product. The success of the assembly line depends on the fact that it reduces the process of production to units so simple that the predicted outcome is assured. The worker's movements are made so elementary and routine that the product inevitably emerges independent of the will or conscious desire of the worker. John McDermott has observed about the assembly line effect: " . . . since each operation uses only a small fraction of a worker's skill, there is a very great likelihood that the operation will be performed in a minimally acceptable way. Alternately, if each operation taxed the worker's skill there would be frequent errors in the operation, frequent disturbance in work flow, and a thoroughly unpredictable quality to the end product."[49] To ensure predictability and efficiency in education, the techniques of industry are introduced with the same effect. Work loses any organic relationship with the end product.

Take, for example, the much publicized program, Individually Prescribed Instruction. Teachers prepare prescriptions—directions for what the child must accomplish. The child, after receiving his prescription, places a recorded disk on some playback equipment, and a disembodied voice asks, "Hello, how are you today?'' (Pause for response.) ''Today we are going to learn the sounds of the letters. Do you have a pencil?'' The child responds and then is directed in the performance of certain tasks. If the child is able to perform these tasks with 85 percent accuracy, he is rewarded with a new prescription. If he fails, he is given remedial training until he meets the performance standard.[50] His progress is carefully plotted by a computer as he passes through the standard work units. Individuality, here, refers to the speed by which one makes his way through the standard work units. Of course, just as corporate management can make the tedium of the assembly line tolerable by scheduling a scientifically determined number of coffee breaks, so can the modern technologist make school work bearable by building into his system an appropriate schedule of other activities. But this would go about as far to create delight in intellectual activity as coffee breaks have in restoring the dignity of work.

In education, as in industry, the standardization of the product also means the standardization of work. Educational activity which may have an organic wholeness and vital meaning takes on significance only in terms of its contribution to the efficient production of the finished product. As in industry, the price of worship at the altar of efficiency is the alienation of the worker from his work—where the continuity and wholeness of the enterprise are destroyed for those who engage in it. Here, then, is one great threat that the production metaphor governing modern curriculum theory poses for American education.

The bureaucratic model, along with its behavioristic and technological refinements, threatens to destroy, in the name of efficiency, the satisfaction that one may find in intellectual activity. The sense of delight in intellectual activity is replaced by a sense of urgency. The thrill of the hunt is converted into an efficient kill. The wonder of the journey is superseded by the relentless pursuit of the destination. And to condition the victim to enjoy being conditioned is certainly less humane than open coercion or bribery.

The tragic paradox of the production metaphor applied to curriculum is that the dehumanization of education, the alienation of means from ends, the stifling of intellectual curiosity carry with them very few compensations. In the corporate structure, the worker who has become a cog in a vast bureaucracy is at least rewarded with an improved financial status and opportunity for leisure. The megamachine in ancient Egypt, where the autonomy of human beings was sacrificed in the great cause of the building of the pyramids, at least produced some measure of increased agricultural production and flood control.[51] What comparable benefits accrue from a corresponding regimentation in education? The particularization of the *educational* product, it turns out, is tantamount to its trivialization. A case in point is what happens to history as it is particularized in the highly regarded and liberally financed ES '70s project. One of the more than 50 pilot schools lists among its educational products the following typical examples in the form of items on a computer-printed Individual Student Progress Report (formerly known as a report card):

Given a list which includes Sibley, Colonel Snelling, Father Galtier, J. J. Hill, Ramsey, Fur Traders, missionaries, soldiers, and settlers of Minnesota and several true statements about their contributions, the student is able to match the listed people with the proper true statements.

Given several statements describing early and present day lumbering in Minnesota, the student is able to identify lumbering in Minnesota by writing E -early lumbering-, P -present day lumbering-, or B -both- in front of the applicable statements.

Educational products manufactured at such a level of particularity, even if multiplied a millionfold, could only be trivial. History (assuming that history is the discipline represented by these performance outcomes) simply is not the accurate recitation of bits and pieces of information. Nor is any discipline a specific finite assemblage of facts and skills. So to define it *is* to trivialize it.

This is not to say that instructional objectives, in and of themselves, are useless. They can add a dimension to educational activity; but they have no meaning outside the context of the means toward their achievement. There are, certainly, a variety of ways to consider the complex interrelationships between means and ends.[52] But the creation of a sharp dichotomy between means and ends or the consideration of means only in the context of efficiency is, pedagogically speaking, a travesty. From an educational point of view, behavior, in and of itself, is of little significance. It is, on the other hand, critically important to know how one comes to behave as he does; whether, for example, a given act derives from mere conditioning or from rational decision-making processes.

Modern curriculum theory, currently being influenced by systems analysis, tends to regard the child simply as input inserted into one end of a great machine from which he eventually emerges at the other end as output replete with all the behaviors, the "competencies," and the skills for which he has been programmed. Even when the output is differentiated, such a mechanistic conception of education contributes only to man's regimentation and dehumanization, rather than to his autonomy.

The mechanistic conception of man, the technology-systems analysis approach to human affairs, the production metaphor for curriculum design all share a common perspective. They represent a deterministic outlook on human behavior. The behavior of human beings is controlled in an effort to make people do the particular things that someone wants them to do. This may take the form of getting people to vote every election day, to buy the latest miracle detergent, or to recite on cue the valences of 30 out of 35 chemical elements. As Von Bertalanffy put it, "Stimulus-response, input-output, producer-consumer are all the same concepts, only expressed in different terms. . . . people are manipulated as they deserve, that is, as overgrown Skinner rats."[53]

NOTES

1. Ellwood P. Cubberley, *Public School Administration* (Boston: Houghton Mifflin Company, 1916), p. 338.

2. Robert H. Wiebe. *The Search for Order 1877-1920* (New York: Hill and Wang, 1967), p. 145.

3. Frederick Winslow Taylor. *The Principles of Scientific Management* (New York: Harper & Brothers, 1911), p. 43.

4. *Ibid.,* pp. 44–45.

5. Nicos P. Mouzelis. *Organisation and Bureaucracy: An Analysis of Modern Theories* (Chicago: Aldine Publishing Company, 1967), p. 85.

6. Cited in: Samuel Haber. *Efficiency and Uplift: Scientific Management in the Progressive Era 1890-1920* (Chicago: University of Chicago Press, 1964), pp. 1–3.

7. Frank Barkley Copley. *Frederick Winslow Taylor: Father of Scientific Management* (New York: Harper & Brothers, 1923). Quoted in: Haber, *ibid.,* pp. 2–3.

8. Haber, *op. cit.,* p. 54.

9. The administration aspect of the bureaucratization of the schools has been ably interpreted by: Raymond E. Callahan. *Education and the Cult of Efficiency: A Study of the Social Forces That Have Shaped the Administration of the Public Schools* (Chicago: University of Chicago Press, 1962).

10. *Ibid.,* p.148.

11. John Franklin Bobbitt. "The Elimination of Waste in Education." *The Elementary School Teacher* 12 (No. 6, February 1912): 260.

12. *Ibid.,* p. 263.

13. *Ibid.,* p. 264.

14. *Ibid.*

15. *Ibid.,* p. 269.

16. Taylor, *op. cit.,* p. 59.

17. Franklin Bobbitt. "Some General Principles of Management Applied to the Problems of City-School Systems." Twelfth Yearbook of the National Society for the Study of Education. Part I (Chicago: University of Chicago Press, 1913), p. 62.

18. *Ibid.,* p. 11.

19. *Ibid.*

20. *Ibid.,* pp. 21–22.

21. J. F. Bobbitt. "High-School Costs." *The School Review* 23 (No. 8, October 1915): 505.

22. Franklin Bobbitt. *The Curriculum* (Boston: Houghton Mifflin Company, 1918), p. 41.

23. *Ibid.,* p. 43.

24. *Ibid.,* p. 45. (Original italics.)

25. *Ibid.,* p. 43.

26. Letter to *The New York Times* 72 (23,946): 12; August 17, 1923 © 1923 by The New York Times Company. Reprinted by permission.

27. Franklin Bobbitt. "The Objectives of Secondary Education." *The School Review* 28 (No. 10, December 1920): 738.

28. W. W. Charters. "The Reorganization of Women's Education." *Educational Review* 62 (No. 3, October 1921): 224.

29. W. W. Charters. "Curriculum for Women." *University of Illinois Bulletin* 23 (No. 27, March 8, 1926): 327.

30. *Ibid.,* p. 328.

31. David Snedden. *Sociological Determination of Objectives in Education* (Philadelphia: J. B. Lippincott Company, 1921), p. 79.

32. David Snedden. " 'Case Group' Methods of Determining Flexibility of General Curricula in High Schools." *School & Society* 17 (No. 429, March 17, 1923): 290.

33. David Snedden. "Junior High School Offerings." *School & Society* (No. 520, December 13, 1924): 740.

34. David Snedden. "Planning Curriculum Research, I." *School & Society* 22 (No. 557, August 29, 1925): 259–65.

35. Snedden, "Junior High School Offerings." *op. cit.,* p. 741.

36. Gilbreth's other brush with immortality was Clifton Webb's portrayal of him as the super-efficient father in the film, "Cheaper by the Dozen."

37. Jacques Ellul. *The Technological Society* (New York: Vintage Books, 1964), pp. 358–63.

38. George S. Counts. *The Senior High School Curriculum* (Chicago: University of Chicago Press, 1926), pp. 12–14.

39. Robert S. Lynd and Helen Merrell Lynd. *Middletown* (New York: Harcourt, Brace & Company, Inc., 1929), p. 197.

40. *Ibid.,* p. 196.

41. Franklin Bobbitt. *How To Make A Curriculum* (Boston: Houghton Mifflin Company, 1924), p. 8.

42. Franklin Bobbitt. "The Orientation of the Curriculum-Maker." *The Foundations of Curriculum-Making.* Twenty-Sixth Yearbook of the National Society for the Study of Education. Part II (Bloomington, Illinois: Public School Publishing Company, 1926), p. 43.

43. Franklin Bobbitt. "A Summary Theory of the Curriculum." *Society for Curriculum Study News Bulletin* 5 (No. 1, January 12, 1934): 2–4.

44. Instructional Objectives Exchange, W. James Popham, Director, Center for the Study of Evaluation, University of California, Los Angeles.

45. W. James Popham. "Objectives and Instruction." American Educational Research Association Monograph on Curriculum Evaluation (Chicago: Rand McNally & Company, 1969), pp. 32–33.

46. *Ibid.*

47. W. James Popham. "Focus on Outcomes: A Guiding Theme for ES '70 Schools." *Phi Delta Kappan* 51 (No. 4, December 1969): 208–10.

48. *Ibid.,* p. 208.

49. John McDermott. "Technology: The Opiate of the Intellectuals." *New York Review of Books* 13 (No. 2, July 31, 1969): 34.

50. "Individually Prescribed Instruction." *Education U.S.A.* Special Report (Washington, D.C.: National School Public Relations Association, 1968), p. 4.

51. Lewis Mumford. *The Myth of the Machine* (London: Secker & Warburg, 1967), p. 12.

52. See, for example: D. S. Shwayder. *The Stratification of Behavior* (New York: Humanities Press, 1965), pp. 144–64.

53. Ludwig Von Bertalanffy. *Robots, Men, and Minds: Psychology in the Modern World* (New York: George Braziller, Inc., 1967), p. 12. Reprinted with the permission of the publisher. Copyright © 1967 by Ludwig Von Bertalanffy.

BIBLIOGRAPHICAL ESSAY

Linda M. McNeil

The search for bibliographical references conveying the ''state of the field'' in curriculum yielded both the expected and the unanticipated. The expected, of course, is the utter lack of agreement among educators, curriculum developers, curriculum analysts, evaluators and policy-makers on the question of what schooling is about. The surprise is the richness and the complexity of the disagreement. The field is so fluid, so enmeshed in funding and politics, so heavily in debt to psychology and other fields, that diverse and even contradictory paradigms exist and jostle each other for dominance in the professional literature. While roots in a social efficiency ideology and ties to public funding make ''accountability'' models of inputs and outputs a prevailing mode for evaluating curricula, that mode is not without critics and a broad range of competing alternatives.

The purpose of this bibliographical essay is to sketch the range of debate on curriculum. The books and articles mentioned by no means comprise a comprehensive listing. They are chosen for their insights, for their relationship to each other, for their representation of basic positions, for their own helpful bibliographies, or perhaps for their frequent citation within the literature. The articles mentioned will be grouped according to the divisions of the present volume and will exclude articles republished here.

I. HOW SHOULD CURRICULUM PROBLEMS BE STUDIED?

It is customary for educators and practitioners to consider curriculum as a design problem; the Tyler rationale (Ralph W. Tyler, *Basic Principles of Cur-*

riculum and Instruction (Chicago: University of Chicago Press, 1949)) consolidated parameters for analysis of the internal components of curriculum construction—goals, implementation, evaluation. Therefore, much of curricular discourse is programmatic, dealing with what to do and how to do it particularly within certain subject fields. The curriculum is studied largely as content or approaches to content within subject fields. In addition, however, there is the academic field of study known as curriculum, the purpose of which is to analyze both the curriculum as a whole and the process of curriculum-making. How one chooses to look at what goes on in schools, at curriculum, depends to some extent on whether one is engaged in producing a curriculum or in observing it and trying to make sense of it.

According to Ian Westbury and William Steimer ("Curriculum: A Discipline in Search of its Problems," *School Review* 79 (No. 2, February 1971)) curriculum does not exist as a "field." Unlike traditional disciplines, curriculum lacks a set of materials, specific professional skills, or a sustained and cumulative research tradition into which to train people. Rejecting Tyler's rationale, the authors try to build on Schwab's work and delineate the field so that it will have logic for both school people and curriculum scholars. Decker Walker in "A Naturalistic Model for Curriculum Development" (*School Review* 80 (No. 1, November 1971)) also sees inpractice curriculum as differing from the Tyler rationale. He describes a far more chaotic dynamic in the making of curricular choices.

The curriculum field has been described as a field of borrowings: it rests on borrowed assumptions and evaluates with borrowed techniques. Much curriculum procedure and product are sold with the claim of making curriculum more "scientific." In "Curriculum Development in Relation to Social and Intellectual Systems" (unpublished), James B. Macdonald argues that curriculum development is not now nor has it been a result of rational, scientific planning, but is the product of social and intellectual forces. He says that the effects of cultural pluralism in curriculum offer more hope than does the enlargement of the technical planning model for meeting the needs of a varied population. In Chapter I of *The Open Access Curriculum* (Boston: Allyn and Bacon, 1971), L. Craig Wilson argues that American education, though supposedly scientific, has "bypassed" twenty years of developments in psychology, research methods, philanthropy, philosophy and social shifts, and has remained closed and authoritarian. He recommends an overtly non-scientific, humanistic "open curriculum."

Also viewing the curriculum field as having changed little, Lawrence Cremin in "Curriculum-Making in the U.S." (*Teachers College Record* 73 (No. 2, December 1971)) discusses William Torrey Harris and the genesis of the curriculum field as a basis for comparing 1950's and 1960's curriculum developments. He sees the earlier paradigms as still dominant, the later ones as too ahistorical to ask the questions needed to transform the curriculum.

Elliott Eisner sees the curriculum field as fragmented, the *ad hoc* accretion of subject field efforts with no overall plan. In "Curriculum Development: Sources for a Foundation for the Field of Curriculum" (*Curriculum Theory Network* 5 (Spring 1970)), he points to the resulting need for generalists and for research into the way curriculum groups actually develop curriculum and the way the "instructional support" structure operates. This support structure is sketched by Ludwig Von Bertalanffy in "The World of Science and the World of Value" (*Teachers College Record* 65 (No. 6, March 1964)) as the effect of imposing technological evaluation modes on education so that technical expertise has superseded moral excellence as a criterion for status. In his words, the absence of a commitment to values has made education into *engineering*, not into the "unfolding of human possibilities." Thus in the utilitarian system of education in the U.S, "truly eccentric, innovative, committed scholarship is impossible."

One dominant thread running through curriculum literature is the relation of theory to practice. "Teaching and Curriculum Planning" by Zvi Lamm (*Journal of Curriculum Studies* 1 (No. 2, May 1969)) is an attempt to classify theories of instruction and to make explicit the relation between theories of instruction and curriculum planning. Mauritz Johnson says that the curriculum influences instruction through the mediation of an instructional plan. "Translation of Curriculum into Instruction" (*Journal of Curriculum Studies* 1 (No. 2, May 1969)) presents his model of the ways curriculum and instruction are interrelated at the point of evaluation. Mark Belth advocates overcoming the reductive debates of theory vs. practice by offering *models* of education that exist and by posing further integration of models (*The New World of Education* (Boston: Allyn and Bacon, 1970)). Wilma Longstreet suggests looking at curriculum as a *process*, thus avoiding theory-practice dichotomies ("Toward a Curriculum Incorporating PROCESS," *Educational Theory* 21 (No. 3, Summer 1971)).

In a different vein, Ivan Illich, Clarence Karier, and Michael Apple are among those who see the curriculum as indicative of the school's role amid many social, political, economic and legal institutions in the society. From their varied perspectives they raise the issue of the school as a distributor of knowledge, and therefore of power (or of powerlessness). They argue that school knowledge is often erroneously assumed to be neutral, existing in itself and of itself, and representing a shared or "common knowledge." They wish to make curriculum problematic and to demonstrate that knowledge included in school curricula indeed comes from somewhere. The curriculum, in other words, has social origins which may or may not have been deliberate but which embody particular social values traceable to groups of individuals whose interests are served by the view of the world thus embodied. They and others call for curriculum research which will examine empirically in-use curriculum for the purpose of showing its origins, its substance and its forms, as mediated through particular administrative procedures, teachers and teaching styles, and student populations. One example of a study based on this view of curriculum-as-problematic is Apple's "The Hidden Curriculum and the Nature of Conflict" (*Interchange* 2 (No. 4, 1971)), which contrasts the actuality of conflict in scientific inquiry and in the social world with the views of consensus and linear progress in these areas as portrayed by most school science curricula. His paper raises the question of how such views of the world become so firmly entrenched in formalized school knowledge. There are beginning to emerge empirical studies which attempt to unravel the politics and practice through which governmental agencies, organized pressure groups, local businesses, individual politicians, parental pressures, local customs, teacher personalities, the training of teachers, and shifts in theory have helped shape curricula. Surely the question of how the curriculum is to be studied must include empirical study of the values, both explicit and tacit, embodied in school curricula and of the sources of those values.

The school's role in the distribution of knowledge within the culture is the subject of studies by British and European educators from a sociology-of-knowledge perspective. Two anthologies present varied implications for this view of school knowledge. *Knowledge and Control: New Directions for the Sociology of Education,* edited by Michael F. D. Young (London: Collier-Macmillan, 1971), treats school knowledge, or curricula, as problematic, as socially derived, and as institutionally distributed within a given historical and political context. Geoffrey M. Esland's "Teaching and Learning as the Organization of Knowledge" and Nell Keddie's "Classroom Knowledge" (see reading #20) are especially interesting as illustrations of the study of curriculum as the product of personal and institutional values and constraints. *Knowledge, Education and Cultural Change,* edited by Richard Brown (London: Tavistock, 1973) also pursues the idea that curriculum is not fixed but problematic. This volume contains several articles analyzing curriculum in specific countries as it relates to social stratification based on the unequal distribution of knowledge. Clearly outside mainstream analysis of curriculum, the view of curriculum as selected knowledge which is the embodiment of the interests of one or more power groups in a society is nonetheless represented by some research. In a historical piece entitled "The Rise of Scientific Curriculum-Making and its Aftermath" (*Curriculum Theory Network* 5 (No. 1, 1975)), Kliebard traces, through the work of Franklin Bobbitt and W. W. Charters, the identification of the curriculum field with technical and scientific pursuits. Boyd Bode's criticism in *Modern Educational Theories* is examined, and two perceptive chapters from Bode's work are reprinted in the same issue.

In *The Use of Imagination: Educational Thought and the Literary Mind* (New York: Barnes and Nobel, 1959), William Walsh describes education as learning to listen, as attaining a sense of the particular, as waiting upon mystery.

How is the curriculum to be studied? As packaged materials designed to elicit behavioral responses? As subject fields and their interrelation or lack of it? As the embodiment of the interests of powerful groups in the society? As institutionalized knowledge? As input into the processing of students toward specified goals? As artifact or accretion-by-default? The range is broad, the debate lively. According to a Swedish researcher, Daniel Kallos, in "Curriculum and Teaching: an Un-American View" (a paper presented at the annual meeting of the American Educational Research Association, 1975), Americans do not yet have adequate ways of studying their curriculum. He argues that current technical research fails to analyze and evaluate the assumptions upon which most curriculum development rests. He cites work being done in Europe which, although few Americans are aware of it, accomplishes more in directing attention to the functions and effects of schooling. The paper is useful for introducing Americans to work in several countries which addresses key questions regarding curriculum. Kallos sees the exporting of American research and measurement techniques as eclipsing the potentially useful importing of European research.

That curriculum is interest-laden is also evident from the work of political theorist Murray Edelman in the analysis of the language employed by school people as they work with children. In "The Political Language of the Helping Professions" (Institute for Research on Poverty Discussion Paper #195–74, University of Wisconsin-Madison), for example, he demonstrates the political relationships assumed when one party to social interaction employs terminology which makes *objects* of the other parties involved. Those with power of authority in a given situation assign a label to those less powerful ("clients") which implies that the latter need "therapy" from the former in order to be "normal," according to a definition of that word supplied by the labeler. Michael Apple has explored the idea (in "Commonsense Categories and Curriculum Thought," *Schools in Search of Meaning* (Washington, D.C.: Association for Supervision and Curriculum Development Yearbook, 1975)) that schools become arbiters of such labels, distributing thereby power or powerlessness. He suggests that once such subject-object labeling occurs in schools, as with terms like "slow-learner," curriculum development then follows such labeling as though it were empirically accurate and meaningful, thus dealing with students as representatives of certain categories rather than as persons. Since such labels are usually borrowed uncritically, as from psychology, they by the nature of their source limit the range of curricular discourse. Dwayne Huebner argues that the prevalence of a technical language in the discussion of school curricula does violence to education. Since education is a human activity, it must be discussed in light of the many dimensions of human life—the technical, but also the ethical, political, economic, aesthetic, and transcendent. He demonstrates the potency of enlarging curricular discourse, in "Curricular Language and Classroom Meanings" (*Language and Meaning,* edited by James B. Macdonald and Robert Leeper (Washington, D.C.: ASCD, 1966)).

II. WHAT PURPOSES SHOULD THE CURRICULUM SERVE?

The aims and objectives perceived for curriculum are inevitably linked to, but not identical to, one's view of the school's role in society. Traditional debates have centered on whether the school's function is to preserve society or change it, or whether schools should aim for the development of the individual or the maintenance of society and its institutions. Thus, psychological arguments are often answered by, or even reinforced by, political or social ones, and vice versa.

In "Curriculum Objectives" (*Journal of Curriculum Studies* 1 (No. 1, November 1968)), F. Musgrove points out that the "cost" of every curriculum is the "other curricula that might have been." He describes present curricula as still based on assumptions of manual labor, puberty at 17, male dominance, life's end at 40 and other out-dated societal values. He would advocate a curriculum aimed at a more flexible notion of social order. (See also, Robert McClintock, "Some Thoughts on 'Permanent Education' " *Notes on Education* 3, December 1973, Teachers College of Columbia University, New York.)

In "Education as Initiation" (in R. D. Archambault (editor), *Philosophical Analysis and Education* (London: Routledge and Kegan Paul, 1965)), R. S. Peters directs discussion of education away from socialization or behavior modification, to a consideration of education as "initiation into public traditions which are articulated in language and forms of thought." In a more analytic piece ("Aims of Education—A Conceptual Inquiry," *Philosophy and Education,* Proceedings, International Seminar, March 23–25, 1966; Ontario Institute for Studies in Education, Monograph #3, 1967)), Peters attempts to make the case that aims are not extrinsic to education, but are "attempts to justify what it means to be educated." (Following Peters's article in the publication are critiques by John Woods and William Dray.)

From these fairly general discussions of aims, one might turn to two excellent analyses of particular educational aims: mental health and the teaching of the scientific method. R. S. Peters calls into question the school's role as a "mental health" agency in "Mental Health as an Educational Aim," in T. H. B. Hollins (ed.), *Aims in Education: The Philosophic Approach* (Manchester, England: Manchester University Press, 1964). His treatment of the topic embraces the controversy of the school as a social control agent, that is, in implementing certain strategies which presume particular definitions of "mental health," and the broader question of the school's presumed responsibility for solving all manner of social ills. In I. Scheffler (ed.), *Philosophy and Education* (Boston: Allyn and Bacon, 1958), J. A. Easley, Jr., discusses the problem of assuming that teaching "the scientific method" should dominate curricular discourse.

The question of individual needs has been central to the discussion of curriculum goals. Kohlberg and Mayer ("Development as the Aim of Education," *Harvard Educational Review* 42 (No. 4, November 1972)) compare three educational ideological bases—romanticism, cultural transmission and Deweyan progressivism—and their psychological underpinnings as a basis for determining curriculum purpose and direction. Reginald D. Archambault in "The Concept of Need and its Relation to Certain Aspects of Educational Theory" (*Harvard Educational Review* 27 (No. 1, Winter 1957)) analyzes the concept of *need* in curriculum discourse as a hypothetical construct, as a basis for educational policy, and as a variant in light of changing norms. He examines the idea of needs as motives or as organic deficiencies, as "good" vs. "harmful," and as individual vs. societal. B. Paul Komisar discusses needs as prescriptive or motivational, and concludes (in B. O. Smith and R. H. Ennis, *Language and Concepts in Education* (Chicago: Rand-McNally, 1961, chap. 2)) that the "needs curriculum" is so based on vague generalities as to be absurd.

A broader discussion of educational objectives is found among several writers in the Autumn 1967 issue of *School Review*. Robert Ebel, for example, says that education is not equipping the learner with a new set of behaviors to meet a pre-determined need, but "increasing the resources of an individual as he seeks to choose his own behaviors wisely." In the 1973 NSSE Yearbook *Behavior Modification in Education,* B. F. Skinner argues that the key to making schools more efficient is translating goals into behavioral outcomes. W. James Popham, in "Educational Needs Assessment" (*Curriculum Theory Network,* Ontario Institute for Education, 1972), also argues that the basic difficulties related to curriculum goals are *procedural*.

An active role for school curriculum in social change is advocated by the current "career education" policies. In *School Review* 82 (No. 1, November 1973)), Sidney Marland, Jr., describes the goals of career education at the level of national policy. In the same issue Robert Nash and Russell Agne cite reasons for the popularity of this national curriculum commitment; they go on to say that it accepts without question the productivity model for citizens in a corporate state. T. H. Fitzgerald calls career education "an error whose time has come." He claims that it ignores the real roots of unemployment, the power of credentialism and the impossibility of true career planning in an uncertain job market. He says career education reduces the child to a "human resource" and ignores the real problems of the allocation of resources in this country. The controversy surrounding career education alone illustrates the difficulty in reaching agreement, whether at the local school or in federal bureaucracies, on the purposes curriculum should serve.

A divergent approach from career education is "general education." In *Seminar Reports* 1 (No. 3, December 7, 1973, Columbia University, New York), Daniel Bell traces the historical developments and something of the decline of general education. He sees at the center of general education two themes: normative questions and political philosophy. In the publication are lively rejoinders, mainly on Bell's view of the changing status of the subject disciplines. (See also Bell's *The Reforming of General Education* (New York: Columbia University Press, 1966).)

Both Bell and Marland would agree that the school ultimately serves a social purpose. Edward Krug traces two dimensions of the school's social mission in the early twentieth century: social control and social service (see especially chapter II, "Social Efficiency Triumphant," in *The Shaping of the American High School*. Vol. 1 (Madison: University of Wisconsin Press, 1964)). He sees the two themes merge in the social efficiency movement, which was a controlling of students as Bell's general education is supposed to be liberating. (See also Volume II of Krug's study which covers the years 1920–1940.) *Phi Delta Kappan* 47 (No. 4, December 1965) is devoted to the overt planning of national goals for schools. The articles deal with both the politics and economics of administering national educational policy.

A social purpose for curriculum is not limited to consensus politics. The Oliver-Newmann-Shaver approach to public issues and controversies (see *Clarifying Public Controversy* (Boston: Little Brown, 1970)) assumes that a basic purpose of schools in a democracy, and especially of social studies curricula, is to make students politically literate and, to the extent possible, politically effective. Fred M. Newmann has carried the purpose of political effectiveness further in his recent book, *Education for Citizen Action: A Challenge for Secondary Curriculum* (Berkeley: McCutchan Publ. Corp., 1975), which proposes involving students directly in political activity in their community so that they may learn "how the system works" rather than "how the system is supposed to work." The book discusses not only the assumptions behind such a goal for curriculum, but some of the practical problems involved when teachers and students become political advocates or participants in a community.

The current surge of group identity and group participation in common causes has affected discussion as to curricular purposes. Just as schools were once assumed to have a role in socializing immigrants or in increasing their social mobility, schools today are also seen as a vehicle for social reform. In *School Review* 80 (No. 2, February 1972), Patricia Minuchin calls for an education for women that will include knowledge of their society and of their individual potential. (In this same issue, see "Education and the Life Cycle," by Bernice L. Neugarten.) In "Education for Liberation" (*School Review* 81 (No. 3, May 1973)), Barbara Sizemore contrasts traditional American ideals assumed in education with a curriculum that would analyze the problems of the oppressed and promote skills for social change through action and dialogue. In the same tradition is Paolo Freire's *Pedagogy of the Oppressed* (New York: Herder and Herder, 1972).

Perhaps less radical politically, though equally radical intellectually, is the book *Existentialism in Education* (New York: Harper and Row, 1956) in which Van Cleve Morris argues for an education for personal responsibility based on a knowledge of one's choices, as opposed to a positivistic education which sets the individual apart from his milieu. The question of the individual's responsibility in a changing world is also addressed by F. Michael Connelly (*Curriculum Theory Network* 6 (Winter 1970–71)) who claims that teachers have become "unwitting allies in what amounts to a curricular lie: that knowledge claims in the curriculum are right and true." He says giving students the *results* of inquiry without the preceding *patterns* of inquiry keeps students forever unable to generate knowledge for themselves, and therefore unable to assume responsibility in their own right.

David Norton too accuses traditional curriculum goals of representing a false view of "reason" and knowledge. In "Learning, Life-Style and Imagination" (*School Review* 78 (No. 1, November 1969)), he shows that imagination, central to both science and art, has been ignored in schooling. David Hawkins also argues that the aims of curriculum are greater than any set of observable behaviors or any one political goal. In "Learning the Unteachable" (in Lee S. Shulman and Evan R. Keisler (eds.), *Learning by Discovery: A Critical Appraisal* (Chicago: Rand-McNally, 1966)), he describes good teaching as being closely akin to the "ceaseless trial" of apprenticeship in which the inherent structural features of the activity (here, science) involve a personal gestalt that transcends verbalizations or linear typologies. Thus, he advocates designing curriculum not for predictability, but for the evolution of thought, thus *unpredictability*. His position is in contrast to those who assume that educational pursuits will have validity if only educators can agree on the ends and if researchers can refine the means toward their accomplishment and the instruments of their measurement.

III. HOW SHOULD KNOWLEDGE BE SELECTED AND ORGANIZED FOR THE CURRICULUM?

Directly related to the discussion of aims and purposes is the organization of school knowledge. The debate usually centers on subject divisions, often with a central core of constants plus elective subjects versus an integrative approach based on problems or issues or central themes, drawing on resources from many fields. In "Selection and Organization of Curriculum Content: An Analysis" (1956 ASCD Yearbook, chapter IV) Arno Bellack discusses basing curriculum on life needs as opposed to organized fields of knowledge. He expresses the need for experiencing many cultural resources in schools and states that the scientific model of thought is not appropriate to all areas of experience in learning even though it is becoming more and more prevalent in curriculum development. In "Conceptions of Knowledge: Their Significance for the Curriculum" (*The Nature of Knowledge: Implications for the Education of Teachers,* a conference sponsored by the E. A. Uhrig Foundation, Milwaukee, November 1961) Bellack discusses two approaches to organizing curriculum—basic disciplines vs. "modes of thought" such as empirical, logical, moral, etc.—and suggests the two can be complementary when knowledge is considered in terms of broad groupings. Also informative regarding philosophical issues underlying knowledge and curriculum organization are W. H. Kilpatrick's "The Essentials of the Activity Movement" (*Progressive Education* 11 (No. 6, October 1934)) and J. E. McClellan's "Knowledge and the Curriculum" (*Teachers College Record* 57 (No. 6, March 1956)). Of interest to those familiar with the structure of the disciplines approach is Kathryn P. Morgan's discussions of Schwab's work: "Some Philosophical Difficulties Concerning the Notion of a 'Structure of a Discipline'," *Educational Theory* 23 (No. 1, Winter 1973).

The concept of structure of the disciplines as a basis for curriculum organization, and therefore curriculum reform, was popularized by Jerome Bruner's *The Process of Education* (New York: Vintage of Random House, 1960, 1963). Though *intradisciplinary* curriculum reform in the post-Sputnik years dominated curriculum discourse, Herbert M. Kliebard explains that the concept set forth by Bruner was at best a nebulous one, and at its worst, a questionable view of knowledge which begged the questions of what constituted "structure" or "discipline," what the "disciplines" had to do with each other, and what relevance education was to have to the individual student ("Structure of the Disciplines as an Educational Slogan," *Teachers College Record* 66 (No. 7, April 1965); see also I. Scheffler, "The Practical as a Focus for Curriculum: Reflections of Schwab's View" in *Reason and Teaching* (Indianapolis: Bobbs-Merrill, 1973)).

Several writers have contributed to the discussion of behavioral objectives as appropriate for organizing curricula. Robert M. Gagné discusses these objectives' internal effects on curriculum in "The Implications of Instructional Objectives for Learning," chapter IV in C. M. Lindvall (ed.), *Educational Objectives*. 3 (Pittsburgh, Pa.: University of Pittsburgh Press, 1964). He specifically deals with behavioral objectives in "Behavioral Objectives? Yes!" (Glen Hass, Joseph Bondi, Jon Wiles, *Curriculum Planning: A New Approach* (Boston: Allyn and Bacon, 1974)). J. Myron Atkin in "Behavioral Objectives in Curriculum Design: A Cautionary Note" (chapter 12 in David A. Payne (ed.), *Curriculum Evaluation: Commentaries on Purposes, Process, Product* (Lexington, Mass.: D. C. Heath, 1974)), however, says that behavioral objectives are an example of letting measurement techniques determine goals, rather than the opposite, which he recommends. (See also Philip G. Smith's "On the Logic of Behavioral Objectives," *Phi Delta Kappan* 53 (No. 7, March 1972).)

Several alternatives to a subject or discipline approach have been proposed. Gene Wise, for example, in "Integrative Education for a Disintegrated World" (*Teachers College Record* 67 (No. 6, March 1966)) says that "compartmentalized curriculum is irrelevant for a society whose traditional sustaining faiths are disintegrating." He would promote an integrative curriculum centered around students' value structure with such headings as "Freedom, Authority and Decision-Making," and "Approaches to the Self and Reality." His view of the total school situation is not far removed from that described in James Mac-donald's "The School Environment as Learner Reality" (*Curriculum Theory Network* 4 (Winter 1969–1970), University of Toronto Institute for Studies in Education), which considers the school as a comprehensive reality or environment which necessarily constrains experience because it is contrived.

Alternative schools attempt to take advantage of the school as an environment yet overcome limits traditional subjects impose on student experience. George Dennison's *First Street School* describes an alternative inner city school (New American Library #3, New York, 1968). Joseph Featherstone, who is known for helping Americans become acquainted with British curricular reforms, has a helpful overview of British primary schools in *An Introduction: Informal Schools in Britain Today* (New York: Citation Press, 1971). The British system of primary education is introduced in R. F. Dearden's *The Philosophy of Primary Education: An Introduction* (London: Routledge and Kegan Paul, 1968); the book has a helpful bibliography and is the first in a series on the subject of the British primary school. (See also John Blackie's *Inside the Primary School* (New York: Schocken, 1971).)

One key word in integrative approaches to curriculum is "experience." A perceptive analysis of the use of "experience" in curriculum discourse is to be found in R. D. Archambault's "The Philosophical Bases of the Experience Curriculum" (*Harvard Educational Review* 26 (No. 3, Summer 1956)). Philip Phenix goes beyond usual curriculum categories in "Transcendence and the Curriculum" (*Teachers College Record* 73 (No. 2, December 1971)).

Several writers have contributed insights into bases for examining curricular organization beyond the usual categories of goals, techniques and evaluation, whether within subject disciplines or integrative curricula. Each deals with the nature of knowledge itself. Kenneth R. Conklin, for example, says that the central focus should be the act of knowing and that teaching must be the putting on display of knowledge and ways of knowing (see "The Aesthetics of Knowing and Teaching," *Teachers College Record* 72 (No. 2, December 1970)). Basil Bernstein examines the relation between "lesson contents and changes in what counts as valid presentation of knowledge" in "On the Classification and Framing of Educational Knowledge," in Young's *Knowledge and Control*. His conceptualization attempts to examine the relationship between social class, hierarchies controlling the distribution of knowledge, and options open to teachers and students for reorganizing content.

IV. HOW SHOULD THE CURRICULUM BE EVALUATED?

Evaluation is a term used to mean grading students, selecting among curricular alternatives, pilot testing new curricula, designing models of financial accountability to taxpayers, or elaborating bureaucratic structures for comparing the measured effectiveness of experimental programs. While the term evaluation appears most commonly in educational literature as the last, just what evaluation research is and what direction it should take are hotly disputed.

Among professional evaluation consultants and those who hire them, the issues are largely procedural. Evaluation is assumed to be the measurement of *effectiveness* of specific content, instructional technique, or structural variations (such as modular scheduling). Refining the instruments of measurement becomes the key question within this view of evaluation. The language of evaluators is largely technological, with "outputs" or products being measured against the "costs" of the means to their achievement. That education is a rational process is assumed, and the dominant mode of measurement is most often expressed in cognitive-psychological language. In other words, to evaluate curricula usually means to compare student achievements.

Here and there, conceptual and theoretical issues in evaluation are also raised in the curriculum literature. In "Language, Rationality and Assessment" (chapter 17 in David A. Payne (ed.), *Curriculum Evaluation: Commentaries on Purposes, Process, Product* (Lexington, Mass.: D. C. Heath, 1974)) Robert E. Stake raises the question of the language to be used in evaluation. He asks that rationality be given a chance "to serve as a reasonable complement to empiricism in the search for 'truth'." Ralph W. Tyler's "General Statement on Evaluation" (*Journal of Educational Research* 35 (No. 7, March 1942)) exemplifies a rational approach. He lays out the purposes of evaluation (periodic check on institution, providing information for the guidance of individual students, etc.), the assumptions behind evaluation (that education is to change behavior, that objectives are the kinds of behaviors desired, that appraisal is to be conducted "on the basis of nearness to objectives"); and then he sets forth his own evaluation procedure.

One article which deals with the historical development of educational evaluation is Jack C. Merwin's "Historical Review of Changing Concepts of Evaluation" in Ralph W. Tyler (ed.), *Educational Evaluation: New Roles, New Means*. NSSE 1969 Yearbook. Part II (Chicago: University of Chicago Press). He relates evaluation theories to dominant theories of education and psychology, discusses the role of evaluation in school planning, and mentions traditional issues in evaluation, such as specific vs. general achievement. A writer who brings some insights to the subject is Harold Berlak in "Values, Goals, Public Policy and Educational Evaluation" (*Review of Educational Research* 40 (No. 2, April 1970). He goes into the issues of political power and social tensions engendered by or reinforced by evaluation results, and attempts to resolve the issue by suggesting that each "expert" must set the boundaries for the specific evaluation task so that the results will not be misapplied.

Most current curriculum evaluation has been seen as feeding information into policy decisions. Herbert J. Walberg defends this position in "Curriculum Evaluation: Problems and Guidelines" (*Teachers College Record*, 71 (No. 4, May 1970)). Most observers of evaluation see it as a form of applied rather than pure research, that is, as research which will alter the curriculum or technique being evaluated. In "Components and Constraints of Curriculum Research," in *Curriculum Theory Network* 5 (Spring 1970), Harry S. Broudy attempts to outline a basis for curriculum research that would actually enhance curricular development. Guy Larkins and James P. Shaver ("Hard-Nosed Research and the Evaluation of Curricula" (*Teachers College Record* 73 (No. 3, February 1972)) elaborate the point that the goals of evaluation research are not those of classical research, that educational research is more often "formative" than "summative," that is, concurrent with and informative to the thing being evaluated. Daniel L. Stufflebeam makes a strong case for evaluation as a link between research and institutionalization of innovation ("A Depth Study of the Evaluation Requirement," *Theory Into Practice* 5 (No. 2, April 1966)). Richard J. Light and Paul V. Smith ("Choosing a Future: Strategies for Designing and Evaluating New Programs," *Harvard Educational Review* 40 (No. 1, Winter 1970)) advocate incorporating evaluation as an integral part of all national level educational "interventions."

Within evaluation literature, it may be helpful to consider two specific issues about which there is considerable controversy: criterion-referenced evaluation and comparative evaluation. *Criterion-referenced* evaluation centers on a predetermined standard of measurement. Robert Ebel in "Criterion-Referenced Measurements: Limitations" (*School Review* 79 (No. 2, February 1971)) states that too much teacher time is wasted in setting specific objectives which are set as absolutes. They are often the result of committee consensus and therefore usually superficial. When such specific objectives come into play, *time* more than student ability usually becomes the major variable. In "Criterion-Centered Research," Alexander W. Astin supports the use of criterion-centered evaluation, saying it forces the researcher to consider the uses to which his evaluation measures will be put. James H. Block counters Ebel directly ("Criterion-Referenced Measurements: Potential," *School Review* 79 (No. 2, February 1971)) by stating that such measures are far more complex than portrayed by Ebel and that such criteria are essential for measuring competency in the basics of the school curriculum.

A second example of debate within the field of evaluation is *comparative* evaluation, the imposing of experimental vs. control or experimental vs. experimental qualifications on two or more curriculum situations in order to decide which to implement in the future; or in order to decide which "produces" the maximum "results" in terms of student achievement or teacher time. Such research is most directly linked with policy and so should be the most closely scrutinized, yet the scrutiny often aims at the techniques of evaluation rather than the assumptions behind them. Rochelle S. Mayer compares pre-school curriculum models in Robert H. Anderson and Harold G. Shane (eds.), *As the Twig is Bent: Readings in Early Childhood Education* (New York: Houghton, Mifflin, 1971), offers a discussion of comparative methods, which may be helpful to anyone wanting an overview of some of the issues involved.

Several writers have considered the problems inherent in comparative evaluation strategies. Among them, Philip Levy ("New Research for New Curricula," *Journal of Curriculum Studies* 1 (No. 2, May 1969)) criticizes the comparative mode for assuming that studying an individual classroom is generalizable beyond the one case and for confusing evaluation with measurement. He contends that some systems of curriculum have *incomparable* outcomes, making the designing of parallel evaluations impossible. Michael A. Wallach's essay review of Patricia Minuchin, Barbara Biber, *et al.*, *"Psychological Impact of School Experience"* (*Harvard Educational Review* 41 (No. 2, May 1971)) describes their comparative evaluation of "modern" over "traditional" elementary schools as inadequate because they have counterposed two types without examining the *quality* of each case within its own type. Such an argument gets into intuitive impressions, which are rarely accepted as "proof" in evaluation studies. Egon G. Guba sees this as a fault within the evaluation paradigm. In "The Failure of Educational Evaluation" (*Educational Technology* 9 (May 1969)) he says that evaluators often use scientific techniques and concepts which do not bear out experiential observation and theory arising from it. When this occurs, it is the research techniques rather than the program being evaluated that should be called into question; often the reverse is true. Edna Shapiro develops a similar argument in "Educational Evaluation: Rethinking the Criteria of Competence" (*School Review* 81 (No. 4, August 1973)). In the same vein, Elliott Eisner states in "Emerging Models for Educational Evaluation" (*School Review* 80 (No. 4, August 1972)) that in educational research little attention is given to whether results that are *statistically* significant also are *educationally* significant; the criteria for the latter are not generated internally by an input-output model of evaluation but must arise outside it. He believes that in educational research, the tendency is to reduce educational problems to forms that fit research paradigms and techniques available, rather than the reverse. Another criticism advanced by J. Thomas Hastings ("Curriculum Evaluation: The Why of the Outcomes," *Journal of Educational Measurements* 3 (No. 1, Spring 1966)) is that research seldom reveals *why* certain test results occur, as well as *that* they occur.

In "An Analysis of Current Issues in the Evaluation of Educational Programs," Herbert Zimiles extends the list of problems within current evaluation research: failure to deal with "incubator" or long-term effects, study of only a portion of the outcomes (usually the intended or anticipated ones), variation of procedures and goals among classes, and others (in Jerome Hellmuth (ed.), *Dis-*

advantaged Child. Vol. 2 (New York: Brunner Mazel, Inc., 1969)). That the important "results of educational experience are not necessarily those that are immediate or measurable" is discussed by J. B. Carroll in "School Learning Over the Long Haul" (in J. D. Krumboltz (ed.), *Learning and the Educational Process* (Chicago: Rand McNally, 1965)).

One problem with traditional evaluation research is what Ernest R. House in "The Conscience of Educational Evaluation" (*Teachers College Record* 73 (No. 3, February 1972)) calls the failure to consider the context of the research. He terms evaluation a form of sophistry; the what's and how's of it are determined by who is funding and what they want to prove. The worth of any evaluation must be determined by looking at its "context of justification," the publicly held opinions of the outcomes. Two writers try to get around such criticisms by an adversary model for evaluation in which an evaluation team would deliberately include opposition opinions. Marilyn Kourilsky makes the argument using a flow chart illustrating the role of the adversary ("An Adversary Model for Educational Evaluation," *Evaluation Comment, Journal of Educational Evaluation* 4 (No. 2, June 1973)); Murray Levine, in "Scientific Method and the Adversary Model," in the same publication draws on law for the language of evidence in evaluation. He sees evaluation as "human intelligence trying to make sense of what it observes," a truism obscured by the "pseudo-precise instruments" of most evaluation studies.

One historical study which places evaluation within a societal framework is Clarence J. Karier's "Ideology and Evaluation: In Quest of Meritocracy" which analyzes enlightenment ideology underlying the philosophy of the "educational state" in twentieth-century America and shows how these ideas made their way into an educational reward system ideologically structured to control and channel people. He suggests that the quest for meritocracy has served more to destroy rather than enhance the dignity of man (in Michael W. Apple, Michael J. Subkoviak, and Henry S. Lufler (eds.), *Educational Evaluation: Analysis of Responsibility* (Berkeley: McCutchan, 1974)).

Not all educational "evaluation" falls within the common paradigm of measuring outcomes. Several other traditions of scholarship offer examples of ways of looking at the worth of educational enterprises: anthropology, phenomenology, critical theory and Marxist sociology, and linguistic analysis. What they have in common is attention to the *nature* and *effects* of school curricula rather than the *effectiveness*.

In "Curriculum as the Accessibility of Knowledge" (paper presented to the Curriculum Theory Study Group, Minneapolis, Minnesota, March, 1970), Dwayne Huebner discusses schooling as "environmental forms that make knowledge accessible" rather than as "content" or "learnings." Using changes in the field of reading curriculum, expansions of pre-school offerings, and the development of materials in the sciences, Huebner illustrates his contention that technological forms of planning and evaluation hide what is going on in schooling. He prefers to discuss curriculum as knowledge embodied in environmental forms which enable men to "open up a world" and discover and move in new possibilities. While the language Huebner uses to describe curriculum strikes one as being different from that of professional evaluators, it is related to the concept of "hidden cirriculum," which takes the curriculum to be more than the explicit content of courses. The hidden curriculum is the latent curriculum of values and information conveyed through procedures and structures and rules in schools. *The Unstudied Curriculum: Its Impact on Children* (edited by N. V. Overly (Washington, D.C.: ASCD, 1970); see especially "The Consequences of Schooling" by Philip Jackson) provides an overview of evaluation from this perspective, a perspective which enables consideration of the unintended outcomes, tacit learnings, and the complex interactional consequences of schooling often overlooked when "evaluation" is limited to measuring proximity to stated curricular goals.

Viewing curriculum as the educative environment also has implications for placing the burden of proof on the school and the school personnel rather than on the student and his or her measured achievement. Gary C. Wehlage, Thomas S. Popkewitz and H. M. Hartoonian, in "Social Inquiry, Schools and State Assessment" (*Social Education* 37 (No. 8, December 1973)) demonstrate an alternative to student achievement evaluation. They advocate assessing the institution and what kinds of possibilities it offers the student for confronting people and events, for interpreting and drawing conclusions from their work, for formulating their own questions, and for facilitation of teacher-student relationships. For those interested in evaluation of the school program from the perspective of what schools offer students, *Evaluation of Achievement: Informal Schools in Britain Today* (New York: Citation Press, 1972) by Douglas A. Pidgeon raises the issue of evaluation in British schools now that they are less standardized; the book's bibliography is extensive. The need for new models of evaluation is echoed in "Models of Schooling and Models of Evaluation," (by Mary Alice White and Jan Duker, *Teachers College Record* 74 (No. 3, February 1973)), which states that pluralistic forms of education in this country call for pluralistic forms of evaluation.

A recent addition to the study of schooling generally and the "hidden curriculum" literature in particular has been the application of anthropological and ethnographic techniques in observing of school situations. Such studies are often limited to nongeneralizable individual situations, but have the advantage of encompassing a present-tense dynamic of the continuing situation. In addition to the work of Philip Jackson (*Life in Classrooms* (New York: Holt, Rinehart, Winston, 1968)) are Philip A. Cusick's *Inside High School: The Student's World* (New York: Holt, Rinehart, Winston, 1973) and Mary Alice White's "The View from the Pupil's Desk" (from Melvin L. Silberman (ed.), *The Experience of*

Schooling (New York: Holt, Rinehart, Winston, 1971)). While none of these falls within the scope of what is usually thought of as "evaluation," they do illustrate the narrowness of basing all evaluation on goal-setting and attainment; often the goals of the teachers and administrators are unintelligible and/or meaningless to the students.

One of the more interesting developments in school research has been the application of new research techniques in order to illustrate the nature and effects of "standardized" testing. The criticism of objective, multiple choice tests has often been that they are geared for middle-class whites and that they therefore are linguistically "foreign" to blacks, to rural or poor whites, to those who speak English only as a second language. Aaron V. Cicourel, D. R. Roth, Robert McKay and others have compiled a book of research studies which take the criticism further: using video-taping of testing situations, they have documented that the testing is not standardized because it erroneously assumes a pure S-R pattern in which the S is a test item that means the same thing to the tester and all tested; the R is a response cued by S and defined alike and, therefore, chosen for the same reason by both tester and tested. In Cicourel *et al., Language Use and School Performance* (New York: Academic Press of Harcourt Brace Jovanovich, Publishers, 1975), the authors present the transcripts of their video-tapes of individual testing situations and reveal that students often have very complicated reasons for choosing a particular answer on a multiple-choice item and that the reason most often has to do with their own personal memories and experience rather than some detached definition. Even children who score so low as to be labeled mentally deficient can often not only *remember* their answers but *supply reasons* for each answer they chose, even though their answer is not the "correct" one. (See also Hugh Mehan's "Assessing Children's School Performance," in Hans Peter Dreitzel (ed.), *Recent Sociology.* No. 5. *Childhood and Socialization* (New York: Macmillan, Inc., 1973).)

V. HOW SHOULD THE CURRICULUM BE CHANGED?

A cursory review of the journals for the past fifty years shows that "change" and "reform" are used almost interchangeably, as though innovation always implies improvement. Dozens of writers have described what they feel to be inadequacies in the curricula that exist and have recommended changes; fewer have dealt with the loci of power over curriculum change, that is, with the issues of who wants and who impedes change and with why change should be valued over the existing curricula. Ioan Davies in "Knowledge, Education and Power" (in Richard Brown (ed.), *Knowledge, Education and Cultural Change* (London: Tavistock, 1973)) offers a general conceptual approach to the questions of who has the power to determine what is taught. He draws on a Parsonian model of categories of existential beliefs, evaluative beliefs and evaluative symbols to examine problems of innovation; then using the "new math" as an example, he shows that a further question must be asked—that of power. Kirst and Mosher ("Politics of Education," *Review of Educational Research* 39 (No. 5, December 1969)) provide an overview of the relationship between power over education and the major research methodologies that have been employed to study education and recommend change.

For an overview of the factors influencing curriculum "innovation" at present, see Volume 3, issues 2 and 3 (combined) of *Interchange*. The lead article by Michael Fullan states that most of the impetus for and substance of curriculum change arises outside the school itself.

The slogan which links research and policy in the development of curricula is "accountability." Presumably, in a time of intense competition for public funds, education can best serve the public if those funds are spent wisely. This has led to the dominance of an accounting model for determining the value of what is not primarily an economic activity—the teaching of children. Robert J. Nash and Russell M. Agne challenge the appropriateness of this model in "The Ethos of Accountability: A Critique" (*Teachers College Record* 73 (No. 3, February 1972)). Other treatments of the accountability rationale for policy determination are Barak Rosenshine and Barry McGaw "Issues in Assessing Teacher Accountability in Public Education" (*Phi Delta Kappan* 53 (June 1972)); Robert E. Campbell, "Accountability and Stone Soup" (*Phi Delta Kappan* 53 (No. 3, November 1971)); Leon Lessinger's *Every Kid a Winner: Accountability of Education* (New York: Simon and Schuster, 1970); Myron Lieberman's "An Overview of Accountability" (*Phi Delta Kappan* 52 (No. 4, December 1970)); and "Educational Innovation and the National Interest," by Herbert M. Kliebard and Joseph E. Schmiedicke (*New York University Education Quarterly* 4 (No. 2, Winter 1973)). Jeannette B. Coltham traces the accountability model to the history of "payment by results" for British teachers in the last third of the 19th century in "Educational Accountability: An English Experiment and its Outcome" (*School Review* 81 (No. 1, November 1972)).

What "accountability" often leads to is the atomization of educational objectives and instructional techniques. Behavioral objectives offer the most common example, along with so-called competency-based teacher evaluation models, which actually do not evaluate teachers except as their performance is thought to be related to incremental patterns in their students' standardized test scores. A danger in such specific goal-setting and narrow standards of measurement is the politicization of all levels of the educational program. W. Robert and Robert B. Howsam in "CBTE: The Ayes of Texas," and Ellis Sandoz, "CBTE: The Nays of Texas" (*Phi Delta Kappan* 55 (No. 5, January 1974)) debate the effects of implementing such an evaluation program in Texas as it related to the training of teachers. M. M. Gubser discusses the effects of employing an accountability framework in Arizona where the subject divisions of the state department of education and later the state legislature were to determine the objectives and instructional techniques of each school subject. An example of the objectives for U. S. History included "the United States remains the envy of the civilized world and is the last best hope of mankind" (*Phi Delta Kappan* 55 (No. 1, September 1973)). The implications of a national level system of policy determination and assessment are treated in "The Science and Politics of National Educational Assessment" (*Teachers College Record* 71 (No. 4, May 1970)).

The relationship between the political system and the educational institutions is not always so overt as in the Arizona case. From the standpoint of Marxist sociology, Jurgens Habermas examines the educational system as reflective of societal values and the interests of those controlling knowledge distribution in *Knowledge and Human Interests* (Boston: Beacon Press, 1971) and *Toward a Rational Society* (Boston: Beacon Press, 1970). In two separate papers Walter Feinberg discusses the way in which assumptions about social stratification, population needs, and technological advance shape the allocation of educational resources. He compares Third World countries with the United States "Educational Equality Under Two Conflicting Models of Educational Development," to be published in *Theory and Society: Renewal and Critique in Social Theory* (Amsterdam and Paris: The Elsevier Publishing Company); and "The Limits of Educational Reform: A Truism Revived," (presented at the American Educational Studies Association, Chicago, 1974).

Often, the discussion of establishing and changing curricula centers on the relationship between research and theory to practice in the classroom. Daniel Kallos, in "Educational Phenomena and Educational Research" (Report #10 from the Institute for Education, University of Lund, Sweden, December 1974), challenges positivism and psychology as paradigms for educational research. In *Innovation and Research in Education* (London: Routledge and Kegan Paul, 1965), Michael D. Young calls for research on innovation to improve schools. John F. Kerr in "The Problems of Curriculum Reform" in J. F. Kerr (ed.), *Changing the Curriculum* (London: University of London Press, 1968) reviews several models of curriculum, then draws on recent British curriculum reform to suggest that curriculum should and can be developed on the basis of theory rather than in piecemeal response to political expediency, economic priorities or social prejudice. Two articles which reveal that curricula based on theoretical research are not panaceas are Brian Jackson's discussion of streaming in *Streaming: An Education System in Miniature* (London: Routledge and Kegan Paul, 1964) and Marshall D. Herron's "Nature of Scientific Inquiry" (*School Review* 79 (No. 2, February 1971)). Herron conducted a study which showed that of those teachers supposedly trained to teach inquiry-based science curricula (PSSC, SMSG, CHEM), only a few could even articulate the meaning of scientific inquiry, and fewer could or wanted to base their teaching on that model, even though all were officially described as using it. His work seems to support Sarason's idea that teachers mediate information, and therefore that curricular change has to be considered as a personal as well as institutional enterprise.

The teacher exists in a social context. Pierre Bourdieu describes the relationship between knowledge and its "intellectual field" and between school knowledge and societal constraints in "Systems of Education and Systems of Thought" (chapter 7 of Michael F. D. Young (ed.), *Knowledge and Control*) and "Intellectual Field and Creative Project" (chapter 6 in *Knowledge and Control*). He discusses the school as the agent of distributing "a whole collection of commonplaces, common speech and language, but also areas of encounter and agreement, common problems and methods of approaching those common problems." While Bourdieu's work is not directly related to changing curricula, it does remind those engaged in developing curricula that the assumptions of a management model of setting goals and implementing them is not a simple or perhaps even feasible task.

CONCLUSION

In conclusion, a note of irony must be sounded: although the aforementioned articles comprise only a tiny fraction of writings about curriculum and evaluation, even the broader body of professional literature itself seems far from adequate in dealing with certain basic curriculum issues. Time after time, the search for articles on a specific, critical subject yielded little. It may be illuminating to list some of these gaps, for they raise serious questions about the interests and purposes served by—and those not served by—educational research.

First is the lack of rigorous historical analysis of curriculum and its shaping. There is little in the curriculum field to parallel the emerging historical studies of the organizational aspects of schooling (especially urban). These studies of school organization have done much to sharpen analysis and debate on the politics and impact of schooling. Presumably, historical studies of curriculum might also serve to illuminate central issues in the field.

Second is the neglect of the conceptual analysis of research methodology. Methodology articles that have been published are usually of the "handbook" variety, or perhaps argue for a new "technique" that will help fine-tune an established instrument of measurement. The field is largely without a body of critical analysis which examines the *assumptions, values,* and *limitations* of different research perspectives. Given such a lack of reflectiveness on their own enterprise, it is little wonder that educators and educational researchers find themselves with so few answers to questions students raise about their rights to educational quality and questions taxpayers pose about "accountability."

Especially lacking is an exhaustive inquiry into the implications that the dominance of psychological models of research and curriculum building have for students.

Except for some cross-national compilations of student achievement scores on standardized tests in individual subject fields, there is virtually no comparison of U.S. curriculum and methods of evaluation with those of other countries, even of countries where considerable educational research is pursued actively and with great sophistication.

Most important, there seem to be as yet few coherent critical studies of the political and economic dimensions of the school curriculum. The student of education could read most education journals without discovering that the school is a political institution, existing in a social context, playing a role in the nexus of economic institutions and juvenile justice agencies of the community and the nation; that "curriculum" is not neutral, a priori "knowledge" borne of consensus. Research into such issues will be complex, and yielding of few generalizable statistical correlations. It will by definition be historically situational, with researchers going into communities and into classrooms to find out what forces are shaping curriculum, to see what is happening to and with students in schools, and to discern the levels at which curriculum decision-making and indecision-making take place. In a technological society in which access to knowledge bears upon one's access to power in the political marketplace, and academic credentials are essential for minimal access to the economic marketplace, the question must not simply be "what has been the course of curriculum research?" or even "where is curriculum research headed?" but "where should curriculum research be going?"

Author Index

649

Subject Index